Migrant Actors Worldwide

Studies in Global Social History

VOLUME 53

Studies in Global Migration History

Series Editors

Johannes Preiser-Kapeller (*Austrian Academy of Sciences*)
Roland Wenzlhuemer (*LMU Munich*)
Elizabeth A. Zanoni (*Old Dominion University*)

VOLUME 16

The titles published in this series are listed at *brill.com/sgmh*

Migrant Actors Worldwide

Capitalist Interests, State Regulations, and Left-Wing Strategies

Edited by

Dirk Hoerder and Lukas Neissl

BRILL

LEIDEN | BOSTON

FRIEDRICH EBERT STIFTUNG

The language editing of this volume was funded by the Friedrich-Ebert-Stiftung (FES). The editors are grateful for this support.

Cover illustration: Loading sugar cane on carts, Hawaii, 1917. From The Frank and Frances Carpenter Collection of the Library of Congress, LOT 11479. Available in the public domain.

Library of Congress Cataloging-in-Publication Data

Names: Hoerder, Dirk, editor. | Neissl, Lukas, editor.
Title: Migrant actors worldwide : capitalist interests, state regulations, and left-wing strategies / edited by Dirk Hoerder and Lukas Neissl.
Description: Boston : Brill, [2024] | Series: Studies in global migration history, 1874-6705 ; Volume 16 | Includes bibliographical references and index.
Identifiers: LCCN 2023044522 (print) | LCCN 2023044523 (ebook) | ISBN 9789004686984 (hardback ; alk. paper) | ISBN 9789004686991 (ebook)
Subjects: LCSH: Migrant labor–History. | Working class–Social conditions. | Sex discrimination–Law and legislation. | Emigration and immigration–History.
Classification: LCC HD5855 .M524 2024 (print) | LCC HD5855 (ebook) | DDC 331.5/44–dc23/eng/20231026
LC record available at https://lccn.loc.gov/2023044522
LC ebook record available at https://lccn.loc.gov/2023044523

Typeface for the Latin, Greek, and Cyrillic scripts: "Brill". See and download: brill.com/brill-typeface.

ISSN 1874-6705
ISBN 978-90-04-68698-4 (hardback)
ISBN 978-90-04-68699-1 (e-book)
DOI 10.1163/9789004686991

This book is printed on acid-free paper and produced in a sustainable manner.

Contents

PART 4
Regional Migration Patterns, Work Regimes, and Workers' Agency

PART 5
Workingmen's and -women's Agency in Globally Interconnected Spaces

Figures and Tables

Figures

Tables

Notes on Contributors

Selda Altan

is an Assistant Professor of History at Randolph College, Virginia and has produced several publications on Chinese labour history and Chinese-Ottoman interactions in the early twentieth century. Her *Chinese Workers of the World: Colonialism, Chinese Labor, and the Yunnan-Indochina Railway* (Stanford University Press, forthcoming) examines labour conflicts during the construction of the French railway between China and Vietnam from 1898 to 1910. Her second project, *A Sisterhood to Save China: Women's Leadership and Labor in the "Gung Ho" Industrial Cooperatives (Indusco), 1938–1952*, highlights the role of women in China's resistance against Japan during the Second World War.

Beate Althammer

studied history, economic history and political science at the University of Zurich, Switzerland, and received her PhD from the University of Trier, Germany, where she also earned her *Habilitation* in 2016. Her research interests include the history of industrial relations, social protest movements, migration, poverty, and welfare in nineteenth and early-twentieth-century Europe. She currently is the principal investigator of the research project "The Borders of the Welfare State: Migration, Social Rights and Expulsion (1850–1933)," based at Humboldt-Universität zu Berlin and funded by the *Deutsche Forschungsgemeinschaft* (DFG).

Nina Trige Andersen

is a journalist and historian affiliated with the Society for Labour History (SFAH). She is a member of the coordination committee of Nordic Labour History and the research councils of the Swedish Labour Movement's Archives and Library (ARAB), Stockholm, and the Centre for Labour History (CfA), Lund. She has published in journals such as *Women's History Review*, *Arbejderhistorie/Arbetarhistoria* (Worker's History), and *Philippine Studies*, and is a recipient of the Rudolf Meidner Prize 2017 and the Kjersti Bosdotter Prize 2018. Her latest book is *Labor Pioneers: Economy, Labor, and Migration in Filipino-Danish Relations, 1950–2015* (Ateneo de Manila University Press, 2019), and *Papirnussere, skrankepaver og blanketfinker: 100 års kamp om organisering og faglig identitet på velfærdsstatens kontorer* (Gads Forlag, 2023) about the Danish trade union for administrative workers in the public sector. Also see www.filippinernesdanmarkshistorie.dk and www.arbejderhistorier.net.

Cecilia Bruzelius
is a Junior Professor of European Public Policy at the Institute of Political Science of the University of Tübingen. Her research focuses on migration and social policy in the European Union.

Geoffrey Ewen
is an Associate Professor in the Departments of History and Multidisciplinary Studies at the Glendon Campus of York University in Toronto, specializing in early-twentieth-century Quebec labour history. His principal areas of interest include the wartime and post-First World War workers' revolts and inter-union rivalry between secular unions and an emerging Catholic labour movement in the years between 1914 and 1925. Between 1987 and 2006, he was active in labour education, teaching working-class history at the Labour College of Canada Residential Program, run by the Canadian Labour Congress.

Katharine Frederick
is Assistant Professor at Utrecht University. Her research focuses on social and economic transformation during the nineteenth and twentieth centuries, with a particular emphasis on how the intersection of globalization, colonization, and industrialization affected the livelihoods and survival strategies of labourers, especially in Sub-Saharan Africa.

Veronika Helfert
holds a PhD in history from the University of Vienna and is a research affiliate at the Central European University (CEU) in Vienna in the project *ZARAH: Women's Labour Activism in Eastern Europe and Transnationally, from the Age of Empires to the late 20th Century*. Her research interests are women's and gender history of protest and revolution, public administration, women's suffrage, and labour history in the twentieth century. Her most recent book (in German) is "*Women, Stand up! A Women's and Gender History of the Austrian Revolution and Council Movement, 1916–1924*" (2021).

Dirk Hoerder
University of Bremen, 1977–2008, and Arizona State University, 2007–2011, taught US and Canadian social history, global migrations, and sociology of migrant acculturation. His publications include *Cultures in Contact: World Migrations in the Second Millennium* (2002), *The Historical Practice of Diversity: Transcultural Interactions from the Early Modern Mediterranean to the Postcolonial World* (co-edited 2003), and Christiane Harzig and Dirk Hoerder with Donna Gabaccia, *What is Migration History?* (2009).

Ritesh Kumar Jaiswal

is an Assistant Professor at the Department of History, University of Delhi. Previously, he was a Swiss National Science Foundation Postdoctoral Visiting Fellow at the University of Zurich. He obtained his PhD from the University of Delhi. During his PhD, he was a Fulbright Fellow at Harvard University, a Volkswagen Global History Fellow at the University of Göttingen, and a junior research fellow at the Indian Council for Social Science Research, Delhi. His research and teaching interests include labour and migration history, Indian Ocean studies, non-indentured and indentured systems of migration, British colonialism, modern Indian history, and global history.

Dácil Juif

obtained her PhD in economic history from the University of Tübingen (2014) and currently is an Associate Professor in Economic History at Universidad Carlos III, Madrid, a research fellow of the Figuerola Institute of History and Social Sciences, and associate editor of the Industrial History Review (RHI-IHR). Her research focuses on the economic history of developing regions and, in particular, on the living standards of mineworkers, the effect of mining activities on well-being, labour migration, the development of tax capacity in former colonies, and long-run human capital formation.

Radhika Kanchana

is a Postdoctoral Researcher at the Centre for the Theory and Analysis of Law (CTAD) at the University of Paris Nanterre in the collective research project "Equality and Law in Personal Status (ELIPS)." She received her PhD from the Institut d'Études Politiques de Paris, France (Sciences Po Paris) in 2016. Her wider research is focused on international migration and inclusion, and the geographical regions of South Asia and the Arab-Gulf region.

Leslie Page Moch

is Professor Emerita of History at Michigan State University where she taught the history of migration and European history from 1996 to 2015 after her tenure at the University of Michigan-Flint. She is the co-editor of several essay collections, author of *Moving Europeans: Migration in Western Europe since 1650* (1992, 2003) and *The Pariahs of Yesterday: Breton Migrants in Paris* (2012), and co-author with Lewis Siegelbaum of *Broad is My Native Land: Repertoires and Regimes of Migration in Russia's Twentieth Century* (2014).

Lukas Neissl
was General Secretary of the International Conference of Labour and Social History (ITH) from 2014 to 2020, and currently is Program Manager in the ERC Advanced Grant "*ZARAH: Women's Labour Activism in Eastern Europe and Transnationally, from the Age of Empires to the late 20th Century*" at the Central European University (CEU) in Vienna. He worked for and was active in trade unions in Austria, Peru and Venezuela.

Christof Parnreiter
is a Professor of Economic Geography at the University of Hamburg, Germany. His research topics include globalization and the geographies of the world economy, global cities, urban research in general, development studies and migration studies. He specializes in Latin American developments. He has published with Karin Fischer, Irmi Maral-Hanak, and Gerald Hödl, *Entwicklung und Unterentwicklung: Eine Einführung in Probleme, Theorien und Strategien* (third edition 2007) and with Michael Hoyler and Allan Watson, *Global City Makers: Economic Actors and Practices in the World City Network* (2018).

Lucas Poy
is an Assistant Professor in Global Economic and Social History at Vrije Universiteit Amsterdam and coordinator of the International Association of Labour History Institutions (IALHI) and the *Red Latinoamericana Trabajo y Trabajadorxs* (REDLATT), both headquartered at the International Institute of Social History, Amsterdam. He has received fellowships and grants from universities and scientific institutions in Spain, Colombia, the Netherlands, and the United States, and belongs to the editorial committee and advisory board of several academic journals, such as the *International Review of Social History*, *Archivos de historia del movimiento obrero y la izquierda*, and the *Journal of Labor and Society*.

Richard Saich
completed his PhD "Social Movements and Resistance to Neoliberalism in America, 1979–2000" at the University of Cambridge in 2023. He is currently a Visiting Lecturer at City, University of London.

Mahua Sarkar
is a Professor of Sociology and Affiliate Faculty of the Women and Gender Studies Institute at the University of Toronto. She has held multiple international fellowships. Her interdisciplinary research and publications focus on a range of topics including contemporary guestwork involving low-resourced

Bangladeshi male migrants, gestational surrogacy as racialized and gendered labour, free and unfree/constrained work under global capitalism, religious nationalisms and the gender question in late colonial Bengal, and the politics of methods in the human sciences. Her current writing project is an advanced monograph entitled *Bidesh Kara (Going Abroad): Bangladeshi Contract Migrants and Contemporary Guest Work.*

Lewis H. Siegelbaum

is a Jack and Margaret Sweet Professor Emeritus of History at Michigan State University where he taught Russian and European history until 2018. He is the author of four books including the award-winning *Cars for Comrades* (2008), and co-author with Leslie Page Moch of *Broad is My Native Land: Repertoires and Regimes of Migration in Russia's Twentieth Century* (2014). He has edited two books and co-edited six others, most recently *Empire and Belonging in the Eurasian Borderlands* (2019). He also co-authored the award-winning online sourcebook *Seventeen Moments in Soviet History*. In 2019, he published *Stuck on Communism: Memoir of a Russian Historian.*

Yukari Takai

is a Research Associate at the Centre for Asian Research at York University in Toronto and a Visiting Research Fellow at the International Research Center for Japanese Studies (Nichibunken) in Kyoto. She has taught gender and migration, North American history, Japanese history and women's history in the United States, Canada and Japan. Currently, she is finalizing a monograph, supported by the Social Science and Humanities Research Council of Canada, on Japanese transmigration in the Pacific world. Takai's recent publication (*Gender & History 31:3*) was honoured as the best article in Canada on the history of migration, ethnicity, and transnationalism in 2020.

Aliki Vaxevanoglou

completed her graduate and post-graduate studies in history and historical sociology at Paris 1 Panthéon-Sorbonne and holds a PhD in social history. She has worked as a researcher in numerous programs for different research centres and universities in Greece and has taught Greek and European History in various post-graduate programs. Since 2000, she is a researcher (currently Senior Researcher) at the Research Centre for Greek Society of the Academy of Athens. Her research, books, and essays concern different aspects of labour history.

CHAPTER 1

Introduction

Migrant Actors Worldwide: Capitalist Interests, State Regulations, and Left-Wing Strategies

Dirk Hoerder and Lukas Neissl

Abstract

In this chapter, the authors first provide a brief summary of migrations worldwide. They outline the inability of governments to understand the demand for labour in their societies and industries as well as migrant strategies to access job options. Further, they examine the role of "the state" in its manifold historic appearances as empire, multi-ethnic conglomerate, or nation and juxtapose the concept of citizens with rights to elite practices of movability of populations. The authors trace these patterns into the distant past and then turn to capital investment strategies – whether privately- or state-owned – and labour and working-class organizations accepting or challenging the power of capital. Both insertion into labour markets and trade unions' responses require analysis of segmented labour markets and job segregation by colour of skin. In conclusion, they discuss the agency of migrant and non-migrant working-men and -women.

Keywords

capital – empire – labour – labour organization – state – workers' agency

In the early decades of the twenty-first century, few topics are as politically charged as "international migration," and seemingly unrelated, the concept of "the superrich."* However, if the individualized catchword "superrich" is

* Most chapters in this volume were first discussed at the 56th Conference of the International Conference of Labour and Social History (ITH) in Linz, Austria, 23–25 September 2021, organized by Susan Zimmermann (Vienna), Lukas Neissl (Vienna), and Dirk Hoerder (Vienna), with Rolf Bauer (Vienna), Josef Ehmer (Vienna), Simon Goeke (Munich), and Marcel van der Linden (Amsterdam).

replaced by "large-scale profit-yielding capital investment strategies" the connection to migration is evident: Capital is being moved to where low-wage labour is available, migrants move – often in large numbers – to where investments and/or wealth accumulated due to specific historic factors create a demand for labour. In contrast, little attention is given to left-wing strategies and, if any, the theme is "the decline of the unions and the left." Over the last two centuries, international wage differentials have grown enormously and, with labour markets divided into more or less segregated segments, large numbers of migrants have been channelled into low-wage sectors and whole segments of resident working classes have been dislocated. These processes have been exacerbated by neoliberal capitalist economies, promulgated by Chicago economists, and supported by state governments since the 1970s.[1]

1 Research Approaches to Labour Migration and Capital Investment Strategies

In this volume, we combine – through case studies employing multiple methods – analyses of migrations worldwide in response to capital formation, concentration, and investment or, vice versa, migrations inducing mobility of capital.[2] Global coverage and local "labour supply," a technical term for men and women charting routes to gain their livelihoods, requires a combination of global and micro-history, the teamwork of specialists for the many different social formations and labour regimes, as well as interdisciplinary approaches concerning migration data and theories, economic history, theories of capital generation and accumulation, the study of labour market practices and assessment of labour market theories, as well as rural and industrial studies.

1 This strain of thought emerged from the Austrian School of Economics' emphasis on individualism, particularly by Friedrich Hayek, and was institutionalized as the Mont Pèlerin Society in 1947. Its main proponent, the University of Chicago economist Milton Friedman, postulated a "natural unemployment rate" in 1951. The scholars – or ideologists – rigorously opposed Keynesian economics and the *ordo*liberal concept of combining societal with market factors to achieve a "social market economy."

2 In the frame of the series "Studies in Global Migration History" this continues approaches taken in Donna R. Gabaccia and Dirk Hoerder, eds., *Connecting Seas and Connected Ocean Rims: Indian, Atlantic, and Pacific Oceans and China Seas Migrations from the 1830s to the 1930s* (Leiden: Brill, 2011); Jan Lucassen and Leo Lucassen, eds., *Globalising Migration History: The Eurasian Experience (16th-21st Centuries)* (Leiden: Brill, 2014); Dirk Hoerder and Amarjit Kaur, eds., *Proletarian and Gendered Mass Migrations: A Global Perspective on Continuities and Discontinuities from the 19th to the 21st Century* (Leiden: Brill, 2013).

It recognizes the global inequalities of power and economic development and migrants' roles in mediating agency between labour markets and life prospects in unequal segments of the globe.[3] The need to globalize and historize transdisciplinary labour history has been widely recognized.[4] Furthermore, the global-local approach also demands research into the role of "the state" whether national, provincial, municipal, or rural, as well as into "the left" whether unions, political parties, or revolutionary organizations. Agency-centred and anthropological approaches attempt to undertake careful analyses of workingmen's and -women's strategies, interactions, and everyday experiences in larger economic-societal-political frames: While events and structures require attention, the emphasis is on processes – on moving individuals, families, or groups. The spaces in or through which migrants move involve webs of social relations, some of them local, others ephemeral in transit, and yet others transcontinental or global.[5]

In this frame, the authors who contributed to this volume combine contemporary and historical perspectives. They analyse income inequalities and structures and mechanisms of exploitation within and between regions and political superstructures. Mobile capital and capitalist strategies force resident workers – "native-born" – and their organizations to re-act or, strategically, pro-act. In an innovative approach, several essays study colonizer-imposed work regimes intended to further the accumulation of profit in the imperialist cores by mobilization and exploitation of workingmen and -women in subjugated societies and emphasize how elites have pursued and adapted these labour regimes to post-colonial economies. While the essays mainly focus on developments from the nineteenth to the twenty-first century, we also refer to the more distant past in this introduction.

Given the global extent of migrations, it is clear that researchers need to decentre "nation" and "state."[6] The still widely used Euro-centric construct of

---

3 Marcel van der Linden, "Enjeux pour une histoire mondiale du travail," *Le Mouvement Social* 241, no. 4 (2012): 3–29; Christian G. de Vito, "History Without Scale: The Micro-Spatial Perspective," *Past and Present* 242, Supplement 14 (2019): 348–372; Christian G. de Vito and Anne Gerritsen, "Micro-Spatial Histories of Labour: Towards a New Global History," in *Micro-Spatial Histories of Global Labour*, ed. Christian G. de Vito and Anne Gerritsen (Basingstoke, UK: Palgrave Macmillan, 2018), 1–28; in general, see Sebastian Conrad, *What is Global History?* (Princeton, NJ: Princeton University Press, 2016).

4 Concerning Marxist approaches, see Marcel van der Linden and Karl Heinz Roth, eds., *Beyond Marx: Theorising the Global Labour Relations of the Twenty-First Century* (Leiden: Brill, 2013).

5 This section is based on Christiane Harzig and Dirk Hoerder with Donna Gabaccia, *What is Migration History?* (Cambridge: Polity, 2009).

6 The literature on the emergence of the nation-and-state combination is extensive. See, for the once new, now traditional approach, Karl W. Deutsch, *Nationalism and*

"nation-state" as developed since the French Revolution and Napoleonic imperialism rests on a contradiction in terms: "State" is conceived as treating each and every inhabitant as a citizen that is equal before the law, whereas "nation" privileges the culture of some citizens, usually a majority, above that of others labelled "minorities" (see Chapter 2 in this volume). This contradiction is not only exacerbated by the fact that state governments and population planners have never considered all inhabitants as having "citizen" status but also that they considered whole population segments as internally portable or even exportable. Methodological nationalism, as will be discussed below, has marred much of the research ever since its emergence in the nineteenth century.

New approaches since the 1970s have discerned the manifold interactions below and above states, whether self-labelled as nations, empires or others.[7] Migrants – with the exception of political or war-time refugees – never departed from a generic nation or overarching state but from the respective localities and regions of their socializations. They relocated (and continue to do so) to specific perceived job options in another locality or region.[8] This requires the study of differentiated and distinct socio-economic geographies, of social and mental spaces.[9]

Social Communication: An Inquiry into the Foundations of Nationality (Cambridge, MA: Massachusetts Institute of Technology, 1953). Benedict Anderson undercut all essentialist constructions of "nation" in *Imagined Communities: Reflections on the Origin and Spread of Nationalism* (London: Verso, 1983); Anthony D. Smith, *The Ethnic Origins of Nations* (Oxford: Basil Blackwell, 1986) and Anthony D. Smith, *Nationalism and Modernism: A Critical Survey of Recent Theories of Nations and Nationalism* (London: Routledge, 1998); Tony Judt with Timothy D. Snyder, *Thinking the Twentieth Century* (London: Heinemann, 2012).

7 Pieter C. Emmer and Magnus Mörner, eds., *European Expansion and Migration: Essays on the Intercontinental Migration from Africa, Asia and Europe* (New York: Berg, 1992); Dirk Hoerder, *Cultures in Contact: World Migrations in the Second Millennium* (Durham, NC: Duke University Press, 2002); Jan Lucassen, Leo Lucassen, and Patrick Manning, eds., *Migration History in World History: Multidisciplinary Approaches* (Leiden: Brill, 2010); Ulbe Bosma, Gjis Kessler, and Leo Lucassen, eds., *Migration and Membership Regimes in Global and Historical Perspective: An Introduction* (Leiden: Brill, 2013); Hein de Haas, Stephen Castles, and Mark J. Miller, *The Age of Migration: International Population Movements in the Modern World* (London: Red Globe Press, 2020).

8 For early formulations, see Julianna Puskas, "Transatlantic Migration from a Hungarian Village on the Basis of Oral Testimonies," in *The Press of Labor Migrants in Europe and North America, 1880s to 1930s*, ed. Dirk Hoerder and Christiane Harzig (Bremen: Universität Bremen, 1985), 59–70; Samuel L. Baily, "The Village-Outward Approach to the Study of Social Networks: A Case Study of the Agnonesi Diaspora Abroad, 1885–1989," *Studi Emigrazione* 19, no. 105 (1992): 43–67.

9 It is impossible to cite all research relevant to our topic globally. We are grateful to many colleagues for advice and references.

Given the fact that men and women, sometimes with their children, move translocally and transculturally, the concept of "transnational," which, at the time of its formulation, was an important step to transcend the fixation on borders and "container states,"[10] never captured migrants' local-parental socialization and specific selection of a destination within family economies.[11] Viewed generically, migrants move within circuits of macro-regional or global investment and profit maximization strategies to increase or maximize the rewards for their labour and capabilities. States have had – and continue to have – only limited influence on both migrants' decisions and capitalist strategies. "Empire" is a catch-all term for power politics, monopolies, corporations, settlers armed with superiority ideologies as well as dispossessed people internally and peoples externally. However, a stateside army- and navy-supported self-positioning as empire advantages capital within the state and, often, out-migrants such as imperial personnel, planters, and missionaries.[12] Historically, the eighteenth-century colonizing world – or worldwide – wars of the seaborne Dutch, British and French elites for territories and labouring populations initiated the global divisions of labour.[13] "Empire" and "imperial" are labels that subsume violence, mutilation, rape, exploitation and dehumanization committed by the power-wielding personnel.[14] In the imperial-military expansion of the nineteenth century, as well as in the unequal power relationships of the present, some

---

10 Nina Glick Schiller, Linda Basch, and Cristina Blanc-Szanton, eds., *Towards a Transnational Perspective on Migration: Race, Class, Ethnicity and Nationalism Reconsidered* (New York: New York Academy of Sciences, 1992), especially Nina Glick Schiller, Linda Basch, and Cristina Blanc-Szanton, "Transnationalism: A New Analytic Framework for Understanding Migration," 1–24; Dirk Hoerder, "Transnational – Transregional – Translocal: Transcultural," in *Handbook of Research Methods in Migration*, ed. Carlos Vargas-Silva (Cheltenham, UK: Edward Elgar, 2012), 69–91.

11 The seminal formulation of family economies was Louise A. Tilly and Joan W. Scott, *Women, Work and Family* (New York: Holt, Rinehart and Winston, 1987).

12 Migrants' decision-making in the frame of family economies is well-studied for labour migrants. In imperial states, the English segment of Great Britain in particular, urban upper middle class, rural gentry, and nobility families sent non-inheriting surplus sons into the (colonizing) army and the colonized economies.

13 For the global historical frame, see John R. McNeill and Kenneth Pomeranz, eds., "Production, Destruction, and Connection, 1750-Present," in *The Cambridge World History*, vol. 7 (Cambridge: Cambridge University Press, 2015). A concept of acquiring labouring populations, "manpowering," in the medieval world – a Eurocentric designation – has been developed by James Belich, *The World the Plague Made: The Black Death and the Rise of Europe* (Princeton, NJ: Princeton University Press, 2022).

14 Caroline Elkins, *Legacy of Violence: A History of the British Empire* (New York: Knopf, 2022). Case studies for particular cases exist for all empires, whether traditional overseas colonizing or continentally annexing.

states provide "investment incentives" through low taxation of profits and high exploitability of, especially migrant, workingmen and -women. Migrant information networks react to such impositions, whether of low wages or poor working conditions, or both (see, among others, Chapter 8 in this volume).[15]

In the present high-income and high-consuming societies, it is low-wage sectors that deliver all of the basic needs: food production and preparation, textiles and clothing, hospital work and health/child/old-age care, housing and other construction, and delivery of food and consumer items. "It so happens" – the veiling term for "this involves intentionally" – that in many of these sectors women's work dominates, which is neglected by states-economies-societies.[16] The neoliberal policies in the frame of globalization have vastly expanded reserve labour pools, transient industries, and transient workers. To maintain this pool, the global opening of borders for low-wage workingmen and -women requires sending states to support the export of labour, i.e., in terms of political theory, the export of citizens: European empires did so in the nineteenth century, whereas North African states, Pakistan, Bangladesh, the Philippines, Central American states and others do so in the present. The receiving states, in turn, maintain highly stratified, segmented, and segregated labour markets and structurally hierarchize their resident populations over migrants.[17] The core tenet of democratic governance, equality before the law, is abandoned when maintenance of the reserve labour pool is the goal as this relies on intended globally unequal – in modern parlance "asymmetrical" – power relations and economic investments.[18]

In this volume, we use a broad definition of migration, including free and unfree labour, temporary and permanent migrants, as well as the full variety of legal status assignments from "classic" labour migrants via refugees or, legally more circumscribed, asylum seekers to temporary migrants and undocumented ones. Since no state or society wants to permanently support refugees, all have to enter the respective labour markets, either immediately after arrival or at a later point in time. To cite a few cases, Palestinian refugees, for

15 For the contemporary unequal distribution of wealth, see Oxfam, *The Inequality Virus: Bringing Together a World Torn Apart by Coronavirus Through a Fair, Just and Sustainable Economy* (Oxfam: Oxford, 2021).

16 Dirk Hoerder, Elise van Nederveen Meerkerk, and Silke Neunsinger, eds., *Towards a Global History of Domestic and Caregiving Workers* (Leiden: Brill, 2015).

17 For an early formulation of labour market theory, see F. C. Valkenburg and A. M. C. Vissers, "Segmentation of the Labour Market: The Theory of the Dual Labour Market – The Case of the Netherlands," *Netherlands Journal of Sociology* 16 (1980): 155–170.

18 For the emergence of world-systems analyses and the relation of power politics and racialization, see Chapter 3 in this volume.

stateside political reasons, have had to live in camps for a long time and some have developed strategies to de-camp; Rohingya refugees from Myanmar, 2017, are being shunted to remote and secluded locations; refugees from Central American US-supported dictatorial regimes are often being pushed back by US southern border forces. "Classic" labour migrants move for economic reasons "pure and simple," they make decisions concerning their life-courses. Those in Western Europe have been styled "guestworkers" in the second half of the twentieth century. While the question might be posed concerning which culture makes its "guests" work, the idea behind the term's invention was political: "Migrants" stay while "guests" are expected to leave. In addition, the same type of migrants, up to the defeat of fascism – German, Austrian, Italian, or any other variant – in 1945, had been called "foreign workers" and, thus, the label could not be used again. While the label "guestworker" is increasingly criticized in German-language research, where it originated, it has received international scholarly acceptance.[19]

Self-decided migrant workers, who are usually designated "free migrants," depart under – often extreme – economic constraints and, instead of being free, these men and women have been and are being coerced out of unsupportable "home" societies. They are, in a way, a homeless social group, an exportable part of a population. Most head for regions of (investment-created) job options that are perceived as better than those in their society of birth – even though they may still be highly exploitative. Migrants, who – in their own words – move "to bread," develop flexible life plans and pursue multiple strategies: If means and goals as well as stateside regulations permit, permanent emigration, and immigration – individually or as a family – is one potential option. Others decide to move in stages to the next income-providing labour market, then to a sea- or air-port location, then to the intended temporary or final destination. They may move in sequence ("chain migration") with early arrivals' savings financing the subsequent trips of kin and friends. Again, others decide for commuting in a wide range of temporal rhythms, depending on the distance between their workplace and home, the job requirements, and the costs involved. (Potential) migrants develop strategies to negotiate, sidestep, or alter migration regulations (see Chapter 20 in this volume). They compare wage levels and working conditions across destinations: In the past,

19 Cindy Hahamovitch, "Creating Perfect Immigrants: Guestworkers of the World in Historical Perspective," *Labor History* 44, no. 1 (2003): 69–94. For a recent critical analysis in the German context, see Veronika Kourabas, *Die Anderen ge-brauchen: Eine rassismustheoretische Analyse von "Gastarbeit" im migrationsgesellschaftlichen Deutschland* (Bielefeld: Transcript Verlag, 2021).

for example, potential South Italian migrants compared working conditions in Montreal, New York, Buenos Aires and elsewhere,[20] Polish migrants from Chicago to Sydney,[21] and Chinese workers between the French and British colonizer realms (see Chapter 8 in this volume).

The decisions of migrants about their lives and the destinations at which they expect or hope to realize their aspirations jointly with official data on the scale of global migrations – probably involving considerable undercount – highlight the ineffectiveness of nation-state approaches. We will outline the extensive theoretical and empirical fallacies of the concept of the "nation-state" below. "Methodological nationalism" as the unquestioned positing of the nation-state as a "natural" base of social, political, economic, and cultural developments has been critiqued for over two decades, at first in a concise theoretical summary by Andreas Wimmer and Nina Glick Schiller. We expand this critique by including analyses of empires, "methodological imperialism," and by designating the emphasis on bordered (state) territories as "methodological territorialism." We add that the positing of "state" – from small units such as Fiji, where imperial powers once "harvested" workers, to imperial ones such as Russia or Britain – comprises "methodological top-down institution-centeredness." Furthermore, the research presented in this volume emphasizes the historical continuities of labour regimes notwithstanding seemingly major changes in political organization, whether from imperial to Soviet Russia or from colonized to independent societies. The combination of labour and migration histories permits refinements of analyses while the inclusion of the major economic actors, those with the power to determine investment flows – whether nineteenth-century plantation owners or late twentieth-century hedge fund managers – permits comprehensive analyses of political-economic interrelations. The separation of politics-policies and economics, once combined in the field of *Politische Ökonomie*, political economy, was a Cold War tool to

20 Samuel Baily, *Immigrants in the Lands of Promise: Italians in Buenos Aires and New York City, 1870–1914* (Ithaca, NY: Cornell University Press, 1999); Donna R. Gabaccia and Fraser M. Ottanelli, eds., *Italian Workers of the World: Labor, Migration and the Making of Multi-Ethnic States* (Urbana: University of Illinois Press, 2001); Donna R. Gabaccia and Franca Iacovetta, eds., *Women, Gender, and Transnational Lives: Italian Workers of the World* (Toronto: University of Toronto Press, 2002).

21 Ewa Morawska, "Labor Migrations of Poles in the Atlantic World Economy, 1880–1914," *Comparative Studies in Society and History* 31, no. 2 (1989): 237–272; Adam Walaszek, "Labor Diasporas in Comparative Perspective: Polish and Italian Migrant Workers in the Atlantic World between the 1870s and the 1920s," in *The Social Construction of Diversity: Recasting the Master Narrative of Industrial Nations*, ed. Christiane Harzig and Danielle Juteau (New York: Berghahn, 2003), 152–176.

juxtapose a (politically) "free West" to an (economically) authoritarian "East." The "South" and its struggles to liberate itself (rather: themselves) from the imperial segments of "the West" was not part of this ideological construct. It was, however, part of the resident and migrant workers' lives.[22]

In this introduction, after a summary of migrations worldwide, we will first outline the inability of governments to understand the demand for labour in their very own societies and industries. Secondly, we will examine the role of "the state" in its manifold historic appearances as empire, multi-ethnic conglomerate, or nation and its moveable populations. Next, we will outline capital investment strategies – whether privately- or state-owned – and labour and working-class organizations accepting or countering the power of capital. In conclusion, we will discuss the agency of migrant and non-migrant workingmen and -women.[23]

Globally, international migration of all kinds involves nearly 258 million people or 3.4 percent of the world's population (2017 data). The number of internal migrations is – and generally has been – higher. Nearly one-third of the international migrants live in Asian countries (79.5 million in a total population of 4.5 billion) or in Europe (77.8 million in a total population of 745 million).[24] Of the migrants, women account for between 42.5 percent (Asia) and 52 percent (Europe). (See Figure 1.1).

2 Labour Demand and Migration in the Present

In the last decade, labour demand and supply have been at the forefront of both regional and global crises. Declining populations in some states and a high percentage of job-seeking young people in others have been and are a

22 Andreas Wimmer and Nina Glick Schiller, "Methodological Nationalism and Beyond: Nation-Building, Migration and the Social Sciences," *Global Networks* 2, no. 4 (2002): 301–334; Andreas Wimmer and Nina Glick Schiller, "Methodological Nationalism, the Social Sciences, and the Study of Migration: An Essay in Historical Epistemology," *International Migration Review* 37, no. 3 (2003): 576–610.

23 Given the intensity of research in the last three decades, it is impossible to cite all the relevant literature. We thus refer to two encyclopaedias: Klaus J. Bade, Pieter C. Emmer, Leo Lucassen, and Jochen Oltmer, eds., *The Encyclopedia of European Migration and Minorities: From the Seventeenth Century to the Present* (Cambridge: Cambridge University Press, 2011); Immanuel Ness, gen. ed., *Encyclopedia of Global Human Migration*, 5 vols. (Oxford: Wiley-Blackwell, 2013).

24 "World Population," Worldometer, accessed 5 March 2022, https://www.worldometers.info/world-population/.

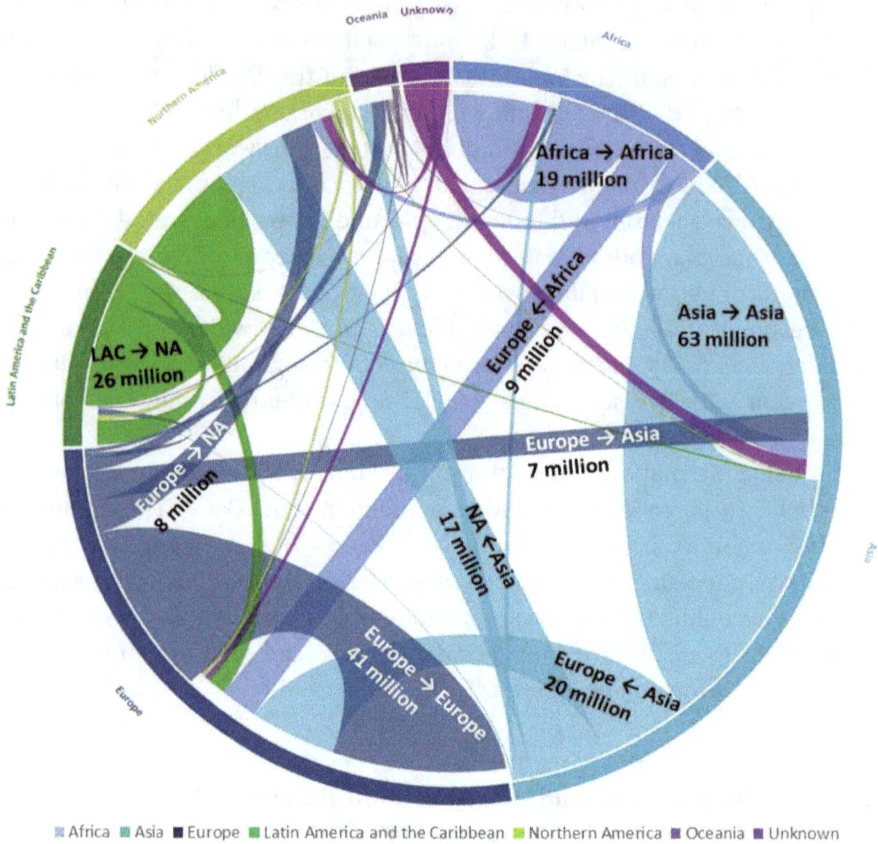

FIGURE 1.1 International migration patterns, 2017, as vectors from origin to destination, by geographical area
Note: NA refers to Northern America, LAC refers to Latin America and the Caribbean
SOURCE: *INTERNATIONAL MIGRATION REPORT 2017* (NEW YORK: UNITED NATIONS, DEPARTMENT OF ECONOMIC AND SOCIAL AFFAIRS, POPULATION DIVISION, 2017), P. 11, FIGURE 5

preoccupation of governments and employers, whether mid-size companies or large capitalist conglomerates. The war of the Assad family (in power since 1970) against a democratization movement in Syria had dislocated more than half of the country's population of 18 million by 2015 and sent millions of refugees to neighbouring countries and Western-Southern-Northern Europe. While highly qualified refugees could enter labour markets quickly, if laws permitted, others became workers in sweatshops in Turkey (Türkiye as from 2022) and other countries of the region, with some displacing resident low-wage workers.

Similarly, when in February 2022, the president of the Russian Federation, Putin, declared war on Ukraine, millions of Ukrainian women and children fled, as did perhaps one million opponents of the war in Russia (estimates of late 2022). At the beginning of the worldwide COVID-19 pandemic, governments rigorously closed borders to prevent the spreading of the virus through travel. As a result, labour migrants on the move were literally stopped in their tracks, while those at their destinations were often ordered to depart.[25]

The topic of aliens, i.e., migrants, carrying "alien germs" into healthy societies had been an anti-immigrant slogan of exclusionists in the late nineteenth-century North Atlantic world.[26] Under the impact of the COVID-19 pandemic, policymakers and public opinion in the highly developed – and mass-consuming – segments of the world economy suddenly became aware that undervalued and underpaid workers were essential to the functioning of the societies' economies. No food without distant plantation labour or local slaughterhouse staff, without airfreighting and transoceanic shipping, without migrant truck drivers and local supermarket sales personnel. No healthcare and other care work without immigrant nurses, doctors, and caregivers for infants and children as well as the infirm and aged. In the face of such pressure, politicians decided that the "system-relevant" migrant workers were to be admitted under quickly imposed regulations, often with quarantine at their own cost. Unless migrantized, racialized, and feminized work sectors are integrated into rule-based labour markets, high levels of underpayment and exploitation will remain systemic.[27]

Throughout history and across the globe, in times of rapid economic development, migrant workingmen and -women from population-exporting states form an essential part of the segmented labour forces in importing states. The latter segregate migrants into 3-D jobs – dirty, dangerous, demeaning – and frame migrants' status below access to citizenship, usually without rights to political participation or organizations to improve working conditions. In Western Europe's guestworker period, trade unions and social-democratic, socialist, and communist parties struggled for (some) inclusion, but industrial

---

25 Katharine Jones, Sanushka Mudaliar, and Nicola Piper, *Locked Down and in Limbo: The Global Impact of COVID-19 on Migrant Worker Rights and Recruitment* (Geneva: International Labour Office, 2021).

26 Alan M. Kraut, *Silent Travelers: Germs, Genes, and the "Immigrant Menace"* (New York: Basic Books, 1994).

27 In the post-Brexit United Kingdom, the anti-immigrant campaign led to a shortage of 50,000 truckdrivers, 5,000 or more slaughterhouse workers, both mainly East European, as well as approximately 100,000 each in the National Health Service and care services, all globally recruited (data from early 2022).

trade unions have been shunted aside by the capital-state complex since Thatcherism and Reaganism. In the oil-producing Arab states and Iran, since the region's economic take-off in the 1970s, the ruling elites had prevented trade union formation. In China, the All-China Federation of Trade Unions is a party organization. In Latin America, the trade union movement is characterized by an enormous degree of heterogeneity. Historically, major trade unions have emerged from above and/or have been integrated into specific national political systems, while independent and autonomous trade unions have often been targeted by repressive capital and state measures. In addition – and comparable to other segments of the globe – a vast proportion of workingmen and -women in the so-called informal sector are traditionally not organized by trade unions.

In Europe, where anti-immigrant sentiments – a kind of updated anti-Semitism – have been growing, large sectors of agricultural food production and its industrial processing rely on more than 5 million migrants, many of them temporary and circular (2020 data): Those from Eastern European societies mostly head for western and northern states, those from North and West Africa mostly for Mediterranean states and France. A large segment is forced to live without documents since the respective governments refuse regularization both of border crossing and legal status. In the EU-28 of 2016, non-regular workers in the agricultural labour force accounted for between 18 and 15 percent of the totals in Italy, Spain, the UK and the Netherlands, and 12 percent in France and Greece.[28] In Central Asia, especially Uzbekistan and Turkmenistan, "the state" – or is it a political-economic elite? – forces the populations into internal seasonal migration for cotton harvesting.[29] In the People's – or Peoples' – Republic of China (PRC), 285.6 million internal migrants drive the urban economies (2020 data). "Internal" in the PRC covers 9.6 million square kilometres as compared to 4.2 million for all EU member states. While at the beginning of Deng Xiaoping's[30] economic reforms of 1979,

28 Johan Fredrik Rye and Karen O'Reilly, eds., *International Labor Migration to Europe's Rural Regions* (London: Routledge, 2021), especially Johan Fredrik Rye and Karen O'Reilly, "New Perspectives on Labor Migration to Europe's Rural Regions," 3–21; Agricultural and Rural Convention, described as "a platform for organizations working together for good food, good farming and better *rural* policies in the EU," 2020 data, accessed 5 February 2022, https://www.arc2020.eu/.

29 In Uzbekistan, forced cotton harvest labour, of which 65 percent were female and which also included children, was abolished in 2020, according to the International Labour Organization (ILO).

30 Deng, in the early nationalist period, had – like most Chinese foreign students at the time – studied and worked in France under the "Diligent Work-Frugal Study Program" which brought some 4,000 Chinese students to France. Turning to radical politics, he

the number of the mostly rural-urban migrants had stood at 6.6 million (1982), by 2010 it involved 6.5 percent of the total population. Since social welfare and public services, including schools for children, are financed and administered through local *hukou*, migrants from afar cannot access registration. However, on the positive side, the options of the state-capitalist reforms have permitted tens of millions of men and women to lift themselves out of poverty through their own agency.[31]

Turning from the "Global North" to the "Global South," a division that requires differentiation, similar patterns are evident.[32] Singapore and Hong Kong, the former a British colony until 1965 and the latter until 1997, attracted and continue to attract hundreds of thousands of migrants, while Malaysia has done so since pre-colonial times, and the Philippines since the introduction of unregulated "special economic zones" in 1995. At the same time, the Philippine state engages in labour export of men into global shipping and of women into domestic and care work in Europe and North America (see Chapter 23 in this volume). European states were labour-export, people-export regions in the nineteenth and early twentieth centuries. The respective governing elites exclude "surplus" men and women from residence and citizenship.

In India, according to the 2011 Census, some 450 million people were internal migrants, approximately 175 million seasonally and circularly, the others for multi-annual or permanent search of incomes individually or as families. A total of 93 percent of them work in the "informal economy" (see Chapter 6 in this volume) and are thus outside the reach of "typical" rural or industrial unions.[33]

---

continued his education at Sun Yatsen University in Moscow. Deng witnessed poverty when a rival faction in the Chinese Communist Party downgraded him to work for four years at a tractor factory in rural Jiangxi province.

31 Ming Lu and Yiran Xia, "Migration in the People's Republic of China," Asian Development Bank Institute, Working Paper 593 (Tokyo, 2016), accessed 5 February 2022, https://www.adb.org/publications/migration-people-republic-china/; C. Textor, Migrant Workers in China: Statistics and Facts (2021), accessed 5 February 2022, https://www.statista.com/topics/1540/migrant-workers-in-china/. On worker mobilization before the reforms, see Felix Wemheuer, *A Social History of Maoist China: Conflict and Change, 1949–1976* (Cambridge: Cambridge University Press, 2019), 193–277.

32 The juxtaposition is a "northern" concept that has not been incorporated in analyses and theorizations from scholarship south of the US border, the Mediterranean, and the Himalayas.

33 At the beginning of the COVID-19 pandemic, millions were sent back to their places of origin without any support. Priya Deshinkar, "Structural Violence and Normalising Human Suffering: Labour Migration during the Covid Pandemic in India," *Journal of South Asian Development* 17, no. 1 (2022): 134–140; Pooja Misra and Jaya Gupta, "Impact of COVID 19 on Indian Migrant Workers: Decoding Twitter Data by Text Mining," *Indian*

In mineral-rich post-colonizer societies, as in post-apartheid South Africa, governments and mining corporations (usually white-owned international capital) supplemented the internal forced mass migration of workers (of black colour of skin) with in-migration from neighbouring societies. In West Africa, Ghana (self-liberated from British colonizer rule, 1957) attracted foreign workers for its fast-growing economy. By the late 1960s, 830,000 men and women (12.3 percent of the population) had arrived, but when world market prices for groundnuts dropped sharply, the government expelled 214,000 of them. As in similar cases, the government thereby shifted the cost of unemployment to the societies of origin, where, if remittances of each of those expelled had supported a family of five, more than one million men, women and children suffered.[34]

In the Arab and Iranian oil-extracting and producing economies, migration began around 1900. British, US, and French ("Western") imperial political tutelage and capital investment regimes induced technical experts and political "advisers" to migrate. When, in 1953, the Persian government led by Swiss-educated Prime Minister Mohammad Mossadegh attempted to change power hierarchies for the benefit of the Iranian state and society, a coup orchestrated by the Western powers' secret service and oil corporation managers ousted him.[35] In the Arab oil-extraction economies, international corporations and

---

Journal of Labour Economics 64 (2021): 731–747. Public media reports, particularly in *The Guardian* (London) and "Indian Migrant Workers During the COVID-19 Pandemic," Wikipedia, accessed 7 February 2022, https://en.wikipedia.org/wiki/Indian_migrant_workers_during_the_COVID-19_pandemic. In general: Ravi Srivastava, "Labour Migration in India: Recent Trends, Patterns and Policy Issues," *Indian Journal of Labour Economics* 54, no. 3 (2011): 411–440. We are grateful to Indu Agnihotri at the Centre for Women's Development Studies, Jawaharlal Nehru University, Delhi, and Silke Neunsinger, Swedish Labour Movement Archives and Library, for refences to migration research in India.

34 Hoerder, *Cultures in Contact*, 550–559. Among many others, also see Margaret Peil, "Expulsion of West African Aliens," *Journal of Modern African Studies* 9, no. 2 (1971): 205–229.

35 One year later, the US Department of State and the CIA ousted the Guatemalan President Jacobo Árbenz Guzmán in a coup because his government intended to nationalize part of the lands, devoted to fruit extraction, of the US-based United Fruit Company (UFC, now: Chiquita Brands International). The UFC (founded 1899) had organized armed interventions in Central America since 1910 and was behind a massacre of approximately 2,000 workers in Colombia in 1928. This capital-worker clash is a theme of Gabriel José García Márquez' novel *Cien Años de Soledad* (One Hundred Years of Solitude). Under the subsequent right-wing governments, a civil war began, 1960–1996, with approximately 200,000 dead, many killed by government death squads, and a larger number of interstate refugees. Another five years later, 1961, the prime minister of the mineral-rich Democratic Republic of Congo, Patrice Lumumba, was murdered by Congolese secessionist and

regional state elites rearranged profit distribution, and hence a brief export stop in the early 1970s was labelled "oil crisis" rather than "capitalist struggle." The high demand for crude as well as the investments required and induced mass labour migrations from population-exporting Egypt, Pakistan, and Bangladesh, as well as Southeast Asian states, including women for domestic work. The oil-consuming segment of the globe with its car cultures and energy-intensive industries is based on the labour of these workers without rights and amenities.[36]

In the Americas, too, labour migration changed considerably over the course of the twentieth century. Until the 1950s, the US and Canada were important destinations for European migrants; thereafter migrants from Latin America and Asia began to fill the labour demand. While most of the latter migrants initially came from Mexico, dependent Puerto Rico, and Cuba, in recent years, migration from Central America has increased. In South America, Venezuela (with its booming oil industry) became an important post-war destination for European migrants, particularly from Italy, Spain, and Portugal. During the 1970s and 1980s, people from all over Latin America, and particularly from Colombia, fleeing (US-backed) dictatorships and civil wars migrated to Venezuela. With falling oil prices, the situation began to change and the severe economic and social crisis of the most recent past led an estimated 6 million Venezuelan citizens to emigrate to neighbouring countries and the US (UNHCR data, 2022). From the Andean region, considerable migratory movements reached the countries of the Southern Cone (Argentina, Chile, and Uruguay) as well as the US and Spain.[37]

Belgian military with connivance both mine corporation managers and British and US secret services.

36 Hoerder, *Cultures in Contact*, 546–550.

37 De Haas, Castles, and Miller, *The Age of Migration*, 145–172; Blanca Sánchez-Alonso, "The Age of Mass Migration in Latin America," *Economic History Review* 72, no. 1 (2019): 3–31; "Migration Data in South America," Migration Data Portal, accessed 3 December 2022, https://www.migrationdataportal.org/regional-data-overview/migration-data-south-america. For the Caribbean see, among many others, Madhavi Kale, *Fragments of Empire: Capital, Slavery, and Indian Indentured Labor Migration in the British Caribbean* (Philadelphia: University of Pennsylvania Press, 1998); O. Nigel Bolland, *The Politics of Labour in the British Caribbean: The Social Origin of Authoritarianism and Democracy in the Labour Movement* (Kingston: Ian Randle, 2001); Lara Putnam, "Undone by Desire: Migration, Sex Across Boundaries, and Collective Destinies in the Greater Caribbean, 1840–1940," in Gabaccia and Hoerder, *Connecting Seas*, 302–337, and Lara Putnam, "Borderlands and Border-Crossers: Migrants and Boundaries in the Greater Caribbean, 1840–1940," *Small Axe* 42 (2014): 7–21. For an overview on labour history in Latin America and the Caribbean, see Rossana Barragán and David Mayer, "Latin America

Societal arrangements across most societies of the globe, Europe included, did not and often still do not provide life chances and perspectives to men and women. Particularly in the age group from 15 to 25 years, when young men and women leave their families of birth for independent lives, millions are coerced to move and hence, to reiterate the obvious, "self-decided migration" often occurs in coercive economic frames.

3 The Role of States in Historical Perspective: Empires, Multi-Ethnic Conglomerates, Self-Declared Nations[38]

For the manifold labour and left organizations, the conceptualization of highly differentiated working classes (not: "the proletariat") was a challenging issue since their emergence. Most state apparatuses, under the guise of "nation," privileged or continue to privilege elites or, more broadly, middle and upper classes. In Europe, at the time of the French Revolution against the aristocracy-church-complex, spokespersons from the middle classes needed historical legitimization and thus the bourgeoisie rooted itself as "the people" in a "natural" peasant culture[39] and carefully avoided any reference to the service and early industrial classes. In the context of the revolutionary struggles in general, a broad overarching unity against the old elite(s) was necessary: When, throughout the nineteenth century, industrial labour forces or working classes grew, the newly established bourgeois states both refused them and the rural classes political membership, i.e., citizen status. Most state-socialized middle-class scholars, a few like Karl Marx and Frederick Engels excepted, excluded the lowly from political theory. Since the same ideological forces also excluded

and the Caribbean," in *Handbook Global History of Work*, ed. Karin Hofmeester and Marcel van der Linden (Berlin/Boston: De Gruyter Oldenbourg, 2018), 83–110.

38 The "Global Collaboratory on the History of Labour Relations" at the International Institute for Social History (IISH) has studied historical shifts in labour relations from, roughly, the rise and subsequent development of capitalism (1500–2000). See Gijs Kessler, Christine Moll-Murata, and Karin M. Hofmeester, eds., "Conquerors, Employers and Arbiters: States and Shifts in Labour Relations, 1500–2000," *International Review of Social History* 61, no. S24 (2016), especially "Introduction," 1–26.

39 Dirk Hoerder with Inge Blank and Horst Rössler, eds., *Roots of the Transplanted*, 2 vols. (New York: Columbia University Press, 1994), 1–110. The complex relation between "state" and "nation" was originally conceptualized by (emigrant) scholars from the multinational Habsburg Empire. During the struggles for liberation from the imperial centre, the trans-european Habsburg family in the increasingly Austrian-German core, intellectuals and activists used their respective "national culture" as strategy. Emil Niederhauser, *The Rise of Nationality in Eastern Europe* (Budapest: Corvina Kiadó, 1976).

women,[40] the “nation” was as much a middle-class male claim and construct as “state” had originally been a territorial claim of a leader with an armed band of (usually unmarried) young men, self- and discourse-styled as “warriors” or “knights.”

The construct of a cultural “nation” congruent with a territorial state never had an empirical basis. The postulated European model cases of France and Great Britain included Basques, people in Brittany, the bilingual Alsatians, or English, Scottish, Welsh, Cornish, Ulster Scots and Irish. The English elite arrogated itself the monopoly of ideology-production, British-imperial, it deprived the colonized Irish of any rights and their descendants had to emigrate as workers. In fact, “colonization” – as term usually applied to overseas annexations – began in Europe in the second half of the fifteenth century with the annexations of the Irish societies, the Northern Russian-Siberian-Central Asian ones as well as Galician-Balkan ones by the respective dynasties and the usage of the subjected populations.[41] The bulk of many-cultured Europe was family-ruled and -owned, Habsburg and Hohenzollern for example. In many-cultured Eurasia the Romanov, correctly the Holstein-Gottorp-Romanov, family held sway and colonized Central Asian and Siberian societies. In many-cultured China, the in-migrant or conquering Jurchen Qing dynasty ruled over Han Chinese and dozens of other cultures. In the colonized segments of the world, later to become the “Global South,” diasporas of Spanish, Portuguese, British, French, Dutch and, later, US migrant (white-skinned) administrative and military men ruled over people of skin colours other than white. When the latter successfully struggled and fought for independence, Western scholars expanded the “nation-state” ideology to Africa, Latin America, and Southeast Asia. Their political theory, which in fact comprised an ideology, was generally conservative and liberal, later neoliberal capitalist. Only ordo-liberals planned to regulate markets according to societal needs.[42]

The classes excluded by elites from state practice and by subservient scholars from political theory began, from the mid-nineteenth century onward, to organize. Workers in general and militants, in particular, found themselves in a quandary: They lived and organized within states but understood that workingmen and -women were exploited regardless of state borders. To the

---

40 Edith Kuiper, *A Herstory of Economics* (Cambridge: Polity, 2022).

41 The conquest of the North American “West” and the peoples living there by the US and Canada was also part of empire-building.

42 Els Bogaerts and Remco Raben, eds., *Beyond Empire and Nation: The Decolonization of African and Asian Societies, 1930s-1970s* (Leiden: Brill, 2013); Lester D. Langley, *The Americas in the Age of Revolution, 1750–1850* (New Haven, CT: Yale University Press, 1996).

bordered nations, they thus juxtaposed an inter-national working class and, as supra-state organizations, the "Internationals."[43] In addition, these new left movements also faced "colonialism" or, in terms of agency, colonizer domination over labouring peoples across the globe. Were workers of colours of skin other than white equal to white-skinned ones? They provided foods or fabrics to working-class consumers in those powerful countries in which the labour and left movements emerged (see Chapter 11 in this volume).

Europe's ideology-producing scholars as well as schoolteachers achieved hegemony, but not rule. Latin American "locals" of European background – intellectuals included or even at the forefront – liberated themselves from the Euro-North American ideological hegemony during the first half of the nineteenth century, while those in Africa and Southeast Asia could do so only in the 1930s and 1940s after the European state and power structures had self-destructed during the First World War or had been destroyed by fascist aggression. The anti- and post-colonial militants, however, generally fought for independence and not for a redrawing of borders. However, in Latin America Simón Bolívar attempted to unite post-colonial polities and, later, in Arabia and Sub-Saharan Africa, some leaders advocated pan-movements aiming at dissolving colonizer-drawn border lines but remaining ephemeral. Most of the newly independent states remained confined in their colonizer shapes, and their political classes frequently remained mentally fettered to nation-state constructs and communicated in the colonizer's language. "Western" state-supported capital investments buttressed this post-colonial continuity.

In states in Asia, neither political theory nor state practice offered different perspectives. Scholars in imperial China, operating in the frame of methodological imperialism, constructed Han Chinese as the basis of society even though the imperial realm – after 1911/12 republican – consisted of many peoples and several other-cultured ruling elites had imposed themselves. Imperial Japan, like family-ruled imperial Europe, consisted of a patchwork of samurai family-run entities with a constructed hierarchy of southerners versus (allegedly inferior) northerners. Neither these elites nor those of other societies of the region considered labouring families, peasant-artisanal-industrial, as full

43 For recent literature on the development of the "Internationals," see Fabrice Bensimon, Deluermoz Quentin, and Jeanne Moisand, eds., *"Arise Ye Wretched of the Earth": The First International in a Global Perspective* (Leiden: Brill, 2018); Jean-Numa Ducange, "The Second International: 1889–1914," in *The Cambridge History of Socialism*, ed. Marcel van der Linden, vol. 2 (Cambridge: Cambridge University Press, 2022), 278–299; Brigitte Studer, *Reisende der Weltrevolution: Eine Globalgeschichte der Kommunistischen Internationale* (Berlin: Suhrkamp, 2020).

members of society. This elite-versus-the-rest-of-society ideology remained intact when insurgent elites restructured the empire. Reacting to a US military threat in 1853/54, Japan's Meiji reformers (since 1868) shifted the cost of industrialization to rural taxpaying families. This forced many, especially from the southern prefectures, to emigrate (see Chapter 20 in this volume). They, like most migrants, provided their labour or, more broadly "human capital," to states more advantageously placed in global power hierarchies. Significantly, labour and left organizations in these "advanced" receiving states usually refused to accept "yellow" migrants as working-class equals.

At this juncture, the power-wielding empires or more correctly, their political-economic elites, had abolished slavery but still needed labour forces for plantations and mines as well as service personnel, especially in the economies of the Indian Ocean rim and Southeast Asia, Latin America, and the Caribbean. The colonizer powers, by direct rule or unequal treaties, extracted workingmen and -women, in particular from Southern China, French-ruled Southeast Asia ("Indochina") and British-ruled South Asia (see Chapter 8 in this volume).[44] When, after a middle-class nationalist period, a new elite and mass movement in China established a communist state in 1949, the peasant and working classes were ideologically upgraded, but power resided with a privileged party apparatus. Thus, across the globe, containerized "nation-states" dominated discourse and held power while imperial cores and colonized macro-regions were inextricably linked by capitalist strategies and working-class experiences. The working classes, however, were compartmentalized by languages and cultures.

4 Portable Working Populations in Historical Perspective

Within states, family-run for centuries or millennia and discursively "national" since the outgoing eighteenth century at best, parlance had caused women, men, and children to lose their individuality by designating them as "populations" in a "territory" rather than as "citizens." Territories, seemingly geographically fixed, were malleable realms of rule, of power. The populations – peasant, craft or worker families producing sustenance, utensils for everyday

44 Hugh Tinker, *A New System of Slavery: The Export of Indian Labour Overseas, 1830–1921* (London: Oxford University Press, 1974); Piet C. Emmer, ed., *Colonialism and Migration: Indentured Labour before and after Slavery* (Dordrecht: Martinus Nijhoff, 1986); David Northrup, *Indentured Labor in the Age of Imperialism: 1834–1922* (Cambridge: Cambridge University Press, 1995).

use as well as luxury items for a miniscule clientele – appear as an anonymous mass. Rulers/ruling families could require service and forced labour, dispose of the masses as war materials, and deport "surplus" men and women.

The portability of populations has been part of human history since the invention or imposition of power apparatuses. In the Persian Empire, rulers such as Dareios and Xerxes (522–465 BCE) forced masses of war captives to move to where their labouring bodies were to be used. A ruler in Babylon planned a zikkurat for the god Marduk and, from around his empire, drafted such a cultural variety of forced workers and war captives that they could not understand each other's tongues. Later mythologists, changing the story, had their God punish the blasphemy of building the "tower of Babel" by confusing the languages of the workers. Other biblical authors knew of King Solomon of Israel, who, wanting to build a huge temple with a sumptuous palace for himself ("First Temple" in the Jewish religion), requested building materials from King Hiram of Tyrus and paid for migrant woodcutters. Then Solomon, "took a census of all the aliens who were residing in Israel [...] seventy thousand of them he assigned as laborers, eighty thousand as stonecutters in the hill country, and three thousand six hundred as overseers to make the people work" (2 Chronicles 2:17). Pharaonic Egyptian and imperial Chinese chronicles also report mass recruitment of workers, be it for the construction of pyramids or canals. Such large construction projects required capital accumulation through taxation and, given the high quality of much of the work, highly skilled workers. Some of these struggled for better conditions. Workers at a tomb near Thebes, Egypt, who did not receive their wages, struck in 1159 BCE. In view of bad harvests, corrupt officials, and high public expenses, they demanded that societal harmony – represented by the goddess *ma'at* – be re-established.[45]

Fast forward: In fifteenth-century Sub-Saharan societies, rulers and elite families had imposed rights-in-persons slavery on their realms' populations. When, in the sixteenth century, European well-capitalized and -armed seafarer merchants reached West Africa's coasts, they expanded the portability of the enslaved across the Atlantic to the Americas and, in the power relationship, turned the rights-in-persons labour regime into "chattel," exploitable things, as a commodity. This transatlantic American, not "African," *slavery* was not merely a condition, as the term suggests, but an active process of enslavement and human trafficking to the plantation mode of production, or "factories in the

45 Toby Wilkinson, *The Rise and Fall of Ancient Egypt* (New York: Random House, 2013), 324–336.

fields,"[46] established in the Caribbean and the Americas with mobile capital of European merchants, gentry, and aristocrats. The enslaving process involved capture with resulting high human loss through marches to the embarkation ports, ex-port of 12 million or more enslaved and, after "wastage" of 3 million chattel or "pieces" during the Atlantic crossing, sale of 9 million people, one-third of them women. The slave-labour regime extended from the British-colonized Atlantic coast and, subsequently, the US South and Mississippi basin via the Caribbean and Central American colonies southward as far as Brazil.[47] Especially on Caribbean plantations, the capitalists had their overseers work millions to death since importing new workers was cheaper than keeping those who were already there in working health or raising slave children to working age.[48] While most cultures in the Americas have partly been created by the enslaved and their children, scholars who were self-segregated and contained in whiteness-ideology have long denied this. This also pertains to the agency of enslaved people in the Americas.[49] The Haitian revolution against French colonizer rule and slavery in Saint-Domingue did, for a long time, not receive adequate historiographical attention. Research and historiography on the region were only decolonized though the contributions of scholars such as W. E. B. Du Bois from the US and George Padmore, Eric Williams, Walter Rodney, Aimé Césaire, Frantz Fanon, C. L. R. James, and Stuart Hall from Caribbean societies.[50]

---

46 Carey McWilliams first used the term in *Factories in the Field: The Story of Migrant Farm Labor in California* (Boston: Little, Brown & Co., 1939).

47 In contrast to methodological nationalist approaches, referring, for example, to US or Brazilian slavery, an integrative approach was first proposed by David Brion Davis in a sequence of three volumes published over four decades: *The Problem of Slavery in Western Culture* (Ithaca, NY: Cornell University Press, 1966), *The Problem of Slavery in the Age of Revolution, 1770–1823* (Ithaca, NY: Cornell University Press, 1975), and *The Problem of Slavery in the Age of Emancipation* (New York: Alfred A. Knopf, 2014).

48 Patrick Manning, ed., *Slave Trades, 1500–1800: The Globalization of Forced Labour* (Brookfield, VT: Variorum, 1996) and Patrick Manning, *Slavery and African Life: Occidental, Oriental, and African Slave Trades* (New York: Cambridge University Press, 1990).

49 Research on slavery was long dominated by US scholars focusing on their own society with – compared to the Caribbean and Brazil – relatively few slaves. A change in perspective to the latter societies reveals the extensive cultural input of enslaved Africa-socialized men and women in the formation of the respective cultures.

50 Adom Getachew, *Worldmaking after Empire: The Rise and Fall of Self-Determination* (Princeton, NJ: Princeton University Press, 2019); Michelle Ann Stephens, *Black Empire: The Masculine Global Imaginary of Caribbean Intellectuals in the United States, 1914–1962* (Durham, NC: Duke University Press, 2005).

Shifting of populations followed a different pattern in the Ottoman Empire. Since the mid-fourteenth century, segments of assumedly disloyal populations in newly annexed regions were uprooted and transported to where their labour was needed, often for grain production near urban concentrations. In this *sürgün* practice, those uprooted would be resettled under conditions that, ideally, would induce them to invite friends and neighbours from their region of birth to join them – by migrating at their own cost rather than with state support.[51]

Europe's "imperial nation-states" of the nineteenth and twentieth centuries deported "surplus" or unwanted populations. The British government, under a scheme to reduce overstock on the internal labour market, planned "assisted migration" to send some 7,000 workers annually to the undersupplied colony of New South Wales, Australia; from the 1880s the Barnardo philanthropy sent poor – in some cases kidnapped – children to the White Dominions as labourers; after 1918, an Empire Settlement Act ex-ported disabled soldiers.[52] The French government, in particular after the Commune uprising in 1871, deported left militants to forced labour in the colonies. The German Emperor allegedly called social-democratic workers "fellows without a fatherland" and, a few decades later, West Germany's population planners, after the Second World War killing fields, hoped to induce surplus women, i.e., those without husbands, to emigrate.[53] All this evidence notwithstanding, the concept of a "surplus" population has never entered the political science of "democratic" societal organization.

---

51 The resettling of populations had also been practiced in this macro-region by the elites of the previous East Roman, Byzantine, Empire. Reşat Kasaba, *A Moveable Empire: Ottoman Nomads, Migrants, and Refugees* (Seattle: University of Washington Press, 2009).

52 From the broad literature: Lydia Murdoch, *Imagined Orphans: Poor Families, Child Welfare, and Contested Citizenship in London* (New Brunswick, NJ: Rutgers University Press, 2006); Gail H. Corbett, *Barnardo Children in Canada* (Peterborough: Woodland Publishing, 1981); Stephen Constantine, ed., *Emigrants and Empire: British Settlement in the Dominions Between the Wars* (Manchester: Manchester University Press, 1990); Melanie Burkett, "Explaining Resistance to Early Nineteenth-Century British Emigrants to New South Wales," *Journal of Migration History* 7, no. 1 (2021): 1–23.

53 Johannes-Dieter Steinert, "Migration and Migration Policy: West Germany and the Recruitment of Foreign Labour, 1945–61," *Journal of Contemporary History* 49, no. 1 (2014): 9–27.

5 Capitalist Investment Strategies, Mass Migrations, and Segmented Labour Markets since the Nineteenth Century

The very title of this subsection should invite critical questions. It does not ask how capital is formed and accumulated, but, like much of scholarship, assumes a status quo, namely existing funds for investment. Second, again like much of scholarship, it is forward-looking, "strategies." Migrants, however, often face retrograde living conditions comprising a lack of jobs, ossified social structures, and neither innovation nor development. They leave stagnant societies-economies-polities without strategies. Furthermore, withdrawal of capital – turning irrigated agriculture into dust belts or industrial regions into rust belts – forces residents to out-migrate. In the nineteenth century, much of Europe – its industrializing western and eastern cores excepted – was an economic disaster zone. At present, the absence of investment in China's rural regions leads to mass departures and the same holds true for much of Africa's rural regions. Large extraction complexes, such as mining or oil, use machinery rather than human labour while agricultural extraction under the plantation regime cannot do without human labour.[54] Viewed positively, labour migrants move from regions with a labour surplus – meaning insufficient food and life chances for some, many, or most – to regions of dynamic development with labour supply shortages. Migrants' decisions provide a balancing effect, men and women decide in gendered frames of reference whether to stay put or to move while states provide frames, usually favouring some over others.

In the century from the 1830s to the 1930s, centres of investment emerged in the Americas along the St. Lawrence River in Canada, the northeast of the US, and Buenos Aires; in Western Europe in a core region from the Netherlands, Belgium and Northeast France, across the Germanies to Silesia and to Budapest and Vienna, in the south to North Italian cities; in European Russia in the region from Moscow northward to St. Petersburg/Leningrad and southward to the Donbas mines. From Europe's peripheries, the mass transatlantic labour migration system emerged, while in the east, a Russian-Siberian migration system extended to the Amur River, the border to China.[55] In both regions,

54 Of the many life-writings of colonized workers, the most widely known is that of Rigoberta Menchú, a Guatemalan indigenous woman. She described internal migration to plantation work, exploitation, state violence, and labour organizing in *I, Rigoberta Menchú*, dictated to anthropologist Elisabeth Burgos (1983). She received the Nobel Peace Prize in 1992.

55 The settlement of farms in North America attracted approximately one third of the migrants in the 1840s, the ratio dwindled to a mere five percent by the 1890s. In contrast, in

the rural-urban migrations vastly outnumbered the transoceanic or transcontinental ones.

In the Southern Atlantic region, the investment into the West Africa-to-Americas human trafficking regime to supply plantation economies with capital-generating labour forces continued until the 1870s. With the formal abolition of slavery in the British Empire (mainly in its Caribbean segment) in 1834/39,[56] new investments in plantations for industrial crops such as rubber, palm oil, and copra in Asia necessitated that a new labour force had to be "found" or fabricated. As a consequence, the Empire's political-economic elites established a regime to generate involuntary workers through debt bondage extending from British-ruled South Asia via French-ruled Indochina to the populations ravaged by the opium trade – a British imperial monopoly[57] – in the southern provinces of the Chinese Empire. The British Empire only decided to end the labour regime in 1917 after nationalist Indian leaders had demanded its abolition in exchange for letting Indian soldiers fight on the Empire's side during the First World War. However, the regime's ongoing and (in-)voluntarily extended contracts lasted into the 1930s.[58]

In the Northern Chinese provinces, Shandong in particular, as in many parts of Europe, rural poverty coerced peasant families from the 1880s into mass outmigration towards the culturally different Manchu lands. Originally agricultural migration, the development of Manchurian mining and heavy industry through imperial Japanese capital with the connivance of regional (Chinese) warlords changed the character to rural-industrial labour migration.

Among these migration systems, especially the transatlantic system has been called a "proletarian mass migration."[59] However, in most migration

---

the Tsarist Empire, the majority of migrants headed to agriculture in the fertile Southern Siberian belt.

56 The London government abolished slavery in 1834 with the proviso that the liberated men, women, and children undergo an "apprenticeship" period with their former owners. For studies on the general history of slavery in the Atlantic region, see Michael Zeuske, *Sklavenhändler, Negreros und Atlantikkreolen: Eine Weltgeschichte des Sklavenhandels im atlantischen Raum* (Berlin/Munich/Boston: De Gruyter Oldenbourg, 2015) and Michael Zeuske, *Afrika – Atlantik – Amerika: Sklaverei und Sklavenhandel in Afrika, auf dem Atlantik und in den Amerikas sowie in Europa* (Berlin/Boston: De Gruyter, 2022).

57 To increase the recruitment reservoir, British government-supported investors had opium produced in Northwest India and forced the Chinese government in the Opium Wars to permit sale of the drug. As intended, mass indebtedness followed.

58 Marina Carter, *Voices from Indenture: Experiences of Indian Migrants in the British Empire* (London: Leicester University Press, 1996); Alessandro Stanziani, *Labor on the Fringes of the Empire* (Basingstoke, UK: Palgrave Macmillan, 2018).

59 Walter F. Willcox and Imre Ferenczi, *International Migrations*, 2 vols. (New York: National Bureau of Economic Research, 1929/1931).

systems, a large majority of the men and women originated from marginal peasant or sub-peasant strata and their trajectory to mines and industries – for women also into service – involved a process of proletarianizing, in some cases delayed through enforced circulation back to rural regions. Such migrants had to adapt peasant forms of resistance to industrial conditions.

So far, this survey, reflecting the state of scholarship, has neither focused on the interior of imperial China nor on North or Sub-Saharan Africa. In the case of China, figures for nineteenth-century rural-urban migrations are not available. The unequal treaties imposed by the European and US colonizer empires did skew but did not stop economic development and it is thus reasonable to hypothesize that urban investments and job options were comparable to those in the urbanizing cores of Europe, Russia, and North America. Concerning Africa, the colonizer empires had divided the populations beginning in the 1830s (Algeria) via tutelage over Egypt (since the late 1840s) to the carving up of "Black Africa" at the Berlin colonizer conference in the 1880s.[60] Given the racist aspect of the division of the world by the white supremacist powers, the term "black" rather than "Sub-Saharan" Africa reflects the attitudes toward the colonized populations. Regional investments, supported by colonizer soldiery and administrators, forced – mainly – men into migrant "wage" labour to extract profits (investors) and taxes (state) from their labour power. State administrators and investors factored in the work of the migrants' wives and children as producers of food and refused to pay family subsistence wages (see Chapters 9 and 17 in this volume). The colonizer empires' structures prevented the emergence of a trans-African investment and migration region.[61]

The investment-labour mobilization nexus, dating from the 1830s, suddenly ended with the financial crisis of the US stock market in 1929.[62] The subsequent decade-long depression – due to the manipulations of (segments of) the miniscule global financial elite – impacted most economies across the world and drastically lowered living standards and life course options of hundreds of millions of people. It also reduced migration since no dynamic economies attracted potential movers and those impoverished were deprived of the

60 The newly established German Hohenzollern Empire (1871), in order to become an imperial player, hosted the "Congress of Berlin" to carve up the Ottoman Empire in 1878 and the "Berlin Conference" for the carving up of Africa in 1884–85.

61 Ewout Frankema and Anne Booth, eds., *Fiscal Capacity and the Colonial State in Asia and Africa, c. 1850–1960* (Cambridge: Cambridge University Press, 2019); Michiel de Haas and Ewout Frankema, eds., *Migration in Africa: Shifting Patterns of Mobility from the 19th to the 21st Century* (London: Routledge, 2022).

62 In the first half of the nineteenth century, the US financial speculation panic of 1837 had economic consequences lasting into the 1840s.

means for migration. In a separate but parallel political development in many European countries, fascist – and in Japan corporatist – governments pursued aggressive and racist projects of economic expansion, with the shared goal of acquiring slave-like working populations, whether Koreans, East Europeans, Somalis or others.

At the end of the resulting Second World War, with much of Europe and Japan, as well as segments of China and Southeast Asia destroyed, new investment and migration patterns emerged.[63] In this context, seven migratory macro-regions may be discerned: North America; Europe west of the dividing line between the "free west" and the "people's republics," both highly problematic terms; Central and Eastern Europe and Siberia; East and Southeast Asia with Oceania; the oil-extracting economies around the Persian Gulf; North and Sub-Saharan Africa; Mexico, Central and South America. These widely used designations involve methodological territorialism. What is, in fact, referred to are the societies in these regions and the people in them pondering whether to stay or to move.

In the northern quarter of the globe,[64] the traditional transatlantic migratory and private investment connections came to an end in the 1950s, with the latter being replaced by US state investment, the Marshall Plan's seed money (1948–1952). The Central-Europe-to-Siberia socialist political and economic sphere separated itself or, perhaps, was separated by the elites of the capitalist political sphere.[65] Both North American and Western European developments continued to require more labour – more workingmen and -women – than available in the respective states. The US economy began to rely on migrant workers from Mexico and later from Central America, who often arrived without documents. In the "body parts" approach to human beings, these were called "braceros," working arms. In England, for centuries, workingmen had been called "hands" and in modern parlance, migration of intellectuals is labelled "brain" drain. Migrants from Mexico left a state with massive oversupply of working people ever since a liberal government in the 1850s had deprived native Mexicans (First Peoples) of commonly held lands and, thus, sustenance, to force them into service and other labour, often unpaid. Since the 1960s, migrants from Central America mainly included

63 Hoerder, *Cultures in Contact*, 508–563.

64 The designation "northern hemisphere" involves methodological territorial expansionism since the north-south dividing line extends from the Gulf of Mexico via the Mediterranean and Caucasus to the Himalayas.

65 Scholars still debate whether the Soviet Union and East European states were intended to be included into the program or whether it was designed to exclude the socialist societies.

refugees from right-wing, US-supported regimes that, internally, were delivering cheap labour forces to US plantation companies. Land ownership and economic power in the Northern Triangle historically have been concentrated in the hands of a small group of elites, leaving a legacy of extreme inequality and widespread poverty.[66] This political regime has been dubbed "banana republic" or "corporate mafia state" – another aspect of "state" that has had no place in traditional Atlantic-world-centred political science.

Labour migrants for Western and Northern European economies were recruited from Mediterranean societies-states. Rather than "braceros," they were designated as "guests," temporary workers, and were without political rights in most receiving states. Unions, however, quickly began organization drives and in some sectors, the West German metal industry for example, the unionization rate of migrant workers was higher than that of native ones. At the same time, investors seeking low-priced labour began, with governments concurring, to export their capital from Western Europe and North America to low-wage states in North Africa, Southeast Asia and, later, the PRC. This forced native workers to change sectors, if other jobs were locally available, or to leave deindustrialized regions altogether.

In the states of the communist "bloc," an undifferentiated western designation, rural-urban migrations followed the pattern of all urbanizing and industrializing societies across the world. However, the ideology of collectivization of farms added political to economic coercion. Migrants did move between socialist states and the Polish and the Yugoslav states kept their outward borders permeable. Prospective Polish migrants could connect to the almost worldwide Polish diaspora (see Chapter 7 in this volume) and the usually skilled labour migrants from Yugoslavia, remaining in their particular economic segments, could transfer their skills. In the Soviet Union, labour migrations eastward had intensified with the investments into mines and industries beyond the Urals, which under the Stalinist regime since the 1930s also involved forced labour. From the late 1950s on, many migrants moved seasonally during the summer months to construction projects with attractive wages in Siberia (see Chapter 12 in this volume).[67]

---

66 Peter J. Meyer, "Central American Migration: Root Causes and U.S. Policy," Congressional Research Service, accessed 20 April 2022, https://crsreports.congress.gov/product/pdf/IF/IF11151.

67 John Randolph and Eugene M. Avrutin, eds., *Russia in Motion: Cultures of Human Mobility since 1850* (Urbana: University of Illinois Press, 2011).

In the southern worlds of the globe, the continuing, if declining imperial domination and the resulting struggles and wars for independences (plural!) involved massive refugee mobilization and, occasionally, deportations. With a specific independence achieved, the diasporic administrative and military colonizer communities had to be shipped back to the former cores in which, given the end of the colonizer power to extract, jobs were not necessarily available. In the newly independent states, withdrawal of colonizer capital resulted in high levels of under- or unemployment and thus significantly increased the potential for internal or inter-state (not: inter-national) migration. Attempts to privilege post-colonial state decisions over (foreign) investment decisions, especially as regards extraction of raw materials, resulted in the delocalization of (foreign) private capital assets, thereby exacerbating economic problems. In Latin America, the Argentine economy and the Venezuelan oil boom attracted mobile workers in periods of economic growth while recessions had the same effect on labour markets as deindustrialization. Similarly, in Sub-Saharan Africa, specific regions – South Africa, Ghana, Rhodesia (after independence Zambia and Zimbabwe) – mostly attracted workers from agriculture (see Chapters 9 and 17 in this volume). In some cases, states forced migrants into temporary and circular mobility to avoid the emergence of labour organizations and class consciousness.

From the post-war 1950s, several societies in Asia – south, southeast, and east – developed dynamism in terms of innovation, investments, and job creation at wage levels attractive both to potential internal migrant low-income workers and migrant profit-searching capital-capitalists. In Kerala, India, for example, the heavy industry – and a responsive state – also permitted development of social security systems. However, scholarship and public information have largely concentrated on so-called tiger states, such as South Korea or Singapore. In these states, the wage levels were low compared to traditional ("western") industrialized regions but not necessarily in terms of the actual means available since living costs in these countries were lower. The resulting shifts of production thus involved job losses in economically highly developed societies and income options in the newly developing ones. When the PRC changed its economic system in the 1980s, job-creating global investors targeted the labour-rich industrializing nodes of the empire. These shifts of production locations, in turn, generated labour demand in ocean shipping to transport the consumer goods to regions where people with purchasing power lived. Crews in transoceanic shipping have largely been recruited from among Philippine men, production of cheap clothing has been assigned to women (and men) in Bangladesh, electronic products often stem from work in Chinese factories, both Taiwan and the PRC, with the Foxconn company a widely criticized mass employer using coercive labour arrangements.[68]

This overview – certainly superficial because of the constraints of space – has used macro-regions as frames to chart developments. However, as noted above, migrants do not move to vaguely circumscribed macro-regions or to states that set frames for legally documented or, often also intended, undocumented entry. Migrants head to specific labour markets and, in consequence, their destinations are local, even when they compare wage levels and cost of living as well as working and living conditions in regions as large as the former colonial empires or the states of the African Copperbelt. Their decision-making is based on their actual local living conditions and – usually with accurate information – on the perceived income and living costs at their intended destination.[69] They factor in the cost of transportation and, perhaps, of state-side admission, as well as the loss of income during their trajectory when they cannot generate income. They reach societies – economies in state frames – in which labour markets are segmented (by skill and language, for example), stratified (by level of skill or education) and segregated (by gender, ethnic culture, colour of skin). Their options are limited to particular slots in these labour markets and, contrary to populist pronouncements, migrants do not pose a threat to native workers unless they arrive with similar qualifications. If, however, frames of reference differ between native and migrant workers, as long as the latter reference their wages or other incomes to their society-locality of origin incomes and cost of living rather than the standards of the receiving economy, competition may and does occur. This issue has posed problems for labour organizations and parties appealing to working-class voters.

68 Pun Ngai and Jenny Chan, "Global Capital, the State, and Chinese Workers: The Foxconn Experience," *Modern China* 38, no. 4 (2012): 383–410; Devi Sacchetto and Rutvica Andrijasevic, "'Disappearing Workers': Foxconn in Europe and the Changing Role of Temporary Work Agencies," *Work, Employment and Society* 31, no. 1 (2017): 54–70; Rutvica Andrijasevic, Devi Sacchetto, and Pun Ngai, "One Firm, Two Countries, One Workplace Model? The Case of Foxconn's Internationalization," *Economic and Labour Relations Review* (2019): 1–17.

69 Information was exchanged by transatlantic letters in the nineteenth century, by return and multiple migrations in the South China-Malaysia and the modern Kerala (India) Gulf economies migrations. Walter D. Kamphoefner, Wolfgang Helbich, and Ulrike Sommer, eds., *News from the Land of Freedom: German Immigrants Write Home,* trans. Susan Carter Vogel (Ithaca, NY: Cornell University Press, 1991); Carl A. Trocki, "Singapore as a Nineteenth Century Migration Node," and Elizabeth Sinn, "Hong Kong as an In-Between Place in the Chinese Diaspora, 1849–1939," in Gabaccia and Hoerder, *Connecting Seas,* 198–247; Kunniparampil Curien Zachariah and Sebastian Irudaya Rajan, *Kerala's Gulf Connection, 1998–2011: Economic and Social Impact of Migration* (Hyderabad: Orient Blackswan, 2012).

As several of the authors in this volume emphasize, the economic rationales just outlined were only one aspect of entwined rationales including family relationships, emotional and psychological aspects and, in some cases, religious preferences. No rational choice theory covers these manifold aspects. In addition to migrants capable of assessing the options in the labour markets of their intended destination by (relatively) accurate information flows, an intensively media-discussed present-day aspect of migration is lack of information about a match between migrants' so-called human capital and the absorptive capacities of labour markets in the destination countries. Without resources to question the propagandistic aspects of the imagery, both potential and actual migrants succumb to the media and stateside projected images of wealthy societies. Again, there are parallels in the past in which Englishmen were lured to the White Dominions by propaganda or rural migrants in many economies of the globe were attracted by the urban facades without information on the working-class living conditions.[70]

6 Class and Organization: How Do Left Unions and Parties React to Labour Migration?

In immigration countries and regions, workers in the higher-reward segments of the labour market and some organizations of the political left tended (and still tend) to see migrants entering the low-wage sectors as a threat. They may respond to the challenge in different, albeit frequently connected, ways: exclusion of the seeming and in many cases badly paid competitors, i.e., attempts to block immigration; institutionalization as the mandated confinement of low-wage workers to certain occupations and economic activities; or solidarity, i.e., attempts to raise lower wages to higher levels, which would have to include demands for a global redistribution to improve conditions in emigration countries (at the expense of capital and/or at the expense of the labouring classes). Viewed from the other side, potential migrants might also choose to stay in their society of birth and struggle for improvement of their underclass position. States – or more precisely: the elites in them – have generally opposed such self-organization. Workers, both resident and migrant, thus had

70 These issues are discussed in Monika Glettler, "The Acculturation of the Czechs in Vienna," in *Labor Migration in the Atlantic Economies: The European and North American Working Classes During the Period of Industrialization*, ed. Dirk Hoerder (Westport, CT: Greenwood, 1985), 297–320, and, for one White Dominion, in Dirk Hoerder, *Creating Societies: Immigrant Lives in Canada* (Montreal: McGill-Queen's University Press, 1999).

to struggle (collectively) against exploitation and, in some cases, even against the destruction of their livelihoods, and for the improvement of working conditions and recognition as citizens. Some workers' organizations demanded and continue to demand a deep restructuring of societies and a redistribution at the expense of capital, reversing the ongoing neoliberal redistribution to the richest ten or even one percent of societies. Colonized peoples had to fight and have to fight to get out from imperial and neo-imperial rule and exploitation, whether traditional European or informal but effective US state-supported capital. In Southeast Asia, movements for self-rule also targeted the impact of imperial Chinese policies and – during the period of Japan's imperial conquests – from this foreign rule. This aspect is receiving increased attention with the PRC becoming a major global economic power.

The probably most famous quote of the Communist Manifesto, "Proletarier aller Länder, vereinigt euch!"[71] is the origin of the internationalist postulate of solidarity of the (historic) labour movement (in the Global North). Our use of qualifying bracketed insertions in the previous sentence is necessitated by the historic emergence and rootedness of both left thought and organizations and the nation-state concept in the Global North. The fundamental assumption of solidarity suggests the existence of a common interest of an inter- or transnational (or even global) working class. Based on the development of a capitalist world market, the international working class (singular!) was supposed to seek its liberation in the collective struggle against capital. However, the complex historical realities shaped by the emergence of (suggested) nation-states in Europe and the processes of racialization inherent to colonialism contested the labour movement's internationalist postulate almost since its inception. Therefore, the history of the labour movement (and the political left in general) has always been characterized by profound divisions over migration. Wherever migrant workers arrive, local workers and their organization had and have to decide whether to include or discriminate against them. The migrants' decision to change societies – in the double sense of the act – reflects the deeply uneven development of regions and states within the capitalist orbit and its former colonialist, now neo-colonialist expansion. In the US, for example, organized labour (with the notable exception of the Industrial Workers of the World after its foundation in 1905) supported the Chinese Exclusion Act of 1882. The American Federation of Labor (AFL) openly discriminated against black workers internally and at the beginning of the twentieth century also

71 English as "Working Men of All Countries, Unite!" in the translation by Samuel Moore from 1888, edited and approved by Friedrich Engels.

campaigned against immigrant workers from Southern and Eastern Europe – of allegedly "dark" or "olive" complexion of skin.

In these debates about the exclusion of migrant workers from (supposedly nationally constrained) labour markets, economic arguments regarding the weakening of the bargaining power of unions of resident workers due to the increased supply of workingmen and -women were frequently linked to (racialized) notions of superiority. Although racism also played a crucial role in the emergence of labour movements structured by the boundaries of states (or "ethnically" defined regions), it took way into the twentieth century for left-wing organizations to acknowledge the (individual and mass) psychological reasons for racialized discrimination, the racialized structuring of labour markets, and the global division of labour with its massive inequalities (see Chapter 3 in this volume).

Nonetheless, there have also always been attempts to develop politics of solidarity between local and (arriving) migrant workers. Trade unions often constituted mass organizations (at least formally) open to all workers and thus could or did provide one of the few important opportunities for political participation for "foreign" migrant workers deprived of rights by nationalist theory and nation-state practice. Therefore, the history of the relationship between resident and in-migrating workers (and their organizations) has always been characterized by conflicting trends of exclusion, discrimination, and solidarity. This volume also aims at exploring these trends in different geographical areas and periods across the world.

In the present, some of the agendas of left unions based in specific states are expanded by "new social movements" or non-governmental organizations (NGOs) which, by avoiding (or attempting to avoid) stateside and national limitations, intend to subject all stages of production and distribution of goods – whether foodstuffs, clothing, or other – regardless of the region involved to common standards of respect for work and of "fair" remuneration. This had been a goal of reformers from the 1870s on and resulted in the founding of the International Labour Organization (ILO), first as a branch of the League of Nations (1919), and since 1946 based in Geneva. The, in the term of the period, "universal" claim to law and regulation of migration, had been developed by the members of the Institut de Droit international, founded in 1893,[72] debated

72 Founding members included in addition to those from Western and Southern Europe, one expert each from Buenos Aires, New York, and Saint Petersburg. Philippe Rygiel, *L'Ordre des circulations? L'Institut de Droit international et la régulation des migrations (1870–1920)* (Paris: Éditions de la Sorbonne, 2021). The Institute received the Nobel Peace Prize in 1904.

at the 1907 Stuttgart Congress of the Second International of social-democratic and socialist parties and unions and again demanded energetically by the members of the Second International in 1912 (see Chapter 11 in this volume). In response to the ravages of the First World War, the ILO Constitution became Chapter 13 of the Versailles Peace Treaty and began with the statement:

> Whereas the League of Nations has for its object the establishment of universal peace, and such a peace can be established only if it is based upon social justice; And whereas conditions of labour exist involving such injustice, hardship and privation to large numbers of people as to produce unrest so great that the peace and harmony of the world are imperilled; and an improvement of those conditions is urgently required: as, for example, by the regulation of the hours of work, including the establishment of a maximum workingday and week, the regulation of the labour supply, the prevention of unemployment, the provision of an adequate living wage, [...] protection of the interests of workers when employed in countries other than their own, recognition of the principle of freedom of association.[73]

Thus, in principle, the demands of left organizations and representatives of the state seemed to be congruent. However, this call for social justice was passed after the workers' agency of 1905 and 1917 in Russia as well as in 1917/18 in other countries, after general strikes in parts of the US and Great Britain as well as Buenos Aires and elsewhere. State representatives labelled this working-class agency "the threat of communism" and intended to stabilize the capitalist system – if with increased rights and equalities – by more peaceful and institutionalized labour relations.

7 Workingmen's and -women's Struggles "from the Bottom Up" – but Why Are They at the Bottom?

Both resident and migrant workingmen and -women have tried to improve their living conditions either individually for themselves and their families or, collectively, for a class within an economic sector or a whole state. Since historians have begun to include labouring families into their studies, this

73 Cited in International Labour Office, Official Bulletin, vol. 1, April 1919-August 1920 (Geneva: 1923).

particular perspective has been called "from the bottom up." However, this raises the question of why workers are generically posited to be at the bottom of society and, specifically, of each and every society. The terminology betrays the implicit acceptance, even by critical historians, of the discursively embedded societal hierarchy of lower-middle-upper classes. While the hierarchy is, of course, socio-economically visible, the notion of being "at the bottom" involves a connotation of being less couth, less educated, and ultimately less capable. For wage labouring men and women such as those of farming families, however, their living spaces are the centres of their lives. The label "bottom" is assigned by observers and interested parties implicitly or even explicitly posited as higher up in the societal hierarchy. It is thus not an acceptable term for scholarly analyses.

Workingmen and -women, whether in agriculture, handicrafts, or factories, undertake their own analyses of power relations and social hierarchies. While they usually do not advocate undifferentiated levelling, an accusation often levied by those more advantageously placed in the societal hierarchy, they do demand fair remuneration in the frame of moral economies that may vary between regions and economic sectors. The minimum demand is a "living wage" in the case of workers or "fair" prices for their products in the case of craft and rural men and women. Most of the struggles analysed by the authors of this volume reflect such basic analyses of family and individual needs in the frame of moral economies and under the recognition that the respective (state-supported) regime of labour and remuneration does not permit healthy lives for adults, prospects for children, and retirement for those beyond working age.

Moral economies, varying between regions, economic sectors, and historical periods are, in a way, the political "theories" of those neither heard nor represented in academic political world views: "Academic" camouflages "middle class," "stateside," or other. A modern term would be "received opinion" – which raises the question: Received by whom? This critique of political theory takes up the previous sections' thoughts on labour and left movements: While these labour and left movements and organizations, ideally, take up the demands and rights of a society's working (and farming) segments, they in turn face the right to live (and prosper) of those who are not part of the specific community but annexed to the powerful states' economic spheres. The demands and rights of migrants as well as of working families in parts of the globe annexed by state power, states' powers, and capitalist regime(s) stand in contrast to those in the annexing, powerful segments of the globe. "Annexed" may refer to nineteenth-century and earlier colonial and imperial domination, to indirect rule of core elites with the help of dependent elites, and to twentieth-century exploitation of raw materials – whether ores or foodstuffs – by international capital backed by the state apparatuses of the Global North and profiting elites in the segments of the Global South.

Given the connotations of terms, often unintended but nevertheless frequently insidious, "Global North" is not merely a label for the Euro-Atlantic world, but included, in a way, powerful socialist states before 1989 and, in the present, states such as the PRC. And, given the catch-all aspect of "global": The moral economies and struggles of labouring families and classes vary from region to region, regime to regime, and over historical formations. However, similarities do exist: The South Indian workers in Ceylon and the French-Canadian and Ukrainian workers in Quebec struggled for living wages and family relations against bosses supported by state institutions (see Chapters 18 and 21 in this volume); the hotel workers in Los Angeles and Copenhagen faced exploitative, increasingly irregularized working and living conditions and developed strategies other than those of the established unions (see Chapters 14 and 23 in this volume). Working families on plantations lost their homes when capitalists shifted production to another colony or decided to invest in different raw materials. Working families in Detroit, US, lost their homes and were forced to migrate when corporation managers shut down the automobile factories and the city's population of 1.85 million (1950, at the end of the wartime boom) "fell" by two thirds to 0.64 million in 2020. Over 1.2 million men, women, and children had to leave on their own, in families, in larger sequential moves. In Kerala, India, the state government developed social security and educational systems but a lack of investors and slow agricultural development resulted in large-scale migrations to the Gulf oil economies: 3.5 million Keralites – one tenth of Kerala's population – lived there in 2010. Working classes were being shifted around under colonizer regimes or are forced to move by themselves in the highly industrialized world around the globe.

PART 1

Perspectives, Approaches, Frames

CHAPTER 2

Pluralist States, Multiple Migrations, International Approaches

Dirk Hoerder

Abstract

This chapter first summarizes the critique of political theory as developed in Europe and by, often immigrant, European academics at US institutions. Thereafter, "inter-national" approaches are discussed that were conceived as "universal" and in the present are sometimes labelled "global." Thirdly, model cases of immigrant inclusion and exclusion by the state are discussed and expanded to states-plus-annexed worlds and capital. This section concludes with a brief foray into the present tiny super-rich elite versus hundreds of millions – many of them labour migrants – having to live in dire straits. In conclusion, projects of improved capital-state-labour relations are discussed with reference to the declaration "Migration in an Interconnected World: New Directions for Action" by the International Organization for Migration and the "Universal Declaration on Cultural Diversity" by the United Nations Educational, Scientific and Cultural Organization.

Keywords

global inequality – immigrant inclusion and exclusion – IOM – political theory – poverty – UNESCO

In this chapter, we will first resume the critique of political theory as developed in Europe andby, at first mostly immigrant, European academics at US institutions.* We then turn to "inter-national" approaches that were conceived as "universal" and, in the present, are sometimes labelled "global." Thirdly, we discuss model cases of immigrant inclusion and exclusion by the state and, fourthly, we turn to states-plus-annexed worlds and capital with a brief foray into the

* I am grateful to an anonymous reviewer for his/her detailed comments.

 | DOI:10.1163/9789004686991_003

present tiny super-rich elite versus hundreds of millions living in dire straits. In conclusion, we discuss the declaration "Migration in an Interconnected World: New Directions for Action" by the International Organization for Migration (IOM) and the "Universal Declaration on Cultural Diversity" by the United Nations Educational, Scientific and Cultural Organization (UNESCO).

1 The Poverty of Political Theory – of European Origin

As outlined in detail in Chapter 1, states in political theory have been constructed as (1) consisting of people with citizenship rights within (2) clearly defined borders and (3) with institutions capable of guaranteeing the secure existence of all. While the concept of sovereign states, version 1.0 realm or property of rulers, dates from the Peace of Westphalia at the end of the intra-European Thirty Years War (1648), version 2.0 includes people as citizens with rights and dates to the French Revolution as well as working-class movements in nineteenth-century Europe and, somewhat later, the Americas. State and nationalist activists in South and East Asia added their experiences and theorizations from the early 1900s,[1] and those in Africa and Southeast Asia, during the struggles and successful achievement of state-specific independences.[2]

Euro-centric theory first emerged among "Western" or "free world" academics and, in the 1950s, international institutions expanded it to cover former-colonial-newly-independent states. Since it has maintained a powerful

---

1 Tim Harper, *Underground Asia: Global Revolutionaries and the Assault on Empire* (Cambridge, MA: Harvard University Press, 2021).

2 This chapter is based on (by year of publication): David Held, *Democracy and the Global Order: From the Modern State to Cosmopolitan Governance* (Stanford, CA: Stanford University Press, 1995); Jay Drydyk and Peter Penz, eds., *Global Justice, Global Democracy* (Winnipeg: Fernwood, 1997); John McMurtry, *Unequal Freedoms: The Global Market as an Ethical System* (Toronto: Garamond Press, 1998); Michael Zürn, *Regieren jenseits des Nationalstaates: Globalisierung und Denationalisierung als Chance* (Frankfurt: Suhrkamp, 1998); Stephen D. Krasner, *Sovereignty: Organized Hypocrisy* (Princeton, NJ: Princeton University Press, 1999); Thomas Pogge, *World Poverty and Human Rights: Cosmopolitan Responsibilities and Reforms* (Cambridge: Polity, 2002); Gary Teeple, *The Riddle of Human Rights* (Aurora: Garamond Press, 2003); Harold R. Kerbo, *Social Stratification and Inequality: Class Conflict in Historical, Comparative, and Global Perspective,* 5th ed. (Boston: McGraw Hill, 2003); Marcel van der Linden and Karl Heinz Roth, eds., *Beyond Marx: Theorising the Global Labour Relations of the Twenty-First Century* (Leiden: Brill, 2013); Elise van Nederveen Meerkerk, *Women, Work and Colonialism in the Netherlands and Java: Comparisons, Contrasts, and Connections, 1830–1940* (Cham, CH: Palgrave Macmillan, 2019); Alexander Etkind, *Nature's Evil: A Cultural History of Natural Resources* (Cambridge: Polity, 2021).

presence in political thought, we recapitulate: The claimed character of states and the concomitant political philosophy is based on the assumption that "citizens" are born within a (clearly demarcated and confined) state-territory and, thus, are part of a given society and its institutions by birth. This position is rigorously statist-static and biologist. A proposal discussed in revolutionary France that in-migrants to the new polity be granted citizenship if they supported the republican system did not gain support, and the shift to Napoleon's imperialism rather led to a nationalist-territorialist ideology. The consequence of this perspective for research has been methodological nationalism, territorialism, and imperialism, as well as a methodological focus on rule and its institutions. This has served to affirm existing conditions and to preclude data-based analyses. The theory cannot accommodate migrants, whose agency changes conditions in the societies of departure and receiving societies.[3]

Concerning "the people" inside a state, administrators and academics occupying or owning the state institutions and discourses constructed a "population," segments of which were considered unfit for political rights or were labelled a surplus that was both portable and ex-portable. In the first century after the promulgation of this statist-static-biologist ideology, women had no citizenship rights of their own; they were part of the nation through male relatives only.[4] The rural and the emerging urban industrial classes were also excluded from any role in the polity but included as basic operators of the economy. As delimitation to the outside, territorial borderlines had been (or were) the result of military victory or defeat or ruling families' negotiations at an arbitrary point in time. These remain in force and are considered inviolable in the twenty-first century.[5]

In such states, administrative personnel occasionally tried to get rid of surplus populations and, in several cases, successfully (from their point of view) exported men and women. Far larger numbers, discontented with state-mandated economic and social conditions and regimes, left of their own decision as their "nation" did not provide food, agricultural territories were insufficient, and population and economic growth did not match. Where rulers imposed new borderlines, men and women living on either side or in annexed territories faced disruption of the previously integrated local economies. The

3 Charles Tilly, "The Emergence of Citizenship in France and Elsewhere," *International Review of Social History* 40, no. S3 (1995): 223–236.

4 Louise A. Tilly, "Women, Work, and Citizenship," *International Labor and Working-Class History* 52 (1997): 1–26.

5 Steffen Mau, *Sortiermaschinen: Die Neuerfindung der Grenze im 21. Jahrhundert* (Munich: Beck, 2021).

imposed new order made their landscapes dis-orderly and many had to out-migrate. In the present, this is the case in border regions to which powerful state actors export enforcement mechanisms, the southern borders of North African states in the case of the EU, and the southern border of Mexico in the case of the US. In the nineteenth century, when some states happily received migrants and provided options for them to use their "human capital," migration worked. "Human capital" refers to the sum of an individual's capabilities, networks, emotions, and spiritualities. The term, sometimes criticized as being too economic in its connotations, captures individuals' transformation of their capabilities and traits, including family relations, into economically viable lives.[6]

The practice of permitting people to enter a state and employ their human capital for both their own interests and that of society was challenged in the latter decades of the nineteenth century. In the receiving states in the Atlantic world, proponents of racist ideologies began to emphasize whiteness as superior and to promulgate programs against in-migrants – and populations of whole societies – of other colours of skin, such as "yellow" for example. By the 1880s, those in England and the US extended the colour scheme to discriminate against "olive" and "dark" people from Southern and Eastern Europe.[7] In East Asia, elites in Japan and China initiated a similar process and debates started from mutually exclusionist self-perceptions of superiority. This racism assumed a hemispheric impact in 1937 with the aggression of imperialist Japanese elites – not of Japan and its population – against China and its population as well as against the peoples of much of Southeast Asia.[8]

2 Universal Human Rights – Including Migration

In the decades of depression, worldwide warfare, and post-war re- or new-construction, the issue of equality of human beings and of who "belongs" and with which rights became pressing to a degree that statesmen and political

6 The term, originally used by economists to measure economic performance, has been expanded by social historians and anthropologists to cover personalities rather than mere quantifiable economic functionality.

7 Donna R. Gabaccia, "The 'Yellow Peril' and the 'Chinese of Europe': Global Perspectives on Race and Labor, 1815–1930," in *Migration, Migration History, History: Old Paradigms and New Perspectives*, ed. Jan Lucassen and Leo Lucassen (Bern: Lang, 2005), 177–196.

8 Andrew Gordon, *A Modern History of Japan: From Tokugawa Times to the Present* (New York: Oxford University Press, 2003).

thinkers of different cultural and political convictions assembled in the "United Nations" – empirically correct: united assembly of states – to negotiate and finally adopt a Universal Declaration of Human Rights (December 1948): "All human beings are born free and equal in dignity and rights. They are endowed with reason and conscience and should act towards one another in a spirit of brotherhood" (Article 1). This had been the goal of the struggles of those relegated to unequal status: Labour movements and working-class cultures had demanded "solidarity," women's organizations called for sisterhood and equal political and social rights, the colonized for self-determination.

In terms of migration and mobility, the Declaration's Article 13 granted the universal right for human beings to decide upon their place of residence. It legitimized migration and considered out-migration a critique of state-society-economy complexes which could or would not provide sustenance or political participation to all. "Everyone has the right to freedom of movement and residence within the borders of each State." And, "Everyone has the right to leave any country, including his [or her] own, and to return to his [or her] country." Wherever people lived, "Everyone has the right to recognition everywhere as a person before the law" (Article 6). However, the "united assembly of states" did neither challenge the state-side seventeenth-century Westphalian-dynastic claim to sovereignty nor the right of states' administrative personnel to decide whom to admit and whom to keep out. Hence, the notion of the freedom to migrate has historically permitted – and still permits – departure but does not grant the right to a secure arrival.

In current debates about migration policy, the "freedom to depart – no right to enter" paradigm has frequently been criticized. A Universal Declaration of Human Rights incorporating the whole process of migration might read: "The freedom of voluntary migration requires conditions in which human beings need not migrate but have the right to migrate and to be accepted into their chosen receiving societies. Forced and involuntary (refugee) migrants, have the right to be accepted into the receiving society of first arrival or of their choice and to participate fully in society, economy, culture, and political system." This, as yet, has not been achieved anywhere in the world, as it is not in the interest of nationalist state projects or of most employers of human labour. In the present – as in the past – migrant arrivals and departures require a fundamental re-conceptualization of the state-citizenship-population relationship, a revolution of theory and practice. But revolutions – a concentrated and energetic form of human agency – do not occur very often.[9]

9 From the voluminous literature see, for example, Joseph H. Carens, *Culture, Citizenship, and Community: A Contextual Exploration of Justice as Evenhandedness* (Oxford: Oxford University Press, 2000); T. Alexander Aleinikoff and Douglas Klusmeyer, eds., *Citizenship*

3 States and Migration

Institutions of states – whether (neo-)imperial, national, immigrant, or other – in the present as in the past hardly ever administer homogenous resident populations. Most states, from their inception, incorporated more than one culture and, with increasing migrations, monocultural state institutions lose contact with many-cultured populations. Resident state personnel may intentionally segregate in-migrants by temporary work regimes or discriminate against out-migrants by depriving them of political and economic rights, such as access to inherence for example. As a result of the absence of political will to address these issues, most modern societies have become segmented entities.[10]

A frequently criticized regime of rigorous segmentation of populations is observed in the capital-rich oil-extracting Gulf states or city-state economies such as Singapore. In contrast, nineteenth-century immigration states considered separation and segmentation as being undesirable and integration as desired. "Integration," at the time, was conceptualized as "assimilation," thereby implying an unconditional surrender of the culture(s) of origin. In practice, "integration" functioned as a stepwise move towards and into the new institutions, structures, and processes – which changed these and the receiving society in the process.[11] Similarly, in the present, states that accept and theorize their past and present immigration, grant access to citizenship, Australia, for example, after four years, and Canada after five years, three of which have to be spent in Canada (legal frame of 2022).[12] The Canadian immigration and citizenship policymakers open-mindedly posited that not every newcomer would self-evidently like Canadian institutions to a degree as to decide to become an immigrant. Thus, they inserted the option to spend part

Today: Global Perspectives and Practices (Washington, DC: Carnegie Endowment for International Peace, 2001); Rainer Bauböck, Bernhard Perchinig, and Wiebke Sievers, *Citizenship Policies in the New Europe* (Amsterdam: Amsterdam University Press, 2009); Catherine Whitol de Wenden, "Citizenship and Migration in a Globalized World," *Rechtstheorie* 51 (2020), 7–13.

10 Wsevolod W. Isajiw, *Understanding Diversity: Ethnicity and Race in the Canadian Context* (Toronto: Thompson, 1999) provides a – critical – introduction to policies in a state often referred to as a model.

11 Dirk Hoerder, "From Migrants to Ethnics: Acculturation in a Societal Framework," in *European Migrants: Global and Local Perspectives*, ed. Dirk Hoerder and Leslie Page Moch (Boston: Northeastern University Press, 1996), 211–262.

12 Both countries select immigrants by qualification in the interest of their economy but, at the same time, ensure relatively easy access to labour markets. While Canada has a special contingent for refugees, Australia's policy is one of detention on isolated islands and has been sharply criticized.

of the post-arrival years in other societies to test alternative options and to assess one's own human and social capabilities in multiple contexts.

However, even such open states-societies make knowledge of their "national history" part of the procedures (or hurdles) to acquire citizenship. Newcomers have to know about various kings, prime ministers, wars, and victories while a knowledge of the actual municipal and district-wide political institutions, present social welfare rights, as well as regulations and duties, is considered less important. On the one hand, this positioning overlooks the process in which migrants add "their" historical memories and thus denationalize narratives and beliefs about a common past. On the other hand, a successful process of "integration" requires both capabilities to navigate the receiving society's actual institutions as well as an institutional facilitating of this process of "acculturation" rather than mere acceptance of and entry into static institutions. To return to the political theory of democratic governance: State-side treatment of in-migrants is a yardstick to measure the depth and extent of democratic structures. Exclusionary treatment of in-migrants often has a corollary in the treatment of out-migrants as, after a certain period, the non-migrating state personnel deprives citizens residing abroad of certain political rights. In consequence, a substantial number of migrants neither have political rights in their state of birth/departure nor in their state of post-migration long-term residence.

Democracy has become fragmented even though some propagandists still pronounce migration as being a "triple-win" with benefits for the receiving state, the state of departure, and the migrant/migrant family (on both ends). Empirical data show that the disenfranchisement of migrants results, especially in metropoles, in the segregation of up to a third of the residents into a non-voting slot – as is the case in Vienna, Austria.[13] These figures are even higher in other self-positioned non-immigration states such as those of the Oil-Gulf or Singapore and governance has increasingly become more partial and deficient. Given states' institutional non-responsiveness, residents and migrants begin to fill the void by developing non-governmental or civil society organizations. However, since in most societies, founding an organization requires high legal competence, in-migrants are again disadvantaged. Many liberal-democratic states, not to mention authoritarian systems, whether the People's Republic of China or a "presidential constitutional republic" such as Angola, have shifted from government by the people and for the people to a

13 Stadt Wien, Integration und Diversität, ed., *Integrations-& Diversitätsmonitor: Wien 2020* (Vienna: City of Vienna, 2020), 55–61.

segmenting, migrant-excluding administrative regime. In contrast, most governments facilitate capital flows across borders and thus accelerate inequality and segmentation.

4 Colonizing States, Capital Accumulation and Mobility, Colonized Working Populations

Governance of the mobility of capital has often or, perhaps, usually been centred on the interest of investors, whether capital managers or owners, with low-wage and low-rights workers being supplied. Sub-standard wages in outsourced jobs and profits accruing to global investors actively hinder the charting of life courses in participatory political structures. Again, the elite-versus-working population dichotomy undercuts equality.

Capital accumulation began in the course of early modern long-distance trade by merchant-shipowners and resource monopolisers across the tri-continental connected "old" world, and subsequently, especially for the Mediterranean macro-region and Western Europe in the elite-ruled North Italian city states.[14] Later, this involved family firms expanding from Southern China into Southeast Asian societies, the northern hemispheric fur trade from Russian-annexed Siberia via Scandinavia to northern North America's annexed native societies, and the Crown-merchant complex operating from Iberian ports outward along African coasts. The powerful newcomers subjugated locally resident populations as producers by establishing exploitative labour regimes. The, often long-distance, entrepreneurs bought cheap and sold dear, including human beings-turned-commodities in the slave trade. By using cheap maritime and land-bound labour, they accumulated capital and – often – reinvested, while territorial nobilities lived off their subjects and – with exceptions – did not invest. Stepwise, merchant entrepreneurs in mining and cloth-making extended their control over resident internal or external labouring populations as producers. If annexed working families still nourished themselves and, often, still owned the means of production, whether traps or

14 The section is based on Dirk Hoerder, *Cultures in Contact: World Migrations in the Second Millennium* (Durham, NC: Duke University Press, 2002); Thomas Piketty, *Le Capital au XXIe siècle* (Paris: Le Seuil, 2013) and Thomas Piketty with Facundo Alvaredo, Lucas Chancel, Emmanuel Saez, and Gabriel Zucman, *Rapport sur les inégalités mondiales 2018* (Paris: Le Seuil, 2018); James Belich, *The World the Plague Made: The Black Death and the Rise of Europe* (Princeton, NJ: Princeton University Press, 2022).

looms, the merchant and resource capitalists as well as rentier ruling families, did not have to invest at this stage of production.

In long-distance trade, local rulers often assigned arriving foreign merchants-investors to self-governing compounds, *Höfe*, *funduqs*, or other quarters, whether in Southeast Asia, the Indian port cities, or northern European Hanseatic quarters. These capital-wielding communities attempted to influence, or even control, local or urban authorities. They changed the focus of producers from their known local markets to purveyors of export goods for distant unknown markets. Some outsourced production from European cities and countrysides to low-wage colonized populations.[15] To maximize their power, court and capitalist elites in Western Europe combined – first in Iberia, then in the London-based court-chartered monopolies beginning with the hemispheric fur trade (Muscovy Company, 1555) for hefty fees and a share of the profits. The Dutch elite estates, politically ruling as States General, followed in 1595/1602 and the French Crown in the 1660s. In imperial China, where the state remained separate, merchants circumvented control by offering a share of their profits to local authorities. This systemic practice, necessary to bridge the state-merchant dualism, has been labelled "bribing" by scholars socialized in tax-and duty-demanding economic frames. In Arabia's caravan trade, the Quraysh ruling elite of Mecca had pooled capital, i.e., joint-stock agreements, as early as the fifth century. In the Mediterranean sea trade, Genoese financial, political, and merchant elite families had combined city power with financial power from the fourteenth century. In the West, the merchant-Crown combine is well studied for Portugal with its agriculturally limited natural resources as well as for the big East India and other corporations whose shares could be traded on a newly established London stock market (still called "the City"). When expanding across the oceans, the seafaring entrepreneurs, rather than keeping to tradition and using quarters assigned by authorities at their destination, erected their own fortified and armed posts along the African coasts and, in the Indian Ocean expanses, extracted toll fees from Arab merchant vessels.

In contrast to merchants, rulers sought income-yielding territories afar to supplement the income requisitioned "at home" from their subjects. Investors realized the advantages of territorial rule when planning to engage local, ideally cheap, labour for export production. While overseas trade remained an, at best tolerated, subsystem in the imperial frame of China, sixteenth-century European North Sea-and Atlantic-centred merchant-investors developed the

15 Christian-European religious orders, for example, had utensils for veneration practices produced in Goa, India, or in Indonesia.

Iberian-Caribbean gunpowder-based rule,[16] including purchase and sale of enslaved labouring men and women from West African societies. Subsequently, Dutch, French, British, and other heavily armed state-private vessels also expanded into the Indian Ocean, and the Southeast Asian and China Seas. This Europe-outward transoceanic mobility fundamentally changed frames of trading from – ideally – mutually beneficial trading protocols that kept transaction costs low to a violent imposition of power with the cost of armament and soldiery borne by the state or, more precisely, the tax-subjected populations. The seventeenth-century territorial plantation economies consisted of core-based capital elites and a migrant support staff, armed with pens and guns. In India, from the colonizer point-of-view, the collection of revenues from producers had to be changed from resident to colonizer rulers and the existing rulers' wealth siphoned off to European coffers. Colonization involved merchant, administrator, military, and policing migrants as diasporas of the powerful.[17] In the worldwide competition between heavily capitalized and armed imperial elites, a turning point occurred in the early 1760s: From the British-French imperial war, Britain emerged victorious. The French government ceded its costly North American possession, Quebec, to keep the profitable sugar-producing slave labour-based plantation islands of Martinique and Guadeloupe. On the other side of the globe, the British East India Company took over Bengal while, to the north, in the Tsarist Empire Catherine II became empress and had her armies begin expansion both against Ottoman Empire and into Afghanistan, i.e., in the British view towards the prosperous and wealthy India. The British military-capital combine in its turn attempted to invade territories of Afghan rulers. Core and capital-rich classes of specific realms of rule (not "nations") competed and expanded globally and either outsourced work (as well as soldiering) or forced segments of the peasant and working classes to become mobile.[18]

Imperial power imposition, at its height, involved in the British case almost one-quarter (458 million) of the world's population and of its territory (1922). The French elite (labelled "the Crown") lost most of its colonial possessions to Britain in the war of 1756–1763, which actually was an early world war. But a century later it had reconstituted itself as the "republican" political and

16 The prior Mediterranean trade empire cannot be discussed here, as much of the capital and expertise involved was Genoa-owned.

17 Dirk Hoerder, "The Weak and the Powerful: A *longue-durée* and Comprehensive Perspective on Diasporas," *Diasporas* 23–24 (2014): 30–49.

18 At this time the imperial elites of Islamic attachment, the Mughals in India, the Safavids in Persia/Iran, and the Ottomans from the Balkans to Egypt lost coherence and power.

financial elite and again acquired "territories," i.e., exploitable populations. In 1924/25 and 1931 respectively, both elites celebrated their power in colonial exhibitions, of which the British one was visited by 27 million, and the French one by 8 million spectators. Colonialism had gained wide appeal and a French propagandist proudly proclaimed: "C'est avec 76.900 hommes que la France assure la paix et les bienfaits de sa civilisation à ses 60 millions d'indigènes" – with 76,900 men France guarantees the peace and privileges of its civilization to its 60 million indigenes. Out of the colonized hundreds of millions of men, women, and children, the armed colonizers recruited involuntarily mobile labour forces, and from the territories, they extracted resources.[19] The memory of the descendants of the colonized, even several generations later – in other words, in the present – stands opposed to the published, often scholarly garnished stories of the colonizer states: The memories of the victimized always differ from those of the perpetrators.

The exhibitions' organizers, stuck in their imperialist bubbles, were probably unaware that at the time, exiled Indian activists were conceptualizing independence (Ghadar Movement)[20] and that in France, Marseilles in particular, workers from occupied Algeria, West Africa, and Indochina were arriving, among them, paying his way as a crew member of a French steamer plying the core-colony-core route, Nguyễn Tất Thành, later known as Ho Chi Minh, in 1911, and Léopold Sédar Senghor, future president of independent Senegal, in 1928.[21]

These early analysts – later turned militants – studied the global disparities, imperial entities, and the separation and segmentation of populations in conquered territories. They understood that the colonizer states' (i.e., public) political economies and the private investors depended on imperial power structures. The dissolution or crash of imperial rule was achieved by colonized peoples' struggles and, if necessary, wars for self-determination. However, empire-introduced and, often, local elite-supported segregations

19 Text from a poster for the Exposition Coloniale Internationale, 1931, Musée du quai Branly, Paris. The whole understanding of the extraction, commerce, and civilizing mission is reflected in the outer friezes and inner frescoes of the Palais des Colonies, that still exists as the Palais de la Porte Dorée in Paris.

20 The activities received an impetus after the British Dominion of Canada excluded workers and agriculturalists arriving since 1903 from Punjab, many of them former soldiers in the British army, from entering at the Pacific ports of "British Columbia" in 1914 ("Komagata Maru incident").

21 Senghor would support the Senegalese (general) strike movement in 1945–1946, and the Dakar-Niger railroad workers' strike, 1947–1948, the first cross-border strike in French West Africa.

and separations of groups may – and often did – last for long after imperial rule had ended and the power-wielding imperial migrants had gone. Their legacies continue to influence migrations – and thus the composition of state populations – to the present (see Chapters 8, 9, 13, 17 and 18 in this volume). Through the wholesale import of labouring bodies to capital-rich cores and the more recent outsourcing of labour to post-colonial – or, in the case of China, post-dependent – societies, as well as through self-decisions to migrate, the independent new states and the former colonizer states remain inextricably entwined.

Concerning the development of capital, already by the late nineteenth century, investors within the highly capitalized dominating segment of the world concentrated their resources in so-called holding companies that conducted business with multiple states, i.e., their respective elites, and exploited workers in the core as much as in the colonies.[22] State-side laissez-faire attitudes to the financial (power) sector resulted in a crash, in October 1929 in New York, with the resulting Great Depression. By the late 1930s, fascist Germany and corporate Japan – or rather their respective elites – aimed at acquiring resources including labouring populations and started the Second World War. After these two men-made [sic] disasters, in the era of US hegemony, multinational companies (MNCs) emerged, that were often US- but also British- and Dutch-capitalized. The corporate capitalists negotiated arrangements with economic and political elites of other, often less powerful states, for oil extraction, with the (frequently British-installed) Arab elites being the most prominent example. Economic theorists – or ideologues – cemented the practice by establishing the neoliberal market discourse to which politicians succumbed.

In addition, a new regime of mass consumerism welded the consuming classes of the "western" and other relatively wealthy segments of the world to low-waged and rights-deprived working populations from afar. Within the "highly developed" economies, the decline of the industrial sector and the export of jobs – and life prospects – was paralleled by growth in service-sector jobs that were unattractive to residents and thus required the import of new labourers. This involved profound changes in labour organization and migration: While workers in traditional settings did have locally socialized skills as well as labour unions, the in-migrating "working guests" or, colloquially, "guestworkers" arrive with different knowledges and cultural competencies. To

22 The connections between labour regimes in the core and in the colonies are well documented in Elise van Nederveen Meerkerk, *Women, Work and Colonialism in the Netherlands and Java: Comparisons, Contrasts, and Connections, 1830–1940* (Cham, CH: Palgrave Macmillan, 2019).

respond to this, labour unions, often with traditional leadership, would have needed to develop new organizational strategies but were often reluctant to do so (see Chapters 14 and 23 in this volume).

5 Jobs in Platform Economies and *Forbes*' List of "The Richest People in the World"

Under neoliberalism, in the US from the (once partly worker-supporting) Democratic Party presidency of Jimmy Carter (1977–1981) through Republican Ronald Reagan's (1981–1989) and Democratic Bill Clinton's presidencies (1993–2001), the global financial sector separated itself from the producing or "real" economy. States, especially Britain with its banking elites in London and (former) dependent island states as well as Panama as a kind of US-dependent state, provided the MNCs with multi-tax shelters: Even the decidedly liberal, and highly renowned London-based *Economist* has begun to publish lists of "crony-capitalists" with no activity in any productive undertaking.

The rapidly growing income inequalities are documented by the Oxford-based NGO Oxfam, the Paris-based World Inequality Laboratory at the École d'Économie (with scholars from more than 70 countries contributing to the World Wealth and Income Database), the Washington-based Institute for Policy Studies' inequality.org, and the UN, as well as the World Bank.[23] According to their research, the richest one percent of the world's population own 45.8 percent of the world's wealth while, at the other end, adults with less than US$ 10,000 in wealth account for 55 percent of the world's population but own a mere 1.3 percent of global wealth.[24] During a phase of the COVID-19 pandemic, from March 2020 to November 2021, some 160 million people, especially women and specifically discriminated in-migrant groups

23 This section is based on the Oxfam Report 2022, https://frompoverty.oxfam.org.uk/world-inequality-report-2022-a-treasure-trove-of-trends-and-new-data/; Capgemini, *World Wealth Report 2022*, https://worldwealthreport.com/; World Inequality Lab, https://inequalitylab.world/en/; inequality.org of the Institute for Policy Studies, Washington, DC, https://inequality.org/facts/global-inequality/; United Nations, Department of Economic and Social Affairs, Population Division, *International Migration 2017* (New York: United Nations, 2017), https://www.un.org/en/development/desa/population/migration/publications/migrationreport/docs/MigrationReport2017.pdf; IOM Global Migration Data Analysis Centre, https://www.migrationdataportal.org/themes/labour-migration, all accessed December 2022.

24 "Wealth" is commonly defined as the value of a household's financial and real (especially housing) assets minus debts.

such as Bangladeshis in Britain, were pushed into poverty. "Labour" – meaning workingmen and -women with their children – lost US$ 4.7 trillion in income, while billionaires gained US$ 3.9 trillion according to the International Labour Organization (ILO) and Oxfam. Globally, declining incomes for the poorest people lead to an estimated additional 21,000 deaths daily.

The world's ten richest billionaires owned US$ 1.3 trillion combined wealth in 2022 and thus surpass most states' total annual goods and services output (*Forbes* and World Bank data). Their wealth is also larger that the possessions of the poorest 40 percent of humanity.[25] If this wealth, half of it gains made during the COVID-19 pandemic period, would be divided equally among the 169 million labour migrants across the globe (Migration Data Portal), each could receive almost US$ 7,700. This amount equals one-and-a-half times the average pre-COVID-19 annual salary of an employee in India, where lockdowns led to wage declines of 3.6 percent in the formal sector, and 22.6 percent in the informal and poorest, i.e., migrant, segments (ILO data). Some 11 million people who lost their jobs had to travel home unassisted with neither food nor transportation.

The global transfer of production from high-wage to low-wage countries and, internally, from formal to informal sectors, has been accelerating for several decades. As a result, migration increases. In high-wage states, investor-and-state decisions displace segments of the working classes; job-receiving states, voluntarily or involuntarily, supply their most abundant and – for some only – resource: low-waged and civic rights-deprived mass male or female workers. While, in the past, Russian serfs and slaves in the Americas were considered moveable, in the present, "free" population segments in many societies are forced into unwanted mobility while others decide, in their own interest, to leave substandard regions or states to seek better options of life in economy-and-state frames accessible to them. Are workingmen and -women actively protesting such conditions – beyond departing? Those supporting families "at home" through remittances often cannot. Are working conditions changing in high-income economies? Polls indicate elevated levels of dissatisfaction (2021, 2022) and increasing numbers who quit their job with many unwilling to re-enter the labour market unless, financially and socially speaking, "yields"

25 In March/April 2022, the atrocities of President Putin's armies in Ukraine led to an outcry against *Russian* oligarchs, but in the (US) *Forbes* list of the richest persons in the world, billionaires from the US and China fill the top ranks with the first Russian being placed in slot 87 of 400 (2022 data). Oxfam, Profiting from Pain, 23 May 2022, https://www.oxfam.org/en/research/profiting-pain.

improve.[26] Will companies take into account that business rationales and individual or family rationales have to match? Does this suggest a fundamental shift in capital-labour relations or is this an ephemeral phenomenon?

The downgrading of both respect and remuneration for workingmen and -women has been intensified by new "platform economies" which offer on-the-moment/for-a-moment jobs with neither perspectives nor rights for sectors with, usually structural, shortages of labour, such as delivery, transportation, fast food, and others in particular. Of 210.5 million men and women employed in the EU-27, 28 million work for more than 500 platforms.[27] The system aims at a regime of "precarization of work by splitting what were once (formally) homogeneous workforces into several groups with different employers, employment contracts, and employment and working conditions." The fragmentation of work involves a new racialization of resident and migrant labour forces and income levels, whereby self-organization or union organization becomes impossible.[28] While pre-platform informal sectors may have offered continuous income-generating activities, platform-dependent men and women can no longer chart their life courses. Migration as a protest? Potential migrants face destination states with arbitrary or systemically discriminatory admission bureaucracies.

6 State-Side Legal Frames, Facilitating Factors, Migrant Agency

Above, we have discussed the "freedom to depart – no right to enter" problem in the Declaration of Human Rights. Rather than repeat debates about migrant rights, whether in the colonized worlds since the late 1800s, in the US since the plight of Mexican farmworkers during the 1930s depression, in Europe since the

26 In the US, in the single month of November 2022, 4.2 million workers quit their jobs while 10.5 million job openings were recorded. "Job Openings and Labor Turnover – November 2022," U.S. Bureau of Labor Statistics, 4 January 2023, https://www.bls.gov/news.release/jolts.nro.htm, accessed 9 January 2023. US, British, French, and German press reports in 2022, ranging from *Forbes* to *Le Monde*, addressed the topic.

27 "Commission Proposals to Improve the Working Conditions of People Working Through Digital Labour Platforms," European Commission, accessed 8 December 2022, https://ec.europa.eu/commission/presscorner/detail/en/ip_21_6605; "Europäische Union: Anzahl der Erwerbstätigen in den Mitgliedstaaten im 3. Quartal 2022," Statista, accessed 8 December 2022, https://de.statista.com/statistik/daten/studie/249104/umfrage/erwerbstaetige-in-den-eu-laendern/.

28 Johanna Neuhauser and Peter Birke, "Migration and Work: Theoretical Perspectives under the Impression of Multiple Crises," *Sozial.Geschichte Online* 34 (2023): 159–187, with extensive citation of the research literature in the field.

beginning of the "guestworker" migrations in the 1950s, in India or China with the mass migrations from rural to urban areas, we will discuss the principles laid down in the report of the Global Commission on International Migration (GCIM), launched by the United Nations Secretary-General and various states' governments in late 2003.[29] Given its framers, it privileges institutional state-side actors in the global economy and hardly addresses migrant agency. In its introductory section, "migration out of choice," the GCIM posits that states – of birth, of residence, of destination – need to establish best-practice frames for migration management:

> Women, men and children should be able to realize their potential, meet their needs, exercise their human rights and fulfil their aspirations in their country of origin, and hence migrate out of choice, rather than necessity. Those women and men who migrate and enter the global labour market should be able to do so in a safe and authorized manner, and because they and their skills are valued and needed by the states and societies that receive them.

However, in the GCIM approach, this only applies to "authorized" border-crossings. Since many states refuse to offer authorized entryways, migrants concerned about their life-chances in ever growing numbers enter unauthorized and subsequently have to live without documents. They are labelled as "illegal" and are thus criminalized by their destination states. Centuries of migration and multi-cultured state populations notwithstanding, the hegemonic political classes of most states, self-containerized in institutional nationalism, have proven incapable of achieving consensus on migration policy.

The GCIM *Directions for Action* recognizes "the role that migrants play in promoting development and poverty reduction in countries of origin, as well as the contribution they make towards the prosperity of destination countries" and demands that "International migration should become an integral part of national, regional and global strategies for economic growth, in both the developing and developed world." The *Directions* do not explicitly deviate from the widely-held assumption that migration occurs one-directional from developing to developed – or resource-gobbling – world. However, large numbers of

29 Global Commission on International Migration, *Migration in an Interconnected World: New Directions for Action. Report of the Global Commission on International Migration,* 5 October 2005, https://www.iom.int/sites/g/files/tmzbdl486/files/2018-07/GCIM_Report_Complete_1.pdf, accessed 18 March 2022.

migrant men and women, following perceived options, move between states-economies-societies with low income-levels.

Migrants' evaluation of options is complex in a frame of institutions and capabilities, job opportunities and spiritualities, language skills and ability to live – or, at least, to function – in more than one culture. Economist migration research, using a single-lane formal-income approach, neglects both informal income and expense management. Desired standards of living and life-course options for children depend on all – not necessarily measurable – incomes and on the allocation decisions on the spending side, which might be called "excome."[30]

To assess options at different destinations – be they intra-regional, trans-continental, or empire-wide – and to assess his or her standing in the globally shifting working populations, a migrant needs accurate information. Men and women crossing the Atlantic or the Southeast Asian Seas in the nineteenth century distrusted government and company tracts and relied on experienced earlier migrants and returnees or on letters with exact information on what to expect and which human resources to bring for a slot in the labour market. However, the accuracy of information provided seems to have declined with time. Since the mid-twentieth century, potential receiving states and employers project – at first via television – an imagery of high-income, easy-consumption societies. If in Nairobi, Paris, London, Beijing, or Mumbai SUVs cruise the streets and wage-receiving street cleaners pick up dog droppings, the respective society, from the perspective of people living in high-underemployment societies, must be sufficiently wealthy to provide jobs for migrants with (over- or under-) estimated skill resources. The imagery projected veils working-class quarters with grey facades and hides outsourced consumer goods production.

The *Directions* do address "push factors" in (malfunctioning) societies of departure and, as regards receiving states, demand the "strengthening of social cohesion through integration" whereby integration is a two-sided process in which the receiving societies need to facilitate language acquisition, labour market access, social contacts, and other important aspects. "Migrants and citizens of destination countries should respect their legal obligations and benefit from a mutual process of adaptation and integration that accommodates cultural diversity and fosters social cohesion."

Pluralism, much debated from the 1970s to the early 2000s, has since been countered by drives for monocultural national identities which stand in

30 Christiane Harzig and Dirk Hoerder with Donna Gabaccia, *What is Migration History?* (Cambridge: Polity, 2009), 62–64.

explicit conflict with the "Universal Declaration on Cultural Diversity" adopted by the UNESCO in November 2001 as the fourth pillar of the generic human rights after political, social, and economic ones.[31] The declaration recognized cultural diversity as a common heritage of humankind, discussed the change from distinctive diversity to shared plurality, and emphasized the importance of cultural diversity as being central for development. In the words of the GCIM's *Directions*, processes of interaction of migrants of different cultures and societies with multiple regional, gender, generational, and economic variants should "be actively supported by local and national authorities, employers and members of civil society, and should be based on a commitment to non-discrimination and gender equity." This requires authorities and institutions to become many-cultured.

Cultures do involve gender and intergenerational hierarchies. In response, the Canadian debate about plural cultures, the (plural) society, and the bi- or multi-cultural state posited that, first, any person may practice his or her pre-migration culture with, second, the proviso: *as long as no other person's cultures or rights are infringed upon*. Thus, for example, immigrant parents may adhere to their culture of socialization but may not prevent their children from living in a different culture.[32]

The GCIM's *Migration in an Interconnected World* demands what should be evident in democracy-proclaiming states: "The legal and normative framework affecting [...] migrants should be strengthened, implemented more effectively and applied in a non-discriminatory manner, so as to protect the human rights and labour standards that should be enjoyed by all migrant women and men." This, the declaration bluntly states, needs to be done "in a more consistent and coherent manner." It is a call never to designate populations as "surplus" and to treat all residents, whether native-born, long resident, or recently entering, equally.

31 United Nations Educational, Scientific and Cultural Organization, *UNESCO Universal Declaration on Cultural Diversity*, 2 November 2001, https://www.ohchr.org/en/instruments-mechanisms/instruments/universal-declaration-cultural-diversity, accessed 18 March 2022.

32 Jean R. Burnet with Howard Palmer, *"Coming Canadians": An Introduction to a History of Canada's Peoples* (Toronto: McClelland and Stewart, 1988) and Jean R. Burnet, *Multiculturalism in Canada* (Ottawa: Canadian Studies Directorate, 1988); Dirk Hoerder, *Creating Societies: Immigrant Lives in Canada* (Montreal: McGill-Queen's University Press, 1999).

CHAPTER 3

World-Systems, Uneven Development, and Migration

Christof Parnreiter with Dirk Hoerder

Abstract

In this chapter, the authors briefly outline the emergence of world-systems approaches first formulated by Immanuel Wallerstein and expanded by Janet Abu-Lughod. They discuss the emergence of connectivities as well as hierarchies over the centuries in global perspective. Conquest and colonization increased inequalities between peoples in macro-regions and long-distance trade often turned into plunder. The racialization of labour forces beginning with slavery involved an ideology of skin colour-coding that underpinned the politico-economic power of European-Atlantic and, subsequently, North Atlantic states. Skin-colour hierarchies have also been developed in other segments of the world. In this frame, migrants, despite being integral and irreplaceable parts of global labour markets, are often excluded from social and political rights in the societies to which they contribute their labour. The authors rely on World Bank data to discuss global migrations due to global inequalities.

Keywords

global inequalities – global migrations – racism – world-systems theory

World-systems analysis approaches global economic interactions and inequalities from a comprehensive interdisciplinary perspective. It focuses on macro-regions and eschews the methodological nationalism that emerges from nation-state-centred studies. Economies of modern states – like those of polities in the Middle Ages (a Europe-centred periodization) – are not merely linked by trade but also by divisions of production. For instance, the components of one US car may be produced in many regional economies across the globe and many printing machines used in the People's Republic of China were produced by the leading offset printing machine maker in Heidelberg, Germany, before the company opened a subsidiary in Shanghai. Opening

 | DOI:10.1163/9789004686991_004

a subsidiary – regardless of the technology involved – requires migration of highly skilled workers, precision engineers, and management personnel as well as of local and regional workers and employees. It involves mobility of capital as well as knowledge transfer. Furthermore, it implicitly indicates inequalities through the production of sophisticated machinery in one segment of the globe and demand for the product in a society not designing and producing such high-level products.

While goods are "transferred," seemingly passive but actually on containerships often manned by mobile Philippine sailors, transborder migrants actively engage in finding a trajectory and creating their own international systems. From a polity-centred perspective, this has been called "voting with one's feet": But the image veils human complexities, since the decision to migrate is taken in the mind and involves emotions. The decisions, in a way, also involve analyses of world inequalities and systems: In which economies can I feed myself or, if not hungry, may I improve my condition? Which states offer entryways, and which societies permit inclusion? Potential migrants have undertaken such analyses throughout history and across societies worldwide. In many societies, the goal to improve one's standing has been part of the social ethos and policymaking. However, if the person who wants to improve his or her prospects happens to cross a border or be of a colour of skin different to that of the local residents, the positive view of improvement often turns negative and ends in (racist) rejection. Inequalities, be they micro-, meso-, or macro-regional, are intricately linked – not merely with capital accumulation but also with nationalism and racism.

In this chapter, we will briefly outline the emergence of world-systems approaches and, secondly, of racism as a tool of power as well as exclusion. We will then discuss global migrations and illustrate migrations due to global inequalities using a few examples and mainly relying on World Bank data.

1 World-Systems Approaches

The standard references for the development of world-systems analysis are Immanuel Wallerstein's magisterial *The Modern World-System* and its backward extension to the thirteenth-century by Janet Abu-Lughod who entitled her study *Before European Hegemony*.[1] In recent research, the emergence

---

1 Immanuel M. Wallerstein, *The Modern World-System*, 3 vols. (New York/San Diego: Academic Press, 1974–1989); Janet L. Abu-Lughod, *Before European Hegemony: The World System A.D. 1250–1350* (New York: Oxford University Press, 1989).

of connectivities as well as hierarchies has been pushed even further back. The eleventh-century Afro-Eurasian world consisted of seven civilizations linked by traveling merchants and their clerks, carters, servants or slaves, and concubines or, less often, wives. Those of the "Americas" – a later designation – remained separate. In the Mediterranean-centred North African, South European, and Western Asian world several types of large-scale long-distance migrations were specific to particular regions and periods. In the Mediterranean, slavery involved men and, over time, mainly women, from North Africa, West Central Asia, and Sub-Saharan Africa. When this regime declined, slave traders, i.e., African captors and European merchant-seamen, from the sixteenth century onwards, commodified human beings from the many African societies. They traded them as "chattel," things or pieces, across the Atlantic to the Caribbean islands, where capitalists of the time invested in a plantation-based export economy serving European consumers. In a different power imposition, migrating Scandinavian raiders expanded southwestward via the shores of the Atlantic as far as Sicily or, southeastward, to Slavic territories and Byzantium, the latter connected to the Chinese economy through caravan trade. From Arabia and subjugated North Africa, Muslim armies established a sophisticated society with Jewish-Christian-Islamic transcultural centres on the Iberian Peninsula. Christian raiders, though called crusaders, were mainly interested in material gain and rule and connected Central and Southeastern Europe to Palestine, while other raiders and migrants brought Western European settlers and military personnel into the territories or, more precisely, life-worlds of Slavic peoples. Another perspective, from the eastern core of the Eurasian world, the Chinese Ming and, subsequently, Qing Empire indicates further large-scale and long-distance migrations specific to regions and periods including Mongol expansion and state-building, Manchu penetration, southward settlement of Han Chinese, internal Hakka migrations, and development of the Chinese diaspora across Southeast Asia. From a South Asian perspective, "India" focuses on the vast commercial linkages along its coasts to the Indian Ocean, the cosmopolitan elites at courts, and the Islamic-Hindu interaction.[2]

In each case of contact, rules of communication had to be developed or imposed. Merchants, distant from their base, generally used trading protocols known to and accepted by all sides which reduced transaction costs. Political rulers generally extracted surplus value from subjects or from subjected

2 Adapted from Dirk Hoerder, *Cultures in Contact: World Migrations in the Second Millennium* (Durham, NC: Duke University Press, 2002), 27–30.

cultural groups – not "peoples" – to arm a band of male followers with which they imposed rule and extracted wealth or, more modestly, the "fruits of labour." According to Abu-Lughod, linkages between the many trading centres across the world led to a long-term slowdown in the development of less powerful and more dependent societies. The rise of "the West" involved the accumulation of profits from worldwide resources, including natural, labour, technical, and intellectual resources. Hence, this development was not the result of superior achievement. Aggressive conquest and colonization made exchange relationships increasingly unequal, and plunder replaced exchange in long-distance trade.

In the nineteenth century, those best supplied with weaponry solidified this economic and power frame into the colonizer-colonized dichotomy. The twentieth- and twenty-first interstate systems[3] of capitalism and the global division of labour are still based on these frames. The present is characterized by the division into core states with high capital concentration and periphery states with raw materials, labour resources, and, often, regimes facilitating the exploitation of geological, natural, and human resources. This system involves dynamic aspects: The core of capital concentration and armed power shifted from Europe to North America and some peripheral societies, through developmental policies and self-help, became ascending semi-periphery countries. Rather than leading to a more favourable position in the global power hierarchies, dynamism, however, may also further reduce the comparative rank of state economies and thus the standard of living of the population – of those with political rights: citizens. Andre Gunder Frank has called this the "development of underdevelopment."[4]

2 Racism

From early on, but in especially with the slave labour regime in the (at first Spanish) Americas, an ideology of skin colour-coding has underpinned the politico-economic power impositions of, first, European-Atlantic and then North Atlantic states: white over black or, more differentiated but still

3 The commonly used term "international" is inaccurate since almost all states (and empires in particular) do not consist of one cultural nation.

4 Andre Gunder Frank, *Capitalism and Underdevelopment in Latin America* (New York: Monthly Review Press, 1967); Andre Gunder Frank and Barry K. Gills, eds., *The World System: Five Hundred Years or Five Thousand?* (London: Routledge, 1993); Andre Gunder Frank, *ReOrient: Global Economy in the Asian Age* (Berkeley: University of California Press, 1998).

dichotomous, white over all other colours of skin. In its early phases, the imposition of this system of classification involved religious aspects: Had – the Euro-centric – God created or reached those living elsewhere and deemed godless? However, this aspect in itself involved the power of definition about who belonged and who did not: "Christian" referred to Rome-centred Latin Church structures and doctrines but it excluded the Coptic and Abyssinian churches as well as – extending from Persia to China – Nestorian Christianity. The close connection between Latin Christianity and western capitalist economies is coming to the fore again in the twenty-first century.

Racism is a form of hostility towards others – aliens, foreigners – that purports to be based on biological differences, and its proponents hierarchically place the biology of white-skinned people over those of other colours of skin.[5] It is the biological extreme of a general hostility to foreigners and, in a more general version, aggressively targets all those outside one's own group and distinguishable by place of birth, language and habits, colour of skin and other physical traits, such as culture, religion, and other aspects. Importantly, however, racism does not aim to *exclude* the alien or foreigner, but to subordinately include him or her into the capitalist division of labour so that he or she can be exploited.[6]

Racialization assumes – as ethnicization often does – that the descriptive elements selected by those labelling define the whole character of other persons and cannot be changed by social factors.[7] Race is thus said to be innate. The adherents of racializing strategies of differentiation combine the othering with positing the superiority of themselves as equally innate. Empirically, this superiority, said to be one of genes and skin colour, is based on capitalist economic power (since the concept of the God-given power of rulers is no longer used). Thus, "whiteness" and the economic regime are inextricably linked. Since the capitalist regime has become dominant – through the development of underdevelopment and for other reasons that cannot be discussed here – the highest level of material consumption has become the yardstick to measure the achievements of "national economies." While neither racializations nor national economies can be supported by data, the existing differences in standards of living connect economies both through exploitation and

5 For an early analysis, see Robert Miles, *Racism* (London: Routledge, 1989).

6 Étienne Balibar and Immanuel Wallerstein, *Race, Nation, Class: Ambiguous Identities* (London: Verso, 1991).

7 While racializing is not limited to European/white societies, it will be discussed as a European and North American strategy in this chapter because of the connected global positioning of power.

migration. People with comparatively lower standards of living – "standard" would need to be defined – observe standards elsewhere and decide to migrate between economies-states. Migration and racism are two strategies in global distribution struggles, in the battles for a share of global wealth. "Capitalism involves not only appropriation of the surplus-value by an owner from a laborer, but an appropriation of surplus of the whole world-economy by core areas" (Wallerstein).[8] Racism serves to institutionalize the hierarchies established by the global division of labour (Étienne Balibar) and defends "privilege," a position before the law, *privi-legium*.

3 Migration in a Racialized World

Migrants intend to achieve *social* mobility through trans-border *geographical* mobility. In the classic, i.e., Euro-centric, understanding this involved creating "new" societies, especially in North America, Australia, and New Zealand. The connotation intentionally was (and is) positive: The fact, that in the spaces of the destination societies, people already lived and were dispossessed, did not enter this his-story. With the decline of both the transatlantic and colonizer migration patterns, developed in the nineteenth century, and with the end of European-North American hegemony over scholarship and the resulting inclusion, on the one hand, of those displaced by the arrival of migrants from Europe and, on the other, recognition that macro-regional migration systems existed in other parts of the world, the popular valuation of migration and migrants is changing to negative perspectives: "They" want a share of "our" wealth; "they" are not comparable to our nineteenth-century emigrants; "they" are refugees from poverty, not from political oppression; "they" thus do not conform to the definition of a refugee according to the Geneva Convention.

Since, in its neoliberal version, the capitalist economy – perhaps its super-rich, oligarchic or, in terms of *The Economist*, plutocratic elite – is no longer delivering acceptable living conditions to all citizens (or populations) in capitalist states, scapegoating of others rather than critical analysis of the regime's shortcomings has become the parlance of the day: The migrants, ethnically, religiously, culturally different newcomers, are threatening the welfare systems of democratic states, and "our" ways of life. Hence, "they" are not entitled to participate. The global systemic inequalities by which rich countries

8 Immanuel Wallerstein, "The Rise and Future Demise of the World Capitalist System: Concepts for Comparative Analysis," *Comparative Studies in Society and History* 16, no. 4 (1974): 387–415, esp. 401.

outsource their wealth generation to societies with lower standards of living generate migrations that bring these inequalities to the doorsteps of the residents of wealthy countries. Some react with "welfare chauvinism" which posits that "welfare is for us, and only for us." While migration increases diversity and thereby encourages creative inputs and development, it nevertheless also demands a sharing of resources.

In the past, racism involved people and peoples in distant, colonized societies and, within Europe, the religious Other, the Jews. In the present, self-proclaimed Christians reinvent anti-Semitism as anti-Islamism or, more general, anti-immigrantism. Both social philosopher Étienne Balibar and world-systems theorist Immanuel Wallerstein argue that xenophobia in past societies is not the ancestor of present anti-immigrant racism. In contrast, modern racism is part and parcel of, in historical sequence, the nation-state, the increasing division of labour, and the core-periphery division and, like all social phenomena it is fluid or flexible as racism may be adapted to the circumstances.[9] Balibar has criticized Marx's terms of "labour" and "class" because, by conflating a historical actor, "the proletariat," with the segment of society reproducing capitalism through their labour, the "working class," the theory loses coherence. Furthermore, he criticized the concept of "nation-state" because of its undefined but aggressive nationalism.[10] Racism may be part of nationalist and working-class stances when, especially in the present, nation-states are in crisis and class positions are undercut by jobs being transferred to other societies. Internal conflicts add to the problems when residents refuse to take on certain types of jobs, such as those in food production or caregiving and therefore need the very in-migrant workers they want to exclude. In these developments, gender is a factor: Many of the jobs shifted to migrants, i.e., the "essential workers" of the COVID-19 pandemic parlance, were traditionally societally assigned to women. Arlie Hochschild called this the "emotional labour" of women in addition to the physical exertion, unregulated hours, and often poor working conditions. The emotions involved in care, whether of infants, children, or the elderly, are thus to be provided by caretakers from other cultural backgrounds.[11] The multiple divisions of labour between women and men in societies, and between the Global South and the Global North, thus frame racism in migrant-receiving societies as well as decisions to migrate in the societies of departure, if migrations are self-willed, or sending societies,

9 Balibar and Wallerstein, *Race, Nation, Class*.

10 Étienne Balibar with Louis Althusser et al., *Lire le Capital*, 2 vols. (Paris: Maspero, 1965).

11 Arlie Russell Hochschild, *The Managed Heart: The Commercialization of Human Feeling* (Berkeley: University of California Press, 1983).

if migrations are state-assisted or even-mandated. Migrations deeply impact family life in the community of origin and individual emotions as well as societal development in the target societies, whether hosting or hostile.

Migrants, despite being integral and irreplaceable parts of global labour markets, are often excluded from social and political rights in the societies to which they contribute their labour. While self-defined immigrant societies may offer belonging and embeddedness, self-proclaimed non-immigrant states, whether Singapore or Austria, refuse participation. "Democratic" states thus divide themselves into a participating segment and a tolerated and necessarily non-participating segment. The basic postulate of modern statism, the equality of all members before the law, is thus undercut by the very state governments. The, in view of the continuing global inequalities continuously growing number and share of migrants is bearing the brunt of the exclusion but still is contributing to the essential functioning of the societies in which they work. Exclusion, as demanded by individual racists and state-wide right-wing parties, would deprive these economies of the labour-power they need.

In some societies, migrants without rights are used in the most difficult types of work in the sectors with the lowest wages, while in others trade unions have struggled for and achieved minimum wages for all, i.e., for all those in traditional sectors but not (not yet?) for those in the new platform economies and delivery sectors such as those of Amazon and similar companies. If low wages are passed on to consumers, the enfranchised citizenship benefits from the exploitation of the disenfranchised and thus benefits from the exploitative system.

4 Global Inequalities: Examples

Migration from the United Provinces of Mexico to the United States of (North) America has been making headlines for decades and is often used as an example of large-scale undocumented migration. The Gross National Product (GNP) per capita in the US is five times that of Mexico. The oft-criticized migrations from Sub-Saharan economies to the EU have as a motivating factor that, according to World Bank's World Development Indicators data, the GNP per capita in the EU is 23 times higher than in the migrants' countries of origin.[12] Within specific regions, Pakistan's GNP per capita is 2.5 times that of

12 "World Development Indicators," World Bank, https://databank.worldbank.org/source/world-development-indicators.

Afghanistan; between regions, Germany's poorest income decile earns 15 percent more than Pakistan's richest income decile (World Bank, Purchasing power parities data for 2013). Hence, a migrant from Pakistan's middle class increases his/her income by migrating into Germany's lower or even underclass. This is also the case for migrations from, for example, the city of Ibadan, Nigeria. The core-periphery polarizations polarize life chances. To improve these, theoretically the global community of states might change the polarization. Practically, individual men and women cross borders to improve their lives and, in a longer perspective, those of their children.

From a historical perspective, collective action, revolutions, and/or wars for independence, led to changes in life perspectives in Mexico between 1910 and 1921, in Russia in 1917, in China in 1911 and between 1927 and 1949, in Cuba between 1953 and 1959, and in Algeria between 1954 and 1962. The state of China, as a newly constituted republic and, subsequently, a communist state, had struggled to escape from the unequal treaties imposed by the colonizer powers that were in effect from approximately the 1840s to 1950s. However, revolutions within countries and their intended benefits were countered by the imposed global terms of trade and, in many cases, by the development of new internal elites. Another route has been taken by states and economies that engaged in investment programs, often with delayed wage increases, to reduce the gap to the wealthy capitalist core. Examples include China and, to a lesser degree, India, the two most populous countries of the world, as well as South Korea, Indonesia, Turkey, Thailand, Malaysia, and Singapore. Still, in 2018, 2.64 billion "citizens of the world" of a total of 7.6 billion were living in (extreme) poverty, again according to the data from international financial institutions. By this date, migrants accounted for 3.5 percent of the world's population while their share of the poor stood at 10 percent. "When a woman from Mexico decides to emigrate in order to make money as a domestic servant, she is designing her own international debt politics. She is trying to cope with the loss of earning power and the rise in the cost of living at home by cleaning bathrooms in the country of the bankers."[13] On the household level, men and women thus try to counter inter-state and global inequalities.

13 Cynthia Enloe, *Bananas, Beaches and Bases: Making Feminist Sense of International Politics* (Berkeley: University of California Press, 1990).

PART 2

Class/Classes: Formations, Outsourcing, Informalizing, Global Hierarchies

CHAPTER 4

Introduction

Dirk Hoerder and Lukas Neissl

The standard view of modern societies – stemming from Western Europe – postulates the threefold upper-, middle- and lower-class division. Since its inception, this view did not come to terms with, on the one hand, rural lower classes including independent small-holding peasants and, on the other, urban craftspeople. These were part of the population but not of the politically enfranchised and economically equal citizenry.

This issue persists to the present: Are workingmen and -women, often divided into residents and migrants, a constituent part of a state, of a nation? Or are they merely a self-mobilizing production factor? Alternatively, are they an entity, moveable en masse by the state, capital, particular companies, or others? At present, although scholars as well as most politicians and the media agree that the working and peasant classes are an integral part of societies and polities, empirical studies do not necessarily support this interpretation to its full extent. The issue becomes very contentious when migrant workingmen and -women demand equal rights and full participation in the receiving society. It is worth emphasizing that the often-used term "host" society implies *temporary* "guest" status.

In the classic state-nation-centred frame, the views of past migrations rested on the assumption of an emigration-immigration dichotomy with emigrants as one-time movers lost to their former state and nation, and immigrants as one-time newcomers becoming residents embedded in their receiving society. Thus, in the century spanning the 1830s to 1930s, Europe's states were labelled emigration countries, and the American states were immigration countries with the US taking the largest share of newcomers. From a global perspective, millions of South Asian as well as Southern and Northern Chinese residents left their countries of birth to find work elsewhere, either within Asia or beyond its shores. Given colonizer rule in Africa, migrations for work were frequently coerced or outright forced and, in many cases, not waged. In the present (2020 data), India experiences the largest out-migration with 17.9 million citizens (of a population of 1.38 billion) living outside its borders while the US still ranks as the foremost in-migration state with 50.6 million foreign-born people in the country (population of 329.5 million). The emigration-immigration terminology raises questions about belonging: Where do migrants feel at home? It also

 | DOI:10.1163/9789004686991_005

raises questions concerning membership: To which state do migrants belong? Do they have rights in their state of departure, perhaps at an intermediate location, and in the state of arrival? Or are they excluded from some, many, or all rights? Are they "in-between" or "uprooted" as cultural essentialists and believers in fixed national identities have argued?

The authors of the following chapters address several aspects of these questions. However, they naturally do not (and cannot) provide a single comprehensive answer to them. All start from the empirical data that many states and economies, both historic and present, do not provide means of living for parts of their resident population – be it due to land as a factor of production for (sub-)peasant classes or jobs in industrial or service economies. In parallel, other state economies have jobs on offer or, more generically, income-generating options, but they lack potential workers. However, these countries do not necessarily seek permanent immigrants but rather working migrants for temporary sojourns. They attempt to acquire moveable or self-moving population segments elsewhere. The relationship of power, political and economic, reflecting the push and pull of migrants has been expressed since ancient times in the image of a big fish swallowing a small fish: In the European Middle Ages, Pieter Bruegel the Elder painted this. Large economies "swallow" the labouring population of their smaller neighbours. However, only a few political scientists and statesmen have attempted to actually study and question unequal power relations, whether internally within states, between states, or globally.

In contrast to state- and employer-side assumptions, migrant men and women are people with their own minds. They make their decisions in family economies and if we assume relatively small families of five members, each migrant discusses his/her options with four kinspeople. Thus, the migrants from India (at present) involve another 72 million people, and the 55 million from Europe (1815–1955) involved 220 million family members. Migrants may decide to move once or repeatedly, they may return and depart again, engage in circular mobility, stay for extended periods of time, and plan to return but never do so. At present, the intensive research on remittances sent by migrants to their families in their societies of origin – a term less emotionally loaded than "home society" – indicates that migration and decision-making in family economies have been integrated into economic research although migration is usually not part of state-centred political theorizing or policymaking.

These issues were in the minds of many when men and women of colours of skin other than white began to migrate into self-labelled "white" societies. Many residents in labour-attracting economies expected the migrants to leave their, now hostile, "host" societies after having contributed their labour power. The issue burst into the public debate again when, at the beginning of the COVID-19 pandemic, states closed their borders to limit the transmission of the SARS-CoV-2 virus. Only then did policymakers and public administrators, to a surprising degree out of touch with basic information, realize that they were shutting out circulating service workers, mostly women and, thus, damaging the care systems for "their" respective state's citizens – the use of the possessive pronoun raises further questions in this context. All of the food industries were similarly affected. In a top-down orchestrated rhetorical turn-around, the migrating and circulating men and women suddenly became "essential" workers whereas, de facto, they continued to be treated as replaceable low-wage labour. Furthermore, in many states, much of construction work – "3-D" = dirty, dangerous, often difficult, and sometimes even demeaning – is currently being outsourced, in this case mostly to migrant men, just as infrastructural work such as constructing the Suez or Panama canals had been in the past. Hence, seemingly whole segments of the labour markets are being outsourced or, more correctly in human terms, whole segments of the working classes are being outsourced. States professing national cultures and political citizenship import or release mobile or mobilized segments of the population and deprive them of citizen status while individuals in the societies, who cannot feed themselves by "nation" or "state" rhetoric, depart of their own decision.

Mahua Sarkar (Chapter 5) places the COVID-19 policy debates and decisions in the perspective of labour migrations. Workers, in her case from Bangladesh, were out-sourced to labour-deficient but investment-rich societies. Compelled by the pandemic-containment lockdowns, according to press reports, 400,000 Bangladeshi workers had to return "home" empty-handed (data from February 2021). Media worldwide showed photos of millions of workers in India who migrated internally and had to return with neither transportation nor food available. Sarkar counters the trope of "essential workers" with sociological analyses of "risk societies" in which some – migrant workingmen and -women, in particular – carry more risks than the residents of the respective state. "Outsourcing the working class" in the present has its antecedents, in the 1970s and 1980s for example, in outsourcing shipbuilding from Western European shipyards (manned since the 1960s by skilled workers from Yugoslavia and Turkey) to, first, Polish and, then, East Asian shipyards or outsourcing steel production and car manufacture from the eastern US and Detroit to locations in India and China. The emergence of "rust belts," as the abandoned regions have been called, or, in China, the restructuring of state-owned companies, dis-locates resident local working families and forces them to re-locate, to accept deteriorating living conditions, or to re-tool. Both the US and China dislocations involved tens of millions of workers. Viewed from the other side, people in or near the "tiger regions" – such as in South Korea, the Shenzhen boom cities, or steel-producing locations in India – experienced a growing job market with resulting improved life perspectives. In China, according to estimates, some 60 million lost their jobs in the state industrial complexes, but 80 million found work in the new Special Economic Zones, with Shenzhen being the most prominent of these. Are the working classes part of the regional societies in decline? Is service work part of a nation-state economy or a segment for "foreigners" without rights? Viewed positively, tens of millions of rural men and women near the investment centres migrated topographically from farm or subsistence plots to factories in cities-in-the-making and socially from rural classes to urban working-class status. The town of Shenzhen, for example, grew from 60,000 inhabitants in 1980 to 6 million in 2000: Making a class? Relocating it? The argument of Mahua Sarkar's study applies to many parts of the world.

The debate, so far, has focused on "work" as conceptualized in the late nineteenth-century industrializing societies: factory work, regular hours, and production routines. At this point, we will not challenge the view of "regular" factory labour but merely remind ourselves that in its early phases, machinery was characterized by stoppages and breakdowns, work autocratically assigned by foremen and/or factory owners, and other irregularities. Far more pertinently than debating the character of factory work, Aliki Vaxevanoglou (Chapter 6) questions the whole dichotomy of "formal" versus "informal" work. Families in many societies – she uses Greece as a case in point – derive their income from multiple sources, sources that statisticians cannot categorize and the input and output of which they cannot quantify. This re-evaluation of current theorizing and parlance permits an unveiling of the long-hidden continuities between patterns of worktime and income generation as well as allocation in medieval Europe or Qing China and most other societies of the past. Vaxevanoglou bridges the constructed dichotomy between the pre-industrial and industrial eras. When the concept of "informal work" was initially introduced as an analytical tool, it was a major step away from the narrow concentration on the factory segment of labour markets and whole economies. However, in the abstract world of theorizing with the power to impose constructs on data and discourses, "informal labour" came to be used to devalue societies which allegedly had not yet reached higher development. The economists of the (in other respects innovative) International Labour Organization participated in this misconceptualization. This raises the question of whether their "formal" funding shaped their questions while scholars in the not yet formalized "developing" world could observe informal arrangements? Focus on "formal" work makes no sense in global terms in the present as six out of every ten workingmen or -women, most of them in the Global South, are "informally" employed or self-employed. Recombining wage labour in state-mandated contractual forms with non-waged but often mutually supportive service labour in families, among kin, or in neighbourhoods or small food production permits a comprehensive understanding of labour relations and types of labour across societies, over the centuries, and of gendered work spheres as well as "child labour" which, in rural family contexts as well as in the crafts, but not in industrial work regimes, are part of self-sufficient lives. Men and women use multiple and flexible income strategies, and these vary between stages in their life cycles. Hence, to improve the accuracy of the discourse in this context, scholars need to abandon the artificial dichotomy of formal and informal work with its types of work and gender implications.

In some societies, combinations of informal and formal work never sufficed to provide sustenance and life prospects to all people living in them. In Europe, Poland and Italy are cases in point. In France, in contrast, couples limited the number of their children early on to keep the available resources and the number of mouths to feed in balance. They did so notwithstanding the prescriptions of the, in the country, extremely powerful Latin Churchmen. In the four British cultures, England-Scotland-Wales-colonized Ireland, families raised more children than could be supported and these population "surpluses" were subsequently sent out or migrated on their own to acquire land – already settled and culturally "owned" – in North America and Australia or, if they were from the gentry and aristocracy, to be offered jobs in imperial administrative and military institutions imposed on colonized societies. Other parts of the world, such as the Southern Chinese provinces, for example, became emigration regions early on, both maritime and southbound, while several northern provinces became emigration regions from the 1880s with those departing moving northbound.

Cecilia Bruzelius (Chapter 7) uses the "classic" two European cases to discuss how the Polish and the Italian state respectively used emigration of – depending on the point of view – citizens or surplus men and women to stabilize their economies and to adjust their national population to their economic potential. She argues that migration is not exogenous to social and economic systems but often – and perhaps in most cases – integral to sustaining political economies. State institutions and their bureaucratic personnel use the emigration of selected segments of the population for population management. When temporary out-migration or permanent emigration becomes part of everyday practices, families often decide on their own who will leave and who will remain. From the view of the state and its decision-makers, exporting underused or unusable labour resources reduces the potential for protest and pressures to adjust structural shortcomings or, positively, permits better allocation of social service resources such as education, healthcare, and old-age provisions to those remaining. Reduction of labour reserves may also increase wages of the non-migrants and/or may stimulate in-migration of workingmen and -women from (neighbouring) societies in which conditions are worse. Beate Althammer (Chapter 16) discusses this aspect by using Polish migration into and within the German Empire as a case.

In the present, the Philippines and Bangladesh as well as Pakistan have become labour-exporting societies. In his ongoing research project "Migration in a World of Inequality," which is not presented in this volume, Immanuel Ness argues that, in contrast to the past when states wanted to achieve positive goals in labour markets, the export of service and construction workers by, for example, the Nepalese state, imposes burdens on families, societies and states: The societies of birth raise children, provide education whether rudimentary or good, pay for special training for prospective skilled and dynamic emigrants, whether domestic workers, caretakers, nurses and doctors, to name only a few, but do not receive taxes from the emigrants' incomes after their departure. Ness's research suggests that this kind of (supported) emigration obstructs development in the sending countries. Beyond the frequently mentioned domestic and care workers, the Global South loses young adults educated in, often, private – and costly – training centres in medicine and healthcare, engineering and business services, and in many other segments. States of departure and the migrants' families thus pay for the logistics of migration while the benefits thereof accrue to the receiving societies. One-third of all Mexican PhDs work in the US and, when, in the 1950s, a Mexican pharmaceutical company developed the first contraceptive pill, US capital bought the company and transferred its expertise – and resulting profits – to the US.

As mentioned above, the southern provinces of imperial China had been emigration regions since the fifteenth century, with migrants initially coming in small numbers from particular districts to settlements in the Southeast Asian islands. In the nineteenth century, to increase the reservoir of exploitable, low-wage-bound labour, the British imperial military, using the "Opium Wars" (1839–1842, 1856–1860) as an instrument, imposed the drug on an unwilling state and its provincial governors. This created the desired indebtedness among drug consumers, who rapidly became addicts, and, as intended, the debt-related involuntary mobility of a labour force for plantations and mines in the British and French as well as Dutch segments of the Indian Ocean and Southeast Asian worlds followed. While the emphasis on debt and oppression, both correct perspectives, highlights the object status of workers, Selda Altan

(Chapter 8) shifts the perspective to a "quest for workers" in which the French and British imperial economies and the respective private investors were competing for workers. She examines the recruitment for the French-colonizer Yunnan-Indochina railway construction, 1898–1910, which was characterized by particularly brutal working conditions that resulted in workers deserting en masse or rebelling. Just as imperial policymakers talked to each other and either learned from or competed with the other, workers compared conditions in the local or regional investment centres of the two empires and made decisions concerning where to go and how to sell their labour. Their accumulated knowledge about the multiple imperial, local, and regional working conditions and wages permitted prospective migrants to act in their own interest. The emerging Chinese – or, at least, regional – working-class subsequently improved its negotiating power and class consciousness. This process involved the formation of a working class that considered opportunity structures rather than merely specific conditions.

Empire and labour are also the topics of Dácil Juif's comparative study of labour recruitment (Chapter 9) in the British Northern Rhodesian Copperbelt (later Zambia), from the 1920s to 1960s and beyond. Given the location of the minerals in sparsely settled regions of subsistence farming and herding, their extraction, funded by imperial capital and supported by the state, required the making-importing-mobilizing of a labour force. To attract workers or to coerce or even force men to migrate to the mines, investors and mine managers, settler-investors in export crops and colonizer administrators cooperated and also frequently pursued distinct interests. On the other side, the potential workers and, of course, their families considered various options or imposed necessities since the colonizer state-imposed taxes had to be paid in money rather than produce. Working families' agency conflicted with the intended colonizer state control of migration. The state-capital combine had to develop a profit-yielding incentive or rely on costly punitive strategies: Were circulating workingmen the most profitable labour force, since women and children staying on the subsistence farm provided food through their labours? Or was permanent family migration and residence in the mining towns preferable because it stabilized an experienced labour force? Managers and administrators in Northern Rhodesia's Copperbelt pursued different strategies from those in Southern Rhodesia (later Zimbabwe) (see Chapter 17 in this volume) as well as compared to those in other important mining regions of Southern and Central Africa. While in Belgian Congo and Portuguese Angola, officials resorted to active recruitment, albeit often through coercion, in British Northern Rhodesia they did so only in the very early stages of industrial copper mining whereby the high-turnover regime with temporary stays in rural areas was not imposed as effectively as in British South Africa. Once women were accepted as urban residents, administrators emphasized their re-productive role but many women took the initiative to produce, enter the market economy, and pursue their own (or their families') interests. Mineworkers' unions only emerged in the 1950s and attained moderate achievements, although in surrounding regions they were either banned or virtually inactive.

To summarize, it is evident from the topics addressed that the perspective from the top down – i.e., from the interests of capitalists or state imperialists – does not permit an assessment of developments on the ground anywhere in the colonizer-colonized segments of the globe. The multiple forms of agency of migrating workers, whether individuals or families, show both regional specifics and, from the workingmen and -women, subcontinental or even comparative imperial assessments of options.

CHAPTER 5

Outsourcing the Working Class

Guestwork in Turbulent Times

Mahua Sarkar

Abstract

Theoretical discussions about "risk" as it relates to the world of work have largely stemmed from the disintegration of stable employment relations in the Global North. This chapter argues that the ideas of "risk" and "uncertainty" are also relevant to the experiences of millions of low-resourced guestworkers or transnational temporary contract workers from the Global South who toil in affluent economies around the world. Focusing on the impact of the COVID-19 crisis on guestwork, it argues that while the pandemic spotlights the exploitation of contract migrants, it also underlines the *significance* of their work in "essential" industries in labour-importing societies. The chapter ends with some reflections on what these contradictory revelations around guestwork and workers might imply for both the immediate and long-term futures of labour mobility regimes that are *designed* to keep migrants from settling in host economies.[1]

1 Versions of this chapter were presented at the *56th International Conference of Labour and Social History* (2021) and the *Development, Power and Policy Seminar* at the University of Toronto Scarborough (2022), as well as to the Critical Migration Studies collective, University of Toronto (2021) and the Department of Sociology, Binghamton University (2022). The author thanks all the participants, especially Ana Maria Candela, Husseina Dinani, Emine Fidan Elcioglu, Gladys Jimenez-Muñoz, Anna Korteweg, William Martin, Marcel van der Linden, and Susan Zimmerman for their support and generous comments. Special thanks are due to Andreas Eckert for his critical engagements with multiple drafts of the paper. Dirk Hoerder and Lukas Neissl's editorial acumen has made the revision process seem easy. The title of the paper derives in part from an unfinished working paper co-authored with József Böröcz. And finally, the paper is dedicated to Lubna Nazir Choudhry – dear friend and colleague – who helped imagine it amidst the pandemic lockdown but is sadly no longer with us for its completion.

 | DOI:10.1163/9789004686991_006

Keywords

automation – circular migration – constrained labour – essential work – guestwork – kafala/kefala sponsorship system – managed migration – non-citizen labour – risk – robots – transnational temporary contract migration – uncertainty

The publication of sociologist Ulrich Beck's influential and much-debated *Risk Society* (1992) and his subsequent *The Brave New World of Work* (2000) seems to have normalized the idea of "risk as a lens" or resource for understanding contemporary human experiences of incertitude, especially as they relate to fluctuations in labour markets. Highlighting a shift from a "uniform system of lifelong full-time work organized in a single industrial location […] to a risk-fraught system of flexible, pluralized, decentralized underemployment" since the late 1960s, Beck's analysis distils the anxieties that many experience into a notion of "risk" that seems both intuitively attractive and capacious.[2] A similar, if somewhat broader, set of reflections is advanced by Zygmunt Bauman in his influential liquid modernity thesis – widely read as a trenchant critique of contemporary welfare society.[3] Both theses underline the contemporary processes of "dis-embedding" individuals from their ascribed social positions without a subsequent "re-embedding" into a new, stable social class and identity location – the twin processes that marked the advent of modernity in the past. Instead, today social bonds seem to be increasingly mutable, while "jobs for life" disappear under dominant market pressures, leaving individuals unmoored, chronically dissatisfied, and searching.[4] What is more, the effects of these large-scale changes somehow appear today as "personal failings" of individuals, rather than processes "connected to public issues or collective interests," as may have been the case in an earlier epoch.[5] The responsibility now seems to lie entirely with individuals, who are expected to "reflexively

2 Ulrich Beck, *Risk Society: Towards a New Modernity* (London: Sage, 1992), 143.

3 Zygmunt Bauman, *Liquid Modernity* (Cambridge: Polity, 2000), 14; Raymond L. M. Lee, "Reinventing Modernity: Reflexive Modernization vs. Liquid Modernity vs. Multiple Modernities," *European Journal of Social Theory* 9, no. 3 (2006): 357; Peter Abrahamson, "Liquid Modernity: Bauman on Contemporary Welfare Society," *Acta Sociologica* 47, no. 2 (2004): 171–172.

4 Will Atkinson, "Not All That Was Solid Has Melted into Air (or Liquid): A Critique of Bauman on Individualisation and Class in Liquid Modernity," *Sociological Review* 56, no. 1 (2008): 4–6.

5 Zygmunt Bauman, *Individualized Society* (Cambridge: Polity, 2001), 41–56, 140–152; Ulrich Beck, *The Brave New World of Work* (Cambridge: Polity, 2000), 53; Atkinson, "Not All That Was Solid," 4–5.

assemble their life paths and identities themselves,"[6] presumably by taking "risks."[7] Recent developments in artificial intelligence, machine learning, and robotics have further impacted the way work is structured in many industries, deepening a general sense of malaise as risks now appear to be less and less calculable, pushing us incrementally into the realm of "genuine" uncertainties.[8]

While these theoretical discussions about the contingencies of work and its futures are largely rooted in the disintegration of stable employment relations in the Global North, not surprisingly, "risk" also permeates lives and livelihoods elsewhere in the world. Across much of the economically underprivileged world, precariousness of work – if not a "wageless life," to echo Michael Denning – has been normalized for a long time.[9] Work characterized by casualized and fluctuating employment and piece rates is hardly an aberration in contexts where informality is the rule.[10] Processes of dis-embedding without adequate re-embedding, and individualization – the transference of risk burdens onto individual decision-making – are palpable across the Global South, both historically and today.[11]

In particular, these processes would seem to resonate closely with the experiences of the millions of migrants who leave – or are forced to leave – their home countries every year to seek better living and working conditions in other parts of the world.[12] Among international migrants, guestworkers or

6 Atkinson, "Not All That Was Solid," 1–2; Beck, *Risk Society*, 135.

7 The modernist conception of risk assumed that "unanticipated outcomes may be the consequence of human action" rather than reflections of "the hidden meanings of nature" as indexed in the ideas of fate or *fortuna*. Deborah Lupton, *Risk* (London: Routledge, 1999), 6–7; Anthony Giddens, *The Consequences of Modernity* (Cambridge: Polity, 1990), 30.

8 "Moderns had eliminated genuine indeterminacy, or 'uncertainty,' by inventing 'risk.' They had learnt to transform a radically indeterminate cosmos into a manageable one, through the myth of calculability." See Sanjay G. Reddy "Claims to Expert Knowledge and the Subversion of Democracy: The Triumph of Risk over Uncertainty," *Economy and Society* 25, no. 2 (1996): 237. I thank Bhaskar Sarkar and Bishnupriya Ghosh for alerting me to the differential usages of the concept of "risk."

9 Michael Denning, "Wageless Life," *New Left Review* 66 (2010): 84–85. Jan Breman and Marcel van der Linden, "Informalizing the Economy: The Return of the Social Question at the Global Level," *Development and Change* 45, no. 5 (2014): 924.

10 Breman and van der Linden, "Informalizing the Economy," 924.

11 An elaborated version of the preceding discussion appears in Mahua Sarkar, "*L'action incertaine: Le contrat de travail temporaire transnational en tant que risque*," in *Action et Incertitude: Les épreuves de l'incertain*, ed. Marc-Henry Soulet (Basel/Berlin: Schwabe Verlag, 2018), 457–460.

12 The total number of international migrants in mid-2020 was 280.6 million. International Organization of Migration, Migration Data Portal, accessed 7 October 2021, https://www.migrationdataportal.org/international-data?i=stock_abs_&t=2020. In 2019, 62 percent of the total number of migrants worldwide moved for work. The majority of transnational

transnational temporary contract workers travel through specific cross-border work-mobility arrangements subject to significant restrictions *designed* to keep them from settling in receiving countries.[13] Elsewhere, I have written about how the legal exclusion of guestworkers from long-term residency and citizenship in host countries impacts their foothold on the slippery continuum between freedom and unfreedom/constraint, pushing them incrementally towards the latter.[14] In my reading, the outbreak of the COVID-19 pandemic reveals a similarly unclear and messy frontier between risk (defined as calculable and, hence, manageable) and uncertainty (what is beyond control) that marks guestwork as an institution. As we shall see below, the COVID-19 crisis has intensified the challenges facing this category of transnational migrant labour, dramatically increasing the quotient of both uncertainty and constraint in their experiences of mobility and work.

My aim in this chapter is threefold. I begin with a brief survey of the specific vulnerabilities of transnational temporary contract migrants or guestworkers as recorded in the media and emerging policy reports, both at the global and regional/national levels, in several significant destination countries/regions worldwide since the outbreak of the COVID-19 pandemic. Does the crisis expose guestworkers to greater degrees of uncertainty, constraint, and possible exploitation than is normal in this form of work-mobility arrangement? In what ways?

Second, drawing on the insights of my own research and existing scholarship, I explore what the present juncture reveals, or perhaps clarifies, about guestwork and workers beyond the problems that are *inherent* in this system

---

migrant workers are found in three sub-regions of the world: 24.2 percent in Northern, Southern and Western Europe; 22.1 percent in Northern America; and 14.3 percent in the Arab States, which include the Gulf Cooperation Council countries (Bahrain, Kuwait, Qatar, United Arab Emirates and Saudi Arabia) plus Iraq, Jordan, Lebanon, Occupied Palestinian Territories, Syrian Arab Republic, and Yemen. International Labour Organization, *Global Estimates on International Migrant Workers* (Geneva: International Labour Office, 2021), 11–15.

13 Approximately 20 percent of all labour migrants in the world reportedly move within the context of overseas temporary contract work or guestworker programs. Kristin Surak, "Guestworkers: A Taxonomy," *New Left Review* 84 (2013): 85–86. Guest/transnational temporary contract work regimes are referred to by various names in the literature. I use these two terms interchangeably in my work and, if any other formulation is applied, it signals the dominant usage in a particular location. For instance, in Singapore, guestworkers are called "foreign workers," "migrant workers," or "foreign migrants."

14 Mahua Sarkar, "Constrained Labour as Instituted Process: Transnational Contract Work and Circular Migration in Late Capitalism," *European Journal of Sociology* 58, no. 1 (2017): 176–177.

of labour mobility. In my reading, the pandemic underscores two important and inter-connected insights: the *significance of* the work done by contract migrants and the extent to which labour-receiving economies are *dependent* on guestwork regimes for a slew of essential services – in agriculture, food production, transportation, delivery services, and care work – as well as in some critical industries. As such, the precariousness, risks, and difficulties associated with guestwork have been well understood for some time now, prompting the description of the work done by contract migrants as "3-D (dirty, dangerous and demeaning)." What I want to underscore here is the ways in which the COVID-19 crisis has *forced* this understanding into mainstream consciousness through the discursive trope of the "*essential worker*."[15] Suddenly, the term seems to be everywhere with debates raging over which occupations can be designated as "essential," and a shifting politics of the merits of such a designation.[16] I am arguing (or perhaps hoping) that the turmoil unleashed by the COVID-19 crisis will help unsettle the condescending – albeit sympathetic – view of so-called "3-D" work, thereby forcing a greater appreciation of these undervalued occupations and the guestworkers who people them.

My third and final aim in this chapter is to offer some reflections on what these contradictory revelations around guestwork – the extreme vulnerability of the workers, the essential nature of the services they provide, and the dependence of labour-scarce economies on such work – might indicate for both the immediate and long-term prospects of this form of labour-mobility arrangements. What risks, if not uncertainties, might guestworkers expect to face in the near and distant future? And what lessons, if any, might histories of mobile labour under global capitalism offer in this regard?

However, before we delve into the COVID-19 pandemic situation and its specific dystopia, a few words about the institution of guestwork seem to be in order.

15 The "essential worker" trope is reminiscent of the ways in which the idea of "the 99 percent" helped coalesce dispersed popular protests over inequality into a coherent critique in the *Occupy Wall Street Movement* a decade earlier. In time, the Occupy movement itself fizzled, but the idea of "the 99 percent" seems to have endured as a resource feeding progressive politics in the US, and beyond. I thank sociologist Emine Fidan Elcioglu for her help in clarifying this point.

16 In the US, for instance, the designation "essential" had contradictory implications. In the pre-vaccine period of the COVID-19 pandemic, it determined which categories of employees were disallowed remote work; after the vaccines arrived, the same designation facilitated access to vaccines.

1 What Is Guestwork?

Guestwork is a specific form of cross-border temporary labour migration that denies migrants the right to seek long-term residency and/or citizenship in destination countries. Within the field of migration studies, such work-mobility regimes are variously referred to as temporary/seasonal/foreign worker programs, guestwork, managed migration, circular migration, or transnational contract work.[17] Often defined as a "fluid pattern of human mobility among countries,"[18] contemporary guestwork involves repeat movements of migrant workers between "home" and often several different destination countries in the course of a single working life. Requiring long periods of separation from families, and very little prospect of settling abroad, this kind of potentially lifelong sojourner mobility is fundamentally different from the permanent emigration that frequently resulted from earlier mass movements of peoples across international borders – be it through enslavement, indenture, or voluntary migration. Instead, circular/managed migrants are perhaps best understood as guestworkers – a term that has gained some traction for its succinct capturing of the ambivalent status of migrants who move legally most of the time, and by "choice" but who, unlike indentured workers, are not allowed to settle in the host society beyond the period of their contracts.[19]

Some scholars differentiate between circular migrations – understood as relatively fluid, repeat movements of labour across international borders – and other kinds of temporary migration involving more or less forced and managed forms of temporary residence. Others, however, insist that all such programs are rooted in a neoclassical understanding of labour as simply yet another

17 Daniel Costa and Philip Martin, *Temporary Labor Migration Programs: Governance, Migrant Worker Rights, and Recommendations for the UN Global Compact for Migration* (Washington, DC: Economic Policy Institute, 2018), 7–8.

18 Kathleen Newland, Dovelyn R. Mendoza, and Aaron Terrazas, "Learning by Doing: Experiences of Circular Migration," *Insight*, Washington, DC: Migration Policy Institute (2008), 2, accessed 1 October 2016, http://www.migrationpolicy.org/research/learning-doing-experiences-circular-migration.

19 Cindy Hahamovitch, "Creating Perfect Immigrants: Guestworkers of the World in Historical Perspective," *Labor History* 44, no. 1 (2003): 70–74. While indentured migration also involve(d) both transnational mobility and a contract, it differs fundamentally from guestwork in terms of the deportability of workers. Historically, many indentured migrants settled in their countries of destination whereas transnational temporary contract workers or guestworkers are *de jure* expected and *obliged* to leave.

commodity in need of efficient allocation for the production of profit rather than a socially embedded category.[20]

Speaking global historically, we may identify three waves of organized guestwork. The first of these may be traced back to the late nineteenth century arrival of Mozambican workers in South African mines and Polish seasonal agricultural workers in Prussia (see Chapter 16 in this volume).[21] Colonial empires had long been in the business of mobilizing large numbers of trans-regional/continental migrant labour – through enslavement, indenture, or conviction – to meet the labour demands in plantations, mines, public works, and other ventures throughout the colonies.[22] However, the ability to ensure the periodic exit of such migrant labouring populations was only made possible at the end of the nineteenth century with the invention of technologies of control designed to monopolize the legitimate means of population movement.[23] The result was the production of a new legal category of "temporary immigrants" in the late nineteenth century amidst a simultaneous rise in "international migration and nationalism" on the one hand, and "restrictive immigration legislation around the world" on the other.[24] These contradictory tendencies only heightened around the First World War when states on both sides of the Atlantic entered into the business of recruiting immigrants, albeit with strict policing regimes in place.[25] In France, for instance, colonial labour forces from Northern Africa, Indochina and Madagascar were joined by workers from China, Italy and Southern Europe to work on the docks, in mines, on military construction sites, as well as in agriculture and factories in a highly unequal and racially differentiated system of labour deployment and remuneration that discriminated against non-white workers.[26]

---

20 Bruce E. Kaufman, "The Institutional and Neoclassical Schools in Labor Economics," in *The Institutionalist Tradition in Labour Economics*, ed. Dell P. Champlin and Janet T. Knoedler (London: Routledge, 2017), 20; Stephen Castles and Deriya Ozkul, "Circular Migration: Triple Win, or a New Label for Temporary Migration?" in *Global and Asian Perspectives on International Migration*, ed. Graziano Battistella (Basel: Springer, 2014), 28.

21 Ulrich Herbert, *A History of Foreign Labor in Germany, 1880–1980: Seasonal Workers, Forced Laborers, Guest Workers*, trans. William Templer (Ann Arbor: University of Michigan Press, 1990); Jonathan Crush, Alan Jeeves, and David Yudelman, *South Africa's Labor Empire: A History of Black Migrancy to the Gold Mines* (Boulder, CO: Westview Press, 1991).

22 Hahamovitch, "Creating Perfect Immigrants," 72–73.

23 John Torpey, *The Invention of the Passport: Surveillance, Citizenship and the State* (New York: Cambridge University Press, 2000), 1–20.

24 Hahamovitch, "Creating Perfect Immigrants," 73–74.

25 Nigel Harris, *The New Untouchables: Immigration and the New World Worker* (New York: I. B. Tauris, 1995), 6–10.

26 Gary S. Cross, *Immigrant Workers in Industrial France: The Making of a New Laboring Class* (Philadelphia: Temple University Press, 1983), 18–44.

The "second phase" in the history of state-sponsored temporary migrant worker schemes began in earnest in the 1930s in the context of war mobilizations, heightened nationalism, and rising wages in Europe and Japan. In the context of reconstruction after the Second World War, such labour importing efforts intensified in Western Europe, with systematic, typically state-sponsored recruitments from a host of countries in Southern Europe and Northern Africa, as well as from Turkey.[27] While the highest concentration of temporary foreign workers as a percentage of the total labour force was in Switzerland (30 percent), the much larger *Gastarbeiter* programs in West Germany and similar initiatives in France together accounted for two-thirds of the entire guestworker population in Western Europe between the end of the war and the mid-1970s.[28] The first formalized temporary labour import arrangements in the US also date back to this period in the form of the *bracero* program with Mexico in 1942, and a similar agreement with British colonial authorities in the West Indies in 1943.

Temporary worker programs also existed within the socialist bloc – albeit on a much smaller scale – in the era after the Second World War. Formally speaking, these "training programmes" for workers were organized within an overarching framework of "economic and technical assistance" designed to transfer skills to socialist ally states in the Global South. However, they were also part of a strategy to ease the problem of labour shortages in "advanced socialist economies" in East-Central Europe, and labour surpluses elsewhere within the socialist world. Prominent examples included migrant labour from Mozambique, Angola, and Cuba in the German Democratic Republic (GDR) and the Soviet Union, and Vietnamese workers in Czechoslovakia.[29]

The third and contemporary wave of guestworker regimes began in the wake of the oil shock in the 1970s involving large-scale importation of non-citizen labour from poorer oil-importing countries – Arabs from the Middle East and North Africa (MENA) region in the 1970s, and more recently from South and Southeast Asia – to the Persian Gulf. According to current estimates, the combined migrant workforce in the Gulf Cooperation Council (GCC) countries – Saudi Arabia, Kuwait, Qatar, Bahrain, the United Arab Emirates (UAE), and Oman – is between 25 and 35 million strong (see Chapter 13 in this volume).[30]

27 Castles and Ozkul, "Circular Migration," 32.

28 Hahamovitch, "Creating Perfect Immigrants," 81–84.

29 Mahua Sarkar, ed., *Work Out of Place* (Berlin/Boston: De Gruyter Oldenbourg, 2018), 7–9.

30 The International Labour Organization (ILO) estimates that, globally, migrant workers constitute 4.9 percent of the labour force of destination countries. This figure is 41.4 percent (or eight times higher) in the Arab States (GCC plus Iraq, Jordan, Lebanon, Occupied Palestinian Territories, Syrian Arab Republic, and Yemen). International Labour Organization, *Global Estimates*, 11.

The unusually high proportion of migrants makes guestworkers the "primary labour force" in these economies – and not simply a complementary or supplementary source of labour – for the first time in the history of guestwork.[31]

By the 1980s, the "tiger" economies of Southeast and East Asia were also increasingly involved in such programs. In the wake of decolonization and the emergence of independent nation-states, and within the context of multiple wars and political struggles in the region, a set of countries – most notably Singapore, Malaysia, and Thailand, and, with lesser success, the Philippines and Indonesia – adopted an export-oriented industrialization strategy that has led to sustained rates of high economic growth. Together these "newly industrializing countries" (NICs), as they used to be known, formed the Association of Southeast Asian Nations (ASEAN) in 1976 to bolster their common political and economic interests, defined in opposition to those espoused by the communist countries in the region – Cambodia, Vietnam and Laos.[32] Beginning with industries "specialising in electronics and electrical components, textiles and garments and footwear," Singapore, Malaysia, and Thailand – the three frontrunners among the ASEAN countries – have over time moved up the production ladder to more advanced manufacturing industries such as aerospace engineering, marine and offshore engineering, robotics, clean air technology, medical technology, oil refining, automobile industry, as well as a host of highly profitable service industries, including specialized financial services, healthcare, and tourism.[33] The rapid pace of development has meant that all three countries have increasingly turned to the large-scale importation of temporary contract workers from neighbouring poorer economies to address their need for both skilled and unskilled labour.[34]

---

31 Mahua Sarkar, "The Flipside of the Integration Question: Guestworker Regimes and Temporary/Circular/Managed Migration in History," *Refugee Watch: A South Asian Journal on Forced Migration*, 49 (2017): 11–12; Martin Baldwin-Edwards, *Labour Immigration and Labour Markets in the GCC Countries: National Patterns and Trends* (London: London School of Economics Global Governance, 2011), 15.

32 Sarkar, "The Flipside," 12; Richard Stubbs, "War and Economic Development: Export-Oriented Industrialization in East and Southeast Asia," *Comparative Politics* 31, no. 3 (1999): 337–355; Giovanni Arrighi, "The Rise of East Asia: World Systemic and Regional Aspects," *International Journal of Sociology and Social Policy* 16, no. 7/8 (1996): 6–44.

33 Economic Development Board, Singapore, https://www.edb.gov.sg/content/edb/en/industries.html; "Malaysia Industry Sectors," Economy Watch, 16 March 2010, accessed 18 February 2017, http://www.economywatch.com/world_economy/malaysia/industry-sector-industries.html; "Thailand Industry Sectors," Economy Watch, 8 April 2010, accessed 18 February 2017, http://www.economywatch.com/world_economy/thailand/industry-sector-industries.html.

34 Amarjit Kaur, "Labour Migration in Southeast Asia: Migration Policies, Labour Exploitation and Regulation," *Journal of the Asia Pacific Economy* 15, no. 1 (2010): 7–8; Prema-Chandra

Since the 1990s, temporary worker programs have also proliferated in Europe, North America, and Australasia and, according to some estimates, over 50 countries in the world operate some form of temporary contract worker programs.[35] This current and third wave of guestwork has also involved large-scale movement of international – mostly female – domestic workers moving on the basis of temporary contracts, mainly from the Global South to the North.[36]

While individual countries and programmes vary in detail, guestwork regimes everywhere typically exclude migrants from fundamental labour rights, such as the choice of employer and job, as well as healthcare in receiving societies. Such legal restrictions, and the high levels of debt that contract migrants routinely incur in securing work permits, can make guestwork one of the more liminal and risky ventures in the human migratory landscape.[37]

2 COVID-19 and Guestworkers: Vulnerabilities

2.1 *UK and US*

There is no denying that while the COVID-19 pandemic has caused widespread loss and disruption of employment, the brunt of it is borne by low-wage minority populations and migrant and contingent workers across the world. Labour force survey data from the UK, for instance, shows that compared to native-born "white British" populations, Black, Asian and minority ethnic (BAME) workers are more likely to lose their jobs due to lockdowns, and lack access to employment protection options such as furloughing. At the same time, some BAME workers – for instance, migrants with visa restrictions – are locked out of public funds mobilized to provide wage coverage to furloughed workers and tide-over loans to businesses.[38]

Similar studies from the US reveal that in April 2020, when the national unemployment rate reached an unprecedented 14.7 percent, the lowest-income workers experienced the highest rates of job loss, with nearly one out

Athukorala and Chris Manning, *Structural Change and International Migration in East Asia: Adjusting to Labour Scarcity* (Oxford/New York: Oxford University Press, 1999), 142.

35 Surak, "Guestworkers," 84.

36 Europe receives over 22 percent of all international domestic workers. ILO, *Global Estimates*, xiii; Sarkar, "The Flipside," 11.

37 Costa and Martin, *Temporary Labor Migration*, 24, 29–31.

38 Yang Hu, "Intersecting Ethnic and Native-Migrant Inequalities in the Economic Impact of the COVID-19 Pandemic in the UK," *Research in Social Stratification and Mobility* 68 (2020): 2–4.

of every four (24.5 percent) part-time workers finding themselves out of work.[39] Notably, 17.4 percent of the total workforce in the US (comprising 28.4 million workers) is foreign-born – a category that includes over 8 million undocumented migrant workers concentrated in contractual/temporary jobs.[40] What is more, the disparities recorded among different racial and ethnic groups in April 2020 – 16.7 percent unemployment among Black workers, compared to 14.2 percent among white workers and 18.9 percent among Hispanics – persisted until the end of the year.

2.2 *The Gulf*

The widespread loss of employment of foreign contract workers has also been reported in the major labour-importing economies across the Persian Gulf and in Southeast Asia, where the proportion of foreigners in the total workforce can range anywhere from 95 percent in Qatar, 90 percent in the UAE and 79 percent in Saudi Arabia, to 38 percent in Singapore.[41] In the early months of the pandemic, the situation in the GCC countries in particular appeared to be dire and millions of workers found themselves stranded with no income, little or no healthcare and, sometimes, even no food. Many were forced to move to unsanitary and crowded labour camps/detention centres – "ideal incubators" for the virus – or risked being unhoused. Not surprisingly, most of the early reported COVID-19 outbreaks across the Gulf states were among migrant populations.

39 In comparison, unemployment figures at the end of 2019 were 3.1 percent among foreign-born workers and 3.8 percent among native-born workers. Congressional Research Service, *Unemployment Rates During the COVID-19 Pandemic: In Brief* (7 December 2020), https://crsreports.congress.gov.

40 Bureau of Labor Statistics, *Foreign-Born Workers: Labor Force Characteristics – 2019*, US Department of Labor, News Release 15 May 2020, https://www.bls.gov/news.release/pdf/forbrn.pdf; Miriam Jordan, "8 Million People Are Working Illegally in the U.S.: Here's Why That's Unlikely to Change," *New York Times*, 11 December 2018, https://www.nytimes.com/2018/12/11/us/undocumented-immigrant-workers.html.

41 Sarah Aziza, "For Persian Gulf Migrant Workers, the Pandemic Has Amplified Systemic Discrimination," *The Nation*, 30 October 2020, https://www.thenation.com/article/world/migrants-coronavirus-persian-gulf/; Bobby Ghosh, "Top World Bank economist explains the impact of coronavirus on foreign workers," *Economic Times*, 7 July 2020, https://economictimes.indiatimes.com/nri/working-abroad/top-world-bank-economist-explains-the-impact-of-coronavirus-on-foreign-workers/articleshow/76827158.cms; Human Rights Watch, *Country Reports: Qatar*, 2020, https://www.hrw.org/world-report/2020/country-chapters/qatar#; Human Rights Watch, *Country Reports: Saudi Arabia*, 2020, https://www.hrw.org/world-report/2020/country-chapters/saudi-arabia#b94615; Human Rights Watch, *Country Reports: United Arab Emirates*, 2019, https://www.hrw.org/world-report/2019/country-chapters/united-arab-emirates.

The widely prevalent and exploitative *kafala or kefala* system of sponsorship[42] that largely exempts employers from accountability compounded the problems since migrant workers could not exit the country without their *kafeel* or sponsor/employer's explicit permission.[43]

In responding to the crisis, the governments of the GCC countries began forcibly deporting thousands of workers – the worst nightmare for many migrants who risk their family's meagre possessions as collateral for the loans that underwrite their overseas sojourns. Travelling back on crowded aircrafts, a fair number of returning workers tested positive for COVID-19 on arrival, while many others travelled penniless as the chaotic deportation process intensified wage theft by employers – a widespread problem that deprived migrant contract workers of their legitimate wage entitlements even before the pandemic.[44] As the crisis continued over months, many overseas contract workers – who are used to supporting their family and kin in their countries of origin – found themselves depending on their families to send money as they struggled to survive. While the full impact of the pandemic on remittance flows from the Persian Gulf to poorer neighbouring countries is yet to be assessed, reports show declining outbound remittances from the region.[45]

2.3 *Southeast Asia*

The picture emerging from the Persian Gulf may be harsh, but it is by no means singular. In Southeast Asia, two economies that rely extensively on migrant labour from neighbouring countries are Malaysia and Singapore.

42 The kafala system of sponsorship ties "individual guest workers to a particular job, and more importantly, to a particular citizen-sponsor or corporate entity (a *kafeel*). This relationship has a contractual facet, in the sense that the men and women who cross the Indian Ocean to work in the Gulf sign contracts that oblige them to work, typically, for two years at a set level of pay. These contracts also oblige the sponsors to pay a certain rate, to cover travel costs, to provide a vacation period." Andrew Gardner, "Engulfed: Indian Guest Workers, Bahraini Citizens, and the Structural Violence of the Kafala System," in *The Deportation Regime: Sovereignty, Space and the Freedom of Movement*, ed. Nicholas De Genova and Nathalie Peutz (Durham, NC/London: Duke University Press, 2010), 203.

43 Martin Chulov, "Migrant Workers Bear Brunt of Coronavirus Pandemic in Gulf," *The Guardian*, 19 April 2020, https://www.theguardian.com/world/2020/apr/19/migrant-workers-bear-brunt-of-coronavirus-pandemic-in-gulf; Aziza, "For Persian Gulf Workers."

44 Sebastian Castelier, "Gulf Migrant Workers Face Crisis of Unpaid Wages Amid Pandemic," *Al Monitor*, 10 August 2020, https://www.al-monitor.com/originals/2020/08/gulf-migrant-workers-wages-covid19-qatar-uae-india-nepal.html.

45 Dilip Ratha, "Remittances during the COVID-19 Crisis: A Year of Recovery and Surprises," *World Bank Blog*, 17 November 2021, https://blogs.worldbank.org/peoplemove/global-remittance-flows-2021-year-recovery-and-surprises.

Malaysia officially hosts some 3.5 million migrant workers and an additional 2–4 million undocumented workers. Together, the two categories of foreign contract migrants constitute up to 40 percent of the country's total, and 60 percent of its low-skilled and semi-skilled workforce.[46] As in the Gulf, when the nationwide lockdown came into effect in March 2020, thousands of workers abruptly lost their jobs, many of whom would never see the wages that were due to them.[47] While the Malaysian government did offer free COVID-19 testing and treatment to contract workers, it also rounded up undocumented migrants, forcing them into crowded detention centres, which became major "hotspots" for subsequent outbreaks of COVID-19.[48]

In an attempt to address rising unemployment among citizens, the Malaysian government banned the hiring of foreign labour in July 2020. However, such restrictions had to be relaxed in the face of severe labour shortages in the agricultural, plantation and construction sectors.[49] Indeed, the Malaysian government has since had to envisage the possibility of "short-term work permits" to employ undocumented workers in these sectors.[50]

If Malaysia's treatment of its foreign migrant workforce amidst the current crisis can be described as incoherent, that of neighbouring Singapore offers a useful elucidation of transnational temporary contract work as an institution and the status of guestworkers.

In the early weeks of the pandemic, Singapore – which recorded some of the first known instances of COVID-19 infections outside China – was hailed as an exemplar of efficient disease management. While the rest of the world was waking up to a nightmarish March, Singapore (along with Hong Kong and Taiwan) appeared to be well on its way to containing the disease through an

---

46 The international migrant stock as a percentage of Malaysia's total labour force at mid-year 2020 was approximately 15 percent. World Bank, *Who is Keeping Score? Estimating the Number of Foreign Workers in Malaysia*, April 2020, viii, https://www.worldbank.org/en/country/malaysia/publication/who-is-keeping-score-estimating-the-number-of-foreign-workers-in-malaysia. Johan Saravanamuttu and Khor Yu Leng, "Migrant Workers: Wake-Up Call for Malaysia – Analysis," *Eurasia Review*, 1 May 2020, https://www.eurasiareview.com/01052020-migrant-workers-wake-up-call-for-malaysia-analysis/.

47 International Labour Organization, "COVID-19: Impact on Migrant Workers and Country Response in Malaysia," 8 May 2020, https://www.ilo.org/wcmsp5/groups/public/---asia/---ro-bangkok/documents/briefingnote/wcms_741512.pdf.

48 Yen Nee Lee, "Neglect of Migrant Workers Could Hurt Malaysia's Economic Recovery," *CNBC*, 4 November 2020, https://www.cnbc.com/2020/11/05/Covid-19-migrant-worker-neglect-may-hurt-malaysia-economic-recovery.html.

49 In 2018, 70 percent of foreign workers in Malaysia were concentrated in manufacturing, plantation, and construction. World Bank, *Who is Keeping Score?*, 21.

50 Lee, "Neglect."

outstanding program of meticulous contact tracing and isolation of new cases among its citizens and residents. Until the beginning of April, there were less than 1,000 recorded cases of COVID-19 on the island.[51]

The situation changed swiftly, however, as the virus surfaced among the foreign migrant workforce, and within two weeks the island state's COVID-19 case count boomed to 17,000 recorded infections – the highest in all Southeast Asia at that time. The proliferation seemed to be concentrated among male work permit holders – 680,000 in total – who, along with a quarter of a million female foreign domestic workers, constitute over 70 percent of the foreign working population.[52]

It bears recalling here that in Singapore work permits are largely reserved for men from so-called non-traditional source countries – such as Bangladesh, India, Myanmar, Nepal, Sri Lanka, Thailand, and the Philippines – who are concentrated in the lowest-paid and most undesired occupations in Singapore's construction, marine, and process industries.[53] Unlike the Employment Pass-wielding foreign professionals, and mid-level skilled technicians with S Passes, work permit holders and foreign domestic workers are denied the right to apply for residency or citizenship, to bring their families with them, or to marry Singaporean citizens and permanent residents.[54] The average basic income of

51 Rene Niehus et al., "Using Observational Data to Quantify Bias of Traveller-derived COVID-19 Prevalence Estimates in Wuhan, China," *The Lancet* 20, no. 7 (2020): 804, https://doi.org/10.1016/S1473-3099(20)30229-2; Jason Beaubien, "Singapore Was a Shining Star in COVID-19 Control Until It Wasn't," *National Public Radio* (US), 3 May 2020, https://www.kawc.org/2020-05-03/singapore-was-a-shining-star-in-covid-control-until-it-wasnt.

52 Rachel Phua and Chew Hui Min, "Can Singapore Rely Less on Foreign Workers?," *Chanel News Asia*, 9 June 2020, https://www.channelnewsasia.com/news/singapore/singapore-foreign-workers-reliance-challenges-12806970; Beaubien, "Singapore Was a Shining Star."

53 Work permit holders can also come from Malaysia, the Peoples Republic of China, and the NAS or North Asian Sources (Hong Kong, Macau, South Korea, and Taiwan). They face fewer restrictions and work in better remunerated industrial and service jobs. Ministry of Manpower, *Work Permit Conditions*, 2017, accessed 21 December 2020, http://www.mom.gov.sg/passes-and-permits/work-permit-for-foreign-worker/sector-specific-rules/construction-sector-requirements.

54 The Employment Pass (EP) brings highly qualified foreign professionals, knowledge workers (P1), entrepreneurs (P2), and skilled personnel (Q) to Singapore. Eligible applicants must have a job offer paying a minimum of S$ 4,500/month to qualify. The S Pass is meant for mid-level skilled technicians, who must earn a minimum of S$ 2,500/month. Both EP and S Pass holders are eligible to apply for permanent residency and citizenship in Singapore. Ministry of Manpower, *Passes and Permits*, accessed 24 January 2022, https://www.mom.gov.sg/passes-and-permits/employment-pass.

such temporary migrants is between S$ 450 and 500 per month.[55] With no access to local labour markets, such workers are required to leave Singapore within seven days if their employment is terminated.

Singapore is not unique in marginalizing its foreign migrant workforce; many labour-receiving societies condemn guestworkers to some form of compulsory social isolation. Separated categorically from "the national population and the benefits of nationality" and overwhelmingly dependent on their employers/hiring companies, they exist as little more than units of "provisional labor" in a state of permanent precarity.[56] In 2005, hundreds of workers went on strike to protest against the "dirty," unsafe, and jail-like dormitories in which they were housed in the Tuas area of the city. Housing discontent was also a major flashpoint in the discourse surrounding the 2013 Little India riots involving hundreds of contract migrants from the subcontinent. Similar reports of foreign workers being housed in severely unsanitary conditions have continued to emerge right into the present.[57]

In recent years, the Singaporean government has constructed forty-odd "purpose-built dormitories" (PBDs) on the outer edges of the city-state. Located far from the city's tourist attractions and public housing estates, these dormitories house over 300,000 low-income foreign migrants. On the face of it, the super-dorms look plush: they offer enviable sea-views, sport movie theatres,

55 Humanitarian Organization for Migration Economics, "Wage Theft & Exploitation Among Singapore's Migrant Workers," *Position Paper*, January 2017, https://static1.squarespace.com/static/5a12725612abd96b9c737354/t/5a1fce6f652dead776d3c970/1512033911372/Position_Paper_Wage-Theft-Exploitation-among-Singapores-Migrant-Workers.pdf; Kirstin Han, "Singapore's Migrant Workers Struggle to Get Paid," *CNN*, 25 February 2018, https://edition.cnn.com/2018/02/24/asia/singapore-migrant-workers-intl/index.html; Lucy Martin, "Singapore: Helping the Migrant Workers Who Pay to Get Jobs," *BBC News*, 13 November 2020, https://www.bbc.com/news/business-54654813.

56 Aziza, "For Persian Gulf Workers." Most workers I have spoken to in the course of my research on low-resourced Bangladeshi male contract migrants in Singapore emphasized the aspect of inadequate living quarters. Some recounted woeful stories of living in containers or in warehouses for months; others recall feeling deeply ashamed of the overcrowded "company houses," situated at the heart of the red-light district in "Galang" (Geylang), which appeared to be "filthy" and the "worst place in Singapore" to these men arriving from rural Bangladesh.

57 Sinapan Samydorai, "Singapore: 300 Indian and Bangladeshi Migrant Workers Stage Sit-in Strike," *Think Centre*, 4 April 2005, http://www.thinkcentre.org/article.php?id=2563; Dewey Sim, Kok Xinghui, and Kimberly Lim, "Coronavirus: After Little India Riot, Singapore Promised Migrant Workers Decent Housing – What Happened?" *South China Morning Post*, 5 February 2020, https://www.msn.com/en-sg/news/singapore/coronavirus-after-little-india-riot-singapore-promised-migrant-workers-decent-housing-what-happened/ar-BB13v04Z.

food courts, mini-marts, gyms, medical facilities and, sometimes, even cricket pitches and beer gardens.[58] However, a closer look reveals that these facilities are also sites of containment and surveillance for a segment of the workforce that the Singaporean state and society consider simultaneously necessary and yet unassimilable, as indexed by the legal exclusion of migrant workers from permanent residency, as well as the consistent criminalization of migrants in mainstream discourse.[59] As the current health crisis demonstrates, the actual living quarters for the workers in these privately run and uber-profitable dormitories are still poorly ventilated and overcrowded – with 10–20 men sleeping in each room, inadequate sanitation facilities that require up to 100 men to share a single communal shower area, and overused, bug-infested kitchens – constituting ideal breeding grounds for infectious diseases.[60] As a result, by the beginning of May 2020, for every new infection involving a Singaporean citizen/resident, there were 82 new instances of illness among migrant workers.[61]

Faced with a debacle spinning out of control, as well as intense international scrutiny, in May 2020 the Singaporean government responded by locking down the workers' dormitories and shifting thousands of healthy migrants into "empty public housing flats and schools" located in residential neighbourhoods. The first measure intensified surveillance and tracking of migrant bodies, transforming the dormitories into veritable "internment camps" while the second once again fomented tense questions around the place of "migrants," with at least some Singaporeans blaming the disease outbreak in dormitories on the "habits" (read: lack of cleanliness, eating practices) of migrant workers. Some have accused migrants of "driving [...] the numbers [i.e., disease case count] up," making Singapore "look bad on the world stage."[62] Clearly, even if

58 "Foreign Worker Dormitories," Building and Construction Authority, https://www1.bca.gov.sg/buildsg/manpower/foreign-worker-dormitories.

59 Charan Bal, "Myths and Facts: Migrant Workers in Singapore," *New Naratif*, 9 September 2017, accessed 24 January 2022, https://newnaratif.com/myths-and-facts-migrant-workers-in-singapore/. Also see *Foreign Employee Dormitories Bill*, speech by Tan Chuan-Jin, Minister for Manpower, 20 January 2015, http://www.mom.gov.sg/newsroom/speeches/2015/foreign-employee-dormitories-bill-second-reading-speech-by-mr-tan-chuanjin-minister-for-manpower-20-january-2.

60 Beaubien, "Singapore Was a Shining Star"; Satveer Kaur-Gill, "The COVID-19 Pandemic and Outbreak Inequality: Mainstream Reporting of Singapore's Migrant Workers in the Margins," *Frontiers in Communication*, 30 September 2020, https://doi.org/10.3389/fcomm.2020.00065.

61 On 1 May 2020, "there were 11 new cases reported among Singapore's permanent residents and 905 new infections among the workers residing in the dorms." Beaubien, "Singapore Was a Shining Star."

62 Rebecca Ratcliffe, "'We're in a Prison': Singapore's Migrant Workers Suffer as COVID-19 Surges Back," *The Guardian*, 23 April 2020, https://www.theguardian.com/world/2020/apr/23/singapore-million-migrant-workers-suffer-as-Covid-19-surges-back; Elga Reyes,

migrant contract workers are tolerated as economic necessities in Singapore, they are not part of the clean, green self-image of the island state.

Figures of COVID-19 infections on the island released in mid-December 2020 further elucidate the astounding chasm between citizens/residents and migrants in terms of health outcomes and structural inequities. Combined results from PCR tests (representing current infections) and serology tests (indicating past infections) revealed that at the end of 2020 more than 47 percent of the foreign workers housed in Singapore's dormitories – some 152,000 in total – had been infected with the SARS-CoV-2 virus.[63] In contrast, the corresponding figure among Singapore's citizens and residents was below 4,000, or <0.1 percent of the over 4 million citizens/residents. To put these numbers into context, nearly 11 percent of the population of London was infected by the end of 2020.[64]

3 What Do We Learn about Guestwork from the COVID-19 Crisis?

The preceding brief survey of the response of several affluent labour-importing societies towards foreign contract workers amidst a pandemic illuminates myriad forms of neglect, mistreatment, and even abuse. However, as many of the reports observe, the COVID-19 pandemic is not the root cause of these problems but has merely intensified already existing exploitation. What is perhaps less apparent from the present-centred discussions in the media is that such exploitation is neither an aberration, nor merely indicative of corruption in the absence of proper implementation of policies. Rather, inordinate exploitation is coded into the very structure and meaning of guestwork, which blurs "the line between consent and coercion," especially when it involves

"Singapore's secrets to a clean and green city," *Eco-Business*, 21 May 2014, http://www.eco-business.com/news/singapore-secrets-clean-green-city/.

63 PCR – polymerase chain reaction – is a test to detect genetic material from a specific organism, such as a virus. It detects the presence of a virus if a person has the virus at the time of the test and it could also detect fragments of the virus even after a person is no longer infected. "COVID-19 and PCR Testing," Cleveland Clinic, accessed on 24 January 2022, https://my.clevelandclinic.org/health/diagnostics/21462-covid-19-and-pcr-testing.

64 Andreas Illmer, "COVID-19: Singapore Migrant Workers Infections Were Three Times Higher," *BBC News*, 16 December 2020, https://www.bbc.com/news/world-asia-55314862; "Singapore's Population Grows to 5.7 million," *Channel News Asia*, 25 September 2019, https://www.channelnewsasia.com/news/singapore/population-number-singapore-foreign-workers-new-citizens-11941034.

underprivileged workers.[65] Moments of crisis such as the ongoing pandemic spotlight what is in fact well understood for over 100 years now in the world of transnational temporary contract work: Utilizing non-citizen labour affords exceptional surplus accumulation. To recall Max Weber's observations on the "tens of thousands" of Polish seasonal workers "brought in to work the sugar-beet fields" by the Junkers in late-nineteenth century Prussia: "[They appear desirable] because by employing them one can save on workers' dwellings, on poor rates, on social obligations, and further because their precarious situation as foreigners puts them in the hands of the landowners."[66] And it is precisely this understanding that is, and historically has been, the *raison d'être* of the institution of guestwork.

Seen from this theoretical and historical vantage point the (mis)handling of guestworkers by a diverse group of labour-receiving countries as outlined above must be read not as oversights or mistakes but as emblematic of the non-responsibility that labour-receiving states practise when it comes to non-citizen workforces. Put in another way, what the pandemic foregrounds is, thus, not so much abuses of guestwork, but rather guestwork *as* abuse.

And yet, for all the horrors that they document, the stories emerging from the ongoing COVID-19 upheaval also testify to another dimension of guest-work as an institution: Foreign migrants may be expendable, but they are also crucial to the functioning of key economic sectors of wealthy labour-receiving societies. We will now briefly turn to this other dimension.

4 Essential Workers, Dependent Economies

In late spring/summer of 2020, confronted with rampant infections among its foreign contract workforce, the Singaporean government announced plans to build new dormitories over the next few years to house up to 100,000 migrant workers. Predictably, the proposal elicited protests from some Singaporeans who abhor the idea of migrants living close to residential areas.[67] The government's response to the familiar litany of complaints, however, was swift. To quote one official: "We really need to appreciate the contributions that our migrant workers have made, *and will continue to make*, in building Singapore

65 Sarkar, "Constrained Labour," 198.

66 Max Weber, "The Nation State and Economic Policy," cited in Surak, "Guestworkers," 84. For similar observations about the *Gastarbeiter* in the second wave, see John Burger, *The Seventh Man* (New York: Viking Press, 1975).

67 Sim, Xinghui, and Lim, "Coronavirus."

and welcome them as part of our community."[68] To this end, the Ministry of Culture even launched a social media campaign – *WelcomeInMyBackyard* – in support of workers relocated to residential neighbourhoods. Apparently, hundreds of "welcome notes have been translated into Tamil, Bengali and Chinese" in a concerted attempt to "shift the perspective on migrant workers [...] The aim is to have migrant workers fully included and integrated into Singaporean society."[69] Recent statements from government officials as well as the business community further underscore the official stance that without foreign migrants Singapore's economy "will suffer" resulting in "fewer jobs for Singaporeans in the long run." And while the government acknowledges the need to wean the country from over-reliance on cheap migrant labour, the official line in Singapore for now is that the island "can never really eliminate its need for [foreign workers]."[70]

Debates concerning the wisdom of welcoming "foreign" circular migrants have raged in Europe as well.[71] Brexit, for instance, is in part a culmination of anxieties around foreign workers taking away jobs from locals.[72] And yet, as recent studies on migrant/seasonal labour in Europe's rural interiors indicate, the production of food in much of Western Europe heavily relies on approximately 5.5 million circular migrants – mostly from Eastern Europe. This mobile workforce is so *essential* that even amidst a continent-wide lockdown, "special arrangements" had to be brokered in many countries to partially maintain the flow of seasonal labour between the two parts of Europe.[73]

In Germany, for instance, farmers negotiated with the federal government to fly in 40,000 Romanian and Bulgarian workers "to harvest asparagus, pick strawberries and plant late-season crops" in lieu of the 300,000 circular

---

68 Excerpt from the speech in Parliament by Lawrence Wong, National Development Minister, quoted in Rina Chandran, "Singapore Calls for 'Mindset' Change as Migrant Workers are Rehoused," *Reuters*, 10 June 2020, https://www.reuters.com/article/us-health-coronavirus-singapore-trfn-idUSKBN23H1EO, emphasis added.

69 Chandran, "Singapore Calls."

70 Phua and Min, "Can Singapore Rely."

71 The definition of "foreign" is complicated by the legal erasure of national borders within the European Union.

72 Nick Robinson, "UKIP: Should the Polish Plumber Be Deported?," *BBC News*, 19 November 2014, https://www.bbc.com/news/uk-politics-30118855; József Böröcz and Mahua Sarkar, "The Unbearable Whiteness of the Polish Plumber and the Hungarian Peacock Dance Around 'Race'," *Slavic Review* 76, no. 2 (2017): 307–314.

73 Svein Inge Meland, "Pandemic Has Revealed Our Dependence on Migrant Workers," *Norwegian University of Science and Technology*, 30 December 2020, https://phys.org/news/2020-12-pandemic-revealed-migrant-workers.html.

migrants who normally come to work during the harvest season.[74] In Italy, where "agriculture is big business," the industry "is almost entirely dependent on foreign labourers, with approximately 350,000 seasonal workers [coming every year] [...] from abroad."[75] Emergency measures in the context of the pandemic have included "regularizing undocumented foreign workers" because few Italian applicants possess the requisite skills for farm work.[76] Even in the Brexit-fraught UK, Romanian migrants had to be flown in "to fill a considerable labour shortfall among skilled agricultural workers."[77] Beyond farming and agriculture, migrant contract workers are crucial to the food processing and care industries in many affluent countries across Europe.[78]

The picture is more complex in the US, where 69 percent of all immigrants and 74 percent of undocumented workers are employed in "essential critical infrastructure" sectors as defined by the Cybersecurity and Infrastructure Security Agency (CISA) of the US Department of Homeland Security.[79] Migrant labour – both undocumented and/or seasonal – has long constituted the bulk of the field workforce in California's US$ 54 billion agricultural industry, and in "apple orchards [...] and dairy farms across the country." In recent years,

---

74 Melissa Eddy, "Farm Workers Airlifted into Germany Provide Solutions and Pose New Risks," *New York Times*, 18 May 2020, https://www.nytimes.com/2020/05/18/world/europe/coronavirus-german-farms-migrant-workers-airlift.html.

75 Michal Bardavid, "Italian Farmers Face Uncertain Future without Staff because of COVID-19," *China Global Television Network*, 1 June 2020, https://newseu.cgtn.com/news/2020-06-01/Italian-farmers-hit-by-lack-of-foreign-workers-due-to-COVID-19-QYnwiYLbmU/index.html.

76 Marco Carlone and Daniela Sestito, "The Italian Farmers Struggling with a Lack of Skilled Workers," *News EU*, 13 May 2020, https://newseu.cgtn.com/news/2020-05-13/The-Italian-farmers-struggling-with-a-lack-of-skilled-workers-Qr1JGAzvgY/index.html.

77 Lena Näre, Synnøve Bendixsen, and Peter Holley, "Notes on the Corona Crisis," *Nordic Journal of Migration Research* 10, no. 2 (2020): 1–4, https://doi.org/10.33134/njmr.332; Frey Lindsay, "Romanian Workers Are Flying in to Fill U.K. Labor Shortages and Remainers Are Loving It," *Forbes*, 17 April 2020, https://www.forbes.com/sites/freylindsay/2020/04/17/romanian-workers-are-flying-in-to-fill-uk-labor-shortfalls-and-remainers-are-loving-it/?sh=6492cd3b5f4b.

78 Anna Noryskiewicz, "Workers from German Meat Packing Plant with Huge Coronavirus Outbreak Claim Grim Conditions," *CBS News*, 26 June 2020, https://www.cbsnews.com/news/germany-coronavirus-outbreak-meat-packing-plant-workers-grim-conditions-tonnies-gutersloh/.

79 Christopher C. Krebs, "Advisory Memorandum on Identification of Essential Critical Infrastructure Workers during COVID-19 Response," 17 April 2020 (Washington, DC: Department of Homeland Security, Cybersecurity and Infrastructure Security Agency), https://www.cisa.gov/sites/default/files/publications/Version_3.0_23_Guidance_on_Essential_Critical_Infrastructure_Workers_4.pdf.

growers have increasingly turned to the H-2A guestworker program to import formally contracted temporary/seasonal workers from Mexico.[80]

Numerous such reports of migrants performing vital services – in food production, health/care work, transportation and delivery services, rubber or palm oil plantations, construction, marine, chemical processing and manufacturing – offer compelling evidence of how guestworkers represent a "hidden backbone" of the labour force in many labour-deficient affluent economies.[81] However, despite this, employers in host societies habitually justify low wages ostensibly because "migrants earn much more than they would" at home, lending credence to "an idyllic picture of a triple-win from labour migration: the employer gets good, cheap labour, the employee earns more than at home, and the family and home country benefit from it."[82] What is lacking in such formulations is a proper appreciation of the costs borne by transnational temporary contract migrants – locked into a pattern of long-term compulsory sojourner mobility on the one hand, and social isolation in host societies on the other. It is an intensely demanding "shadow life"[83] that uproots guestworkers from home but affords them no satisfaction of "arriving."[84]

What, then, can – and should – be done to resolve this obvious contradiction in the status of guestworkers, namely their fundamental expendability on the one hand, and the essential nature of their services on the other?

5 Conclusion: Lessons for an Uncertain Future

As the discussion above shows, at the most obvious level, the COVID-19 pandemic has exposed the fragility of global supply chains of migrant contract labour. It has further illuminated the tension between the dependence of affluent host economies on guest/seasonal workers and the ideological construction of guestworkers as a flexible and expendable workforce subject to deportation in periods of economic downturn. And while calls to replace migrants with local workers resound once again in many a labour-importing

80 Philip Martin and Daniel Costa, "The H-2A Farm Guestworker Program is Expanding Rapidly," *Economic Policy Institute*, 1 August 2017, https://www.epi.org/blog/agricultural-guestworkers-expanding-h-2a-program/.

81 Hillary Leung, "Singapore Was a Coronavirus Success Story – Until an Outbreak Showed How Vulnerable Workers Can Fall Through the Cracks," *Time*, 29 April 2020, https://time.com/5825261/singapore-coronavirus-migrant-workers-inequality/.

82 Johan F. Rye quoted in Meland, "Pandemic Has Revealed."

83 Meland, "Pandemic Has Revealed."

84 Bauman, *Liquid Modernity*, 33–34.

society amidst the current crisis, it is not clear whether citizen workers are in fact ready to "get their hands dirty" in demanding manual work, even where higher wages are on offer. The claim that low-skilled foreign migrants deprive citizens of work is, thus, overstated. More often than not today – as during the first wave of guestworker regimes in the late nineteenth and early twentieth centuries – local and migrant workers occupy different rungs or sectors of the labour force, even within a single industry. Existing evidence further suggests that in industries where the involvement of migrant workers "complements" that of locals, opportunities and income levels improve discernibly for the latter.[85]

In recent years, employers in some affluent economies have increasingly turned to automation in their search for a solution to the persistent problem of a reliable supply of labour. In the US, automation has been used for some time now for harvesting crops such as wheat, soybean, and cotton, while more recently, farmers have also begun introducing robots in packing plants. However, robots are still too clumsy to handle sensitive fruits such as plums, berries, and peaches and vegetables such as asparagus and fennel. Consequently, at least for the foreseeable future, guestworkers remain the preferred crop pickers.[86]

Automation is also expensive, making it inaccessible to most small-and medium-sized enterprises. An overwhelming majority of firms in the construction and manufacturing sectors in Malaysia and Singapore, for instance, are relatively small. For such firms, the transition from a labour-dependent production model – in which the average annual salary of most manual foreign workers is less than S$ 10,000 (US$ 7,500) – to one with large-scale automation involving hundreds of thousands of dollars in initial layout which is estimated at US$ 250,000 for a two-robot system installation[87] is a daunting, if not an impossible prospect.[88]

---

85 Walter Theseira, "Speech on the Fortitude Budget," *Channel News Asia*, 4 June 2020, accessed 26 November 2020, Channelnewsasia.com; Caglar Ozden, Ximena Del Carpio, and Mauro Testaverde, "South-South Migration: Foreign Workers in Malaysia," *World Bank Blog*, 6 December 2013, https://blogs.worldbank.org/peoplemove/south-south-migration-foreign-workers-malaysia.

86 Miriam Jordan, "As Immigrant Farmworkers Become More Scarce Robots Replace Humans," *New York Times*, 20 November 2018, https://www.nytimes.com/2018/11/20/us/farmworkers-immigrant-labor-robots.html; Danielle Pacquette, "Farmworker vs. Robot," *Washington Post*, 17 February 2019, https://www.washingtonpost.com/news/national/wp/2019/02/17/feature/inside-the-race-to-replace-farmworkers-with-robots/.

87 Two robots operating during two shifts, 5 days a week, for 50 weeks a year. Tanya Anandan, "Industrial Robotics," https://www.robotics.org/content-detail.cfm/Industrial-Robotics-Industry-Insights/Calculating-Your-ROI-for-Robotic-Automation-Cost-vs-Cash-Flow/content_id/5285.

88 Darwin Lau, "A Fully Automated Construction Industry? Still A Long Way Ahead," 22 August 2020, https://www.archdaily.com/945761/a-fully-automated-construction-industry-still-a-long-road-ahead.

These caveats notwithstanding, it is probably not unreasonable to expect that automation will restructure many industries in the not-too-distant future and the COVID-19 crisis may well provide "a digitization booster" ushering in greater use of artificial intelligence and robotics worldwide.[89] How might such a projected boom in robotics and other forms of artificial intelligence-driven mechanization affect the world of work, and especially the future of guest-work? The forecasts emerging from different corners of the world seem to yield a mixed picture.

A recent study from Malaysia, for instance, argues that while automation will likely displace 54 percent of all jobs in Malaysia within two decades, a great majority of the affected jobs will likely be semi-skilled. In other words, it will be Malaysian workers – accounting for 86 percent of the semi-skilled workforce – who will bear the brunt of this transformation and not the low-skilled foreign migrants.[90] On the other hand, a 2018 study undertaken by the Organization for Economic Cooperation and Development (OECD) suggests that across 32 participating countries, "close to one in two jobs" (46 percent) are at significant risk of being transformed, possibly even eliminated, by automation (a probability of a degree of automation of between 50 and 70 percent) in the foreseeable future. What is more, the risk of automation is most likely to affect low-skilled jobs in manufacturing, agriculture and the service industries – i.e., precisely the sectors that hire migrant contract workers.[91] A third set of projections – from the World Economic Forum (WEF) – meanwhile anticipates a significant loss of approximately 500,000 jobs in the construction industry in the near future, a major employer today for transnational contract workers worldwide, and a vastly transformed industry in which fewer highly skilled workers will co-exist with robots and cobots (collaborative robots).[92]

---

89 Zoe Thomas, "Coronavirus: Will COVID-19 Speed up the Use of Robots to Replace Human Workers?" *BBC News*, 19 April 2020, https://www.bbc.com/news/technology-52340651; International Federation of Robotics, "IFR Presents World Robotics Report 2020," 24 September 2020, https://ifr.org/ifr-press-releases/news/record-2.7-million-robots-work-in-factories-around-the-globe.

90 Theng Theng Tan and Jarud Romadan, "The Economic Case Against the Marginalisation of Migrant Workers in Malaysia," *London School of Economics Blog*, 1 October 2020, https://blogs.lse.ac.uk/seac/2020/10/01/the-economic-case-against-the-marginalisation-of-migrant-workers-in-malaysia/.

91 Ljubica Nedelkoska and Glenda Quintini, "Automation, Skills Use and Training," OECD Social, Employment and Migration Working Papers 202, March 2018, https://doi.org/10.1787/2e2f4eea-en.

92 Kayla Matthews, "5 Ways Robotics will Disrupt the Construction Industry in 2019," *Robotics Business Review*, 23 January 2019, https://www.roboticsbusinessreview.com/news/5-ways-robotics-will-disrupt-construction-industry-in-2019/. The WEF is the international organization for public-private cooperation. "Our Mission," World Economic Forum, accessed 24 January 2022, https://www.weforum.org/about/world-economic-forum.

It would seem that the OECD and WEF projections signal a near future that largely undercuts the need for non-citizen transient labour in most affluent economies, especially where migrant workers already occupy positions that are either undesired by citizens or "complement" the work done by the latter. The forecast from Malaysia, on the other hand, indicates a slower structural transformation towards an automated future that might still require significant reliance on cheap migrant labour for the foreseeable future. The public debates raging over similar questions in Singapore would seem to reinforce this latter projection, especially since the island state lacks adequate internal labour resources. We might also note here that the GCC countries – still the most important destination for guestworkers – are not significant actors in the automation frontier, yet.[93]

In the long run, automation may indeed spell the end of this current wave of guestwork, if not guestwork itself as a form of constrained labour-mobility regime. In the short to medium term, however, there is still much that can be done to improve the existing system of large-scale temporary labour migration and contract work. And here, we may draw on two important lessons that the COVID-19 pandemic foregrounds – regarding *the essentialness of guestworkers in labour-deficient economies* and their widespread *reliance on workforces from elsewhere* – to formulate possible strategies. The first – essentialness of guestworkers – must be mobilized to demand better wages, safer and more secure working and living conditions, and the right to adequate redress and legal protection for transnational temporary contract workers *qua workers*. This mobilization ought to happen ideally at the global level, rather than be left to the vagaries of local circumstances. It is worth underscoring here that most of the abuses that foreign contract workers face pertain to labour rights infringement and, as such, they ought to be addressed within a viable framework of decent work extending to *all* workers – local and migrant, legal and undocumented, formal and informal. To paraphrase one recent comment from Singapore, labour-receiving societies must rethink their expectation of having a "first world standard of living delivered at third world prices."[94]

The second lesson indexes the dangers inherent in decoupling "essential [...] jobs that must take place in [a particular country] from [worker] residency in [that country]." For too long, labour-receiving societies seem to have functioned as gated, rich communities that expect to simply outsource a significant

93 Lee, "Neglect"; Theseira, "Speech." According to the World Bank, Saudi Arabia, the UAE, and Kuwait were among the top ten remittance sending countries in 2017. Labor Force Data, https://data.worldbank.org/indicator/SL.TLF.TOTL.IN.

94 Theseira, "Speech."

segment of their essential but undervalued workforce from poorer – sometimes neighbouring – societies. The disruptions brought on by the pandemic have thrown into sharp relief the impracticality and inequities underlying such arrangements. To the extent that human societies will always likely need some forms of human labour beyond the highly skilled, perhaps the appropriate long-term strategy should be to grant transnational temporary contract workers – especially those who provide essential services – the right to permanent residency in the host societies to which they so handsomely contribute.

Examples of such transformation of the legal status from temporary labour to permanent residents/citizens are not uncommon in the history of labour migration under capitalism. In the late nineteenth and early twentieth centuries, indentured workers often settled in the host society at the end of their contract period, while the history of guestwork itself records the partial "integration" of at least some guestworkers who played a significant role in the postwar rebuilding effort in Western Europe. And indeed, today, moves to fast-track naturalization of migrants, especially those providing essential services amidst the current crisis, are part of a portfolio of strategies under consideration by some states, such as Portugal and Canada.[95]

The COVID-19 pandemic has certainly highlighted much that is structurally amiss with guestwork/temporary migrant worker regimes. At the same time, it is possible to see it as yet another historic opportunity for states to rectify the fallacy of attempting to outsource significant segments of the working class. It would indeed be a pity if affluent labour-deficient economies across the globe failed to seize this opportunity to grant all their workforces – migrant and citizen – the stability and respect they deserve. For, a stable working class is *essential* for every functioning society.

95 Immigration, Refugees and Citizenship Canada, "New Pathway to Permanent Residency for over 90,000 Essential Temporary Workers and International Graduates," Government of Canada, 14 April 2021, https://www.canada.ca/en/immigration-refugees-citizenship/news/2021/04/new-pathway-to-permanent-residency-for-over-90000-essential-temporary-workers-and-international-graduates.html; Chantal da Silva, "Portugal Is Giving Citizenship Rights to Migrants and Asylum Seekers So They Can Access Healthcare Amid Coronavirus Outbreak," *Newsweek*, 11 May 2020, https://www.newsweek.com/portugal-citizenship-rights-migrants-asylum-seekers-health-care-coronavirus-1503178.

CHAPTER 6

Is There Informal Labour?

The Concept, the ILO's Ideology, and Greece as an Example

Aliki Vaxevanoglou

Abstract

Current irregular migration and "informal" labour are inextricably linked. Based on extensive on-the-ground research and interviews with documented and undocumented migrants and their employers in Greece, this contribution focuses on the "informal" labour field in which undocumented migrants work. It discusses the concept of the "informal economy" as a historical object and thus explores the origin, diffusion, and relevance of a very ambiguous notion. Finally, it examines the specific implications of this concept in the case of Greece and present-day migration.

Keywords

Greece – informal economy – informal labour – International Labour Organization (ILO) – petty commodity production – undocumented migration

1 Introduction: Irregular Migration and "Informal" Labour

With the end of the bipolar world in 1989, the phenomenon of irregular labour migration increased worldwide.[1] In the wealthiest countries, it quickly became a political, social, ideological, and ethical issue,[2] as a result of which studies on the subject multiplied. 20 years later, in 2009, clandestine migration in the

1 Catherine Wihtol de Wenden, *Atlas des migrations dans le monde: Réfugiés ou migrants volontaires* (Paris: Autrement, 2005), 4–5.

2 Among others, see Étienne Balibar et al., *Sans-papiers: L'archaïsme fatal* (Paris: La Découverte, 1999).

 | DOI:10.1163/9789004686991_007

European Union (EU) was estimated to involve between 1.9 and 3.8 million people, representing 0.39 to 0.77 percent of the European population.[3]

Within Europe, this corresponds to a new kind of migration that differs significantly from its post-war equivalent which was legal, systematically organized by states, and mostly intended to provide unskilled, salaried labour forces to the industrial sector of the richest countries.[4] After 1970, the global economic restructuring and the concomitant offshoring practices led to the adoption of deterrent migration policies that were prohibitive for low-skilled workers.[5] Consequently, a large proportion of migrants in Europe officially became undesirable and migration laws institutionalized the category of the "undocumented worker."[6] Apart from irregular entry and residence, the lack of administrative documents prevents migrants from working in the formal economy and current undocumented migration is closely linked to various forms of "informal" work that comprises undeclared, untaxed, and unprotected work.[7] In Europe, this dual phenomenon of irregular migration and "informal" labour mainly concerns the countries of the South and their substantial "informal" economies.[8] Therefore, with an "informal" economy ranging between 28.5 percent in 1999 to 39.3 percent in 2013 of the total economy[9] and a considerable "informal" labour market,[10] Greece has attracted and continues to attract significant numbers of irregular migrants.

---

3 Dita Vogel, Vesela Kovacheva, and Hannah Prescott, "The Size of the Irregular Migrant Population in the European Union: Counting the Uncountable?," *International Migration* 49, no. 5 (2011): 89, table 4, https://doi.org/10.1111/j.1468-2435.2011.00700.x.

4 Peter Stalker, *Les travailleurs immigrés: Étude des migrations internationales de main-d'œuvre* (Geneva: International Labour Office, 1995), 19–21.

5 Balibar et al., *Sans papiers*, 13–14.

6 Franck Düvell, "Paths into Irregularity: The Legal and Political Construction of Irregular Migration," *European Journal of Migration and Law* 13 (2011): 275–295, https://doi.org/10.1163/157181611X587856.

7 According to the International Labour Organization's (ILO) definition of informal labour, "Informal Economy Workers," accessed 12 January 2022, https://www.ilo.org/global/topics/wages/minimum-wages/beneficiaries/WCMS_436492/lang--en/index.htm.

8 Emilio Reyneri, *Migrants' Involvement in Irregular Employment in the Mediterranean Countries of the European Union* (Geneva: ILO, 2001), 21–43.

9 Frederick Schneider and Mai Hassan, *Size and Development of the Shadow Economies of 157 Countries Worldwide: Updated and New Measures from 1999 to 2013* (Bonn: Institute for the Study of Labour/IZA, 2016), 37, table A 4.1.

10 Estimates of the size of the Greek "informal" labour market vary, ranging from 24 to 46.7 percent of the total. See European Commission, *European Platform Tackling Undeclared Work: Member State Factsheets and Synthesis Report* (Brussels: European Commission, 2016), 4, table 1.4 and Mihails Hazans, *Informal Workers across Europe: Evidence from 30 European Countries* (Bonn: Institute for the Study of Labour/IZA, 2011), 33, table 3.

This chapter is based on the findings from long-term field research and interviews with undocumented, poorly documented, or regular migrants as well as with employers of migrants in Greece.[11] It focuses on "informal" labour and, more precisely, on the lower levels of the work hierarchy, where undocumented migrants operate. Its primary aim is to treat the "informal economy" as a historical object by investigating the origins, meaning, and reality of an ambiguous concept that has globally been imposed as self-evident. Information on this topic was collected from statistical data (censuses, survey data), the archives of the ILO and other international or supranational organizations. To round off the analysis, the significance of the "informal" economy in the case of Greece, and of current migrants, is discussed.

2 Migration in Greece: Facts and Stereotypes

After the disintegration of the socialist regimes in 1989, Greece for the first time experienced large-scale undocumented migration, mostly originating from the neighbouring Balkan countries. No suitable policies or legislation was in place to cope with this new phenomenon, and laws governing migration, residence, and work were largely lacking.[12] Nevertheless, undocumented migrants were immediately incorporated into the so-called informal economy. Some ten years later, in 2001, it was assessed that 10 percent of the population living in Greece were migrants and that they represented 15 percent of the active population – figures which constituted the highest percentages among all countries in the EU at the time. According to the estimates, half of the migrants were Albanians and of the total foreign population living in Greece, more than 50 percent was undocumented.[13] Despite remaining in a situation of administrative irregularity for years, these migrants were incorporated into the Greek "informal" sector.[14] Hence, Greece became a new kind of migration country in Europe,

11 For a detailed description of this research, see Aliki Vaxevanoglou, "Invisible Workers: Migrants, the Informal Economy, and its Transformations," [in Greek] *Greek Society* 12 (2022): 251–298.

12 Franck Düvell, "Clandestine Migration in Europe," *Social Science Information* 47, no. 4 (2008): 481, https://doi.org/10.1177/0539018408096442.

13 Stavros Zografakis and Charalambos Kasimis, "Greek Economy and Migrants: Yesterday, Today, Tomorrow," [in Greek] *Competitiveness for Development: Policy Proposals,* ed. Michalis Masourakis and Christos Gortsos (Athens: Hellenic Bank Association, 2014), 383–384.

14 Russell King, Gabriella Lazaridis, and Charalambos Tsardanidis, eds., *Eldorado or Fortress? Migration in Southern Europe* (London: Palgrave MacMillan, 2000), 60–62.

and a similar model is found in other Southern European countries such as Portugal, Italy, and Spain, each characterized by an important and dynamic "informal" economy.[15] After 2000, a second major arrival of migrants reached Greece, now originating from a multiplicity of more distant countries such as Afghanistan, Iraq, Iran, Pakistan, Syria, Bangladesh, Nigeria, Congo, Ethiopia, Somalia, Mauritania, Senegal, etc. Just like the migrants of the first major wave of arrivals, these migrants, largely being *sans-papiers*, were also absorbed by the "informal" sector. Around 2010, Greece had by far the highest share of irregularly employed migrants within the EU.[16]

More precisely, in 2011, the Greek National Census recorded 911,929 foreigners residing legally in the country, a figure corresponding, once more, to 15 percent of the active population.[17] This census failed to register clandestine migrants who, out of fear of being arrested, were hiding – even from the enumerators. However, in the same year, a very cautious estimation suggested a figure of 391,478 undocumented migrants. As this figure almost exclusively comprised young people, without family and children in Greece, this number may well have represented 10 percent of the active population. The same source underlined a remarkable shift that did not concern the size of the irregular resident population, which stayed the same, but rather its ethnic composition. Over the first decade of the twenty-first century, the Albanian undocumented migration in Greece diminished substantially due to the regularization campaigns that were implemented, and mostly, to the new system of free entrance visa, while the irregular residents of African and Asian origin have increased in large numbers. The research found that at least one-third of all irregular residents had lived and worked in Greece for more than eight years.[18]

Thus, Greece is neither simply a transit country, i.e., an inevitable gateway to reach the "promised lands" of the North,[19] nor solely a country of "containment" and "warehousing"[20] meant to protect the complacency and

15 Reyneri, *Migrants' Involvement*, 27–43.

16 Friedrich Schneider and Colin C. Williams, *The Shadow Economy* (London: Institute of Economic Affairs, 2013), 96, figure 5.

17 Zografakis and Kasimis, "Greek Economy," 383–384.

18 Thanos Maroukis, "Update Report Greece: The Number of Irregular Migrants in Greece at the End of 2010 and 2011, Database on Irregular Migration," Hellenic Foundation for European and Foreign Policy, accessed 12 January 2022, https://www.files.ethz.ch/isn/144536/Briefing-Notes_21_June-2012_Thanos-Maroukis1.pdf, esp. 2 and 4.

19 Franck Düvell, "Transit Migration: A Blurred and Politicised Concept," *Population, Space and Place* 18, no. 4 (2012): 415–427, https://doi.org/10.1002/psp.631.

20 Angeliki Dimitriadi and Antonia-Maria Sarantaki, "Borders and the Mobility of Migrants in Greece," *Research on the Common European Asylum System* no. 28 (Chemnitz: CEASEVAL, 2019), 13, 20.

the well-being of the wealthiest European countries against "undesirable migrants." Instead, Greece is a destination country; just like the migrants of the first large arrival, most undocumented migrants from Asia and Africa continue to work in Greece, thereby reaffirming the typology of employment for irregular migrants. This typology also runs along gendered lines as men toil in agriculture, construction, small manufacturing firms, tourism, catering, or cleaning services, while the much smaller number of women are employed in a narrower range of occupations, such as housemaids, nurses, workers in tourism, catering, cleaning, nightclubs, or the sex trade.[21] In both categories, the majority of migrants follow "old-fashioned" patterns of migration, embedded in a family strategy. Their main goal is to save money and send it back to their countries of origin.[22]

Furthermore, the far-reaching consequences of the 2008 economic crisis in Greece – i.e., the worsening of the situation in the local labour market, the 26.4 percent decrease in the Gross Domestic Product (GDP), and the resulting significant increase in poverty[23] – have neither influenced the size of the migrant flows, nor their employment.[24] While largely remaining undocumented, migrants in Greece work "informally" in arduous, dangerous, and badly-paid jobs, for private individuals and, above all, for small family units.[25]

The current undocumented migrants are at the heart of several fundamental contradictions that characterize modern affluent societies. They find themselves caught between different political trends and attract many stereotypes which prevent their systematic study. Unwillingly, they exemplify a whole series of situations that are – either explicitly or implicitly – conflicting or paradoxical. Despite any deterrent policies – such as the very strict legalization campaigns for undocumented migrants,[26] the harmonization of Greek legislation with European regulations, or the new systems of policy and securing

21 King, Lazaridis, and Tsardanidis, *Eldorado*, 14–19.

22 Vaxevanoglou, "Invisible Workers," 260. See also Reyneri, *Migrants' Involvement*, 20–21.

23 From 2007 to 2016, the estimated level of poverty increased between 100 and 200 percent. Eirini Andriopoulou, Alexandros Karakitsios, and Panos Tsakloglou, *Inequality and Poverty in Greece: Changes in Times of Crisis* (Bonn: Institute for the Study of Labour/IZA, 2017), 1, 5, 25.

24 Thanks, of course, to the adequate adaptation of migrants to the new conditions of the labour market. Zografakis and Kasimis, "Greek Economy," 389.

25 Vaxevanoglou, "Invisible Workers," 263.

26 According to all researchers, these campaigns were ineffective as well as circumscribed by a "philosophy of restriction." Zografakis and Kasimis, "Greek Economy," 393–396.

against clandestine migration across the European borders[27] – the fact is that, for decades, large numbers of migrants have been working continuously in the "informal" sector of the Greek economy without being legalized. In fact, the major stereotype is the very concept of the "informal economy."

Therefore, to proceed with the relevant discussion, scholars need to examine the concept of "informal economy," not as an obvious reality, but rather as a notion conceived and diffused in a specific historical context.

3 Informal Economy: A Brief History of a Notion

3.1 *The Diffusion and Institutionalization of the Term*

Coined in 1971 by the English anthropologist Keith Hart,[28] the concept of an "informal" economy was immediately adopted by the International Labour Organization (ILO) in its large-scale research programs, titled "World Employment Programme" (WEP), concerning many countries in Africa,[29] Latin America,[30] and Asia.[31] As early as 1974, the World Bank had also embraced the concept of "informality."[32]

Thanks to the significant means at the disposal of the ILO and the numerous researchers affiliated with ILO research programs, the concept of "informality" was rapidly disseminated throughout the scientific world via international organizations' research programs, conferences, and publications.[33]

---

27 Examples of such systems are Frontex – the European Border and Coast Guard Agency – instituted in 2005 and the forty-kilometre-long fence constructed in the Evros border region in 2011.

28 Keith Hart, paper presented in September 1971 at the large conference on "Urban Unemployment in Africa" organized by the Institute of Development Studies (University of Sussex) and published later as "Informal Income Opportunities and Urban Unemployment in Ghana," *Journal of Modern African Studies* 11, no. 1 (1973): 61–89.

29 ILO, *Employment Income and Equality: A Strategy for Increasing Productive Employment in Kenya* (Geneva: ILO, 1972). Subsequently, the term "informal" was applied by experts of the ILO's World Employment Programme (WEP) in other African countries such as Mauritania, Togo, Mali, Rwanda, Cameroon, etc.

30 For instance, see Programa Regional del Empleo para América Latina y el Caribe (PREALC), *Situaciones y Perspectivas del Empleo en Salvador,* 2 vols. (Geneva: ILO, 1975).

31 Among others, see A. N. Bose, *The Informal Sector in the Calcutta Metropolitan Economy,* WEP, 2–19, Working Paper 5 (Geneva: ILO, 1974).

32 Indicatively see, Dipak Mazumdar, *The Urban Informal Sector,* Employment and Rural Development Division, Development Economics Department, SWP211 (Washington, DC: World Bank, 1974).

33 It is impossible to mention all the relevant research programs and publications.

"Informality" was swiftly promoted as a scientific term for the study of poor countries, and the first theses on the subject appeared.[34]

While it is impossible to extensively describe the phenomenon here, the term "informal" spread through a network of development economists and analysts who specialized in poor countries, worked for international organizations and collaborated with universities or research centres.[35] They formed "a veritable industry in the academic social sciences, with a complex and often ambiguous relationship to governmental, international, and private agencies, actively engaged in promoting economic growth, alleviating poverty, and fostering beneficial social changes in 'developing' regions of the world."[36] Despite having different responsibilities and objectives, these institutions framed a network of highly paid consultants and senior executives who functioned as organic intellectuals and would construct a particular worldview with hegemonic aspirations.[37]

The European Economic Community (EEC) subsequently also adopted the term and, in the late 1980s, as part of the process of convergence of the economies of the EEC member countries, the European Commission funded research programs on the "informal" economy of Southern European countries, which were later extended to all EEC countries.[38] Their main conclusion was that the more state-regulated and organized the societies examined were, the smaller their "informal" economy was. During the 1990s, estimates of "informal" economies in Europe varied widely, with Germany, for example, only having 8.7 percent of "informal" work, while Greece attained percentages as high as 30.2 percent.[39]

---

34 The first thesis in French on the informal economy was Jean-Pierre Lachaud, "Contribution à l'étude du secteur informel en Côte-d'Ivoire: Le cas du secteur de l'habillement à Abidjan" (PhD diss., University of Bordeaux, 1976).

35 Ray Bromley, "Introduction. The Urban Informal Sector: Why Is It Worth Discussing?," *World Development* 6, no. 9–10 (1978): 1036, https://doi.org/10.1016/0305-750X(78)90061-X.

36 Frederick Cooper and Randall Packard, eds., *International Development and the Social Sciences: Essays on the History and Politics of Knowledge* (Berkeley: University of California Press, 1997), 1.

37 See the works of Robert W. Cox, starting with "Social Forces, States and World Orders: Beyond International Relations Theory," *Millennium: Journal of International Studies* 10, no. 2 (1981): 126–155, https://doi.org/10.1177/03058298810100020501.

38 Philippe Barthélemy et al., *Underground Economy and Irregular Forms of Employment (Travail au noir): Final Synthesis Report* (Luxembourg: Office for Official Publications of the European Communities, 1990).

39 Collin C. Williams and Janice Windebank, *Informal Employment in the Advanced Economies. Implications for Work and Welfare* (London: Routledge, 1998), 100, table 7.1.

With the collapse of the socialist bloc, the concept of an informal economy in Europe increasingly gained interest. The massive influx of migrants into Europe's rich countries, and especially into the regions of the South, not only revitalized their economies but also foregrounded relevant research programs and publications.[40] The term was now inescapable and, in 1993, the Fifteenth International Conference of Labour Statisticians – which has met every five years since 1923 under the auspices of the ILO – took on the task of defining informality.[41] Thus, "informal" was institutionalized on a global scale as a scientifically valid term. It is indicative that today, major international organizations devote important funds to measure "informal economy" worldwide.[42] However, in view of this background, the question remains as to what exactly represents the famous "informal" economy.

3.2 *The "Informal" Economy and Its Specific Structure*

Initially, the notion of an "informal" economy – *économie non-structurée* in French publications – was meant to approach a strange phenomenon: Despite Africa's urban explosion and the stagnation of wage labour, apparent or disguised unemployment was only increasing slightly.[43] In the beginning, the new concept, strictly confined to the urban sector, was described with great precision in many specialized studies – starting with Keith Hart's. For Hart, the informal economy does not just include "underemployed shoeshine boys and sellers of matches," nor does it consist solely of people living on odd jobs. On the contrary, the informal economy is a complex, robust, and highly organized system that structures African cities. Hart underlined the importance of varied sources of income where formal employment, even if badly paid, provided a stable income and could be combined with informal work.[44] The urban informal sector is dynamic, profit-making, productive, and inventive. It provides goods and services for a large, though often poor, section of the population.[45]

---

40 Among countless studies, articles, and books, see Reyneri, *Migrants' Involvement.*

41 ILO, "Resolution Concerning Statistics of Employment in the Informal Sector, adopted by the Fifteenth International Conference of Labour Statisticians, in January 1993," in *Papers of the Governing Body* (Geneva: ILO, 1993), 51–64.

42 "Share of Informal Employment," ILO, accessed 12 January 2022, https://www.ilo.org/re-Search/informality/map1_en.html and "Informal Economy and the World Bank," World Bank, accessed 12 January 2022, https://openknowledge.worldbank.org/handle/10986/18799.

43 Philippe Hugon, "L''informel' ou la petite production marchande revisités quarante ans après," *Mondes en développement* 166, no. 2 (2014): 18, https://doi.org/10.3917/med.166.0017, esp. 17.

44 Hart, "Informal Income," 68, 78.

45 ILO, *Employment Income,* 5.

Its links with the formal sector are diverse and complicated, and some authors have proposed several sub-categories of informality, according to economic standards (modern, intermediate, traditional), according to legal considerations (the degree of informality), or socio-economic criteria (subsistence units, transitional units, small and medium scale enterprises).[46]

Most importantly, the "informal" sector corresponds to a particular system strongly structured around small family units working in the primary, secondary, or tertiary sector, sometimes combining all three sectors.[47] The family is the productive unit, possessing its own means of production (land, herds, workshop, or shop), while its members constitute the workforce.[48] Field research studied family ownership of enterprises, small-scale activities, and high labour intensity.[49] These family units produce goods and services for the market, on a small scale, with the primary aim of creating jobs and income for the people involved, with little or no division between labour and capital. Labour relations are based on family, kinship, or neighbourhood ties, rather than on contractual agreements with formal guarantees. The family unit may also use the support of an external and "salaried" labour force. However, most of these remunerated workers are relatives, friends, and neighbours and, if possible, the stable employment of "strangers," without social references of kinship, neighbourhood, or recommendation is avoided. Thus, production units of the informal sector bear the characteristic features of household enterprises,[50] and the informal economy is largely embedded within family relations. In this context, marginalized people, such as external migrants, are those who do not have significant links with the family system.

Initially, just like Hart, the ILO and other research projects stressed that employment in the informal economy is not peripheral. On the contrary, it is at the very heart of the economy,[51] often emerging in "economically efficient and profit-making activities." Several researchers indicated that small-scale enterprises are not a barrier to growth: They do not compete with large enterprises but rather complement them as they are involved in the circulation, distribution, and repair of goods manufactured in the formal economy.[52] Many studies

46 Hugon, "L'"informel'," 17–22.

47 ILO, "Resolution Concerning Statistics," 56.

48 Alejandro Portes and William Haller, "The Informal Economy," in *Handbook of Economic Sociology,* ed. Neil J. Smelser and Richard Swedberg (New York: Princeton University Press, 2005), 404.

49 Indicatively, see ILO, *Employment Income,* 6.

50 ILO, "Resolution Concerning Statistics," 52.

51 PREALC, *Situaciones.*

52 ILO, *Employment Income,* 5.

emphasized "the close articulation of informal labour with firms in the capitalist economy [...]: such activities do not generally correspond to traditional subsistence production, but embody continuously changing requirements and opportunities in the 'modern' economy."[53] In El Salvador and the Dominican Republic, for example, marginal services (street vendors of all kinds, and other petty urban trades) account for 10 percent of the informal workforce – not including, of course, criminal or illegal activities. By contrast, 90 percent of informal employment is evidently linked to the modern economy and 44.3 percent of this percentage is in repair services (painters, plasterers, plumbers, electricians, shoemakers, etc.), while most food processing businesses are also small and belong to the informal sector.[54] These studies have underlined the flexibility and dynamism of informal enterprises, which can detect gaps and opportunities in the formal economy and develop around them.[55]

3.3 *Evolution*

However, according to Alejandro Portes and William Haller, the dynamic dimension of the informal economy – illustrated in Hart's study and other analyses – subsequently disappeared with the bureaucratic institutionalization of the term. The ILO effectively re-identified the informal economy with poverty,[56] thereby supporting the – then – dominant version of development based on the mass industrialization of classical capitalism. "Informal economy" acquired a miserabilist connotation and was considered to exclusively concern people who were not employable in the modern economy.[57] In both ILO and World Bank publications and research, the concept of an informal economy was overly simplified and used synonymously with terms such as underemployment, exclusion, poverty,[58] and hence the dominant view was that it had

53 Alejandro Portes, "Unequal Exchange and the Urban Informal Sector," in *Labor, Class, and the International System*, ed. Alejandro Portes and John Walton (New York: Academic Press, 1981), 81.

54 Norman Long and Paul Richardson, "Informal Sector, Petty Commodity Production, and the Social Relations of Small-Scale Enterprise," in *The New Economic Anthropology*, ed. John Clammer (London: Macmillan, 1978), 180.

55 Alejandro Portes, Manuel Castells, and Lauren A. Benton, eds., *The Informal Economy: Studies in Advanced and Less Developed Countries* (Baltimore: Johns Hopkins University Press) 1989, 15–25.

56 Portes and Haller, "The Informal Economy," 404.

57 Paul E. Bangasser, *The ILO and the Informal Sector: An Institutional History* (Geneva: ILO, 2000), 16.

58 Portes and Haller, "The Informal Economy," 404.

to be eliminated. Until 1987, the directive adopted by the World Bank and the International Monetary Fund was to "formalize the informal sector."[59]

However, rather than being a euphemism for poverty or marginalized people, the term "informal" was initially intended to approach a "specific form of relationships of production, while poverty is an attribute linked to the process of distribution."[60] In the course of the dissemination and trivialization of the term "informal" by international organizations, the aspect of the specific structure of the so-called informal sector was erased. Furthermore, these small family units – petty commodity production units[61] – obviously have a centuries-old history as a system of production and work organization, in the industrialized countries before the Industrial Revolution, in countries with late or limited industrialization, such as those in Southern Europe, or in countries that have not undergone industrialization. Their basic characteristics can also be found in the work of the English historian, Rodney Hilton, who described petty commodity production units in the countryside and in towns of Europe's late Middle Ages.[62] The institutionalization of the notion of informality has not only rendered the economies of poor countries opaque but also tends to swallow up whole sections of our history.

The overconsumption, overuse, and over-exploitation of the term "informal" have emptied it of its original, specific content, making it commonplace, i.e., the expression of a mere ideology.[63] Although "informal" is an extremely feeble analytical concept, it nevertheless has a heavy ideological load and is based on many untenable assumptions, and of course, stereotypes. In fact, one of the basic criteria of informality is the violation of official labour laws, state's labour laws.[64] However, this interpretation derives from countries with strong states, which have a long tradition of labour regulative, normative, and legislative action; it is projected onto countries with weak states[65] – that is, onto countries whose state does not control and regulate all economic transactions and, moreover, is unable to tax and protect all the labour activities of its

59 Bruno Lautier, *L'économie informelle dans le tiers monde* (Paris: La Découverte, 2004), 17–21.

60 Portes, Castells, and Benton, *The Informal Economy*, 12.

61 Caroline O. Moser, "Informal Sector or Petty Commodity Production: Dualism or Dependence in Urban Development," *World Development* 6, no. 9–10, (1978): 1041–1064.

62 Indicatively, see Rodney Hilton, *The English Peasantry in the Later Middle Ages: The Ford Lectures for 1973 and Related Studies* (Oxford: Clarendon Press, 1975).

63 Jacques Ellul, *Exégèse des nouveaux lieux communs* (Paris: Calmann-Lévy, 1966), 17.

64 Bruno Lautier, Claude de Miras, and Alain Morice, eds., *L'Etat et l'informel* (Paris: L'Harmattan, 1991), 105–142.

65 Lautier, de Miras, and Morice, *L'Etat et l'informel*; Portes and Haller, "The Informal Economy," 409–411.

population.[66] Could the "informal" simply be the distance that separates the states of poor countries from the states of rich countries?

This seemingly neutral and inoffensive term, carrying very important political, and ideological connotations, is highly imprecise and misleading, and the heterogeneity of what is grouped under the general heading of "informal" is disconcerting: from peddlers to small or medium family units.[67] Hence, "informal" has become a kind of catch-all term and anything that is not wage work (stable, declared, taxed, and protected) is classified as informal. Moreover, what used to be called crafts, micro-enterprises, self-employment, family labour and solidarity, survival strategy, or petty commodity production, has come to be identified with the "informal sector." From pure Marxists to the most liberal neoclassicals, all now employ the same term[68] and the adoption of the concept of "informal" by very different schools of thought has severely reduced the pre-existing intellectual diversity.

When the term was widely diffused by the ILO and other international organizations in the 1970s, it was reformulated and transformed into an exclusively moralistic concept. Through its association with poverty, informality embodied a "counter-model," a dark and "cursed" part of the world which had to be eradicated. Informality was contrasted with an ideal pattern – which was certainly real, but historically exceptional: the optimal working conditions prevailing at the time in the richest countries. Henceforth, "informal" became the way in which the rich countries of the North would interpret any economic activity that failed to conform to their production and labour standards, i.e., industrialization in large units, overwhelming predominance of wage labour, contractual remuneration and, above all, stable salaried work, which was guaranteed and protected by the state, institutions, trade unions, and legislation.[69] According to this paradigm, wage labour was to become the sole or main source of workers' income throughout the world.[70] However, even today, when agriculture is included in the "informal sector," for most countries in Sub-Saharan Africa, as well as Southern and Eastern Asia the share of "informal"

---

66 Bertrand Badie, *L'État importé: Essai sur l'occidentalisation de l'ordre politique* (Paris: Fayard, 1992).

67 Hugon, "L'"informel"," 28.

68 Bruno Lautier, "L'étrange altérité du travail: Parcours d'un socio-économiste du développement," *Revue Tiers Monde* 214, no. 2 (2013): 41–42, https://doi.org/10.3917/rtm.214.0035.

69 For a critique of the ILO's perception of labour, see Robert W. Cox, "Labor and Hegemony," *International Organization* 31, no. 3 (1977): 385–424, https://doi:10.1017/S0020818300026448.

70 For instance, see ILO, *Employment Income*.

employment exceeds 90 percent.[71] The "ideal" archetype of formal labour was and remains unattainable in poor countries.

During the 1970s, the ILO, World Bank, international organizations, and the theoretical schools involved with these issues considered salaried labour as the inevitable future of poor countries' populations,[72] a predetermined future that was destined to precisely reproduce the historical model of the rich countries in their own historical process. Consequently, all poor countries would be metamorphosed, through a rather painful stage of large-scale industrialization, into countries of salaried workers employed in industrial plants or the service sector. This never happened. And the whole argument overlooked the fact that although modern economic growth in the West was indeed linked to industrialization, the guarantee and protection of wage-earners was not automatic but rather came about after long social struggles by the workers.[73]

4 Economic Policy versus Political Economy

4.1 *The European Institutionalization of the "Informal"*

In this context, during the late 1980s, the concept was integrated into the process of economic convergence among the EEC countries. For Southern Europe, it was assumed that the overwhelming majority of "informal" employment (undeclared, untaxed, and unprotected) was due to multi-jobbing workers, paid work at home, part-time employment, and the traditional or innovative cluster based on family and small businesses. The vast majority of "informal" employment was thus thought to be due to a "peculiar" structure of labour organization and income-generating activities that just sought to counterbalance insufficient or inexistent incomes from formal labour.[74]

Following these assumptions, some sociologists in the 1990s argued about a "South European pattern of capitalist development" that pertains to agricultural countries which were industrialized late (and only partly). However, unlike the Northern countries, these countries largely have not experienced

---

71 Jacques Charmes, "The Informal Economy Worldwide: Trends and Characteristics," *Margin: The Journal of Applied Economic Research* 6, no. 2 (2012): 113, https://doi.org/10.1177/097380101200600202.

72 Lautier, "L'étrange altérité," 41.

73 Robert Castel, *Les métamorphoses de la question sociale: Une chronique du salariat* (Paris: Fayard 1995).

74 Enzo Mingione and Mauro Magatti, *The Informal Sector: Report to the European Commission's Employment Task Force (Directorate-General* V) (Brussels, October 1994) (unpublished report), esp. 11–14.

massive proletarianization. Migration abroad occasionally permitted the "de-bottlenecking" of a system in which small family units dominated, and thanks to migrants' remittances, enabled them to steadily reproduce themselves. Again, unlike the Northern countries, the political power in the South of Europe did not manage to shape a stable alliance with the entrepreneurial world. On the contrary, by providing various benefits, the political power persistently protected the productive role of small family enterprises and their extensive social basis.[75]

4.2 *The Concept of "Informal" Labour and Greece*

Greece constitutes an extreme example of this South European pattern. However, for ideological reasons, the importance of small family units and non-salaried work relations has never been thoroughly investigated, except for very few studies evaluating the real importance of this kind of work for family incomes. Thus, in 1960, the proportion of salaries and wages was estimated to represent only 30.9 percent of the total family income, in 1970 it stood at 34.1 percent, in 1980 at 36 percent, and in 1994 at 34.7 percent.[76]

Informality essentially corresponds to a multi-source income strategy. In 1987, it was estimated that at least half of the Greek population has additional income from second employment or agricultural revenue. This happened despite the fact that since 1983 – always as part of the convergence process of the EEC member countries' economies and the harmonization of Greek legislation with European regulations – having a second job was forbidden by a new law and therefore became "informal." However, in Greek society, the extent of "informal" labour lends it a crucial social importance that tacitly legitimizes it as a normal, unexceptional phenomenon.[77]

More precisely, the labour market is characterized by the limited percentage of workers and families fully dependent on wage income. Research also underlined the importance of kinship and extended family networks in performing social welfare functions which are usually provided by the state in Northern

75 A distinction was made between a northwestern zone (Northern Portugal, the Basque region, Catalonia, and Lombardy) in which the pacing and degree of industrialization were higher, and a southeastern zone (Southern Spain, most of Portugal, Southern Italy, and Greece) in which agrarian structures were extensively reproduced. Enzo Mingione, "Labour Market Segmentation and Informal Work in Southern Europe," *European Urban and Regional Studies* 2, no. 2 (1995): 121–143, https://doi.org/10.1177/096977649500200203.

76 Konstantinos N. Kanellopoulos et al., *Distribution, Redistribution, and Poverty* [in Greek] (Athens: Centre of Planning and Economic Research, 2004), 35 table 2.1.

77 Koula Kassimati, *Survey on the Social Characteristics of Employment* [in Greek] (Athens: National Centre of Social Research, 1989), 32, 36.

Europe. "Informal" employment was and is always structured by family strategies and networks. This deep embeddedness of labour activities within kinship constitutes the main difference between the "formal" and the "informal" economy paradigms.[78]

4.3 *Current Undocumented Migrants and "Informal" Labour*

In 2016, an ILO report funded by the EU estimated the Greek "informal" economy at around 25 percent of its GDP. It was stressed that this was due to the high level of self-employment which amounted to 32 percent (14 percent in the EU-28) and the large share of micro-enterprises. Micro-enterprises with 1 to 9 employees represented 96 percent of all enterprises in Greece, employing 55 percent of the labour force (compared to less than 30 percent in the EU-28). Greek citizens, as well as legal and undocumented migrants, were found to be holders of "informal" jobs and it was also assessed that secondary "informal" employment played a major role.[79] Apparently, the same structure has been reproduced for decades.

As a matter of fact, the large-scale post-1989 arrival of migrants allowed the well-integrated "informal" family units to flourish to a remarkable degree.[80] However, this very flexible, poorly paid, unregistered, and undocumented workforce radically changed the way in which the classical "informal" system functioned. These undocumented migrants were not related to the family system and their informal job was their unique source of income, not just a complementary one. Thus, the marginal part of the "informal" economy broadened immensely, and a new kind of "informal" precarious workers proliferated.

These marginal jobs in the informal economy are not identical to the various modern forms of flexible work or atypical jobs that are now institutionalized by the European states[81] – atypical jobs which the aforementioned ILO report did not consider as they came to be relabelled "formal" employment and thus only concern Greek citizens and documented or poorly documented migrants. Many impoverished Greeks are currently working side by side with migrants. Both, for example, are employed by illegal, semilegal, or legal "Temporary

---

78 Enzo Mingione, "Labour Market Segmentation and Informal Work," in *Economic Transformation, Democratization and Integration into the European Union: Southern Europe in a Comparative Perspective*, ed. Heather D. Gibson (Basingstoke, UK: Palgrave, 2001), 152, 161–163, 182–184.

79 ILO, *Diagnostic Report on Undeclared Work in Greece* (Geneva: ILO, 2016), 9, 24, 50.

80 Zografakis and Kasimis, "Greek Economy," 390–391.

81 Stefan Clauwaert and Isabelle Schömann, *The Crisis and National Labour Law Reforms: A Mapping Exercise* (Brussels: European Trade Union Institute, 2012).

Employment Agencies." Through these "special agencies," large private companies and also public institutions in the service sector hire migrants or Greeks to do cleaning work, firing them after six months only to hire a new batch of migrants or Greeks for another six months.[82] Nevertheless, Greek citizens keep their civil rights – especially the right to vote – and whatever labour rights they may still have. Meanwhile, the phenomenon of "agency workers" is escalating worldwide[83] and the partial withdrawal of states from the field of labour protection blurred the distinction between the marginalized people in the formal and those in the informal economy.

Initially, for migrants, the main, if not sole, connection with Greek society was the employer who provided them with labour. The interviews from the fieldwork capture a variety of experiences, in which the best coexists with the worst: from unpaid wages and mistreatment to honest and friendly dealing – the whole range of possible behaviours can be identified.[84] Some migrants – mostly Albanians – having a similar cultural pattern with Greek popular strata, were successfully integrated into the system of the "traditional" informal economy. Through marital ties with Greeks or by mobilizing their network of Albanian relatives, they created their own "informal" family units.[85] However, most migrants remain on the margins of Greek society in adverse working and living conditions and simply manage to acquire modest savings.[86]

Some recent estimates of the entire Mediterranean region, for example, indicate that in Greece, 90 percent of the wage workers in the agricultural sector are undocumented foreigners,[87] who move within the Greek territory following the demand for agricultural work. They are housed in abandoned warehouses and shacks made of zinc or plastic and their daily wages range from € 15 to 30.[88] However, farm production in Greece has been based on the labour power of these undocumented migrants for decades, thereby enabling

---

82 Vaxevanoglou, "Invisible Workers," 267–268; Thanos Maroukis, "Temporary Agency Work, Migration and the Crisis in Greece: Labour Market Segmentation Intensified," *Transfer: European Review of Labour and Research* 22, no. 2 (2016): 179–192, https://doi.org/10.1177/1024258916634620.

83 Judy Fudge and Kendra Strauss, *Temporary Work, Agencies and Unfree Labour: Insecurity in the New World of Work* (London: Routledge, 2014).

84 Vaxevanoglou, "Invisible Workers," 274–276.

85 Theodoros Iosifides et al., "Forms of Social Capital and the Incorporation of Albanian Immigrants in Greece," *Journal of Ethnic and Migration Studies* 33, no. 8 (2007): 1343–1361, https://doi.org/10.1080/13691830701614247.

86 Vaxevanoglou, "Invisible Workers," 274–276.

87 Alessandra Corrado, Carlos de Castro, and Domenico Perrotta, *Migration and Agriculture Mobility and Change in the Mediterranean Area* (London: Routledge, 2017), 10.

88 Vaxevanoglou, "Invisible Workers," 275.

the reproduction, restructuring, and expansion of agricultural units. Indeed, migrants have saved the agrarian economy from a harsh downturn. The same applies to plant nurseries, greenhouses, fisheries, and stockbreeding which were initially dependent on Albanian migrants, and later, on migrants from Asia and Africa. Migrant work became a structural factor for the rural economy and society in Greece,[89] and this "labour model" expands to other European countries.[90]

Similarly, many *sans-papiers* migrants work, more or less continuously, in construction, tourism, catering, care, and cleaning for private individuals or companies; they are also employed in family stores, petty workshops, and mostly in clothing sweatshops,[91] a phenomenon that is also proliferating in Northern Europe.[92] Owned by Greeks, these illegal workshops operate as subcontractors for *haute couture* firms or mass consumption brands. They employ only undocumented migrants, principally from Bangladesh, Afghanistan, Pakistan, and Iran. At the time of the field research, many of the interviewees had already been working in these jobs for years and, during the financial crisis, these workshops mushroomed in the degraded neighbourhoods of Athens.[93]

The results of the migrants' undeclared, exhausting, and underpaid labour are systematically recorded in the Greek Annual Censuses of stockbreeding, agriculture, fisheries, construction, tourism, and the clothing industry. Officially, however, the workers themselves are invisible in national censuses and hence the data presents a false image of the productive process from which a significant segment of the labour factor is missing, while a distorted perception of the labour market – and of Greek reality – is imposed. The invisibility of migrant labour is a cultural, social, and historical phenomenon and is obviously dependent on political power. However, despite any proclamations to the contrary, all governmental parties – including the left – eschewed the matter, letting Greek society solve the problems that have arisen as it sees fit; the same

89 Charalambos Kasimis and Apostolos Papadopoulos, eds., *Migrants in Greece: Employment and Integration into Local Communities* [in Greek] (Athens: Alexandria Publications, 2012), 43–44.

90 Johan Fredrik Rye and Sam Scott, "International Labour Migration and Food Production in Rural Europe: A Review of the Evidence," *Sociologia Ruralis* 58, no. 4 (2018): 928–952, https://doi.org/10.1111/soru.12208.

91 Vaxevanoglou, "Invisible Workers," 265–266.

92 Varun Aggarwal, Federica La China, and Lucia Vaculova, *Irregular Migration, Refugees, and Informal Labour Markets in the EU: The Rise of European Sweatshops?* (Brussels: European Institute for Asian Studies, 2016).

93 After a police raid, these workshops close for a little while and then reopen. Vaxevanoglou, "Invisible Workers," 266.

was true for trade unions' attitudes to labour legislation.[94] Moreover, defending the labour rights of migrants would objectively burden their employers, who are citizens, members of trade unions, and voters.

5 Conclusion

The concept of "informal labour" – obfuscating crucial social phenomena – was institutionalized during the 1970s by the ILO and other international organizations and subsequently adopted by supranational organizations such as the EU. It constitutes a concrete example of the ideological hegemony of international organizations.

Initially a stimulating research hypothesis, the "informal economy" was quickly upgraded within the ILO to a concept of strategic importance, a political issue. During this process, and despite intense internal disagreements, the most conformist interpretation prevailed, and the term was reduced to a banal synonym for poverty, underemployment, and exclusion. Through the powerful networks of international and supranational organizations, their research programs, their senior executives, and their collaborators, the notion of an "informal economy" spread among social scientists and policymakers of most countries in the world.[95] The concept was subsequently channelled into the "ideological apparatuses"[96] of the respective states, i.e., their media, education systems, etc. Especially in the West, the "informal economy" concept, recorded in textbooks, encyclopaedias, and dictionaries, was included in the body of scientific knowledge; it became an unquestionable certainty, reproduced automatically, spontaneously, and stereotypically. Thanks to the amnesia about the conditions of its genesis,[97] the "informal economy" was widely accepted as the chief attribute of the poorest countries, an obvious, self-evident, and inherent attribute. Within a decade, the simplistic notion of informality was "successfully socialized."

However, by using the criterion of non-wage labour, what is labelled "informal economy" encompasses very disparate situations, including both the

94 Zografakis and Kasimis, "Greek Economy," 383.

95 It is impossible to quote here the relevant, voluminous information drawn from the ILO archives. The same applies to the abovementioned "internal disagreements" within this organization.

96 Louis Althusser, *Positions (1964–1975)* (Paris: Les Éditions sociales, 1976), 67–125.

97 Pierre Bourdieu, *Sur l'État: Cours au Collège de France 1989–1992* (Paris: Seuil-Raisons d'agir, 2012), 578.

makeshift jobs or the backbreaking labour of marginalized people (such as undocumented migrants) and the activities of those who are perfectly integrated into the family unit system. Furthermore, there is a great deal of fluidity between non-wage and wage employment, as people may work jointly in the formal and the informal sectors or work temporarily in the informal sector while trying to find a formal job, whereas wage-earners may open small family businesses that allow them to shorten their wage career. Above all, an "informal" economy is not without form. Organized around small productive units in rural and urban areas, it is strongly structured by family ties. Lastly, what is called the "informal economy" constitutes the main form of labour organization in most countries of the world.

Although suitable for modern Western societies, the dichotomy between formal and informal labour fails to explain the complexity of work in the rest of the world. In fact, informality is a "systemic concept,"[98] rooted in a particular theoretical paradigm. This particular paradigm concerned the (then) burning issues of the poorest countries and especially former colonies, many of which at the time were vigorously claiming political independence and equitable development, that is, a better future. Within the United Nations (UN) and the ILO, these countries represented – numerically, politically, and symbolically – a considerable force. In fact, "informality" is not only linked to the strengthening of international and supranational organizations that imposed the concept; it is also intrinsically related to the decolonization process and the "development saga" of the 1960s and 1970s.

Since the end of the Second World War, while the political geography of the world was mutating and the United States was claiming a hegemonic role on a global scale, the problems related to the poverty of the so-called "Third World" countries were of major concern to the West and all international organizations. The economic development of the poorest countries became the main priority for the international diplomatic agenda.[99] At the ideological level, the concept of economic development replaced the older European concept of "civilizing mission" that had characterized the colonial era.[100] However,

98 Pierre Bourdieu with Loïc J. D. Wacquant, *Réponses: Pour une anthropologie réflexive* (Paris: Éditions du Seuil, 1992), 71.

99 Daniel Speich Chassé, "Technical Internationalism and Economic Development at the Founding Moment of the UN System," in *International Organizations and Development, 1945–1990*, ed. Marc Frey, Sönke Kunkel, and Corinna R. Unger (London: Palgrave MacMillan, 2014), 33.

100 Cooper and Packard, *International Development*, 1.

hegemony always needs forms of legitimacy and consensus,[101] and the UN turned into a crucial forum for the debates and policies that would accompany this global transformation. The concept of economic development, as well as the technical and financial assistance of the United States and international organizations to poor countries, were seen as "apolitical politics."[102] Moreover, the idea of development had the inestimable advantage of being equally attractive to leaders of "underdeveloped" societies and the people of the developed world. Thus, citizens all over the world acquired common expectations: They could share the joys of prosperity, but also be part of the intellectual universe and the moral community that flourished around the global development initiative of the post-war decades.[103] However, the idea of development was not neutral but rather implied a specific relationship of financial, technological, political, ideological, and cultural dependence between the rich industrialized countries and the poor emerging ones.[104] Nonetheless, development became the key to a new conceptual framework, which also provided the broader intellectual and ethical context for the dissemination of the concept of informality.

The "informal economy" notion – bearer of an implicit ideology that is never revealed as such – swiftly evolved into a myth, i.e., a depoliticized concept. This notion displays all the characteristics of a modern myth, as defined by the French semiotician Roland Barthes more than 60 years ago. The essential principle of the modern myth is to deprive the object of which it speaks of its history, and, more precisely, to transform this history into nature. Another property of the modern myth is that it always perceives dissimilarity as a caricature of itself, a failed duplicate. Furthermore, the myth will confess some lesser "evil" to cover up the main "evil."[105] Tautological, egocentric, self-referential, arrogant, and pretentious, the myth of the informal economy erased the history of the poorest countries and the relevant power relations.

Modern myth will state facts, and never explain,[106] thus evacuating reality, which sinks, bleeds, and evaporates. Modern myth sacrifices reality to save

---

101 Robert W. Cox, "Gramsci, Hegemony, and International Relations: An Essay in Method," *Millennium: Journal of International Studies* 12, no. 2 (1983): 162–175, https://journals.sagepub.com/doi/abs/10.1177/03058298830120020701.

102 Michele Alacevich, "Planning Peace: The European Roots of the Post-War Global Development Challenge," *Past and Present* 239, no. 1 (2018): 219, 263, https://doi.org/10.1093/pastj/gtx065.

103 Cooper and Packard, *International Development*, 1.

104 The bibliography concerning the history of development is extensive. For example, see Corinna R. Unger, Iris Borowy, and Corine A. Pernet, eds., *Routledge Handbook on the History of Development* (New York: Routledge, 2022).

105 Roland Barthes, *Mythologies* (Paris: Éditions du Seuil, 1957), 216–229.

106 Barthes, *Mythologies*.

ideology, and this is precisely what happened with the notion of informality in poor countries, where, despite obstacles and predictions, "informal" labour relations have been reproduced on a wider scale.[107] This is even more the case in countries where the structural adjustment programs of the International Monetary Fund or the World Bank have imposed, among other things, the "formalization of the informal."[108] The generally disastrous results of these interventions led, around 1987, to a reversal in the meaning of informality for the two organizations mentioned above: As formal employment declined and the role of the state as job provider and protector of the workforce weakened, the narrative of informality shifted. From being seen as the cause of poverty (according to international organizations), informality was transformed into a universal panacea for resolving the problems of poverty and unemployment. The informal sector was given a positive social role: to absorb "like a sponge" the unemployed that structural adjustments had multiplied.[109] In reality, it is the flexibility of the labour market – whether formal or informal – that constitutes the new diktat of international and supranational organizations and the workers most "prone" to flexibility are impoverished citizens and undocumented migrants.

In contrast to the concept of "informal economy" and its particularly intricate history briefly outlined here, the category of "undocumented migrants" was institutionalized in Europe through the emigration laws of the wealthiest countries – thereby enforcing the conception of Europe as a "fortress" and of migrants as an "invading army."[110] Nevertheless, in other countries, the real world turned out to be far more complicated and this complexity has not been officially acknowledged by their governments and trade unions. Despite the application of deterrent policies, unofficially they tolerated undocumented migration and therefore offered one more "informal" benefit to small family units, but also to sweatshop owners and to the agencies of temporary employment. Incidentally, they also tolerated undocumented migrants who were able to work and send money home. Through this process, a segment of the workers in Europe was transformed into a new type of labour force, a "pure" labour force without political, trade union, or civil rights.[111]

107 Charmes, "The Informal Economy Worldwide," 103–132.

108 Lautier, *L'économie informelle,* 17–21.

109 Indicatively, see Tony Addison and Lionel Demery, *The Alleviation of Poverty under Structural Adjustment* (Washington, DC: World Bank, 1987).

110 King, Lazaridis, and Tsardanidis, *Eldorado*, 24.

111 Balibar et al., *Sans-papiers,* 89–116.

CHAPTER 7

Utilizing Population Movements

How States Use Emigration to Regulate National Economies

Cecilia Bruzelius

Abstract

International migration is sometimes thought of as exogenous to national social and economic systems, despite the fact that regulation of migration can be a way of enabling and conditioning markets. This chapter considers the socio-economic rationales behind states' regulation of national populations' emigration, by examining emigration policy in two European countries with long traditions of emigration – Italy and Poland – from the early twentieth century until today. The analysis indicates that emigration has deliberately been used to regulate domestic labour markets and accumulate resources, and the ways in which the two countries have approached this together with the potential reasons for these political choices are discussed in this chapter.

Keywords

emigration – labour export – migration policy – populations

1 Introduction

States' preferences concerning migration and their attempts to regulate migratory processes are much less frequently studied from the perspective of countries of origin, or "sending states," than countries of destination.[1] This chapter is concerned with how, and to what ends, states regulate their populations' emigration. In line with the focus of this volume, I concentrate specifically on the socio-economic rationales behind emigration policy – although it should

1 Suzy K. Lee, "The Three Worlds of Emigration Policy: Towards a Theory of Sending State Regimes," *Journal of Ethnic and Migration Studies* 43, no. 9 (2017): 1453–1471; Michael K. Miller and Margaret E. Peters, "Restraining the Huddled Masses: Migration Policy and Autocratic Survival," *British Journal of Political Science* 50, no. 2 (2020): 403–433.

 | DOI:10.1163/9789004686991_008

be noted that political rationales such as nation-building are hardly separable from those aimed at creating national economies. Such an analysis is relevant given that migration sometimes is treated as separate from, and often in contradiction to, national socio-economic policy.[2] Nevertheless, scrutinizing the rationales behind emigration policy reveals that states' regulation of migration can be considered part and parcel of their attempts to create and control markets. It also reminds us that regulating migration to achieve socio-economic ends is not limited to controlling foreigners' in-and outmigration, the most common view of migration policy, but may also involve states making their own populations mobile. Adopting such a perspective on the attempted uses of emigration by states equally highlights the transnational facets of national, social, and economic policies that are habitually thought of as limited to the internal territories of the state.

The chapter focuses on Europe with a view on how state uses of national populations' emigration have changed over time. The reason for this is twofold. First, most of the recent research on emigration politics and policy focuses on a selection of countries in the Global South but less often on Europe and rarely takes a longue durée perspective. Second, existing research on European states' management and uses of emigration tends to not go beyond historical research focusing on the late nineteenth and early twentieth centuries and typically focuses on single countries.[3] Comparisons across countries and over longer periods of time are, however, important to identify patterns and begin to understand how, when, and why states use emigration to achieve specific economic ends. Against this background, this chapter explores the socio-economic rationales behind two European states' regulation of citizens' emigration over time, focusing on Italy and Poland and examining the period from the late nineteenth century, when both countries began regulating emigration, to the present. The two countries were selected as examples of countries with long histories of emigration in which emigration policies evolved over time.[4]

---

2 Cecilia Bruzelius and Isabel Shutes, "Towards a Mobility Perspective in Social Policy Research," *Global Social Policy* 22, no. 3 (2022): 503–520.

3 Pawel Kaczmarczyk, Enrique Aldaz-Carroll, and Paulina Hołda, "Migration and Socio-Economic Transition: Lessons from the Polish Post-EU Accession Experience," *East European Politics and Societies* 34, no. 4 (2020): 911; Nancy L. Green and Francois Weil, eds., *Citizenship and Those Who Leave: The Politics of Emigration and Expatriation* (Urbana: University of Illinois Press, 2007).

4 Examining other European countries also helps to understand socio-economic rationales: See, for example, labour market policies of Germany, the Netherlands, Portugal and Spain: Barend Peter Hofstede, *Thwarted Exodus: Post-War Overseas Migration from the Netherlands* (Gravenhage: Martinus Nijhoff, 1964); Christoph Raas, *Institutionalisierungsprozesse auf einem internationalen Arbeitsmarkt: Bilaterale Wanderungsverträge in Europa zwischen 1919*

The comparison serves to illustrate *the desired socio-economic ends* and *the policy with which* states have used emigration and to tease out the reasons *why* they did so. To achieve the latter objective, I develop a set of broad expectations that guide the subsequent chronological description and comparative analysis of the country cases. My analysis is based on secondary literature.

I argue that sending states have encouraged and utilized their own populations' international movement to regulate their labour market supply and to accumulate resources, so as to stabilize their economies. Moreover, I discuss how these policy choices reflect certain demographic contexts, path dependencies in migration and associated policy, as well as economic and social levels of development within and between countries.

2 Controlling Human Mobility to Enable and Condition Markets

Populations both constitute and generate resources, making them an integral aspect of both the state and the capitalist economy. Therefore, the regulation of human mobility was integral to the historical emergence of both the modern state and the capitalist economy. The transition from private to state regulation of internal and, later, international mobility was an essential aspect of the transition from feudalism to capitalism, facilitating the transition from local to national markets.[5] Allowing as well as limiting migration across internal and external borders was simultaneously a means to satisfy the demands of capital and to address the social challenges associated with the capitalist economy. Free movement within European states and empires was considered a way to guarantee a sufficient supply of labour in industrializing regions, but also as a means of reducing pauperism. Concurrently, the mobility of the poor was heavily regulated to alleviate the burden of poverty relief systems on the migrant-receiving localities or, to put it in Polanyian terms, to protect the institutions that provided the necessary embeddedness of markets. In contrast, the development of colonizer powers' national welfare states was closely tied to

und 1974 (Paderborn: Ferdinand Schöningh, 2010); Johannes-Dieter Steinert, *Migration und Politik: Westdeutschland – Europa – Übersee 1945–1961* (Osnabrück: Secolo Verlag, 1995).

5 Karl Polanyi, *Origins of Our Time: The Great Transformation* (Boston: Beacon Press, 2001 [1944]), 59–69; John Torpey, *The Invention of the Passport* (Cambridge: Cambridge University Press, 2000).

forced population movements within the colonial state from the periphery to the centre.[6]

International migration serves similar functions today. Advanced economies have come to rely on labour in-migration to satisfy labour demands in the secondary labour market sector and also draw on highly skilled workers to fill gaps in the primary labour sector. Migration can, thus, serve both complementary and substitutive functions vis-à-vis other socio-economic institutions and policies,[7] and as a deliberate strategy for achieving socio-economic goals and stabilizing national economies.

To consider migration as a socio-economic policy, the politically expected and intended outcomes of migration have to be analysed more than the actual outcome of migrations or migration policies. Accordingly, in this chapter, I concentrate on the socio-economic goals that states have explicitly sought to achieve by regulating migration although the extent to which "the state" is the actor in formulating and implementing policy is debatable, given the multiple actors and interests involved in shaping state policy. Migration policies nevertheless need to be justified in terms of basic functional imperatives of the state, which are also reflected in broad policy objectives such as national interest. I will correspondingly refer to the state interchangeably with "governments."[8]

3 Regulating Citizens' Emigration to Achieve Socio-Economic Ends

My focus on state uses of emigration concentrates on the exit of national populations, rather than the well-studied entry of foreigners. Regulating citizens' emigration does not merely comprise managing the domestic supply and demand of labour but also extends to the international distribution of national populations, thereby implicating specific socio-economic opportunities. Considering this, emigration may serve to stabilize national economies in two key ways, both of which also serve political goals: First, by addressing

6 Gurminder K. Bhambra and John Holmwood, "Colonialism, Postcolonialism and the Liberal Welfare State," *New Political Economy* 23, no. 5 (2018); Green and Weil, "*Citizenship and Those Who Leave.*"

7 Michael J. Piore, *Birds of Passage: Migrant Labour and Industrial Societies* (Cambridge: Cambridge University Press, 1979); Alexandre Afonso and Camilla Devitt, "Comparative Political Economy and International Migration," *Socio-Economic Review* 14, no. 3 (2016): 591–613.

8 David Fitzgerald, "Inside the Sending State: The Politics of Mexican Emigration Control," *International Migration Review* 40, no. 2 (2006): 259–293; Martin Ruhs, *The Price of Rights* (Princeton, NJ: Princeton University Press, 2013), 135.

social challenges resulting from the market economy (and as we shall see, also planned economies) and second, by supporting the *accumulation* of capital and human resources. To begin with the social challenges, emigration may be a way to cope with a fluctuating demand for labour and, in times of recession or economic shock, it can be a safety valve to reduce the oversupply of labour and ease associated social pressures, and thereby also reduce political tensions.[9] This is not only a question of labour market regulation, but also a way to live up to promises of employment and welfare: If states not only allow but also assist unemployed parts of the population in departing to destinations where job opportunities exist, then the social and economic conditions of those who stay may concurrently improve as competition for work declines and wages accordingly increase. Likewise, in times of economic boom and labour shortages, states may look towards emigrant human capital abroad and encourage returns.

A second major function that emigration can serve is the accumulation of financial and human capital. Such economic opportunities result from having emigrant communities, with whom special "home" states and societies often retain ties. In a backward linkage, emigrants typically remit money to their country of origin, which contributes to political and economic stability. Remittances are a source of foreign capital and can additionally strengthen those in power if citizens erroneously attribute their increased well-being to their government. Remittances may also be a source of private social protection in the absence of sufficient public social provision. A significant presence of citizens abroad can also unlock opportunities for cross-border trade, as, for example, emigrants abroad may be consumers of domestic products. Such economic opportunities provide an impetus for states to facilitate transnational political and economic relations with emigrant communities as "a means of gaining access to the wealth of the richer receiving countries" in ways that "serve national goals." Moreover, emigrants may improve their skills while abroad, which could bring desirable human capital to the country of origin.[10]

In this context, the question arises concerning under what conditions states would rely on citizens' emigration for these purposes. To begin with, there must be real or perceived problem pressure, which is likely to relate to the state of the

9 Albert Hirschman, "Exit, Voice, and the State," *World Politics* 31, no. 1 (1978): 90–107; Frances Fox Piven and Richard Cloward, *Regulating the Poor: The Functions of Public Welfare*, 2nd ed. (New York: Vintage Books, 1993).

10 Roy Germano, *Outsourcing Welfare: How the Money Immigrants Send Home Contributes to Stability in Developing Countries* (Oxford: Oxford University Press, 2018); Lee, "The Three Worlds," 1456.

economy and the demand and supply of labour. However, how the economic situation is interpreted, and what approaches are considered appropriate for addressing it, depends on various contextual factors. Notably, we may expect demographic conditions to influence a state's preferences concerning emigration: In a context of perceived "overpopulation," emigration may seem a more viable option to regulate markets than in a context of demographic decline. Next, emigration offers a complement and substitute to domestic social and economic policy, which is why we may see states opt to ensure their citizens' access to dependent employment abroad under conditions of underdeveloped or dysfunctional domestic policies.[11] Moreover, we can expect past migratory movements to shape emigration policy, as the resulting social networks shape further practices of migration as well as migration policy choices.[12] Where emigration is already an established practice (irrespective of state policies), states may try to further enable and manage it to maintain the movement and reap the most benefits. Furthermore, if countries turn to emigration to achieve socio-economic goals at one point in time and establish practices for doing so, it is – from a path-dependency perspective – more likely that they will pursue similar policies in the future. Finally, the international context matters. Enabling national populations not only to leave but also to reside abroad heavily depends on the demand for – and treatment of, in so far as this is important for the countries of origin – foreign labour in destination states. This shapes both the respective immigration policies and sending states' ability to negotiate access to foreign labour markets.[13] Equally, and connecting to the previous point about migration trajectories, migratory movements will take place in greater numbers when there are social and economic differences *between* countries – making corresponding emigration policy more likely.

Next, I examine how emigration has been governed and which socio-economic functions of emigration were intended in Italy and Poland. My empirical focus is on the policies aimed at regulating outbound moves as well as returns of national populations, and, in addition, at maintaining ties with

---

11 Afonso and Devitt, "Comparative Political Economy"; Neil G. Ruiz, "Made for Export: Labor Migration, State Power, and Higher Education in a Developing Philippine Economy" (PhD diss., MIT, 2014).

12 Douglas S. Massey, "The Social and Economic Origins of Immigration," *Annals of the American Academy of Political and Social Science* 510 (July 1990): 60–72.

13 Georg Menz, *The Political Economy of Managed Migration* (Oxford: Oxford University Press, 2009); Roberto Ventresca, "Italian Migration Policies at the Beginning of the European Integration Process: Fruitless Attempts?," in *Peoples and Borders: Seventy Years of Migration in Europe, from Europe, to Europe [1945–2015]*, ed. Elena Calandri, Simone Paoli and Antonio Varsori (Baden-Baden: Nomos, 2017), 57–76.

emigrant populations. Which justifications for their policies do policymakers articulate? I exclude policies of forced emigration, such as deportation schemes, from this examination and the starting point of the investigation is the turn of the nineteenth century when European states actively began to manage emigration. The Polish case study, however, begins in 1918, as Poland was not a sovereign state between 1795 and 1918.

4 Italy

Comprehensive attempts to regulate emigration in Italy began at the turn of the nineteenth century after emigration had become a mass phenomenon and the Italian state had been unified in 1861. The rationale behind the first law of 1888 (Law 5866) was to ensure a safety valve to ease widespread pressures of unemployment and social tensions. While this law primarily marked a shift from the attempt to limit emigration to permitting it, the subsequent law on emigration in 1901 (Law 23) was more ambitious in that it established the General Emigration Agency (*Commissariato Generale dell'Emigrazione*) whose sole purpose was to organize emigration. This involved rationalizing outflows, implementing training programs for emigrants, and managing diaspora relations to further transnational trade. The agency subsidized private organizations that managed and assisted emigration and it also provided training programmes for prospective emigrants that were tailor-made to match the needs of the destination countries' labour markets. The programme included evening and holiday schools for illiterate adults, courses for teachers of emigrants, and vocational training in mechanics, building trades, agriculture, and other occupations. This so-called "selective emigration" policy grew more pronounced as the US – the main destination of Italian emigration – became more selective in admitting immigrants. Another important dimension of the law of 1901 was the protection of emigrants' welfare. It has, in fact, been suggested that emigrants were one of the first social groups to benefit from the beginnings of Italian welfare-state measures as the formal right to emigrate and work abroad was accompanied by attempts on the part of the Italian state to ensure that potential migrants could safely exercise this right. However, once abroad, the Italian state, in reality, did little for its citizens and left the task of caring for Italians to the Catholic church.[14]

14 Guido Tintori and Michele Colucci, "From Manpower Export to Brain Drain? Emigration and Italy, between Past and Present," in *Routledge Handbook of Contemporary Italy: History, Politics, and Society,* ed. Andrea Mammone, Ercole Giap Parini, and Giuseppe Veltri

This policy change coincided with a shift from seeing emigration primarily as a demographic phenomenon to a circulation of the labour force and revenues across borders. Correspondingly, the state began to estimate the value of revenues sent back by emigrants. These, it was concluded, amounted to significant resources for several regions of origin and were an important source of capital for the accelerating industrialization in Italy. To access these means for the national economy, the state sought to facilitate money transfers and channel them through Italian banking and finance networks. The Bank of Naples, with Naples being the main port of departure, was made the single official bank for administering remittances.[15]

These emigration policies and rationales remained almost identical after the fascist seizure of power in 1922. The fascists also continued previous governments' financial support for colonialization projects: Emigration policy was not merely to be a way of regulating domestic social problems, but also to facilitate turning emigrants into tools for exports and colonial expansion. In the spirit of both objectives, the fascists initiated the Credit Institute for Italian Labour Abroad (*Istituto di Credito per il Lavoro Italiano all'Estero*, ICLE) in 1923, which financed the establishment of Italian private companies abroad on the condition that they employ Italian workers. Moreover, the ICLE was meant to "intensify the savings of Italians abroad."[16]

In the years after the Second World War, Italy's economy suffered not only from war-time losses and destruction but also from scarce investment in the agricultural and industrial sectors. To confront the resulting unemployment and ease mounting social tensions, which could strengthen the anti-government opposition, especially the Communist Party, the government again turned to emigration. The policy aimed to reduce unemployment and guarantee the inflow of foreign currencies through remittances. According to government forecasts, remittances in 1953 would amount to ten percent of the country's total imports. Italian manpower was also exchanged by the Italian

(New York: Routledge, 2015), 38; Elizabeth Cometti, "Trends in Italian Emigration," *Western Political Quarterly* 11, no. 4 (1958): 825; Caroline Douki, "The Liberal Italian State and Mass Emigration, 1860–1914," in Green and Weil, *Citizenship and Those Who Leave*, 104–105.

15 Douki, "The Liberal Italian State," 102–106; Guido Tintori, "Italy: The Continuing History of Emigrant Relations," in *Emigration Nations: Policies and Ideologies of Emigrant Engagement*, ed. Michael Collyer (Basingstoke, UK: Palgrave Macmillan, 2013), 135–137.

16 Tintori, "Italy"; Mark I. Choate, *Emigrant Nation: The Making of Italy Abroad* (Cambridge, MA: Harvard University Press, 2008); Philip V. Cannistraro and Gianfausto Rosoli, "Fascist Emigration Policy in the 1920s: An Interpretative Framework," *International Migration Review* 13 no. 4 (1979): 673–692.

state for raw materials and energy: In 1946, Belgium was to receive a specified number of Italian workers per week in return for guaranteed delivery of coal.[17]

Pursuing emigration as a socio-economic strategy became more difficult in the post-war period, as those states that had previously accepted Italian labour in large numbers now pursued strategies of full employment for their own labouring population and hence were much more protective of their labour markets. In response, under a program of "assisted emigration," the Ministry of Foreign Affairs and the Ministry of Labour signed a series of migration agreements that allowed destination countries to select workers. Between 1946 and 1956, this involved almost every West European state as well as overseas destinations. The Italian government also used the Marshall Plan to fund its emigration policies, amongst them the continuation of the ICLE and its loan program for Italian companies abroad through which approximately 20,000 emigrants received assistance from 1950 to 1955.[18]

Since bilateral agreements were not sufficient to reach the minimum Italian emigration goals and unemployment remained high despite economic reforms, the Italian government subsequently turned to multilateral international solutions to reduce the unemployed population segment in the state. From 1948 onward, through the Organization for European Economic Cooperation (OEEC), the Italian government tried to assert that the "jobless must be considered as an international pool, to which every European state can refer to attain needed manpower amounts." However, the real breakthrough in the government's attempts to ensure Italians' access to work abroad came with the negotiations on the European Common Market Treaty (1955–1957), which coincided with a new peak of unemployment in Italy. Italian negotiators argued that Italy's oversupply of labour was a problem for all of Europe and made free outlets for Italian workers a key demand. As a result, free movement for workers was included in the Treaty.[19]

Throughout the 1950s, the Italian government also actively supported emigration by acting as an intermediary between foreign companies and Italian workers in local labour exchanges. In the 1960s, after the free movement of workers had been achieved, Italian emigration legislation was mainly focused on emigrants' social rights, and several amendments and supplements were

---

17 Ventresca, "Italian Migration Policies," 59–60 and fn. 48; Willem Maas, *Creating EU Citizens* (Boston: Rowman and Little, 2007), 25.

18 Cometti, "Trends," 828–832; Ventresca, "Italian Migration Policies"; Tintori, "Italy," 139.

19 Ventresca, "Italian Migration Policies," 63; Cometti "Trends," 829; Frank Roy Willis, *Italy Chooses Europe* (New York: Oxford University Press, 1971), 157.

made to bilateral agreements to ensure their access to social insurance and healthcare abroad.[20]

With the so-called oil crisis in 1973, the period of assisted emigration and bilateral agreements came to an end and thereafter, emigration policy focused more on maintaining ties and, later, on encouraging returns. In the 1970s, the responsibilities for emigration policy were largely devolved to Italy's 20 regions, which established Emigration Departments and developed programmes dedicated to linkages to communities abroad, ranging from social subsidies to vocational training and co-development projects. An additional intent involved training and attracting emigrant descendants to return to Italy for work. Other goals involved creating import-export channels and encouraging tourism, thus effectively turning emigrant communities into "business communities."[21] Similar policies were also pursued at the national level: In 2012, the technocratic government of Mario Monti created an online platform (*Innovitalia*), meant to "maximise the impact of human capital" of Italian "brains" abroad and to "promote research and business opportunities" in partnership with the motherland.[22]

Since the 1990s, and more intensively since the 2000s, the Italian governments (under the Ministry of Foreign Affairs and the Ministry of Labour) and the Italian regions have increasingly pursued return programmes, suggesting a shift in the political perception of emigration. In the wake of the 2008 financial crisis, long-standing ideas about the benefits of emigration were supplemented by concerns surrounding an Italian "brain drain." When, with the crisis, Italian emigration unencouraged by the government increased in numbers, concerns that the "best of Italy" was being lost grew salient. As a result, political measures to encourage their return became a political topic with the so-called Law Against Exodus of 2010 (Law 238) providing tax incentives to returnees as well as public housing and pension benefits. As a reflection of the perceived brain drain, national and regional return programs exclusively focus on the return of the highly skilled, with an emphasis on individuals who have advanced their human and social capital abroad. Examples are the "Brain Back Umbria" and the "Welcome Talent" in Milan.[23]

20 Willis, *Italy Chooses*, 156; Tintori and Colucci, "From Manpower Export," 43.

21 Tintori and Colucci, "From Manpower Export," 43–44.

22 Tintori, "Italy," 145.

23 Tintori and Colucci, "From Manpower Export," 44; Guido Tintori and Valentina Romei, "Emigration from Italy After the Crisis: The Shortcomings of the Brain Drain Narrative," in *South-North Migration of EU Citizens in Times of Crisis*, ed. Jean-Michael Lafleur and Mikaolaj Stanek (Amsterdam: Springer, 2017): 60.

5 Poland

After independence in 1918, Polish governments in the interwar period actively sought to increase emigration to deal with economic underdevelopment, extensive poverty and unemployment, and overpopulation – especially in the countryside. As a first measure, it included the right to emigrate in the constitution. Subsequent emigration policy involved not only attempts to protect those departing but, regardless of political leaning, governments in the interwar period used emigration as an explicit strategy to regulate the labour market. In legislation, emigrants were defined as those "who leave in search for work, or for the purpose of work." Concurrently, the government discouraged the many prewar Polish emigrants who wanted to return to the (now independent) country, due to the fear of a mass influx of people to an economy that had little to offer.[24]

The Polish state facilitated emigration by providing information through designated offices of the State Employment Agencies, subsiding railway tickets and baggage fees, and the abolition of passport fees. Amongst other measures, a special fund was established for the training of potential emigrants. To ensure access to foreign labour markets, the Polish state concluded bilateral agreements with multiple European and overseas countries. Although the state made attempts to ensure emigrants' socio-economic rights, Poland's weaker bargaining role and urgent economic problems resulted in many compromises. Germany, to which Poland prohibited emigration for political reasons until 1926, remained an important destination because of the geographical proximity and well-established patterns of migration.[25]

The successive Polish governments also concluded agreements with Latin American countries, both to increase emigration and to establish Polish enclaves abroad, through which domestic markets could be expanded. To these (never particularly successful) ends, the Polish state financed companies abroad – much like the ICLE – that would employ emigrants. Again, similarly to Italy, the government made the most of the ample remittances, which did, indeed, become a crucial source of foreign capital. In 1929, the Treasury Ministry established the Polish Bank of Aid (today the Bank Pekao S.A.) with

24 Anna Kicinger, *Polityka emigracyjna II Rzeczpospolitej*, CEFMR Working Paper 4 (Warsaw: University of Warsaw, 2005); Alina Janowska, *Emigracja zarobkowa z Polski 1918–1939* (Warsaw: Państwowe Wydawnictwa Naukowe, 1981), 100.

25 Janowska, *Emigracja*; Kicinger, *Polityka emigracyjna*, 41, 53–57.

branches across multiple countries, whose main tasks were to administer emigrants' savings.[26]

Central to the emigration policy in the interwar period was the protection of emigrants' welfare and the key law of 1927 covered the preparations for their departure, transit, and stay abroad. A special assistance fund, mentioned above, was used for emigrant education and welfare institutions abroad. The bilateral agreements sought to protect Polish emigrants, for example, by providing compensation in case of industrial accidents and by pension insurance coverage.[27]

While emigration to the West was in principle heavily restricted during the post-Second World War period and Communist rule, governments in practice used bilateral agreements from the 1970s onwards to facilitate the emigration of workers. Poland signed agreements with the German Democratic Republic (GDR) (1988) and Czechoslovakia (1984), but also the Federal Republic of Germany in 1979. Since unemployment officially did not exist, the main benefit of labour export until 1989 was to compensate for the negative trade balance by remittances, i.e., foreign exchange.[28]

In the aftermath of the fall of the Soviet Union and the advent of Poland's transition to a market economy, the government once again used emigration as a means of regulating unemployment and, to this end, continued to rely on bilateral agreements: In the 1990s it had concluded 18 agreements with 15 countries whereby, in terms of numbers, the most important of these was signed with Germany in 1991. It allowed for the movement of agricultural workers and, in fact, mainly regularized migrations already taking place. The Polish Ministry of Labour and Social Policy portrayed the bilateral arrangements as part of their labour market policy to fight unemployment. It divided the number of job slots available under the programs between the country's regions according to the respective level of unemployment. The government additionally justified the program with the argument that access to foreign labour markets would contribute to the improvement of the professional and language

26 Kicinger, *Polityka emigracyjna*, 56; Tara Zahra, *The Great Departure: Mass Migration from Eastern Europe and the Making of the Free World* (New York/London: W. W. Norton, 2017), 123–128; Zbigniew Landau and Jan Tomaszewski, *Bank Polska Kasa Opieki S.A. 1929–1989* (Warsaw: Szkoła Główna Handlowa w Warszawie, 1991), 14.

27 Kicinger, *Polityka emigracyjna*, 38–43.

28 Michael Okolski, "Przepływ siły roboczej w świetle niemiecko-polskiej umowy dwustronnej opracownikach sezonowych," in *Polscy pracownicy na rynku Unii Europejskiej*, ed. Pawel Kaczmarczyk and Wojciech Lukowski (Warsaw: Scholar, 2004).

skills of the Polish workforce. Such bilateral programs remained in place until the early 2000s.[29]

By the beginning of the twenty-first century, Poland continued to struggle with a severe oversupply of labour and very high unemployment, which in 2002 – just prior to Poland's EU accession in 2004 – amounted to more than 20 percent.[30] The right of EU citizens to take up work in other member states was consequently seen as a key benefit of Union membership. Against this background, the government and, in particular, the Ministry of Labour, actively lobbied for the opening of EU labour markets, initially before 2004 and, subsequently, before the end of the two-year period of mobility restrictions in May 2006.[31]

Immediately after accession, large numbers of citizens left the country and by 2007, 2.3 million Poles lived abroad (6.6 percent of the population)[32] – far more than had been expected. In response, the first emigration policy adopted, namely the "Closer to work, closer to Poland" program of 2006, was intended to assist Polish emigrants abroad and to smoothen the emigration experience. In the view of the government, this was necessary to "protect Polish citizens against dangers and threats related to the often unprepared labour emigration."[33] To achieve this, additional consulates were established and access to their services was simplified. Thus, as in the past, efforts to protect emigrant workers' welfare have remained at the core of Polish emigration policies. However, in many EU destination states, some ten years after the accession, free movement and the rights of mobile EU citizens became contentious political topics. In this context, the Polish government has repeatedly defended Polish citizens' equal treatment abroad, notably in response to the United Kingdom's assaults on EU citizens' social rights and the run-up to Brexit.[34]

However, shortly after the 2006 program was launched, the negative aspects of emigration became salient to political debates on the free movement of

29 Okolski, "Przepływ siły roboczej."

30 Kaczmarczyk, Aldaz-Carroll, and Hołda, "Migration and Socio-Economic Transition," 8.

31 Kicinger, *Polityka emigracyjna*, 53.

32 Agnieszka Fihel, ed., *Recent Trends in International Migration in Poland: The 2011 SOPEMI Report*, CMR Working Papers 52/110 (Warsaw: University of Warsaw, 2011), 25.

33 International Centre for Migration Policy Development, *Return Migration: Background, Practice Examples and Policy Options for Intra-EU Mobility – Focus on Poland* (Vienna: International Centre for Migration Policy Development, 2019), 34.

34 Nigel Morris, "David Cameron Faces Strong Resistance in Poland over EU Migrant Benefit Limits," *Independent*, 9 December 2015, https://www.independent.co.uk/news/uk/politics/david-cameron-faces-strong-resistance-poland-over-benefit-curbs-eu-migrants-a6767096.html.

workers. The Polish economy experienced rapid growth and unemployment dropped from 19.1 percent in early 2004 to 7.1 percent in late 2008 which prompted employers to complain about labour and skill shortages. As a result, the prevalent political view shifted from considering emigration as a chance to reduce unemployment to one in which it was leading to a loss of the economically most valuable professionals.[35]

In this context, the Polish government made an about-turn in its policy from promoting outmigration to (at least discursively) encouraging emigrants' return. At no earlier point in time, except when in 1989 the government had encouraged the repatriation of ethnic Poles, had the government pursued outright return migration policies. In 2007, the new "Return Program" (*Powotry*), in the words of the Ministry of Labour and Social Affairs, was a labour market issue: "Among the most important tasks for the government administration, local authorities and economic entities is the creation of conditions which would favour the return to the country of, *in particular people who could contribute to the improvement of the* [*economic*] *situation in Poland*."[36]

Officially, the government's position in the early 2020s is that return should be enabled and offices provide information as well as support for reintegration for those who do return. Selected groups, especially the highly skilled, are actively encouraged to return, for example through financial support to resettle. At the same time, potential problems relating to un-or low-skilled workers who have also left the country seem not to be acknowledged.[37] The government did develop policies aimed at establishing relations with emigrant communities, following recommendations of experts from the Migration Working Group in 2008. The latter group of experts anticipated that large-scale return migration would occur, which may have reduced the perceived need for return policies. As many Poles continue to reside abroad, the Ministry of the Economy pursues outreach activities to encourage investment in Poland by Poles abroad.[38]

---

35 Magdalena Lesińska and Justyna Pokojska, *Analiza dyskursu medialnego w Polsce na temat emigracji poakcesyjnej (2004–2013)*, CMR Working Papers 87/145 (Warsaw: University of Warsaw, 2015); Maciej Szczepański, "Analiza polityki państwa wobec migracji powrotnych: Przypadek Polski," in *Polityka państwa wobec migracji powrotnych własnych obywateli: Teoria i praktyka,* ed. Magdalena Lesińska, CMR Working Papers 44/102 (Warsaw: University of Warsaw, 2010).

36 Szczepański, "Analiza polityki," quote 26, italics added.

37 Szczepański, "Analiza polityki"; "Nawa Return Program," accessed 11 May 2022, https://nawa.gov.pl/en/scientists/polish-returns.

38 Szczepański, "Analiza polityki," 28; Kaczmarczyk, Aldaz-Carroll, and Hołda, "Migration and Socio-Economic Transition," 18; Magdalena Lesińska and Izabela Wróbel, "Diaspora Policies, Consular Services and Social Protection for Polish Citizens Abroad," in *Migration*

6 A Comparative Perspective: Emigration to What Ends?

The comparison presented in this chapter shows that both Italy and Poland have tried to manage emigration to "shape their nation's economic goals."[39] This is also evident in the institutional configurations of emigration policy, as labour and social affairs ministries have often been the designated authorities in charge. With policy tools ranging from actively assisting outmigration to efforts to encourage certain emigrants' return, Italy and Poland have attempted to achieve multiple socio-economic objectives with the help of emigration and emigrants. For one, the emigration policy has been a tool for regulating labour markets. Both countries demonstrate how "sending states may commodify and market the labour of their citizens globally so as to fulfil basic state requirements of political and economic viability."[40] Enabling and encouraging emigration has been explicitly framed as ways to deal with labour, but also with perceived population oversupply, as well as to reduce social tensions perceived to challenge not only the social order but – as in Italy – also the political order and incumbent governments. Emigration policies, especially bilateral agreements, have been aspects of governments' unemployment policies. In addition, as a social policy aim, emigration has been promoted to reduce poverty. When, however, labour and population shortages began to be felt, return policies became part of governmental labour market strategies, although never as prominent as assisted emigration policies. In other words, like unemployment insurance spending, emigration policies have to some extent been cyclical in relation to the economy – a form of migration Keynesianism under which a workforce is geographically reshuffled.

Beyond labour market regulation, both states have controlled the emigration of their citizens – both in the sense of actively encouraging it ex-ante and managing it post factum – to generate resources.[41] First, by providing institutional channels for remittances, preserving ties to foreign communities, and

and Social Protection in Europe and Beyond (Volume 2), ed. Jean-Michel Lafleur and Daniela Vintila (Cham, CH: Springer, 2020), 367.

39 Federico Romero, "Migration as an Issue in European Interdependence and Integration: The Case of Italy," in *The Frontier of National Sovereignty: History and Theory 1945–1992*, ed. Alan S. Milward et al. (London/New York: Routledge, 1992), 33.

40 Christina Siracusa and Kristel Acacio, "State Migrant-exporting Schemes and their Implications for the Rise of Illicit Migration: A Comparison of Spain and the Philippines," *Journal of International Migration and Integration* 5, no. 3 (2004): 342.

41 Magdalena Lesińska, "The Dilemmas of Policy Towards Return Migration: The Case of Poland After the EU Accession," *Central and Eastern European Migration Review* 2, no. 1 (2015): 77–90.

encouraging transnational trade and investment, the Italian and the Polish states have sought to capitalize on emigrant communities and boost the inflow of foreign capital. In some instances, emigration has even been a means of accumulating natural resources – Italian workers were directly traded for raw materials in the immediate post-war period! Second, emigration has also been used as a means of human capital accumulation. The Polish government considered bilateral agreements not only as a way to reduce unemployment but also as a possibility for Polish workers to gain skills abroad. In the present, return policies have been implemented in both countries – more so in Italy than in Poland – to profit from skills acquired abroad that are perceived as valuable for the national economy. Third, in close connection to accumulation, emigration has also been considered a way of extending domestic markets through transnational economic opportunities and exchanges. In fact, in the first half of the twentieth century, sending populations abroad was explicitly seen as an alternative to colonialism[42] as "colonies" of nationals in foreign lands were meant to generate revenues for the motherland. In the present, this idea seems to linger, as the emphasis on Italian business communities abroad of successive recent Italian governments indicates.

Finally, the protection of emigrants' rights has been an integral aspect of Italian and Polish emigration policy. The efforts seeking not only to grant citizens access to foreign labour markets but also to support their chances of success once there, may be read as a way to legitimize these policies. They may also be understood as an effort to avoid mere short-term emigration that is not sufficiently economically beneficial for the sending country. If migrants return soon after departure, the problems that gave rise to emigration policies are not alleviated. On the other hand, permanent settlement abroad entails a loss of state investment in human capital and, furthermore, remittances usually decline the longer migrants reside abroad.[43] By defending the rights of their citizens abroad, countries of origin can maintain ties and foster loyalties to be able to tap into resources in other countries.

7 Making Sense of Emigration Policy

When do countries choose to rely on emigration to address socio-economic challenges? In terms of perceived or real problem pressures, it is evident that

42 Zahra, *The Great Departure.*

43 Barbara Schmitter Heisler, "Sending Countries and the Politics of Emigration and Destination," *International Migration Review* 19, no. 3 (1985): 472.

policies not only address labour market challenges but also demographic concerns. Overpopulation was a concern in both Italy and Poland in the early twentieth century. In contrast, at the time, countries such as Sweden, which faced high emigration coinciding with concerns about depopulation, did not assist emigration to address economic and social challenges. In fact, demographic concerns at times seem to trump economic concerns when it comes to emigration policy: The Italian government's introduction of return policies in response to concerns surrounding the brain drain occurred during the great recession, when emigration could, in principle, have been perceived to perform the same function as it had done earlier. However, it also coincided with a growing concern in Italy about low fertility and an ageing society.

Next, emigration can be understood as both an outcome of and a strategy for resolving challenges resulting from comparatively underdeveloped domestic social and economic policy. These two features may reinforce each other as emigration may temporarily solve or, at least, make socio-economic challenges less acutely evident. Both Italy and Poland began their emigration policy trajectories in times when their economic development lagged relative to that of neighbouring countries. Regarding Italy, it has been argued that the economic strategies pursued in the first part of the twentieth century, which were based on protectionism and centred on non-labour-intensive sectors, stunted development and resulted in the emigration of a sizable part of the population. Other scholars observe that Italian political elites concentrated their efforts "on the strategic assets that ... Italian citizens abroad might secure," while "reducing to a minimum any commitments in the social ... sphere" and refusing to address the economic and structural causes behind emigration.[44]

The international context has also clearly shaped both countries' emigration strategies as demand for workers, especially from other European countries, made state emigration strategies possible. In the first part of the twentieth century, Italian and Polish workers were sought by neighbouring countries that industrialized earlier; during the two world wars, receiving states imposed heavy restrictions; in the period after the Second World War, internal European labour migration quickly expanded.[45] Similar economic divergences as well as skewed patterns of migration remain in early twenty-first-century Europe.

Destination countries' preferences also conditioned emigration strategies: In the era before the Second World War, the Italian government responded

44 Tintori and Colucci, "From Manpower," 45.

45 Dudley Kirk, "European Migrations: Prewar Trends and Future Prospects," *The Milbank Memorial Fund Quarterly* 25, no. 2 (1947): 128–152.

to destination countries' new quota systems with a "selective emigration" strategy and by training emigrants to match the demands of foreign labour markets. In the more restrictive post-war area, bilateral agreements that allowed destination countries to select workers for specific sectors and tasks were a prerequisite for enabling outmigration. This limited Italy's and Poland's ability to use emigration as a tool for reducing unemployment and poverty, since mainly workers with specific skills could migrate under the bilateral agreements. Italy found a way out of this dilemma by insisting on the free movement of workers within the EU. However, the disadvantage of free movement – from the point of view of the state – is that although sending countries no longer have to negotiate for their citizens to be able to access foreign job markets, they also lose the capability to select which people to send. Correspondingly, emigration policies have primarily shifted towards managing relations with emigrant communities and encouraging and assisting the return of the economically desired ones. Thus, while the free movement of workers was an explicit strategy for resolving high unemployment for both Italy and Poland before European integration, it does, once in place, make emigration, if anything, more of an implicit than explicit socio-economic policy.

Finally, path-dependent elements are evident in both countries' emigration policies. Notably, emigration as a labour market and an accumulation policy has persisted not only between elected governments of different political leanings but also across distinct political regimes – democratic, fascist, and communist governments. This may be due to several factors. First, emigration policies with the aim of reducing unemployment have often been attempts to manage already occurring migration. Polish migration to Germany is a case in point; here the continuation of migration despite both states' attempts to prohibit it made it preferable for both states to try to regulate it (and thereby avoid irregular migration). Second, large-scale emigration has shaped collective self-understandings and established transnational communities that have made emigration a thinkable and plausible, and relatively legitimate, policy option. Research on Poland in the first half of the twentieth century indicates that the long-established tradition of emigration resulting from the partitioning of the country generated an "emigration ethos,"[46] which perhaps facilitated the political decision to rely on emigration. Similarly, Guido Tintori noted that the perceived economic benefits of an Italian diaspora in a global market may be one reason why Italy has continued to portray itself as an emigration nation (even

46 Kicinger, *Polityka emigracyjna*, 5. This may be compared to the proclaimed "immigration ethos" of countries such as Australia, Canada, and the US.

after statistically becoming a net-immigration country) as well as to frame Italian emigrants as "brains" (even though skilled emigrants are a minority).[47]

8 Conclusion

This chapter has demonstrated how two European states from the late nineteenth century onward have encouraged and utilized their own populations' international movement to shape their political economies. The purpose of the comparison has been to demonstrate how they have done so and propose the potential rationale behind the state policy. Further comparative research is needed to better understand why states pursue certain emigration policies.[48] At present, this corresponds to the regulation of citizens' emigration for economic purposes in countries around the globe, with Mexico and the Philippines being the most-cited cases.[49] This political economy perspective on the politics of (e)migration showcases not only certain political uses of national population movements but also illustrates that national citizenship is not necessarily a privileged category: Where nationals are primarily treated as economic resources that may be shifted geographically according to national economic and political needs, as defined by political elites, the whole notion of citizenship is challenged. Moreover, it showcases that the reach of national welfare states is not limited to national territories: Italy and Poland included foreign labour markets and lands in their planning of how to resolve social and economic challenges. In fact, when countries simultaneously assist the emigration of their citizens and attempt to defend emigrant workers' rights, even citizenship rights, a new understanding of social and industrial citizenship is required as the common nation-state-bound conceptualization of citizenship is inadequate to capture such practices.[50]

---

47 Tintori, "Italy," 140.

48 Lee, "The Three Worlds."

49 Robyn Magalit Rodriguez, *Migrants for Export: How the Philippine State Brokers Labor to the World* (Minneapolis: Minnesota University Press, 2010); Kaczmarczyk, Aldaz-Carroll, and Hołda, "Migration and Socio-Economic Transition."

50 John Crowley, "The National Dimension of Citizenship in T.H. Marshall," *Citizenship Studies* 2, no 2 (1998): 165–178.

CHAPTER 8

The Quest for Chinese Labour

Colonial Competition for Coolies and the Emergence of the Modern Chinese Worker

Selda Altan

Abstract

The scholarship on the nineteenth-century coolie trade has shown that the study of post-emancipation labour regimes can yield valuable insights into understanding the continuous impact of global labour circulations. In particular, indenture helps to elucidate the transition from slavery to wage labour and the creation of racial hierarchies in colonized territories. Building on the scholarship on bonded labour regimes, this chapter traces the roots of the modern Chinese worker in the nineteenth-century coolie trade and reconstructs the transnational context of class formation in China. It demonstrates that the coolie trade in the age of colonial competition precipitated the creation of a labour market in China through colonial coercion. Ironically, the proliferation of overseas work opportunities and the shared knowledge of the coolie experience carried labour to the centre of anti-colonial and anti-dynastic struggles in China while offering a critique of the debilitation of global labour movements by racial thinking.

Keywords

Chinese workers – colonialism – coolie trade – labour – labour markets – race

1 Introduction

The coolie trade refers to labour importation from densely populated countries or regions with complex "informal" labour arrangements (see Chapter 6 in this volume) to territories where local populations do not meet the labour demand for agricultural production or infrastructural development. Although Europeans used the term "coolie" since the sixteenth century to denote Asian unskilled workers, in its nineteenth-century articulation, "coolie" came to

 | DOI:10.1163/9789004686991_009

designate a particular category of South Asian and Chinese workers who were mass-recruited under contractual agreements that fixed the term of employment and enforced penal sanctions if workers violated the contractual terms. While English and Spanish merchants called indentured workers coolies and *culís,* in some French sources *engagés* was used to refer to such workers, including those from Africa.[1]

What distinguishes the coolie trade of the nineteenth century is the colonial character of the business. In the absence of a free labour market where workers were readily available for employment in adequate numbers, colonizer governments created the conditions of free emigration to their colonial territories from countries over which they had economic and political leverage. At the same time, colonists cooperated with local actors who used coercion and deception to extract workers from their close-knit rural communities. The trade's coercive character, the contracts' binding nature, and the coolies' dreary transportation/working conditions are the main reasons why many scholars have seen the coolie trade/indenture system as a reincarnation of slavery. However, as will be discussed in this chapter, the mediation of recruitment by extensive labour networks and the competition between different colonial powers for cheap labour, combined with the coolies' collective and individual resistance, curbed the power of colonizers, motivating them to liberalize the labour markets from the intervention of local actors.

In the late nineteenth century, China was under the burden of extreme financial sanctions imposed after military defeats by European powers and Japan. With its limited industrial production, it had to open its borders to foreign powers for railway projects, mining, and other industrial investments while simultaneously suffering from the parasitic British-imposed opium trade.[2] The rising number of foreign investments in treaty ports undermined the handicraft industries in the interior. Chinese peasants, the largest section of society, were still working with traditional farming methods. Apart from a few profit-generating crops such as opium poppy, mainly cultivated in the provinces of Sichuan and Yunnan but not comparable in quality and quantity

1 "Engagé" was originally the term for white migrant workers. See Alessandro Stanziani, "Beyond Colonialism: Servants, Wage Earners and Indentured Migrants in Rural France and on Reunion Island (c. 1750–1900)," *Labor History* 54, no. 1 (2013): 64–87.

2 Britain defeated China in two Opium Wars, 1839–42 and 1856–60, as did France in the Sino-French War of 1884–85. This forced China into an unequal treaty system. Defeat in the Sino-Japanese War of 1895 followed, and the last blow came when the allied foreign army detachments suppressed the anti-foreign Boxer Uprising in 1900 and forced the Qing government to pay an enormous indemnity.

to British opium imports from India, the decline in agricultural production was significant. At the same time, a trend in the accumulation of land in the hands of individual landlords made life difficult. Burdened by increasing taxes used to finance reform programs and foreign debts, for many Chinese peasants the prospect of selling their small pieces of land and joining the ranks of the urban proletariat was more appealing, if not inevitable. The consequent mass escape from the countryside supplied the growing urban centres in Southeast China with surplus labour to be exported to European colonies despite the government ban on foreign travel.

The coolie trade showed variation over time and place.[3] Especially in Qing China, given the existence of a sovereign government, the countries seeking Chinese labour had to limit their recruiting excesses in response to Chinese official and popular reactions.[4] By the turn of the twentieth century, colonizing powers succeeded in creating a "free" labour market in China, meaning that they had removed the obstacles to Chinese workers' global mobility without recognizing them as free wage earners in the European sense. Still, the process by which the coolie trade gained the characteristics of government-regulated contract labour increased the value and hence the competitive power of Chinese labour. Building on the shared experience of the coolie age, early-twentieth-century Chinese workers fought for their interests through multiple channels while sowing the seeds of Chinese working-class identity in an increasingly globalized labour market. The coolie experience was also used in literary works to construe the modern Chinese worker, now defined as a free wage earner who developed a class identity through this particular global experience.

2 The Coolie Trade: Expanding and "Liberalizing" the Labour Market

The coolie trade turned into a flourishing business in the 1840s when Britain intensified its efforts to bring the slave trade from Africa to an end. Even in its inception, the trade was imbued with colonial competition, especially in sugar production. After the equalization of import duties by the Imperial Sugar

3 Matthias van Rossum, "Coolie Transformations – Uncovering the Changing Meaning and Labour Relations of Coolie Labour in the Dutch Empire (18th and 19th Century)," in *Bonded Labour: Global and Comparative Perspectives (18th-21st Century)*, ed. Sabine Damir-Geilsdorf et al. (Bielefeld: Transcript Verlag, 2016), 83–102.

4 The Qing was the ethnically Manchu dynasty that ruled China from 1644 to 1912. China became a republic in 1912.

Duties Act in 1846, British colonies, deprived of reduced import duties and a large workforce, lost their competitive edge over sugar planters in Brazil and Cuba, who still used slave labour. A British report of 1862 pointed out that, among its possessions, only Mauritius had a competitive power over other sugar producers. Planters in Mauritius had imported "cheap" Indian coolies since 1834 and this had put the colony in a better position compared to Spanish Cuba, where "dear" immigrant Chinese complemented slave labour.[5]

Cuban planters began to import Chinese labour in 1847 when the anti-slavery measures of the British navy in the Atlantic increased the costs of the slave trade. Not surprisingly, the company that initiated the coolie trade to Cuba was a London-based business of the Zulueta family, formerly engaged in the slave trade.[6] They adjusted their slave trade infrastructure for the new circumstances of the "free" labour era and from 1847 to 1873, British traffickers and Spanish Cuban buyers shipped approximately 150,000 Chinese coolies to Havana, which constituted an enormous growth factor for the Cuban economy.[7]

This momentum was maintained by keeping the coolies under a strict labour regime. The Cuba commission sent by the Chinese government in 1873 to investigate the conditions of the coolies found that Chinese workers were treated like enslaved people. They were not allowed to leave the premises without "walking" papers and were kept as prisoners for corvée labour until the authorities verified the authenticity of their documents.[8] The authorities also limited the workers' mobility by paying them in "script," redeemable only in plantation stores, rather than currency, thereby tightening workers' bondage to the plantation owners. In addition, planters used underhanded methods to extend labour contracts to a degree that the most common form of protest among Chinese workers in Cuba was suicide.[9]

5 Henry Taylor, "State of the West Indies in 1862" (Colonial Office, July 1862), 9.

6 Lisa Yun, *The Coolie Speaks: Chinese Indentured Laborers and African Slaves in Cuba* (Philadelphia: Temple University Press, 2008), 15. The Zulueta family was originally based in Cádiz, Spain, but when the liberal government of 1820–23 collapsed, the family moved to London with other liberal exiles. They were active in banking, slave trade, and the plantation business. Kathleen M. López, *Chinese Cubans: A Transnational History* (Chapel Hill: University of North Carolina Press, 2013).

7 Yun, *Coolie Speaks*, 16–17.

8 Margaret Mih Tillman et al., "Chinese Immigrants in Cuba Repository Collection," *Chinese America: History and Perspectives* 2016, 13–26.

9 *The Cuba Commission Report: A Hidden History of the Chinese in Cuba: The Original English-Language Text of 1876* (Baltimore: Johns Hopkins University Press, 1993).

In Peru, the newly independent government also encouraged coolie importation to strengthen its position in the global economy and provided substantial subsidies to traders who would bring contract labourers to the country while compensating planters for each enslaved person they freed. As a result, from 1847 to 1874, approximately 100,000 Chinese arrived in Peru, mainly from Portuguese Macau, to be employed in cotton and sugarcane plantations, guano mining, and railroad construction.[10] As in Cuba, the efforts to keep production costs to a minimum centred on disciplining migrant workers and limiting their mobility. The Peru commission sent by the Qing government in 1887 observed the payment of low wages and work abuses including corporal punishment, imprisonment, and the illegal extension of coolie contracts through forgery.

Despite strict measures, wage variation in different plantations indicates that the planters' effort to limit the movement of coolies did not always work. Especially free Chinese, who had fulfilled their contract terms, were able to increase their salaries, sometimes significantly, by seasonally moving from small to large plantations. Still, Chinese dealers retained great power over workers and, for instance, during the Chilean invasion of 1879–1883, Chinese intermediaries captured hundreds of dispersed coolies and returned them to planters. In return, they not only secured payments for each escapee but could also open plantation stores to sell goods needed by the same captured Chinese workers.[11]

With its influence over densely populated India and coastal Chinese cities, Britain emerged as the leader of the nineteenth-century coolie trade, a business that offered higher profits than the African slave trade. As Lisa Yun aptly states, "while mobilizing to abolish the transatlantic slave trade, the British were establishing themselves as dominant traffickers of Indian and Chinese coolies."[12] This goal was impossible to achieve without liberating Asian labour markets from the power of their existing governments. However, when European colonists needed workers to maintain their plantation economies after the gradual abolition of slavery, significant labour mobility already existed. For men in the Fujian and Guangdong provinces, working abroad in Southeast Asia had long been a common way of making a living.[13] In the eighteenth and early nineteenth centuries, these Chinese immigrants formed

10 Michael J. Gonzales, "Chinese Plantation Workers and Social Conflict in Peru in the Late Nineteenth Century," *Journal of Latin American Studies* 21, no. 3 (1989): 385–424.

11 Gonzales, "Chinese Plantation Workers," 387.

12 Yun, *The Coolie Speaks*, 6.

13 Guotong Li, *Migrating Fujianese: Ethnic, Family, and Gender Identities in an Early Modern Maritime World* (Leiden: Brill, 2016).

professional guilds, merchant houses, and labour gangs using their clan, hometown, or ethnic connections. Britain had to compete with these networks as much as it had to compete with other colonizer powers in the region.

To sustain their plantation economies in the face of competition from local producers in Southeast Asia, who had the advantage of stable labour supply from China, the British and Dutch colonizer governments implemented a series of structural reforms that tacitly aimed to create a labour market out of the control of local labour gangs or village chiefs. For example, the Dutch administration in Java banned subcontracting via village heads in favour of individual labour contracts in 1819. This move came after the unsuccessful attempt to tax individual landholding peasants based on land value rather than harvest yields.[14] The Cultivation System imposed in 1829 required almost half of the population in Java to produce cash crops in return for wages. The colonial administration paid wages to peasants for their mandatory labour and then extracted the land tax from them. A reduction in the government demand for corvée labour also facilitated the transition to contract-wage labour. Still, these measures did not fully liberalize the labour market and, in many parts of the colony, labour gangs and debt bondage were still the only ways for planters to maintain a steady supply of labour. More than structural changes in the region's existing recruitment regime, it was the population growth in the late nineteenth century that turned the region into a "mass exporter of labor."[15]

Britain's efforts to create a labour market in China and Southeast Asia began at the same time and British Hong Kong was one of the first destinations for the "floating population" that escaped the mayhem of the Taiping Rebellion in 1850–1864.[16] Until August 1852, British vessels shipped 73 percent of all Chinese migrants from Hong Kong to various destinations in Southeast Asia. When the British Passengers Act in 1855 limited coolie shipments within British territories, Portuguese Macau subsequently emerged as the new hub. However, British shipping companies and the British colonial government continued as leading coolie traders. As early as 1840, a Colonial Land and Emigration Commission had been created with members selected from the Royal Navy and, until its abolition in 1878, this body monitored the compliance of the British coolie traders through the Passengers' Acts of 1855 and 1863. These regulations were

14 Ulbe Bosma, *The Making of a Periphery: How Island Southeast Asia Became a Mass Exporter of Labor* (New York: Columbia University Press, 2019), 74.

15 Bosma explains the population growth through improved healthcare and longer life spans.

16 The Taiping Rebellion was a millenarian movement led by Hong Xiuquan, a person of Hakka ethnicity, who wanted to create a Christian kingdom in China. The rebellion resulted in a death toll of approximately 20–30 million.

indispensable to protect the labour market from any monopolistic intervention, especially from the existing regional labour networks.

The British employment of Indian workers in their Southeast Asian possessions complicated the labour scene dominated by Chinese emigrants. Before the Straits Settlements – modern Penang, Dinding, Malacca and Singapore – became a crown colony in 1867, the British East India Company had built the region's infrastructure with convict labour from India, and later from Hong Kong. The work of Indian convicts in these "penal colonies" aided the colonial administration to counterbalance the Settlements' contending Chinese population. However, after the Indian Rebellion of 1857, the colonial administration feared that a potential convict riot among former Indian mutineers in the Straits Settlements would "rouse the passions" of lower-class Chinese.[17] Even without any influence from Indian rebels, the secret societies in command of Chinese emigrants clashed with the police in 1871–1872[18] and this agency induced the colonizer government to regulate the labour market in coolies.

The British Committee that arrived in the Straits Settlement in 1876 to investigate the Chinese labour question emphasized the need for government intervention to limit the power of local labour brokers. In 1877 and 1880, special ordinances under the guise of protecting the emigrants imposed new regulations. A government "Protector of Chinese" was appointed to oversee the engagements between employers and coolies. Although not sufficient to eliminate labour brokers, the regulations "freed" many Chinese from the gang-like labour networks and put them under the colonial administration's direct supervision. By the 1880s, Chinese coolies bound for the Straits Settlements had some independence to sign contracts they deemed advantageous. However, they continued to join labour squads to protect their interests if need be. As late as 1890, British reports still complained that "brokers drove up prices, obstructed the free flow of labor, and contributed to the labor shortage by pocketing money, providing unnecessary services [funerals], speculating on labor contracts, and forming a ring that excluded outsiders."[19] Like the Dutch colonial government, the British administration occasionally had to yield to the regional recruiters to maintain its colonial economy.

17 Anand A. Yang, *Empire of Convicts: Indian Penal Labor in Colonial Southeast Asia* (Oakland: University of California Press, 2021), 184.

18 Persia Crawford Campbell, *Chinese Coolie Emigration to Countries Within the British Empire* (London: P. S. King & Son, Ltd., 1923), 9–10.

19 Cited in Adam McKeown, "The Social Life of Chinese Labor," in *Chinese Circulations: Capital, Commodities, and Networks in Southeast Asia,* ed. Eric Tagliacozzo and Wen-chin Chang (Durham, NC: Duke University Press, 2011), 78.

3 The French Empire's Involvement in Coolie Recruitment and Trade

Unlike the British and the Dutch, French planters initially preferred Indian *engagés* (French for indentured labour) to Chinese coolie workers. The rumours of the approaching abolition of slavery in French colonies motivated French settlers to recruit Indian coolies to Réunion Island in 1828 as the labour demand in sugar production soared.[20] At the time, Asian emigration was not a significant issue in the French Empire, but both the success and complications of Indian recruitment to Réunion prompted the government to regulate the conditions of Asian migrants through a decree from 3 July 1829 for Indian and Malay workers and from 10 November 1843 for authorizing the recruitment of Chinese coolies for public projects. The colonial administration managed the first round of recruitment itself but left later shipments to private operators.

As in Cuba, Chinese coolies worked side by side with enslaved people from Africa and *engagés* from India – whereby the distinction between the two was ambiguous. The legal conflicts from the period indicate that French landowners in Réunion were not happy with the unruly character of Indian and Chinese coolies and, for this reason, they tried to counterbalance Asian workers with *engagés* from Africa. However, when the French government banned African recruitment in 1859 due to accusations of "disguised slavery," Réunionnais planters had to rely on Asian workers and France signed a treaty with Britain on 10 August 1861 to recruit Indian coolies.[21]

When Asian coolies appeared as an attractive alternative to slave labour, settlers in the French Caribbean Indies, having failed in their effort to attract European immigrants, pressured the government for the authorization of Asian emigration, arguing that white immigrants failed to adjust to the colony's difficult climate. In response, two decrees promulgated on 13 February and 27 March 1852 specified the regulations for labour importation from non-European countries. One purpose was to expand the successful experiment with Indian coolies in Réunion to the French colonies in the Americas. Asian labour importation to the French Caribbean took off immediately and from 1853 to 1888, 76,339 Indian and 2,129 Chinese contract labourers were transported to Guadeloupe, Martinique, and French Guiana.[22]

20 L. Maillard, *Notes sur l'île de la Réunion (Bourbon)*, 1862, 184.

21 Marcel Rémond, *La main-d'œuvre dans les colonies françaises* (Paris: Librairie Cerf, 1902), 52–57.

22 David Northrup, "Indentured Indians in the French Antilles," *Outre-Mers: Revue d'histoire* 87, no. 326 (2000): 245–271.

As in the case of former Spanish slave traders who subsequently became coolie dealers, French businesses previously engaged in the slave trade seized the opportunity to profit. When US entrepreneurs arrived in East Asia in 1848–1849 to recruit labourers to support their westward expansion, the French media expressed excitement about the increasing maritime activity around the South China Sea.[23] The demand for coolie workers was so high and the number of vessels so limited that 10,000 contracted workers from Canton (Guangzhou) were waiting to be transported from Hong Kong.[24] A French ship from Bordeaux transported Chinese coolies from Hong Kong to San Francisco at the rate of 350 francs per person, which yielded a handsome profit. The shipments to Cuba and Peru were even more profitable. The value of a coolie who was shipped first class was S/. 450 in Peru, and S/. 300 and S/. 100 respectively for those in the second and third class.[25] The profit rate exceeded 50 percent after factoring in the costs, including food, clothing, medical examination, and administrative expenses such as consulate certificates, customs fees, and emigration office charges.[26]

To facilitate transactions with labour suppliers from India, China, and Oceania in the coolie trade to the Caribbean, the former slave traders of Le Havre, France, and plantation owners in the French West Indies formed a financial institution in 1856 headed by shipowner Louis Victor Marziou. In this scheme, as the regional historian Jean Legoy narrates, French shipowners sent their agents (usually long-haul captains) to China's coolie markets in Macau, Hong Kong, Canton, Amoy (Xiamen), and Shanghai to contact Chinese brokers. In many instances, the latter worked through unlawful means given the Chinese government's restrictions on labour recruitment and foreign travel. These brokers supplied coolies at 30 francs each to French agents, who took them to the French consul as a witness to the reading of contracts in Chinese and French before the recruits signed them. Once the coolies arrived in the

23 Jean Legoy, "Le Havre et le transport des coolies au milieu du XIXème siècle," *Recueil de l'association des amis du vieux Havre* 39 (1982), 1–16.

24 Robert L. Irick, *Ch'ing Policy Toward the Coolie Trade, 1847–1878* (Taipei: Chinese Materials Center, 1982), 26.

25 The currency was Peruvian sol and, at the time, 1 US$ equalled 1.08 soles. The coolie boats had different compartments, some with better ventilation, more space, and other amenities. While this helped to reduce mortality and disease rates during the trip, it also meant that contract buyers had to pay higher prices to hire these coolies. In addition to the standard medical examination, buyers also personally evaluated the fitness of new arrivals and selected their workers accordingly.

26 "Coût du coolie mis à bord," annexed to the telegram dated 18 November 1878. Archives Nationales Section Outre-Mer, Guyane 55 F3 (06–10).

colony, they were distributed to plantations at varying prices and on free-market terms until, in 1858, the government fixed the prices paid by planters to avoid speculation and overpricing.

The bustle of coolie importation to the French Caribbean did not last long. When the government contributions were cut and sugar prices started to fall in the wake of the US Civil War, very few navigation companies were eager to carry back the coolies whose contract terms ended.[27] In the 1870s and 1880s, thousands of Indian coolies were stranded in French territories, mainly because they could not find vessels for their return. Similarly, the repatriation of Chinese coolies from Cuba and Peru caused diplomatic debates in the 1870s. While the Qing government insisted on the repatriation of Chinese workers at the expense of these countries, the governments of Cuba and Peru were not willing to assume the costs.

4 The Qing Government's Attempts to Negotiate Terms of Recruitment and Work

In addition to declining profits from shipping operations, coolie recruitment in China started encountering significant challenges due to the Chinese government's restrictions that were passed in response to popular outrage about involuntary recruitment. In the spring of 1866, the administration of La Compagnie de l'Approuague in French Guiana requested the help of the French consulate in Shanghai to recruit Chinese coolies. The company had been granted 200,000 hectares of land in French Guiana with the authorization to import 1,000 workers to be employed in gold mining, agriculture, and forestry operations. When recruitment from Africa and India did not bring the expected results, it contracted with the Shanghai-based Remi, Schmidt et Cie to procure between 300 and 400 Chinese coolies. According to the company's claim, the French Consul-General refused to authorize recruitment. The Minister of the Navy and Colonies responded to the company's complaint by stating that the French diplomatic missions did not have any involvement in the privately operated coolie trade other than to monitor the implementation of emigration regulations.[28]

In the same year, 1866, the Qing government announced new measures against the coolie trade and could rely on foreign governments' cooperation.

---

27 Northrup, "Indentured Indians," 260–261.

28 Guyane 55: F3 (06–10).

France and Britain believed that the coolie trade should be handled in free-market terms since they were aware that their increasing involvement would entail further Chinese intervention. The fact that Remi, Schmidt et Cie was in liquidation by the time of the correspondence indicates that foreign companies were not making the profits they expected from the coolie trade, especially when they lacked official backing and Chinese cooperation. While the "free market" was to be free from local interference, it did not function without colonizer patronage.

The difficulty in finding workers in China compelled French colonists to look for alternative channels, most of which were recommended by entrepreneurial Chinese. In late 1874, a Chinese businessman named Salomon who lived in Surinam contacted the planters of Cayenne (French Guiana) and offered to procure a certain number of Chinese coolies whose contract terms were about to expire in Surinam. At the time, escape from plantations was a common form of coolie resistance[29] and, in many cases, the runaways found refuge in the plantations of a neighbouring country. To prevent potential disputes with these, the government of French Guiana put Mr. Salomon in contact with the Chamber of Agriculture and Commerce, a private body, and authorized coolie arrivals on the condition that they possessed the necessary paperwork as proof of their perfect freedom of movement. In other words, the competition for cheap labour provided canny intermediaries with opportunities to turn their influence over labourers into a lucrative business and this very competition was used by migrants to improve their work conditions by moving between plantations in different countries. (For Japanese intermediaries, see Chapter 20 in this volume.)

While French colonists were trying to keep their plantations supplied with labourers from Asia, Britain was committed to using its control over Indian coolies to its advantage. In 1890, it restricted coolie importation to French plantations in the Indian Ocean on the grounds that Indian coolies were mistreated by French planters. While Britain probably needed the Indian coolies in its colony of Mauritius at the time, this naturally does not mean that the coolie complaints were fictitious.

In fact, since the beginning of the trade to French Réunion, the coolies had to deal with challenges ranging from unsanitary conditions to racial prejudice. According to official reports, the arrival of new and diverse ethnic groups precipitated the outbreak of previously unknown diseases on the island and

---

29 David Northrup, *Indentured Labor in the Age of Imperialism, 1834–1922* (New York: Cambridge University Press, 1995), 127.

mortality rates were high. Resistance among the coolies was common and they brought forward complaints about unpaid wages, ill-treatment, contract violations, and excessive work hours.[30] In 1868, from an island population of 180,000, a total of 19,069 individuals were in prison, and another 10,694 had been sent to "discipline workshops," i.e., forced labour. Overall, 75 percent of the sentences were imposed on coolies, 80 percent of whom were Indian which meant that one-third of the Indian workers were in prison at any given moment.

The first response of the French planters to British restrictions was to look for workers from Africa because, by the late 1880s, anti-Chinese bigotry as embodied in the "yellow peril" discourse had permeated the colonial world. French colonists observed that many Chinese coolies opened businesses after the termination of their contracts and became "prosperous" without assimilating into the community.[31] The fact that Chinese workers and merchants sent most of their income generated in Euro-America to their families in China decreased this immigrant community's economic value in the eyes of French and British politicians. Nevertheless, the resistance of Africans on the coast increased costs to levels the French colonists considered unbearable. As a result, they accepted Chinese coolie recruitment as inevitable despite unrelenting scepticism towards the Chinese.[32]

Francis Vetch, a Réunion-born merchant based in Fuzhou, managed the coolie shipments in 1901. In a new approach, Vetch sought workers in the agricultural interior of China, especially among the Catholic converts, with the help of missionaries and French consuls. Vetch did not have much difficulty in the wake of the Boxer Rebellion, during which Chinese converts were subject to persecution by the anti-Christian crowds. Soon, due to the efforts of such entrepreneurs, China's labour market which was initially concentrated in treaty ports had expanded into the rural hinterlands where foreign railroad and mining companies also needed "free" labour. Moreover, the influence of Christian priests countervailed the power of Chinese foremen who tended to act like "little mandarins" if given too much power.[33]

30 Joseph Cooper, *Un continent perdu, ou l'esclavage et la traite en Afrique (1875)* (Paris: Librairie Hachette, 1876), 53–54.

31 Édouard Madier de Montjau, *De l'émigration des chinois au point de vue des intérêts européens* (Paris: Maisonneuve et Cie, Éditeurs, 1873), 14.

32 Fauvel, "La main-d'œuvre chinois dans nos colonies," *Revue de Géographie* 53 (December 1903): 112–127.

33 Fauvel, "La main-d'œuvre chinois," 119.

5 Qing Officials React to Workers' Mistreatment and Labour Resistance

As discussed, the most significant impact of the post-slave emancipation competition for cheap labour was the opening of a labour market in Southern China, a policy facilitated by the turmoil during the Opium Wars and the Taiping Rebellion (1839–1860). The Chinese official restrictions on labour mobility were the last obstacle to the growth of this "free" market. The Treaty of Nanking – imposed by Britain after the First Opium War and signed in 1842 – opened Amoy, Fujian, Ningbo, Shanghai, and Canton as treaty ports. It also eliminated Chinese intermediary companies (*hongs*) by letting British merchants "carry on their mercantile transactions with whatever persons they please."[34] Immediately after the Qing government signed similar treaties with other powers, Chinese dealers sent mass coolie shipments to French Réunion, Spanish Cuba, Brazil, and Peru. However, as soon as the profit potential of the new business became obvious, they began to employ illicit methods such as kidnapping and deception to procure coolies for foreign companies: Attracting people to distant places with much higher travel costs and greater personal risks was more difficult than convincing them to migrate to relatively closer and more familiar Southeast Asia.

While Qing China's officials were discontented with the illicit recruitment operations of foreign companies in treaty ports, they came to value the remittances sent by the overseas Chinese. In addition, sending the poor and criminals abroad was a convenient way of eliminating potential social problems such as unemployment.[35] Local populations, of course, showed no similar acceptance of the kidnappings, especially after the horrendous stories of coolie uprisings on foreign vessels began to spread. In 1852, the attempt of the coolie trader Francis Darby Syme (of Syme, Muir and Company) to set free a coolie broker named Lin Huan from prison triggered a large riot in Amoy.

Lin Huan had been taken into custody for holding a man against his will to sell him to a British coolie trader, and it was typical for British companies to use their privileges to protect their brokers. Amoy's elites and officials had long been campaigning against the notorious coolie trade and had been posting warning placards throughout the town. On 22 November 1852, a crowd rushed

34 *Treaties, Conventions, Etc., Between China and Foreign States* (Statistical Department of the Inspectorate General of Customs, 1908), 161.

35 Jiali Peng, "Shijiu shiji qishi niandai hou zhongguo laoli ziyuan wailiu he 'zhu zai' fanmai de gaochao [The high tide of China's labour outflow and 'pig' trade after the 1870s]," *Zhongguo jingji shi yanjiu*, no. 4 (1987): 125–144.

to the coolie "barracoons," but it was stopped by British marines who killed 12 people. In protest of the Lin Huan incident, the Chinese merchants closed their shops and refused to open them until justice was served. During the trial, the coolies testified that they were promised work in Fuzhou but instead put in depots for overseas shipment and were not allowed to leave. Many others testified witnessing the beating of the coolies. After the incident, the coolie shipments from Amoy came to a gradual halt and moved further south, to Canton, Hong Kong, and Macau.

Similar incidents occurred in Shanghai in mid-1859. Tensions were high due to frequent kidnappings by local brokers, and the families of the kidnapped had been patrolling the port, hoping that they could release their relatives from foreign ships. On 29 July, after the *Gertrude*, a French coolie ship rented to the Spanish, left the port, a group of coolie relatives attacked two British sailors and killed one. The crowds continued to attack foreigners in the following days until the magistrate beheaded the Chinese kidnappers and displayed their heads on poles to appease the masses.

Amid common resentment against the coolie trade, expressed in public protests and widely circulating placards in Canton, Amoy, and Shanghai, Britain continued to lead the changes to create a free labour market. The Beijing Convention, signed in 1860 after the Second Opium War, confirmed the liberty of Chinese individuals who chose to enter into engagements with British subjects and "ship themselves and their families on board any British vessel at any of the open ports of China."[36] In the same convention, the two countries agreed on regulations regarding emigration. However, kidnapping and deception remained widely used methods since the Chinese refused to be traded like enslaved people. In the words of Shelly Chan, "the free Chinese emigrant was not found but had to be made."[37]

The Qing government included an addendum to the convention it signed with Britain and France six years later. While agreeing not to hinder voluntary engagements, it declared its commitment to punish illegal recruitment operations with the death penalty. Even if France and Britain did not ratify the agreement, the Qing imperial government used the addendum of 1866 as the emigration law of the country.[38] While the regulation did not end the coolie trade and kidnappings, it expanded the role of Qing officials and foreign

36 *Treaties, Conventions, Etc., Between China and Foreign States*, 240.

37 Shelly Chan, *Diaspora's Homeland: Modern China in the Age of Global Migration* (Durham, NC: Duke University Press, 2018), 22.

38 Ta Chen, *Chinese Migration, With Special Reference to Labor Conditions* (Honolulu: University of Hawai'i Press, 2015), 18.

consuls. In 1873, the Qing government was able to terminate the coolie trade in its most blatant form, first in Hong Kong and then in Macau. After this date, the trade functioned like "free contract labour," although foreigners continued to see Chinese workers as indentured coolies regardless of their vocational skills or official protection. Recognizing and treating Chinese workers as free wage earners would entail uncontrollable labour mobility, which could disrupt production and trigger racial conflicts in the colonies. As a result, the liberalization of the Chinese labour market came with further restrictions on labour migration as in the case of the Chinese exclusion laws in the US.[39]

The Qing emigration policy thus underwent a significant change from limiting emigration to the proactive defence of Chinese emigrant interests abroad. The addendum of 1866 not only regulated the recruitment and embarkation of coolies in China but also their assignment and work conditions in their final destinations. A further purpose was to guarantee the repatriation of Chinese workers from colonial territories at the expense of foreign employers. Two years later, the Burlingame-Seward Treaty secured the right of free movement for Chinese residents in the US. In 1877, China opened consulates in Cuba and Peru to protect Chinese emigrants. The final step for the liberalization of emigration came with the decree of 13 September 1893, which allowed Chinese emigrants in foreign countries to return home at will. While Chinese emigrants, workers, and merchants alike, had previously returned to China, local officials often extorted money from them or, during their absence, stripped their relatives or neighbours of legal protection. The 1893 decree aimed to encourage emigrant return so that their savings could be used in China.[40]

Already in the negotiations between China and Britain in 1859, the Qing government posited that coolies sent to plantations had special arrangements. Prince Gong, the head of the Qing Foreign Affairs Bureau, stated that although the coolies were "employed by foreigners and received monthly salaries, they are not selling their labor to foreigners, they should be considered as if China were loaning them to foreign countries to use."[41] The Qing government, while cooperating with foreign governments to create a labour market based on voluntary work contracts rather than deception and coercion, came to realize that globally circulating Chinese workers would provide China with the opportunity to position itself as a sovereign state in the new global order. Even

39 The Chinese exclusion laws were a series of laws that aimed to prevent Chinese labour migration to the US. They were in place from 1882 to 1943.

40 Ching-Hwang Yen, *Coolies and Mandarins: China's Protection of Overseas Chinese During the Late Ch'ing Period* (Singapore: Singapore University Press, 1985), 249–280.

41 Cited in McKeown, "The Social Life of Chinese Labor," 73.

if Qing officials recognized the freedom of Chinese workers to sign work contracts with foreign employers, they reserved their right to intervene in these engagements if national interests were at stake. This official protection would significantly empower Chinese workers in the new century.

Notwithstanding these regulations for the liberalization of emigration, Chinese officials did understand and appreciate the potential profits from the global coolie trade. In 1879, a representative of the China Merchants' Steam Navigation Company contacted the French consulate in Shanghai on behalf of the company director Tong King-Sing (Tang Jingxing) to inform the consul about plans to transport Chinese emigrants to the Sandwich Islands (Hawai'i) and bring back Chinese passengers from San Francisco. The prominent reformist bureaucrat Li Hongzhang founded this navigation company in 1872 to break the monopoly of foreign navigation companies in China's coastal cargo traffic. Although the company was technically a private enterprise, it enjoyed considerable government support in the form of low-interest loans and the exclusive right to ship the grain tribute tax to Northern China. As the coolie trade turned into a profitable business, the company was planning to benefit from the worldwide Chinese circulation by forming a branch of the main company specializing in the transportation of Chinese passengers.

The foreign traders, for their part, expressed concerns about the unpredictable reactions of Chinese passengers. In 1848, Chinese convicts aboard the *General Wood* from Hong Kong to Penang started a rebellion that resulted in the killing of the captain and many passengers.[42] Similarly, in 1852, Chinese coolies onboard the *Robert Bowne*, bound for San Francisco, killed the US captain and most of the crew, presumably because the captain asked them to cut their queues for sanitary reasons.[43] Returning to China without the legally-required queues was impossible for coolies. In sum, the consul was hopeful that the handling of coolie transportation by Chinese merchants would mitigate the accusations that the coolie trade was a new form of slavery and that it would eventually alter the negative public opinion in China. The government's backing of the China Merchants' Steam Navigation Company would ease the entire process of coolie importation from recruitment to transportation. However, the later operations in the Chinese labour market suggest that instead of actively steering the coolie trade, Chinese officials opted to leave the

42 Yang, *Empire of Convicts*, 180.

43 "The Massacre on Board the Ship Robert Bowne," *New York Times*, 5 August 1852. A queue was a Manchu hairstyle required to be worn by male subjects of Qing China. The failure to comply with this mandate would result in the penalty of execution for treason.

market to its own devices, except for cases in which workers expressly asked for their intervention.

6 The Coolie Experience and the Making of the Modern Chinese Worker

Scholars have characterized the late-nineteenth-century changes in Qing emigration policy as a leap in China's integration into the modern world order through the active use of its sovereign rights. However, less studied is how the experience of Chinese overseas workers shaped emerging socio-political identities in early-twentieth-century China when the Qing Empire was shaken by revolutionary nationalism. The nationalism of this period found its voice in the discourse of "dual enslavement." Leading late-Qing revolutionaries such as Zou Rong and Sun Yatsen asserted that China was enslaved by both the ruling Manchu dynasty and foreign imperialists who used the dynasty's weakness to exploit China's resources and human power.[44]

Writers in the nationalist press argued that colonialism had taken a new form and no longer did it require territorial occupation or the "massacring of peoples" but rather it worked by exploiting a land's essence and the fruits of people's labour.[45] For example, the prominent Vietnamese nationalist Phan Boi Chau appealed to solidarity from his Chinese audience by reminding them that it was Chinese immigrants from southern provinces who had increased the quality of the Vietnamese land with their agricultural knowledge and labour. How could they have stayed silent about the appropriation of their labour by French colonizers? What happened in Vietnam (French colonization) was about to occur in China unless the Chinese acted against their subordination in solidarity with other colonized peoples.[46]

Concurrently, Chinese nationalists highlighted the global hatred of and racism against Chinese labour to mobilize workers against colonial intrusions.

44 Zou Rong, "The Revolutionary Army," *Contemporary Chinese Thought* 31, no. 1 (1999): 32–38. Sun Yatsen argued that China should be called a "hypo-colony" because it was not enslaved by one but all countries. Sun Yatsen, *San Min Chu I: The Three Principles of the People* (Taiwan: China Cultural Service, 2003), 17.

45 Xia Yi, "Wei dianyue tielu zaocheng jinggao quan dian [A Warning to Yunnan on the Completion of the Yunnan–Vietnam Railway]," in *Yunnan zazhi xuanji* (Beijing: Zhishi chanquan chubanshe, 2013), 515.

46 Boi Chau Phan, "Ai yue diao dian [Grief Over Vietnam and Condolence for Yunnan]," in *Yunnan zazhi xuanji*, 641–642.

In 1904, during the Russian expansion into Northern China, an article warned workers that foreign occupation would entail great risks for labourers. It stated,

> you do not know that in foreign countries they will not allow us Chinese to work. This is because their labor organizations, although they talk about international unity, they speak only for the white race and do not include us, the yellow race. Because of our temperament, our willingness to work hard for little money, and our refusal to observe the regulations when we work in foreign countries, they look upon us as though we are snakes and serpents and hate us so much that they can barely restrain themselves from killing us.[47]

The article shows an accurate knowledge of the latest working-class struggles and the challenges of racism. According to the author, the implication for workers of China's colonization would be enslavement or, worse, mass killings. Chinese workers as hate objects for colonizing countries and their working classes became a cause célèbre for nationalists.

The "enslavement" strain of argument soon incorporated the nineteenth-century coolie experience – not only in political debates but also in literature – as Chinese authors evoked the trauma of nineteenth-century indenture to highlight the dangers of colonialism.[48] References to the coolie experience mushroomed, especially in 1902, when the US indefinitely extended Chinese exclusion laws, and again in 1904 when the US Congress refused to renew the Gresham-Yang Treaty, which granted settled Chinese labourers in the US the right of return after visiting their country. In May 1905, the Shanghai Chamber of Commerce protested against the exclusion laws by calling for a boycott of US companies and merchandise. Once the boycott started in July, vast numbers attended meetings in at least ten big cities, including Shanghai, Canton, and Amoy, where speeches, pamphlets, and short novels narrated the horrors of the coolie age.[49]

While the boycott centred more on the status of merchants and students than workers, a novel titled *The Golden World* published two years after the anti-US boycott testifies that there were voices in defence of workers. A female

47 Cited in S. A. Smith, *Like Cattle and Horses: Nationalism and Labor in Shanghai, 1895–1927* (Durham, NC: Duke University Press, 2002), 53.

48 Elizabeth E. Weber, "Reimagining Coolie Trajectories: The Triumphant Return as Political Statement in Late Qing 'Coolie Fiction,'" *Literature Compass* 13, no. 5 (2016): 300–310.

49 Mae Ngai, *The Chinese Question: The Gold Rushes and Global Politics* (New York: W. W. Norton, 2021), 294–296.

character in the novel addresses a gathering of women, advocating that, as the mothers of Chinese nationals, they must fight for Chinese workers irrespective of their class status because if the workers would gain their rights, merchants and students would also receive them. Many workers supported the boycott through strikes or in unison with their employers or affiliated secret societies.[50]

A paradoxical aspect of the campaign was that French companies benefited most from the boycott as US entrepreneurs recruiting for the construction of the Panama Canal had to turn to French companies for labour importation. At the time, France was building the Yunnan-Indochina railway and was in dire need of labour as the malarial climate of Yunnan province required constant replacements for those deceased. The difficulties encountered by the French company in labour recruitment for a project inside China suggests that, by the early twentieth century, Chinese workers had learned their lessons from the notorious coolie trade and many Chinese in major coolie recruitment centres refused to work for the railway. Those who signed contracts deserted the worksites immediately after they saw the conditions; many appealed to Qing officials for help in payment disputes, and a few mistreated workers wound up attacking or even killing their foreign employers.[51]

In provinces as far afield as Fujian, protests occurred against recruitment for the Yunnan railway. In 1905, Cen Chunxuan, the governor of the provinces of Guangdong and Guangxi, banned recruitment in Canton after complaints and frequent public protests. At the time, China did not have a national labour law. However, many railway and mining agreements signed with foreign governments, including the Yunnan Railway Treaty of 1903, included clauses that required fair wages, reasonable working hours, and ethical treatment of Chinese workers. These agreements defined Qing officials as authorities in cases of worker strikes. Although the agreements left sanctions to the initiative of individual officials, it was clear that strikes and labour conflicts were now factored into government considerations when foreign investors were involved.

French diplomats worried that the negative image caused by the labour conflicts in Yunnan would harm their recruitment operations for overseas projects. In fact, foreign newspapers, like the Chinese press, defined the treatment of the Chinese in Yunnan as a "grave scandal."[52] A French inspector who visited

50 Smith, *Like Cattle and Horses*, 48.

51 Selda Altan, "Politics of Life and Labor: French Colonialism in China and Chinese Coolie Labor During the Construction of the Yunnan-Indochina Railway, 1898–1910," *International Labor and Working-Class History* 101 (2022).

52 D. W. Crofts, "A Grave Scandal," *North China Daily News*, 20 June 1906.

Southern China in 1904 reported that France lagged in regulating Asian emigration and employment. In English and Dutch colonies, work was subject to strict regulations that did not leave the treatment of workers to the discretion of employers. In contrast, the French companies viewed workers as a commodity with an endless supply. As a result, Chinese workers chose to sign contracts with British and Dutch companies and avoided the French ones.

This shows that by the early twentieth century, Chinese workers were cognizant of the global competition for their labour and this knowledge enabled them to demand better contract terms by comparing the terms proposed by different colonizer powers. They also knew how to navigate the Chinese labour market by manoeuvring both Qing officials and public opinion into protecting their interests. Hence, even though foreign governments had opened the Chinese labour market by force, the market had already developed its own dynamics based on the experience of the coolie age. While foreign governments and businesspeople continued to view Chinese workers in terms of the nineteenth-century coolie system, the modern Chinese worker had already emerged – in a deterritorialized labour market.

7 Conclusion

To date, scholars of Chinese labour history have studied the emergence of a Chinese working class with reference to local dynamics such as culture, hometown networks, or membership in secret societies. Many have argued that Chinese labour struggles before the May Fourth Movement, an anti-imperialist and cultural movement that originated out of student protests in Beijing on 4 May 1919, were subsumed under nationalist activism, and hence did not have an autonomous character.[53] The "dual enslavement" discourse and the coolie narratives that were reinvigorated in the early twentieth century contributed to the ascendancy of a victimization paradigm in scholarship, which also underestimated Chinese workers' agency.

However, this comparative perspective on the coolie trade in the nineteenth century and the increasing worker activism in the early twentieth century suggest a different picture. Despite the imposition of a particular labour regime that combined the characteristics of slavery and wage labour, Chinese workers developed the means to protect their interests beyond their national borders.

53 The May Fourth movement was a socio-political movement led by Chinese intellectuals between 1917 and 1921 for national independence and cultural rejuvenation. The Chinese Communist Party was born out of the May Fourth activism among workers and students.

On the one hand, these means included the use of the Qing state's sovereign powers or regional labour networks while on the other, they also took the form of less organized or individual responses, such as individual absenteeism or mass desertion and selective acceptance of labour contracts. The study of class formation within the limits of national histories and mass movements has obscured the minuscule struggles of mobile workers as instances of a larger movement. Class formation in any country cannot be understood without discussing labour mobility and migration in the very age when capital dismantled national borders for its borderless expansion. The Chinese coolies' global experience reminds us that labour exploitation gains new layers and triggers alternative forms of resistance once it overflows the factory grounds and expands into inter-racial and cross-border spaces.

Unfortunately, we do not have accurate figures as to how many Chinese left China for work and how many came back from the 1830s to 1911. According to Adam McKeown, in the century from 1840 to 1940, approximately 20 million Chinese – including 750,000 as indentured labourers – emigrated, 90 percent of them to Southeast Asia.[54] We know that in the period under review in this chapter, and even without including the migration to Southeast Asia, at least 1.3 million Chinese travelled to foreign countries with the hope of returning to their villages financially better equipped to create a new and better life for their families.[55] If we remember that in these migrations they gained invaluable insight into the meaning of being a labourer through their encounters with foreign employers and alternative labour regimes, it becomes clear that the making of the Chinese working class cannot be understood without considering the stories brought back by the returnees. Thus, this chapter highlights the significance of the Chinese labour market's colonial "liberalization" in the nineteenth century as the broader context of class formation in China.

---

54 Adam McKeown, "Chinese Emigration in Global Context, 1850–1940," *Journal of Global History* 5, no. 1 (2010): 95–124.

55 According to Chinese scholars the number of Chinese coolies contracted to foreign countries from 1801 to 1925, including those in Southeast Asia, amounted to 2.3 million. Hansheng Chen, ed., *Huagong chuguo shiliao* [Documents Concerning the Overseas Emigration of Chinese Laborers], vol. 4 (Beijing: Zhonghua shuju, 1981), 169–172; 194; 240. For the emigration motives of Chinese peasants, see Michael Williams, *Returning Home with Glory: Chinese Villagers around the Pacific, 1849 to 1949* (Hong Kong: Hong Kong University Press, 2018).

CHAPTER 9

African Agency versus State and Capital Control

Migration to the British Northern Rhodesian Copperbelt in Comparative Perspective, 1920s to 1960s

Dácil Juif

Abstract

Migration played a key role in supplying labour for African large-scale mining throughout the twentieth century. In this chapter, we assess workers' agency versus state-capital control of migration, residence in mining towns, and labour mobilization in Northern Rhodesia's Copperbelt compared to the other main mines of Southern and Central Africa. While in the Belgian Congo and Portuguese Angola officials resorted to active recruitment – often under coercion – in British Northern Rhodesia they only did so for a few years during the advent of industrial copper mining. A high turnover with temporary stays in rural areas was promoted in the British colony but not imposed as effectively as in South Africa. Although women were welcome in urban areas for their reproductive role, they also carried out a range of marketed activities. African mineworkers' unions only emerged in the 1950s and attained moderate achievements, although in surrounding mining regions they were either banned or virtually inactive.

Keywords

circular migration – mining – Northern Rhodesia – Southern and Central Africa – stabilization – trade unions – women

1 Introduction

The region of Southern and Central Africa contains the most mineral-rich soils on the continent, and in several countries, industrial mining started about a century ago or even earlier. Since the areas where minerals were extracted on a large scale were originally sparsely populated, the African labour force was, at least in the early stages, predominantly composed of migrants. By migrant workers, we refer to movers within colonial or national borders as well as

 | DOI:10.1163/9789004686991_010

cross-border movers. Some of these moves were "permanent," usually as a family, and others "circular," bringing single-male migrants to jobs and back to their rural homes, resulting in labour turnover of various durations. The period studied covers the start of large-scale mining activities until the independence of Northern Rhodesia in 1964.

Research has shown that the duration of the mining industry's reliance on circular migrant labour and the distances these migrants travelled varied throughout Southern and Central Africa and also over time.[1] Although companies and states looked at surrounding mines for examples, country-and time-specific geological, economic, and political conditions influenced the choice of implementation of labour stabilization policies or reliance on circular migrant labour. This chapter provides a comparative assessment of certain aspects of relations between African migrant workers, colonial states, and capital. A key contribution is the assessment of the Copperbelt province of Northern Rhodesia in the mirror of the other main historical mining areas of the larger region: the Katanga mines in the Belgian Congo, the diamond mines of Lunda in Angola, and the Rand gold mines of South Africa (see Figure 9.1).[2] The present chapter expands on previous work by adding an understudied Portuguese colonial mining setting to the comparative assessment of mining labour provision, and by discussing the role of women and workers' mobilization in shaping labour conditions.[3]

The industrial mining settings studied here display important similarities including the period of extraction (since the late nineteenth or early twentieth century) and the role of large monopolistic companies. At the same time, they

1 For example, Dácil Juif, "Migration and Stabilization: Mining Labor in the Belgian Congo, Northern Rhodesia, and South Africa," in *Migration in Africa: Shifting Patterns of Mobility from the 19th to the 21st Century*, ed. Michiel de Haas and Ewout Frankema (London: Routledge, 2022), 203–228.

2 We will focus on South African gold mining labour because there is much more information available than on diamond mine labour in the period studied. Gold mining began in Southern Rhodesia from 1890 as smaller-scale European capitalist endeavours. Botswana will not be included in the analysis since diamond mining operations began only after its independence.

3 Little comparative research on Sub-Saharan Africa is available. Ralph Austen, *African Economic History: Internal Development and External Dependency* (London: James Currey, 1987); Carolyn Brown, "Mining," in *General Labour History of Africa: Workers, Employers and Governments, 20th-21st Centuries*, ed. Stefano Bellucci and Andreas Eckert (Woodbridge, UK: James Currey, 2019), 151–176; Simon Katzenellenbogen, "The Miners' Frontier: Transport and General Economic Development," in *Colonialism in Africa 1870–1960*, vol. 4: *The Economics of Colonialism*, ed. Peter Duignan and L. H. Gann (Cambridge: Cambridge University Press, 1975), 360–426.

entail differences in local conditions that make the comparison worthwhile, such as the respective colonizing power and, after 1910, independent South Africa, the presence and power of white populations, and the main mineral extracted (gold, copper, or diamonds).

The first industrial mining operations in the region began after the discovery of vast diamond deposits in Kimberley in 1867 and gold in the Witwatersrand in 1886 (both in South Africa). Soon, the industry became concentrated in the hands of a single company, the *Anglo American Corporation of South Africa*. A few decades later, after the colonizer powers' "Scramble for Africa," rich diamond deposits were discovered in the northeastern region of Portuguese Angola and were exploited from 1917 until 1977 by an international, monopolistic company, Diamang (*Companhia de Diamantes de Angola*) until its partial nationalization before the complete pull-out in 1988. When the value of copper and other non-precious metals in international markets rose at about the same time, the Central African Copperbelt emerged as a major industrial mining region. In the Belgian Congo, copper was exploited by the Belgian *Union Minière du Haut Katanga* (UMHK) from 1911 until the nationalization of the mining industry by the independent Congo's president in 1967. In British Northern Rhodesia, where copper production started in the late 1920s, two companies, the *Rhodesian Selection Trust*, a British corporation with American financial backing, and the *Anglo American Corporation*, a South African conglomerate, controlled mining in the country until they were nationalized in 1969.

This chapter brings together insights from secondary literature and empirical findings from primary sources, including statistical yearbooks and demographic surveys, correspondence between companies and governments, and mining company records on African labour. First, it discusses how labour was provided in different settings. We follow the contemporary officials' differentiation between "voluntarily" labour-seeking migrants and "recruited" migrant labour.[4] Forced labour for public works and other purposes was common in colonial Africa,[5] which raises the question concerning the possible extent to which mining in this region also relied on coercion to secure sufficient labour.

---

4 Whether or not Africans voluntarily sought to work for Europeans may be debated, given that the options available to them were often restricted and taxation and land alienations acted as push factors. See, for instance, Charles Feinstein, *An Economic History of South Africa: Conquest, Discrimination, and Development* (Cambridge: Cambridge University Press, 2005). Moreover, in Portuguese Angola, men sometimes volunteered for mine work because they would otherwise have been forced to do so under worse conditions.

5 Marlous van Waijenburg, "Financing the African Colonial State: The Revenue Imperative and Forced Labor," *Journal of Economic History* 78, no. 1 (2018): 40–80; Alexander Keese, "Searching for the Reluctant Hands: Obsession, Ambivalence and the Practice of Organising Involuntary

We discuss the coercive recruitment by the Northern Rhodesian mining companies in conjunction (or not) with the colonial state, how it changed over time, and how it compared to the mineral-rich neighbouring Lusitanian and Belgian colonies, and to South Africa. We argue that endemic labour scarcity, state ideology, and the response to international pressure, for example on the part of the International Labour Organization (ILO), help explain the observed variation.

Second, when discussing labour migration to the mines, we highlight the occasional dissonance between how colonial and mine authorities envisaged labour mobility and its actual reality. The government ideology concerning whether one-time movement and permanent settlement of workers with families or temporary circular movement of single workers was desired, varied considerably between mining settings and over time. However, due to African agency, the reality of the permanent versus temporary nature of residence in mining towns sometimes varied from what the state and companies planned or from what most contemporary intellectuals thought to be the case.[6]

Third, we explore the role of women in mining camps. Although their presence in towns has been considered an indicator of real "stabilization" or permanent urbanization, women in colonial Africa, and more so in mining, were largely excluded from the formal wage labour force and therefore usually resided in mining towns as workers' wives or companions. Colonial authorities (and companies) considered the role of women in the industrial capitalist labour system to be purely, or largely, reproductive. In this context, questions arise as to whether or not they carried out market activities and what level of decision-making power they had within their households. We try to approach these and other questions despite the near absence of data on women's roles in primary sources.

Fourth, we discuss how communication between capital (and state) on the one hand, and workers on the other hand, took place. Labour mobilization and strikes were important means for miners to transmit their discontent. The relations between African labour and management were sometimes also mediated

---

Labour in Colonial Cuanza-Sul and Malange Districts, Angola, 1926–1945," *Journal of Imperial and Commonwealth History* 42, no. 2 (2013): 238–258.

6 For example, after the Great Depression, reports into the causes of the 1935 Copperbelt strikes revealed that despite the British colonial aim to tie residence permits in urban areas to work contracts, a considerable number of men – and women – had not returned to their rural areas despite having lost their jobs. James Ferguson, *Expectations of Modernity: Myths and Meanings of Urban Life on the Zambian Copperbelt* (Berkeley: University of California Press, 1999).

by appointed tribal elders and, after the Second World War, by trade unions. However, there were important differences across mining areas and African trade unions were only legal and active in Northern Rhodesia for little more than a decade, while the other states examined here completely suppressed industrial labour organizations. We discuss the possible reasons for the (non-) emergence of African mineworkers' trade unions from a comparative perspective as well as their effectiveness in attaining improvements in workers' living standards.

In the next section, we address the issue of labour recruitment and retainment including the involvement of coercion from the beginning of mining activities until ca. 1940. The third section deals with labour stabilization and the presence of women in mining areas, mainly after the Second World War, and the emergence of African trade unions as well as the effects of their actions on wages and welfare.

2 Mining Labour Systems in Comparative Perspective until the 1940s

2.1 *Labour Recruitment and Coercion in Southern and Central Africa*

As mentioned, the mining industry required large amounts of labour that was not always readily available onsite. Therefore, men were recruited from distant places and brought to work at the mines. If willingness to engage in wage labour for Europeans was lacking, coercion – sometimes at gunpoint – was used. Recruitment was more abusive in some cases, and more so in the earlier period of mining.

When mining commenced in British Northern Rhodesia in the late 1920s, it was easier to obtain "free" labour – in the sense that it was not forced to work – because, compared to other areas, Africans had less access to resources to generate food or cash. This was a deliberate colonial policy: White settlers took the best land, and railroads were situated to serve them and market their products, thereby bypassing African areas.[7] In addition, the British colonial government successfully collected indigenous taxes in cash only. The Bemba and Bisa tribes of the east of Northern Rhodesia made up the most important source of mining labour throughout colonial times. Since their home region was particularly unsuited for agriculture and market access was very poor,

7 Frederick Cooper, *Decolonization and African Society: The Labor Question in French and British Africa* (Cambridge: Cambridge University Press, 1996), 44.

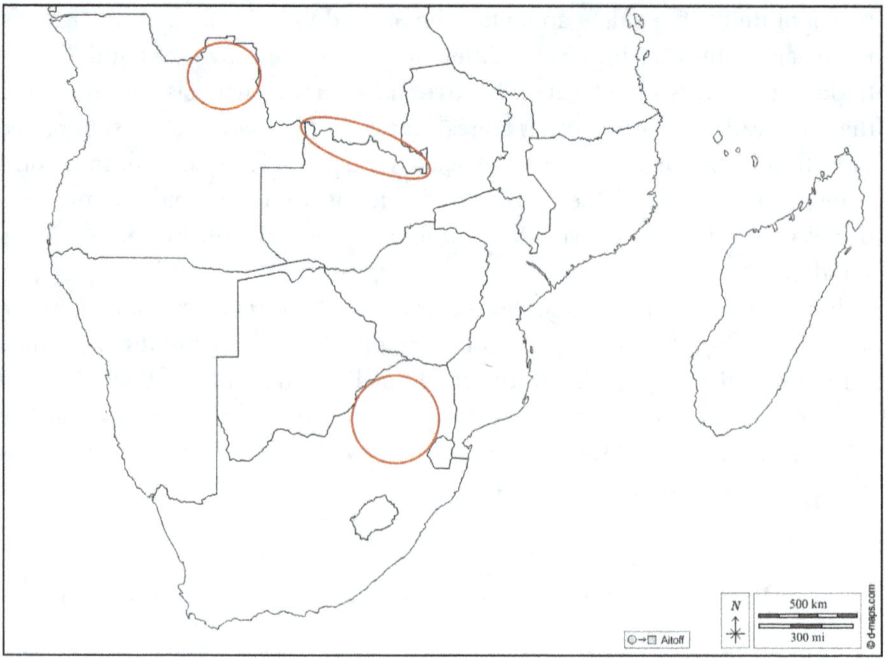

FIGURE 9.1 Location of the mining areas discussed (encircled in red)
SOURCE: MODIFIED FROM HTTPS://D-MAPS.COM/M/AFRICA/AUSTRALE/AUSTRALE06.GIF

they had to resort to searching for wage labour elsewhere to earn money to pay the taxes imposed on them by the colonial power. For the same reason, Northern Rhodesian Africans had already been working for wages in surrounding colonies controlled by other European powers; for example, at the Katanga (Belgian Congo) mines, which had opened across the border 15 years earlier.

During the mine construction boom around 1930, the Northern Rhodesian mines successfully pressured the government to prohibit recruitment by the Belgian UMHK to increase the pool of native labour. Even with this political intervention from British authorities, the companies still had to recruit a substantial part of their workforce in relatively distant places in the east of Northern Rhodesia and Nyasaland[8] and they even formed a recruiting organization, the Native Labour Association in 1930. However, the high levels of

8 Fergusson, *Expectations*, 49.

TABLE 9.1 Percentage of voluntary manual workers at UMHK, Diamang and Northern Rhodesian mines

	UMHK	Diamang	Northern Rhodesia
1921	23		–
1929	45	50	30–40
1934	98	66	ca. 100
1939	76	55 (1938)	ca. 100
1944	74	62	ca. 100
1949	92	57	ca. 100
1959		59	ca. 100
1964		66	ca. 100

Note: "Voluntary" refers to workers who were not recruited but arrived on their own account

SOURCES: ANNUAL REPORTS UMHK – DEPARTMENT OF INDIGENOUS LABOUR, SEVERAL YEARS; DIAMANG INDIGENOUS LABOUR SECTION ANNUAL REPORTS (SPECIAL THANKS TO LEO DOLAN FOR SHARING THESE DATA); FERGUSSON, *EXPECTATIONS*, 49

unemployment during the Great Depression in the years following 1931 ended any recruitment.[9]

Other mining areas had to rely on recruitment to a larger extent than Northern Rhodesia. For instance, the Katanga Copperbelt, where land was neither well suited for agriculture nor for herding, was very sparsely populated.[10] From the start of mining activities in the 1910s, a government-assisted recruiting agency, the Bourse du Travail du Katanga (BTK), recruited labour for the mines in Belgian colonial territory, particularly in the province of Kasai in the centre of the Congo and the Lomami district of Katanga. Other private recruiters operated on behalf of UMHK in neighbouring colonies. Coercive labour recruitment by the mine police force in collaboration with the military was common for the Congo in the 1910s and 1920s[11] and even during the

9 Elena Berger, *Labour, Race and Colonial Rule: The Copperbelt from 1924 to Independence* (Oxford: Clarendon Press, 1974), 12.

10 Dácil Juif and Ewout Frankema, "From Coercion to Compensation: Institutional Responses to Labour Scarcity in the Central African Copperbelt," *Journal of Institutional Economics* 14, no. 2 (2018): 313–343.

11 Adam Hochschild, *King Leopold's Ghost: A Story of Greed, Terror and Heroism in Colonial Africa* (Boston/New York: Houghton Mifflin Harcourt, 1998), 275.

Great Depression the UMHK continued to rely on the active recruitment of new workers (see Table 9.1). Many forcefully recruited workers deserted, often already during the journey to the mines (approximately 10 percent in the early 1920s) and to counteract this, from 1922 onwards, breaking a work contract became illegal and punishable by imprisonment and fines.[12] Coercive recruitment by UMHK private recruiters outside Belgian territory includes the case of Angolans by Robert Williams and Company in the province of Moxico (ca. 300 to 500 miles from the mines) between 1917 and 1921. Perrings documents how, although stipulated differently in an interstate agreement with the Portuguese, outright coercion was employed in recruitment and deserters were brutally punished. Due to the deplorable recruitment practices and the high mortality in the mine camps, out of the 3,479 Angolans recruited in this period, 536 men died on company premises, and a further 778 deserted.[13]

Similarly, in Portuguese Angola, the colonial state introduced the coercive contracted labour regime (*shibalo*) – prevalent in other parts of the colony – per agreement with the Diamang company in 1921 to the Lunda district: Generally, locals not satisfying the conditions for exemption were forcefully recruited for labour in public road and railway construction, but in this case, the company had exclusive access to *shibalo* labour.[14] Similar to the Congolese case, African village headmen (*sobas*) were ordered to round up recruits, including minors, for the mines through the state's indigenous police force (*cipaios*). Diamang and UMHK continued to recruit labour throughout the colonial period, but the UMHK gradually reduced coercive recruitment since mine work became increasingly attractive. Correspondingly, desertion rates declined at UMHK (from 9.5 percent in 1922 to 2–3 percent directly after the Second World War),[15] and at Diamang (from 10–25 percent in the 1910s and 1920s to just 2.8 percent in 1937). However, the reduction in this latter case was mainly due to the company hiring personnel or paying local public employees (*chefes do posto*) to accompany recruits on their way to the mines. From 1948 onward, the introduction of motorized transport contributed to the arrival of contracted labour at the mines.[16]

12 Raymond Leslie Buell, *The Native Problem in Africa,* 2 vols. (New York: Macmillan, 1928), 2:553–554.

13 Charles Perrings, "'Good Lawyers but Poor Workers': Recruited Angolan Labour in the Copper Mines of Katanga, 1917–1921," *Journal of African History* 18, no. 2 (1977): 237–259.

14 Todd Charles Cleveland, "Rock Solid: African Laborers on the Diamond Mines of the Companhia de Diamantes de Angola (Diamang), 1917–1975" (PhD diss., University of Minnesota, 2008), 93.

15 Annual Reports UMHK – Department of Indigenous Labour.

16 Cleveland, "Rock Solid," 71.

South Africa's gold mines relied on a sophisticated system of organized recruitment to continuously replenish its transient workforce. This included agreements with foreign governments and recruitment stations throughout Southern Africa, as far as Nyasaland and Northern Rhodesia.[17] The system expanded throughout the twentieth century. At a peak in the early 1970s, 70 percent of the workforce in the Rand gold mines had been recruited north of South Africa, while the remaining workers were recruited within South Africa, Lesotho, and Swaziland.[18] In South Africa, recruitment in distant cheap labour pools was a strategy for companies to save costs, as they were exempted from having to compete with South African manufacturing wages. While there is little evidence of outright coercion being used, some sending regions' colonial governments, particularly in the case of Portuguese Mozambique, profited from taxing returning migrants and imposing fees on the South African mines' recruitment company.[19]

As to the reasons for the difference in reliance on forced recruitment, we already mentioned the availability of labour in Northern Rhodesia. In addition, the British government seems to have been more compliant than other metropolitan powers with international labour guidelines in their colonies.[20] Britain ratified the 1930 ILO Forced Labour Convention[21] as well as the 1936 Convention on "Recruiting of Indigenous Workers," and earlier ones such as the Slavery Convention. The Forced Labour Convention elicited controversy since several representatives argued that reliance on fully free labour alone was not practicable in colonial societies. While Britain promptly ratified the convention, the French government refused to ratify it until 1937 and the Belgian one until 1944.[22] While all empires decreed the end of coerced labour

17 Juif, "Migration and Stabilization."

18 Jonathan Crush, Alan Jeeves, and David Yudelman, *South Africa's Labor Empire: A History of Black Migrancy to the Gold Mines* (Cape Town: David Philip Publishers, 1991).

19 Kleoniki Alexopoulou and Dácil Juif, "Colonial State Formation Without Integration: Tax Capacity and Labour Regimes in Portuguese Mozambique (1890s-1970s)," *International Review of Social History* 62, no. 2 (2017): 215–252.

20 Cooper, *Decolonization*, 219.

21 The convention initiated an internationalized approach to the labour question in colonies. Colonizer states had imposed different types of unfree labour: the labour tax (*taxa bracal* in the Portuguese Empire or *prestations* in the French Empire), military conscripts used for public work projects, forced cultivation of crops, and punitive labour. The rules were intended to make the allegedly "primitive" populations "learn how to work," their implementation required rudimentary infrastructures for administrative and commercial purposes, and they could be employed to punish "vagrants" and other "wrongdoers." Keese, "Searching," 242.

22 Cooper, *Decolonization*, 30.

after the Second World War, the authoritarian Portuguese government only initiated the abolition of forced labour in 1961.[23]

Northern Rhodesia's mining companies felt less of a need to resort to coercive recruitment since local men voluntarily offered their labour to a sufficient extent (despite mine management's complaints to the government that labourers left for work in neighbouring colonies). The lack of alternative cash income sources to pay taxes, and the fact that companies pressured the colonial government to prohibit recruitment by UMHK for Katanga in 1929 contributed to alleviating the scarcity of labour. In addition, Britain faced demands from war allies (particularly the US) regarding the elimination of coercive labour. At the same time, however, the British Colonial Office gave much more decision-making power to local governments that were reluctant to remove penal sanctions for contract breaches in Northern Rhodesia.[24]

2.2 *The Circular Migrant Labour System*

When the Northern Rhodesian copper mines started to operate in the late 1920s, many officials and mine managers held that a rapidly circulating male labour force reduced labour costs, maintained tribal authority and culture, and forestalled social risks of proletarianization. Moreover, it was argued that a migrant labour system would reduce inequalities between the countryside and towns, as urban-earned wages would only be paid upon return to the rural areas. In the employers' view, migrant labour meant that wages could be lower than the real social cost of subsistence, because African subsistence production in the villages, especially the labour of women, subsidized the raising of children and care of the elderly. Given the general lack of faith in the future of the mining industry and the fear of another slump like the Great Depression of the early 1930s, the prevailing view was that workers should easily be able to return to their former tribal life.[25]

In support of the circular migrant labour system, in 1936 the Governor of Northern Rhodesia, Sir Hubert Young, held that recruitment of migrant labour with deferred payment of their wages should be promoted to make sure that

---

23 Keese, "Searching," 240.

24 The British continued to rely on penal sanctions for breaking contracts in several colonies, including the Rhodesias, until the 1950s. In distinction to civil suits to which violators would be subject in the Western countries, sanctions typically involved jailing of workers who "deserted," because, allegedly, Africans were unreliable workers and their way of life meant that they could not be sued. Cooper, *Decolonization,* 167.

25 Elena Berger, "Government Policy towards Migrant Labour on the Copperbelt, 1930–1945," *Transafrican Journal of History* 2, no. 1 (1972): 83–102, here 86.

the workers returned to their villages. He did, however, accept that a small number of skilled Africans settled permanently in the Copperbelt, as long as the majority was repatriated to their home villages by the mines at regular intervals.[26] By 1937, the repatriation of workers every two years was an accepted government aim.[27]

Nonetheless, Rhodesian mining companies opposed expensive organized recruitment and repatriation as men in the 1930s were willingly flocking to the towns in large numbers. The mine managers also resisted the government's mandate which ordered that a share of the workers' wages should be transferred to the rural areas. A 1942 report for the general manager of Mufulira Mines Ltd. stated that transferral gave workers the "wrong impression of the wage they received" and that it reduced their purchasing power because prices were higher in villages.[28] However, opinions concerning stabilization remained divided among employers. For example, Ernest Oppenheimer, chairman of the (mainly) South African company Anglo American Corporation, even in 1940 wanted workers to be encouraged to return home after approximately 18 months to avoid any expenses in housing and management that a policy of long-term settlement would imply.[29]

Mine managers looked at surrounding industrial mines for alternative models of labour policy. UMHK was already reducing labour turnover from the mid-1920s by a policy of settling a large portion of its workforce with families around the mines where they would be subject to tight regulation and control of most aspects of their lives.[30] After 1927, the company only hired workers for three-year contracts, and the majority were re-engaged when their contracts expired. Several inspectors reported back to Northern Rhodesia's government and mines about the situation of UMHK labour, and they generally praised the conditions in which workers and their families lived from the mid-1920s onward. For example, a quarterly report on "Rhodesian Natives in the Katanga" sent by the British Vice Consul in October 1929 stated that "the conditions under which natives work could hardly be bettered as regards feeding, hospitals, housing, and general treatment. Conditions have much improved since I arrived here in 1925." As a compound manager of the Roan Antelope mine

26 Berger, *Labour, Race*, 35–36.

27 Berger, "Government Policy," 92.

28 ZCCM Archives, 10.7.10B; cited in Juif and Frankema, "From Coercion to Compensation," 332.

29 Berger, *Labour, Race*, 70.

30 Dácil Juif, "Paternalism, Profitmaking and African Agency: Mining and the Spread of Education in the Belgian Congo," in *Cliometrics of the Family: Studies in Economic History Series*, ed. Claude Diebolt et al. (Cham, CH: Springer, 2019), 305–332.

(part of Mufulira Copper Mines Ltd.) wrote to the Native Labour Association in 1938, "in terms of welfare, Union Minière is undoubtedly ahead of us. Practically the whole work is carried out by the Roman Catholic priests and sisters [...] Women and children at U.M. are treated as being the mine's strength and under their discipline and control. Schools are provided and women participate e.g., in horticulture."[31]

In Angola's Diamang mines, wives and children were also encouraged to join workers. According to Cleveland, "Diamang officials displayed great enthusiasm for the relocation of entire families – or partial families for men with multiple wives – to its mines. Administrators from both settings determined that workers accompanied by wives and/or children deserted less frequently and were generally more 'stable.' Many wives accompanied their husbands to Diamang's mines to handle the evening cooking and cleaning duties, while at other times children went to assist with these daily tasks, with or without their mothers."[32] Even though approximately 23 to 40 percent of contracted men were joined by their wives in the 1940s, the labour conditions for all family members were so harsh that retention rates were very low and hence the company failed to develop a long-term, fixed African labour force.

On the opposite side of the spectrum, the South African system of gold and diamond mining labour was clearly rotatory and almost exclusively housed single male workers in compounds until the 1970s. In the 1930s, contract periods commonly ranged from ten to twelve months and workers returned to their tribal homes for periods between contracts. At the Rand gold mines, married quarters were only provided for 1,474 especially skilled African workers out of a labour force of approximately 200,000 men in 1930.[33] Similarly, in Southern Rhodesia, where white settlers strongly influenced institutional development, "circular migration remained dominant through the end of the colonial period and deep into the early post-colonial era."[34]

An important question is whether the circular migrant labour system was favoured and respected by Africans. African workers in the early twentieth century probably only aimed to sell their work to Europeans in small units of time,

31 ZCCM Archives, 10.7.10B; cited in Juif and Frankema, "From Coercion to Compensation."

32 Todd Charles Cleveland, "Minors in Name Only: Child Laborers on the Diamond Mines of the Companhia de Diamantes de Angola (Diamang), 1917–1975," *Journal of Family History* 35, no. 1 (2010): 95.

33 Berger, "Government Policy," 90.

34 Kate Frederick and Elise van Nederveen Meerkerk, "From Temporary Urbanites to Permanent City Dwellers? Rural-Urban Labor Migration in Colonial Southern Rhodesia and the Belgian Congo," in *Migration in Africa*, ed. de Haas and Frankema, 275.

to obtain enough money to build up herds, invest in agricultural improvement, marry, or, in the case of Northern Rhodesia, pay the hut tax. However, independently of government policy and whether they received longer or shorter contracts, a significant portion of workers – 31 percent according to a 1931 estimate – had chosen to settle in the mining towns of Northern Rhodesia with their families.[35] The Forster Commission of Enquiry into a strike in 1940 noted that many women were present and that companies encouraged this. The Commission did not recommend changes in a system that assumed rapid turnover of six to eight months on average.[36] Throughout the 1940s, the Northern Rhodesian Government remained reluctant to hasten stabilization and feared that substantial improvements in urban facilities would not only encourage the permanent settlement of existing residents but also lead to a large influx of people from the villages.[37]

In sum, the government of Northern Rhodesia lacked the administrative machinery to enforce its plan – largely against the interests of the mine managers – of a fully migrant labour system, common in South Africa, with organized recruitment, deferred payment, and the prohibition to settle in towns without a work contract. However, different from Katanga, neither mine companies nor the state wholeheartedly invested in a stabilized workforce until after the Second World War.

2.3 *Communication between Africans and Capital: Towards Trade Unionism*

African miners in Northern Rhodesia and across Africa went on strike before African trade unions were allowed. The Copperbelt strikes of 1935 and 1940, where 7 and 17 miners respectively died from police bullets (others were hurt), raised the issue of African unionization among governments and international organizations. Workers were not without representation, as the Northern Rhodesian mine companies had established councils of tribal elders or "tribal representatives" in their compounds, who not only mediated in domestic quarrels but also met with compound managers to report grievances or receive information. However, these representatives were not among the leaders of the strikers, as the workers felt that they had drifted to the side of management.

The commissions of enquiry into these strikes blamed "agitators" (including migrants from southern colonies who had developed industrial consciousness elsewhere) but recommended addressing "African advancement" to higher

35 Cooper, *Decolonization*, 46.
36 Cooper, *Decolonization*, 131.
37 Berger, *Labour, Race*, 68.

positions reserved for Europeans (as many of the discontented workers were already performing this type of work without recognition). However, because of the rotating and largely illiterate workforce, the Forster Commission of 1941 did not yet recommend trade unions to be established in this part of Africa. This attitude lasted through the Second World War and, after a strike in 1945, the Northern Rhodesian governor rejected a trade union bill arguing that "African workers are not yet thought to be sufficiently advanced to be able to satisfactorily organize a Trade Union and take proper part in Trade Union activities."[38]

While the reasons for the introduction of African trade unions in British Africa have been debated, the theory that British authorities were forced to introduce them as a result of unrest has largely been dismissed. It has also been described as a progressive act of the Colonial Office from a belief in its social value and a desire to improve labour conditions. Elena Berger holds that, in Northern Rhodesia, the deteriorating relations between the government and the European Northern Rhodesia Mine Workers' Union (M.W.U.) were the main cause that prompted officials to promote African trade unionism.[39] The M.W.U. insisted on "equal pay for equal work,"[40] and the government (and, at this stage, also the mine companies) feared that this would convince Africans of this principle, while the authorities wanted to promote "African advancement" to skilled jobs without paying European wages.[41] Finally, in 1946, the Secretary of State in London announced that it intended to assist African workers in forming trade unions, and in 1947, a Scottish trade union representative was sent by the Colonial Office to instruct Africans in the Copperbelt on industrial action. In 1949, all trade unions were amalgamated and the African Mineworkers' Union (A.M.U.) came into being. In its early years, the union faced many difficulties, including language barriers, in furthering African advancement.[42]

In comparison to neighbouring mining areas, the Northern Rhodesian A.M.U. was relatively active whereas in the Belgian Congo, although trade unions were authorized from 1946, adherence remained comparatively low throughout colonial times. In Katanga, workers seem to have been appeased

38 Berger, *Labour, Race*, 84.

39 Berger, *Labour, Race*, 87.

40 This was demanded by European workers across Southern Africa on the assumption that, at equal pay, employers would always prefer a European over a black worker.

41 Berger, *Labour, Race*, 95.

42 Berger, *Labour, Race*, 91–96.

by the paternalistic system, as missionaries partnered with state and company management, and schooling was used to guide the masses in the desired direction, while carefully ensuring that a revolutionary spirit was not awakened.[43] In Northern Rhodesia, workers possibly also originated from or had experience working in areas where labour consciousness and unrest were more common, which was not the case in Katanga.

In colonial Angola's Diamang mines, "there is little evidence that the company's African work force engaged in overt resistance, such as strikes or trade unionism, so commonly pursued by African mineworkers elsewhere across southern Africa." Instead, employees "engaged in a wide variety of acts, often hidden, to improve their living and working conditions without fear of the violent reprisals that open, collective action would have surely elicited."[44] In South Africa, where mobilization of black mine workers had already taken place in the 1920s, European workers and voters inhibited African labour organization at a time when trade unions were emerging in other parts of Africa.

In a broader African comparative perspective, according to Charles Orr, in regions south of the Equator, where large-scale mining dominated, industrial relations were less developed than in North and West (British and French) Africa, where small-scale farming, commerce and industry predominated.[45] He ascribes this to the deeply rooted attitudes of paternalism and the power and wealth of employers. European unions in these settings (but not in the Congo or in Angola, where white unions were absent until after the Second World War and independence, respectively) usually did not integrate Africans but regarded them as potential job rivals. European employers, governments, armed forces, and white workers were thus holding back African mobilization and violently repressed insurrections. At times, tribal enmities also played a role in this context.

43 John Higginson, *A Working Class in the Making: Belgian Colonial Labor Policy, Private Enterprise, and the African Mineworker, 1907–1951* (Madison: University of Wisconsin Press, 1989).

44 Cleveland, "Rock Solid," VIII, 144–165.

45 Charles A. Orr, "Trade Unionism in Colonial Africa," *Journal of Modern African Studies* 4, no. 1 (1966): 65–81.

3 Stabilization, Women, and Trade Union Struggles in Northern Rhodesia

3.1 *Stabilization in Northern Rhodesia*

During the Second World War, the labour question and especially stabilization became an issue for state officials who, however, postponed major changes to the post-war period. Since the 1940 Copperbelt miners' strike – even though British colonial policy was generally to leave decisions to the officer on the spot – tension arose between the Colonial Office on the one hand and the local government and companies on the other.[46] According to the view of the Colonial Office, permanent urbanization had to be accepted and the living standards of Africans in cities had to be improved. In contrast, local government officials were much more rural-oriented and largely uninformed about urban Africa – in the realm of compound managers – and held on to indirect rule and the preservation of tribal life.[47]

The Colonial Office's position was in line with international bodies, among which stabilization had become the consensus. From 1947 onward, the ILO, joined by the Inter-African Labour Conferences in 1948, and some organisms of the UN reopened a discussion on migration and stabilization.[48] Although necessary, migration risked fostering social "evils" – family separation, prostitution, and the drainage of male labour power from agriculture. Furthermore, it had the disadvantage of leaving industrial work in the hands of a floating population rather than a disciplined class. To address this, migration, therefore, had to be carefully regulated and should be reduced by inducements to stabilization such as family wages, family housing, and the provision of social services to urban areas.

While the policy was being debated, workers settled in urban regions. J. Clyde Mitchell from the Rhodes Livingstone Institute[49] noted that in Luanshya and the Roan Antelope mine town 24.4 percent and 7.5 percent, respectively of the African population in 1951 had been born and brought up in town, while

---

46 For example, the Colonial Office feared that penal sanctions to enforce contracts might lead to ILO criticism and that restrictions on African labour unions were likely to drive industrial organizations underground or into the political field.

47 Berger, "Government policy," 96.

48 A UN document cited the "abnormal mobility of labour in Africa" and associated it with low wages and lower productivity. Cooper, *Decolonization*, 365.

49 The Rhodes-Livingstone Institute (RLI) was founded in 1937 to remedy the ignorance of African life that had made the 1935 mine strike such a shock. Clyde Mitchell, "African Urbanization in Ndola and Luanshya," *Rhodes-Livingstone Communication*, no. 6 (Lusaka, 1954), 17, and table XVII.

a further 20 percent of the inhabitants could be classified as "temporarily urbanized."[50] Until stabilization became official policy, Africans living in town were not accepted as permanent residents and housing at the mines, much of which was of poor standard and quite unsuitable for families, was tied to employment.

Finally, in the mid-1950s, the model of the workers' families residing in the cities became official policy and the following years saw a large urban influx with much improvisation in terms of housing and substantial unemployment in the public townships adjacent to mining compounds. Between 1950 and 1960, for instance, the population of the main Copperbelt towns (Luanshya, Ndola, Kitwe, Mufulira, and Chingola) increased from 175,000 to 288,000, whereby the share of women in the population (all ages) ranged from 43 to 45 percent.[51] According to Fergusson, urban workers continued to retain strong rural ties for several reasons: affective relations, uncertainties about urban security when confronted with ill health or old age (given the lack of social security), and the possibilities of families to combine wage labour with agriculture or petty trade to enhance collective opportunities. As a result, children were still sometimes sent back to the countryside to be brought up there.[52]

Stabilizing labour was a political choice that was not made everywhere in Southern and Central Africa. While Northern Rhodesia did so in the 1950s, the Belgian colonial authorities stuck to the policy of stabilization introduced in the 1920s in Katanga (and Diamang tried to attract workers accompanied by family members), South Africa defended a migrant African labour force and "separatism," which directly contradicted the international consensus of the time. In South Africa, an escalation of urban strikes during the Second World War and the gold miners' strike of 1946 sharply confronted the government and the voting white public with black urban and industrial labour. After the nationalist victory in the 1948 elections, the South African government made determined use of police powers to reinvigorate the migratory system[53] and expelled large numbers of city dwellers to rural areas and to a life deemed to

50 Berger, "Government Policy," 100.

51 1950 Demographic Sample Survey of the African Population of Northern Rhodesia, and Demographic Survey of eight main towns in Northern Rhodesia 1960, carried out by the General Statistics Office of the Federation of the Rhodesias and Nyasaland.

52 Fergusson, *Expectations of Modernity*. Even in the 1970s, urban dwellers had not cut ties and returned to their rural hinterlands during the crisis that hit the copper mining sector particularly hard. Deborah Potts, "Counter-Urbanisation on the Zambian Copperbelt? Interpretations and Implications," *Urban Studies* 42, no. 4 (2005): 583–609.

53 The length of stay of foreign circular migrant workers in the mines varied by origin and in time but was never more than two years in a row. Juif, "Migration and Stabilization."

be "African." The South African government also considered that fracturing the working population into segments with different access to urban legal status and housing would allow for better control.[54]

3.2 *The Role of Women in Northern Rhodesian Mining Towns*

Stabilization brings us to the role of women in industrial-mining cities. On the one hand, allowing men to be joined by their wives was initially a strategy of Northern Rhodesian mining companies to compete for labour with other employers, and the managers soon recognized its benefits regarding workers' productivity. In 1943, the Anglo American Corporation compound manager admitted: "the married employee is undoubtedly more content than the single, he is better fed, looked after and clothed and has the rudimentary of a sense of responsibility which tends to make him a more stable and efficient worker."[55] Moreover, the relocation of reproduction to mining towns would allow to "socialise the children who would become workers to the demands of industrial work discipline."[56] On the other hand, management resented the costs of housing and feeding women and children, which resulted in many families living in mine compounds under inadequate conditions until the 1950s.

The activities performed by women were supposed to be "reproductive," i.e., providing for the maintenance of mine workers, thereby enhancing workers' productivity and reducing the labour costs for the company (e.g., cooking their meals). These activities included subsistence agricultural production to supplement workers' meagre rations, fetching workers' rations provided by the company, cooking their meals, preparing their baths, etc. The Roan Antelope Mine at Luanshya, which most actively and successfully encouraged the presence of wives, established a system of agricultural plots on otherwise unused company land for use as gardens in the early 1930s and other mines subsequently followed this example.[57]

Using oral history, George Chauncey challenged the view derived from official company and state reports that adult women in the Copperbelt during colonial times had all arrived as workers' wives and were financially dependent on their husbands. Instead, he argued that customary wives, who had usually

54 Cooper, *Decolonization*, 263.

55 Cited in Jane Parpart, "The Household and the Mine Shaft: Gender and Class Struggles on the Zambian Copperbelt, 1926–64," *Journal of Southern African Studies* 13, no. 1 (1986): 38.

56 George Chauncey Jr., "The Locus of Reproduction: Women's Labour in the Zambian Copperbelt, 1927–1953," *Journal of Southern African Studies* 7, no. 2 (1987): 136.

57 This was also common practice at Diamang and UMHK mines (see Higginson, "A Working Class" and Cleveland "Rock Solid").

married the workers in the rural areas, arrived but also single women, who stayed at relatives' homes, and "temporary wives," liaisons that were formalized in the mining towns. At times, customary wives engaged in beer brewing, marketed their agricultural produce, and sometimes housed visitors, whereby all these activities comprised sources of additional cash income. For single women, domestic and sexual services were the main marketed activities. Some of the single women decided to temporarily marry a man, as this would give them access to company housing and land and permit them to expand the range of their economic activities. On their part, the companies would certify these temporary unions, as they reasoned the workers would be better cared for.[58]

Because of the relatively small numbers of women, and the advantages that married status brought men (having a single-family house and a domestic attendant), temporary wives enjoyed a relatively strong position within the couple and, for example, made demands regarding the splitting of workers' wages. Some women were also very successful in their own marketed activities, and the financial independence that resulted from such activities went against the companies' – as well as the colonial governments' – aims of women providing for workers. Therefore, these marketed activities were sometimes curtailed in mining towns.[59]

From the advent of mining activities, Rural Native Authorities expressed great concern over urban marriages not being approved by relatives. The migration of single women to mine towns challenged the structure of rural societies, in which marital relations and bride services played a substantial role.[60] The government subsequently endorsed the tribal authorities' concerns and, at the same time, feared that the presence of too many women could accelerate

58 According to Parpart, "The Household," women also played a role in class struggles and they actively participated in the strikes of 1935, 1940 and 1952, 1955 and 1956. Moreover, the pressures and costs of married life appear to have been a significant factor pushing miners towards unionization, and women participated in trade union meetings.

59 For instance, in 1929 and 1933, the Roan and Nkana mines prohibited home brewing in their compounds. The reason for this, however, was mainly due to concerns about the effects of alcohol consumption on labour productivity. Chauncey, "The Locus," 144–145. Additionally, the establishment of full-scale businesses in the compounds was not allowed, and thus some women established groceries and restaurants in the nearby municipal townships run by the colonial government. Chauncey, "The Locus," 153. Government officials also repeatedly, although often unsuccessfully, tried to crack down on prostitution, which was a major source of income for single women. Parpart, "The Household," 39.

60 Chauncey describes how in the matrilocal Bemba society, as women left the villages, fathers were deprived of the "free work" of the men who married their daughters.

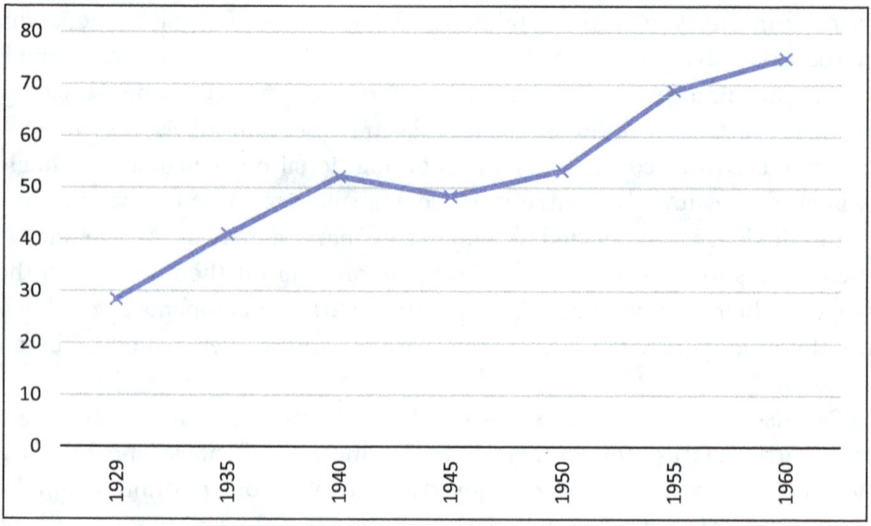

FIGURE 9.2 Share of married workers in the Northern Rhodesian mines in percent
SOURCE: DATA FROM FERGUSSON, *EXPECTATIONS OF MODERNITY*

proletarianization. In the late 1930s, the government decided to actively support the Native Authorities by allowing them to set up control posts and impose fines on women who tried to leave for the urban areas without being in possession of a marriage certificate issued by the Native Authorities. This system continued for more than a decade, although companies did not cooperate and did not restrict the access of women without marriage certificates to the compounds. In 1936, the government also set up Urban African Courts, whose members were appointed by rural elders, chiefly to increase the level of control over urban Africans, especially women.

In the 1950s, corporate and colonial policy took a turn. The official rhetoric of stabilization – of the British colonial government and international organizations – stressed that women were key to creating an African urban working class: They would determine the cultural standard of the home and the upbringing of children. "The African woman," the Inter-African Labour Conference (IALC) concluded in 1955, "has an essential part to play in the consolidation of family life and in the development and maintenance of social and cultural standards."[61] By 1960, the share of married workers in the Northern Rhodesian mines had increased to 75 percent from 30 percent in 1929 (see Figure 9.2).

61 Cooper, *Decolonization*, 366.

Companies also became keener to create a stable and predictable African workforce with European values. To placate discontent among African workers (and to save labour costs), they advanced Africans to skilled positions (see below). At the same time, the policy towards women changed and became geared towards creating model families. African social welfare workers were appointed to teach miners' wives to adapt to urban lives and to be good housewives, and they mediated in domestic quarrels to promote marital stability. By reserving housing and resources for the model workers' families, and condemning prostitution and adultery, the compound staff made life more difficult for non-married women.

3.3 *African Trade Union Struggles in Northern Rhodesia: Wage Increases, Colour Bar, and African Advancement*

As mentioned above, African trade unions in Angola, Congo, and South Africa were either illegal or largely inactive in the period under review. In British Northern Rhodesia, the colonial visions of post-war society made both the state and capital the targets of an escalating series of claims from African labour (and political movements). If the industrial worker was to be productive like a European, he should be paid like one; his wife should be able to raise a family without having to engage in "African" economic pursuits. The A.M.U.'s central struggle focused on African advancement or access to certain jobs and wages. Mining companies were also seeking more flexibility to assign Africans to semi-skilled and skilled jobs and pay them less than whites. While the European M.W.U. fought to protect their jobs, claiming "equal pay for equal work," the latter policy was out of the question for employers, and the attempts of mine management to negotiate with the white union so that job categories were opened for lower-paid Africans only partially succeeded.

In 1952, a three-week strike instigated by the A.M.U. ended in arbitration through which African miners achieved substantial gains in across-the-board wage increases. While the starting rate for Africans was raised from 45 shillings per ticket of 30 shifts to 80, the debate concerning African advancement accomplished nothing[62] and the board of enquiry into the strike justified the continued existence of the "dual wage structure." The differences were extreme: In 1953, for example, the mines were paying 5,700 European miners a total of 10,055,981 GBP in wages, allowances, and bonuses (including profitability bonuses) whereas 36,147 Africans were receiving 4,470,287 GBP in wages and rations.[63]

---

62 Cooper, *Decolonization*, 341.

63 Northern Rhodesian Chamber of Mines Yearbook of 1956, pp. 69 and 76.

In January 1955, the A.M.U. initiated another strike that lasted for nine weeks. The union, in part because of the lack of progress over African advancement, was losing support and needed to show militancy. After companies' attempts to defeat the union, the Anglo American Corporation and the Rhodesian Selection Trust signed an agreement with the European M.W.U. which opened 24 job categories to Africans and the number of employment groups was raised from 9 to 12. At the end of 1956, 428 Africans (less than 2 percent of the workforce) had been promoted to these advanced jobs.

By the end of the 1950s, a conflict-ridden and frenzied time of social change,[64] African mine workers could compare their material gains with two reference points. African average wages (including cash wages and rations) in the mines went up over 300 percent from 61 GBP in 1950 to 200 GBP in 1958 compared to a ca. 50 percent rise in prices, i.e., real wages increased by 70 percent.[65] At the end of the 1950s, Northern Rhodesian copper miners earned (adjusted for purchasing power), on average, approximately 23 percent more than their counterparts in the Belgian Congo, at least *six times* more than Diamang miners, and 56 percent more than miners in South Africa, where African trade unions were banned and a strong formal colour bar relegated Africans to unskilled jobs.[66] However, despite these gains, the top wage paid to an African as late as 1962 was 50 shilling and 4 pence, whereas the bottom wage paid to a European was 64 shilling.[67] As a result, although African miners in Northern Rhodesia were better off than other African miners in the region, they were still much worse off than European miners. The issues of the colour bar had not been resolved when Northern Rhodesia became independent in 1964 and dual wages were not formally abolished until 1969.

4 Conclusion

This chapter illustrated the relations between African mining workers, the state, and capital in Northern Rhodesia in comparison with other mining areas of Southern and Central Africa from the beginning of industrial mining activities until the independence of the British colony. With this juxtaposition of

64 In 1956, a series of largely political strikes took place in the Copperbelt which induced the government to proclaim a state of emergency.

65 Juif and Frankema, "From Coercion to Compensation," Figure 4.

66 Juif and Frankema, "From Coercion to Compensation," Figure 4; Diamang Indigenous Labour Section Annual Report; Cooper, *Decolonization*, 346.

67 Cooper, *Decolonization*, 346.

historical cases, we aimed to bring contrasts in the organization of migrant mining labour to the fore and to shed light on the role played by colonial policy and government ideology, among other local conditions.

While in the Belgian Congo, Portuguese Angola, and South Africa the mining companies – often in close cooperation with the state – resorted to active labour recruitment throughout the studied period, in British Northern Rhodesia they only did so for a few years during the advent of industrial copper mining in the region. The use of coercion in recruitment was common in the early years in the Belgian Congo and for a longer period in Angola, but less so in Northern Rhodesia and South Africa. Apart from the lower labour scarcity, this was also related to the higher level of British compliance with international labour guidelines.

Moreover, while the Congolese copper company, the Belgian colonial state, and the Portuguese diamond mines embraced labour stabilization, the Northern Rhodesian government promoted – and the Rhodesian mining companies partly preferred – a circular migrant labour force that combined urban residence of a maximum of two years with stays in rural areas. However, measures to ensure that workers returned to their tribal areas at regular intervals, including recruitment and repatriation by the companies as well as a deferred wage payment system, could not be imposed as effectively as in South Africa, given lower state capacities and employers' resistance. Although in the Copperbelt women were welcome companions of workers for their reproductive role, they also carried out a range of market activities at the fringes of company and government oversight.

Concerning the communication between African miners and capital, Africans expressed their discontent during strikes which took place on both sides of the Copperbelt as well as in South Africa since the 1920s. However, while they were ruthlessly suppressed in South Africa and African workers' mobilization was prohibited, the Katanga miners were probably appeased by the paternalistic system, and in Lunda, even though discontent was widespread, there is little evidence of open resistance on the part of the miners. In Northern Rhodesia, African mineworkers' unions emerged in the late 1940s, were promoted by the British Labour government, and attained moderate achievements in terms of wage increases before independence. Future work in this area could contrast the labour conditions and well-being of migrant mining workers, within this region or a wider area, with the use of more internationally comparable measures.

PART 3

Empires and Labour Regimes – and "the Left"

CHAPTER 10

Introduction

Dirk Hoerder and Lukas Neissl

As in the case of the analysis of class or classes, present-day research on labour regimes starts and often remains framed, "containerized," in state-bordered approaches. Studies of colonial labour practices, however, consider the role of the respective specific colonizer or larger imperial power. This topic can also be pursued deep into the past, including labour regimes in Pharaonic Egypt, Assyria, biblical Israel, Song China, the empires of the savannah belt in Sub-Saharan Africa before the arrival of intruders from Europe, Tsarist Russia's annexation of Siberia and Central Asia in the seventeenth and eighteenth centuries, and others.

However, in this section the authors discuss the period of intensive industrialization after the economic crisis of 1873, lasting until 1877 or, even as "the long depression" to the early 1890s. Its main cause – among multiple factors – was financial overexpansion: It was one of the recurring financial "bubbles" of which the most recent one disrupted lives and developments in 2008/9. The 1873 crisis started in Vienna, the capital of the Habsburg Empire, and in the overextended German Empire and rapidly involved the rest of Europe and the US, before reaching into colonized societies such as British India and British South Africa.

The crisis followed the "liberalization" of investment laws and resulting speculative manipulations and insolvencies. High levels of unemployment reduced consumption or – viewed from the perspective of the unemployed and their families – meant impoverishment and, often, hunger. "Liberalization" is a problematic term. While the aim of reducing bureaucratic regulation and increasing options for initiatives has positive connotations, signalling this in everyday parlance hides its negative aspects, including the fact that the realization of options requires resources, whether financial means or, for workers, negotiating power. State-legislated liberalization provided additional advantages to those with resources, capital among others, and reduced options for those who lacked resources from the beginning. Economic liberalization in this form meant the promotion of economic elites and was deeply undemocratic – intentionally so.

Social reformers realized this early on, as did the short-changed workers. The latter began their struggles, and working families with nothing but their labour

 | DOI:10.1163/9789004686991_011

power as a resource in a liberalized market began to organize. Even more so, workers in the colonized world, whose very right to dispose of their labour was denied, began anti-colonizer struggles. Since the beginning of colonization, the imperial states supported "their" investors, whether by small-scale appropriation of the land of the colonized, and thus their means of production and livelihood, or by large-scale investment in extractive industries such as plantations or mines, both producing for export and undercutting options to secure livelihoods locally. To cement their position and advance their interests, elites have always needed a "deep" state.

During the depression of the 1930s, reformers and, after the destructions generated by the corporatist and fascist aggressors of 1937 (in China) and 1939 (at a global scale), ordoliberals in large segments of the industrialized world from 1945 onwards attempted to combine liberal market and production policies with a frame of societal responsibility for all members of a state. However, at this time, the struggle for more equal distribution of options remained a "privilege" of those short-changed in already wealthy societies whereas those in colonized societies first had to struggle for liberation from the yoke imposed on them. Reform could begin only after independence but, in many new states, was not pursued by those newly in power.

While colonizer elites – whether political, economic or both – could easily pursue their strategies based on superior guns in the colonies and subservient police forces "at home," workers in the colonizing states faced the dual challenge of exploitation in their unsupportable home and the issue that "their" elites imported labour from places where "home" was characterized by even more unsupportable living conditions. Working families saw the advantage of migrating – or of being migrated – which left working-class organizations, whether parties or unions, in a quandary. Could they struggle for the equality of a (postulated) international working class in, globally, highly unequal positions of economic development and exploitation? Or would they have to drop their worldwide aspirations? This dilemma led to sometimes acrimonious debates in the Second International, 1889–1914. Lucas Poy (Chapter 11) addresses these debates by switching the perspective from scholars' fixation on countries in the Global North with highly developed socialist and other left movements to the margins, here represented by socialists in Argentina. In this context, it is important to note that, at this stage, we will not enter into a discussion of why people who are "at the centre" of their lives should be designated as being "on the margins" and we will rather adhere to the way of thinking and terminology of the times. The Argentine socialists, in their majority immigrants themselves, questioned how they should react to more recent immigrants with less working-class organizational experience who (potentially) undercut their level of wages and living standard.

From the minutes of the international socialist congresses in Amsterdam and Stuttgart, 1904 and 1907, Poy reconstructs how the delegates from capitalist core countries considered themselves as ideologically advanced. Rather than analysing the global inequalities of imperial military, political and economic power, they saw their societies – and thus themselves – on top: civilized versus uncivilized countries; workers engaged in a conscious class struggle versus those not struggling; backward workers without an inkling of class consciousness. While they differentiated between "artificial," i.e., capitalist-induced, and "natural" migration, they also implied that workers in, and migrants from, the economically and culturally "lesser" developed countries were, as yet, unprepared or even unfit to participate in class struggles. Delegates from emigration countries, such as the Hungarian part of the Habsburg Empire, countered that emigration was a legitimate strategy for workers who need and want to improve their situation. A delegate from another region "on the margins," industrializing Japan, indicated that the "capitalist-induced" migrants, whom the core socialists maligned, happened to be of colours of skin other than white and "yellow" in particular. The position of capitalist-core-country delegates was deeply racist. In the end, a compromise resolution was formulated by "advanced" but thoughtful socialists from the continental Habsburg Empire of many peoples, which included the "highly" developed and capitalist Austria and Northern Italy as well as the "lesser" developed emigration regions of the Balkans and Galicia/Ruthenia (today Ukraine). The entire structure of this empire was based on an (uneasy) balance between peoples, and it would collapse only a few years later when, in the capitalized German-language segment, the political elite with the emperor as spokesperson declared war against self-determination-seeking Serbians. At the international socialist congresses, as in the Habsburg Empire, the issue of economic and racial hierarchies was placed at the centre stage by representatives from the margins. The delegates from colonizer/imperial countries – Dutch, British, French and, more recently, US American – stood by their own "advanced" position and represented views shared by most of the workers who had elected them.

The issues that left organizations faced and that the members of the Second International debated have by no means been resolved at the beginning of the twenty-first century. In the contemporary setting, workers in high-wage countries or, among them, in higher-placed segments of the labour markets tend to see those in low-wage sectors as a potential threat, and often rightly so. At the time of the writing of this book in March 2022, the P&O Ferries Company, operating between the British Isles and the European continent, stopped its business, fired 800 employees, and announced that a subcontractor, paying lower wages to foreign seamen, would take over. The company, owned through a financial holding company by the ruling family in Dubai, had already flagged out its ships from Britain to Cyprus. Its management argued that the British government had permitted a competing ferry company to operate under a work regime that did not respect the British legal framework.

Workers, unions, and left parties may respond to the perceived – or real – challenge posed by poorly-paid workers, imported by capitalist companies, by questioning the entire economic order, which would require revolutionary change. Alternatively, they might consider three different, albeit frequently connected ways to act: 1) exclusion, i.e., the attempt to block in-migration; 2) institutionalization, i.e., the confinement of low-wage workers to certain occupations and economic activities; or 3) solidarity, i.e., the attempt to raise lower wages to higher levels. The latter, both in the present and in the past, would need to include demands for global redistribution of wealth to improve conditions in emigration countries and in low-wage sectors "at home." Such redistribution might be advocated at the expense of capital, i.e., the propertied classes, and/or, almost unavoidably, also at the expense of the respective working classes. Redistribution or, far more cautiously, reform of the historical or contemporary labour regimes may also be pursued by state governments and elites in reaction to changing political and economic circumstances and interests.

In a survey of labour migration within the Eurasian landmass that successively comprised the Russian Empire, the Soviet Union, and the Russian Federation from the end of serfdom in 1861 to the recent past, Lewis Siegelbaum and Leslie Page Moch (Chapter 12) highlight incentives to leave home for work and measures to control mobility. They take a chronological perspective on the major migrations: The resettlement of peasants on land set aside for cultivation, arrangements for seasonal migration, rural-to-urban migration, wartime evacuation, and settlement for major resource development and infrastructure projects. The authors argue that although measures to incentivize and control labour migration before 1917 and after 1991 share strategies with contemporary migration regimes elsewhere, the Soviet state outstripped contemporary others in its ambitions, efforts, and institutions developed to control the migration of working people. The Commonwealth of Independent States (CIS), or perhaps more pointedly, neo-capitalist Russia, demonstrate to what extent regimes imposed on the macro-regional working population show similarities regardless of the political frame.

Radhika Kanchana (Chapter 13) argues that such similarities also exist in the region from Arabia to India, which was once part of the British Empire. When oil was discovered in the declining Ottoman Empire, the British and French imperial governments sought to further its dissolution and acquire parts of its territories. In pursuit of this interest, the British imperial elite in 1918 re-formed the (former) Ottoman oil-containing provinces of Baghdad, Basra, and Mosul as "their" state Iraq. Mosul, at the time of this empire-imposed state formation, was still held by Ottoman troops and Kurdish and Arab forces struggled for self-determination. The imperial Royal Air Force quelled this struggle with bombs and poison gas. On the resulting Iraqi-Arab "protectorate" state with its developing crude oil extraction and refining, the British imperialists, to the detriment of the local populations, imposed a labour regime that imported and advantaged subjects from their profitable colony-viceroyalty India. When in the early 1930s, Iraq and the Arab states achieved political independence – economic-capitalist "independence" (within the framework of the capitalist world market) only came about in the 1970s – the new states continued the labour regime with reversed roles, i.e., advantages for the local population and import of workers, first from Arab countries, especially Egypt and Palestinian camps with large surplus labour forces, and subsequently from the culturally more divergent Pakistan and Southeast Asia. As was the case under British overrule, these imported workers had no rights, suffered from miserable working conditions, and only received low wages. This labour regime, at present usually attributed to reactionary Muslim monarchies in western parlance, is a holdover from British colonizing interests.

As an imperial latecomer – and in this respect similar to imperial Germany after 1871 – the United States "of America," or more geographically correctly "of a part of North America," with few exceptions did not acquire territories for the purpose of colonization and pursued policies of "open access" to markets worldwide instead. In the second half of the nineteenth century, the main thrust was towards the populous societies of East Asia. The "liberal" market policies, supported by the US navy, first "opened" Japan, weakened under the late Tokugawa shogunate, in 1853, and, secondly, jointly with the other imperial powers, several of imperial China's port cities. Some of the resulting unequal treaties were rhetorically disguised as "gentlemen's agreements." In the twentieth century, the direction of US policies turned to focus on its "backyard," Mexico and the Central American states. It imposed a (neo)liberal economic regime with the resulting restrictions on workers for the benefit of big US companies and their capital investors. Just as the British and US secret services had ousted the Persian/Iranian reformer Mossadegh, in 1954 the Central Intelligence Agency (CIA), jointly with the State Department and the United Fruit Company (presently: Chiquita United Brands), ousted the reformist Guatemalan president Juan Árbenz Guzmán, whose policies would have changed the existing labour regime. In the following decades, especially under the presidency of Republican Ronald Reagan from 1981 to 1989, the US intensified its push for neoliberal economic regimes which impoverished working families to a degree that – as socialists in Amsterdam and Stuttgart had noted eight decades earlier – out-migration remained the only option available to improve standards of living. All headed north, many to California, where subcontracting companies turned them into cheap and replaceable workers, as Richard Saich (Chapter 14) demonstrates. The neoliberal Californian labour regime and the emergence of California as one of the leading economic centres of global capitalism strongly rested on the exploitation of migrant workers from Central America. However, by their own agency and "social movement unionism" they succeeded in improving their negotiating power. Among other factors, it was the specific dynamics of labour militancy of migrant workers that led to the revitalization of trade unions in California in the 1990s, as they did in Denmark (see Chapter 23 in this volume). The dialectics of labour and capital require careful analyses.

As the chapters show, the issue of developed-undeveloped, which the socialist delegates debated in 1907, remains unresolved to the present. Central American states have been kept in "underdevelopment." At the time of the completion of this volume, the issue of oil production (as climate-damaging fossil fuel) and energy supply (due to the war against Ukraine) is at the top of the news headlines. The century-long connection between energy and food production, oil extraction and plantation economy, and imperialism remains unchanged. The, since the nineteenth century, developing countries have used the wealth arising from their low-wage extraction economies to build their industrial capacity, and subsequently transform themselves into developed countries. Tool-making factories and, more recently, digitally controlled manufacturing, and resulting capital accumulation, have changed the former division into multiple world-systems to the Global North (developed) versus Global South (un-, underdeveloped) dualism, and neo-imperialism has deeply entrenched this divide. A century ago, the labour and socialist leaders present in Stuttgart had no intention to change the global hierarchies, while in the present, the economic elites meeting annually in Davos have no intention to change the current inequalities. The ideology-driven economy of growth, advocated in the Global North and the global financial institutions, relies on commodity supply – commodified labour included – from the economies, and this ultimately means peoples of no or little growth.

CHAPTER 11

Organizable and Unorganizable Migrants

Racism and Internationalism in Early-Twentieth-Century Social Democracy

Lucas Poy

Abstract

Following an initiative of the Argentine Socialist Party, the Second International discussed the "question of migration" during its congresses in Amsterdam (1904) and Stuttgart (1907). While the topic was not entirely new, on this occasion parties from the non-European "peripheries" played an important role and the discussion soon gave rise to a polarization of opinions on the racial problem and the movement of Asian workers. The chapter explores the positions of US and European delegates and juxtaposes them to those from Japan and other allegedly peripheral societies. Drawing upon secondary literature, socialist newspapers from different countries and archive materials of the Second International, the chapter shows how the "question" of migration, and the problems it posed to labour and socialist movements, sparked complicated arguments on the interplay between racism, solidarity, and internationalism.

Keywords

internationalism – migration – racism – Second International – socialism

The "local and global" of labour migration and working-class organization were reflected when, on 13 February 1902, delegates from different trade unions organized a meeting in downtown Buenos Aires "to discuss the best way to counteract the propaganda made in European countries, and especially in Italy, to direct the immigration flow to Argentina."[1] As it reported on the meeting, the official organ of the local Socialist Party reminded its readers that the party's "minimum program," approved during the founding congress of 1896,

1 This chapter is part of a broader research project on social democracy and migration on a global scale. Earlier versions of some of the sections appeared, in Spanish, in *Revista Izquierdas* (Santiago de Chile) in 2021.

 | DOI:10.1163/9789004686991_012

included an article calling for the "suppression of all artificial encouragement of immigration."[2] Convinced that the matter was worthy of international discussion, the party leadership submitted a draft resolution to the forthcoming congress of the Second International, to be held in Amsterdam in August 1904. The proposal was included in the agenda but was eventually postponed to the following international meeting, which took place in Stuttgart in 1907. On that occasion, the topic occupied a prominent place: A special commission met for three days, and leaders from different parties engaged in a sometimes unpleasant and acrimonious debate. In only a couple of years, the issue triggered a global discussion, prompting interventions and collecting experiences from places as distant as Sydney, Buenos Aires, Amsterdam, New York, Budapest, Warsaw, and Tokyo.

It is hardly surprising that the topic attracted the attention of socialist leaders and activists from all over the world, as the first decade of the twentieth century was the heyday of an era of unprecedented mass migration. Between 1850 and 1914, approximately 55 million Europeans migrated to the Americas, Asia, and Oceania, and an even larger number, around 80 million people, migrated within Europe.[3] Furthermore, the migratory movements in other regions were also substantial: between 1846 and 1940, approximately 50 million people migrated from Southeast Asia to India and Southern China and another 50 million from Central Asia, Siberia, and Japan to Northeast Asia and Russia. In Adam McKeown's words, "it was a world on the move, flowing into factories, construction projects, mines, plantations, agricultural frontiers, and commercial networks across the globe."[4]

At the same time, this period of intense globalization and movement of capital and labour coincided with a consolidation of nation-states, imperialist endeavours, and nationalism. Labour and socialist movements emerged in this interaction between the global and the local that shaped national, ethnic and class identities. The experiences of migration and its influence in the shaping of the working classes were very diverse across different geographies. While migrants could cross many borders without significant restrictions during this period, some countries such as the United States and Australia had already established serious restrictive measures toward migrants of certain origins,

---

2 *La Vanguardia* (Buenos Aires), 1 March 1902.

3 T. J. Hatton and Jeffrey G. Williamson, *The Age of Mass Migration: Causes and Economic Impact* (New York: Oxford University Press, 1998); Dirk Hoerder, *Cultures in Contact: World Migrations in the Second Millennium*, (Durham, NC: Duke University Press, 2002).

4 Adam McKeown, "Global Migration, 1846–1940," *Journal of World History* 15, no. 2 (2004): 167.

notably from China and other Asian countries.[5] Moreover, trade unions and labour activists played a significant role in the discussions and campaigns that led to the establishment of these restrictions.[6] In this context, the regular encounters of socialist organizations at the congresses and meetings of the Second International provide a unique vantage point to explore how leaders and activists of different regions engaged with each other in fraternal but still bitter and tense discussions.[7]

As this chapter will show, although the Stuttgart congress approved a radically worded resolution that opposed most restrictions to transnational migration, during the debate many voices expressed much more restrictive views, underpinned by perspectives that drew up a hierarchy of migrants according to their origin. By exploring the different perspectives that arose during the discussion, this chapter goes beyond the usual cursory references to the approved "Stuttgart resolution," thereby enriching our knowledge of the positions of international socialists regarding these issues. In particular, it focuses on how actors from the socialist "peripheries" initiated the discussion and influenced its resolution. Moreover, it argues that the debate in Stuttgart went beyond the "question" of migration and the problems it posed to labour and socialist movements, sparking more complicated arguments on the interplay of racism, whiteness, stances on free and unfree labour, solidarity, and internationalism.

Classic works of the 1960s and 1970s addressed the place of the "national" and "colonial" questions in the history of socialism and highlighted the tensions that ran through the Second International even during its heyday in the

5 Carl Strikwerda, "Tides of Migration, Currents of History: The State, Economy, and the Transatlantic Movement of Labor in the Nineteenth and Twentieth Centuries," *International Review of Social History* 44, no. 3 (1999): 367–394; Adam McKeown, *Melancholy Order: Asian Migration and the Globalization of Borders* (New York: Columbia University Press, 2011).

6 Among many others: Alexander Saxton, *The Indispensable Enemy: Labor and the Anti-Chinese Movement in California* (Berkeley: University of California Press, 1971); Jonathan Hyslop, "The Imperial Working Class Makes Itself 'White': White Labourism in Britain, Australia, and South Africa Before the First World War," *Journal of Historical Sociology* 12, no. 4 (1999): 398–421; Lyam Byrne, "Coolies or Comrades? Labor Socialism and the Contradictions of Internationalism, 1909–22," *Labour History* 113 (2017): 157–181; Inés Valdez, "Socialism and Empire: Labor Mobility, Racial Capitalism, and the Political Theory of Migration," *Political Theory* 49, no. 6 (2021): 902–933.

7 On the significance of socialist congresses as observation points to examine ideas and practices about internationalism, see Kevin J. Callahan, *Demonstration Culture: European Socialism and the Second International, 1889–1914* (Leicester: Troubador Publishing, 2010) and Pierre Alayrac, *L'Internationale au milieu du gué: De l'internationalisme socialiste au congrès de Londres (1896)* (Rennes: Presses universitaires de Rennes, 2018).

first decade of the twentieth century.[8] Despite its obvious links with these discussions, however, the question of migration received relatively little attention, apart from the classic writings by Claudie Weill, who briefly examined the way in which the congresses of the Second International and its social democratic successor, the Labour and Socialist International, addressed the movement of migrant workers.[9] In his chapter in *The Cambridge History of Socialism*, edited by Marcel van der Linden, French historian Jean-Numa Ducange called for a "specific study of the nationalities and colonial question, and more generally, of the question of racism." Moreover, he argued that "just as labour history has taken to a global approach, we should do the same when we write the history of the Second International."[10] Following on these ideas, and drawing upon secondary literature, socialist newspapers and archival material, I argue that the renewed interest in the history of transnational socialism could profit from the insights of migration history to explore one of the least researched discussions of the experience of the Second International.

8 Georges Haupt and Madeleine Rebérioux, eds., *La deuxième Internationale et l'Orient* (Paris: Cujas, 1967); Georges Haupt, Michael Löwy and Claudie Weill, *Les Marxistes et la question nationale, 1848–1914* (Paris: Maspero, 1974). See also Jean-Numa Ducange, *Quand la Gauche pensait la Nation: Nationalités et socialismes à la Belle-Époque* (Paris: Fayard, 2021). For a thorough and recent state-of-the-art on the historiography of the Second International, see Kevin Callahan, "A Decade of Research on the Second International: New Insights and Methods," *Moving the Social* 63 (2020): 185–199.

9 Claudie Weill, *L'Internationale et l'autre: Les relations inter-ethniques dans la IIe Internationale* (Paris: Arcantere Editions, 1987); Claudie Weill, "Die Frage der Migrationen im internationalen Sozialismus: Stuttgart (1907) – London (1926)," *Moving the Social* 26 (2001): 55–64. After the ITH Conference 2021, where this paper was originally presented, Daan Musters published an important article addressing the migration debate in the years of the Second International. Whereas Musters' article focuses on the perspectives of American and German socialists, the present chapter engages further with the stances of socialists acting in the peripheries of the International, such as Argentina, Australia, the Dutch Indies, and Central Europe (Daan Musters, "Internationalism, Protectionism, Xenophobia: The Second International's Migration Debate (1889–1914)," *International Review of Social History* 68, no. 1 (2023): 75–105). Other authors that discussed the topic include Patricio Geli, "El Partido Socialista y la II Internacional: La cuestión de las migraciones," in *El Partido Socialista en Argentina*, ed. Hernán Camarero and Carlos Herrera (Buenos Aires: Prometeo, 2005) and Ole Merkel and Moritz Müller, "Proletarier mancher Länder, vereinigt euch? Der schleichende Niedergang des Internationalismus in der 'Kulidebatte' der II. Sozialistischen Internationale (1883–1910)," *Arbeit – Bewegung – Geschichte: Zeitschrift für historische Studien* 20, no. 1 (2021).

10 Jean-Numa Ducange, "The Second International: 1889–1914," in *The Cambridge History of Socialism*, ed. Marcel van der Linden, vol. 2 (Cambridge: Cambridge University Press, 2022), 280.

1 Socialists and Immigration in Non-European Regions: The Good, the Bad, the Ugly

The Argentine proposal to the Amsterdam congress conveyed all the contradictions that ran through the socialist milieu of turn-of-the-century Buenos Aires, mostly composed of socialists of European descent struggling to organize a local working class heavily shaped by migration flows. Many local socialist leaders were recent European migrants themselves, mostly from Italy, Spain, and Germany and this fact, combined with a clear racial bias toward the indigenous population, explains why they did not promote restrictive measures towards European migrants but rather postulated a more obscure distinction between "natural" and "artificial" immigration.[11] For Argentine socialists, European immigration was a factor in the development of the local, assumedly "backwards," working class, although it could become detrimental if too extensive.

"Whereas it is desirable," Argentine socialists argued, "to receive a foreign contingent which really improves the situation of the working class, the schemes that promote artificial currents of migration, incited by capitalist and political greed, must be severely condemned."[12] The assessment was followed by a line of action, and in the countries receiving immigrants, socialist parties were expected to reject public expenses meant to artificially favour immigration, whereas in the "exporting" European countries they had to strictly control agencies and middlemen. Moreover, labour parties needed to share information to prevent migrants from being deceived by false promises. The rest of the text was a contribution towards that goal, as it described the harsh situation of workers in Argentina. In closing, the document also indicated that most immigrants were reluctant to obtain Argentine citizenship, with one of the reasons being that they were interested in preserving their original nationality.[13] The proposal thus called for a campaign to "ensure that the voluntary acquisition of citizenship in a country does not deprive the right to keep the citizenship of origin once the subject or citizen has returned to his or her homeland."[14]

Although it was included on the agenda, the Argentine proposal did not occupy an important place at the Amsterdam congress. Due to lack of time, it

11 Geli, "El Partido Socialista y la II Internacional."

12 *La Vanguardia* (Buenos Aires), 19 December 1903. Unless otherwise noted, all translations into English in this chapter are by the author.

13 Lucas Poy, *El Partido Socialista argentino, 1896–1912: Una historia social y política* (Santiago de Chile: Ariadna Ediciones, 2020).

14 *La Vanguardia* (Buenos Aires), 19 December 1903.

had not been discussed in a special session and was therefore included among other pending business during the last day's plenary meeting.[15] A draft presented by the commission was in line with the text sent by the Argentinians, albeit with some additions. It highlighted the fact that migrants were "victims of the capitalist regime" but also mentioned that they usually "had the prospect of replacing strikers." Concerning practical steps, the motion condemned "all legislative measures aimed at preventing migration" and declared that it was necessary to "enlighten the emigrants artificially attracted by capitalist promoters, and to counteract the false information." It also requested that socialist parliamentarians ask for a "control of abuses" and, taking up the Argentine proposal, demanded that immigrants be granted political rights in the countries of destination without losing them in their lands of origin.

However, this draft was met with a counterproposal that was drawn up during the session by American (in the period always referring to the United States), Australian, and Dutch socialists. Conveying the perspective of socialists from regions with a history of significant racial tension between white and non-white workers – with the Dutch delegates expressing the point of view of the white colonists of the Dutch East Indies – the document commenced with a warning about "the dangers to the working class which arise from the immigration of foreign workers," namely "a lowering of wages, a ready supply of strike-breakers and sometimes bloody conflicts." It formally rejected "all laws which tend to exclude foreign workingmen who have been forced to emigrate through oppressive conditions" and hoped that, under socialist influence, immigrants would eventually join the local trade unions and demand the same rate of wages. However, it went on to say that "workers of backward nationalities, such as Chinese, Negroes, etc., are often imported by capitalists in order to harm the local workers by working for a minimum wage, and those who allow themselves to be exploited live in a kind of slavery." The proposal concluded that social democracy should "combat with all means at its command the application of this method to destroy labour organizations and lower the standard of living of the working class, whereby the progress and the ultimate realization of socialism would be retarded."

During the brief debate that followed, it became clear that the main issue at stake would be that of the "people of colour." Representing the Socialist Party of America, Morris Hillquit argued that the labour movement must distinguish

15 The reconstruction of the discussion is based on the German and French minutes: *Internationaler Sozialisten-Kongress zu Amsterdam: 14. bis 20. August 1904* (Berlin: Buchhandlung Vorwärts, 1904); *Congrès socialiste international, Amsterdam 14–20 août 1904* (Geneva: Minkoff, 1985).

"between workers of civilized countries and those of uncivilized countries, between workers who are in the process of class struggle, or at least in the process of developing class consciousness, and those who do not yet have the slightest precondition for it." He recalled, of course, that American trade unions have been very vocal and active in the campaign for the prohibition of Chinese migration. "This may sound reactionary," Hillquit argued, "but it is indispensable if we do not want to destroy the whole movement, for it is a vital interest of our labour movement to keep out *coolies* and negroes."[16]

To be sure, the arguments of Hillquit and his comrades called into question the celebratory and internationalist mood of the closing plenary session of the congress. An uncomfortable atmosphere spread throughout the room as several delegates from France, the United States and Japan took the floor to criticize the motion, even recalling Marx's call for proletarians of all lands to unite, rather than divide, themselves. Others, such as Fritz Paeplow, from the German Sozialdemokratische Partei Deutschlands (SPD), put forward a more moderate perspective which revealed that tensions and resentments also lingered on among European socialists. Paeplow argued that "Marx would never have demanded that the most backward workers be let in without any consideration for the concrete conditions of their own country, to demand, for example, that the German construction workers allow their situation to be made significantly worse by the unrestricted immigration of Italian workers." He admitted, however, that he could not side with Hillquit's motion, as the trade unions of each country had the duty to educate the immigrant workers and to bring them into their organizations. In view of the lack of time, the Scottish trade unionist and founder of the British Labour Party, James Keir Hardie, asked to postpone the question until the next congress. The motion was accepted, and the debate finished with a general statement calling the unions to "make the acceptance of foreigners as easy as possible."

Hence the question remained open, and the participants readied their arguments for a more serious controversy. Three years later, in a report published in the *Official Bulletin of the Socialist Party of America*, Hillquit mentioned that

16 On American socialism and the question of migration, see Charles Leinenweber, "The American Socialist Party and 'New' Immigrants," *Science and Society* 32 (1968): 2–25; Sally Miller, *Race, Ethnicity, and Gender in Early Twentieth-Century American Socialism* (New York: Garland, 1996); Paul Heideman, *Class Struggle and the Color Line: American Socialism and the Race Question, 1900–1930* (Chicago, IL: Haymarket Books, 2018); Lorenzo Costaguta, "Geographies of Peoples: Scientific Racialism and Labor Internationalism in Gilded Age American Socialism," *The Journal of the Gilded Age and Progressive Era* 18, no. 2 (2019): 199–220; Musters, "Internationalism, Protectionism, Xenophobia."

the question of migration was of "vital importance" for American socialists and asked his fellow comrades if they could "passively tolerate the capitalist practice of artificially stimulating emigration and importing cheap labour from foreign countries."[17] Two months later, the National Executive Committee passed a resolution to be presented at the 1907 Stuttgart congress. Written by Hillquit, it argued that certain labour migration was unavoidable "under a highly developed system of capitalism," and that in other cases migration was "artificially stimulated by steamship and railroad companies, land speculators and other capitalist promoters." So far, the argument was analogous to the one developed by the Argentinians. However, Hillquit moved on to argue that there was a *third* type of migration, namely "the deliberate importation of foreign labour by the capitalist class for the purpose of increasing the competition between the workingmen of the importing country, lowering their wages and breaking the power of their organizations." This type of imported labourers could be "individually hired by contract in other capitalist countries or imported in masses from countries yet hardly touched by the capitalist mode of production."[18]

This line of argumentation was complemented by the Dutch socialists who had already supported the American resolution in the previous congress. In a long article published in the socialist newspaper *Het Volk* in August 1907, Henri van Kol set out to provide a thorough examination of the topic.[19] Not surprisingly, he also stressed the necessity of distinguishing between migrants of different types, thereby creating a hierarchical taxonomy. Although he acknowledged the tensions created by migrations inside Europe, he argued that no restrictions were necessary in this case, as "in civilized countries there can be no lack of assimilation and fraternization between workers of different nationalities." However, things were different regarding migrants from other origins, and Van Kol was even more explicit than Hillquit about the need to

17 *The Socialist Party Official Bulletin*, III, 5, January 1907.

18 *Congrès socialiste international: Stuttgart 6–24 août 1907* (Geneva: Minkoff, 1985). See also Morris Hillquit, "Immigration in the United States," *International Socialist Review* 8, no. 2 (August 1907).

19 "De Landverhuizing en de Internationale Sociaal-demokratie," *Het Volk* (Amsterdam), 6 August 1907. Concerning Van Kol, who lived in the Dutch East Indies for a long time, and his approaches to the colonial question, see Fritjof Tichelman, "Pays-Bas: La social-démocratie hollandaise et l'Indonésie," in *La deuxième Internationale*, ed. Haupt and Rebérioux, 212–240. More broadly, regarding Dutch social democracy and Indonesia, see Erik Hansen, "Marxists and Imperialism: The Indonesian Policy of the Dutch Social Democratic Workers Party, 1894–1914," *Indonesia* 16 (1973): 81–104; Erik Hansen, "The Dutch East Indies and the Reorientation of Dutch Social Democracy, 1929–40," *Indonesia* 23 (1977): 59–85.

impose restrictions based on racial and cultural features. "The problem is quite different," he argued, "when faced with peoples whose civilization differs from the European, whose standard of living is much lower; when the gradual integration of workers, standing on a different stage of development, in the trade union organization is not yet conceivable in a long future." When it came to "the Negroes of Africa, the Chinese of Asia and the natives of the islands of the South," Van Kol pointed out, it was necessary to "consider the real situation, however reluctantly, if the whole future of socialism is not to be jeopardized."[20]

Van Kol developed an argument that would become crucial in the debate: it was not a matter of race, he argued, but one of culture and education, of course, "determined" by the economic situation. "The decisive factor," he said, "is neither skin color nor place of residence, but only the stage of economic evolution reached by different groups of workers." These workers, according to him, were incapable of organization and would become "willful tools in the hands of our opponents." Asking for restrictions against them was therefore a duty of self-preservation and even a favour to the "backward" workers themselves because excluding them would serve the interests of international social democracy and the social movement in general. He permitted himself a note of condescension, arguing that Western socialists should "support and protect these backward peoples and make them susceptible to higher development" but stressed again that until this level of development was reached, it was a matter of survival to keep these workers away from the labour market.[21]

2 The Response from Central and Eastern European Socialists

Whereas the contributions from the United States and the Netherlands, by Hillquit and Van Kol, went further than the original Argentine proposal and helped define the more restrictive and racist positions in this debate, socialists from several emigration regions (within Europe), on the opposite side of the political spectrum, made a plea for open borders and argued against restrictions.

Among several texts that appeared in the months immediately preceding the Stuttgart congress, there was a report signed by "B. Gornberg" (Boris Markovich Frumkin), a leader of the Jewish Bund.[22] As it had become customary in the

20 "De Landverhuizing en de Internationale Sociaal-demokratie."

21 "De Landverhuizing en de Internationale Sociaal-demokratie."

22 "Emigration and Immigration: A Report to the International Socialist Congress in Stuttgart, 1907," translation from Yiddish included in Uri Herscher and Stanley Chyet, eds., *On Jews, America, and Immigration: A Socialist Perspective* (New York: American

debate, Frumkin started by noting that labour migration was inseparable from the development of capitalism on a global scale. He soon moved on to argue that this movement of various peoples was not just driven by the forces of supply and demand, for capitalists also played an active role in trying to maximize their profits and reducing wages by attracting "workers from less developed countries, workers who demand less, are less organized, and will make do with little due to hunger, need and persecution."

So far, his reflections were not so different to the ones examined above. However, Frumkin soon made clear that "in the final analysis this abnormal situation, too, arises from capitalist production," and moved on to claim that it could not be solved under this regime. He also highlighted several political problems lying ahead, namely that apart from creating a large reserve workforce, migration helped capitalists develop "antagonistic feelings between native and immigrant workers," thus endangering socialist internationalism. Moreover, in the second part of his report, Frumkin criticized the politics of reformist trade unions, arguing that it called forth "the most blatant chauvinism, stirs up national and racial antagonisms, and awakens class-egotism in its most naked form."[23]

Drawing on these considerations, the Bund concluded that immigration and emigration were intricately linked with the nature of the capitalist economy and conceived all types of restrictive legislation as "essentially reactionary," thus calling for socialists to reject them altogether. Instead, they should focus on campaigning against restrictive laws, exposing their true nature, and fighting against the "feelings of demoralization which anti-immigration agitation breeds in the labouring masses." From the Bund's point of view, restrictive legislation "obscures the class-consciousness of the workers, draws the proletariat away from the class struggle, introduces dissension among the workers, and creates an atmosphere for the development of national and racial enmities." Other, more practical, campaigns were proposed, such as fighting for a "normal working day" and a minimum wage, but also against middlemen and shipping companies. Moreover, immigrants should always enjoy political rights and trade unions needed to be reorganized, "to assure that newly arrived workers will have access to them."[24]

Jewish Archives, 1980). For a recent account of the history of the Bund, see Frank Wolff, *Yiddish Revolutionaries in Migration: The Transnational History of the Jewish Labor Bund* (Leiden: Brill, 2020).

23 "Emigration and Immigration: A Report."

24 "Emigration and Immigration: A Report."

Although shorter and focused on the situation in his own country, an article published in the most important theoretical periodical of the SPD, *Die Neue Zeit*, by the Hungarian socialist Jószef Diner-Dénes developed similar arguments.[25] Like Frumkin, Diner-Dénes examined the question from the point of view of a region of emigration and focused on the situation of emigrants.[26] Referring to the large numbers of emigrants coming from Hungary, not only to the United States but also to neighbouring countries and regions, he tried to explain that it was a legitimate endeavour of a working class in need. The aim of his text, ultimately, was to question the interpretation developed by foreign trade unions that considered Hungarian immigrants as "backward" and unable to organize. Like Frumkin, however, Diner-Dénes did so without completely questioning the notion that immigrants from different countries had different "cultural" levels. Indeed, he concluded that:

> despite all the noise of the American opponents of emigration, it can be said that it is becoming less and less dangerous for American workers from year to year. First, because the ratio of qualified workers who emigrate, who were either already organized or are easy to organize, is improving steadily. Furthermore, the percentage of Slovak and Ruthenian emigrants is also declining sharply in comparison with the more culturally advanced Hungarian and German emigrants, among whom there are far fewer illiterate people.[27]

If the stances of Hillquit and Van Kol represented the most restrictive position, and those of Frumkin and Diner-Dénes outlined the opposite perspective, a lengthy article by Otto Bauer in *Die Neue Zeit* (1907) developed an intermediate position. Bauer, an Austrian in the Habsburg Empire, self-defined as "of many peoples" and living in Vienna at the time of large-scale Czech, Slovak, Jewish, and Hungarian immigration, was a theoretical leader of the International, but his analysis was also important because his ideas would form the basis of the resolution adopted at the Stuttgart congress.[28]

---

25 "Auswanderung und Einwanderung in Ungarn: Bericht, verfaßt im Auftrag der Sozialdemokratischen Partei Ungarns," *Die Neue Zeit* 45 (1907): 621–634.

26 Annemarie Steidl, "Migration Patterns in the Late Habsburg Empire," in *Migration in Austria*, ed. Günter Bischof and Dirk Rupnow, (New Orleans: University of New Orleans Press, 2017): 69–86.

27 "Auswanderung und Einwanderung in Ungarn."

28 "Proletarische Wanderungen," *Die Neue Zeit* 41 (1907): 476–494. *Die Neue Zeit* published other articles about this question during these months that I cannot address here due to space constraints.

Bauer addressed the issue by combining the region of origin and the reason for migrating in a typology. In the first place, he mentioned emigration "from economically backward countries." The second case was the migration of "the industrial worker [who] decides to migrate to foreign countries if higher wages beckon him there." Bauer also acknowledged a third type of migration not driven by economic but by political reasons, using the example of Eastern European Jews. Bauer then moved on to assess the consequences for the labour movement. In his view, the level of salaries was not only determined by the supply and demand on the labour market, but also by the cultural qualities of the workers. Introducing a criterion not very different from the one put forward by Van Kol, Bauer went on to argue that

> the more backward the cultural circles the immigrants come from, the easier they bear the arbitrariness of the entrepreneur – hence the preference of Prussian Junkers for Slavic farm labourers – the more likely they are to accept the most oppressive working conditions, such as those Russian and Polish Jews who immigrate to England, where they form a docile material for the development of a shameful sweat system [...] The more backward the immigrants are, the more difficult it is for them to fit into the trade union organizations.[29]

Using this argumentation, Bauer provided an approach that combined "economic" and "cultural" elements in a vision that could fit the views of the readership of *Die Neue Zeit*. He reasoned that "immigration from industrial-capitalist economic areas is far less dangerous than immigration from agricultural countries." The danger of the former was "insignificant," because of its small numbers and because of this "cultural" development. While acknowledging that the development of capitalism would "gradually" help workers of different countries "acquire the psychology of the modern industrial worker," Bauer stressed that this was a long historical process, with phases that could not be "arbitrarily shortened."[30]

Naturally, socialists were called to promote different approaches towards each type of migration. In the first case, "immigration from industrial-capitalist economic areas," Bauer strongly argued that it represented no risk – on the contrary, it might have beneficial effects, and therefore socialists should "demand full freedom of movement for the workers of the modern industrialized

29 "Proletarische Wanderungen."

30 "Proletarische Wanderungen."

countries." However, the situation was different for other types of migrants and contract labour, consciously organized by employers to lower wages and break strikes, needed to be rejected outright, and fought against in the countries of emigration. The most complicated case, Bauer commented, was "immigration from agricultural regions." While he admitted that pure restriction was not possible and should be rejected, the labour movement should "seek to combat its dangers through its planned political and trade union action." In his conclusion, Bauer returned once again to the argument concerning the "cultural backwardness" of certain classes of workers and developed the idea that real international solidarity actually meant supporting foreign workers in their countries of origin to prevent them from migrating.[31]

3 Showdown at the Stuttgart Congress 1907

"Unlike what happened in Amsterdam [...], this time the subject of labour migration interested many delegates," emphasized an Italian reporter present at the Stuttgart congress.[32] Indeed, the commission that discussed the problem met for three days and the debate included many more interventions and proposals than three years earlier.[33] It soon became clear that the motion put forward by the Americans would become the centre of the debate, insofar as the main question at stake was the restriction of migration from non-European regions. This argument was further stirred by one of the youngest delegates in the room, the Australian Victor Eugene Kroemer. He stressed that the question of migration was more important in Australia than in the rest of the world because capitalists there promoted "yellow labour" to weaken the position of Australian workers, who enjoyed a higher "standard of life." Kroemer claimed that "white immigrant workers organize themselves swiftly," while "coloured workers reject organization." The Australian labour movement was therefore eager "to keep out all those workers who cannot be expected to adopt the white way of life." The young delegate did not miss the opportunity to mention that Australian workers did not have "any hostility in principle against the

31 "Proletarische Wanderungen."

32 *Avanti*, 25 August 1907.

33 The reconstruction of the discussion is again based on the German and French minutes, *Internationaler Sozialisten Kongress zu Stuttgart 18.-24. August 1907* (Berlin: Buchhandlung Vorwärts, 1907), and *Congrès socialiste international: Stuttgart 6-24 août 1907*, as well as different socialist periodicals: *L'Humanité*, 21 and 22 August 1907, *Arbeiter-Zeitung*, 22 August 1907, *Vorwärts*, 22 and 23 August 1907.

Chinese and the Japanese," but stressed that they were "obliged to fight against an immigration that is nothing but a capitalist manoeuvre." He concluded by saying that Australian workers must protect themselves against the immigration of Asian workers "in the interests of the progress of socialism."[34]

Kroemer's intervention made a deep impression. Straightforward as it was, it did not help to promote the case that Americans and Dutch delegates had put forward in a more nuanced way. As delegates took the floor to distance themselves from this perspective, Morris Hillquit made his best effort to defend the American proposal. "We do not have any race prejudice," he started, "but we are realistic." Hillquit moved on to explain that the Chinese and the Japanese, "the yellow race in general" were "involuntary strike-breakers" and presented a disastrous competition to local workers. He tried to convince his fellow delegates by arguing that the backwardness of these migrants revealed itself in terms of organization. Unlike the Belgians or the Italians who migrated to France, Hillquit argued, the Chinese were "too backward to be organized." He concluded that the American proposal was the most revolutionary one, for "it was the only one that ensures the development of the labour movement."

József Diner-Dénes reminded Hillquit that only a few years ago the Hungarian immigrants in the United States had been considered "impossible to organize." As he did in his article in *Die Neue Zeit*, he countered Hillquit's argument but without disregarding the idea of cultural backwardness: "the countries that are *unorganizable* today," he pointed out, "will not be tomorrow. In backward countries, development no longer takes as long as it does in those countries that were the first to develop, such as England and Germany." On the other side of the spectrum, Mark Lucas, from South Africa, took the floor to defend Hillquit, arguing that it was necessary to "prevent the importation of cheap labour, otherwise our trade unions will be broken."[35]

The chair of the commission, the Austrian, Moravia-born social democrat Wilhelm Ellenbogen, tried to set the tone of a possible compromise resolution,

---

34 On the Australian labour movement and the "White Australia" policy, see Ann Curthoys and Andrew Markus, eds., *Who Are Our Enemies? Racism and the Australian Working Class* (Sydney: Hale & Iremonger, 1978). Specifically on the Australian early socialist movement, see Verity Burgmann, "Racism, Socialism, and the Labor Movement, 1887–1917," *Labor History* 47 (1984): 39–54.

35 Although the engagement of socialists from Southern Africa in this debate was scarce, the question of migration of white and non-white labour in the region was very significant and the literature on the topic is rich. See, among others, Hyslop, "The Imperial Working Class Makes Itself 'White'"; William Kenefick, "Confronting White Labourism: Socialism, Syndicalism, and the Role of the Scottish Radical Left in South Africa before 1914," *International Review of Social History* 55, no. 1 (2010): 29–62.

drawing on Otto Bauer's arguments. According to him, there were two different tendencies in the discussion: one coming from "immigration countries" and the other from "emigration countries." Following a line of compromise quite common in Second International congresses, he claimed that it was the task of the commission to "take the best of both views," something that could be achieved if "we proceed negatively and exclude everything from the outset that is unacceptable to socialists, like for example all exclusion laws and corporative measures." He recommended to rather focus on several "positive measures," mostly in the hands of the trade unions, such as organizing and educating migrant workers and campaigning for a few legal measures, such as the minimum wage, the control of the shipping companies, etc.

A much more sensational intervention, which made a significant contribution to closing any options still open for the American resolution, came from the Japanese delegate Kato Tokijiro. So far, the discussion had focused on the "problems" that Asian migration created for white workers, and never on the grievances of Asian workers themselves. Speaking in German, Kato addressed the core of the question when he asked why the Japanese were depicted as the main enemy and deported from the United States, while "the Italians, the Slovaks, the Jews, etc., who made an identical competition to American workers" were not. "It seems to me," he continued, "that race plays a significant role and that the Americans are being influenced by the famous fear of the yellow peril." He reminded his fellow delegates that Japanese workers were "just as much under the thumb of capitalism as other peoples, and only bitter necessity drives them out of their homeland to seek their bread in a foreign land" (see Chapter 20 in this volume). Socialists had the duty of "taking in these poor brothers, to protect them and to fight capitalism together with them." Japanese workers, Kato concluded, were no different to workers of any other nationality – recalling Marx, he claimed that it would be contrary to the principles of socialism to exclude them from working-class organizations.

The current of opinions was so strongly against the Americans that even Willem Vliegen from the Dutch delegation had to distance himself from their position. His argumentation, full of racism and condescension, pursued a different approach: He claimed that the American socialists showed an "exaggerated pessimism," for the workers from "inferior peoples" performed "inferior work" and therefore were not a serious competition. Moreover, according to him, the United States, Southern Africa, and Australia were regions with scarce white populations, and hence the pressure on wages could not be so significant. He also mentioned that emigration could improve the condition and wages of the workers who remained in their home country. The ideas set forth by Van Kol in *Het Volk* some weeks before the congress, however, were still clear in the wording of the resolution presented by the Dutch delegation. It argued that "some categories of workers from backward countries (...) are often imported by capitalist entrepreneurs in order to reduce wages, smash the trade unions, or lower the standard of living of the workers" and therefore it was urgent to exclude workers "on contract," to set limits to the working day and to reform the transport system. The Dutch socialists concluded by stressing that as long as these measures had not yet been implemented, and as long as these emigrants were still at a lower stage of development, i.e., completely unfit to participate in the trade union and political battles, they must be banned – even in their own interest – because they would be an obstacle to all progress, and they would delay the victory of socialism for a long time to come.

As in Amsterdam three years before, the German Paeplow acknowledged some of the points made by the Americans and other supporters of a restrictive resolution. He claimed that "it was impossible to accept that, in the countries where the labour movement is more developed [...], the fruit of all these efforts will be enjoyed by a mass import of workers with no needs, instruments of the dominant capitalist class." He put pressure on the French delegates, reminding them that in France "a certain percentage of public works must be carried out by native workers, and the French comrades, who here so eloquently represent the complete freedom of immigration, have most probably voted for these stipulations."[36] Paeplow even pointed out that "the mass importation of Italian and Slavic workers makes it exceedingly difficult to improve the condition of German agricultural workers."

When the debate ended, the commission decided to cast a vote between the American resolution, on the one hand, and the three proposals by Ellenbogen, Vliegen, and the Bund on the other. The American proposal was easily rejected, and a sub-commission with Ellenbogen in charge was subsequently appointed to draft a final resolution based on the three selected proposals.[37] The lengthy resolution finally approved by the congress mostly followed the arguments presented by Bauer in *Die Neue Zeit*.[38] It started with a remark almost unanimously emphasized by delegates of all tendencies that "immigration and

36 For further context, see John J. Kulczycki, *The Foreign Worker and the German Labor Movement: Xenophobia and Solidarity in the Coal Fields of the Ruhr, 1871–1914* (Oxford: Berg, 1994).

37 The commission was formed by Ellenbogen, Vliegen, Schippel, Diner-Dénes, and Balabanoff.

38 The final resolution and all the drafts are available in the archive of the Second International at the International Institute of Social History: https://hdl.handle.net/10622/ARCH01299.

emigration of workingmen are phenomena as inseparable from the substance of capitalism as unemployment, overproduction and underconsumption of the workingmen," all of them means that were frequently used to "reduce the share of the workingmen in the product of labour." It moved on to tackle the main issue that had been at stake by saying that the congress did not "consider exceptional measures of any kind, economic or political, as the means for removing any danger which may arise to the working class from immigration and emigration, since such measures are fruitless and reactionary; especially not the restriction of the freedom of migration and the exclusion of foreign nations and races."

After this, the resolution shifted the pendulum in the opposite direction. "On the other hand," it continued, the congress declared "it to be the duty of organized workingmen to protect themselves against the lowering of their standard of life which frequently results from the mass import of unorganized workingmen" and considered it was a duty to "prevent the import and export of strike-breakers." The approved resolution went on to acknowledge "the difficulties which in many cases confront the workers of the countries of a more advanced stage of capitalist development through the mass immigration of unorganized workingmen accustomed to a lower standard of life and coming from countries of prevalently agricultural and domestic civilization." Only after these explanations were presented, the resolution continued that "the congress sees no proper solution of these difficulties in the exclusion of definite nations or races from immigration, a policy which conflicts with the principle of proletarian solidarity."

In conclusion, the resolution recommended a few practical measures. The first part addressed the countries of immigration and included the prohibition of the export and import of workers "who have entered into a contract which deprives them of the liberty to dispose of their labour power and wages," the promotion of legislation to shorten the working day, as well as campaigns for a minimum wage, to regulate the sweating system, to control hygienic conditions, and to abolish restrictions "which exclude definite nationalities or races from the right to sojourn in the country and from the political and economic rights of the natives." It also included a series of demands for trade unions, to ensure that they integrate immigrant workers. The second part referred to the countries of emigration. The measures included "active propaganda for trade unionism," "enlightenment of the workingmen and the public at large of the true conditions of labour in the countries of immigration," and a call for concerted action of trade unions of all countries in matters of migration. The last part demanded strict control of steamship agencies and emigration bureaus and thorough regulation of the transportation system.

4 Conclusion

Following the initiative of the Argentine Socialist Party, the Second International discussed the "question of migration" during its congresses at Amsterdam and Stuttgart. The topic was not new, as the transnational movement of workers within Europe – for instance, Italian workers in Switzerland and France, or Belgian labourers in the north of France[39] – had already created tensions and discussions among socialist parties in the previous decade and within the International Socialist Bureau. What was new in 1903–1904 was the engagement of socialist groups from the non-European "peripheries," which submitted the main proposals that shaped the debate, and the fact that they discussed the transnational movement of non-white workers. Even though it took an internationalist line, it questioned attempts to put limits on workers' mobility, and called for the joint organization of the native and immigrant working class, the Stuttgart congress's resolution did not entirely hide the tensions that had arisen during the debate and included several remarks about the limits that should be imposed on labour import strategies promoted by the capitalist class.

These complex international discussions revealed a peculiar interaction between the global and the local. This chapter showed that the proposal that Argentine socialists sent to the International Socialist Bureau responded to several difficulties they encountered in their local action: On the one hand, trade union activists sympathetic to the party were worried because the arrival of new European immigrants depressed the wages of local workers; on the other, the Socialist Party faced the problem that many of these migrants were not naturalized and therefore could not participate in elections, and sought a change in legislation in European countries so that immigrants who acquired Argentine citizenship would not lose that of their countries of origin. Their motion, however, opened an international debate that went far beyond these local concerns. As it quickly became clear, the "question of migration" was intertwined with very fundamental political problems regarding which socialist parties of different countries had divergent positions, because the situations and contexts they faced at the local level were quite different.

The discussion soon gave rise to a polarization of opinions on the racial problem and the immigration of Asian workers. The Argentine proposal had been submitted by white socialists who were first-or second-generation

39 See, among others, Gerard Noiriel, *Le massacre des Italiens: Aigues-Mortes 17 août 1893* (Paris: Pluriel, 2009); Bastien Cabot, *"À bas les Belges!": L'expulsion des mineurs borains (Lens, août-septembre 1892)* (Rennes: Presses universitaires de Rennes, 2017).

European migrants and who were concerned about the influx of European immigration. Since they were not worried about racialized "others," they never considered serious restrictive measures. However, things took a different turn when American, Australian, and Dutch socialists engaged in the discussion in Amsterdam in 1904. It was above all American socialists who moved beyond the distinction between "natural" and "artificial" immigration with a reference to the possibly indentured position of certain migrants, to openly state that the problem was where the migrants came from as well as the colour of their skin. In so doing, they were supported by delegates from British colonies, such as Australia and Southern Africa, where the question of restricting Asian – and African – immigrants played a central role in shaping local labour movements, and by a section of Dutch socialist leaders, led by Henri van Kol, who represented the views of white colonists in Indonesia and had also developed a strongly paternalistic and racist stance with regard to the colonial question.

The restrictive motions put forward by the Americans and the Dutch galvanized the debate and pushed their adversaries into a common front that concealed many tensions and divergences, including resentments among Western European socialists. It soon became evident that the most clearly restrictive proposals had little chance of success in a venue that celebrated internationalist appeals to the unity of the proletariat and was dominated by socialists from Western European countries where the immigration of workers of Asian or African origin was not (yet) an issue in local debates. At the same time, the tone of the discussions revealed that even those who were unwilling to go along with Hillquit and Van Kol developed condescending positions towards non-European populations.[40] All the participants in the debate linked capitalist development with "cultural advancement" and the latter with a greater willingness to organize politically and in trade unions. As in the imperial discourse of the time, non-whites were seen as unprepared for self-government and democracy as well as unfit for labour and socialist organization.[41]

---

40 Musters developed an interesting typology that distinguished between "protectionist" and "xenophobic" nativism, but which poses the risk of losing sight of the extent to which both were tightly embedded. Musters, "Internationalism, Protectionism, Xenophobia."

41 Sebastian Schickl, *Universalismus und Partikularismus: Erfahrungsraum, Erwartungshorizont und Territorialdebatten in der diskursiven Praxis der II. Internationale 1889–1917* (St. Ingbert: Röhrig Universitätsverlag, 2012). See also Ulbe Bosma's assessment of the social Darwinist assumption of a "hierarchy of human races," in terms of their "propensity to operate in modern civilization." Under this assumption, "black labour was enslaved, Asian labour indentured, whereas the apex was firmly held by the free white well-educated northern European." Ulbe Bosma, "Beyond the Atlantic: Connecting Migration and World History in the Age of Imperialism, 1840–1940," *International Review of Social History* 52, no. 1 (2007), 117.

This interpretation made it possible to develop arguments with a strong racist basis but to present them as if they were a question of "cultural" backwardness. The "otherness" of coloured workers – and of "unfree" labour in general – was shaped by their alleged inability to build labour organizations, thus developing a reason for discrimination that was not seen as incompatible with socialist internationalism. To a certain extent, the distance adopted with respect to these "others" actually fostered the unity among socialists of European origin because by concluding that workers from certain origins were "unorganizable," the delegates present at the Amsterdam and Stuttgart congresses were also celebrating themselves as the vanguard of the international proletariat.

Classic accounts of the history of the Second International have explored the deep tensions hidden behind compromise and radically worded resolutions, for instance concerning topics such as militarism and colonialism. A closer examination of the articles in socialist periodicals and the minutes of congresses shows that the question of migration provides a further example of this pattern, complicated by discussions about race and colonialism. Moreover, the chapter engaged with more recent historiographical trends that examine how the congresses of the Second International displayed and conducted "inter-national" sociability and symbolism among socialists of different countries. The discussions around migration not only expressed the potential and the limits of this inter-national solidarity among the representatives of European socialism – more importantly, they revealed to what extent the very framework of this international solidarity encountered serious tensions when confronted with the presence of non-white workers from the peripheries. A further exploration of the subject of migration and racism within the ranks of the Second International (and its heirs after the First World War), going beyond its European core, and incorporating the experiences of colonial and semi-colonial countries, will allow for an appreciation of the complications involved and enrich the new interest in the history of international socialism.

CHAPTER 12

Labour Migration Regimes in Imperial Russia, the Soviet Union, and the Russian Federation

Lewis H. Siegelbaum and Leslie Page Moch

Abstract

This chapter surveys labour migration within the Eurasian landmass that successively comprised the Russian Empire, the Soviet Union, and the Russian Federation from the end of serfdom in 1861 to the recent past. It highlights incentives to leave home for work and measures to control mobility defined as *regimes of labour migration*, taking a chronological perspective on major migrations: the resettlement of peasants on land set aside for cultivation, arrangements for seasonal migration, rural-to-urban migration, wartime evacuation, and settlement for major resource development and infrastructure projects. It argues that although the measures to incentivize and control labour migration before 1917 and after 1991 share strategies with contemporary migration regimes elsewhere, the Soviet state outstripped its contemporaries in its ambitions, efforts, and institutions developed to control the migration of working people.

Keywords

limitchiki – migration regimes – Northern increment – propiska – regular and irregular migrants – resettlers – seasonal migrants

The story of labour migration within the Eurasian landmass that successively comprised the Imperial Russian state, the Soviet Union, and the Russian Federation is partly familiar to those who are aware of how labour migration progressed in other global regions but is nonetheless also characterized by some unique aspects. In this context, it is the Soviet part of the story that deviates most from what was observed elsewhere in the world. In this chapter, we will argue that measures to incentivize and control labour migration undertaken before 1917 and again after 1991 share certain similarities with institutions and strategies elsewhere, but that the Soviet state engaged in a series of practices that set it apart in several important ways. This, to our knowledge, first study to

 | DOI:10.1163/9789004686991_013

focus specifically on labour migration in Imperial Russia, the Union of Soviet Socialist Republics (USSR), and post-Soviet Russia is the product of extensive research using both primary and secondary sources. The former include archival and published sources from the late Imperial period on the transportation by sea and rail of labour migrants to Siberia and the Russian Far East as well as the memoir of a tsarist resettlement administrator in the field; the writings of Soviet leaders on labour migration policy, directives for settling Red Army veterans in the 1930s, and the internal workings of the Evacuation Council during the Great Patriotic War; and finally contemporary press coverage of labour migration issues.

In what follows, we refer to both the incentives for people to leave home for work and measures to control such mobility as *regimes of labour migration* and the ways people seeking to improve their or their family's lives by working away from home responded to such regimes as *repertoires of migration.* As we argued in *Broad Is My Native Land*, regimes and repertoires of migration are intricately connected, shaping each other in a kind of dialectical dance. Here, we focus on the regimes of labour migration, which encompass the resettlement of peasants on land set aside for cultivation, arrangements for seasonal migration, rural-to-urban migration, and even evacuation during wartime and in the case of major infrastructure projects. It should be borne in mind that these forms of migration were powerfully affected by the vastness of the Eurasian steppe, geographical factors such as river patterns and climate, and the available means of transportation. We will proceed in chronological order, beginning with Imperial Russia after the emancipation of the serfs in 1861.

1 Imperial Russia

Many historians have described the Imperial Russian state as a "service state" meaning that in return for their service, state servitors received noble status (hereditary above a certain level as defined in the Table of Ranks that Peter the Great introduced in the early eighteenth century) and access to peasants' labour. Nobles extracted such labour either in the form of quitrent (*obrok*) payments that could be fulfilled in kind or in cash, or as labour obligations (*corvée*, or in Russian, *barshchina*). However, despite large grants to nobles of peasant-inhabited lands, especially under Catherine the Great (1762–1796), not all peasants were enserfed. By the mid-nineteenth century, roughly half of the peasants within the European provinces of the empire retained the status of so-called state peasants who were at least nominally free to purchase land, enter into contracts, and appear in court. For the serfs, labour mobility was not only feasible but often a necessity related to the fulfilment of obligations to their owners which required outside earnings in field or city.

Likewise, emancipation did not signal absolute freedom to move. Concerned that noble landowners would retain a labour force at their disposal and seeking to prevent the dissolution of village life, the state officials who devised the Emancipation Decree incorporated two kinds of continuing obligations into the document. One consisted of redemption payments over a period of 49 years that were to be paid to former serf owners by peasants, organized as a village commune (*obshchina*). From this provision arose the second constraint on labour mobility: the village commune bore collective responsibility for such payments, which subsequently necessitated its permission for individual members of the commune to spend extended periods of time labouring elsewhere.[1] The village commune thereby assumed a critical role in the regime of labour migration.

Provided with passports by the commune, peasants periodically left their villages to seek work that would supplement what they and other family members could eke out at home. This activity most commonly occurred on a seasonal basis corresponding with the agricultural cycle. Peasant "out-migrants" (*otkhodniki*) tended to travel in two different directions. Men and women from villages in the Central Industrial provinces around Moscow found work in the increasingly factory-based textile industry that was often located outside of the city. Additionally, peasant males from the same provinces worked seasonally as peatcutters, brickmakers, and stonecutters. Second, peasants from the Central Black Earth provinces gravitated to the large agricultural estates in what was then known as New Russia (today, Ukraine). These sugar-beet and wheat-growing estates thrived on the burgeoning international trade and the expansion of the empire's railroad system that funnelled crops to the port cities of Odessa, Kherson, and Nikolaev.[2] "Toward the end of the nineteenth century," as we noted, "more than a million male peasants traveled annually, by cart, railroad, and steamer, but mostly on foot, to large outdoor hiring markets

1 For two classics covering the *longue durée* of peasants in Imperial Russia, see Jerome Blum, *Lord and Peasant in Russia: From the Ninth to the Nineteenth Century* (Princeton, NJ: Princeton University Press, 1961) and Geroid T. Robinson, *Rural Russia under the Old Regime: A History of the Landlord-Peasant World and a Prologue to the Peasant Revolution of 1917* (Berkeley: University of California Press, 1967).

2 Lewis H. Siegelbaum, "The Odessa Grain Trade: A Case Study in Urban Growth and Development in Tsarist Russia," *Journal of European Economic History* 9, no. 1 (1980): 113–151.

located at important crossroads and railroad stations where they negotiated wages with agents of estate owners and grain merchants."[3]

The seasonality of labour was not confined to agriculture. For instance, the development of coal mining and metallurgy in the Donets Basin (Donbas) of Eastern Ukraine not only depended on large infusions of capital from Belgium, Britain, Germany, and France but also on strong, young men from the same Central Black Earth provinces that sent labourers into the wheatfields. By the turn of the century, at least 50,000 made the journey annually. Among them was Nikita Khrushchev's father, Sergei, who would travel from Kursk province to the Donbas where he worked on the railways and as a miner.[4] Others included both agriculture and mining in their annual itineraries: "Leaving their families behind ... they would work the harvest in the steppe in August and September, then head for the mines where they would be employed through the winter months, returning to their farms in March or April, typically at Easter."[5]

Further afield, increasing numbers of peasants were migrating eastward beyond the Urals to settle in that vast part of the empire they tended to call Siberia and, before the turn of the century, a million had already done so. The imperial state sought Orthodox Slavic peasants to colonize and cultivate sparsely inhabited territory as a means of forestalling further encroachment by Chinese and Korean migrants.[6] A law of 1889 released peasants from the necessity to seek permission from their communes to depart; they did, however, need to identify a specific place of settlement in their applications to the Ministry of State Domains. For its part, what came to be the Resettlement Administration, formed in 1896, identified, surveyed, and marked off plots of land for settlement. It also maintained waystations/checkpoints at Chelyabinsk and Syzran' and provided reduced fares on steamships and trains.[7] For intrepid settlers, the

3 Lewis H. Siegelbaum and Leslie Page Moch, *Broad Is My Native Land: Repertoires and Regimes of Migration in Russia's Twentieth Century* (Ithaca, NY: Cornell University Press, 2014), 69.

4 William Taubman, *Khrushchev: The Man and His Era* (New York: W. W. Norton, 2003), 18–20.

5 Siegelbaum and Moch, *Broad Is My Native Land*, 69.

6 On the Chinese and Koreans, see Lewis H. Siegelbaum, "Another Yellow Peril: Chinese Migrants in the Russian Far East and the Russian Reaction before 1917," *Modern Asian Studies* 12, no. 2 (1978): 307–330; Alyssa M. Park, *Sovereignty Experiments: Korean Migrants and the Building of Borders in Northeast Asia, 1860–1945* (Ithaca, NY: Cornell University Press, 2019); Sören Urbansky, *Beyond the Steppe Frontier: A History of the Sino-Russian Border* (Princeton, NJ: Princeton University Press, 2020).

7 For a comprehensive contemporary history, see V. V. Kir'iakov, *Ocherki po istorii pereselencheskago dvizheniia v Sibir' (v sviazi s istoriei zaseleniia sibiri)* (Moscow: I. N. Kushner & Co., 1902).

Volunteer Fleet offered transportation by sea from Odessa to Vladivostok via the Suez Canal, the Indian Ocean past Indochina and China, comprising a voyage of 45 days. However, most travelled overland by a combination of horse-drawn cart and railway, with the progressive extension of the Trans-Siberian Railroad between 1891 and 1916 greatly facilitating the journey for millions of peasants.[8]

Judging from the memoirs of Aleksei Tatishchev, service in the Resettlement Administration involved a lot of travel and occasionally adventure. Inspection tours to assess the condition of settlements and expeditions to identify potential settlement sites punctuated daily work regimens in Vladivostok, Tashkent, and eventually, Tiflis.[9] In administering Siberian settlement, the state eventually realized the advantage of relying on the traditional peasant practice of sending out a scout (*khodok*) to locate lands for settlement. In this way, a repertoire of peasant migration became part of the state's regulatory regime. A law of 1904 essentially deputized such individuals, granting them and their clients various privileges including assisted passage, tax and military draft deferments, and housing loans on the condition that they abide by the Resettlement Administration's rules. As amended in 1907, these rules assigned scouts to specific parcels chosen by land organization commissions that consisted of zemstvo personnel as well as the Resettlement Administration's own considerable staff of agronomists, surveyors, and hydrologists. Maps and handbooks containing a lot of advice supplemented the state's efforts to reduce both "irregular" (*samovol'nyi*) settlements and the number of returnees.[10]

The high point of settlement came in the years 1907–1909 when the checkpoints recorded some 2 million peasants en route to land parcels east of the Urals. The Stolypin reforms initiated in November 1906 made it easier for peasant families to detach themselves from collective responsibilities. Couched by Prime Minister Petr Stolypin as a "wager on the strong and the sober," the reforms targeted the equalizing functions of the commune, the result of which was an increased outflow not only to Siberia but also to jobs in the expanding

8 On journeys by sea, see "O perevozke krest'ian-pereselentsev raznykh gub. v Iuzhno-Ussuriiskii krai iz g. Odessy v g. Vladivostok na sudakh Dobrovol'nogo flota v 1897 g., vol. 1, 1897," Rossiiskii Gosudarstvennyi Istoricheskii Arkhiv (RGIA), f. 391, op. 2, d. 211; on Trans-Siberian arrangements, see Komitet Sibirskoi Zheleznoi Dorogi, ed., *Kolonizatsiia Sibiri v sviazi s obshcheim pereselencheskim voprosom* (St. Petersburg, 1900).

9 A. A. Tatishchev, *Zemli i liudi: V gushche pereselencheskogo dvizheniia (1906–1921)* (Moscow: Russkii put', 2001).

10 For details, see Lewis H. Siegelbaum, "Those Elusive Scouts: Pioneering Peasants and the Russian State, 1870s-1950s," *Kritika: Explorations in Russian and Eurasian History* 14, no. 1 (2013): 43–48.

urban sector.[11] Indeed, the city was the primary beneficiary of labour as the urban population tripled between 1860 and the First World War, primarily due to the arrival of newcomers.[12]

Among immigrant women, domestic service attracted the largest group, about one-quarter of female workers in Moscow as of 1900. They lived under the same roof as their employers. Women in other lines of work – the needle trades, tobacco, and textiles – were primarily on their own. As for prostitutes, the police kept a close eye on them, or at least on their health, certified on the notorious "yellow card." A quarter of the men, at least in 1902 Moscow, relied on the *artel*, a self-organized group of compatriots, to facilitate urban survival. Although ties to the village remained strong, the city increasingly offered workers not only employment but opportunities for community in the form of factory-provided housing, mutual aid societies and, at least after the 1905 Revolution, trade unions.[13] In this manner, the changing migration regime meshed with the expanding demand for urban labour.

2 The Soviet Union

What most distinguishes the Soviet period are the far greater efforts by state authorities to mobilize supplies of labour. By mobilization we mean the organized physical displacement of people to exercise a specific economic function. Although Soviet authorities engaged in such efforts during the Civil War (1918–1921), labour mobilization really came into its own with the onset of the First Five-Year Plan for industrialization (1928–1932), the collectivization of agriculture, and the establishment of an extensive system of labour camps (the Gulag). Some of these labour migration regimes persisted into and beyond the Great Patriotic War (1941–1945); others faded by the end of the 1930s. The other side of mobilization was restriction, again to an unprecedented degree. Concurrently with mobilization, the state also instituted a hierarchy of

11 Abraham Ascher, *P.A. Stolypin: The Search for Stability in Late Imperial Russia* (Stanford, CA: Stanford University Press, 2001).

12 Joseph Bradley, *Muzhik to Muscovite: Urbanization in Late Imperial Russia* (Berkeley: University of California Press, 1985); Michael Hamm, ed., *The City in Late Imperial Russia* (Bloomington: Indiana University Press, 1986).

13 Barbara Engel, *Between the Fields and the City: Women, Work, and the Family in Russia, 1861–1914* (Cambridge: Cambridge University Press, 1994); Rose Glickman, *Russian Factory Women: Workplace and Society, 1880–1914* (Berkeley: University of California Press, 1984); Laurie Bernstein, *Sonia's Daughters: Prostitutes and Their Regulation in Imperial Russia* (Berkeley: University of California Press, 1994).

desirable places in which the most appealing locations were reserved for the worthiest citizens and forbidden to the less worthy as punishment. Although neither mobilization nor restriction worked perfectly, the aspiration to replace the market mechanism to control the labour supply was a hallmark of the Soviet state.

The Civil War occasioned the resort to a variety of institutions and justifications for restricting workers' mobility as well as mobilizing labour. From October 1918, people identified as "bourgeois elements" were enjoined to perform "compulsory labour service" (*trudovaia povinnost'*), usually involving publicly visible physical tasks such as street cleaning. Soon, the provisions were extended to virtually all able-bodied adults. A series of decrees by the Council of Labour and Defence followed, culminating in the formation of a Main Committee for Compulsory Labour (*Glavkomtrud*), headed by the secret police (Cheka) chief, Feliks Dzerzhinsky. The committee conducted more than 20 mobilizations of workers, "some fixing workers to particular 'militarized' enterprises, and others ordering their transfer to areas of labour deficit."[14] The mobilizations covered a variety of industries such as mining, metal processing, and shipbuilding and enlisted corresponding trade unions to identify "labour deserters." They represented the flip side of turning units of soldiers into "labour armies," the brainchild of Commissar of War Lev Trotsky that was intended to counteract the continued disintegration of the economy. As Lenin told the Eighth Congress of Soviets in December 1920, "no socialist country is possible . . . if it cannot move tens and hundreds of thousands of workers wherever they are needed."[15] Although the Soviet government abandoned such measures after its victory over the Whites, they and the notion of labour service that it used to justify them remained enshrined in the narrative of the "heroic period of the Great Russian Revolution" and the policies retrospectively known as War Communism.[16]

The subsequent period, known as that of the New Economic Policy, is of import here not only for the reinstitution of state-supervised peasant settlement but also for its projected scale. In 1925, the Central Executive Committee of the Soviets set up an All-Union Resettlement Committee, essentially

14 Lewis Siegelbaum, "Militarization of Labor," at Seventeen Moments in Soviet History, http://soviethistory.msu.edu/1921-2/militarization-of-labor. See also Leon Trotsky, "The Manpower Crisis and How to Solve It: Theses Adopted by the Party Central Committee. January 22, 1920," in *The Origins of Forced Labor in the Soviet State, 1917–1921*, ed. James Bunyan (Baltimore: Johns Hopkins Press, 1967), 95–101.

15 V. I. Lenin, *Polnoe sobranie sochinenii*, 55 vols., 5th ed. (Moscow, 1970), vol. 42, 150.

16 L. Kritsman, *Geroicheskii period Velikoi Russkoi Revoliutsii* (Moscow: Gosizdat, 1925).

re-establishing the tsarist Resettlement Administration along with many of its personnel. This followed the formation of the Central Colonization Committee designed to settle nomadic peoples and populate designated areas of the country for agricultural and industrial development. Characteristically, however, the Soviet government not only sought to manage resettlement but also to organize it on a grand scale. The Resettlement Committee, for example, drew up plans for moving over 5 million people in the span of ten years from areas of excess population to regions of "Union significance," defined as the Far East, Siberia, the mid-Volga, and Karelo-Murmansk.[17] Policies and practices governing other kinds of labour migration – peasants taking up work and residence in cities, the seasonal nexus between the central agricultural provinces and the Donbas, and even (for the time being) forced labour in remote locations – resembled their tsarist predecessors. This similarity is owing to the restitution of market mechanisms in hiring and wage determination as well as the limited monetary resources at the disposal of the state.

With Stalin's "Great Break" of 1929, an era of unprecedented migration commenced. People ricocheted from rural areas undergoing collectivization and "dekulakization" to industrial construction sites and burgeoning cities. Some were recruited, others were expelled, and still others found themselves confined to carceral locations. Although it was known as the period of the First Five-Year Plan, the moniker of the plan puts a tidy face on this mishmash of peregrinations as neither before nor since had the Soviet state indulged in such fantasies of control. Nevertheless, the "grand strategies of the state" to transform the country did alter the landscape. On the steppe just to the east of the Urals, a giant steel mill arose, built by both recruited and coerced labourers, many of whom became residents of the city of steel. That city, Magnitogorsk, grew from nothing to nearly 200,000 inhabitants in three short years. Throughout the country, cities absorbed 12 million new residents between 1928 and 1932, with 4.1 million counted in 1931 alone.[18]

The Soviet state responded to the sheer volume of urban in-migration with "an aggressively restrictive regime of migration containment."[19] To pre-empt

17 E. H. Carr, *Socialism in One Country, 1924–1926*, 2 vols. (Harmondsworth: Penguin, 1970), vol. 1, Note A.

18 Stephen Kotkin, *Magnetic Mountain: Stalinism as a Civilization* (Berkeley: University of California Press, 1995), 29–105; Sheila Fitzpatrick, "The Great Departure: Rural-Urban Migration in the Soviet Union," in *Social Dimensions of Soviet Industrialization*, ed. William G. Rosenberg and Lewis H. Siegelbaum (Bloomington: Indiana University Press, 1993), 15–40.

19 Siegelbaum and Moch, *Broad Is My Native Land*, 121.

"spontaneous" departures of peasants from the villages, it introduced "organized recruitment" (*orgnabor*) in 1931, a system designed to steer recruits to particular construction projects and other worksites identified by the State Planning Committee (Gosplan). The following year, it inaugurated the distribution of residence permits (*propiski*) to all adults who resided in "regime" cities and carried out "socially useful labour." Initially applied to Moscow, Leningrad and Kharkiv, the number of such cities was expanded to eleven by April 1933 and eventually to 28. In addition, beginning in December 1932, all urban residents were issued internal passports that tracked their movements and served as a prerequisite for obtaining residence permits. By August 1934, some 12 million citizens possessed such a document out of a total urban population of some 44 million individuals of all ages.[20]

The two documents worked in tandem to define legally permitted urban residents and at the same time cleanse cities of undesirable, socially marginal, and "socially harmful elements." Those subjected to expulsion included kulaks who had fled collectivization in the countryside, people engaged in illegal trade, and disenfranchised former elites known as *lishentsy*. Together, the passport and propiska enhanced the legibility of Soviet society, created hierarchies of citizens and cities, and shaped how citizens regarded themselves in relation to other legally defined groups.[21]

However, the state failed to achieve its aim of stemming the tide of "irregular" (*samovol'naia*) labour migration. Throughout the remaining years of the 1930s, thanks to the inexhaustible demand for their labour and their reliance on informal connections, millions of peasants made their way to the cities without proper documentation. They also moved around a lot, as Moshe Lewin notes, "changing jobs, creating unwanted surpluses in some places and dearth in others."[22] However, the state did manage to alter patterns of migration and settlement and also established distinctions among Soviet citizens: those who could boast of urban residence (and even more so, the privileged status associated with living in a regime city), those who became collective and state farmers, and those who eked out an existence on the margins as individual farmers

20 Sheila Fitzpatrick, *Stalin's Peasants: Resistance and Survival in the Russian Village After Collectivization* (Oxford: Oxford University Press, 1994), 92–96.

21 David Shearer, "Elements Near and Alien: Passportization, Policing and Identity in the Stalinist State, 1932–1952," *Journal of Modern History* 76 (2004): 835–856; Emily J. Elliott, "Migrants and Muscovites: The Boundaries of Belonging in Moscow, 1971–2002" (PhD diss., Michigan State University, 2019), 29.

22 Moshe Lewin, *The Making of the Soviet System: Essays in the Social History of Interwar Russia* (New York: New Press, 1985), 221.

(*edinolichniki*).[23] Except for the latter category, these distinctions persisted for decades.

Collectivization tore the social fabric of the countryside, inserting urban-derived cadres, extruding many well-to-do elements, and anchoring the rest in place. The analogy to enserfment is inapt, although millions of peasants certainly felt trapped by the application of the labour-day (*trudodni*) system of responsibilities and payment, even when mitigated by seasonal departures. To provide leadership, the Union of Agricultural Collectives (*Kolkhoztsentr*), aided by trade unions, recruited volunteers – the so-called "Twenty-Five Thousanders" – who in addition to serving as collective farm chairmen also performed technical and clerical functions.[24] The other side of the coin was the expulsion of peasants who ostensibly resisted the confiscation of their property or disrupted that of others. They were defined as kulaks or kulak supporters, and local authorities received quotas from above to help them determine how many to expel. Between 1930 and 1932, dekulakization resulted in the exile of over 380,000 families (1.8 million individuals) from their native villages, two-thirds beyond their native region.[25]

This regime of compulsory, punitive migration transported over a million "special settlers" by rail, together with their horses and farm equipment in 715 convoys. Their destinations in the Far North, the Urals, Siberia and Kazakhstan, presided over by commandants appointed by the Commissariat for Internal Affairs (*Narodnyi Komissariat Vnutrennykh Del*, NKVD), were often previously uninhabited and bereft of housing … until the settlers themselves constructed it. It was a labour migration because the settlers toiled in forestry, agriculture, railroad and port construction, mining, and metallurgy as well as in ancillary occupations such as school teaching and clerical work. They also cultivated garden plots just as their former neighbours did on collective farms. Beginning in 1935, the NKVD carried out numerous deportations of Poles, Germans, Finns, Koreans, and other nationalities deemed unreliable from border regions – in effect ethnicizing the sobriquet of kulaks, which meant their relocation as

---

23 Natalie Moïne, "Passeportisation, statistique des migrations et contrôle de l'identité sociale," *Cahiers du Monde russe* 38, no. 4 (1997): 587–599.

24 Lynne Viola, *The Best Sons of the Fatherland: Workers in the Vanguard of Soviet Collectivization* (New York: Oxford University Press, 1987).

25 Lynne Viola, *The Unknown Gulag: The Lost World of Stalin's Special Settlements* (Oxford: Oxford University Press, 2007).

special settlers. These substantial operations continued into the Great Patriotic War (1941–1945) and indeed for a few years beyond.[26]

The distance from home comprised an important part of the punitive nature of this regime. However, the absence of guards, barbed wire, and other appurtenances of the Gulag – the labour camps set up shortly after the October Revolution but vastly expanded after 1929 – set the Special Settlements apart. The inmates of the Gulag, who were tried and found guilty of either political or civil crimes, also laboured in forestry, metallurgy, and, most notoriously, mining. From 1930 until Stalin's death in 1953 precipitated the dismantling of the system, some 18 million Soviet citizens spent time in the camps of whom an estimated 1.8 million did not survive.[27]

All the while, previous labour migration regimes continued to function. In the case of voluntary resettlement, a synergy developed between it and the removal from collectivized villages of those who would become special settlers. Red Army veterans, with varying degrees of volition, served as a key component of these new resettlers. For example, between October 1933 and April 1934 the Resettlement Committee relocated some 59,000 Red Army and collective farm families to southern districts of Ukraine and Russia. Other such families resettled farther afield in Eastern Siberia and the Russian Far East.[28] We traced the daily progress of these operations in the archives which numerous officials meticulously recorded. They also organized transport, provided food and other supplies for the journey, and arranged for the reception of the convoys. The Resettlement Committee shared responsibility for these logistics with the security police, the army, and the Commissariat of Transport. The execution of this migration regime proved so complicated that responsible officials received bonuses when such transports went off without disaster.[29]

On 24 June 1941, two days after Nazi Germany launched its invasion, the Soviet government and the Central Committee of the Communist Party created a Council for Evacuation. There had been some precedent for relocating industry and essential workers during the First World War. For example,

---

26 N. L. Pobol' and P. M. Polian, eds., *Stalinskie deportatsii, 1928–1953 gg.* (Moscow: Materik, 2005); Terry Martin, "The Origins of Soviet Ethnic Cleansing," *Journal of Modern History* 70 (1998): 813–861.

27 Golfo Alexopoulos, *Illness and Inhumanity in Stalin's Gulag* (New Haven, CT: Yale University Press, 2017); Stephen G. Wheatcroft, "Victims of Stalinism and the Soviet Secret Police: The Comparability and Reliability of the Archival Data. Not the Last Word," *Europe-Asia Studies* 51, no. 2 (1999): 315–345.

28 Report by the Director of the Southern District Sectors, 14 October 1934 in Rossiiskii Gosudarstvennyi Arkhiv Ekonomiki, f. 5675, op. 1, d. 48a, ll. 1–16.

29 Siegelbaum and Moch, *Broad Is My Native Land*, 43–44.

as reported in Eduard Dune's memoir, in August 1915 the tsarist government evacuated to Moscow Riga's Provodnik rubber factory, along with its skilled workers (among them, Dune's father) and their families.[30] However, the scale of the Soviet effort was, and remains, unparalleled. The joint party-state resolution called for "the evacuation of the population, institutions, military and other freight, factory equipment and other valuables" from areas threatened with enemy occupation.[31] In articulating its policy, which amounted to a new regime of labour migration, the Evacuation Council emphasized both "distribution" (*razmeshchenie*) and "employment" (*trudoustroistvo*).[32]

During the latter half of 1941 alone, evacuation authorities presided over the dismantling, transport and reassembling of over 2,500 industrial enterprises of which some 1,500 were large-scale. Historians have estimated that, all told, the trains carried some 16.5 million people to the east – to the Volga, the Urals, Siberia, Kazakhstan, and Central Asia. In addition to factories, the evacuation entailed food supplies, laboratories, educational institutions, and cultural organizations.[33]

The evacuation regime bore all the hallmarks of a massive bureaucratic operation in which hard-pressed officials often made spur-of-the-moment decisions that could have dire consequences for those rescued from Nazi occupation. When, in May 1942, a resettlement official called regional authorities to persuade them to accept evacuees from besieged Leningrad, only one of the seven agreed to accept the full complement, two others accommodated some evacuees, two refused to take any, nobody answered the phone at another regional headquarters, and the last had no telephone connection.[34] Nonetheless, this vast program enabled the millions of evacuees not only to survive but also to contribute incalculably to the success of the war effort. It was one of the most important inspirations for our earlier observation that "World War II is the central event of migration history in the twentieth century."[35]

The war profoundly altered the configuration of labour, most evidently in exacerbating its inveterate shortage. Already in 1945, the Supreme Soviet's Presidium introduced a new system of incentives for individuals to work in the

30 Eduard Dune, *Notes of a Red Guard* (Urbana: University of Illinois Press, 1993), 5.

31 For the resolution, see KPSS *v rezoliutsiiakh i resheniiakh s"ezdov, konferentsii i plenumov TsK, 1938–1945 gg.*, vol. 7 (Moscow, 1985), 212.

32 Rebecca Manley, *To the Tashkent Station: Evacuation and Survival in the Soviet Union at War* (Ithaca, NY: Cornell University Press, 2009), 31.

33 Manley, *To the Tashkent Station*, 1, 50; Mark Harrison, *Soviet Planning in Peace and War, 1938–1945* (Cambridge: Cambridge University Press, 1985), 72.

34 Gosudarstvennyi Arkhiv Rossiiskoi Federatsii (GARF), f. A-327, op. 2, d. 50, ll. 24–25.

35 Siegelbaum and Moch, *Broad is My Native Land*, 264.

Far North and other climatically inhospitable regions rich in oil, gas, and minerals. Facilities such as Vorkuta, Magadan, and Noril'sk, historically dependent on Gulag labour, thus began to absorb voluntary workers. They received wages according to regional coefficients ranging from 1.0 to 2.0 of a standard wage as well as additional vacation time, travel expenses, provision of housing and an accelerated pension schedule.[36] These provisions constituted what came to be known as the Northern Increment. The progressive closure of the Gulag system and the influx of free labourers occasioned the physical transformation of the camps into modern cities and the founding of new ones. The population of these regions nearly doubled between 1960 and 1985, increasing from 4.7 million to 9.2 million.[37]

Brochures from the late 1950s and early 1960s with titles such as "Come settle in _____ oblast/republic" testify to efforts to woo new agricultural settlers to Petrozavodsk, Tomsk, Khabarovsk, Sakhalin, and other underpopulated areas. They typically listed benefits and contained glowing accounts of "how resettlement improved my life." But the Virgin Lands program, launched in 1953 to settle the arid West Siberian and Northern Kazakh steppe, dwarfed them all. As Nikita Khrushchev's pet project, it initially attracted several hundred thousand families, although inadequate housing, unreliable harvests, and friction with both earlier settlers and the indigenous population provoked large numbers to seek better lives elsewhere.[38]

While recruiters continued their efforts to attract workers and peasants to remote areas, the cities of the country's core regions – and particularly their large enterprises – went begging for labourers. In Moscow, the Likhachev (ZIL) and Lenin Komsomol (AZLK) Automobile Factories, the Moscow State Construction and Assembly Trust (*Mosstroi*), and others adapted an existing practice on an expanding scale. They petitioned the Committee for the Utilization of Labour Resources of the Russian Soviet Federative Socialist Republic (RSFSR) to increase the "limit" on the number of workers they employed, arguing that this was necessary to meet their previously agreed-upon production plans.[39] Once granted permission, such enterprises were

36 Iu. V. Roshchin, *Migratsiia naseleniia v sub'be Rossii* (Moscow: Avangard, 2008), 155–156.

37 Tsentral'noe statisticheskoe upravlenie pri Sovete ministrov RSFSR, *Narodnoe khoziaistvo RSFSR v 1985 g.* (Moscow, 1986), 33.

38 Siegelbaum and Moch, *Broad is My Native Land*, 61–62.

39 In 1967, the Central Administration for Organized Recruitment and Resettlement under the Council of Ministers of the USSR was transformed into the State Committee for the Utilization of Labour Resources with its branches in the union republics and with local offices in oblast executive committees.

free to recruit workers, usually for a period of three years. These additional workers, popularly known as *limitchiki,* received a temporary propiska, dormitory housing, workplace education and healthcare, and the possibility of permanent employment. Thus, was born the Soviet equivalent of the German *Gastarbeiter*.[40]

The limitchiki came from the "overpopulated" central Russian provinces. In the early 1970s, over one in three was a woman; by the middle of the decade women comprised nearly 45 percent. Overwhelmingly young, limitchiki generally worked in those arduous and unskilled occupations that urbanites eschewed, which subsequently lent a derogatory connotation to the term. They soon were legion. By 1980, they made up an estimated one-third of the workforce at hiring enterprises and 15 percent of the total labour force in large cities. In construction, three out of four workers may have been limitchiki.[41]

However, despite any progress made as a result of the implementation of various initiatives, the thirst for labour proved insatiable and, failing to attract sufficient numbers of Soviet workers, officials from the committee for labour resources looked abroad. In 1981, they concluded a protocol with the government of Vietnam establishing a "transnational network" of labour migration that by the end of the decade brought tens of thousands of Vietnamese men and women to Soviet coal mines, car plants, textile mills, and other industrial facilities, mostly in the RSFSR. Moscow's Likhachev factory received several thousand.[42] The Soviet hosts covered travel expenses and provided linguistic and vocational training at no cost to the recipients. This reliance on bilateral agreements and even some of their stipulations are familiar to historians of post-war Western European labour migration.[43] Soviet authorities also contracted with their Bulgarian counterparts, already in 1967, to supplement their own contingent of workers receiving the Northern Increment. The far northern

40 Dietrich Andre Loeber, "Limitchiki: On the Legal Status of Migrant Workers in Large Soviet Cities," *Soviet and Post-Soviet Review* 11, no. 1–3 (1984): 301–308; Elliott, "Migrants and Muscovites," 5.

41 Loeber, "Limitchiki," 303–304; Victor Zaslavsky, *The Neo-Stalinist State* (Armonk, NY: M. E. Sharpe, 1981), 144–146, 188–189.

42 Cynthia Buckley, Everett Peachey, and Erin Hoffman, "The Tenacity of Transnational Networks: Vietnamese Migrants in the Soviet Union and Russian Federation," Abstract at https://paa2012.princeton.edu; Elliott, "Migrants and Muscovites," 99–100; George Ginsburgs, "The Case of Vietnamese Gastarbeiters in the Soviet Union," *Osteuropa-Recht* 35, no. 3 (1989): 166–187. The agreement of 1981 followed upon programs dating back to the 1960s that brought thousands of Vietnamese workers to the USSR for vocational training but probably also involved factory labour and other routine jobs.

43 Leslie Page Moch, *Moving Europeans: Migration in Western Europe since 1650* (Bloomington: Indiana University Press, 2003), 177.

region of the Komi Autonomous Soviet Socialist Republic (ASSR) thereby received substantial contingents of Bulgarian lumberjacks and construction workers who built entire "Bulgarian villages" to accommodate themselves.[44]

These respective arrangements were prefigured by an earlier example of the "friendship of the peoples" (*druzhba narodov*) concluded between the Soviet Union and the People's Republic of China. As recounted in Khrushchev's memoirs, during his trip to China in 1954 he proposed that his Chinese counterparts provide "a million or more Chinese workers be sent to Siberia to help us take advantage of the vast timber resources there." At first demurring, Mao eventually assented and, according to Khrushchev, approximately 200,000 went.[45] If true, the presence of Chinese workers in the Russian Far East reprised that of their compatriots who toiled as navvies on the Trans-Siberian Railroad, dug for gold, and performed other menial tasks that kept the regional economy humming in the late Imperial period.[46] In this manner, Soviet regimes of labour migration could harken back to Imperial antecedents. They also survived the bumpy transition to capitalism that began in the mid-1980s under the watchword of *Perestroika*.

3 The Russian Federation

The post-Soviet Russian state scaled back its ambitions and capacity to manage labour migration. Rejecting the Soviet mania for long-term planning, it turned to market mechanisms and acceded to the prerogatives of private enterprise. The transition to capitalism – replete with hyperinflation, goods shortages, and wage arrears – had dire consequences for most wage earners as well as former Soviet citizens dependent on state subsidies to make their residence in outlying parts of the country viable. At the same time, the upsurge of nationalism in the other former Soviet republics persuaded ethnic Russians and other non-titular ethnic groups to flee to the relative safety of the Russian Federation. The fact that the Russian Federation's economy rebounded sooner

44 Brian LaPierre, "Bai Ganyo Goes to the Workers' Paradise: Bulgarian Guestworkers in the USSR, Personal Diplomacy, and the Economics of Soviet Empire," unpublished paper presented at the 2020 Association for Slavic, East European, and Eurasian Studies (ASEEES) annual [virtual] convention, 4–5.

45 Nikita Khrushchev, *Khrushchev Remembers: The Last Testament*, trans. and ed. Strobe Talbott (Boston: Little, Brown & Co., 1974), 283–285. We were unable to corroborate Khrushchev's account.

46 Siegelbaum, "Another 'Yellow Peril'," 307–330.

than those of the other former Soviet Socialist Republics (SSRs), coupled with its lack of visa requirements for those crossing what had been internal Soviet borders, resulted in a major influx of not only refugees but also labour migrants to Russia's largest cities.

A fundamental fact about Soviet migration policy had been its treatment of movement within the Soviet Union as all of a piece which meant that crossing a border within the USSR had no special regulation, whether at a border between oblasts or SSRs. Hence, moving from Tajikistan to Moscow, say, required no more documentation than from one provincial city to another within the RSFSR. We previously referred to this arrangement as "Transnationalism in One Country."[47] After 1991, although the borders became international, the policy remained the same until the early 2000s and hence citizens within what had become the Commonwealth of Independent States (CIS) could continue to use their Soviet passports and other Soviet-originated documents.[48]

Institutionally, the Russian Federation distinguished itself from Soviet practice by forming a Federal Migration Service (FMS) in 1992. The FMS was responsible for executing the two main laws regulating immigration: "On Refugees" and "On Forced Migrants," with the latter referring to people of Russian nationality who wished to settle in the Russian Federation. Subsequently, the FMS also would concern itself with implementing laws regulating labour migrants from within the CIS. The FMS itself would subsequently undergo significant institutional revision and even obliteration in 2000–2002. For several years thereafter, it answered to the Ministry of Interior, whereby this arrangement proved inadequate. From 2004 onward, the office of the President of the Russian Federation assumed a governing role, naming the FMS's top officers and initiating policy revisions.[49]

Irina Ivakhnyuk of the Russian International Affairs Council discerns four stages in the evolution of migration policy and trends up to 2009. During the first stage (1991–1995), when refugees and forced migrants constituted the lion's share of immigrants, the state scrambled to set up an institutional framework and appropriate laws to deal with the influx. A laissez-faire ideology occupied centre stage, reflected in the replacement of the propiska for urban residence with a registration system not dependent on one's employment. Aside from

47 "Transnationalism in One Country?: Seeing and Not Seeing Cross-Border Migration Within the Soviet Union," *Slavic Review* 75, no. 4 (2016): 970–986.

48 On these and other details concerning the transition, see Irina Ivakhnyuk, *The Russian Migration Policy and its Impact on Human Development: The Historical Perspective.* UN Human Development Reports, Research Paper 14 (New York: United Nations, 2009).

49 Ivakhnyuk, *Russian Migration Policy*, 30–31.

this difference, however, registration resembled the Soviet-era permit procedures, inspiring one specialist to comment "The propiska is dead, long live the propiska."[50]

Changes in the nature and volume of migration heralded the second stage (1996–2002). The relative stagnation of the economies of the "near abroad" and Russia's open borders precipitated a deluge of temporary labour migrants – temporary because bureaucratic strictures blocked paths to legal employment and Russian citizenship. Data from the turn of the millennium reveal a chasm between the numbers of migrants officially registered (deemed "regular") and those circumventing regulations ("irregular" migrants). Indeed, in toto, the latter outnumbered the former by about 14 to one. By country of origin, Ukraine sent the largest group of regulars (some 39 percent) followed distantly by Moldova, Tajikistan, and Armenia. However, when it came to estimates of irregulars, Ukraine's proportion dropped to 27 percent.

Tellingly, the largest gap between the numbers of regular and irregular migrants was for groups such as the Kyrgyz who were estimated to have sent 20 times the number recorded, i.e., 350–400,000 compared to 20,000.[51] "Like the Kyrgyz" means people from Central Asia and the Caucasus, including those from within the Russian Federation such as Chechens. The racialization of these former Soviet peoples into "people of colour" was closely linked to the reimagining of Moscow and other major cities in the Russian Federation as Slavic and white. This mental regime in turn contributed to the ethnicization of low-status and low-wage labour, thereby creating a syndrome familiar to students of post-colonial societies. Regarded by legal authorities and the general public as suspects if not as security risks, such non-white groups primarily worked in services, petty trade, and construction.[52]

There is a striking similarity between the proportions of these "regular" and "irregular" migrants to "organized" and "unorganized" Soviet-era seasonal

---

50 Ivakhnyuk, 26–29; Hilary Pilkington, *Migration, Displacement and Identity in Post-Soviet Russia* (London: Routledge, 1998), 40.

51 Ivakhnyuk, *Russian Migration Policy*, 32–33, 39–40. The disproportion is similar for Georgia and Azerbaijan. For more on the Kyrgyz and the intermediaries on whom they rely, see Madelaine Reeves, "Diplomat, Landlord, Con Artist, Thief: Housing Brokers and Mediation of Risk in Migrant Moscow," *Cambridge Journal of Anthropology* 34 (2016): 93–109.

52 Meredith Roman, "Making Caucasians Black: Moscow Since the Fall of Communism and the Racialization of Non-Russians," *Journal of Communist Studies and Transition Politics* 18, no. 2 (2002): 1–27; Jeff Sahadeo, *Voices from the Soviet Edge: Southern Migrants in Leningrad and Moscow* (Ithaca, NY: Cornell University Press, 2019), 93–115. Sahadeo argues that "southerners" already faced discrimination and racism in Soviet times.

migrants (*otkhodniki*) engaged in agriculture and forestry. Kateryna Burkush's work on Soviet Ukrainian migrants during the 1960s-1970s indicates that about one in five was "organized" via orgnabor, but for migrants from the Transcarpathian region only one in twelve relied on the authorities' arrangements. The similarity of ratios, however, masks one important difference. So-called unorganized (or, more accurately, "self-organized") workers, who made their own arrangements with collective farms earned considerably more in money and kind than their compatriots who played by Soviet rules. However, Ivakhnyuk shows that the reverse was true for immigrants at the end of the millennium as they not only earned less but were more likely to be subjected to violence and coercion. A reported two-thirds had their passports confiscated by their employers, who ruled this labour migration regime.[53]

The third stage in Ivakhnyuk's schema (2002–2005) opened with a law "On the Legal Status of Foreign Citizens on the Territory of the Russian Federation." Primarily inspired by security concerns, the law laid out myriad "administrative procedures and barriers, often duplicating each other" to tighten control over migrants. However, it soon proved unworkable and while the quotas set for each region often went unmet, thanks to pervasive bribery and other forms of corruption, the actual numbers of migrants did not wane. The laws on migration provoked criticism that they were "no more than framework regulations that do not guarantee wages, [or] social and labour rights for migrant workers." Evidently, even President Putin recognized the necessity to abandon reliance on the punitive approach.[54]

A fourth stage (from 2006 onwards) thus followed in reaction to the failures of the third, simplifying procedures and otherwise expanding the opportunities for legal entry of CIS citizens. Migrants now could search for jobs immediately upon arriving in a Russian city, register their residence irrespective of whether or where they worked, change jobs without seeking permission from legal authorities and in other respects integrate themselves into the general labour market. "Liberalization" and "humanization" serve as the watchwords for the revised policy presided over by the FMS. Official data suggest that it

53 Kateryna Burkush, "Inglorious Heroes of Labor: Transcarpathian Seasonal Workers during Late Socialism" (PhD diss., European University Institute, Florence, 2018); Kateryna Burkush, "Seasonal Migration: Problem or Solution? Soviet Initiatives of Stimulating and Managing Seasonal Labor Migration in the 1950s-1980s," unpublished paper presented at Fifth Annual GHI-Berkeley Young Scholars Forum on Histories of Migration: Transatlantic and Global Perspectives, October 2021; Elena Tiuriukanova, *Forced Labour in the Russian Federation Today: Irregular Migration and Trafficking in Human Beings* (Geneva: ILO, 2004); Ivakhnyuk, *Russian Migration Policy*, 44–45.

54 Ivakhnyuk, *Russian Migration Policy*, 49.

immediately resulted in a sharp increase in work permits issued, with over half a million going to Uzbeks alone in 2008. Meanwhile, to counter population decline among Russians, a presidential decree of June 2006 offered liberal, indeed unprecedentedly generous, benefits to "compatriots" living abroad to "resettle" back in the homeland.[55]

Economic and political perturbations notwithstanding, these regimes continued to prove their effectiveness for another decade or so in the sense of maintaining an adequate, low-wage labour force that earned enough to send remittances back home. The COVID-19 pandemic disrupted this arrangement and the imposition of lockdowns in the cities, the closing of Russia's borders, and a corresponding trimming of staff and wages led to a sharp decline in the number of temporary migrants employed and perhaps as many as 5 million returned home. While the unprecedented situation affected almost all industries, construction and agriculture suffered the most, followed by hospitality.[56]

4 Conclusion

Russians perennially like to ask themselves whether they belong to Europe, are Eurasian, or represent a "species of [a] nation unto itself." This survey of labour migration regimes over the past century and a half provides evidence to support each of these identities. The abolition of serfdom removed a major impediment to the mobility of labour and capital, thereby pointing in the direction that major European countries had traversed. However, so long as the village commune – an institution lauded by Slavophiles for its uniquely Russian qualities – continued to impede members' departures in search of greener pastures or wage work, it would stifle that progress. That, at least, was what motivated Prime Minister Stolypin in 1906 to introduce measures to encourage peasant householders to consolidate their lands, colonize lands to the east, and otherwise strike out on their own.

55 Ivakhnyuk, 53–54, 60.

56 "Russia Hit by Fall in Migrant Workers from Central Asia," *Financial Times*, 8 May 2021, https://www.ft.com/content/c7c17f5e-e7b2-45bb-97d7-d5b456fb2bec. See also Damelya Aitkhozhina, "As Russia Faces Economic Downturn, Migrant Workers are Paying the Price," *Open Democracy*, 9 September 2020, https://www.opendemocracy.net/en/odr/russia-faces-economic-downturn-migrant-workers-are-paying-brutal-price/; "Russia Eyes Measures to Tackle Migrant Labor Shortage," *Moscow Times*, 10 February 2021, https://www.themoscowtimes.com/2021/02/10/russia-eyes-measures-to-tackle-migrant-labor-shortage-a72894.

Regardless of whether, given more time, Stolypin's "wager on the strong" could have prevented revolution or rather contributed to the peasantry's proletarianization and revolutionary disposition, the October Revolution ushered in seven decades of Soviet exceptionalism. Among the most exceptional aspects were those encompassing the Stalin era of *sui generis* attempts to mobilize labour via state *dirigisme* on an unprecedented scale. So ambitious were these efforts that they provoked all manner of deviance, violence, and recrudescence. Moshe Lewin termed this syndrome "the contamination effect" whereby "the quicker you break and change, the more of the old you recreate. Upon deeper examination, institutions and methods which seemed to be entirely new display the often quite astonishing reemergence of many old traits and forms."[57]

The Gulag, the most extensive carceral regime, became a synecdoche for the Stalin era as a whole. However, other regimes for imposing and controlling labour migration outlived it and came into their own in the last decades of Soviet power. Organizing seasonal labour, restricting residence in cities, and attracting workers to remote regions of the country all bore the stamp of "made in the Soviet Union" and all of it came crashing down in 1991 with the end of Soviet power. All of it, that is, except for treating cross-border travel as if the newly independent states of the Commonwealth were still part of the same country. The bilateral agreements that created this migration regime greatly facilitated temporary labour migration, providing Russia's new capitalists with a plentiful source of low-wage workers living in the penumbra of legal society. In this post-colonial sense, the Russian Federation of the twenty-first century is more European than any of its predecessors.

57 Lewin, *Making of the Soviet System*, 276. Among the examples of the syndrome given by Lewin "the ruralization of the cities" (220–221) is the most relevant.

CHAPTER 13

Producing (Im-)mobile Capital and Labour in the Arab-Gulf Region

From the British Empire to Independent States

Radhika Kanchana

Abstract

The United Arab Emirates (UAE), Saudi Arabia, Bahrain, Qatar, Kuwait and Oman, which are all members of the Gulf Cooperation Council (GCC), stand out globally for their significant reliance on migrant labour and face widespread criticism owing to their generally harsh and abusive work conditions, especially at the lower-wage tiers. The economies in the Arab-Gulf region show a clear pattern whereby capital is concentrated and immobile, and (foreign) labour is imported and subsequently immobilized to achieve a maximum in cheap and flexible manpower. The chapter argues that this is not merely due to the authoritarian and conservative Islamic regimes but that present-day policies (or "no policy" as policy) need to be contextualized in deeper social and historical roots, especially the British colonial legacy including slavery and the long-existing kafala system.

Keywords

Arab-Gulf states – British colonial policy – guestworker – labour – migration

This chapter aims to situate the current migration policies of the Arab-Gulf states in their wider historical and global underpinnings. Capital is concentrated and immobile, primarily among the citizen-elite. And, (foreign) labour is imported and subsequently immobilized to achieve maximum usage of cheap and flexible manpower. This, I argue, is not merely due to authoritarian and conservative Islamic regimes. The present-day migration policies (or "no policy" as policy) need to be contextualized in their deeper social and historical roots, including slavery and long-standing *kafala* practices and, especially, the British colonial legacy. The historic Islamic practice of the kafala was, in fact, adapted to specific contexts and needs when the British Empire exercised

 | DOI:10.1163/9789004686991_014

control over much of the Arab-Gulf region until the 1970s, albeit in varying degrees of formal/informal protectorate status.

I argue that a direct link exists between the current system and that which the British imperial regime established to manage its foreign and local workforce to suit its priorities. This is evident from the 1920s onward when, at the time of the newly emerging oil industry, the Empire strictly regulated the flows of capital and labour with international investment and new visa requirements. The imperial administrators developed elaborate mechanisms to maintain the composition of the nationalities they preferred among the workforce. They wanted "subjects" of British India – under direct imperial control – and, in particular, skilled and semi-skilled Indian labourers. They also wanted to cement their control over the native Arab population and reduce, allegedly for protection and security reasons, the native rulers' powers.

When they became independent, the six member states of the Gulf Cooperation Council (GCC) – Oman, Bahrain, the United Arab Emirates (UAE), Saudi Arabia, Kuwait, and Qatar – continued the policies of the Empire which were successful from the point of view of capital yields and labour demands, albeit this time intending to favour their citizens. The current GCC policies show the extension of the British co-optation of a "local" tradition for the purpose of control over migrant workers. Within the same region, Iran and Iraq testify to similar influences from the period of the "protectorates." I rely on both published and my own research[1] and explore the sources of present-day policies by considering a larger perspective beyond local and regional factors. The chapter seeks to interrogate the multiple influences and the extent of continuities across time and space as regards temporary worker policies. The reasons for the evolution of these policies are located both in immediate regional factors and in the larger imperial-capitalist frame.

1 Which Factors Influence Current Policies? The Exceptionalism Explanation

The current policy situation in the Arab-Gulf region, negatively connoted because of the abusive conditions imposed on migrants, is framed by the GCC states' heavy reliance on importing migrant labour. The GCC economies receive the highest inflow of labour globally and have an exceptionally high

1 Radhika Kanchana, "The Expediency of the Contemporary Guest Worker Migration Policies that Curb Mobility: The Arab-Gulf Countries and the Indian Migrants" (PhD diss., Institut d'Études Politiques de Paris/Sciences Po, 2016).

share of in-migrants in their total populations. According to 2015 data, the number of migrants in the GCC countries – an estimated 25 million – represents 10 percent of global migrants. The migrant share of the total population of these countries amounts to about 32 percent in Saudi Arabia and, at the highest level, to approximately 90 percent in Qatar. The GCC states' migration "policy" is thus designedly that of "no policy." The governments exclusively insist on labour import restricted to temporary labour with near-zero naturalization practices that make it all but impossible for migrants, regardless of their class or other criteria, to receive citizenship, even though laws are in place that (theoretically) could facilitate this.

Scholars have long noted that such so-called "guestworker"[2] policies, used in many regions across the contemporary world, have proven to be anything but temporary[3] since the receiving "national" economies start to irreversibly depend on cheap and "temporary" foreign labour.[4] In the private sector of the GCC countries, the share of foreigners ranges from a "low" of approximately 60 percent in Saudi Arabia, and values above 90 percent in the UAE and Kuwait, to nearly 99 percent in Qatar. It needs to be emphasized that despite the popular image of the "guestworker," in the GCC countries, the term not only applies to low-wage blue-collar workers but also to migrants in other occupational categories such as businessmen or professionals. Furthermore, it even applies to people and their families who have been residing in the respective country for multiple generations. The guestworker policies in the Arab-Gulf region impose rigorous limits on the mobility of foreign workers, who thus suffer acutely from discriminatory conditions in *v*arying degrees, depending on their respective social status in the host country.

One intended consequence of this practice is that capital stays firmly and almost exclusively concentrated in the hands of the citizen-elite. For migrant resident entrepreneurs and professionals, strict restrictions apply concerning investments in businesses or other property and all of their options are mediated via complicated mechanisms through a citizen-sponsor/partnership or special-purpose instruments such as free zones.

---

2 Kristin Surak, "Guest Workers: A Taxonomy," *New Left Review* 84 (2013): 84–102.

3 For instance, see Stephen Castles, "Guest Workers in Europe: A Resurrection?," *International Migration Review* 40, no. 4 (2006): 741–766; Cindy Hahamovitch, *No Man's Land: Jamaican Guestworkers in America and the Global History of Deportable Labour* (Princeton, NJ: Princeton University Press, 2011); Philip L. Martin, "Temporary Worker Programs: US and Global Experiences," *Canadian Issues* 122 (2010): 122–128.

4 Alan Richards and Philip L. Martin, "The Laissez-Faire Approach to International Labor Migration: The Case of the Arab Middle East," *Economic Development and Cultural Change* 31, no. 3 (1983).

In this context, labour is also firmly immobilized and foreign manpower is maintained at a level that is as cheap and as flexible as possible. The labour market in the GCC states is thus highly segregated, with blatant hierarchies along ethnonational lines and with allocations to certain economic sectors. Similar segmentation exists in Singapore and other labour-importing states. In addition, the GCC governments have felt compelled to implement corrective policies in response to perceived demographic imbalances. Hence, from time to time, they have introduced policies to "nationalize" selected sectors of the labour market, to encourage population growth through nativist policies, or to control the national-origin composition of foreign labour. For instance, a decisive shift from Arab to Asian labour was imposed in the 1970s,[5] with, more recently, a shift to sourcing workers from Southeast Asia. Such ad-hoc policy decisions further increase the vulnerability of migrant workers' situations in the host country. Moreover, they significantly impact the societies of origin, both in terms of the family economies and those of whole states such as Egypt.

A widely used explanation for these specific regional policies and their perpetuation is what may be called the exceptionalism position: The GCC states are authoritarian Islamic monarchies and oil-rich rentier states. They are unwilling to change the system and distribute wealth beyond their citizenry. However, there are, of course, other authoritarian states and concentrations of wealth, if not in a citizenry, then in a financial elite, as critical economists have noted in the last decades, whether among the "super-rich" of the West, the "oligarchs" of the East, or political "potentates" in Africa.[6]

An additional dimension of the exceptionalism claim is the region's history concerning slavery, especially in the erstwhile pearling industry, and the discriminatory kafala tradition based on debt relationships. The elites of the region played an active and prolonged role in the global slave trade and slave labour was central to sectors of their economies. The Gulf region's industry of pearling – diving for pearls – was a centre in the global trade for pearls although it subsequently waned in the 1930s due to the competition from Japanese cultured pearls. Local use of slave labour, however, lasted into the 1960s.[7]

In the common understanding, the kafala system involves workers being tied, originally via debt to a creditor, and in the present to a citizen-sponsor, which is a relationship that conjures up an image of a form of modern-day

5 J. S. Birks, I. J. Seccombe, and C. A. Sinclair, "Labour Migration in the Arab Gulf States: Patterns, Trends and Prospects," *International Migration* 26, no. 3 (1988): 267–286.

6 Oxfam, *The Inequality Virus: Report 2021* (The Hague: Oxfam, 2021).

7 Pedro Machado, Steve Mullins, and Joseph Christensen, eds., *Pearls, People, and Power: Pearling and Indian Ocean Worlds* (Athens, Ohio University Press 2020).

slavery. In practice, a kafala migrant only secures employment and residence status via a citizen-sponsor. This sponsor or *kafeel* (either a citizen or an institution) controls the foreign worker's legal status, and thereby, the temporality of his (or her) sojourn.[8] However, the kafala was and is a long-standing Islamic practice that is adapted to specific contexts. It was traditionally used as an instrument of guarantee or bond assuring the repayment of a debt and, in the desert, it also was a Bedouin custom to ensure safe passage. Furthermore, it has served as an alternative frame to that of the adoption of a child. Hence, the tradition is neither a rigidly fixed phenomenon nor are similar practices limited to the Arab-Gulf region/or the Islamic world, as being tied to a recruiting firm was a characteristic of Western Europe's early phases of guestworker programs in the 1950s and 1960s. Similarly, the "bondage" of children was practised between courts in medieval Europe to prevent one ruler or ruling family from attacking the other. In contrast, in the present, kafala underpins the GCC states' use of foreign temporary labour and, since its application largely remains informal, it expands governments' flexibility to manoeuvre.[9]

2 Explanations beyond the "Local" Factors: The British Empire and Its Policy in the Colonial Period

While the local or regional factors discussed above are valid, the narrative on GCC exceptionalism requires greater historical depth and the addition of an imperial perspective. The British-Raj or India segment of the British Empire exercised wide political and administrative control over much of the Arab-Gulf region from the 1820s to the 1970s. The formal and informal protectorate status was divided into two phases: First, the period approximately lasting until the

8 Radhika Kanchana, "Is the Kafala Tradition to Blame for the Exploitative Work Conditions in the Arab-Gulf Countries?," in *South Asian Migration in the Gulf: Causes and Consequences*, ed. Mehdi Chowdhury and S. Irudaya Rajan (London: Palgrave Macmillan, 2018), 61–79. Among the recent scholarship on the kafala in the GCC region, see Noora Anwar Lori, *Temporary Workers or Permanent Migrants? The Kafala System and Contestations over Residency in the Arab-Gulf States*, Working Paper 12, Institut Français des Relations Internationales, Center for Migrations and Citizenship (Paris/Brussels: Institut Français des Relations Internationales, 2012); Mohammed Dito, "Kafala: Foundations of Migrant Exclusion in GCC Labour Markets," in *Transit States: Labour, Migration and Citizenship in the Gulf*, ed. Abdulhadi Khalaf, Omar AlShehabi, and Adam Hanieh (London: Pluto Press, 2014); Ray Jureidini and Said Fares Hassan, "The Islamic Principle of *Kafala* as Applied to Migrant Workers: Traditional Continuity and Reform," in *Migration and Islamic Ethics: Issues of Residence, Naturalisation and Citizenship*, ed. Ray Jureidini and Said Fares Hassan (Leiden: Brill, 2019), 92–109.

9 Kanchana, "Is *Kafala*," 63.

1920s, when imperial interests dominated and the requirements for entry documentation for workers were introduced. Second, the period from the 1950s, when commercial oil-centred interests took precedence over or clashed with political interests. This chapter focuses on this early administrative structure up to the time when India and the Gulf states became independent. It explores the reasons for the specific labour policy implemented and the elements of continuity over time. The imperial legacy needs to be included in the analysis of both the capital investment decisions and the regime of labour regulation. In the frame of its imperial power, the British administration established the means to manage local and migrant foreign workforces in accordance with priorities and policies. These imperial practices, purportedly for protection and security reasons, represent the precursors of policies in the present, in particular those of the second phase.

In the first phase, for almost a century from the 1820s to 1916, the British Empire imposed its influence on the Arab-Gulf region via treaties with Arab sheikhdoms, so-called Sovereignty Agreements. These agreements excluded the Al-Ahsa region in Arabia, where oil was found later. The essential aspect of the treaties involved the local rulers' surrender of their external sovereignty to London in exchange for protection from the Empire. In the context of the competition between empires, Britain's imperative at the time was to prevent any (other) external influence or interference in the region. It treated the region as a buffer zone and, given its proximity to British India, as strategically important for access to India. The policy thus aimed at preserving the exclusiveness of the British presence on the Arabian shore of the Gulf.[10]

These strategic interests dictated the early structures of the policies concerning migration and residence: The treaties required British consent when a local ruler wanted to permit the residence of a foreigner, which traditionally had required an endorsement by the local notables. Thus, the contemporary local elites, which included a few Indian and other already established merchants, recommended and requested permission for the entry of any foreign national from the British Political Resident.[11] In the 1920s, local authorities introduced formal entry documents to privilege the interests of the British and

10 James Onley, *The Arabian Frontier of the British Raj: Merchants, Rulers, and the British in the Nineteenth-Century Gulf* (Oxford: Oxford University Press, 2008); Radhika Singha, "The Great War and a 'Proper' Passport for the Colony: Border-Crossing in British India, c.1882–1922," *Indian Economic and Social History Review* 50, no. 3 (2013): 289–315.

11 The British Political Resident was appointed by the British India Government to handle its relations with the Gulf region (known as the Political Agent for the Lower Persian Gulf from 1820, which later expanded the role).

their subjects, which positioned imperial control over the natives' interests or influence.

In the case of Indian nationals, for example, in contrast to the established historical migration patterns of merchants and traders in the region, the employment of workers and service personnel in this phase was shaped by the British administration. For its expanding bureaucratic infrastructure in the region, it imported labour from the colonies and dominions, e.g., from the Indian Political Service (IPS) cadre to fill the more important posts in the administrative staff and other services. In all colonies, foreigners were present in all classes and professions: civil administration, customs and postal service, police, and armed forces. The largest number, however, was recruited for personal and domestic services as drivers, clerks, cooks, and other domestics. Other migrant groups included people from the Levante.

The different scenario in the second phase of British imperial influence from around the 1950s was directly related to the discovery of oil reserves.[12] International companies were formed under Oil Concessions or Commercial Agreements to explore the drilling for oil under specific conditions favouring the British and the ruling elites' interests. The sequence of oil discoveries began in Bahrain with the concession to drill given to the Bahrain Petroleum Company (BAPCO) dating to 1929 and the actual discovery of oil in 1932. Companies were subsequently established in Kuwait in 1934 (Kuwait Oil Company, KOC), in Qatar in 1936 (Petroleum Development Qatar, PDQ), in Oman in 1935 (Petroleum Concessions Ltd., PCL), in Saudi Arabia in 1943 (Arabian American Oil Company, ARAMCO), and in the "Trucial States" in Abu Dhabi in 1939 (Petroleum Development (Trucial Coast) Limited, PDTCL). The latter states were a British-created conglomerate of small sheikdoms, whose rulers signed "truces" with the Empire, and which would subsequently become the UAE in 1971. Initially, capital investment in the companies was sourced from British capital with some input from other European powers, whereby the Empire's attempt to restrict US capital investments proved unsuccessful.

The capital inflows triggered large-scale infrastructural and other developments in the Arab-Gulf region as a result of which the patterns of migration changed since the local workforce was neither sufficient in terms of their

12 Ian J. Seccombe and Richard I. Lawless, "Foreign Worker Dependence in the Gulf, and International Oil Companies: 1910–50," *International Migration Review* 20, no. 3 (1986): 548–574; Ian J. Seccombe and Richard I. Lawless, "The Gulf Labour Market and the Early Oil Industry: Traditional Structures and New Forms of Organization," in *The Gulf in the Early 20th Century: Foreign Institutions and Local Responses*, ed. Richard I. Lawless (Durham, NC: University of Durham, Occasional Papers Series 31, 1986), 91–124.

numbers nor skills to cater to the needs of the rapidly developing oil and related industries. For the imperial powers, Britain in particular, contrary to the primacy of political interests in the earlier decades, commercial ones began to determine the agenda. From the 1950s, these new economic imperatives led to the consolidation of the structures and rules governing the entry and duration of stay of foreigners.

While the earlier "sovereign" agreements had involved the rulers and the British government, a new instrument, Concession Agreements (CA), also included companies: These agreements were tripartite and included private investors. The CAs specified the terms and conditions of exploitation of oil resources including the recruitment of manpower. Thus, the CAs became the key instrument defining the migration "flows" into the region and it was the British government that insisted on the so-called nationality clauses in the CAs to ensure control over migrants. This is evident from the agreements between the British government and the respective oil company made before the finalization of a CA. The agreement between the British authorities and the Kuwait Oil Company in 1934 is a case in point since the official CA contained a clause giving preference in hiring to local Kuwaitis and, in a second tier, to Arabs recruited in the neighbouring states. However, in negotiations preceding the agreement, His Majesty's Government in the UK had ensured the recruitment of workers from British India by the company.[13]

In effect, this nationality clause produced a system of "reservations" since it promised preferential recruitment of local Arab workers provided, however, that these had the required skills. De facto, it ensured the prerogative of the British to staff the better-paying positions and to hire loyalists to the British Empire or beneficiaries of the commercial cause – especially British nationals, men from the dominions, and subjects from other colonies. The staff was invariably three-tiered. The senior level, broadly comprising the professional and highly skilled posts, was primarily occupied by British nationals (and sometimes Americans and continental Europeans). The junior levels, comprised of the semi-skilled, artisanal, clerical, or other professional ranks, were, for instance, filled in by Indians, Persians, and others. Finally, the low-paid and low-skilled levels tended to exclusively be staffed through local recruitment.

This pattern not only segregated locals to the lowest level of the job pyramid, but the British interest-driven policy also distorted intra-Gulf and larger regional mobility. As a consequence, local workers felt compelled to migrate to

13 Sharon Stanton Russel, "Uneasy Welcome: The Political Economy of Migration Policy in Kuwait" (PhD diss., MIT, 1987).

other states where their work and income prospects would not be frozen to the lower wage tier. In addition, the British-imposed regime of CAs was meant to restrict the hiring of workers from groups considered undesirable according to imperial interests because of their potential political activities. This applied, for example, to Persians in the case of Bahrain as well as to Iraqis and Palestinians in the case of Kuwait. In this way, the Empire intended to counter the contemporary political dynamics of the pan-Arab and pro-socialist movements.

The overseas labour recruitment practices of the oil companies mirrored the imperial selective nationality patterns and they recruited their personnel abroad using two methods whereby the first, formal method involved recruitment offices based abroad. Almost all companies opened recruitment offices in Bombay. However, this method was undercut by the British-India government which had amended the Emigration Act of India (1883) in 1922 and placed restrictions on labour migration. The act served the interests of plantation and mining investors for bound (indentured) labour in the Indian Ocean segment of the Empire, which was institutionalized since the 1830s (the decade of the abolition of slavery in the British Empire). India's new nationalist leaders (often in exile) strenuously opposed the system and the miserable working conditions resulting from it, which even led to an international outcry against the regime of indenture.[14] The companies, in addition, had to assume the responsibility to adhere to government-mandated obligations, such as quotas, and to administrative and other formalities.

Under these imperial constraints, the companies generally favoured the second method, namely the recruitment of workers through informal channels. Elite groups, for example, local businessmen (including Indian traders), applied for a No Objection Certificate (NOC) from the British Political Resident to import a given number of workers in return for a commission fee. After entry into the country and securing the promised job, the workers paid the sponsor. Hence, the NOCs were a common instrument.[15] In the case of Kuwait, to cite one example, the British Foreign Office remained in charge of its external affairs until independence in 1961 and continued to impose the requirement

14 Usha Mahajan, "Slavery, Indian Labour and British Colonialism," review of *A New System of Slavery: The Export of Indian Labour Overseas, 1830–1920*, by Hugh Tinker, *Pacific Affairs* 50, no. 2 (1977): 263–271.

15 The British Foreign Office "scrutinised visa applications very carefully, in order to exclude as many as possible of the opportunists and tricksters any oil state attracted, for whose misbehaviour the British might have been blamed." Peter Lienhardt and Ahmed al-Shahi, eds., *Disorientations: A Society in Flux: Kuwait in the 1950s* (Reading, UK: Ithaca Press, 1993).

that potential in-migrants first had to find a local host to sponsor their entry into the country.

Hence, a review of the historical developments in the region indicates that the British administration – both in London and through its residents – framed and adapted the requirements for entry and residence that are now considered hallmarks of the restrictive GCC work regime. The regime, already in place in the first phase, was thus merely adapted and significantly expanded in scope and scale during the second phase, whereby in the latter, company interests would often prevail over the political interests of the imperial administration. For example, Persian workers were actively recruited despite the restrictions in place. During and after the Second World War, the increased demand for oil tipped the balance of interests further to the side of the companies and, during the war years, they had even competed with the manpower demands of the British army and navy. Private companies managed to secure their labour supply, sometimes under the cover of military-civil needs: Capital found ways to circumvent or, at least, bend the political-imperial rules. It thus won control over foreign labour, sometimes with explicit support from the political regime.

While the two phases, roughly to the 1920s and from the 1950s onwards, were distinct in some respects, the structures that were initially established were simply consolidated and expanded during the second phase. In the process, the management of labour and its supply, which had centred on the needs of the British-India administration, came to fit the interests of the British-controlled or-sponsored petroleum companies.

3 Policies in the Neighbouring Regions

While the scope of the research for this chapter is focused on the Arab-Gulf region, the developments in Iran and Iraq, the regional neighbours in this period that were also under British imperial control, show strong commonalities.[16] Furthermore, similarities can also be traced in the case of Burma (modern-day Myanmar) under British colonial administration.

16 Selected references: Touraj Atabaki, "Far from Home, But at Home: Indian Migrant Workers in the Iranian Oil Industry," *Studies in History* 31, no. 1 (2015): 85–114; John Chalcraft, "Migration and Popular Protest in the Arabian Peninsula and the Gulf in the 1950s and 1960s," *International Labor and Working-Class History* 79 (2011): 28–47; Stefan Tetzlaf, "The Turn of the Gulf Tide: Empire, Nationalism, and South Asian Labor Migration to Iraq, c. 1900–1935," *International Labor and Working-Class History* 79 (2011): 7–27.

In Iran and Iraq, oil was discovered as early as 1909 and 1911. The capital invested was organized as the Anglo-Persian Oil Company (APOC), which was subsequently renamed as the Anglo-Iranian Oil company (AIOC) in 1935 and, for Iraq, as African & Eastern Concessions Ltd. and, subsequently, with additional capital investments from France and Germany, as the Turkish Petroleum Company (TCP) and, finally in 1929 as the Iraq Petroleum Company (IPC). Whereas Iran was placed under informal rule, Iraq fell directly under the British mandate from 1920 to 1932, following the capture of Baghdad during the First World War in 1917. For the refinery in the city of Abadan (Iran, near the Persian Gulf), the bulk of the skilled and semi-skilled workers was recruited from India. In fact, Indians had been among the initial workforce immediately after the oil discovery and founding of the company in 1910. The British viceregal government in India eventually assumed all the administration of labour migration from India. The employment of Indians only ended with the nationalization of the AIOC in 1951 and the Abadan refinery eventually closed down in 1958. In 1953, when the Iranian government and Prime Minister Mohammad Mossadegh attempted to nationalize the oil companies, in western parlance the "Abadan crisis," he was deposed in a coup known as "Operation Ajax" that was orchestrated by the US and British secret services. The developments in Iraq mirrored the Iranian developments in terms of the control mechanisms in place for privileging favoured imported labour from India to the detriment of the local workforce.

Further to the east, Burma *was* administered as a province of British India (1826–1948) and the imperial viceregal government encouraged the migration of Indians to the colony[17] from the mid-1800s and, much more intensely, from the First World War onwards as rural labourers, domestic workers, sepoys, professionals, and in other domains. In addition, the Raj supplied the labour demands of the Rangoon refinery. Links between the Burmah Oil Company and the APOC in Iran allowed the British authority to implement its macro-regional labour management. It produced similar mechanisms with the same overarching interest of enforcing control or discipline over migrant workers through the maintenance of group hierarchies and differentiated rights.

17 Selected references: Radha Mohan, "Immigration Policy of Burma in Relation to India: A Brief Survey," *Indian Journal of Political Science* 16, no. 2 (1955): 165–170; Edith L. Piness, "The British Administrator in Burma: A New View," *Journal of Southeast Asian Studies* 14, no. 2 (1983): 372–378; Ritesh Kumar Jaiswal, "Ephemeral Mobility: Critical Appraisal of the Facets of Indian Migration and the Maistry Mediation in Burma (c.1880–1940)," *Almanack* 19 (2018): 80–118.

These cases of societies and polities experiencing the same British colonial administration and, incidentally, the same expansion of investment into the petroleum industry, share not only imperial approaches to labour mobilization but also show interlinkages. Indian labourers hired at Burma's Rangoon refinery were at times directly transferred to the Iranian Abadan refinery. The British authorities co-opted traditional tribal customs, such as the kafala, and introduced intermediaries for the contractual regime to ease the burden of their role in recruitment and reduce bureaucratic hassles. The imperial administrations in Iran and Iraq and, even as far as Burma, shared similarities with the labour practices and mechanisms of the Arab-Gulf region, and indeed were its forerunners.

Hence, it was the British administration that first used the kafala system for migrant control in Iran and the workers who were recruited were not allowed to bring their families, albeit with some exceptions for high-ranking clerks. The Shaw Wallace & Co. Ltd., an India-based British Indian trading company that acted as an agent for, e.g., providing labour for Persia's APOC, recruited under the so-called "free contract system," which involved additional constraints, such as a reduction of the contract period from three years to one. The imperial insistence on the nationality clause in the CAs served "immediate economic and political expediency."[18] When designing such "ethno-national bases of labour differentiation and discrimination,"[19] imperial politics and oil-industry profit interests worked hand-in-hand to develop common mechanisms for maximizing dominance over and control of the subdued labour, as Touraj Atabaki noted, "like foreign soldiers, foreign workers were brought under the discipline of colonial rule and subject to its priorities."[20] Forms of forced labour were thus a familiar "colonial weapon" for the maximum profit of the overseas colonial enterprise, with the least amount of accountability.

4 Conclusion

This empirically researched chapter on the role of British-introduced colonial structures in founding the Arab-Gulf states' contemporary migration policies highlights three convergences.

18 Russel, "Uneasy Welcome," 100.

19 Gennaro Errichiello, "Foreign Workforce in the Arab-Gulf States (1930–1950): Migration Patterns and Nationality Clause," *International Migration Review* 46, no. 2 (2012): 389–413.

20 Touraj Atabaki, "Indian Migrant Workers in the Iranian Oil Industry 1908–1951," in *Working for Oil: Comparative Social Histories of Labor in the Global Oil Industry*, ed. Touraj Atabaki, Elisabetta Bini, and Kaveh Ehsani (London: Palgrave Macmillan, 2018), 189–226.

First: The Arab-Gulf states' guestworker policies involve far more than a "local" story. The British-era link shows that the current abusive GCC migration policies are not a case of exceptionalism, popularly attributed to the GCC states being Islamic monarchies, but also one of imperially-introduced institutions to regulate migration to suit the Empire's prerogatives during both the pre-oil and early oil eras before the emergence of the current states. The Empire developed systemic mechanisms to give precedence to its nationals and its preferred subjects – such as labour from British India – to the detriment of local native populations and influences.

Second: The old imperial policies are lingering on in the "new" and current policies. For example, the Arab-Gulf region still is an essentially closed labour market and recruitment generally occurs via the contractors or sponsors, the *kafeels*, rather than being direct. The colonial/imperial administration privileged the elite interests of the time, be they those of the British state or those of the local rulers acceptable to the imperial authorities. The GCC states, which continue this profitable regime, have expanded the profitability to their citizens and the same historically established structures now serve the new elites as they previously favoured the former elites with the only difference being that instead of foreign capitalists, their Arab national inheritors are now at the top of the hierarchy. The migrant non-nationals in both the colonial and independent phases, irrespective of their occupational or class level, permanently remain at the bottom of the hierarchy in temporary and disposable spaces, internally stratified according to their nationality, ethnicity and length of stay.

Third: The Arab-Gulf region's case in the past and at present is intimately connected with larger international economic and migration processes. It was and is part of the international political economies of the slave trade, colonial capital flows, and the expansion of the oil industry. As a result, all cases outlined in this chapter show a common frame or regime to achieve a labour pool malleable to colonial imperatives.

The present scenario of restrictive guestworker migration policies in the Arab-Gulf region, which continue to exploit workers for the profit of the elites, is therefore not an exceptional one. Rather, it is part of the larger historical and global frame, in this case, a British imperial legacy in the guise of a nation-state.

CHAPTER 14

The Making of a Neoliberal Labour Regime in California

Immigration, American Empire, and Union Organizing in the 1980s and 1990s

Richard Saich

Abstract

In the 1980s, California became an important economic hub within an increasingly integrated global economy. However, economic restructuring made work more precarious, particularly in the growing services sector. The shift to neoliberal modes of governance exacerbated inequality and poverty and undermined social protections that had been institutionalized by liberal reformers since the 1930s. This chapter argues that California's neoliberal labour regime of the 1980s was sustained in large part by the exploitation of (im-)migrant workers from Mexico, Guatemala, El Salvador, and Nicaragua and that migration from these countries was shaped by the impact of the Reagan administration's foreign and economic policy in Central America. These structural features shaped the context of labour organizing in complex and sometimes unexpected ways and ultimately contributed to the revitalization of unions in California. In fact, the mobilization and militancy of immigrant workers was a crucial contributing factor to the labour resurgence in the state in the 1990s.

Keywords

California – Central America – Mexican immigrants – neoliberal labour regime – service sector

1 Introduction

In 1980, the Reagan administration launched a campaign to restore American power in the world and re-establish the primacy of "free market" capitalism within the global economy. This was achieved through US sponsorship of authoritarian governments and the imposition of economic reforms by

 | DOI:10.1163/9789004686991_015

American-backed multilateral financial institutions. The former destroyed leftist opponents and weakened democratic opposition to liberalization while the latter promised recalcitrant governments the loans they needed to cope with their growing indebtedness. Historian Greg Grandin has described the effects of this strategy in the western hemisphere as constituting a "third conquest of Latin America."[1] This chapter traces the effects of these policies back to the US.[2] It shows how the "Reagan offensive" in Latin America in turn reinforced the neoliberal political economy that was then taking shape in the US. By proposing a multi-scalar analysis of transnational processes of economic restructuring and immigration, it reveals the role of the US "empire" – historical structures of political, military, and economic domination – in sustaining neoliberal labour regimes in the United States. Finally, it argues that these processes created the conditions for a new terrain of struggle between capital and labour. To illustrate this point, it examines the "social movement" unionization campaigns launched by migrant workers in California in the 1980s and 1990s.

2 The Neoliberal Transition in California

In recent years, political and intellectual historians have begun to unearth the history of the policy entrepreneurs, think tanks, business groups, and politicians who engineered the rise of neoliberalism in the US.[3] Through their growing influence in the Republican Party in the 1960s and 1970s, these groups aimed to cut taxes, dismantle government regulations, and roll back welfare provisions and with the election of Ronald Reagan as president in 1980, these proposals subsequently became official government policy. The fact that these political developments were catastrophic for the cause of organized labour

1 Greg Grandin, *Empire's Workshop: Latin America, the United States, and the Rise of the New Imperialism* (New York: Owl Books, 2007), 159–195.

2 Odd Arne Westad, *The Global Cold War: Third World Interventions and the Making of Our Times* (Cambridge: Cambridge University Press, 2005), 331.

3 For a sample of this literature, see Kim Phillips-Fein, *Invisible Hands: The Making of the Conservative Movement from the New Deal to Reagan* (New York: W. W. Norton, 2009); Angus Burgin, *The Great Persuasion: Reinventing Free Markets Since the Depression* (Cambridge, MA: Harvard University Press, 2012); Daniel Stedman Jones, *Masters of the Universe: Hayek, Friedman, and the Birth of Neoliberal Politics* (Princeton, NJ: Princeton University Press, 2012); Philip Mirowski and Dieter Plehwe, eds., *The Road from Mont Pèlerin: The Making of the Neoliberal Thought Collective* (Cambridge, MA: Harvard University Press, 2015); Gary Gerstle, *The Rise and Fall of the Neoliberal Order: America and the World in the Free Market Era* (Oxford: Oxford University Press, 2022).

within the US is well-known. Union density plummeted, membership declined from 29 percent of the entire workforce in 1973 to approximately 16 percent in 1991, and for many, work became increasingly precarious and insecure.[4] The defeat of the Professional Air Traffic Controllers Organization (PATCO) by Reagan in the early 1980s is often credited as being a major turning point in this national political narrative.[5]

However, neoliberal reforms were also associated with the transformation of the global division of labour. With the advent of the "post-Fordist" economy, industrial production itself became globalized, and this yielded a fundamental shift in the balance of power between labour and capital.[6] In the early 1990s, these economic developments were increasingly described as the product of "globalization," a seemingly inexorable process that erased national borders, eliminated trade barriers and brought about a flattening and homogenizing of social and cultural life. The "deterritorialization" that allegedly characterized neoliberal development, however, was not as uniform and homogenous as both cheerleaders and critics of globalization often implied. Rather, it comprised multiple differentiated labour regimes. As anthropologist Aihwa Ong noted, deterritorialization did not create one smooth homogenous space and the claims by Michael Hardt and Antonio Negri "about the formation of a unified space of counter-Empire" by "the mobile multitude" as a movement of resistance "blithely neglects analysis of the actual, multiple, and segregated conditions of workers in the Empire's networks." Ong's suggestion that neoliberalism creates "situated modes of labor control" provides a more empirically grounded theory of how resistance to neoliberalism is generated.[7] The historical evolution of neoliberal labour regimes was thus the product of changes in national and state policymaking, the evolution of complex global production

4 Nelson Lichtenstein, *State of The Union: A Century of American Labor*, rev. ed. (Princeton, NJ: Princeton University Press, 2013), 213.

5 Joseph A. McCartin, *Collision Course: Ronald Reagan, the Air Traffic Controllers, and the Strike That Changed America* (Oxford: Oxford University Press, 2013).

6 Folker Fröbel, Jürgen Heinrichs, and Otto Kreye, *The New International Division of Labour: Structural Unemployment in Industrialised Countries and Industrialisation in Developing Countries* (Cambridge: Cambridge University Press, 1980); Alain Lipietz, *Mirages and Miracles: The Crisis in Global Fordism*, trans. David Macey (London: Verso, 1987).

7 On deterritorialization, see Gilles Deleuze and Félix Guattari, *Anti-Oedipus: Capitalism and Schizophrenia*, trans. Robert Hurley, Mark Seem, and Helen R. Lane (Minneapolis: University of Minnesota Press, 2008); Gilles Deleuze and Félix Guattari, *A Thousand Plateaus: Capitalism and Schizophrenia*, trans. Brian Massumi (London: Bloomsbury, 2013); Michael Hardt and Antonio Negri, *Empire* (Cambridge, MA: Harvard University Press, 2000); Aihwa Ong, *Neoliberalism as Exception: Mutations in Citizenship and Sovereignty* (Durham, NC: Duke University Press, 2006), 121–138.

systems, and the articulation of social relations embedded within localized sites of struggle. In California, the Service Employees International Union would seize upon local developments to struggle against the outsourcing of service work to migrants or immigrant workers. (For similar developments in Denmark, see Chapter 23 in this volume.)[8]

In California, the liberal-labour alliance had brought the Democratic Party to power with the election of Pat Brown as Governor in 1958. Brown implemented many of the social reforms that are retrospectively associated with the New Deal order, such as labour rights protections and more generous welfare provisions.[9] In fact, California foreshadowed national trends towards the neoliberal transition when, at the onset of the urban crisis, divisions within the state's Democratic Party and the mobilization of Conservative voters in the suburbs provided an opening for Ronald Reagan to defeat Brown in the race for the governorship in 1966.[10] Although some scholars have tended to emphasize Reagan's pragmatism as governor, he had already assembled the fundamental components of the neoliberal programme by 1971 with a comprehensive assault on welfare spending. Although Reagan was succeeded by the liberal Democrat Jerry Brown as Governor in 1975, the Democrats soon found themselves hobbled by the passage of Proposition 13 in 1978, which was a citizen's initiative to suppress property taxes.[11] The fiscal constraints imposed by this so-called "tax revolt" meant that state and local officials would increasingly turn to federal grants for funding, although these dried up after the election of Reagan to the Presidency in 1980. Following the 1982 gubernatorial election, Republican George Deukmejian pursued a neoliberal agenda

---

8 For some theoretical background on the term "labour regime," see Elena Baglioni et al., eds., *Labour Regimes and Global Production* (Newcastle, UK: Agenda Publishing, 2022), 1–25. This conceptual framework is useful for integrating local, transnational, and global labour histories as proposed by Marcel van der Linden, "Labour History: The Old, the New and the Global," *African Studies* 66, no. 2–3 (2007): 169–180.

9 Steve Fraser and Gary Gerstle, eds., *The Rise and Fall of the New Deal Order, 1930–1980* (Princeton, NJ: Princeton University Press, 1989).

10 Gerald Horne, *Fire This Time: The Watts Uprising and the 1960s* (Charlottesville: University of Virginia Press, 1995); Matthew Dallek, *The Right Moment: Ronald Reagan's First Victory and the Decisive Turning Point in American Politics* (New York: Free Press, 2000), 150–172; Lisa McGirr, *Suburban Warriors: The Origins of the New American Right* (Princeton, NJ: Princeton University Press, 2001).

11 Jonathan Bell, *California Crucible: The Forging of Modern American Liberalism* (Philadelphia: University of Pennsylvania Press, 2012), 245–256; Wallace Turner, "Reagan Urges Huge Cut in California Relief Rolls," *The New York Times*, 4 March 1971, https://www.nytimes.com/1971/03/04/archives/reagan-urges-huge-cut-in-california-relief-rolls-would-reduce.html.

that encompassed the privatization of health services, cuts to mental health services, and the further tightening of welfare rules.[12] Deukmejian's victory signalled the final dissolution of the New Deal coalition and the ascendancy of neoliberal governance in California.

The neoliberal turn was subsequently evident even in cities that remained under Democratic control because much of the urban tax base – the prosperous middle-class citizens – migrated to the suburbs.[13] For liberals such as Tom Bradley, the mayor of Los Angeles, this presented problems and he turned to an alliance with downtown business interests as a means of growing the urban economy. Under such an alliance, the city government would use "tax increment financing" to promote development.[14] Los Angeles was drawn into the competition to attract domestic and foreign capital, particularly from Japanese investors.[15]

3 The Restructuring of California's Economic Sectors and Labour Markets

In the 1990s, commentators began to describe Los Angeles as a "global city," a major centre of world trade and international financial capital. In the previous two decades, the state of California had grown to become the seventh largest economy in the world – larger than most nation-states – and by 2005 its US$ 1.5 trillion economy made it the fifth largest in the world.[16] This economic growth, however, had been achieved at the cost of intensifying inequality

12 Jennifer Wolch, "From Global to Local: The Rise of Homelessness in Los Angeles during the 1980s," in *The City: Los Angeles and Urban Theory at the End of the Twentieth Century*, ed. Allen J. Scott and Edward W. Soja (Berkeley: University of California Press, 1996), 395.

13 Thomas J. Sugrue, *The Origins of the Urban Crisis: Race and Inequality in Postwar Detroit* (Princeton, NJ: Princeton University Press, 1996); Kevin M. Kruse, *White Flight: Atlanta and the Making of Modern Conservatism* (Princeton, NJ: Princeton University Press, 2007).

14 Raphael J. Sonenshein, *Politics in Black and White: Race and Power in Los Angeles* (Princeton, NJ: Princeton University Press, 1993), 163–169.

15 Scott Kurashige, *The Shifting Grounds of Race: Black and Japanese Americans in the Making of Multiethnic Los Angeles* (Princeton, NJ: Princeton University Press, 2008), 284–285; Mike Davis, *City of Quartz: Excavating the Future in Los Angeles* (London: Verso, 2006), 70–83.

16 Jon David Vasche, "A Perspective on the California Economy," *California State Legislature, Office of the Legislative Analyst*, December 1988, 47; U.S. Bureau of the Census, *Statistical Abstract of the United States: 1990*, 110th ed. (Washington, DC: 1990), https://www.census.gov/library/publications/1990/compendia/statab/110ed.html; Kevin Starr, *California: A History* (New York: Random House, 2005).

and while many Californians were growing wealthier, increasing numbers of workers were having to accept lower wages and deteriorating working conditions. As early as the 1960s, the state began to experience deindustrialization, as manufacturing jobs were moved to locations with lower labour costs. Although automation and computerization in other industries brought about higher levels of productivity, the benefits of those advances were shared by fewer workers. In August 1991, the closure of the General Motors Van Nuys plant in the San Fernando Valley of Los Angeles, following a prolonged battle by unions and community groups to save it, marked the end of an era.[17] The new "post-industrial" economy brought wealth to the suburbs, but it did little for the urban poor.

Significantly, the transition to a "post-industrial" economy did not involve the wholesale elimination of traditional sectors but rather their restructuring. For instance, as one of California's most important sectors, agriculture remained part of the diversifying economy, although the inflationary pressures of the 1970s resulted in a deep crisis in this area. Falling commodity prices as a result of high interest rates in the 1980s and the perennial problem of securing sufficient water supply in the arid West prompted many farmers to sell their land to larger more capital-intensive firms or commercial land developers.[18] Others switched to producing high-value but labour-intensive fruits and vegetables for export which created demand for migrant labour.[19] In the textile industry, thousands of jobs were offshored and manufacturers in the Southern US adopted automation as a way to respond to intense foreign competition. However, the garment industry in California continued to expand with the proliferation of small shops employing predominantly female and undocumented workers. Production in these industries could continue in Los Angeles because of the comparative advantage in transport costs.[20] The spectacular

17 Edward W. Soja, "It All Comes Together in Los Angeles," in *Postmodern Geographies: The Reassertion of Space in Critical Social Theory* (London: Verso, 1989), 201–204; Kevin Starr, *Coast of Dreams: A History of Contemporary California* (London: Penguin, 2006), 238.

18 Richard White, *"It's Your Misfortune and None of My Own": A New History of the American West* (Norman: University of Oklahoma Press, 1991), 560–561; Ruth Wilson Gilmore, *Golden Gulag: Prisons, Surplus, Crisis, and Opposition in Globalizing California* (Berkeley: University of California Press, 2007), 67–68.

19 Patricia Zavella, "The Tables Are Turned: Immigration, Poverty, and Social Conflict in California Communities," in *Immigrants Out! The New Nativism and the Anti-Immigrant Impulse in the United States,* ed. Juan F. Perea (New York: New York University Press, 1997).

20 Julia C. Bonham, "Robotics, Electronics, and the American Textile Industry," in *Hanging by a Thread: Social Change in Southern Textiles,* ed. Jeffrey Leiter, Michael Schulman, and Rhonda Zingraff (Ithaca, NY: Cornell University Press, 1991); Soja, "It All Comes Together in Los Angeles," 207–208, 215–217; Ong, *Neoliberalism,* 121–138.

rise of Silicon Valley and the development of new information technologies depended upon electronics manufacturing and assembly which employed migrant workers, particularly Latina, Vietnamese, and Filipina women. From its very beginning, while the semiconductor industry pursued outsourcing, offshoring, and anti-union strategies, the inflow of undocumented workers allowed firms to also limit labour costs and continue production in California.[21] Many other new jobs were still being created in this period, but they were primarily within sectors that had also been historically less organized, such as health and personal care.[22]

The largest area of growth was in the services sector and, between 1959 and 1980, the Los Angeles region added 750,000 service sector jobs, accounting for nearly 40 percent of all job growth and almost double the number of manufacturing jobs.[23] While the office boom in Los Angeles facilitated an expansion of the cleaning and building services industry, parallel to the practice of offshoring in the manufacturing sector, outsourcing assumed large proportions in the domestic services sector. Private building managers, working for large corporations, began to contract out cleaning and other facilities-management functions to external private firms that were operating in a non-union environment and larger service companies sought savings by reducing worker pay and benefits. As a result, union membership and worker power within the cleaning industry plummeted.

This coincided with greater labour market segmentation and in the 1970s and 1980s economists began to talk about the "dual labour market." The term described an occupational structure that was characterized by the division of the job market into well-paying and low-paying service jobs, a phenomenon that occurred as urban centres lost low-skilled jobs and gained high-skilled

21 Margaret O'Mara, *The Code: Silicon Valley and the Remaking of America* (New York: Penguin, 2019); Karen J. Hossfeld, "'Their Logic Against Them': Contradictions in Sex, Race, and Class in Silicon Valley," in *Women Workers and Global Restructuring*, ed. Kathryn Ward (Ithaca, NY: Cornell University Press, 1990); David N. Pellow, *The Silicon Valley of Dreams: Environmental Injustice, Immigrant Workers, and the High-Tech Global Economy* (New York: New York University Press, 2002), 137–168; Glenna Matthews, *Silicon Valley, Women, and the California Dream: Gender, Class, and Opportunity in the Twentieth Century* (Stanford, CA: Stanford University Press, 2003), 147–182, 243–247.

22 Eileen Boris, *Caring for America: Home Health Workers in the Shadow of the Welfare State* (Oxford: Oxford University Press, 2012), 4–19; Gabriel Winant, "'Hard Times Make for Hard Arteries and Hard Livers': Deindustrialization, Biopolitics, and the Making of a New Working Class," *Journal of Social History* 53, no. 1 (2019): 107–132.

23 Wolch, "From Global to Local: The Rise of Homelessness in Los Angeles during the 1980s," 392.

jobs in FIRE: finance, insurance, and real estate.[24] Between 1972 and 1982, Mayor Bradley oversaw a boom in office construction in Los Angeles, with office space increasing by 50 percent. Major sub-centres emerged in Century City, Newport Beach, and Orange County.[25] Furthermore, by the late 1980s, Los Angeles was home to a large contingent of corporate headquarters, banks, and corporate law firms.[26] The commercial and residential development boom in turn fuelled the growth of informal employment in the construction industry in addition to the new demand for workers in low-wage service jobs in janitorial, hotel, restaurant, and domestic work. By the 1990s, the workforce in these industries was predominantly Latinx – a term used for Latin American migrants – that were resident in the US.[27]

As a result of the fiscal restraints imposed by Proposition 13, outsourcing and subcontracting were increasingly embraced, not only by private firms but also by government agencies to reduce the size of their budgets. Neoliberal economists also provided a rationale for transferring jobs from the former to the latter by arguing that the public sector was less efficient than the private sector.[28] However, in the private sector, workers experienced greater job insecurity. Since unions were relatively more resilient in the public sector, privatization also had the effect of further weakening the labour movement. Working conditions deteriorated because of these practices, even in those industries that historically had greater union density. When corporate building managers began to contract out cleaning and other facilities management functions to external smaller private firms and large service companies, these, in turn, sought savings by reducing worker pay and benefits.

24 Saskia Sassen, *The Global City: New York, London, Tokyo* (Princeton, NJ: Princeton University Press, 1991), 64–67, 197–214.

25 Edward W. Soja, "Los Angeles, 1965–1992: From Crisis-Generated Restructuring to Restructuring-Generated Crisis," in *The City: Los Angeles and Urban Theory at the End of the Twentieth Century*, ed. Allen John Scott and Edward W. Soja (Berkeley: University of California Press, 1996), 441; Edward W. Soja, *My Los Angeles: From Urban Restructuring to Regional Urbanization* (Berkeley: University of California Press, 2014), 49.

26 Soja, "It All Comes Together in Los Angeles," 210.

27 Kurashige, *The Shifting Grounds of Race*, 292.

28 Peter Drucker is often credited with popularizing privatization in the American context in his 1969 book *The Age of Discontinuity: Guidelines to Our Changing Society* (New York: Harper & Row, 1969). In the 1980s, it was promoted by American conservatives such as Robert W. Poole, *Cutting Back City Hall* (New York: Universe Books, 1980); John D. Donahue, *The Privatization Decision: Public Ends, Private Means* (New York: Basic Books, 1989); Germà Bel, "Retrospectives: The Coining of 'Privatization' and Germany's National Socialist Party," *Journal of Economic Perspectives* 20, no. 3 (2006): 187–194.

4 California and Transnational Migration

The neoliberal labour regime in California was sustained by the exploitation of mainly undocumented migrant workers. In fact, Mexican labour had long been crucial to the state's economy. During the Second World War, American officials had feared that agricultural production in the US West and Southwest would be disrupted by labour shortages and hence the government reached an agreement with Mexico to establish the Bracero Program to facilitate the importation of Mexican contract labour.[29] Following the end of the Bracero Program in 1964 and the passing of the Hart-Cellar Act in 1965, which abolished the national origins quota system (in place since the early twentieth century), the in-migration of both documented and undocumented workers continued. From 1965 to the early 1990s, the supply of "low-skilled" workers was boosted by the immigration of perhaps 5 million people to Los Angeles alone.[30] While Mexican migration had become institutionalized by the social networks that were necessary for the functioning of the programme, at the same time, political instability and war in East Asia and Central America also accelerated immigration from other countries. Given the economic restructuring of the 1970s and 1980s described above, newly arriving immigrants were as likely to be working in labour-intensive jobs in urban areas as they were in the agricultural sector.

Many managers in labour-intensive industries tended to favour immigrant workers because they perceived them as being easily controlled, a perception informed by a historical set of racist assumptions about Latin Americans. However, it also reflected the highly unequal power relations produced by the economic relationship between the two regions and the legal prerogatives of the US state. When the Bracero Program was terminated, the economic incentives for continuing established patterns of migration remained, although such migration was now classified as illegal by US authorities.[31] In the 1960s and 1970s, many Mexican workers regarded employment in the US as a temporary arrangement, and they were "target earners" who frequently returned to their home country.[32] Growing anti-immigrant sentiment in the 1970s and 1980s prompted an expansion and militarization of border enforcement and

29 Mae M. Ngai, *Impossible Subjects: Illegal Aliens and the Making of Modern America* (Princeton, NJ: Princeton University Press, 2014), 127–166.

30 Soja, "Los Angeles, 1965–1992," 442.

31 Ngai, *Impossible Subjects*.

32 Ruth Milkman, ed., *Organizing Immigrants: The Challenge for Unions in Contemporary California* (Ithaca, NY: ILR Press, 2000), 13.

the subsequent intensification of "security" measures increased the number of apprehensions of undocumented immigrants, thereby creating the impression of a crisis. This in turn precipitated the passage of the Immigration Reform and Control Act (IRCA) in 1986, which, ironically, further disrupted the established pattern of return immigration, thus increasing the undocumented population within the US as well as the turn to "defensive naturalization" in the 1990s.[33]

When unionized workers were ousted from secure employment due to restructuring, employers could turn to this new pool of labour and by the mid-1990s, approximately 50 percent of foreign-born residents in Los Angeles were from Mexico and 10 percent were from El Salvador and Guatemala. As Michael Piore suggested in his influential study *Birds of Passage* (1979), the dynamics of the secondary labour market were influenced by social and institutional "pull" factors (demand for low-wage labour) as much as the "push" factors (such as wage differentials between the US and countries in the Global South).[34] The move by employers to adopt "flexible" employment practices expanded the secondary labour market, thereby absorbing new immigrant workers, and the willingness of some employers to avoid paying taxes and flout labour laws simply accelerated this process. As sociologist Janice Fine has argued, "In Los Angeles, as well as in many other locations, the growth of low-wage immigrant employment was a consequence, not a cause, of declining job quality."[35]

Because the IRCA made it illegal to hire undocumented immigrants, it also had the effect of reducing the bargaining power of Mexican immigrants, depressing their wages, and intensifying exploitation.[36] Workers often lacked awareness of their rights and were unlikely to approach government agencies to address their grievances. The threat of deportation was a particularly potent weapon in the hands of employers.[37] If individuals sought to organize their fellow workers, then managers could simply fire them or report them to the INS

33 Douglas S. Massey, "America's Immigration Policy Fiasco: Learning from Past Mistakes," *Daedalus* 142, no. 3 (2013): 5–15.

34 Michael J. Piore, *Birds of Passage: Migrant Labor and Industrial Societies* (Cambridge: Cambridge University Press, 1979).

35 Janice Fine et al., "Celebrating the Enduring Contribution of Birds of Passage: Migrant Labor and Industrial Societies," *Industrial and Labor Relations Review* 69, no. 3 (2016): 774–782.

36 Douglas S. Massey and Kerstin Gentsch, "Undocumented Migration to the United States and the Wages of Mexican Immigrants," *International Migration Review* 48, no. 2 (2014): 482–499.

37 In the 1980s, empirical research by Rita J. Simon and Margo DeLay found that legal status was the most important factor in predicting the hourly rate of pay for immigrant women from Mexico. Rita J. Simon and Margo DeLey, "The Work Experience of Undocumented Mexican Women Migrants in Los Angeles," *International Migration Review* 18, no. 4 (1984): 1212–1229.

(Immigration and Naturalization Service). As a result, it was often assumed by employers and union leaders alike that immigrants could not be organized. These conditions resulted in the formation of an ethnic niche within the "secondary" labour market as employers used existing immigrant networks to recruit new workers.[38]

5 Connections: US Imperialism in Latin America

Immigration from Central America should not only be understood in relation to the domestic labour regime and the transnational linkages that sustained it, but also in relation to the long history of US imperialism in Latin America. Patterns of transnational migration to Los Angeles can be conceptualized as "blowback," that is the unintended consequences of the Reagan administration's attempt to impose neoliberal modes of governance in the Global South. This occurred in two interrelated ways, namely due to the effects of US economic and foreign policy. In the words of Juan Gonzalez, "Quite simply, our vast Latino population is the unintended harvest of the U.S. empire."[39]

During the 1970s, American banks had "recycled" petrodollars from oil-exporting countries by extending their lending to countries in the Global South, including Mexico. The Volcker shock of 1980, a policy of high interest rates imposed by the US Department of the Treasury, sent the interest on these loans spiralling out of control and, as a result, the Mexican government was unable to service its debts when recession hit in 1982. The Reagan administration, together with the international financial institutions, saw the crisis as an opportunity to leverage neoliberal policy reforms in the Global South while the new generation of technocratic political leaders in Mexico was receptive to demands for "structural adjustment," especially since many of them had been trained in economics departments in the US.[40] The result was a "lost decade" or, in the words of one economist, "the most traumatic economic event in Latin America's economic history." Workers' earnings in Mexico plummeted, and the

38 Roger Waldinger, "Not the Promised City: Los Angeles and Its Immigrants," *Pacific Historical Review* 68, no. 2 (1999): 257–265.

39 Walter LaFeber, *Inevitable Revolutions: The United States in Central America,* 2nd ed. (New York: W. W. Norton, 1993); Juan Gonzalez, *Harvest of Empire: A History of Latinos in America,* rev. ed. (New York: Penguin, 2011); Chalmers Johnson, *Blowback: The Costs and Consequences of American Empire,* 2nd ed. (New York: Henry Holt, 2004); Naomi Klein, *The Shock Doctrine: The Rise of Disaster Capitalism* (London: Penguin, 2008).

40 Sarah Babb, *Managing Mexico: Economists from Nationalism to Neoliberalism* (Princeton, NJ: Princeton University Press, 2001).

poverty rate rose dramatically from 40.5 percent to 48.3 percent in the single decade from 1980 to 1990.[41] Economic dislocation was particularly acute in rural areas in the northern states, creating a strong incentive for people living there to emigrate to the North in search of better economic opportunities. The conditions created in Mexico are therefore either directly or indirectly associated with what Saskia Sassen has called "counter-geographies of globalization," which comprises gendered and racialized circuits of migration and exchange that existed outside of formal legal frameworks and were often not discussed within official discourse, but which were nonetheless fostered by the conditions created by neoliberal globalization. Sassen also points out that migrant women were often constructed as an economic "burden" to receiving countries but were nonetheless at the centre of a wide range of profit-making activities, both in the formal economy (for example nursing, electronic and textiles manufacturing, etc.) and the shadow economy (for example in the sex industry).[42]

Immigration from Guatemala, El Salvador, and Nicaragua differed from immigration from Mexico insofar as it was, in addition, the direct outcome of US foreign policy. The Reagan Administration's policy in the 1980s was in many ways an extension of pre-existing Cold War imperatives in the US's "backyard." In 1954, the Central Intelligence Agency (CIA) orchestrated a coup against the democratically elected government of Guatemala, removing reformist president Jacobo Árbenz. The US government provided financial and military assistance to the new Guatemalan regime as it pursued a decades-long attempt to suppress left insurgents and US military advisors played a key role in providing counterinsurgency training to Guatemala's paramilitary death squads.[43] Influenced by the ideas of the neoconservative intellectual, political scientist and diplomat Jeane Kirkpatrick, the Reagan administration embraced the principle that the US should support authoritarian client states irrespective of their human rights record.[44] Thus, the Reagan administration provided

41 José Antonio Ocampo, "The Latin American Debt Crisis in Historical Perspective," in *Life After Debt: The Origins and Resolutions of Debt Crisis*, ed. Joseph E. Stiglitz and Daniel Heymann (Basingstoke, UK: Palgrave Macmillan, 2014).

42 Saskia Sassen, "Women's Burden: Counter-Geographies of Globalization and the Feminization of Survival," *Journal of International Affairs* 53, no. 2 (2000): 503–524.

43 Piero Gleijeses, *Shattered Hope: The Guatemalan Revolution and the United States, 1944–1954* (Princeton, NJ: Princeton University Press, 1992); Stephen Schlesinger and Stephen Kinzer, *Bitter Fruit: The Story of the American Coup in Guatemala*, 2nd ed. (Cambridge, MA: Harvard University Press, 2005).

44 Jeane J. Kirkpatrick, "Dictatorships & Double Standards," *Commentary Magazine*, November 1979; Jeane J. Kirkpatrick, *Dictatorships and Double Standards: Rationalism and Reason in Politics* (New York: American Enterprise Institute and Simon & Schuster, 1983); Jeane J. Kirkpatrick, *The Reagan Doctrine and U.S. Foreign Policy* (Washington,

financial and military aid to the right-wing junta in El Salvador, which was then embroiled in a violent civil war. In the context of domestic criticism from the Democratic-controlled Congress, negative public opinion, and domestic protest movements, Reagan adopted an official policy of "democracy promotion" to legitimize authoritarian regimes and provide a fig leaf for American strategic interests in Latin America.[45] Reagan also utilized trade initiatives such as the Caribbean Basin Initiative to strengthen US hegemony in the region.[46] Most controversially within the US, Reagan's National Security Council sought to undermine the Nicaraguan Revolution following the overthrow of the Somoza regime by providing covert support for the Contra rebels.[47]

As had earlier been the case in South American countries, authoritarian regimes became the means to establish economic policies that accorded more closely with neoliberal ideology.[48] The human costs of these conflicts were high, with a quarter of a million deaths in the period from 1974 to 1996, over a million people displaced within their home countries, and over 2 million Nicaraguans, Salvadorans, and Guatemalans seeking refuge in the neighbouring countries of Costa Rica and Honduras or further northward in Mexico, the US, and Canada. The Reagan administration refused to grant Salvadorans and Guatemalans refugee status as a group because to do so would amount to public recognition of the complicity of the US in their oppression by corrupt governments and

---

DC: Heritage Foundation, 1985). Odd Arne Westad points out that "[t]he Reagan approach was in many ways a continuation of the policies and methods developed by Carter's National Security Adviser Zbigniew Brzezinski and his staff." The transition from detente to greater intervention in foreign policy thus paralleled the transition from economic management to deregulation in domestic policy. Westad, *The Global Cold War*, 331–363.

45 Thomas Carothers, *In the Name of Democracy: U.S. Policy Toward Latin America in the Reagan Years* (Berkeley: University of California Press, 1993); Christian Smith, *Resisting Reagan: The U.S. Central America Peace Movement* (Chicago, IL: University of Chicago Press, 1996); Robert Pee and William Michael Schmidli, eds., *The Reagan Administration, the Cold War, and the Transition to Democracy Promotion* (Basingstoke, UK: Palgrave Macmillan, 2018).

46 William M. LeoGrande, *Our Own Backyard: The United States in Central America, 1977–1992* (Chapel Hill: University of North Carolina Press, 2000), 151.

47 John Canham-Clyne, "Business as Usual: Iran-Contra and the National Security State," *World Policy Journal* 9, no. 4 (1992): 617–637; Malcolm Byrne, *Iran-Contra: Reagan's Scandal and the Unchecked Abuse of Presidential Power* (Lawrence: University Press of Kansas, 2014). The Contras also received aid from other US allies, including Saudi Arabia. Richard Sobel, "Contra Aid Fundamentals: Exploring the Intricacies and the Issues," *Political Science Quarterly* 110, no. 2 (1995): 287.

48 On Friedman, the "Chicago Boys" and Chile, see Klein, *The Shock Doctrine*, 49–71; Ruth Blakeley, *State Terrorism and Neoliberalism: The North in the South* (London: Routledge, 2009).

hence they were subsequently classified as "economic migrants," along with most other Latin Americans. In contrast, like the first generation of Cubans before them, Nicaraguans were considered to be legitimate refugees fleeing a "pro-Soviet regime" although few of these refugees were able to regularize their status.[49]

6 Labour Organizing in California: Social Movement Unionism

While recognizing the interrelationship of the structural features of the labour market in Los Angeles, patterns of transnational migration, and US imperialism in Central America, historians also need to focus on the agency of the workers. In fact, employers in the services sector themselves badly underestimated the willingness of migrant workers to organize, which may in part be explained by the historical collusion of labour unions in the US with white supremacy and racial discrimination against migrant workers since the late nineteenth century.[50] However, such attitudes began to falter in the face of their mobilization in the 1960s. Perhaps the most significant campaign in this respect was the successful drive of the United Farm Workers to organize agricultural workers in the context of the new social movements, in this case, the rise of the Chicano movement.[51] In 1968, activists Bert Corona and Chole Alatorre founded El Centro de Acción Social Autónoma-Hermandad General de Trabajadores (CASA), an organization dedicated to defending the rights of both documented and undocumented migrant workers. The veterans of these movements helped to transmit knowledge and skills to a new generation of

---

49 Susan Bibler Coutin, *Nations of Emigrants: Shifting Boundaries of Citizenship in El Salvador and the United States* (Ithaca, NY: Cornell University Press, 2007). Relatively few Argentines or Chileans had been able to migrate to the United States. María Cristina García, "Latino Immigration," in *The Oxford Handbook of American Immigration and Ethnicity*, ed. Ronald H. Bayor (Oxford: Oxford University Press, 2016), and María Cristina García, *Seeking Refuge: Central American Migration to Mexico, the United States, and Canada* (Berkeley: University of California Press, 2006). According to García, "From 1983 to 1990, only 2.6 percent of Salvadoran asylum applicants were successful, and only 1.8 percent of Guatemalan applications for the same period were granted."

50 Gwendolyn Mink, *Old Labor and New Immigrants in American Political Development: Union, Party, and State, 1875–1920* (Ithaca, NY: Cornell University Press, 1986).

51 Randy Shaw, *Beyond the Fields: Cesar Chavez, the UFW, and the Struggle for Justice in the 21st Century* (Berkeley: University of California Press, 2008); Vicki L. Ruíz, *From Out of the Shadows: Mexican Women in Twentieth-Century America*, 10th anniversary ed. (Oxford: Oxford University Press, 2008), 116–118.

organizers who worked hard to overturn anti-immigrant feelings within the US labour movement.

Increasingly, some sections of the American Federation of Labor-Congress of Industrial Organizations (AFL-CIO, the largest labour federation in the US) began to recognize the need to extend organizing efforts to new groups of workers as the only way to offset dwindling memberships and declining union density. Although progress was slow, the first signs of change were evident following the passage of the IRCA, when the AFL-CIO created the Labor Immigrant Assistance Program (LIAP) and the California Immigrant Workers Association (CIWA). These organizations helped workers to file for amnesty, granted benefits to workers short of full union membership, and would provide important institutional support for labour organizing in future years.[52] However, in some cases, institutional support was not even necessary and two breakthrough campaigns in the early 1990s, both involving successful spontaneous ("wildcat") strikes by Latinx workers, showed that immigrant workers were not as easily intimidated as employers believed.[53]

The migrants had had widely differing experiences in their home countries and these diverse circumstances that led them to emigrate to the US meant that some were more likely to be responsive to unionization than others. It is likely that the disruption of circular migration by anti-immigrant sentiment and the changed legal frame in the US may have boosted the militancy of Mexican workers. In the past, these workers would have returned home when unable to find work or when dismissed from their jobs. However, with the

52 Robert Lazo, "Latinos and the AFL-CIO: The California Immigrant Workers Association as an Important New Development," in *Latino Employment, Labor Organizations, and Immigration,* ed. Antoinette Sedillo López, vol. 4 (New York: Garland, 1995), 100–121.

53 In 1991, 900 workers at American Racing Equipment in Rancho Dominguez engaged in a spontaneous strike led by leaders from Honduras, El Salvador, and Mexico. The "wildcat" strike led the International Association of Machinists and Aerospace Workers to create a new union local at the plant and to negotiate a contract on behalf of the workers. David Sickler, "Multi-Union Organizing: Speech by David Sickler 12/7/95 at UCLA," *Labor Research Review* 1, no. 24 (1996): 106–107; Carol Zabin, "Organizing Latino Workers in the Los Angeles Manufacturing Sector: The Case of American Racing Equipment," in *Organizing Immigrants: The Challenge for Unions in Contemporary California,* ed. Ruth Milkman (Ithaca, NY: ILR Press, 2000). In October 1991, Jesus Gomez began organizing fellow drywall workers when his employer refused to address an underpayment in wages and, in June 1992, 1,800 of these workers began a spontaneous strike that secured the support of various organizations and unions and, eventually, a contract. Ruth Milkman and Kent Wong, "Organizing the Wicked City: The 1992 Southern California Drywall Strike," in *Organizing Immigrants: The Challenge for Unions in Contemporary California,* ed. Ruth Milkman (Ithaca, NY: ILR Press, 2000).

militarization of the border, the risks of repetitive, circular journeys significantly increased. Consequently, undocumented workers had a greater investment in their – initially intended to be temporary – receiving communities and became more willing to join unions to improve their working conditions and protect their rights. Guatemalan, Salvadoran, and Nicaraguan immigrants tended to come from a much broader range of socio-economic backgrounds than Mexican immigrants. Many were well educated and had experience with unions in their home country, as a result of which they possessed skills that were useful for labour activism. They also understood that they were being exploited, but the threats of employers in the US paled in comparison to the violence and intimidation they had been subjected to in Central America – in "home countries" that did not provide a home. The willingness of these migrant and immigrant workers to organize likely reflected the fact that their earlier life experiences provided a different perspective on the risks involved. As one organizer remarked: "In this country, they fire you. But they don't take you out in the middle of the night and disappear you."[54] Many labour activists from Central America had experienced a great deal of upheaval and trauma before they began working and organizing in the US.[55] Equally, for some, their identification as Latinx workers within the US was a source of cultural strength and solidarity.[56]

Another important component of the resurgence of the labour movement in California was the growing awareness that new strategies were needed to organize within the neoliberal labour regime. Labour leaders within the Service Employees International Union (SEIU) were instrumental in developing such new approaches following the launch of their Justice for Janitors campaign in the mid-1980s to fight back against de-unionization. Founded in Chicago in 1920 and affiliated with the American Federation of Labor (AFL) rather than the Congress of Industrial Organizations (CIO), the union had always represented non-industrial workers. In the mid-1980s, the union changed direction under the reformist leadership of John Sweeney. It doubled its dues, expanded its national staff, and dedicated a quarter of its income to organizing, five times

54 Kevin Baxter, "Labor of Love: A Passionate Yanira Merino Refuses to Let Fatigue or Threats Stop Her Push to Empower Workers," *Los Angeles Times, Life and Style,* 18 February 1996.

55 Andrew Gomez, "An Oral History of the Justice for Janitors Movement: On Trauma, Central America, and the Undocumented," *InterActions: UCLA Journal of Education and Information Studies* 11, no. 1 (2015).

56 Maria A. Gutierrez de Soldatenko, "Justice for Janitors Latinizing Los Angeles: Mobilizing Latina(o) Cultural Repertoire," in *Latino Los Angeles: Transformations, Communities, and Activism,* ed. Enrique Ochoa and Gilda L. Ochoa (Tucson: University of Arizona Press, 2005), 225–245.

what was typical for unions at the time. Many of the people joining the drive were New Leftists of one persuasion or another, veterans of the new social movements of the 1960s and 1970s. The SEIU was therefore well positioned to respond to the changing demographics of the American working class and to extend its efforts to organize groups of workers who had previously been considered unorganizable – by organizers who did not speak their language.

In the mid-1980s, the SEIU launched the Justice for Janitors campaign, a unionization drive that initially focused on Pittsburgh, Philadelphia, Denver, and Seattle, before turning to Southern California in 1988. As outlined above, Los Angeles witnessed a boom in office construction between 1972 and 1982 and this commercial and the consequent residential development created a demand for workers in low-wage service jobs. When the campaign reached Los Angeles, organizing efforts in smaller companies were initially moderately successful, but it soon became clear that the structure of the cleaning industry proved resistant to traditional tactics.[57] The National Labor Relations Act (NLRA), still the legal core of labour relations, had been formulated during the New Deal years of the 1930s in the context of (industrial) stable and clearly defined employer-employee relationships. Under the NLRA, workers wanting to organize a union could do so by signing cards or a petition asking for an election of representatives to be held by the National Labor Relations Board (NLRB). However, these conditions no longer existed in the heavily subcontracted building services industry of the 1980s.

The cleaning companies, which were often small, held contacts with the – usually capital-intensive – companies owning the buildings. These big corporations inserted short-notice cancellation clauses into the contracts to be able to switch to an even cheaper rival service company. The small entrepreneurs thus regularly lost or gained accounts at different worksites. As a labour-intensive industry, workers' wage rates were a major determinant of the success or failure of the cleaning company. Although the independent contractor was the formal employer, ultimately working conditions and pay were determined by the company owing the buildings, which was protected from secondary boycotts under the NLRA rules. In this context, the traditional method of deploying union officials to organize and win NLRB elections at separate worksites was unlikely to be effective and therefore union strategists decided to organize

57 Roger Waldinger et al., "Helots No More: A Case Study of the Justice for Janitors Campaign in Los Angeles," in *Organizing to Win: New Research on Union Strategies*, ed. Kate Bronfenbrenner et al. (Ithaca, NY: Cornell University Press, 1998), 110.

the entire industry. To do so, they would need to convince workers of the efficacy of the union even before it had won formal recognition.[58]

This realization led union organizers to embrace a strategy known as "social movement unionism." Throughout the 1990s, the Justice for Janitors campaign won a string of victories across California using this approach, eventually bringing about a transformation of the cleaning industry and reversing union losses in the previous two decades. Rather than rely solely on the legal framework constructed by the New Deal, Justice for Janitors organizers began to use nonviolent civil disobedience, community alliances, and the "court of public opinion" to persuade managers to give in to worker demands.[59] However, the SEIU was not the only union experimenting with these new methods of organizing, as the Hotel Employees and Restaurant Employees (HERE) union, the International Ladies Garment Workers Union (ILGWU), and the Asian Immigrant Women Advocates (AIWA) were all beginning to use these tactics in their campaigns. In all these cases, the participation of the rank-and-file workers was crucial because success no longer depended upon a small number of union officials in negotiation with the employers, but rather on a broad mobilization capable of disrupting business as usual. The militancy of the workers themselves was therefore a vital ingredient in the success of the labour resurgence in the 1990s.

7 Conclusion

A historical analysis of the evolution of neoliberal labour regimes demonstrates how domestic policymaking and global economic restructuring interacted in such a way as to fundamentally alter the balance of power between capital and labour in the late twentieth century. In global terms, we should not think of the neoliberal era as disconnected from an earlier era of colonial domination, but rather as a continuation of domination by other means.

The case of California shows that to fully explain how this happened it is necessary to operate on multiple overlapping scales of analysis: local, transnational, *and* global. Broader transnational historical developments, such as the economic crisis in Mexico and conflicts elsewhere in Central America, shaped the particularities of the Californian economy and its reliance on immigrant

58 John Howley, "Justice for Janitors: The Challenge of Organizing in Contract Services," *Labor Research Review* 1, no. 15 (1990): 64–69.

59 Andy Banks, "The Power and Promise of Community Unionism," *Labor Research Review* 1, no. 18 (1991): 18.

labour in important ways. To understand how labour struggles were fought in this terrain, historians must consider the deep interconnection between neoliberal political economy, histories of immigration, and the global reach of American Empire.

This approach throws into relief the agency of workers at the margins of the post-industrial economy and their successful organizing efforts in the state of California in the 1990s. Workers secured several important victories during the high tide of neoliberal ascendency and the political and cultural resources that these workers brought to the campaigns helped to fuel the renewal of the Californian labour movement. Hence, while the Reagan offensive in Latin America geographically displaced the conflict between labour and capital, it did not end it.

PART 4

Regional Migration Patterns, Work Regimes, and Workers' Agency

CHAPTER 15

Introduction

Dirk Hoerder and Lukas Neissl

Within the frame of global movements of capital and macro-regional migration systems, people in search of making a livelihood develop innumerable meso- and micro-systems of mobility. The proximity of the destination, accessible cheap transport, and options to visit their family staying behind or to return home frequently are some of the factors influencing their decision-making. The destination generally is a centre of investment with, often distant, investors, in the nineteenth and early twentieth centuries the European colonizer states and, later, the US. Investments might also be made by local elites. The destinations may include regions in which local farmers or craftspeople require additional labour when they intensify market-oriented production without smaller or larger investments from outside the family or community. Information "flows" connect the community and region of departure with the region and community of arrival. The term "flow," transposed to society from nature, flowing water, reflects continuous "natural" movement in considerable quantities or volumes. This usage masks the fact that the movement of human beings – with or without the capacity to perform labour – is not inherently natural. Rather, it requires agency from assessing the standard of living at the place of origin, perhaps the place of birth, via collecting information on potential destinations or, if kin and neighbours are already migrating, decisions to join and follow their routes.

The assessment of standards of living focuses on the income differential between the communities of departure and arrival as well as the costs involved. Do workingmen and -women move as adolescents, ready to leave the authority of parents, kin, or caretakers? In such cases, the emotional costs would be low. Are they pushed out, since neither the family nor they themselves can provide food in a job-deprived local economy? Do they migrate once they have formed a family and leave partners and children behind? In these instances, the emotional costs would be high. Do they separate from a family in, perhaps dire, straits in order to send remittances back? This might mean poor living conditions at the (usually gendered) place of work, whether mine or factory, household or care institution, latifundia or plantation. Costs and rewards of migration differed and still differ, between men and women, and between adults, adolescents and children. Such decisions had to be made regardless of location

 | DOI:10.1163/9789004686991_016

and culture in the context of values regarding family, local embeddedness, and migration traditions. Prospective migrants in particularly power-deprived locations in the powerful Tsarist or British Empire, for example, had to make such decisions. Buenos Aires, Vienna, Teheran, Delhi, and Edo/Tokyo as well as many other metropoles, cities, and towns attracted capital – or, perhaps more correctly – extracted surplus value from the workers present, accumulated this surplus as capital, invested it, and attracted further workers from surrounding rural economies or from afar. Cities, generally, also offered newcomers more options for life projects or, at least, chances of survival, than small communities of origin. To connect cost and emotions it is worth noting that migration into a larger community expanded the marriage market for young people and, perhaps, reduced the power of parents and kin concerning the decision of whom to marry. All of this holds true throughout history, albeit in varying frames of culturally chosen or imposed preferences.

In the previous section, the authors analysed larger regions, Central America and Southern California, the societies of the Indian Ocean rim and the Arab-Gulf region, the Eurasian world of Russia through varying political systems and with its numerous investment foci and urbanizing regions, and the attempts of committed socialists to develop policies covering developed and lesser developed regions with a hierarchy of standards of living. In this section, the authors focus on more limited interconnected regions: Poland (then divided between the sovereigns of the three neighbouring empires) and imperial Germany (then still a conglomerate of small and large states), as well as rural and urban regions in British-imperial Southern Rhodesia and British-imperial Southern India and Ceylon. In each case, economic investment and political power intersected. Furthermore, in each region, the rural-urban divide, which might also be termed a low- and high-investment divide or a low-option versus multiple-option divide, required migration decisions and determined, in political-economical frames, the costs and benefits of such decisions. Since labour migrants, both men and women alike, usually have nothing to fall back on, their migration decision had to have a positive or, at least, neutral outcome. They could not afford failure – those who did fail ended in graveyards and were and are lost to dominant historical memory; those who just scraped by often had neither the energy nor the opportunity to struggle for better conditions. This raises the question of whether such issues enter decision-making processes about investments at the top of the economic-political hierarchy. Slave owners in the nineteenth century knew that importing human working bodies from West African societies was more profitable than providing those already present with life-preserving working conditions. Similarly, many investment owners in the twenty-first century know that subcontracted labour yields higher profits than a regularly employed workforce. At the time of writing, the Amazon company is bitterly fighting against the lawful attempts of its workers to form unions.

In the late nineteenth century, men and women and their children in the many Polish-speaking societies, divided and annexed by the dynastic ruling elites of Hohenzollern, Habsburg, and Romanov in several stages in the late eighteenth century saw economic options afar rather than on the nearby, brutally exploitative nobles' latifundia. Those in the Hohenzollern section, or "in Germany," took note of job options in the western mines and industries of the Ruhr District: Employers needed them, political authorities attempted to exclude them, and most labour unions of German workers had no interest in them. Beate Althammer (Chapter 16) highlights the fact that the traditional German-Polish juxtaposition is undifferentiated. The German (or Hohenzollern) authorities, and in terms of location of power more correctly, the Prussian authorities divided men, women, and children of Polish culture according to imposed imperial rule into "foreign Poles" from the Habsburg and Romanov-held territories and *Reichsangehörige* (inhabitants of the Empire) living in the Prussian-held territories. The latter, usually bilingual because of the intermingled German-Polish-language lives east of the Oder River, had the right to move. While the Prussian authorities have been depicted as powerful, their attempted restrictions on the migrations of foreign Poles were often tentative and were not applied by regional (Prussian) authorities in the Rhine Province with a high labour demand. The Prussian (Berlin) policy of nation-driven, perhaps racist, exclusion broke with the traditional West and Central European liberal migration practices and the exclusion of those labelled ethnically "Polish" paralleled the move in the US to exclude those labelled "Chinese." The latter, like the Poles, had regional identifications and dialects. Significantly, in nationalist frames of mind, generic ethnic labels are usually imposed from the top down. Following other recent studies, Althammer describes the system as a prototypical guestworker regime and, through sensitive case studies, outlines how individual workingmen and -women – sometimes with support from their employers – resisted exclusionary decisions by local authorities. These, in turn, often consulted the central government without receiving precise answers. Thus, individuals' resistance impacted policies, albeit to a lesser extent than the policies in turn impacted individual workers' options.

In a way, the study of the migration of agriculturalists from rural to urban regions in British-ruled Southern Rhodesia seems to be distant from Central Europe, both geographically as well as in terms of power relationships. However, while the cases and cultures are distinctive, they also show similarities. In both regions, the underlying issue, namely how to mobilize labour from the capital side-of-view and how to survive on the labour side-of-view, was the same. What is different are the strategies of imposing rule as well as the positions and impositions of the local authorities. In the Prussian case, local magistrates attempted to mediate between workers' (emotional) needs and rights and the central government's discriminatory regulations; in the Southern Rhodesian case, the local (white settler) institutions imposed restrictions that the central (in this case distant imperial white) government had not intended. However, both white London and the white settlers did agree that black Africans, in general, should be deprived of their agricultural lands, i.e., their means of production, and be forced to move to "reservations" where they could not survive. As a result, the men would thus have to migrate into the wage service of urban whites, as Katharine Frederick (Chapter 17) shows. These Reserves were not barbed-wire camps as in later European forced-labour practices, but large encampments with subsistence agriculture. The reservation plots would be worked by women and children, while the hunger-enforced out-migration of men would supply labour to the colonizers. Labouring men had to move back and forth between these areas, which forestalled permanent urban residence. This system was linked to settler demands for racial segregation in cities but simultaneously undercut the settlers' and investors' interest in a stable labour force. Of the women relegated to the Reserves, some decided to migrate to cities, although economic opportunities were limited, and some undertook independent economic activities to supplement their household incomes. Like the Prussian authorities' central-local differences, the British imperial-settler differences undermined any attempts at coherent policymaking. The emerging urban black working-class quarters permitted mutual support but, under the power conditions, black working-class mobilization faced significant hurdles. Strike action in the 1940s set in motion some gains for black industrial workers, but white workers' unions rigorously defended white privilege. While the socialist delegates at the Stuttgart (1907) congress (Chapter 11) debated and implicitly rejected the notion of an international working class, the black workers in Southern and Northern Rhodesian cities as well as in the mines (Chapter 9) experienced segregated class compositions, and investments and resulting industrial growth from the late 1940s onwards did not change the situation. A real change would only come with independence – at least this was what most of those struggling for independence hoped at the time.

As in these two regions, migration between insufficient rural subsistence production and waged labour, in this case on plantations and in households, connected South Indian workers with imperial investments in Ceylon and with Sinhalese workers. Ritesh Kumar Jaiswal (Chapter 18) outlines how in this setting, too, the frame was set by political colonizer authorities, namely the British India government and the British rulers in Ceylon. The former attempted to – depending on the point of view – get rid of a labour surplus or help below-subsistence families to find supplementary waged work through migration while the latter hoped to provide cheap labour to plantation investors whose taxes supported them. The former sought minimally acceptable working conditions to forestall discontent that might turn into anti-colonial struggles. Both faced, earlier than the Rhodesian branch of the imperial government, nationalist demands for proper treatment of workers. However, "the" nationalists did not unite to oppose the colonizers since one section was Sinhalese, the other Indian, and both pursued distinct goals. Thus, ethnicity rather than white-versus-coloured racism became a factor in their agendas: jobs in Ceylon for Sinhalese to the detriment of migrant workers from India. Sinhalese workers, however, did not want the kind of jobs the South Indian migrants had to take and they refused to labour under the working conditions which – in this case British – plantation managers and investors imposed. Given the two competing strategies for independence and ethnicized labour forces, no joint anti-capitalist or anti-investor struggle did and could emerge. Rather, native Sinhalese – whipped up by a nationalist, as yet colonized political elite and a nationalist-chauvinist press – rioted against in-migrant Indian shopkeepers, domestic workers, and others.

Again, these issues are comparable to many other struggles across cultures and centuries: jobs assigned to "foreigners" by (absentee) employers who intentionally provided miserable working conditions. None of the elites in question – nationalist Sinhalese, British Ceylonese, nationalist Indian, or British Indian – was ready to address the systemic issue. The British India government did demand that Indian migrants in Ceylon receive living wages and, when the Ceylonese elites did not respond, curtailed or forbade out-migration. Ceylonese planter-investors petitioned for a reopening of the short and cheap migration routes across the Gulf of Mannar, without, however, intending to improve the working conditions. Instead, they blamed middlemen, *kangani*, who connected labour demand in Ceylon and supply in South India, for extortionist practices. While these mediators ideally acted as facilitators, in practice many used their position to enrich themselves – as did plantation owners by imposing the practice of compelling workers to purchase necessities in overpriced plantation stores. The *kangani* system, widely used in the societies of the Indian Ocean rim as well as in the Southeast Asian plantation regime, had its equivalent in nineteenth-century industrialists in the west of Germany sending trusted workers back to Poland to recruit additional workers. Again, cultures and geographies notwithstanding, the aspects of labour relations and regimes, temporary and long-term migration, and of exploitation and agency were similar.

While we have argued that *the* state or *the* class remain constructs that cannot be used as a tool of analysis, the studies in this section demonstrate that comparative empirical analyses may discern similarities across societal differences.

CHAPTER 16

Foreign Polish Labour Migrants in the German Empire

A Reassessment

Beate Althammer

Abstract

The migration of "foreign" Polish labourers from tsarist Russia and Habsburg Galicia to imperial Germany, and especially to eastern Prussia, has occupied academic research since its onset at the end of the nineteenth century. Labour scholars have lately even identified this case as one of the first "guestworker" programs in global history – a specifically modern type of managed migration aimed at providing cheap and flexibly disposable labour. However, blind spots remain. After outlining the regulatory system that the Prussian government designed for the recruitment of foreign Poles, this chapter discusses some misconceptions that have arisen in recent scholarship. The focus subsequently shifts from the agrarian Prussian east to the industrialized west and examines how the system functioned there. The final section highlights the cases of individual Polish workers whom Prussian authorities targeted for expulsion because of their irregular presence. Their stories illustrate migrants' diverse routes and aspirations as well as the ways in which official policy was resisted.

Keywords

expulsion – guestworkers – immigration control – Polish migration – Prussia

1 Introduction

The migration of "foreign" Polish labourers from tsarist Russia and Austrian Galicia to the German Empire, and particularly to rural eastern Prussia during the Wilhelmine period, is a well-established theme in historiography. Contemporary scholars had already paid attention to the topic, most famously young Max Weber who, in the early 1890s, thoroughly analysed the structural changes that induced Prussia's Junker class to draw on labour from the Russian and Austrian parts of Poland, while he simultaneously embraced anti-Polish stereotypes. Like many educated Germans of his time, Weber imagined this migration as an "invasion of eastern nomadic swarms" that threatened to depress German lands "to a lower, eastern cultural stage," and against which the "eastern border of Germanness" had to be defended in a "struggle for existence."[1] While such chauvinism has lost favour since Weber's times, it has nevertheless informed a critical scholarship that describes Prussia's foreign Polish labourers as an exemplary victim group trapped between capitalist exploitation, rising xenophobia, and state coercion at a historical juncture in which Wilhelmine Germany was aspiring to become a global power. In the 1950s, the East German historian Johannes Nichtweiß wrote a well-researched monograph on the use of these migrants as seasonal farm workers.[2] In the 1980s, West German historians Klaus Bade and Ulrich Herbert published influential works that described the case as the first incidence of large-scale labour importation to Germany.[3] At the same time, the East Germans Lothar Elsner and Joachim Lehmann highlighted it as foundational to the "reactionary traditions of imperialist foreign-labourer policy" still alive in the West.[4] Many studies have since returned to the subject, for instance as an illustration of imperial Germany's inner-European colonialist and increasingly *völkisch* attitudes.[5]

What has primarily attracted attention in the discourse is the regulatory system that the Prussian state imposed from the 1890s onwards with the aim of channelling large numbers of foreign Poles into its agricultural sector but simultaneously preventing their permanent settlement. This policy has also sparked the interest of international labour scholars who have discovered the Prussian case as one of the earliest "guestworker programs" in global history. Cindy Hahamovitch has even singled it out as *the* earliest such program, although nearly coeval with the commencement of the import of Mozambicans to the

---

1 Max Weber, "Die ländliche Arbeitsverfassung (1893)," in *Gesammelte Aufsätze zur Sozial- und Wirtschaftsgeschichte* (Tübingen: Mohr, 1924), 444–469, quotes 452, 457, 468.

2 Johannes Nichtweiß, *Die ausländischen Saisonarbeiter in der Landwirtschaft der östlichen und mittleren Gebiete des Deutschen Reiches: Ein Beitrag zur Geschichte der preußisch-deutschen Politik von 1890 bis 1914* (Berlin: Rütten & Loening, 1959).

3 Via English translations, their works have partly become accessible to an international readership, see Ulrich Herbert, *A History of Foreign Labor in Germany, 1880–1980: Seasonal Workers, Forced Laborers, Guest Workers*, trans. William Templer (Ann Arbor: University of Michigan Press, 1990); Klaus Bade, *Migration in European History*, trans. Allison Brown (Malden, MA/Oxford: Blackwell, 2003).

4 Lothar Elsner and Joachim Lehmann, *Ausländische Arbeiter unter dem deutschen Imperialismus 1900 bis 1985* (Berlin: Dietz, 1988), 11.

5 Sebastian Conrad, *Globalisierung und Nation im Deutschen Kaiserreich* (Munich: Beck, 2006), 124–167.

mines of South Africa,[6] and several authors have recently taken up her exposure of Prussia as a pioneer of guestworker regimes. This strand of research, of course, emphasizes the euphemistic character of the term "guestworker," a translation of the German *Gastarbeiter* that originated after the Second World War. It designates labourers from poor backgrounds who are demanded by economically booming countries as temporary cheap labour power but rejected as members of society. They constitute a distinctively modern type of transnational migrants actively recruited abroad for hard and low-paying jobs and who are subsequently expected to return home, with the state monitoring their circulation. The Prussian example, Hahamovitch asserts, "perfectly captures the essence of the guestworker programs that would dot the globe over the next 100 years."[7] Kristin Surak concurs that the German case is "emblematic," and Mahua Sarkar that it is "particularly illustrative" of this development.[8]

In light of all these valuable works, one might ask if there is anything left to say on the subject. Why return to such a well-known matter? This chapter argues that there are three reasons to do so. First, many recent contributions rely on selective secondary literature, and in the course of retelling the story, some questionable assumptions have slipped in that deserve discussion. Second, the existing scholarship mostly takes a macro perspective that traces overarching processes, with the effect that the migrants turn into an anonymous mass. The term "import" (*Einfuhr*) that keeps reappearing is especially revealing. While present-day academics use it with a critical intention to convey how unscrupulous Junkers and bureaucrats reduced foreign labourers to a commodity, this approach tends to reproduce dehumanization as it ignores the wishes, experiences, and strategies of the migrants themselves. Certainly, scholarship has dealt with recruitment and working conditions, but mostly on a generalizing level that stresses exploitation, repression, and the inability of "imported" workers to fight back. In this perspective, these were "completely excluded" from the surrounding German society and helplessly "at the mercy of their masters."[9] There are some exceptions. Simon Constantine, for instance,

6 Cindy Hahamovitch, *No Man's Land: Jamaican Guestworkers in America and the Global History of Deportable Labor* (Princeton, NJ: Princeton University Press, 2011), 14.

7 Cindy Hahamovitch, "Creating Perfect Immigrants: Guestworkers of the World in Historical Perspective," *Labor History* 44, no. 1 (2003): 69–94, quote 76.

8 Kristin Surak, "Guestworkers: A Taxonomy," *New Left Review* 84 (2013): 84–102, quote 88; Mahua Sarkar, "The Flipside of the Integration Question: Guestworker Regimes and Temporary Circular/Managed Migration in History," *Refugee Watch: A South Asian Journal on Forced Migration* 49 (2017): 1–25, quote 4.

9 Roland Gehrke, "Between Economic Interest and Nationalism: The Policy Regarding Polish Seasonal Rural Workers in the German Empire before 1914," in *Migrations in the*

has explored the situation of foreign Polish labourers within the local environment of Mecklenburg estate villages, which enables him to draw a more nuanced picture of everyday relationships.[10] Christiane Reinecke provides some glimpses into the agency of migrant farm workers in the Brandenburg countryside, showing how they could dodge official regulations.[11] Yet such close examinations remain rare. A third deficit is that the existing scholarship predominantly deals with rural East Elbia because the majority of Germany's foreign Polish labourers toiled there. However, industrialized regions further west undoubtedly seemed more attractive to many. We know very little about how the Prussian policy functioned in the central and western provinces, where restrictions were even tighter but incentives to stay greater.

While Russian and Galician Poles also left their relatively poor homelands in great numbers for other destinations, especially the United States, in the period before the First World War (see Chapter 7 in this volume),[12] this chapter solely focuses on the peculiar regulations that Germany's dominant power, Prussia, developed for them. The second section provides an overview of these regulations and the third discusses certain questionable assumptions in recent scholarship. The fourth part turns to Prussia's most western province, the Rhine Province, specifically to the highly industrialized Düsseldorf district, and sketches how the regional authorities struggled with implementing the central government's policy. The last section presents selected cases of individual migrants whom the authorities targeted for expulsion because they were living in disaccord with government rules, but who successfully resisted. In large parts, the chapter draws on archival sources produced by the Prussian bureaucracy.[13] The aim is not to refute established scholarly interpretations but rather to complement them. It is true that the Prussian state envisioned something like a guestworker program *avant la lettre*, but guestworkers often have turned out not to be the perfect immigrants that the creators of such

German Lands, 1500–2000, ed. Jason Coy, Jared Poley and Alexander Schunka (New York/Oxford: Berghahn, 2016), 110–130, quote 119–120.

10 Simon Constantine, *Social Relations in the Estate Villages of Mecklenburg, c. 1880–1924* (Aldershot, UK: Ashgate, 2007), 107–134. The Grand Duchies of Mecklenburg did not fully adopt Prussia's regulations.

11 Christiane Reinecke, *Grenzen der Freizügigkeit: Migrationskontrolle in Großbritannien und Deutschland, 1880–1930* (Munich: Oldenbourg, 2010), 95–105.

12 Ewa Morawska, "Labor Migrations of Poles in the Atlantic World Economy, 1880–1914," *Comparative Studies in Society and History* 31, no. 2 (1989): 237–272.

13 This research is a component of the project "The Borders of the Welfare State: Migration, Social Rights and Expulsion (1850–1933)," funded by the *Deutsche Forschungsgemeinschaft* (DFG) – 411657768.

programs hoped for. They elude restrictions, begin to argue, and some set their minds on staying permanently. In the pioneering Prussian case, additional difficulties arose from the fact that the government rules had a tentative character and did not fit well with conventional norms.

2 The Prussian Regulations: A Brief Overview

Prussia's anti-Polish migration policy originated in frictions with its own Polish minority in the annexed eastern provinces that it ruled over since the partitions of Poland in the late eighteenth century. These troubles intensified after the foundation of the German nation-state in 1867/71, which incorporated the Prussian part of former Poland despite Polish protests. Ethnic Poles constituted the largest national minority in the German Empire, amounting to approximately ten percent of the Prussian population. Mostly Catholics, they also belonged to a religious minority within Protestant Prussia and became strongly involved in the "culture war" (*Kulturkampf*) of the 1870s. The Prussian government under Otto von Bismarck attempted to fight their opposition by enforcing linguistic assimilation but only achieved a radicalization of Polish national feelings, which in turn stoked up government repression and German nationalist agitation. While Prussian Poles may have experienced discrimination, they nevertheless were Prussian citizens, and the state could not get rid of them. What the government did try to do, however, was to stop this vocal minority from growing via immigration from the Russian and Austrian parts of Poland. In 1885, Bismarck initiated mass expulsions of the Polish inhabitants of the eastern provinces who could not prove that they had Prussian (or another German) citizenship. Of approximately 44,000 persons identified as foreign Poles, around 31,000 were forced to leave, largely irrespective of their social status and duration of residence.[14] While the government's calculus was that the removal of disruptive immigrants would help Prussia absorb its Polish minority, the measure aroused widespread indignation instead, also among German Catholics, left-wing liberals, and socialists, not to mention international critique. German nationalists, by contrast, hailed this stroke against the "Polonization" of eastern Prussia.

From the national viewpoint, it appeared imperative to inhibit renewed Polish immigration, but economic interests were opposed to this objective.

14 Helmut Neubach, *Die Ausweisungen von Polen und Juden aus Preußen 1885/86* (Wiesbaden: Harrassowitz, 1967); Matthew Fitzpatrick, *Purging the Empire: Mass Expulsions in Germany, 1871–1914* (Oxford: Oxford University Press, 2015), 93–122.

East-Elbian agriculturists emphasized that they needed foreign Polish labourers for two reasons. Firstly, native farm workers (both German and Polish speakers) were abandoning the rural east. They made up a substantial share of the last great surge of German emigration to the United States in the 1880s while many more left for Berlin and industrial regions, above all the Ruhr area. Others chose farm work in central Germany, where wages were higher than in the east. Secondly, East-Elbian agriculture was in a process of restructuring. American and Russian exports had depressed the profitability of cereal production, inducing landowners to shift to alternative crops, especially sugar beet, but the cultivation of sugar beet was labour-intensive with strong seasonal fluctuations. Although historians have often described nineteenth-century East Elbia with its large *Rittergüter* (knights' estates) as semi-feudal, these were rapidly transforming into rationalized agribusinesses.[15] One consequence of capitalist modernization was that rural labourers who had formerly been bound to their estates as cottagers were set "free" and turned into wage workers who were only hired for the required periods. For natives, the dearth of year-round income was an additional reason to move west, and this again made agrarians cry for migrants from beyond the Russian and Austrian-Galician borders: They seemed the perfect solution to an increasing scarcity of relatively cheap and seasonally flexible labour.

After Bismarck's resignation in 1890, the Prussian government gave in to "capitalist" interests and readmitted cross-border recruitment, albeit with restrictions aimed at safeguarding "national" concerns. The interior minister authorized that in the four eastern provinces both agricultural and industrial enterprises could employ foreign Poles, but only from 1 April to 15 November, and on condition that these had to leave Prussia for the remainder of every year (the so-called *Karenzzeit*).[16] The same applied to the central and western provinces with the additional limitation that here only agricultural but not industrial employment was permitted. After various slight modifications, a ministerial instruction from September 1899 summarized the rules and specifically outlined the obligations of employers who wanted to hire foreign Poles.[17] Employers had to obtain official permission and sign a declaration stating that

15 Oliver Grant, "'Few Better Farmers in Europe'? Productivity, Change, and Modernization in East-Elbian Agriculture, 1870–1913," in *Wilhelminism and its Legacies: German Modernities, Imperialism, and the Meanings of Reform, 1890–1930*, ed. Geoff Eley and James Retallack (New York: Berghahn, 2003), 51–72.

16 Nichtweiß, *Die ausländischen Saisonarbeiter*, 43–44.

17 Ministerial Order, 4 September 1899, Geheimes Staatsarchiv Preußischer Kulturbesitz (GStA PK), I. HA Rep. 77, Tit. 1176, no. 6: 13–19.

they would register the workers with the local police upon arrival, provide for their medical examination, vaccination, and proper accommodation, inform the police about dismissals and runaways, and reimburse costs should police-enforced transportation back to the border become necessary. This instruction henceforth served as the principal guideline for the Prussian bureaucracy, but already in 1900, the *Karenzzeit* shrank further to the weeks from 20 December to 1 February – barely more than a Christmas holiday. Nevertheless, the compulsory departure from Prussia each winter remained an essential feature as it underscored that foreign Polish workers were transient "seasonal workers" by definition. Moreover, the regulations completely banned foreign Poles from domestic service as well as from positions as apprentices and journeymen in the crafts. In 1905, the government extended the same rules to Russian Lithuanians of the Catholic faith because of their historical and assumed ideological liaison with Poland, whereas a milder version applied to Ruthenians (Ukrainians) from Galicia since their national and confessional orientation appeared less concerning.

After the turn of the century, a special infrastructure for monitoring the foreign labour force emerged. Under the auspices of the Prussian ministry of agriculture, a quasi-official agency named *Deutsche Feldarbeiterzentrale* (later *Deutsche Arbeiterzentrale*) was established in Berlin with branch offices primarily along the eastern borders. Until the 1920s, it did not occupy a dominant role in recruitment, which remained very heterogeneous, but it became responsible for managing a system of legitimation cards initiated in 1907.[18] From 1909, all foreign workers in Prussia theoretically needed such a card. The *Feldarbeiterzentrale* issued them at its border offices and maintained a central registry. Alternatively, workers could apply for cards within the country via the local police. The system served several purposes. On the one hand, it addressed the problem that German officials had difficulties with reading foreign-language documents, particularly those in Cyrillic script, and that many migrants did not possess any proper papers. Although Germany had largely abolished passport obligations in 1867, travellers (both natives and foreigners) had to be able to produce some kind of identity document, and proof of identity was also necessary for local registration as a resident irrespective of origin. The legitimation cards were supposed to help with these general requirements. On the other hand, the aim was to put foreign workers under special control as apart from the usual personal data, the cards noted the current employer, and the police had to ascertain correct termination

18 Nichtweiß, *Die ausländischen Saisonarbeiter*, 134–143.

before approving job changes. Above all, however, the system served to earmark Poles: Their cards were red, as opposed to yellow for Ruthenians and, initially, white for other foreign workers.

3 Historiographic Interpretations

The card system in conjunction with the *Karenzzeit* and the restrictions on permitted occupations have led historians to conclude that Prussia's foreign Polish workers were not "free workers" because they were deprived of the freedom to market their labour power.[19] International scholars conclude the same with regard to more recent guestworker regimes. Although they volunteer, guestworkers are unfree in this view because they lack the freedom to choose and switch jobs, to protest without risking deportation, and ultimately to settle down and stay.[20] The Prussian case appears as an emblematic precedent because it created precisely such a coercive constellation in which Poles either had to accept exploitation as temporary labourers with no prospects of advancement or total banishment. Another parallel that present-day academics see is that of racism. The scholarship on guestworker regimes stresses that guestworkers typically come from the Global South and that racist prejudices foster their exploitation, while their marginalized situation in turn entrenches racist prejudices. The same has been said for the Prussian case, although Poles are just as "white" as Germans. Herbert, for instance, argues that widespread anti-Polish sentiments shaped a climate in which the maltreatment of Polish workers seemed natural and that the state's special regulations encouraged such increasingly racist attitudes.[21]

While these observations are intriguing, they tend to exaggerate the gulf between the local population and Polish migrants. In East-Elbian Prussia, life was also hard for the natives: wages were low, farm work was backbreaking, landlords had a long tradition of treating their labourers as subalterns, and agricultural workers enjoyed little social rights, for instance no right to strike.

---

19 For instance, Ulrich Herbert, *Geschichte der Ausländerpolitik in Deutschland: Saisonarbeiter, Zwangsarbeiter, Gastarbeiter, Flüchtlinge* (Munich: Beck, 2001), 36.

20 Apart from the works already mentioned see, Luis F. B. Plascencia, "State-Sanctioned Coercion and Agricultural Contract Labor: Jamaican and Mexican Workers in Canada and the United States, 1909–2014," in *On Coerced Labor: Work and Compulsion after Chattel Slavery*, ed. Marcel van der Linden and Magaly Rodríguez García (Leiden: Brill, 2016), 225–265.

21 Herbert, *Geschichte*, 42–44.

Although these difficult conditions provided the impetus for many to leave in search of better prospects, the majority stayed, and locals often worked together with foreign Poles. We must also keep in mind that, at least in the province of Posen, the estate owners and inhabitants themselves were largely Polish. Furthermore, most farm labourers from beyond the (relatively near) borders would probably have returned home for family visits during the winter slack anyway, just like seasonal migrants throughout Europe commonly did.[22] Besides, officials recurrently noted that those who did not want to go home found ways to spend the break elsewhere, for instance in adjoining German states that had only partially adopted the Prussian regulations. In any case, many sources contradict the image of Polish farm workers as helpless victims. Especially breaking contracts continued to be a notorious response to unsatisfactory conditions of both native and foreign rural labourers, even though the latter risked expulsion. It seems that the risk was not very high.[23] Employers often did not bother to report runaways, and there were always others willing to hire them in times of labour shortage. The police, in turn, did not necessarily expel the contract-breakers they caught but rather tried to get them re-employed. Moreover, not all workers signed contracts that bound them for the entire season. Apart from switching farms, they also had other means of resistance. Open strikes were risky, but it was often sufficient to slow down work to exert pressure and, in the case of outright abuse, workers could go to court. In 1906, for instance, a group of Russian Poles won a lawsuit against the estate owner Georg von Arnim-Güterberg who had cheated them out of part of their pay.[24] They were not only aided by a local lawyer, but also by their German foreman who testified on their behalf. The victory was all the more significant as von Arnim belonged to an influential noble family and presided over the Brandenburg chamber of agriculture.

Although studies concerning everyday practices are still too sparse for definite conclusions, it seems safe to say that farm labourers from the Russian and Austrian parts of Poland searched for work in Prussia because it seemed relatively attractive to them and that they possessed a considerable degree of negotiating power. Many spent a few seasons abroad to earn money for building

22 Concerning the Ruthenians, the Prussian government acknowledged this. Ministerial Order, 27 September 1905, Landesarchiv Nordrhein-Westfalen, Abteilung Rheinland (LAV NRW-R), BR 04, no. 900: 332–333.

23 According to reports for the year 1905, Prussian authorities expelled just 208 Austrian-Hungarian seasonal workers for breach of contract. GStA PK, I. HA Rep. 77, Tit. 1176, no. 7, adh. 1.

24 Landgericht Prenzlau, 19 January 1906, GStA PK, I. HA Rep. 77, Tit. 1135, no. 1 Fasz. 7a.

a better life at home, or for emigrating to America.[25] Of course, information circulated throughout the migrant community about where to find reasonable conditions, and nobody could be forced to go to known tyrants. Herein lies a major difference to later guestworker programs: no centrally organized "program" existed in Wilhelmine Prussia.[26] The government neither recruited nor distributed the workers, nor did it dictate the terms of the contract. It did not even object when foreign Poles returned to the same place every spring and hence became familiar with local circumstances but only tried to enforce the outlined framework regulations. This means that migrant farm labourers did not enjoy the "protection" that state-run guestworker programs typically promise, yet they remained relatively free to choose where to work.

Nevertheless, the regulations broke with European conventions of the nineteenth century, which Prussia itself had long embraced. For decades, the Prussian bureaucracy had promoted liberal principles such as the freedom of movement with little discrimination between native and foreign subjects. The exclusion of entire categories of people from settlement and from large sectors of the labour market contradicted the established norms of transnational interchange. Whereas immigration acts that banned certain foreign, especially overseas ethnicities were beginning to emerge in other world regions (e.g., the US Chinese Exclusion Act of 1882), nothing similar was on the agenda in Europe and Imperial Germany generally still adhered to common practice, with the drastic exception of Prussia's restrictions on foreign Poles. When questioned, the government pointed to the sovereign right of states to expel undesirable aliens from their territory, a right that all European countries claimed. Conventionally, however, expulsion responded to individual circumstances such as destitution, delinquency, or political troublemaking, and not to origin. In internal correspondence, the Prussian bureaucracy expressed the difference with the terms "subjectively" as opposed to "objectively" undesirable foreigners whereby Polish workers were ranked as "objectively" undesirable, irrespective of their personal comportment. This implied a problematic ethnonationalist departure from liberal concepts, which the government was well aware of, and for this reason, it more or less veiled its policy.

---

25 Edward Pietraszek, "Zwischen Geldverdienen und Aufstieg: Polnische Arbeitsmigranten in Deutschland von 1870 bis 1939," in *Vom Wandergesellen zum "Green Card" Spezialisten: Interkulturelle Aspekte der Arbeitsmigration im östlichen Mitteleuropa*, ed. Klaus Roth (Münster: Waxmann, 2003), 107–133.

26 Only in 1927 did Germany and the reconstituted Poland sign a treaty on the recruitment of Polish farm workers that stipulated a state-controlled program.

Historians have often spoken of "special laws" or "legal regulations" and, as their corollary, of the "illegal employment" of Poles in Wilhelmine Prussia.[27] This terminology is imprecise and overlooks a crucial point as no pertinent law existed, but only a succession of ministerial orders to the regional authorities that were mostly marked as "secret" and remained unpublished. Following the instruction of 1899, all district governments did publish police ordinances, which informed employers under pain of fines that they needed official permission for hiring foreign Polish workers and had to report all arrivals and departures. However, acceding to complaints from fined employers, the Prussian high court quickly dismissed these ordinances as invalid because they lacked a legal basis.[28] The judiciary thus confirmed that it was not illegal to hire foreign Poles just like any other person; nor was it illegal for foreign Poles to take up employment. The legitimation cards introduced in 1907 changed nothing in this respect. A published ministerial order declared them obligatory and stressed their quality as official documents, meaning that falsifications were liable to prosecution.[29] Yet simply ignoring the cards did not violate any law. All that the executive branch could do was to coax employers to cooperate voluntarily and threaten to expel non-legitimized foreign workers. A peculiar feature of Prussia's "guestworker regime" was, therefore, that it fitted uneasily with the existing legislation, and parliamentary approval for legal adjustments would have been hard to obtain in the pre-war era.

One clear error that has slipped into recent scholarship, probably attributable in parts to the pervasive "gender-neutral" masculine phrasing of much of the earlier historiography, is the belief that Prussia's regulations concerning foreign Polish workers only allowed the recruitment of "single men" who, moreover, were allegedly "banned from speaking German."[30] Hahamovitch and Sarkar both hold that these were core elements of the Prussian regime designed to keep migrants and the native population strictly segregated. However, the government did not forbid Poles to speak German and never excluded women from taking up work in Prussia – females made up nearly

27 For instance, Elsner and Lehmann, *Ausländische Arbeiter*, 27, 35–36; Herbert, *Geschichte*, 42–43, 45.

28 Kammergericht Berlin, 3 June 1901 and 3 July 1902, LAV NRW-R, BR 04, no. 900: 118–119, 195–196.

29 "Verfügung betr. die Zulassung ausländischer Arbeiter zur Arbeit in der Landwirtschaft und in den gewerblichen Betrieben in Deutschland," 21 December 1907, *Ministerialblatt für die preußische Innere Verwaltung* 69 (1908): 17–19.

30 Hahamovitch, "Creating Perfect Immigrants," 76; Hahamovitch, *No Man's Land*, 15; Sarkar, "Flipside," 5.

half of the foreign Polish seasonal farm labourers.[31] It is also not quite correct that the recruited workers (of either gender) had to be "unmarried,"[32] as the instruction of 1899 rather stated that only individuals, not family units, were permitted, with exceptions for the eastern border provinces. From 1906, the exception became the rule: families could now sign up without geographic limitation as long as they did not bring along children of (or below) school age.[33] The exclusion of children evidently served to bolster the non-settlement goal while simultaneously aiming to avoid troubles with providing schooling and medical care for them. The large-scale participation of women, however, distinguished the Prussian case from many guestworker schemes of the mid-twentieth century.

A final occasional (yet significant) misconception is the confusion between foreign and native Poles. A recent article on guestworker regimes, for instance, remarks with regard to Prussia's "labour imports" that "about 300,000 Poles burrowed in Ruhrgebiet mines" by 1913, thereby suggesting that 300,000 Ruhr miners were *foreign* Poles.[34] This was not the case. Several monographs on the so-called Ruhr Poles may have contributed to the confusion by placing the terms "guestworkers" and "foreign workers" in their titles, although their protagonists were (as the authors well knew) Prussian and German citizens.[35] The locals certainly tended to perceive these internal migrants from the eastern provinces as strangers, and the latter themselves tended to uphold their Polish identity, but labelling them as foreigners or guestworkers is inappropriate as it obscures the radically different position of Prussian and non-Prussian Poles. While the former had a statutory right to work and stay where they liked throughout the Empire, the latter did not. It is thus necessary to use and reserve the adjective "foreign" for those Poles who did not enjoy the rights of

31 For a discussion on their situation, see Kathrin Roller, *Frauenmigration und Ausländerpolitik im Deutschen Kaiserreich: Polnische Arbeitsmigrantinnen in Preußen*, 2nd ed. (Berlin: Bertz, 1994).

32 Among others, Herbert, *Geschichte*, 22, 26; Reinecke, *Grenzen*, 87, 89.

33 Ministerial Orders, 17 May 1906 and 28 February 1911, LAV NRW-R, BR 04, no. 901: 114, 192.

34 Surak, "Guestworkers," 88.

35 Richard Charles Murphy, *Guestworkers in the German Reich: A Polish Community in Wilhelmine Germany* (Boulder, CO: East European Monographs, 1983); John J. Kulczycki, *The Foreign Worker and the German Labor Movement: Xenophobia and Solidarity in the Coal Fields of the Ruhr, 1891–1914* (Oxford: Berg, 1994). The classic study on the Ruhr Poles is by Christoph Kleßmann, *Polnische Bergarbeiter im Ruhrgebiet 1870–1945: Soziale Integration und nationale Subkultur einer Minderheit in der deutschen Industriegesellschaft* (Göttingen: Vandenhoeck & Ruprecht, 1978).

Prussian-German citizens, even though the two groups were indeed not always distinguishable at first glance.

4 Implementing the Regulations in the West

Since the large-scale recruitment of foreign Poles was a phenomenon of agrarian Northeast Germany, the Prussian regulations primarily aimed at this region, and here their implementation became routine. Despite countless transgressions, the basics worked fairly well because they respected farmers' interest in labour supply, because the *Karenzzeit* matched the agricultural cycle, and because the journey to and from Russian Poland and Galicia was not too far. East-Elbian agrarians had reasons to support the rules, while workers lost little by complying. However, in urban and industrial centres, the constellation was different. The government banned foreign Poles from industrial employment in all but the eastern border provinces due to (well-founded) fears that these might join the westward movement of natives. According to data collected by the county administrators, the goal was achieved, as Table 16.1 shows for the Rhine Province, which, next to Westphalia, encompassed Germany's industrial heartland. Overall, the Rhine Province attracted more foreign workers than any other Prussian province: 209,697 out of 790,189 (27 percent) in 1910 (first row in Table 16.1); but only 4,864 of these workers seemed to be Russian and Austrian Poles (last row in Table 16.1).[36] While the distribution partly reflected geographical location, the government policy also had a twofold impact. On the one hand, the anti-Polish regulations contributed to actually keeping foreign Poles away; on the other hand, they induced workers, employers, and even local authorities to conceal or overlook politically undesired origins. Moreover, officials trained in the west had no practice in distinguishing between various peoples from the east and they had little interest in singling out foreign Poles, as these were not causing any particular problems in everyday life. Although the regional state authorities, namely the provincial governor and the district presidents, began taking the regulations seriously from the late 1890s onwards, it was not easy to get the message through to the local level.

In the Düsseldorf district, the first attempt at systematic implementation started in 1898 when the police identified several hundred foreign Poles

36 Data taken from Klaus Bade, "Arbeiterstatistik zur Ausländerkontrolle: Die 'Nachweisungen' der preußischen Landräte über den 'Zugang, Abgang und Bestand der ausländischen Arbeiter im preußischen Staate' 1906–1914," *Archiv für Sozialgeschichte* 24 (1984): 163–284.

TABLE 16.1 Foreign workers in 1910: Total and major "national" groups

	Prussia					Rhine Province				
	Agriculture		Industry		Total	Agriculture		Industry		Total
	Male	Female	Male	Female		Male	Female	Male	Female	
Total	190,148	148,165	420,176	31,700	790,189	24,402	9,335	168,473	7,487	209,697
Netherlanders	22,435	7,143	75,158	5,208	109,944	17,354	6,113	48,366	3,032	74,865
Italians	712	93	92,288	1,623	94,716	228	35	53,235	721	54,219
German Austrians	6,621	4,258	79,774	11,821	102,474	889	408	19,198	1,283	21,778
Austrian Czechs	1,330	962	25,065	3,108	30,465	90	63	6,754	444	7,351
Belgians	584	282	6,864	575	8,305	546	266	5,737	491	7,040
Russian and Austrian Poles	116,588	109,557	25,925	1,865	253,935	1,826	1,679	1,251	108	4,864

employed in industrial establishments and began expelling them. However, the action was halted halfway through, ironically at the request of the Berlin ministries who worried about diplomatic inconveniences.[37] While the Russian and Austrian governments accepted the return of seasonally unemployed farm workers over winter, they protested against summary expulsions of citizens of their countries who had a permanent livelihood in Prussia. Berlin thus repeatedly urged the regional authorities to proceed cautiously – a difficult balancing act. Employers' protests also played a role. Especially the Gerresheim glass factory near Düsseldorf remonstrated against the removal of its Russian-Polish workers, and apart from the temporary suspension of removals, the management obtained a lasting concession mediated by the district president: The interior minister agreed that Gerresheim glassworkers employed before 1896 could definitely stay – an exemption that was soon extended beyond this particular factory.[38]

Upon receipt of the ministerial instruction from September 1899, the Düsseldorf district president embarked on a new effort. Like his colleagues across the country, he published a police ordinance that obliged employers to obtain a permit for hiring foreign Polish workers and to register them with the police.[39] With this ordinance, the general public learned for the first time that the hiring of such workers was exclusively permitted in agriculture, and charged with enforcement, the local authorities again found several hundred foreign Poles in industrial enterprises. When admonished, employers usually professed that they had either been unaware of the foreign citizenship or of the Polish nationality of these persons. The Gerresheim glass factory, for instance, claimed that some recently hired workers had produced documents identifying them as Russians, but not as Russian *Poles*.[40] Elsewhere, foreign Poles had passed as Prussians because they possessed deregistration certificates from a former Prussian place of residence or German invalidity insurance cards. For a while, the district president insisted on the removal of the discovered Poles and ordered some employers to be fined for non-compliance with the police ordinance. But then came the high court rulings that declared such ordinances

37 Interior Minister to Düsseldorf District President, 30 January 1899, LAV NRW-R, BR 04, no. 900: 1; Press clippings concerning a speech of the Austrian Minister President on 29 November 1898, GStA PK, I. HA Rep. 77, Tit. 1176, no. 4 adh. 1.

38 Interior Ministry to Düsseldorf District President, 3 March 1899, and Ministerial Order, 23 July 1901, LAV NRW-R, BR 04, no. 900: 4–5, 114.

39 "Polizeiverordnung," 20 August 1900, *Amtsblatt der Königlichen Regierung zu Düsseldorf* (1900): 369.

40 Landrat Düsseldorf to District Government, 9 January 1901, LAV NRW-R, BR 07, no. 8883.

invalid, and after a local court had also acquitted a fined employer,[41] the district president revoked the Düsseldorf ordinance in 1904. Consequently, employers no longer felt obliged to scrutinize the nationality of job seekers, and the revocation could even be mistaken as a lift of the ban on foreign Polish workers.

Up until the First World War, the Düsseldorf district president periodically reminded the local authorities of their continuing duty to enforce the ministerial regulations. Nevertheless, these sometimes sank into oblivion, and even if officials remained alert, control was difficult and time-consuming in large cities where thousands of people moved in and out every year. When the police did, by chance, detect a Pole who was working outside the government-defined perimeters, they usually first advised him or her to depart voluntarily, and if this did not happen, formal expulsion followed. Statistical data on expulsions that differentiates between the reasons for these is rare, but sporadic information suggests that irregularly employed foreign Poles did make up a substantial share of the total in the Düsseldorf district. For the year 1905, for instance, the local authorities reported 101 expulsions of Austrian-Hungarian citizens, 34 of whom they listed as "objectively undesirable" Polish workers, while the rest were classified "subjectively undesirable" for causes ranging from criminality to dependency on public poor relief to strike agitation.[42] About most of the affected, we know the names at best. Some, however, protested and thus left deeper traces in the archives.

5 How to Challenge Expulsion

Although foreigners could not appeal to courts against expulsion orders, they could appeal to superior executive authorities, and many did. Typically, not rural seasonal labourers used this method of resistance but town dwellers who had already forged social ties in their new homes of choice. The authorities were bound to evaluate every petition and, at least in the west, foreign Polish workers who had done nothing to make themselves "subjectively undesirable" had comparatively good chances of success. The following examples serve to illustrate favourable circumstances and supporting arguments.

41 Amtsgericht Ratingen, 24 September 1903, LAV NRW-R, BR 04, no. 900: 141.

42 LAV NRW-R, BR 07, no. 15950.

5.1 *Arriving Early*

In February 1906, the textile worker Agate Balnat received police orders to leave the city of Elberfeld and the Prussian state territory.[43] She was a Catholic Lithuanian and thus, as per the ministerial order from May 1905, the regulations concerning foreign Poles applied to her. First, her employer unsuccessfully interceded on her behalf. Then she herself, although illiterate, sent a petition to the exterior minister, who was the wrong addressee but forwarded it to the interior ministry, from where it reached the Düsseldorf district president with the request to report. Balnat inter alia related that she had lived in Prussia since 1895, first as a maid in East Prussia and since 1899 in Elberfeld. This was a useful hint: as mentioned above, Berlin had granted an exemption for foreign Poles employed before 1896, and already in an earlier case, the Düsseldorf district president had negotiated that this should also benefit Lithuanians. Albeit Balnat had no proof of her time in East Prussia, the authorities bothered to investigate, unfortunately with the result that she had arrived there *in* and not *before* 1896, and hence the provincial governor turned her petition down. However, Balnat did not surrender and in September 1906 she sent another submission to the Emperor. Again asked to report, the district president informed that in the meanwhile there had been other appeals against the removal of Lithuanian workers, especially from the Essen chamber of commerce.[44] Therefore, he now advocated postponing the arrival deadline for Lithuanians to 1905 or 1906, which would also settle Miss Balnat's case. Reluctantly, the interior minister agreed.[45] Interesting is that these deliberations display a marked willingness of the Düsseldorf authorities to stretch the reading of ministerial concessions. What originally had been an exception in favour of one particular factory that wanted to retain longstanding workers gradually turned into a provision in favour of all Polish and Lithuanian immigrants who had worked *anywhere* in Germany since before 1896 and 1907 respectively.

5.2 *Switching Occupations*

Prussia's regulations applied to foreign Polish *workers* but not to other wage earners such as shop assistants or the self-employed. This offered a way out for migrants with a strong interest in staying, and sometimes the authorities advised them accordingly. This happened to Hermann Katzka who, in February 1904, sent a petition to His Majesty Wilhelm II from Brussels.[46] He originated

---

43 Landeshauptarchiv Koblenz (LHAK), 403, no. 6820.

44 There were also protests in the press, for instance in the *Kölnische Zeitung*, 3 October 1906.

45 Ministerial Order, 19 August 1907, GStA PK, I. HA Rep. 77, Tit. 1176, no. 6: 52.

46 LHAK, 403, no. 6818.

from Russia, he wrote, but at the age of 16 had moved to Austria, where he learned the tailoring trade. Afterwards, he moved to the Düsseldorf district, first to Barmen and in 1901 to Duisburg. While he was planning his wedding with a native woman, the police suddenly threatened him with expulsion simply because of his Russian-Polish origin. He had thus moved to Belgium, his fiancée followed him, and they got married. Now, with their new-born baby, the couple desperately wanted to return to the wife's "fatherland," and Katzka implored the Emperor to grant them permission to do so. As usual, the Emperor's cabinet forwarded the petition to the interior minister, the minister handed it over to the provincial governor, and the governor requested a report from the district president. The latter answered that Katzka's expulsion had been mandatory because he was working as a journeyman tailor but added that his return should be admissible if Katzka wished to settle down as a self-employed artisan. The governor consented, and Katzka was notified that his expulsion would be rescinded under the named condition.

5.3 *Denying Polishness*

Equally remarkable were the official reactions in the case of Faiga Adler.[47] Her parents were Jewish traders from Russian Poland who had established themselves in Barmen. Berlin also had reservations about Jewish traders but issued no general ban against them, and the local authorities did not object to the Adler family. However, in 1913 it surfaced that 16-year-old Faiga had found employment in a factory, whereby she turned into a "foreign Polish worker." Subsequently, the district president, provincial governor and interior minister extensively discussed whether the girl, or the whole family, had to be expelled, but concluded that a change of occupation would do, and Bernhard Adler promised to employ his daughter in his own business. Yet in the spring of 1914, Faiga was still in the factory. Her father argued that the family needed her income and that he could not keep busy all his children in his small trade. Moreover, he insisted that he was not a "national Pole," but had German ancestors. The district president, in line with the mayor, backed Adler's petition to permit Faiga's industrial employment. From the perspective of the "Polish question," he reasoned, it did not really matter where the girl worked and although there was no proof of German ancestry, the family's Polishness indeed appeared doubtful. Their names sounded rather German-Jewish than Polish, and upon request of Barmen's mayor, the German Consulate in Warsaw had confirmed that Poles and Jews usually regarded each other as distinct nationalities. When

47 LHAK, 403, nos. 6823 and 6824.

the provincial governor also supported Adler, the interior minister grudgingly gave in. This case highlights the fundamental uncertainties that were still unresolved on the eve of the First World War. Did the regulations on foreign Polish workers apply to the children of residents with other occupations? To what extent did they apply to Jews from Poland? For lack of definitive answers to such questions, some leeway in decision-making remained.

5.4 *Marrying a German*

Faiga Adler and Agate Balnat would have had another option for securing a right of residence: By marrying German citizens, they themselves would have become irremovable citizens. Such relationships of course ran counter to Prussian policy, but they nonetheless occurred, and in contrast to overseas colonial constellations,[48] the government did nothing to impede "mixed marriages" between German men and Polish women. More controversial was what to do in the opposite case. Immigrant men could not gain citizenship via marriage; instead, women – as was the gendered legal situation throughout Europe from the nineteenth deep into the twentieth century – lost their original citizenship when they chose a foreign husband and risked banishment from their own "fatherland," as Mrs. Katzka experienced. Prussian authorities often acted pitilessly in this respect, albeit to varying degrees. The Düsseldorf district president generally held that there was no need to expel foreign Polish workers once they had married a native woman, at least when the wife was not a Prussian Pole.[49] Marriage could hence quasi regularize irregular situations, as happened with Johann Rozanek.[50] Rozanek was a Russian Pole who, according to his own account, had come to Germany in 1901. In 1906, he moved to the city of Düsseldorf, but without registering as an inhabitant, and the authorities only noticed his presence in 1909, when he wedded a woman from Malmedy (on the Belgian border of the Prussian Rhine Province). Since he was a construction worker, the official regulations prescribed his expulsion, but the mayor and the district president endorsed his plea to stay. The couple had lived together for years before marrying, they had a child, and Rozanek additionally supported the wife's mother and little sister – relatives who would become destitute if he was forced to leave. Apart from financial considerations, the crucial argument, in this case, was that due to his family, Rozanek was becoming

48 Birthe Kundrus, *Moderne Imperialisten: Das Kaiserreich im Spiegel seiner Kolonien* (Cologne: Böhlau, 2003), 219–280.

49 District President to Provincial Governor, 26 October 1904, LAV NRW-R, BR 04, no. 900: 227–229.

50 GStA PK, I. HA Rep. 77, Tit. 1176, no. 1 R, vol. 5: 191–194.

"Germanized." The interior minister once more granted an exemption from the rules but urged that the Düsseldorf police should control immigration more closely in future.

5.5 *Pleading Hardship*

A last example takes us back to the Gerresheim glass factory, which was a hotspot since the first attempt to implement the ban on foreign Polish workers in 1898. The company had expanded rapidly during the late nineteenth century and preferentially recruited workers from eastern Prussia and western Russia. These were mostly skilled workers from towns with a glassmaking tradition. Some brought along their families, others married in Gerresheim, and their sons often became glassmakers as well.[51] As an investment in a stable labour force, the factory offered company housing, and its site on the outskirts of Düsseldorf resembled a little multilingual town of its own. Despite repeated admonishments, the management never stopped also employing Russian Poles, a fact that the authorities once more rediscovered shortly after Gerresheim's incorporation into the city of Düsseldorf in 1909. The police now summarily issued expulsion orders, against which 14 glassworkers petitioned the Emperor in October 1910.[52] Berlin forwarded the petitions to the district president who turned them down. Subsequently, some departed, but several families refused to go. At the centre were the Najnert and Nowakowski families, who had arrived in Gerresheim between 1901 and 1903.[53] They had settled down in company flats, were covered by social insurance, their children attended local schools and spoke fluent German. Although living in modest conditions, they had much to lose and hence insistently brought forth reasons why it was impossible for them to leave, from illnesses and childbirths to the graves of deceased relatives that needed attendance. This went on for years. The Düsseldorf mayor kept handing over their protests to the district president with sympathizing comments and the district president acknowledged that expulsion to distant Russia would cause serious hardship for these families. The provincial governor and the interior minister urged that the irregular situation must end, but then accepted further delays. Meanwhile, the families' social integration progressed. One of the Nowakowski sons married a Prussian-Polish woman, and soon another baby was born. Johann Najnert

51 Klaus Stelling, "Zur Herkunft der Gerresheimer Glasmacher nach ihren Geburtsorten im 19. Jahrhundert," *Düsseldorfer Jahrbuch* 60 (1986): 97–132.

52 Interior Minister to Düsseldorf District President, 5 November 1910, GStA PK, I. HA Rep. 77, Tit. 1176, 1 W, vol. 6.

53 LHAK, 403, nos. 6823 and 6824.

began drawing an invalidity pension and in 1913, his grown-up children applied for naturalization. The district president was even inclined to grant naturalization but made it dependent on fitness for military service. With the outbreak of the First World War, the still undecided matter was shelved. While the surviving sources do not tell us what became of these glassworkers, it seems likely that they achieved a secure residence status in the end: In 1921, a ministerial order generally precluded the expulsion of foreigners who had lived in Prussia since before April 1914.[54]

As in other cases, the Najnert and Nowakowski families primarily escaped deportation because the local authorities sided with them. Although their employer also interceded on their behalf, economic interests played a minor role. Among the more than 2,000 workers of the glass company, foreign Poles constituted a minority, and the factory did not need these particular individuals. Rather, the struggle was about humanitarian considerations and guarding a certain autonomy against Berlin. Neither the Düsseldorf mayor nor the district president ever opposed the government's anti-Polish policy in principle, and in general reports, they sometimes reproduced xenophobic stereotypes. Confronted with individual fates, however, the necessity to remove evidently harmless people in the national interest became questionable. Though perhaps not yet "Germanized," these glassworkers seemed well adapted to Rhenish life. Indeed, some reports described them as nearly perfect immigrants – not because they constituted cheap and flexibly disposable labour power, but because they worked hard, cared for their families, and abstained from political activities "since their quality as foreigners has emerged."[55]

6 Conclusion

While the cases presented in the last section of this chapter ended satisfactorily for the affected individuals, many others did not, and the selection does not mean to relativize the highly problematic impact of the Prussian regulations on foreign Polish workers. Most disastrous was the differentiation of migrants not only by citizenship, but also by a set of geographic, linguistic, confessional, and social criteria, which amounted to the construction of new ethnonational discriminations with an inherently racist tendency. The stigmatization of Poles

54 "Ausweisung lästiger Ausländer," 21 October 1921, *Ministerial-Blatt für die Preußische innere Verwaltung*, 82 (1921): 372–376.

55 District President to Provincial Governor, 29 January 1912, GStA PK, I. HA Rep. 77, Tit. 1176, no. 1 R, vol. 6: 46–47.

as noxious to the German nation ultimately fed into their subjugation as inferior humans under Nazi rule.[56] However, such fatal developments were not predetermined or envisioned before the First World War. The aim was not even to create a particularly cheap and exploitable labour reserve in the interest of capitalists. The regulations were certainly convenient for East-Elbian agrarians, but in their absence, these would still not have paid and housed masses of farm workers all year round. For industrialists, this sort of state intervention was inconvenient because it encroached on their freedom to hire whom they liked. As court rulings confirmed, the state could not force them to cooperate. Although the category of the "illegally employed alien" did not yet exist, it started becoming conceivable precisely at the moment when Prussian officials realized that they lacked instruments to make employers assist with sorting out unwanted foreigners. Indeed, arguably the most direct consequence of Prussia's special regulations was that they furnished the bureaucracy with experiences that served it well when a short while later, during the interwar period, systematic immigration controls in the name of national labour-market protection became common throughout Europe.

Poles were not "imported" to Prussia but had their own reasons for coming. While they mostly sought temporary work in the eastern provinces as officially permitted, some wandered west, and once established with relatively good jobs and family households, they wanted to stay. Typically, the authorities only noticed their presence with some delay, if at all, and many workers and small employers evidently were not even aware of the restrictions on their residence and employment in Prussia. When it emerged that someone was an irregularly employed "foreign Polish worker," the police tried to expel him or her, but this became harder the longer a person had lived in the region, and once native wives or locally raised children were involved the practical and moral problems deepened. Even though the regulations aimed at preventing such situations from the start, they nevertheless occurred, and when local authorities sympathized with protesting candidates for expulsion, the higher ranks of the bureaucracy were likely to grant exceptional leaves to remain. However, the condition was that the petitioners had not made themselves "subjectively" undesirable, and this required, among other things, abstinence from both Polish nationalism and labour activism.

The social democratic labour movement could potentially have been a powerful alley for foreign workers. By 1912, the *Sozialdemokratische Partei*

56 Herbert, *Geschichte*, 10; Hans-Erich Volkmann, *Die Polenpolitik des Kaiserreichs: Prolog zum Zeitalter der Weltkriege* (Paderborn: Ferdinand Schöningh, 2016).

Deutschlands had become the strongest party in the Reichstag, and its representatives frequently condemned the Prussian government's migration policy with largely the same arguments that present-day scholars use. They accused capitalists of importing foreigners in order to depress local working conditions and the state of backing exploitation with police coercion. Party and union leaders usually propagated equal rights for foreigners as the imperative countermeasure. However, the issue of free immigration already caused dissent in theoretical debates, and in everyday practice, solidarity often proved difficult.[57] Rural East Elbia was far away from the social democrats' strongholds, which were urban and Protestant. Unionization was minimal even among German farm workers, and the labour movement never seriously approached foreign seasonal migrants. More efforts were made in industrial regions. In the partly Catholic Rhine-Ruhr area, for instance, social democratic and Christian unions competed for winning over Italian construction workers. Generally, however, foreigners appeared hard to organize, and this in turn stoked resentment among native union members.

One good reason for migrants' reluctance to associate themselves with the labour movement was its riskiness, irrespective of national origin. Simple union membership and even strike participation were usually tolerated, but when foreigners exposed themselves as social democratic (let alone anarchist) "agitators," they ran into danger of receiving orders to leave the country. The Rhenish authorities, too, were rigorous in this respect. In 1910, for instance, at the same time as he defended Rozanek and the Gerresheim glassmakers, the Düsseldorf mayor mercilessly expelled a Dutch worker, Johann Jochem. This man had also lived in Gerresheim for years, was married to a German woman and father to a locally-born child. Yet in this case, the mayor refused to see anything worth considering in his appeals because Jochem had "lately made himself undesirable as a follower and agitator of social democracy."[58] In the eyes of a Rhenish mayor, being a leftist "agitator" was clearly a greater sin than being a Pole. For foreign Poles, however, it was doubly unadvisable to become associated with leftist tendencies, as this would preclude any chance of exemption from the rule declaring them "objectively undesirable." Hence, while the threat of expulsion certainly limited the scope of action for foreigners in general, and for foreign Polish workers in particular, this should still not induce us to underestimate the scope of action they could and did use.

57 Martin Forberg, "Ausländerbeschäftigung, Arbeitslosigkeit und gewerkschaftliche Sozialpolitik: Das Beispiel der Freien Gewerkschaften zwischen 1890 und 1918," *Archiv für Sozialgeschichte* 27 (1987): 51–81.

58 District President to Provincial Governor, 1 October 1910, LHAK, 403, no. 6822: 238–239.

CHAPTER 17

Colonial Boom Towns

Migration and Insecure Urban Tenure in Industrializing Southern Rhodesia

Katharine Frederick

Abstract

This chapter employs a "systems" approach to trace the development of rural-urban labour migration in British colonial Southern Rhodesia during the mid-twentieth century and uncover why black urban labourers struggled to establish permanent roots in burgeoning industrial cities. The economic and institutional characteristics of the colony influenced the socio-economic opportunities of black Africans in both rural and urban areas. As the colony underwent industrialization from the mid-1940s onward, rural men increasingly migrated to industrial urban centres in search of manufacturing wages that far exceeded the perpetually depressed agricultural wages. However, relatively few were able to establish permanent urban tenure together with a family over the ensuing decades, which resulted in cities with extreme gender imbalances among the black community. This was largely a consequence of the broader institutional makeup of colonial Southern Rhodesia, which primarily served the socio-economic interests of a small white settler community, often at the expense of the colony's black inhabitants.

Keywords

colonial institutions – industrialization – migration – Southern Rhodesia – urbanization – wages

1 Introduction*

This chapter explores the mid-twentieth century growth of rural-urban migration into urban centres of industrializing British-ruled and white

* This research was carried out as part of the ERC-funded project *Race to the Bottom?* (ERC-CoG grant 771288). The author thanks Elise van Nederveen Meerkerk, Ewout Frankema and Michiel de Haas for their comments in the course of the project.

 | DOI:10.1163/9789004686991_018

settler-dominated Southern Rhodesia, which would eventually be proclaimed independent by the settler community under the Universal Declaration of Independence in 1965 but would only be internationally recognized as independent Zimbabwe in 1980.[1] Using an array of economic and sociological reports prepared or commissioned by the colonial government of Southern Rhodesia, this chapter examines the underlying causes of the persistently temporary character of rural-urban migration in the colony as well as the obstacles to worker agency faced by black industrial labourers, which perpetuated deep socio-economic division along racial lines.[2]

Viewed in a longer timeframe, urbanization was not new to the people of the region. In the Kingdom of Great Zimbabwe, considerable urban settlements developed between the eleventh and fifteenth centuries. However, this development subsequently stalled and only Bulawayo was still a major town when, in the late-nineteenth century, the British Empire imposed its colonial rule on the region. Salisbury (renamed Harare in 1982) was established by settlers in 1890 and soon became the administrative centre of Southern Rhodesia. From around 1900, European immigrants increasingly clustered in both Bulawayo and Salisbury,[3] and Africans began taking up urban employment, particularly in services, but often only remained for a few months before returning home to rural areas.[4] In the decades that followed, the colony developed large mining, farming, and manufacturing sectors, eventually ranking among the most industrialized colonies on the continent. By the 1960s, only South Africa had a larger manufacturing sector measured as the share of industry in the total gross domestic product (GDP): 16 percent in Southern Rhodesia compared with 20 percent in South Africa.[5] From the 1940s onward, industrialization

---

1 Named after Cecil Rhodes who acquired the region in 1893, while "Zimbabwe" ("stone house" in the Shona language) reflects the medieval urban culture.

2 For a discussion on the case of Southern Rhodesian urbanization and industrialization in comparative perspective, see Katharine Frederick and Elise van Nederveen Meerkerk, "From Temporary Urbanites to Permanent City Dwellers? Rural-Urban Labor Migration in Colonial Southern Rhodesia and the Belgian Congo," in *Migration in Africa: Shifting Patterns of Mobility from the 19th to the 21st Century*, ed. Michiel de Haas and Ewout Frankema (London: Routledge, 2022), 256–280, and Katharine Frederick, "The Production of Precarity: Industrialization and Racial Inequality in Colonial Zimbabwe," *Revista de Historia Industrial/Industrial History Review* 31, no. 85 (2022): 51–86.

3 M. A. H. Smout, "Urbanisation of the Rhodesian Population," *Zambezia* 4, no. 2 (1975): 80–82.

4 Robert Percival Plewman et al., eds., *Report of the Urban African Affairs Commission, 1958* (Salisbury: Government Printer, 1958), 6.

5 Gareth Austin, Ewout Frankema, and Morten Jerven, "Patterns of Manufacturing Growth in Sub-Saharan Africa: From Colonization to Present," in *The Spread of Modern Industry to the Periphery Since 1871*, ed. Kevin Hjortshøj O'Rourke and Jeffrey Gale Williamson (Oxford: Oxford University Press, 2017), 353.

spurred urban growth, and black[6] male migrants increasingly travelled from rural areas to the colony's emerging cities to seek wage work in manufacturing and services. Although several other forms of migration emerged during the same period – including migration to mining-oriented urban areas in various parts of Southern Africa, as discussed in Chapter 9 in this volume – this chapter specifically focuses on the rapid increase in urban migration caused by the industrial expansion in colonial-era Southern Rhodesia.

Viewed from the present, Sub-Saharan African cities have been expanding rapidly in the last few decades, thereby closing the gap with more urbanized world regions. However, a longer temporal view reveals that profound urban transformations were already underway during the colonial era as a result of the above-mentioned migrations. While the estimated share of the Sub-Saharan African population living in cities averaged below five percent in 1920, this figure had nearly tripled by the 1960s, as colonialism ended across most of the continent.[7] Despite this, Sub-Saharan Africa's rate of urbanization stood at less than half of the world average at the time (Table 17.1). However, Southern Rhodesia exceeded Africa's continental average by the 1960s after having experienced particularly rapid urban growth from the 1940s (Table 17.2).

1.1 *Temporary Tenure in Colonial Boom Towns*

As was the case in many other colonies, early rural-urban migrations in Southern Rhodesia were of a highly temporary nature, with labourers typically returning to rural areas after relatively brief stints working in town.[8] In this highly migratory context, few women and children resided in towns and cities, comprising a scant five percent of the black population of Salisbury, for example, in the early decades of the century. Thus, the development of an urban-born proletariat was retarded. This chapter investigates the factors that influenced the character and intensity of rural-urban migration, with the

6 The term "black" or "black African" is used in this chapter to identify people of African descent. This is a conscious choice to draw attention to the deeply discriminatory ideologies, based on origin and skin colour, that guided the development of exploitative institutions in colonial Southern Rhodesia, where the interests of "white" European settlers were consistently framed against those of "black" Africans.

7 Bill Freund, *The African City: A History* (Cambridge: Cambridge University Press, 2007), 65.

8 For example, Peter Duignan and L. H. Gann, "Introduction," in *Colonialism in Africa 1870–1960*, vol. 4: *The Economics of Colonialism*, ed. Peter Duignan and L. H. Gann (Cambridge: Cambridge University Press, 1975), 13, and Walter Elkan and Roger Van Zwanenberg, "How People Came to Live in Towns," in *Colonialism in Africa 1870–1960*, vol. 4: *The Economics of Colonialism*, 666–669; Freund, *The African City*, 91.

TABLE 17.1 Urbanization rates per world region, 1960–2018

Region	1960	1970	1980	1990	2000	2010	2018
North America	69.9	73.8	73.9	75.4	79.1	80.8	82.2
Europe & Central Asia	55.5	60.9	65.0	67.6	68.7	70.7	72.2
Latin America & the Caribbean	49.5	57.3	64.5	70.7	75.5	78.5	80.6
Middle East & North Africa	34.9	42.7	49.6	54.9	58.6	62.7	65.4
East Asia & the Pacific	16.9	18.8	21.3	28.1	36.6	47.6	55.6
South Asia	16.7	18.6	22.3	25.1	27.4	30.8	34.0
Sub-Saharan Africa	14.7	18.1	22.3	27.4	31.4	36.0	40.2
World	33.6	36.6	39.3	43.0	46.7	51.6	55.3

SOURCE: WORLD DEVELOPMENT INDICATORS. HTTPS://DATABANK.WORLDBANK.ORG/HOME.ASPX

TABLE 17.2 Urbanization in Southern Rhodesia, 1936–1961

Year	Rate
1936	3.6%
1946	5.9%
1949	10.0%
1951	12.7%
1956	14.3%
1961	17.0%

Note: Urbanization rates are imputed from available indexes
SOURCES: PLEWMAN ET AL., *REPORT*, 162; ERIC GARGETT, *THE ADMINISTRATION IN TRANSITION: AFRICAN URBAN SETTLEMENT IN RHODESIA* (GWELO: MAMBO PRESS, 1977), 38; LOVEMORE ZINYAMA AND RICHARD WHITLOW, "CHANGING PATTERNS OF POPULATION DISTRIBUTION IN ZIMBABWE," *GEOJOURNAL* 13, NO. 4 (1986): 378; FREDERICK AND VAN NEDERVEEN MEERKERK, "FROM TEMPORARY URBANITES TO PERMANENT CITY DWELLERS," 257

TABLE 17.3 Sex ratios in Southern Rhodesia, 1962

Locality	Number of males per 100 females (total population)	Number of males per 100 females (age >16)
Salisbury	186	276
Bulawayo	163	211
All Southern Rhodesia	108	111

SOURCES: CENTRAL STATISTICAL OFFICE, *FINAL REPORT OF THE APRIL/MAY 1962 CENSUS OF AFRICANS IN SOUTHERN RHODESIA* (SALISBURY: CENTRAL STATISTICAL OFFICE, 1964), 45; FREDERICK AND VAN NEDERVEEN MEERKERK, "FROM TEMPORARY URBANITES TO PERMANENT CITY DWELLERS," 261

aim of uncovering *why it remained largely temporary (often circular) in nature throughout the colonial period.*

Amid rapid mid-century industrial and urban growth, colonial officials in several African colonies – including the United Party government in Southern Rhodesia – began to favour the permanent urban settlement of married labourers with their wives and children in order to create, in their parlance, a "stabilized" urban labour force. Despite this shift in official attitudes in (some) segments of the Rhodesian government, permanent residence in urban areas remained rare for black workers in the decades after the rise of rural-urban migration. Few male migrant labourers established an urban family, and most of those who did start a family left their family members behind in rural areas. A government study in 1958 found "ample evidence" that more black African families would settle in town if economic conditions, including sufficient housing, allowed this.[9] Thus, by the 1960s, urban sex ratios were still markedly skewed, with far more men relative to women in the major industrial centres of Salisbury and Bulawayo relative to the colony as a whole (see Table 17.3). Migration to the urban environment thus remained a temporary experience long after urbanization and industrialization commenced in the colony.

From a comparative perspective, Southern Rhodesia's development diverged markedly from colonies in other legal and political frameworks, such as the Belgian Congo, where the permanent urban settlement of industrial

9 Plewman et al., *Report*, 18.

workers already commenced in the 1940s and progressed far more rapidly. The core differences can be traced to the geopolitical conditions and colonial institutions of each colony. The Belgian Congo's isolation from nearby colonies helped encourage an earlier industrial take-off and also impeded large-scale cross-border migration which influenced urban labour markets and enabled migrant industrial workers to settle permanently. Perhaps more importantly, colonial institutions in the largely metropolitan-controlled Belgian Congo were influenced much less by settler interests than in the colony of Southern Rhodesia, which was granted a semi-autonomous status by London in 1923, thereby allowing the locally controlled colonial government to freely craft policies that typically strongly favoured white settler interests at the expense of black Africans.[10] In contrast to the Belgian Congo, the experience of black labourers in early-industrializing settler-dominated South Africa was far more similar to Southern Rhodesia. In fact, the Southern Rhodesian government would mirror several earlier implemented South African policies, including land alienation and taxes, that pushed black labourers into low-paid industrial wage work, along with "colour bar" rules that excluded black workers from better-paid skilled occupations dominated by white workers, and "pass laws" that prohibited black workers from living in urban areas that were deemed the exclusive domain of white families. In both the cases of South Africa and, as will be shown, Southern Rhodesia, such measures led to an entrenched system of black urban labour migration.[11]

1.2 *Theories on Limited Labour "Stabilization"*

Contemporary economists debated the causes of the limited permanent settlement of African workers in places such as Southern Rhodesia. Essentialist theories alleged that this was linked to the innate characteristics of black Africans including their presumed inertia, lack of consumptive incentives, and cultural attributes such as migration as a "rite of initiation" and thus inherently temporary, or attachment to rural communities. Others suggested that temporary urban migrants were essentially "target workers" who laboured in cities with the express (and limited) goal of saving money to invest in the family farm as a means of maximizing livelihood security.

10 Frederick and van Nederveen Meerkerk, "From Temporary Urbanites to Permanent City Dwellers," 256–280.

11 Charles H. Feinstein, *An Economic History of South Africa: Conquest, Discrimination, and Development* (New York: Cambridge University Press, 2005), 128–135; Dácil Juif, "Migration and Stabilization: Mining Labor in the Belgian Congo, Northern Rhodesia, and South Africa," in *Migration in Africa*, ed. de Haas and Frankema, 203–228.

More complex theories, critical of imperial and colonizer rule, pointed to poor working conditions and living standards in cities as disincentives to settle permanently,[12] and recent research suggests that wages and urban living costs were crucial determinants of urban tenure. In West Africa and the Belgian Congo, relatively high wages enabled families to settle in industrializing towns and larger urban zones, thus leading to relatively balanced urban sex ratios. In contrast, much lower wages in East African cities – generally set at rates to sustain a single male worker – deterred family settlement in towns for much of the colonial period, resulting in distorted urban sex ratios akin to the case of Southern Rhodesia.[13] The resulting reinforcement of male labour mobility and reliance on women's and children's labour on family plots slowed the emergence of working-class agency and retarded the development of better working and living conditions. Following this reasoning, this chapter highlights the interactions between industrialization, urbanization, and opportunity constraints in a settler colony, where the interests of black Africans were subordinated to the demands of a minority of white settlers of European descent.

In the relatively unique institutional context of semi-autonomous Southern Rhodesia, local colonial – rather than broader imperial – institutions and policies played a central role in influencing and, in many cases, restricting the economic opportunities available to black Africans in both rural and urban zones. This, in turn, influenced labour migration decisions, as well as the capacity of black urban labour migrants to remain permanently in cities. Qualitative and quantitative sources reveal that insufficient wages were, as in the case of East Africa, a key driver of persistent urban labour transience in Southern Rhodesia. Moreover, although urban labour organizations serving black workers began to develop from the 1940s onward, they remained considerably less powerful relative to white unions, which wielded immense political influence and fought to "protect" white labourers from competition with black workers.[14]

12 For an overview of various assumptions and arguments, see, e.g., Walter Elkan, "Migrant Labor in Africa: An Economist's Approach," *American Economic Review* 49, no. 3 (1959): 188–197; Tom Soper, "Labour Migration in Africa," *Journal of African Administration* 11 (1959): 93–99; Marvin P. Miracle and Bruce Fetter, "Backward-Sloping Labor-Supply Functions and African Economic Behavior," *Economic Development and Cultural Change* 18, no. 2 (1970): 240–251.

13 On East and West African rural-urban labour migration, see Felix Meier zu Selhausen, "Urban Migration in East and West Africa Since 1950: Contrasts and Transformations," in *Migration in Africa*, ed. de Haas and Frankema, 281–307. For the Belgian Congo, see Frederick and van Nederveen Meerkerk, "From Temporary Urbanites to Permanent City Dwellers," 256–280.

14 For Southern Rhodesia's urban racial inequality compared with other settler and non-settler colonies in Sub-Saharan Africa, see Frederick, "The Production of Precarity," 51–86.

1.3 *Migration Systems: Beyond "Push" and "Pull"*

Since the mid-twentieth century, both colonial officials and scholars have explored the drivers and characteristics of migration movements in colonial contexts, with an emphasis on "push" and "pull" factors. For example, colonial taxes could *push* rural inhabitants to migrate toward burgeoning towns, mines, or plantations to seek wage work in lieu of subsistence agriculture,[15] as could more forceful push factors such as outright land dispossession.[16] Meanwhile, migrants could be drawn, or *pulled*, toward particular locations by attractive characteristics, including relatively high wages[17] and perhaps even the excitement of new urban environments.[18]

Although some push and pull factors did influence migratory movements, the tendency to treat them in isolation has obscured the complex relationships between sending and receiving areas, which are crucial for understanding the dynamics of migration. Theorists of migration have proposed a more comprehensive "systems approach" that incorporates developments in both sending and receiving regions to uncover feedback mechanisms that may enhance or limit further migration.[19] Akin L. Mabogunje has argued that rural-urban

---

15 For early studies, see Elliott J. Berg, "The Economics of the Migrant Labor System," in *Urbanization and Migration in West Africa*, ed. Hilda Kuper (Berkeley/Los Angeles: University of California Press, 1965), 160–181, and Elliott J. Berg, "The Development of a Labor Force in Sub-Saharan Africa," *Economic Development and Cultural Change* 13, no. 4 (1965): 394–412; William J. Barber, *The Economy of British Central Africa* (Oxford: Oxford University Press, 1961). For a critique of Barber, who viewed the interference of tax collectors as a positive impulse to the monetization of indigenous African economies, see Giovanni Arrighi, "Labour Supplies in Historical Perspective: A Study of the Proletarianization of the African Peasantry in Rhodesia," *Journal of Development Studies* 6, no. 3 (1970): 197–234. Direct taxes particularly affected migrant labour markets in Southern and East Africa. See, e.g., K. Swindell, "Labour Migration in Underdeveloped Countries: The Case of Sub-Saharan Africa," *Progress in Human Geography* 3, no. 2 (1979): 250; Ewout Frankema and Marlous van Waijenburg, "Structural Impediments to African Growth? New Evidence from Real Wages in British Africa, 1880–1965," *Journal of Economic History* 72, no. 4 (2012): 916–921; Kleoniki Alexopoulou and Dácil Juif, "Colonial State Formation Without Integration: Tax Capacity and Labour Regimes in Portuguese Mozambique (1890s-1970s)," *International Review of Social History* 62, no. 2 (2017): 215–252.

16 Arrighi, "Labour Supplies," 197–234; Samir Amin, "Underdevelopment and Dependence in Black Africa: Historical Origin," *Journal of Peace Research* 9, no. 2 (1972): 114–115.

17 For real wages in Sub-Saharan Africa, see Frankema and van Waijenburg, "Structural Impediments to African Growth," 895–926.

18 Akin L. Mabogunje, "Systems Approach to a Theory of Rural-Urban Migration," *Geographical Analysis* 2, no. 1 (1970): 1–18, here 10.

19 Hein de Haas, "The Internal Dynamics of Migration Processes: A Theoretical Inquiry," *Journal of Ethnic and Migration Studies* 36, no. 10 (2010): 1587–1617; Oliver Bakewell, "Relaunching Migration Systems," *Migration Studies* 2, no. 3 (2014): 300–318.

migration in Africa can best be analysed as an organic "system" consisting of rural sending and urban receiving zones that operate within a broader "environment" comprised of institutions, policy, market conditions, and technological characteristics that directly influence the migratory system(s). Hence, changes in one part of the system can affect the constituent parts and thereby alter the character of the system as a whole.[20]

Maintaining a multi-factor systems perspective is particularly helpful for elucidating how and why African rural-urban migration responded to shifting institutional environments in a colonial context. It not only takes individual preferences into account but also engages more structural factors such as industrial development, wage structures, and broader policies that may have helped or hindered migratory movements and, in the case of Southern Rhodesia, the ability of migrants to remain permanently in towns.[21] Moreover, it incorporates the changes that the migration process itself brings to both sending and receiving communities, which could reshape the contours of the existing rural-urban migration system.[22] The particular geopolitical positioning of Southern Rhodesia enabled integration with the migration systems of other nearby colonies, and this influenced the character of its rural and urban labour markets and migratory developments. Furthermore, colonial institutions influenced an array of economic and social institutions with profound implications for economic opportunities in both rural and urban areas.

In broad lines, the overarching migration system was characterized by three sub-systems that often overlapped and competed by providing different opportunities to potential migrants: rural-rural migration, rural-urban migration, and rural-mine migration.[23] The development of rural-urban migration can only be fully understood by considering how sub-systems interacted. Consequently, although the focus of this chapter is on the migration of rural dwellers to industrializing cities, migration *between* rural areas also plays an important role in the analysis as part of the larger migration system in and around Southern Rhodesia.

---

20 Mabogunje, "Systems Approach," 2–4.

21 Mabogunje, "Systems Approach," 4.

22 De Haas, "Internal Dynamics," 1591.

23 While mining towns may also be classified as "urban," in this chapter the term is exclusively used to denote manufacturing centres. Mines in Southern Rhodesia were heavily served by labourers from other colonies, and for the sake of brevity, the rural-mine migration sub-system of Southern Rhodesia is not treated extensively here. For rural-mine migration in the nearby Northern Rhodesian Copperbelt, see Chapter 9 in this volume.

The following analysis spans the period from the turn of the twentieth century, when the colony's institutional foundations were laid, through mid-century when industrialization and urban migration ramped up, to the 1970s when temporary urban migration continued to persist several decades after the colony's initial industrial boom and urban expansion.

2 Political Economics in a Settler Colony

2.1 *Institutionalizing Inequality*

In much of Sub-Saharan Africa, particularly in colonies with relatively large settler populations, colonial governments restricted the economic agency of rural African subjects with two main aims: to lay claim to valuable land and to push Africans onto wage-labour markets for the benefit of European employers seeking cheap labour sources.[24] From the early years of colonial rule, Southern Rhodesia's colonial government began actively restricting African peasants' access to land, levying taxes, applying discriminatory price controls, and imposing segregation policies to achieve these ends. The severely limited opportunity structures that consequently emerged obstructed the permanent settlement of black families in cities once the colony began industrializing from the 1940s onward. This section outlines the development of these policies.

Following the foundation of Southern Rhodesia in the last decade of the nineteenth century, a relatively substantial population of European settlers began migrating to the colony and establishing family farms and larger commercial enterprises.[25] The arrival of settlers initially provided lucrative marketing opportunities for African farmers, who profited from the rising demand for grain.[26] However, the white settlers soon chafed at the stiff competition they faced both in agricultural markets and for labour since black cultivators who could earn incomes as free agents were unwilling to work for settlers on plantations or in mines. In this context, the colonial government instituted measures that stymied African marketing opportunities and pushed many onto wage labour markets.[27]

---

24 See, e.g., Ian Phimister and Rory Pilossof, "Wage Labor in Historical Perspective: A Study of the De-proletarianization of the African Working Class in Zimbabwe, 1960–2010," *Labor History* 58, no. 2 (2017): 216–217.

25 Ian Phimister, *An Economic and Social History of Zimbabwe, 1890–1948: Capital Accumulation and Class Struggle* (New York: Longman, 1988), 4–20, 100–101.

26 Phimister, *Economic and Social History*, 25.

27 Arrighi, "Labour Supplies," 209–210.

Already in the first decade of the twentieth century, a process of land alienation was initiated as the Southern Rhodesian government created Native Reserves for African (re)settlement, thereby instituting the territorial segregation of Africans and Europeans. Africans living outside of these designated areas were obliged to pay land and grazing fees that many could not afford, which effectively forced them onto the Reserves. Some were pushed off their land to make way for European settlers seeking fertile and well-situated farms. Reserve lands, in contrast, were often dry, infertile, and disconnected from emerging urban centres, thereby cutting peasant producers off from access to markets.[28] By the early 1920s, nearly two-thirds of all black inhabitants of Southern Rhodesia were residing in the Reserves.[29]

Once the political power of the growing white settler community was further bolstered by the British government's acceptance of a semi-autonomous "Responsible Government" in 1923, this ongoing process of racial segregation and land dispossession was further cemented by law: The Land Appropriation Act of 1930 formally established distinct "Native" and "European" areas, along with remaining unassigned zones. While white settlers accounted for only five percent of Southern Rhodesia's population in 1930, the officially designated European area covered just over half of the colony's territory; in contrast, the land allotted specifically to black Africans, who made up 95 percent of the total population, amounted to less than one-third of the territory (see Figure 17.1 and Table 17.4).[30] Worse still, per-capita land allotments on the Native Reserves would progressively fall from 19 hectares in the early 1930s to only 9 by the 1950s as populations increased.[31] Moreover, geographic mobility was tightly restricted as black Africans were only permitted in European zones, which included cities, under strict conditions of employment by a white settler.

At the same time, the imposition of an array of taxes, payable in cash, further eroded the economic position of black Africans and, while Africans bore a considerable share of the fiscal burden, the government primarily used the funds obtained to support white settler farms and enterprises.[32] Moreover, the Maize Control Acts, instituted in the 1930s, would artificially depress grain prices paid

28 Zinyama and Whitlow, "Changing Patterns," 368–369.

29 Phimister, *Economic and Social History*, 65–67, 83.

30 Barry N. Floyd, "Land Apportionment in Southern Rhodesia," *Geographical Review* 52, no. 4 (1962): 577; Phimister and Pilossof, "Wage Labor in Historical Perspective," 217; Zinyama and Whitlow, "Changing Patterns," 368–369.

31 Rory Pilossof, "Labor Relations in Zimbabwe from 1900 to 2000: Sources, Interpretations, and Understandings," *History in Africa* 41 (2014): 351.

32 Phimister, *Economic and Social History*, 83; Arrighi, "Labour Supplies," 210.

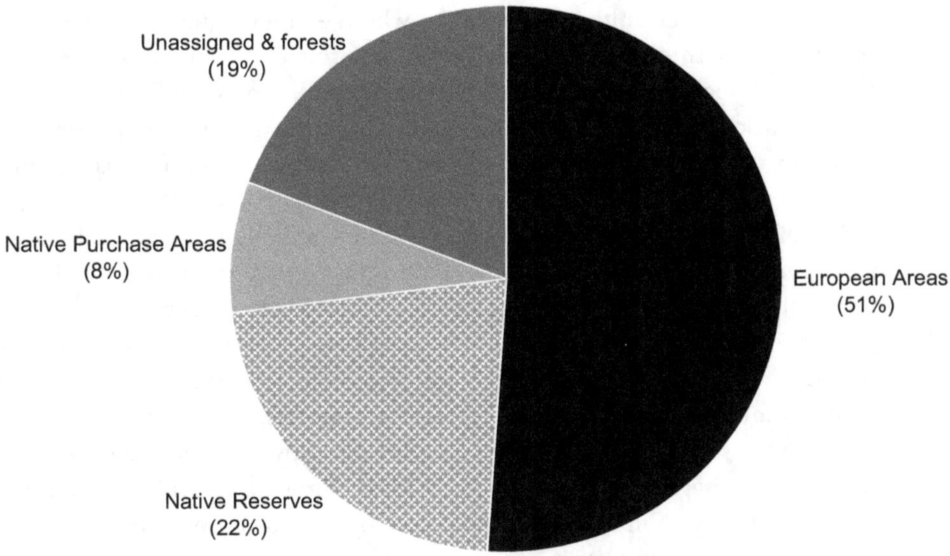

FIGURE 17.1 Land apportionment in Southern Rhodesia, 1930
SOURCE: BARRY N. FLOYD, "LAND APPORTIONMENT IN SOUTHERN RHODESIA," 577

TABLE 17.4 Composition of the population, Southern Rhodesia, 1901–1961

	Black African		European descent		Total
1901	530,000	98%	11,032	2%	541,032
1911	700,000	97%	23,606	3%	723,606
1921	847,000	96%	33,620	4%	880,620
1931	937,000	95%	49,910	5%	986,910
1945	1,640,000	95%	82,386	5%	1,722,386
1951	1,970,000	94%	136,017	6%	2,106,017
1961	2,885,000	93%	225,000	7%	3,110,000

Note: For black Africans: 1901=1902, 1961=1960; for Europeans: 1945=1946. Early colonial censuses often estimated population figures, providing only a rough picture of shares. Recent estimates suggest that the black African population of Southern Rhodesia may have been even larger. See, e.g., Frankema-Jerven African Population Database, v. 1.0: Ewout Frankema and Morten Jerven, "Writing History Backwards and Sideways: Towards a Consensus on African Population, 1850-present," *Economic History Review* 67, no. S1 (2014): 907–931

SOURCES: FLOYD, "LAND APPORTIONMENT IN SOUTHERN RHODESIA," 577; PETER J. M. MCEWAN, "THE EUROPEAN POPULATION OF SOUTHERN RHODESIA," *CIVILISATIONS* 13, NO. 4 (1963): 429 (TABLE 1); FREDERICK, "THE PRODUCTION OF PRECARITY," 59

specifically to black cultivators, many of whom earned a quarter of the price paid to white farmers for the same agricultural produce.[33] Diminished incomes thus forced poorer farmers toward wage labour and, consequently, the proportion of black men of Southern Rhodesian origin on the wage labour market continuously increased through the first half of the twentieth century, rising from less than a quarter in 1920 to approximately 60 percent in 1951.[34]

Initially, many laboured on European farms, although agricultural wages were perpetually depressed. Low agricultural wages were intrinsically linked to a colonial policy of encouraging migration flows of cheap contracted labourers from neighbouring colonies that had fewer employment opportunities – particularly Mozambique and Nyasaland – a system facilitated by recruitment agreements between colonial authorities.[35] To promote this system, the Southern Rhodesian government even provided free transport support services beginning in the 1930s.[36] Most "foreign" contracted labourers were specifically channelled into rural employment by government agencies, which helped limit any significant growth in rural wages. Low rural wages were worsened by existing discriminatory labour regulations, including the draconian Masters and Servants Act (1901) that essentially outlawed bargaining tools for agricultural workers. At the same time, settlers represented by the powerful Rhodesia National Farmers Union lobbied against any legislation that favoured black agricultural workers.[37]

2.2 *Industrialization and Early Urbanization*

Against this backdrop of mounting economic pressures on Southern Rhodesia's rural black population, the colony began to undergo rapid industrial growth, which stimulated rural-urban migration by the mid-1940s. Prior to the 1940s, mining and commercial agriculture had been heavily encouraged by the colonial government, overshadowing nascent urban manufacturing initiatives.[38]

33 Phimister, *Economic and Social History*, 185–189.

34 Arrighi, "Labour Supplies," 204, 221–222.

35 Phimister, *Economic and Social History*, 50, 85; D. G. Clarke, *Contract Workers and Underdevelopment in Rhodesia* (Gwelo: Mambo Press, 1974); Social Welfare and Housing Secretary for Labour, *Report of the Secretary for Labour, Social Welfare and Housing for the Year Ended 31st December, 1960* (Salisbury: Government Printer, 1961), 11–12.

36 Peter Scott, "Migrant Labour in Southern Rhodesia," *Geographical Review* 44, no. 1 (1954): 36; Clarke, *Contract Workers and Underdevelopment in Rhodesia*, 25.

37 Clarke, *Contract Workers and Underdevelopment in Rhodesia*, 43–44.

38 William Gervase Clarence-Smith, "The Effects of the Depression on Industrialization in Equatorial and Central Africa," in *The Economies of Africa and Asia in the Interwar Depression*, ed. Ian Brown (London/New York: Routledge, 1989), 173–175.

However, supply shortages during the Second World War prompted the government to boost domestic manufacturing, and by 1940 the state had underwritten the development of factories producing both light and heavy industrial products, ranging from yarn to artillery. Within a decade, the colony boasted nearly 500 factories, with many situated in Salisbury and Bulawayo, and their output grew by almost 25 percent each year in the second half of the 1940s. British and South African investors poured capital into Southern Rhodesian manufacturing, particularly consumer goods factories, and the value of regional exports of textile products to neighbouring colonies grew swiftly from £65,000 in 1948 to over £4 million in 1953.[39] Within a few years, manufacturing earnings outstripped both mining and settler agriculture.[40]

As industrial development increased, demand for industrial workers soared, and so did rural-urban migration as black male labourers from rural Southern Rhodesia increasingly headed to industrial centres, especially Salisbury and Bulawayo. Between 1936 and 1951, urbanization rates more than tripled (see Table 17.2). As in the agricultural sector, a large share of the black urban labour force came from neighbouring colonies in the early decades of industrialization, particularly in the case of Salisbury.[41] By the mid-1950s, roughly half of the black urban labour force in Southern Rhodesian towns hailed from neighbouring colonies, particularly Nyasaland and Mozambique (Table 17.5). Many of these cross-border migrant labourers remained in town for relatively short periods before either returning home or moving on to other employment opportunities further south in the mines of South Africa. For example, during the 1950s, migrants from Nyasaland typically departed after four to five years of work.[42]

The presence of foreign manufacturing employees undoubtedly partly influenced the highly temporary character of rural-urban labour migration in Southern Rhodesia. However, while the share of cross-border migrants in the Rhodesian industry would eventually peak and decline after the late 1950s,[43] urban tenure continued to remain elusive for most black Southern Rhodesian

39 Ian Phimister, "Secondary Industrialisation in Southern Africa: The 1948 Customs Agreement Between Southern Rhodesia and South Africa," *Journal of Southern African Studies* 17, no. 3 (2007): 437. For a comprehensive overview of the development of Southern Rhodesia's industrial sector, see Phimister, *Economic and Social History*, 239–257.

40 Plewman et al., *Report*, 9.

41 Plewman et al., *Report*, 16 (Table VII).

42 Scott, "Migrant Labour in Southern Rhodesia," 45–46.

43 For shares in the late-1950s versus late-1960s, compare Plewman et al., *Report*, 16 (Table VII) and Peter Harris, *Black Industrial Workers in Rhodesia: The General Problems of Low Pay* (Gwelo: Mambo Press, 1974), 13.

TABLE 17.5 Africans in employment in Southern Rhodesian towns, 1956

Town	Colony of birth						
	Southern Rhodesia	Northern Rhodesia	Nyasaland	Portuguese territories	Other	Total	% Foreign migrants
Salisbury	41,203	2,181	28,987	28,972	701	102,044	59.6%
Bulawayo	42,841	7,928	10,262	5,224	1,150	67,407	36.4%
Umtali	7,496	93	618	5,568	77	13,852	45.9%
Gwelo	8,737	425	1,030	517	77	10,768	19.0%
Que Que	2,890	474	960	457	15	4,796	39.7%
Gatooma	2,049	460	1,137	584	35	4,265	52.0%
Fort Victoria	3,031	41	116	167	17	3,372	10.1%
Total	*108,247*	*11,602*	*43,110*	*41,489*	*2,072*	*206,520*	*47.6%*

SOURCES: PLEWMAN ET AL., *REPORT*, 16 (TABLE VII); FREDERICK AND VAN NEDERVEEN MEERKERK, "FROM TEMPORARY URBANITES TO PERMANENT CITY DWELLERS," 259

industrial workers for many decades thereafter. Indeed, as the next section illustrates, the array of colonial policies and institutions that limited the economic mobility of Africans in Southern Rhodesia arguably played a central role in impeding the permanent settlement of black urban labourers in Southern Rhodesia's cities.

3 Barriers to Urban Permanence in Industrial Towns

3.1 *Rural and Urban Opportunity Constraints*

The persistently temporary character of rural-urban migration in Southern Rhodesia's industrial cities was, at least in part, an unintended consequence of very different economic opportunities for rural versus urban labourers. From the early days of industrialization, wage rates for black workers in urban areas became increasingly attractive in comparison to agricultural wage opportunities in rural areas as the colony underwent its first rapid industrial push (see Figure 17.2). This was partly a result of the systematic depression of agricultural wages in rural areas (as discussed above). From the 1940s, strike action by black railway and industrial workers had helped to promote upward wage momentum – albeit very modest in comparison to the wages paid to white workers (see discussion below) – as well as the recognition of black workers' unions. The immense wage disparity that increasingly emerged between rural and urban areas resulted in large numbers of black migrants leaving rural areas to seek more remunerative wage work in urban areas. This, in turn, created exceedingly strong competition in urban labour markets. Persistently high urban labour supplies – driven by government policies that actively diminished *rural* opportunities – raised the constant spectre of urban unemployment, thereby undermining the prospects for permanent urban tenure.

Although this oversupply of urban labour broadly undermined the security of black urban labourers, it must be noted that the decision of many black workers to venture to town in lieu of working in the lower-paid rural sector illustrates worker agency on an individual level, which ran contrary to the demands of both agricultural employers and colonial officials in rural areas. For example, the Secretary of Internal Affairs noted in the early 1960s: "One

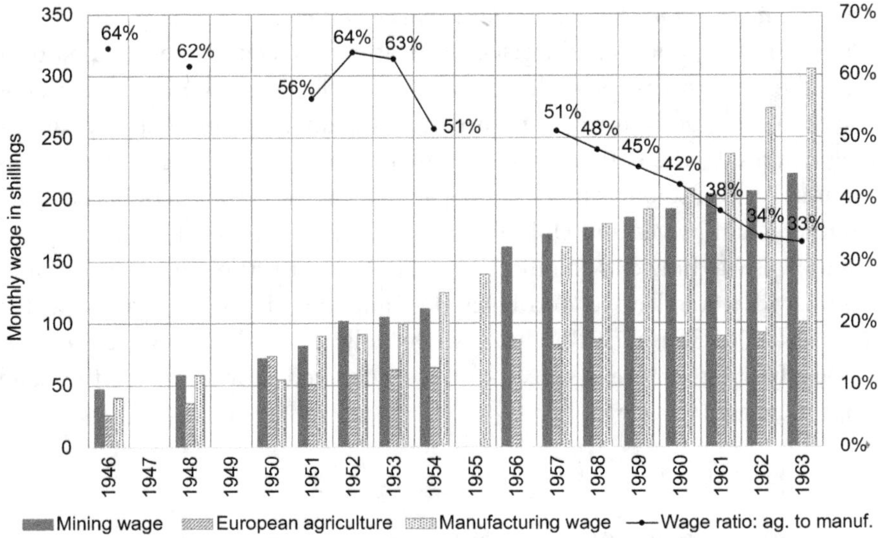

FIGURE 17.2 Average nominal wages for African labour, Southern Rhodesia, 1946–1963
Note: The agriculture-manufacturing wage ratio for the outlier year 1950 has been excluded to illustrate the broader trend more clearly
SOURCES: PAUL MOSLEY, *THE SETTLER ECONOMIES: STUDIES IN THE ECONOMIC HISTORY OF KENYA AND SOUTHERN RHODESIA, 1900–63* (CAMBRIDGE: CAMBRIDGE UNIVERSITY PRESS, 1983), 160 (TABLE 4.9B); FREDERICK AND VAN NEDERVEEN MEERKERK, "FROM TEMPORARY URBANITES TO PERMANENT CITY DWELLERS," 264

District Commissioner reports that although there is large-scale unemployment in his urban areas, European farmers are having difficulty in obtaining farm labour, as the young indigenous men do not appear to favour work on farms" and that, in general, "the local indigenous labourer was not offering himself for such work."[44]

However, despite their relatively privileged position in comparison to black rural wage workers, black industrial workers faced considerable hurdles in the city and the earnings for most black urban workers remained far too low to sustain an urban-situated family. While married men often earned more than single men, incomes were simply not sufficiently high to meet the cost of supporting non-labouring dependents in the city. The majority of those who did settle in town with a wife and children fell below the poverty line, even in Salisbury's New Highfield area, where the city's relatively more affluent black inhabitants lived (Table 17.6).[45] Most single men, in contrast, were within or above the poverty line. This incentivized labour migrants to venture to the city alone, maintaining a "dual existence," split between stints of urban employment and rural life on the Reserves.[46]

3.2 *Labour Stabilization: Policy versus Practice*

While colonial policies and legislation relating to black workers shifted over time, they almost always tended to negatively affect the economic security of black Africans, both in rural and urban areas, albeit in different ways at different times. In the early decades of colonial rule, authorities in many Sub-Saharan African colonies had encouraged temporary migration of black urban labourers, with wives and children left on the Reserves or in their colony of origin. This was linked to colonizer anxieties that the settlement of black families in cities would lead to "detribalization" and undermine segregation, which in the case of Southern Rhodesia was widely demanded by white settlers, especially in urban areas which had been deemed "European" by the Land Apportionment Act (1930).[47]

44 Secretary for Internal Affairs and Chief Native Commissioner, *Report of the Secretary for Internal Affairs and Chief Native Commissioner for the Year 1962* (Salisbury: Government Printer, 1963), 32.

45 D. G. Bettison, "The Socio-Economic Circumstances," 188, 193.

46 Introductory note of the Native Reserves Land Utilization and Good Husbandry Bill of 1948 cited in Ian Phimister, "Rethinking the Reserves: Southern Rhodesia's Land Husbandry Act Reviewed," *Journal of Southern African Studies* 19 (1993): 231.

47 Mamdani Mahmood, *Citizen and Subject: Contemporary Africa and the Legacy of Late Colonialism* (Princeton, NJ: Princeton University Press, 1996), 6–7; Richard Gray, *The Two*

TABLE 17.6 Percentage of households in income brackets relative to the Poverty Datum Line (PDL), Salisbury, 1957

	Extremely impoverished	Below PDL	Within PDL	Above PDL	Extremely affluent
Single men	5%	22%	37%	17%	13%
Families in New Highfield	47%	18%	20%	2%	13%
Families in "other areas"	57%	19%	17%	3%	3%

SOURCES: D. G. BETTISON, "THE SOCIO-ECONOMIC CIRCUMSTANCES OF A SAMPLE OF AFRICANS IN SALISBURY, JULY, 1957," IN PLEWMAN ET AL. *REPORT*, 181, 188 (TABLES 1, 6, AND 7); FREDERICK AND VAN NEDERVEEN MEERKERK, "FROM TEMPORARY URBANITES TO PERMANENT CITY DWELLERS," 259; FREDERICK, "THE PRODUCTION OF PRECARITY," 74

However, as noted in the introduction, policies regarding black urban labourers began to shift by the middle of the century as urban populations expanded with industrialization from the mid-1940s. Southern Rhodesian officials became increasingly concerned with purported moral hazards in cities primarily comprised of men in "the irresponsible 18–35 age group" as well as diminished labour productivity due to high turnover.[48] In the post-war years, more permanent urban settlement of black labourers was thus widely promoted by the colonial administration in Southern Rhodesia, as well as other British colonies.[49] By the early 1950s, Southern Rhodesia's semi-autonomous government began actively implementing policies that were intended to simultaneously stimulate longer urban tenure among black urban workers and to relieve pressure on increasingly overpopulated rural Reserve lands.[50] In practice, however, these aims were complicated by the settler-beholden government's concurrent commitment to white settler interests. Moreover, those

Nations: Aspects of the Development of Race Relations in the Rhodesias and Nyasaland (London: Oxford University Press, 1960), 256.

48 Howman Committee, "Report on Urban Conditions in Southern Rhodesia," *African Studies* 4, no. 1 (1945): 11–13.

49 Frederick Cooper, *Decolonization and African Society: The Labor Question in French and British Africa* (Cambridge: Cambridge University Press, 1996), 365–367.

50 By the 1940s, nearly two-thirds of the Reserves were reportedly overcrowded. Phimister, *Economic and Social History*, 237–238.

policies that were implemented often disregarded the preferences and social realities of the black labourers themselves.[51]

First, the Native Land Husbandry Act of 1951 sought to rigorously divide black Africans into either rural peasant producers with tenured land on the Reserves or urban industrial labourers living permanently in towns with their families.[52] The carrying capacity of the Reserves was capped, and the black urban industrial worker was to have "his tentacles pulled out of the soil" by divesting him of his rights to land on the Reserves.[53] However, the government only focused on the rural side of the equation – that is, systematically granting land tenure to rural Reserve dwellers and stripping urban industrial workers of land rights – but failed to legislatively facilitate more permanent urban tenure and economic security for black urban workers.[54] The ramifications of institutionalized land dispossession in a context of urban insecurity became apparent in the late 1950s when a recession cut industrial employment opportunities, precipitating a crisis for the landless – and now widely unemployed – black urban workers.[55] By the end of the 1950s, the Land Husbandry Act had been implemented on less than half of the Native Reserves but had reportedly divested over 100,000 families of access to land.[56] The Act inflicted economic insecurity on tens of thousands and failed to achieve the government's labour stabilization goals in both rural *and* urban areas as evidenced by persistent sex imbalances: As of the mid-1950s, women vastly outnumbered men in Rhodesian villages, mirroring the situation in towns.[57] The Act proved a failure and was eventually overturned in the early 1960s.

The government subsequently took further steps in its effort to engineer urban labour stabilization. In 1958, the colonial administration banned the employment of Africans from other colonies in Southern Rhodesian

51 Barry N. Floyd, *Changing Patterns of Land Use in Southern Rhodesia*, vol. 1 (Lusaka: Rhodes-Livingstone Institute, 1959), 274.

52 For official perspectives on the plan, see Minister of Native Affairs, April 1951, cited in Plewman et al., *Report*, 21.

53 Phimister, "Rethinking the Reserves," 231; William R. Duggan, "The Native Land Husbandry Act of 1951 and the Rural African Middle Class of Southern Rhodesia," *African Affairs* 79, no. 315 (1980): 229.

54 Floyd, *Changing Patterns*, 271–275.

55 Some scholars surmise that the recession caused the eventual abandonment of the Land Husbandry Act as industrial labour demand decreased, thereby reducing the interest in stabilizing the urban labour force. Robin Palmer, *Land and Racial Domination in Rhodesia* (Berkeley/Los Angeles: University of California Press, 1977), 243–244.

56 Phimister, "Rethinking the Reserves," 236; Zinyama and Whitlow, "Changing Patterns," 377.

57 J. Clyde Mitchell, *An Outline of the Sociological Background to African Labour* (Salisbury: Ensign Publishers, 1961), 80.

manufacturing centres to simultaneously relieve employment competition for native-born black industrial workers and attempt to funnel cross-border migrant labour to settler-owned plantations and mines, which struggled to attract Southern Rhodesian workers.[58] The share of the black urban labour force comprised of men born in the colony grew from 52 percent in 1958 to 82 percent by 1969.[59] However, despite these developments, permanent urban tenure still remained out of reach for many.[60]

3.3 *Racial Wage Disparities*

The insufficient wages for black urban workers, which persisted well into the 1970s, remained at the heart of the problem, making a shift toward genuine urban "stabilization" virtually impossible despite government interventions. Low black urban wages were a direct result of deep racial wage disparities that had been virtually codified by decades of legislation that strongly favoured the interests of white urban labourers. Although urban wages were (comparatively) much higher than what workers could earn in rural wage work, they, too, were kept artificially low. Wages for white industrial workers, in contrast, rose precipitously as the industrial sector expanded (Figure 17.3), and by 1972 white workers earned over 10 times as much as black workers.[61] While black labourers made up 80 percent of the industrial labour force between the 1940s and 1960s, they took home only 30 percent of the sectoral wage bill.

While Southern Rhodesian officials justified the wage gap on the basis of productivity differences,[62] contemporary sociologists such as Giovanni Arrighi instead pointed to strong white bargaining power and legislation that barred black Africans from higher-paid occupations.[63] Moreover, lower-skilled jobs were reportedly often "reserved" at "European" wage rates in state-run companies to ensure that unskilled white workers would not face direct competition from "similarly unskilled blacks for employment."[64] Thus, the government's

---

58 D. G. Clarke, "International Labour Supply Trends and Economic Structure in Southern Rhodesia/Zimbabwe in the 1970s," *Working Paper World Employment Programme* WEP2-26/WP20 (1978): 51.

59 Plewman et al., *Report*, 16 (Table VII); Harris, *Black Industrial Workers*, 13.

60 See Percy Ibbotson, "Urbanization in Southern Rhodesia," *Africa* 16, no. 1 (1946): 73–82; David Bettison, "Factors in the Determination of Wage Rates in Central Africa," *Rhodes-Livingstone Journal* 28 (1960): 22–46; Bettison, "The Socio-Economic Circumstances"; Harris, *Black Industrial Workers*; Eric Gargett, *The Administration in Transition: African Urban Settlement in Rhodesia* (Gwelo: Mambo Press, 1977); Arrighi, "Labour Supplies."

61 Harris, *Black Industrial Workers*, 11.

62 For example, see Plewman et al., *Report*, 73.

63 Giovanni Arrighi, *The Political Economy of Rhodesia* (The Hague: Mouton, 1967), 49–50.

64 Harris, *Black Industrial Workers*, 15–16.

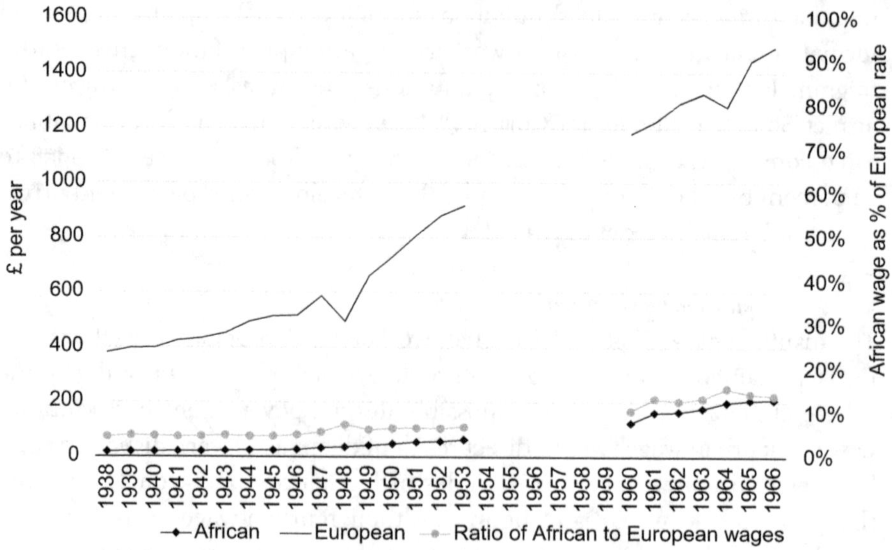

FIGURE 17.3 Average annual white European and black African nominal wages per worker, Southern Rhodesian manufacturing sector, 1938–1966
Note: The "European" category includes small numbers of "Asian" and "coloured" labourers for the years 1960–1966. In the context of Southern Rhodesia, the term "coloured" was applied to individuals of mixed-race ancestry
SOURCES: CENTRAL AFRICAN STATISTICAL OFFICE, *THIRTEENTH REPORT ON THE CENSUS OF INDUSTRIAL PRODUCTION, 1938–1953* (SALISBURY: CENTRAL AFRICAN STATISTICAL OFFICE, 1955), 26, 34, TABLES II AND III; CENTRAL STATISTICAL OFFICE, *THE CENSUS OF PRODUCTION IN 1966. MINING, MANUFACTURING, CONSTRUCTION, ELECTRICITY AND WATER SUPPLY* (SALISBURY: CENTRAL STATISTICAL OFFICE, NO DATE), 53, TABLE 6; ALSO SEE FREDERICK AND VAN NEDERVEEN MEERKERK, "FROM TEMPORARY URBANITES TO PERMANENT CITY DWELLERS," 274; FREDERICK, "THE PRODUCTION OF PRECARITY," 70

sensitivity toward blue-collar settler interests helped perpetuate occupational segregation and racial wage discrimination into the 1970s.

An additional barrier to permanent urban tenure was a persistent shortage of suitable housing for black labourers.[65] The colonial government attempted to remedy the housing problem with the Natives (Urban Areas) Accommodation and Registration Act (1946, 1951), which placed the burden of housing on employers. However, linking employment and habitation did little to alleviate urban insecurity for black workers since temporary unemployment

65 Ibottson, "Urbanization in Southern Rhodesia," 79.

could result in homelessness. The Act also provided broad regulatory powers to city authorities who began tracking down and evicting black women "illegally" living with urban workers without government-issued marriage certificates.[66] Housing posed an even larger problem for married men with families since the majority of the housing projects were intended for single men.[67]

Settlement of black families in urban areas gradually increased from the 1970s onward as wages began to rise – albeit starting from very low levels. However, those families that did manage to come to town continued to face considerable poverty, with the majority of men still unable to afford to comfortably support an urban family: As of the mid-1970s, nearly 90 percent of Southern Rhodesia's black industrial labour force reportedly still earned wages that were insufficient to maintain an average-sized family in town.[68] Consequently, many urban labourers fostered ties with their rural home communities, and even among those who managed to establish an urban household, rural links remained an economic safety valve, providing the ability, for example, to send children to live with rural relatives to reduce the economic burden of additional mouths to feed. Consequently, the maintenance of rural-urban links, which the colonial government had already sought to cut in the 1950s with the failed Native Land Husbandry Act, remained crucial for the survival of black urban households some 40 years after rural migration to cities had commenced.[69]

4 Conclusion

The case of Southern Rhodesia illustrates how migration systems both respond to and transform opportunities within rural and urban zones. These varying opportunities are intrinsically bound to broader economic and institutional structures, particularly in an interventionist colonial context. Here, economic opportunities in rural zones were sharply curtailed during the early twentieth century as exploitative colonial policies put immense economic pressure on black rural inhabitants, while large-scale migratory inflows of cheap rural

66 Ian Phimister and Brian Raftopoulos, "'Kana Sora Ratswa Ngaritswe': African Nationalists and Black Workers – The 1948 General Strike in Colonial Zimbabwe," *Journal of Historical Sociology* 13, no. 3 (2000): 311–312.

67 Plewman et al., *Report*, 50.

68 Peter Harris, "Industrial Workers in Rhodesia, 1946–1972: Working-Class Elites or Lumpenproletariat?," *Journal of Southern African Studies* 1, no. 2 (1975): 149.

69 Gargett, *The Administration in Transition*, 20, 25, 29.

labourers from neighbouring colonies diminished agricultural wages. The ensuing flow of black male labourers into industrializing cities generated fierce competition for urban jobs and enhanced the risk of urban employment. Although wages were higher in towns, urban labourers necessarily maintained ties with rural zones given that they could not start or maintain a family in the city. The makeup of colonial Southern Rhodesia's institutions, which overwhelmingly favoured white settler interests, retarded both permanent urban residence of black industrial workers and the emergence of black African unions. The colonial government's eventual attempt to legislate a freeze on rural and urban movements failed as the economic prospects allotted to black urban labourers were far too meagre to weather the forced breakdown of the existing system of flexible rural-urban movement. Social and geographic mobility between rural and urban zones would consequently remain vital for black urban labourers until their economic opportunities increased to such a degree that they could permanently sustain a family in town, a development that was delayed until well beyond the end of the colonial period.

CHAPTER 18

"Ceylon for Sinhalese!"

"Depression Politics" and Indian Migrants in Ceylon

Ritesh Kumar Jaiswal

Abstract

The Great Depression had a significant impact on the political economy of colonial Ceylon which led to consequential changes in the prices, production, global circulation, and consumption of tea and rubber. The changing political economy intersected with the emergence of national politics that involved intense anti-migrant and anti-Indian rhetoric. The anti-colonial and anti-immigrant ethnonationalism merged and brought about crucial transformations in relations between capital and labour as well as patterns of Indian migration and intermediation. This chapter scrutinizes the role of the press, propaganda, colonial policies, and nationalist politics in fanning xenophobia and violence and exacerbating the existing labour conditions and immigrant-native relations. The varied responses of the colonialists, nationalists, intermediaries, and migrants in Ceylon to these changes initiated by the Great Depression and its consequences are also important aspects of the examination.*

Keywords

British Empire – Ceylon – colonialism – ethnonationalism – Great Depression – India – Indian labour – Indian migration – kangany system – plantations – return migration – Sinhalese – xenophobia

* Earlier drafts of this chapter were presented at the ETH-UZH Colloquium on Extra-European and Global History, Zurich, 29 September 2022; XIIIth V. V. Giri-AILH Labour Conference, Noida, November 2021; Labour and Mobility Roundtable, organized by Georgetown University and the University of Virginia, January 2021. I am grateful to the commentators for their feedback, and I am especially thankful to Prof. Dirk Hoerder and Dr. Judith Vitale for their comments. I would also like to acknowledge the Swiss National Science Foundation and the University of Zurich for academic and research support.

 | DOI:10.1163/9789004686991_019

Migrations from India across the Bay of Bengal from 1850 to 1940, despite being equal in scaleto the simultaneous transatlantic migration during the same period, remain largely ignored in both Indian and global history. The British colonial territories of Burma (Myanmar), Ceylon (Sri Lanka), and Malaya (Malaysia and Singapore) were the destinations of more than 90 percent (approximately 27 million) of the total of 30 million recorded journeys during the colonial period. Adding Chinese migrants, the Bay of Bengal region witnessed one of the world's largest migration flows. Ceylon was the second-largest recipient of Indian migrants after Burma, recording 9 to 9.5 million journeys from India between 1850 and 1940. These migrations, due to conditions at home and at the destination as well as under the *kangany* system, were largely circular with less than 10 percent of the migrants settling permanently.[1] The transformations induced by interwar developments, especially the Great Depression, amplified this ephemerality. This chapter examines the politics around Indian migrants in Ceylon and the transformations in the migration patterns, intermediation, and labour conditions during the Great Depression and the rising ethnonationalism of the 1930s.

The Great Depression of the 1930s was a crucial period in the history of colonial Indian migration to the British colonies around the Bay of Bengal. It involved a significant transformation in the political economy of agriculture and industry in the region and shaped the changing relations of labour and capital. This led to shifting patterns of migration and (im)migrant-native relations. Most crucially, this involved the rise of ethnocentric nationalism involving exclusionist positions and xenophobic sentiments. During the 1930s, extreme reactions in the form of mob violence and riots targeting migrants and their "unrestricted" mobility arose. Migrant Indian labourers, especially the non-estate ones, were the most visible and vulnerable targets.

The emerging anti-Indian and anti-migrant sentiment paced the decolonization process by providing Ceylon nationalists with a solid foundation and popular support for their larger political goals of self-government and independence. Political discourses of the time engaged a range of actors including Indian and Sinhalese nationalists, colonialists, and migrants (labouring and non-labouring). The political manoeuvres of this period led to the formulation of colonial policies of return, repatriation, and restrictions on migration and exclusion of migrants from various workspaces. These policies altered

1 Ritesh Kumar Jaiswal, "Mediated (Im)mobility: Indian Labour Migration to Ceylon under the Kangany System (c. 1850–1940)," in *The Palgrave Handbook of Bondage and Human Rights in Africa and Asia*, ed. Gwyn Campbell and Alessandro Stanziani (New York: Palgrave Macmillan, 2020), 157–188, 166–167.

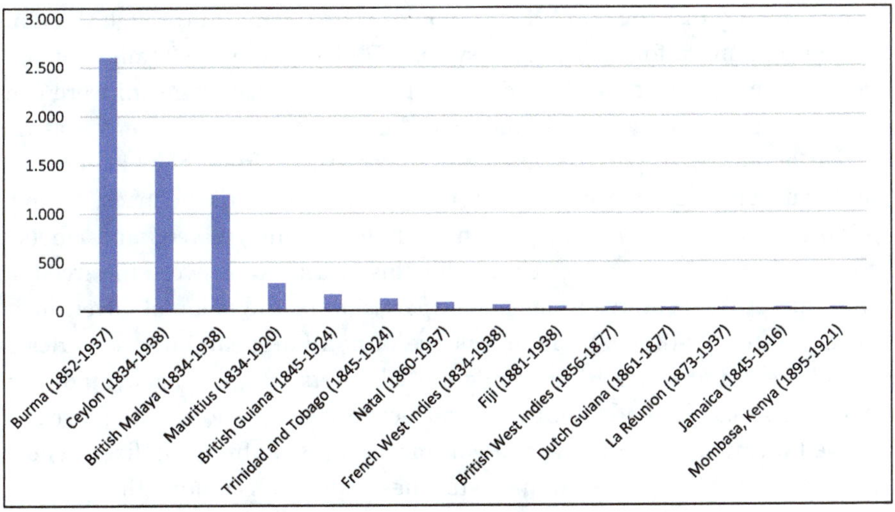

FIGURE 18.1 Net Indian immigration in thousands
Note: The figures reflect the net Indian immigration or the total stock, not the higher total flow, of migrants in the years mentioned. This figure can best be used for broader comparisons of net immigration to Burma, Ceylon, and Malaya vis-à-vis the other colonies, as there are multiple problems concerning the statistics of migration across the Bay of Bengal, such as double counting as the migrants oscillated between India and the destination colonies
SOURCE: KINGSLEY DAVIS, *POPULATION OF INDIA AND PAKISTAN* (PRINCETON, NJ: PRINCETON UNIVERSITY PRESS, 1951), SECTION ON MIGRATION

patterns of migration, systems of recruitment and intermediation as well as the migrants' everyday work and life. This chapter addresses the context, content, and consequences of rising ethnonationalism and the politics around Indian migrants in Ceylon during the period of global turmoil through the lens of popular and political discourses around colonialism, the economics of migration, and the work and life of migrants.

1 Background[2]

Unlike the formally regulated indenture system of migration which largely involved three-to-five-year bound labour, the majority of migration journeys

2 The following abbreviations will be used to refer to institutions and publications: AARCOL: Annual Administration Report by the Controller of Labour; ARAGOIC: Annual Report

across the Bay of Bengal to British colonies were organized through the non-indentured and informal *kangany* system. Derived from the Tamil language, *kangani* means "headmen," "foremen," or "overseers." The kangani were generally men of "high standing" and "good" caste from the same region as the estate labourers. As "patriarchal" figures they recruited from their kin networks and maintained caste restrictions at the plantations. Until the 1920s, colonial administrators described the system as "free and unregulated," and labelled the migrants as "free."[3] The reasons for this classification were the freedom from direct legal interventions and supervision of the colonial government at the source (until 1922); the prevalence of non-European intermediaries in recruitment and supervision of migrant labourers by the kangany; independent networks of friends, family and villagers migrating and working together; as well as mostly monthly verbal contracts signifying free will, fixed tenure, and easy exit.[4] Recent research locates these migrations among the free non-European migration in the larger attempt to counter the dichotomy of "free European" and "unfree non-European" migrations and to attribute agency to non-European migrants.[5] This chapter highlights the shifts in the colonial and nationalist interpretations of the kangany system of migration to Ceylon and the intermediaries involved. It also assesses how Ceylonese nationalists used the colonial reiteration of "free and unregulated" Indian migration to pursue their larger goals and agenda.

Indian migrants to Ceylon came from diverse regional-linguistic backgrounds, castes, and classes, and they engaged in a wide range of occupations. In contrast to the indenture system of migration to the colonies in the Pacific and Western Indian Ocean, and the Caribbean, where the bulk of the workforce were northern Indian migrants from the Bhojpuri belt engaged as plantation labourers, the majority of the migrants to Ceylon were Tamil and Malayalee speaking migrants. They mostly came from the Trichinopoly, Tinnevelly,

of the Agent of Government of India; BL: British Library; C&I Dept.: Commerce and Industry Department; CLC: Ceylon Labour Commission; EHL Dept.: Education, Health and Land Department; GOI: Government of India; IEA: Indian Emigration Act; L&O Branch: Land and Overseas Branch; NAI: National Archives of India; NAUK: National Archives of the United Kingdom; R&A Dept.: Revenue and Agriculture Department.

3 In addition to "free migration," the Indian emigration to Ceylon (and Burma) was categorized under "other migration," "unregulated migration," etc. *Annual Report of Emigration from Madras to Colonies, 1880–1900,* R&A Dept., Emigration Branch, NAI.

4 Jaiswal, "Mediated (Im)mobility," 157–188.

5 Adam McKeown, "Global Migration, 1846–1940," *Journal of World History* 15, no. 2 (2004): 155–189; Ulbe Bosma, "Beyond the Atlantic: Connecting Migration and World History in the Age of Imperialism," *International Review of Social History* 52, no. 1 (2007): 116–123.

Ramnad, Salem, Madurai, Tanjore, Malabar, Travancore, and Cochin regions of Southern India and largely were landless agricultural labourers from the lower and the so-called "untouchable" castes of the Pallar, Pariahs, Vellala and Ambalakarar. The majority of these migrants were engaged as workers in almost equal proportions on estate (coffee until 1880 and then tea and rubber) and non-estate works. The latter included domestic servants, peons (day labourers), porters, rickshaw pullers, and grass cutters, mainly engaged in the urban sphere. However, not only labour moved but also stocks of capital and reserves of commercial, industrial, and professional skills. A substantial proportion of the non-labouring migrant classes in Ceylon, as in Malaya and Burma, included those engaged as petty and big traders and merchants, shopkeepers, moneylenders, professionals (bankers, doctors, lawyers, teachers, etc.) as well as employees of colonial administrations of many ranks and colonial army personnel.

Concerning the gender aspects, the non-estate migration to Ceylon was characterized by a highly disproportionate sex ratio, mainly because of the precarity of work. Given that they were unassisted migrants, archival data is sporadic and scarce. In contrast, for the assisted migrations of plantation labour, a relative sex ratio parity was achieved between 1911–1931. The shift from coffee to tea plantations from the 1880s onwards led to the promotion of *family emigration* due to increased demand for women labour for much of the fieldwork.[6] The percentage of women among the estate labour migrants subsequently increased from 34 percent in 1871 to 48 percent in 1921.

The increased settlement of women and the improvement of the sex ratio on Ceylon estates was a *continuous process*. The vast expansion in the cultivation area as well as the nature of the work at the tea plantations required a substantial increase in the annual in-migration of male and female workers. However, while the number of migrants – both male and female – almost doubled from the coffee to the tea period, the gender ratio at first glance remained stable at 10–25 percent women in the total annual arrivals. Although it is also worth noting in this context that a lesser proportion of women and children emigrated back to India.[7]

6 Major Orde Browne (Labour Adviser), *Report on the Labour Conditions in Ceylon, Mauritius and Malay* (NAUK, 1942), para 25.

7 N. E. Marjoribanks and A. K. G. Marakkyyar with Ahmad Tambi Marakkayar stated that "women more often settle in their new homes, their daughters grew up, marry, and settle there too." *Report on Labour Emigrating to Ceylon and Malaya*, C&I Dept., Emigration Branch, Government Press, Madras, 1917, NAI.

With the advent and vast expansion of tea plantations, the demand for women workers increased as they were cheaper than male workers and were seen as a crucial element to contribute to the development of a settled productive and reproductive workforce. With the rising demand for tea in "the West" and its increased significance for the colonial economy, Assam witnessed a similar trajectory.[8] Women's and children's "nimble fingers" were considered particularly suited for the plucking of tea leaves. Moreover, women who were subject to patriarchal norms in South India were seen as "more controllable" and therefore less likely to challenge the authority of men at all levels of the plantocracy.[9] For women, an important reason to migrate involved the loosening of the socio-religious, caste, and domestic restrictions they faced at "home" while the various women-centred tasks at plantations and relatively higher wages provided them with income.[10] The remuneration of women's productivity not only made them economically independent entities but also regular contributors to family economies.

In the regions of origin, women's mobility amplified as a result of rural impoverishment and the narrowing of traditional occupational opportunities. Crucial factors involved deindustrialization, reduced access to common resources, the emergence of absolute property rights of male heads of the household, a series of judicial, legislative and administrative measures which provided the paterfamilias with greater control over the labour and mobility of other family members and closed the escape routes from oppressive marriages.[11] Increased instances of fraud, misrepresentations, trafficking, seduction and abduction induced coerced migrations of women as well as men.

---

8 Andrew B. Liu mentions that for Assam plantations networks intensified and the geographical expanse of labour recruitment expanded. Colonial officials and planters specifically promoted women and children's migration and introduced pro-natal policies including maternity benefits and bonuses for bearing children once they realized that they needed to recreate the conditions of village family life to secure a self-reproducing population. *Tea War: A History of Capitalism in China and India* (New Haven, CT: Yale University Press, 2020), 141.

9 Rachel Kurian and Kumari Jayawardena, "Indebtedness and Socio-cultural Hierarchies on the 19th century Ceylon Plantation: Unfree Labour and Capitalism in South Asia," 2nd Leiden Slavery Studies Association 'Slaving Zones' Conference, June 2017, 14–15.

10 Orde Browne's report (para 82) compared the rates of wages paid on estates in Southern Indian with those of Ceylon. His data from 13 districts showed a balance in favour of Ceylon rates of approximately 22 percent in the case of men and 60 percent in case of women, while juvenile workers in Ceylon earned approximately 80 percent of Indian men's wages.

11 Samita Sen, "'Without His Consent?': Marriage and Women's Migration in Colonial India," *International Labor and Working-Class History* 65 (2004): 99–100.

Thus, while alternative economic and sexual choices and the remuneration of their productivity encouraged women to escape from oppressive families, unhappy marriages, and declining economic opportunities in India, the Ceylonese plantation regime often pushed them into the exploitative contractual debt-bondage regime, the stranglehold of intermediaries and multiple patriarchies, exhausting productive and reproductive chores, lower wages, sexual violations, separation of families, and abysmal living and health conditions. Thus, the structures of coercion and freedom, of voluntariness and involuntariness on both sides of the coast, simultaneously informed women's decisions to emigrate, to stay at the plantations, and to settle down or to return.

2 The Context: Migrant Labour after the Abolition of the British Regime of Indenture

After the abolition of the indenture system of labour migration to the British Empire's colonies in the Caribbean, Pacific and Western Indian Oceans in 1917, the emigration of Indian labourers to Ceylon, Malaya, and Burma continued through the informally regulated kangany and *maistry* systems. The British justified the continuation of this type of migration by geographical proximity and by persisting historical ties and cultural affinities between the regions. However, under pressure from Indian nationalists opposing the exploitation of Indian labourers, the British government on both sides of the Bay of Bengal regulated all aspects of the labour migration to Ceylon and Malaya through the Indian Emigration Act of 1922 and corresponding Ordinances at the destinations. Labour migration to Burma remained unregulated and largely exploitative since Burma was administered as a province of British India until 1937.

The Indian Emigration Act of 1922 and the corresponding Ceylon Ordinance I of 1923 regulated the kangany system of recruitment, migration, and the conditions of workers in Ceylon. In Annual and Bi-annual Reports, the Agent of the Government of India (GOI) in Ceylon and the Controller of Labour informed the colonial governments and the Indian and Ceylonese public about the legality of migration and conditions of work. In a confidential memorandum in 1928, Purshottamdas Thakurdas, a member of the Standing Emigration Committee in India, proposed an investigation into the opportunities for employment of surplus labourers from South Indian districts within India, especially in Punjab, Sind, parts of the United Provinces, and the Bombay Presidency. He opposed emigration to colonies such as Ceylon and Malaya where unskilled

Indian workers neither received just wages nor were accorded equal political rights vis-à-vis other classes and "natives."[12]

For its part, the Southern Indian Chamber of Commerce focused on improving conditions for Indian estate labourers in Ceylon.[13] In this context, the chamber stressed rising indebtedness, low wages, lack of proper housing and education facilities, and the absence of provisions against unemployment, sickness, or old age. It aided repatriation and decried the growing propaganda against the Indian workers by Ceylonese politicians, mainly those of the dominant Sinhalese group. Indebtedness, which was considered the "greatest evil" under the kangany system, was the greatest stumbling block in the labourers' path to economic independence. In consequence, the Agent of the GOI stated in his annual report of 1927 that "the kangany system has outlived its usefulness" and the Overseas Indian Association demanded a "dispensing with all the services of the kanganies and abolition of the kangany system to secure the welfare of the labourer."[14]

The kanganies, earlier portrayed as paternalistic leaders of the migrant labourers and useful labour recruiters, in colonial reports of the 1920s were condemned as extortionist overlords pushing the labourers into debt and as upholders of all persisting ill practices on the Ceylonese plantations. However, the kangany intermediaries, who often did exploit workers for their personal economic gain, had, in fact, been customized by both planters and officials to handle labour recruitment or dismissal, supervision over the production process, disbursement of wages, collection of funds advanced, and control of labour relations and personal affairs. The kanganies often stood under immense pressure and contractual obligation to the "white employers" and, in cases where they were unable to meet these obligations, they were held liable for punishments under the provisions of the Breach of Contract Law of 1859. The shift in the characterization of the intermediaries not only permitted the colonizers to take legal recourse to control the powers of the kanganies over their dependent workforce but also to shift the blame for the deplorable conditions under the plantation regime onto their shoulders. Thus, the twentieth-century colonial reform measures, largely concerned with lowering the cost of recruitment and establishing an extensive surveillance regime, aimed at

12 *Suggestion by Purshottamdas Thakurdas in Regard to the Policy Underlying the Emigration of Indians Overseas*, Overseas Branch, 1928, NAI.

13 *Ceylon-Memorandum on the Question of Indian Estate Labour by Overseas Indian Association*, L&O Branch, EHL Dept., 1936, NAI.

14 *Ceylon-Memorandum on the Question of Indian Estate Labour by Overseas Indian Association* (1936), NAI.

undermining the power and control of kangany intermediaries. The reform measures were also meant to pacify the Indian nationalists by improving the conditions of Indian migrant workers and freeing them from their perennial debts. In the end, however, they achieved nothing concrete.

3 Economic Depression and Its Repercussions on Wages and Mobility

The Great Depression brought critical changes to the regime of commodity production. In the early 1930s, the largest tea exporting colonies were India, followed by Ceylon and Java with the bulk imported by the UK and re-exported to European and American markets. However, the global demand for tea and rubber shrank and rubber prices fell from 3.75 to 3 pence per lb, and tea prices in Ceylon's mid-and low-country fell from 14.6 pence per lb in 1929 to 7.6 pence per lb in 1932.[15] Between 1930 and 1933, the export value of Ceylonese tea fell from approximately Rs. 182 to 117 million, and that of rubber from 47 to 22.9 million.[16] As a result, wages fell as did the demand for Indian migrant labourers in Ceylon. In addition, in 1932 officials planned to abolish the Minimum Wage Ordinance of 1927, which had been applied since 1929 by the Planters Association of Ceylon and the Ceylon Estate Proprietary Association. However, the governor, who noted that this would put the "plantation workers at the mercy of the employers," instead called for a "reduction of the minimum wage based on the fact that prices of rice as well as the cost of living, which were determinants of the minimum wage, had fallen."[17] The British GOI gave its consent, assuming that the reductions would not reduce the labourers' "effective emoluments."

Throughout the 1930s, the price of rice kept decreasing and so did and workers' wages (see Figure 18.2). While the first plan to reduce wages in 1930 was abandoned, from 1931 on, the planters adjusted wages downward in tune with the falling price of rice. These and subsequent wage cuts affected workers differently in low-, mid-and up-country estates (see Table 18.1).[18] The living conditions of working families had been poor even before the wage reductions. Many of the estates did not have dispensaries or maternity relief and as regards

15 *Orde Browne's Report, Appendix III* (NAUK, 1942).

16 *ARAGOIC for 1932*, 1933, NAI; *Confidential Memorandum on Position of Indians in Ceylon*, L&O Branch, 1934, NAI.

17 *Confidential Report of the Agent of GOI in Ceylon of Events During the Period August-December, 1932*, L&O Branch, January 1933, NAI.

18 *Annual Reports of the Agent of GOI in Ceylon for 1932*, 1933, NAI.

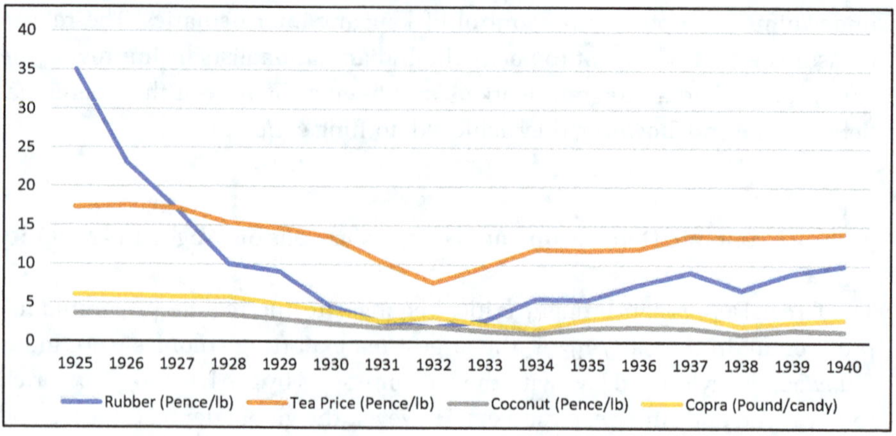

FIGURE 18.2 Average prices of principal commodities, Ceylon, 1925–1940
SOURCE: BROWNE, *REPORT*, APPENDIX III

the 400 schools for the children of the labourers, the authorities focused on their labour rather than on curricula. Although sewage lines had been laid in some estates from 1922 to 1927, many lines were still unhealthy and like "small dungeons."[19]

In 1933, an international agreement on the regulation of the export of tea and on limiting the extension of the tea-growing areas was signed by the governments of British India, Ceylon, and the Dutch East Indies.[20] The scheme was a manifestation of the growing anxieties of the European tea empires and intended to form a trans-imperial cartel to reduce the gap between supply and demand and to increase prices. The Dutch planters in Java could dispose of their crop to the tea factories at a price barely covering the cost of plucking and they thus wanted a rapprochement of British-Dutch tea interests for the benefit of the industry as a whole.[21] As a result, exports of tea from the major tea empires were regulated by licenses and the tea seed trade was prohibited.[22]

19 *Report by Mr. D. Xavier on the Condition of Indian Labourers in Ceylon*, EHL Dept., Overseas Branch, August 1931, NAI.

20 *Tea Restriction-Ceylon, Part-II*, CO 54/915/12, NAUK, UK.

21 *Tea Industry: Visit of Mr. G. J. Vehry to India and Ceylon*, CO 54/914/6, 1932, NAUK, UK.

22 The Ceylon government, however, also passed an ordinance to provide for the regulation and control of the export of tea from Ceylon, *Tea (Control of Export) Ordinance 11 of 1933*, *Tea Restriction-Ceylon, Part-II*, CO 54/915/12, NAUK, UK, *Tea Restriction-Ceylon, Part-III*, CO 54/915/12, NAUK, UK.

TABLE 18.1 Comparative data of wages of Indian estate labourers, in cents

Wages	1929			May 1931–February 1932			10 May 1933–June 1934		
	Men	Women	Children	Men	Women	Children	Men	Women	Children
Up-Country	54	43	32	49	39	29	41	33	25
Mid-Country	52	41	31	47	37	28	37	30	21
Low-Country	50	40	30	45	36	27	35	28	20

SOURCE: *CEYLON BLUE BOOK*, 1939, CO 59/152, NAUK, UK

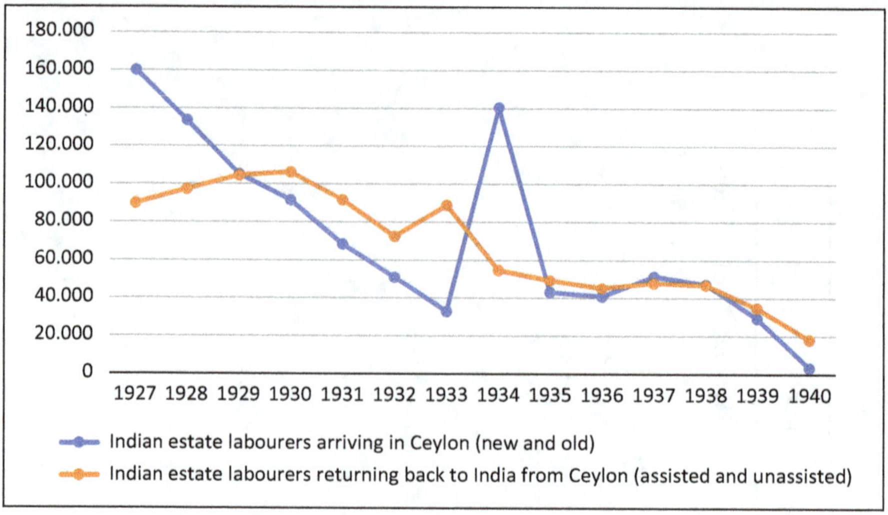

FIGURE 18.3 Annual estate labour immigrants and emigrants, 1927–1940
Note: Returnees included those repatriated under the Ceylon Government Scheme of 1923–1924 as well as under the Ceylon Government Special Scheme for repatriation due to the depression in the rubber (1930) and tea industries (1932)
SOURCE: *ARAGOIC FOR 1923–25, 1937, AND 1939*; BROWNE, *REPORT*, APPENDIX VI, CO 825/37/8, NAUK, UK

The reduction of rubber and tea production naturally led to a progressive decline in demand for estate workers. Colonial statistics reveal a massive decrease in Indian emigration to Ceylon, an increase in returns, and the initiation of schemes of repatriation as well as restriction of recruitment. The highly mobile non-estate migrants faced reduced emigration and increased returns,[23] with the latter also being due to the growing hostility of "natives," who, especially in Colombo, saw them as competitors for various kinds of urban unskilled work.

During the depression, schemes for the repatriation of "superfluous" or "discontented" labourers were instituted. As did much of labour regimentation, these schemes had a long history. In 1907, for example, the *Ceylon Destitute Immigrants Regulation Ordinance* targeted those who were suspected of being or becoming destitute or were considered undesirable. They had to show that

23 Compiled from *AARCOL for 1938, Ceylon*, 1939, NAI; *AARCOL for 1933, Ceylon*, 1934, NAI; *AARCOL for 1925, Ceylon*, 1926, NAI; *ARAGOIC for 1939*, Overseas Section, 1940, NAI. According to the reports, the number of Indians outside estates cannot be ascertained with any accuracy.

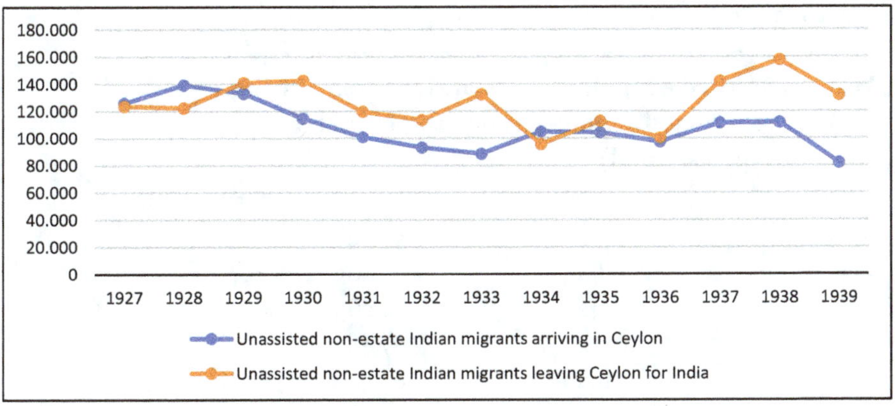

FIGURE 18.4 Unassisted migrations
SOURCE: *ARAGOIC FOR 1939*, APPENDIX V

they were in possession of Rs. 150 before landing at Ceylon or ask relatives in Ceylon to act as security.[24] In 1923, repatriation schemes had begun for those who had been in Ceylon for less than one year and, in 1924, for those who were sick or indigent.[25] In 1931, the government introduced a system of free repatriation of rubber estate labourers who were "unsatisfied" or "unwilling" to work at the new reduced wage rate and, in 1932, for tea estate workers. The Ceylon government introduced special schemes in 1933 and 1935 for the repatriation of labourers discharged from those tea estates partially closed under the "care and maintenance basis" and for whom further employment at acceptable wages could not be found. Of approximately 6,000 applications for repatriation by labourers dissatisfied with their wages, only half were approved in 1932.[26] By the end of 1936, the *Controller* at his discretion repatriated "surplus" workers out of the Immigration Fund and another, more liberal repatriation scheme for such labourers went into effect in January 1937.[27]

These repatriation schemes did not consider the interest of labourers who wished to stay, in particular those who had settled on the island for a long time

24 *Ceylon Immigration Commission – Questions in the Legislative Assembly, Memorandum of Various Organization*, L&O Branch, 1935, NAI; *Ceylon Destitute Immigrants Regulation Ordinance 1907 Amendment*, L&O Branch, 1937, NAI.

25 *ARAGOIC for 1936*, L&O Branch, 1937, NAI.

26 *ARAGOIC for 1932*, 1933, NAI; *Repatriation of Indian Labourers from Ceylon on Account of the Depression*, March 1932, Overseas Branch, 1932, NAI; *Reduction in Minimum Wages and Repatriation of Indian Estate Labourers*, L&O Branch, 1933, NAI; *Ceylon-Surplus Indian Labour Repatriation and Recruiting Licenses Cancellation*, L&O Branch, 1935, NAI.

27 *ARAGOIC for 1936*, 1937, NAI.

TABLE 18.2 Repatriation and returns, 1924–1929

Year	Assisted emigrants repatriated at public expense (total)	Estate labourers leaving unassisted (total)
1924	571	50,448
1925	1,851	53,203
1926	2,442	61,265
1927	2,302	87,481
1928	3,492	93,596
1929	3,183	101,228
1930	7,462[a]	98,728
1931	15,707[a]	75,866
1932	14,336[a]	58,157
1933	43,343[a]	46,626
1934	2,304	52,481
1935	6,252	43,036
1936	5,306	39,747
1937	10,322	37,606
1938	3,004	43,803
1939	2,975	31,714

Note: Includes those repatriated under the rubber scheme of 1930 and the tea scheme of 1932, apart from the regular repatriation schemes under the ordinances of 1923 and 1924

SOURCE: BROWNE, REPORT, APPENDIX VI, CO 825/37/8, NAUK; AAR-COL 1938, 38

and had lost touch with their "homeland." Many were unwillingly repatriated. Those who stayed became even more vulnerable objects of repression at the hands of employers and kangany intermediaries as they not only had to work for lowered wages but also had shorter and more irregular days of work.

Furthermore, when dissatisfied labourers decided to quit the estates and return to India, they needed a discharge certificate as a mandatory document for return and re-employment on Ceylonese estates should conditions improve. Together with the superintendents, the kanganies illegally held back the certificates until, or even after, all debts were paid off, in particular when a shortage of new migrant workers was assumed.

While new recruitment of labour for rubber estates and mid-and low-country tea estates was restricted in 1930/31, the government maintained that complete cessation of recruitment was "unnecessary" and thus planters and the colonial state continued to assist some migrants.[28] While these measures followed assumed economic rationales, they occurred in the context of increasing rural-to-urban migrations of Ceylonese, resulting in rising unemployment among urban natives. Increasingly, demands were voiced to employ natives in workspaces occupied by Indian migrants, including estate labour.

In the imperial and global economic context, the government of Ceylon formed a *Ceylon Tea Propaganda Board* in October 1932 to promote demand in the global market.[29] In Britain, an *Empire Marketing Board* promoted "empire products" and intra-empire trade through pamphlets, advertisements, and commissioned paintings. In addition, the newly formed *International Tea Committee* was to study ways and means for increasing tea consumption.[30]

The international agreement of 1934/35 to restrict the output of tea and rubber gradually helped to restore the supply and demand equilibrium. Both rubber and tea prices increased and, thus, the prospects of employment on estates in Ceylon improved. However, the demands for re-opening recruitment of new labour were accompanied by pressure from Indian nationalists on the British GOI to raise estate labour wages to pre-May 1933 levels (see Table 18.1). In June 1934, the Planters Association and the Ceylon Estate Proprietary Association agreed to this proposal but recruiting licenses were issued only to kanganies on estates in dire need of labour.[31] Labour supply was high: During the first seven months of 1934 nearly 96,545 labourers emigrated to Ceylon as compared to 11,811 in the entire year of 1933.[32] However, the output restriction scheme, the excessive recruitment in 1934, along with a malaria epidemic and the "most severe and prolonged drought in the history of Ceylon" meant that, from September 1935, no recruiting licenses were issued to kangany intermediaries and migration from India to Ceylon was again confined to non-recruited or old assisted and unassisted migrants.[33]

---

28 *Annual Report of the Agent of GOI, Ceylon for 1932*, 1933, NAI; *Repatriation of Indian Labourers from Ceylon on Account of the Depression* (1932), NAI.

29 *Tea Propaganda Ordinance 19 of 1932*, CO 54/909/7, NAUK, UK.

30 *Administration Report of the Tea Controller, Ceylon, for the Fifth Year of Restriction*, April 1937 to March 1938, Ceylon Government Press, Colombo, 1939, CO 852/207/5, NAUK, UK.

31 *Confidential Report of Important Events by the Agent of GOI in Ceylon During the Period August-December 1933*, EHL Dept., L&O Branch, *1934*, NAI.

32 *Confidential Memorandum on Position of Indians in Ceylon* (1934), NAI.

33 Note by the Agent of GOI in January 1938, in *Ceylon-Indian Estate Labourers, Illegal Recruitment from Ceylon and Steps Taken to Check It*, L&O Branch, 1937, NAI; *ARAGOI for 1935*, EHL Dept., L&O Branch, L&O & KW, Ceylon, 1936, NAI; *Confidential Report of Important Events by the Agent of GOI in Ceylon During the Period August-December 1934*, L&O Branch, 1934, NAI.

4 "Depression Politics": Rising Anti-Indian Immigration Sentiments and Negotiations

The depression political economy was instrumentalized by national politicians who sought to use anti-migration and anti-migrant rhetoric as a tool for their agendas of mass nationalism, self-government, and decolonization. Since the beginning of the depression, the dominant Sinhalese group, strongly represented in the *Legislative Council of Ceylon*, demanded the retrenchment of Indian migrants from various workspaces.[34] Even for estate work, which Ceylonese looked down on, they urged that locals replace Indians. The rising economic competition soon escalated into open conflicts. In particular, Malayalees, who formed an essential part of the non-estate migrant Indian labouring population in urban spaces, were targeted.[35] Nationalists blamed the rising unemployment among Sinhalese on the Malayalee's "unrivalled proficiency as cheap and efficient domestic workers." Physical violence ensued and press and propaganda statements increased tensions. While Labour Party leader A. E. Goonersinghe accused Malayalees of being responsible for men of the country's unemployment, starvation and death, the Malayalees recognized the importance of forming a union to channel their struggles against rising xenophobia, leading to the foundation of the Malayalee Mahajan Sabha.[36]

In December 1934, the left-wing leader of the Sri Lanka Freedom Party, S. W. R. D. Bandaranaike, "in the view of the serious and increasing unemployment among Ceylonese workers," requested the British governor to "appoint a Commission to consider and report upon the problem of non-Ceylonese workers in Ceylon, particularly with a view to the restriction and effective control of immigration."[37] In the heated debates in the State Council, the British Ceylonese Government asserted that it pursued a preferential policy towards Ceylonese labourers, provided they were "efficient and available," and that it urged other employers to adopt a similar policy. However, the British Ceylonese Government opposed a complete restriction on the immigration of unskilled labourers since they had been the reason for "the prosperity of the country

34 *Position of Indians in Ceylon*, Overseas Branch, 1930, NAI.

35 *Anti-Malayalee Outbreaks in Colombo*, Overseas Branch, 1931, NAI; *Cuttings from Times of Ceylon*, December 1931, NAI.

36 *Ceylon Anti-Malayalee Agitation-Memorial-Ceylon Malayalee Mahajan Sabha (Confidential)*, L&O Branch, 1936, NAI.

37 *Ceylon-Indian Estate Labourers, Illegal Recruitment from Ceylon and Steps Taken to Check It* (1937), NAI.

for the last hundred years and were considered to be 'self-adjusting' to the demands, rather than undercutting prospects of Ceylonese employment."[38]

The (Jackson) Commission, appointed to ascertain whether any restriction on Indian immigration was required, asserted that banning Indian immigration was *not needed at the time*, i.e., until "efficient" local labourers in "sufficient numbers" were available. The entry of Ceylonese into new sectors of work would be a slow and gradual process and would require a change in their outlook and habits. The government was to provide employment agencies, assist Ceylonese in overcoming their inability to perform particular kinds of work and open a training school for domestic servants as well as promote co-operative labour societies.[39]

The commissioners asserted that the economic recession was a temporary phenomenon and that complete immigration restriction would, in the long run, not only ruin the economic prosperity of the country but also sever economic ties with India, antagonize Indian opinion, and most probably invoke retaliatory measures on the part of the British Indian Government. The conclusions of the report reflected the British Empire's anxieties concerning a decline in revenues if planters would fail to supply the global demand for tea and rubber.

5 The Ceylonese Response to Estate Labour Shortages

The increase in export quotas led to new demands for estate labour recruitment from India as early as the first quarter of 1937 and, by the end of the year, on rubber estates where fewer Indians were employed, the labour shortages were significant. Together with the press, the Ceylon British Government as well as the Sinhalese Minister of Labour attempted to evoke a sense of dignity and pride among the Sinhalese for estate work. Depots at various places, recruiting agents touring Sinhalese villages and explaining advantages such as free housing, free medical aid, and a gift of two rupees to each labourer on arrival only resulted in the agent's comment in 1938: "the results despite all these attempts have been disappointing."[40]

38 *Confidential Report of Important Events by the Agent of GOI in Ceylon During the Period August-December, 1934*, NAI.

39 *Confidential Report of Important Events During the Period January-July, 1938*, NAI; *Ceylon Immigration Commission Report*, L&O Branch, 1937, NAI.

40 *Reduction in Minimum Wages and Repatriation of Indian Estate Labourers* (1933), NAI. The first recruiting depot, opened in late 1937 in Akmeemana in the Southern Province, registered 80 labourers within the first fortnight but fewer since then. *Confidential Report*

Given the Sinhalese's unwillingness to perform estate work, protracted negotiations were conducted in the autumn of 1937. The Planters Association estimated a shortage of up to 20,000 labourers; Sinhalese politicians demanded that recruited Indian workers should be subject to indenture; and the Executive Committee of Labour in Ceylon, with permission from the Sinhalese-dominated State Council, subsequently approved the recruitment of 5,000 labourers. The Council feared that if Ceylon failed to produce its exportable quota of tea and rubber, it would not only face loss of revenue but also face the risk of having its export quota reduced.[41] Sinhalese nationalists, on the other hand, continued to view Indian non-estate labour as a menace to Ceylon and called for restrictions and quotas. Thus, Ceylonese nationalists and officials maintained a position of convenience desiring and despising Indian migrants at the same time.

6 The Indian Position on the Kangany System and the Labour Demands in Ceylon

When the British GOI re-opened recruitment in September 1937, Indian nationalists expressed strong opposition to any attempt to revive the indenture system (abolished in 1917) as well as to any discrimination against any class of Indians. Similarly, the Ceylon Indians, the Ceylon Indian Association, the Ceylon Malayalee Mahajan Sabha, and the All-Ceylon Head Kanganies' Association as well as the Agent of the GOI all disapproved of restrictions imposed on any particular class of Indians: "Either you deny yourself entirely the benefit of all Indian labour of all classes or you allow free entry to all Indians."[42] As a consequence, the British colonizers feared that any selective emigration of Indian labour to Ceylon would create political chaos.

The working and living conditions of Indian migrant workers in Ceylon received wide publicity: aggravated by the depression and persisting racial discrimination at all levels, Indian nationalists' demands for equal opportunities

of Important Events During the Period August-December, 1937 by Agent of GOI in Ceylon, Overseas Branch, 1938, NAI.

41 *Ceylon-Indian Estate Labourers, Illegal Recruitment from Ceylon and Steps Taken to Check It* (1937), NAI. *Confidential Report of Important Events by the Agent of GOI in Ceylon During the Period January-July 1938* (1938), NAI.

42 *Ceylon Immigration Commission – Questions in the Legislative Assembly, Memorandum of Various Organizations* (1935), NAI; *Ceylon Indian Estate Labourers – Illegal Recruitment from India and Steps Taken to Check It* (1937), NAI.

for migrant labourers and an end to the kangany system received widespread attention. Under pressure from Indian nationalists, the British GOI conveyed to the Ceylonese government that recruiting would be re-opened and licenced only when they received satisfactory assurance of (1) the removal of racial discrimination and the enfranchising of Indian estate labourers settled in Ceylon to village committees, and (2) the restoration of wages in the mid-and low-country estates to the level that prevailed between May 1931 and February 1932.[43] This was to end the kangany system, at least at the level of recruitment.

The British Ceylon Government and Sinhalese nationalists, on the other hand, criticized the British GOI on the grounds that (1) the village committee franchise was more of political value than of material benefit to the labourers; (2) stopping recruitment was damaging the interests of many "hungry labourers of South India," and (3) that the "poor labourers of South India anxious to emigrate would do so even illegally by paying bribes or other methods." The European plantocracy in Ceylon asserted that restrictions would damage planters but leave Sinhalese nationalist politicians unaffected.

In response, the Agent of the GOI in Ceylon asserted that the general policy of the British GOI was to permit emigration only to those colonies where Indians were treated "satisfactorily." He pointedly added that approximately 25 percent of the total planted acreage of tea, 58 percent in the case of rubber, was owned by Sinhalese, who would suffer economically. The agent added that the issue at stake was not merely that of the workers wishing to migrate to Ceylon but also of the approximately 700,000 workers that were already there. It was asserted that the conditions of the workers in Ceylon had steadily improved in terms of the availability of work, wages, and conditions of bargaining since the stoppage of recruitment in 1935. Securing political rights, as demanded by Indian nationalists, would offer better opportunities to own land and settle down in Ceylon.[44] The agent's responses reflected the increasing pressure from the Indian nationalists for just and equal treatment of Indians in Ceylon and for better employment options for workers in India. Through their strong stand against the exploitation and discrimination of Indian workers overseas, especially in Ceylon and Malaya, the Indian nationalist politicians achieved mass support and thereby strengthened the anti-colonial struggles in India.

43 *Ceylon-Indian Estate Labourers, Illegal Recruitment from India and Steps Taken to Check It* (1937), NAI.

44 Note dated 29 January 1938 prepared by the Agent of GOI on Ceylon on the stoppage of recruitment of Indian Labour to Ceylon Estates, *Ceylon-Indian Estate Labourers, Illegal Recruitment from Ceylon and Steps Taken to Check It* (1937), NAI.

7 New Restrictions and Newer Forms of Malpractices

While restrictions on recruitment had been dictated by circumstances in Ceylon, from late 1937 the British Government of India took the nationalists' demands into account and the interests of workers and their families: Assisted migration was prohibited, but migration of non-recruited labourers returning to estates of their previous employment in Ceylon – called *palaiyal* – and of their close relatives (spouses, children, parents, brothers, and unmarried sisters) was permitted. Non-recruited migrants were allowed to proceed to Ceylon provided (1) a direct application for assisted passage was made to the Ceylon Emigration Commissioner; (2) a certificate from the village headman was required; (3) if the intending migrant's family objected to his/her departure, a certificate from the magistrate of his/her area had to be obtained. The Protector of Emigrants, at his discretion, judged the authenticity of the certificates and either granted or refused permission for emigration.[45]

However, the British GOI was aware that a large number of labourers reaching Ceylon as non-recruited were, in fact, "irregularly recruited," i.e., "induced" by kanganies and returnee labourers without valid recruiting licences. This practice had a long history. Planters and estate superintendents were behind it and, as early as 1904, had established the Ceylon Labour Commission (CLC) through the Coast Agency Committee, a sub-committee of the Planters' Association, headquartered at Kandy. Its commissioner was himself a planter with his headquarters being at Trichinopoly. The CLC financed kangany recruiters, exercised supervision over them and advertised the advantages of employment on the estates by means of handbills and leaflets in vernacular languages and by magic lantern shows. While the Ceylonese government initially contributed funds to the CLC, by 1914, 86 percent of the estates had agreed to pay a fee of 40 cents per acre under cultivation of tea, rubber, or coconut to fund the CLC operations which by then, together with the Coast Agency, recruited all the labourers for the Ceylon estates.

For applicants, the procedures were complex and personal particulars, immigration certificates, identification certificates and discharge certificates were required to prove *palaiyal*-status. If these were missing, the Protector of Emigrants categorized applicants as *emigrants*. This technically included

45 *Note Dated 4th February, 1938 by the Agent of GOI in Ceylon on Non-Recruited Assisted Emigration*, L&O Branch, 1938, Delhi Records-2, NAI; *Unofficial Notes with Compliments from the Principal Information Officer, GOI*, 1939, EHL Dept., Overseas Section, NAI; *Confidential Report of Important Events During the Period August-December, 1937 by Agent of GOI in Ceylon*, 1938, NAI.

workers who had been in Ceylon for less than five years. In collusion, kanganies, depot agents and estate superintendents circumvented restrictions and rules by forging documents or sending a certificate of prior employment to a labourer recruited in India. Moreover, unlicensed kanganies certified single women or minors, who had never been to Ceylon, as "sham relatives" of co-emigrants or those already in Ceylon.

When Ceylonese officials alleged that colonial authorities were bribed by "poor labourers desperate to emigrate," the Agent of the GOI commented that it was rather the Ceylon planters or their kanganies who bribed village headmen or Ceylon recruiting depot servants.[46] An Indian member of the Ceylon State Council demanded a censure of the Emigration Commissioner for allowing indirect recruitment without licenses and despatch of approximately 24,000 emigrants from India in the few months from July to September 1937.[47] Despite renewed attempts at supervision and control, the surreptitious practices in labour recruitment continued. In 1937, despite the ban on new recruitments, the number of estate labourers coming to Ceylon increased by 25 percent compared to 1936, in total numbers from 40,803 to 51,472.[48] When the Agent of the GOI in Ceylon stated that, all controls notwithstanding, unlicensed recruiters, estate superintendents, depot agents, as well as the Emigration Commissioner, jointly veiled the irregular practices, the Emigration Commissioner claimed that he was not responsible for checking illegal activities.[49]

8 Towards Closure of Recruitment: Reasons, Pretences, and Debates

Since, in practice, only migrants but never the plantation authorities and officials were subject to scrutiny, Indian nationalists demanded action. Under pressure, the GOI enacted the Indian Emigration (Amendment) Act No. XXI in September 1938. It authorized the government to prohibit the emigration of all persons or any specified class of person from departing by sea out of British India to any specified country for unskilled work unless they possessed the prescribed permit or were exempted by general or special order of the central

46 *Ceylon-Indian Estate Labourers, Illegal Recruitment from Ceylon and Steps Taken to Check It* (1937), NAI.

47 *Confidential Report of Important Events During the Period August-December, 1937 by Agent of GOI in Ceylon*, 1938, NAI.

48 *AARGOIC for 1938.*

49 *Ceylon Labour Commission Monthly Review* for November 1937; *Note Dated 4th February, 1938 by the Agent of GOI* (1938), NAI.

government. "Anyone who departs or attempts to depart; or whoever causes or assists or attempts to cause or assist any person to depart" was liable to punishment.[50]

At the same time, in Ceylon, the number of popular protests against non-estate Indian immigration under the slogan "Ceylon for Sinhalese and Sinhalese alone" significantly increased. Policies to exclude Indians from civil services, whether municipal, medical, port administration or other, had already been practised undercover or openly since 1923.[51] By decree of 1 August 1939, the Ceylon government dismissed all non-Ceylonese (those not born in Ceylon) employed after 1934 on daily pay from government departments with a month's notice, free repatriation, and a retirement bonus. They were to be replaced by unemployed Ceylonese.[52] Under pressure from the Indian side, the Ceylon government agreed to treat non-Ceylonese employees with over ten years of service with an interruption of no more than one year on the same footing as Ceylonese workers. Due to the absence of systematic records concerning each worker's work and journeys, these rules were applied arbitrarily and even high-level political interventions, such as a visit by Pandit Nehru, did not change the Ceylon colonial government's stance. In fact, the dismissal order was extended to daily-paid municipal workers, contract workers, teachers in assisted schools, and to railway employees.[53]

Popular antagonism against Indians was whipped up through the press, public speeches, anti-Indian pamphlets, street songs, and processions. Officials trivialized riots against Indians as "unexpected and isolated incidents of rowdyism on part of some bad characters."[54] In the State Council, one member, Mr Bandaranaike, stated that he would be "glad to see every Indian turned out of Ceylon." In Colombo, Indians were abused and A. E. Goonersinghe organized picketing campaigns and boycotts to drive away Indian traders and shopkeepers. The Colonial Secretary, Malcolm Macdonald, conveyed that "the desire of the Ceylon Government to give preference to Ceylonese in Government service

---

50 *Indian Emigration (Amendment) Act XXI of 1938*, L&O Branch, 1938 NAI.

51 "India Bans Migration of Workers," *News Chronicle*, 1 August 1939, PJ Dept., IOR: L/PJ/8/203, BL, UK.

52 *Ceylon – Indian Daily Paid Employees in Government Department Dismissal – Ban on Emigration for Unskilled Work*, Overseas Branch, 1939, NAI; *ARAGOIC for 1939*, 1940, NAI.

53 *ARAGOIC for 1939*, 1940, NAI; *Ceylon – Disabilities of Indians – Appointment of Ceylon Public Commission – Definition of Ceylonese*, L&O Branch, 1937, NAI; *Disabilities of Indians in Ceylon*, EHL Dept., L&O Branch, 1936, NAI; *Ceylon – Indian Daily Paid Employees in Government Department Dismissal – Ban on Emigration for Unskilled Work* (1939), NAI.

54 *Ceylon – Riots in Colombo, Attack on Indian Shops*, L&O Section, 1938, NAI; *Ceylon – Anti-Malayalee Agitation*, L&O Branch, 1936, NAI.

is natural and inevitable."[55] While all this created further uneasiness among Indian labourers in Ceylon, the aggressive boycott of Indians only ended with the declaration of war and the promulgation of defence regulations in 1939.[56]

These widely discussed developments created a mass base for Indian nationalists' demands for both the safety and fair working conditions of Indians in Ceylon and for restricting further emigration to Ceylon. Working and living conditions, payment of wages, food, housing and sanitation, education, repatriation, malpractices connected with discharge certificates, separation of families on estates, and perennial indebtedness, all demanded redress.[57] Debts, usually to kangany or estate shopkeepers, were mainly the result of purchases of overpriced necessities or perhaps minor luxuries. Estate labourers, in their turn, sent petitions to the office of the Agent in Ceylon, complaining against ill-treatment and injustices, in particular the refusal to provide discharge certificates, as well as non-payment, irregular deductions, and the withholding of wages for alleged debts to the kanganies.[58]

In 1939, Indians in Ceylon numbered around 800,000 or 14.5 percent of the total population. Of these, nearly 679,000 or more than 85 percent were estate workers and their dependents with whom the Sinhalese did not directly compete.[59] Thus, the Sinhalese nationalists' accusation of Indians being the cause of Sinhalese unemployment had no factual basis. However, given both the political and economic developments of the 1930s, the GOI in consultation with the Government of Madras, from where the bulk of the emigrants came, imposed a complete ban on the emigration of unskilled Indian labourers to the island in August 1939. This ended almost a century of mobility and settlement of Indians in Ceylon.[60]

A side effect of the ban was that it helped the Indians in Ceylon to increase their bargaining power vis-à-vis their employers and to ensure better living and

55 *Note on Unrest Among Indian Labour on Estates in Ceylon*; *Indians in Ceylon – Sinhalese Urge Boycott, The Times*, 11 July 1939, PJ Dept., IOR: L/PJ/8/203, BL, UK, 392.

56 *ARAGOIC for 1939*, 1940, NAI.

57 *Unofficial Note with Compliments from Director of Public Information* in *ARAGOIC for 1937*, 1938, NAI.

58 *Annual Reports of the Agent of GOI in Ceylon, 1930 to 1939*, NAI; *AARCOL for 1938*, 1939, NAI; *Agent of GOI in Ceylon and His Assistant Visits to Estates – Question of Legal Authority to Interview Labourers*, EHL Dept., Overseas Section, 1938, NAI.

59 Data taken from *Indo-Ceylon Talks, Hindustan Times*, Delhi, 6 November 1940, Public and Judicial Dept., IOR: L/PJ/8/203, BL, UK; *ARAGOIC, 1939*, 1940, EHL, Overseas Branch, NAI, para 3, Appendix IV.

60 *Ceylon – Indian Daily Paid Employees in Government Department Dismissal – Ban on Emigration for Unskilled Work* (1939), NAI.

working conditions. The Agent of the GOI in Ceylon noted this new consciousness and reported an increased number of strikes. The Deputy Controller of Labour, on his part, emphasized that the ban had no prejudicial effect on the tea and rubber estates. He estimated that one labourer was required per acre of tea, and one labourer for three acres of rubber. Based on the total acres of tea and rubber plantations, a total of 529,000 (411,500 on tea and 117,600 on rubber) labourers were required in Ceylon, at a time when 535,000 were present (460,000 Indians, 75,000 Sinhalese).[61] The planters also saw no negative consequences: The number of labourers remained unchanged since few workers departed for fear of not being able to return. Shortages would thus only occur if a sudden increase in production would be mandated or if the estate owners under care and maintenance (tea 80,000 acres, rubber 120,000 acres) decided to resume production.[62]

Still, representatives of the planters hypocritically criticized the ban on the grounds that it caused the separation of families. In fact, the separation of families had been and was a standard feature of the plantation regime and the annual reports of the Agent of the GOI frequently noted petitions of workers for redress. Public opinion in India favoured the ban but resented its sudden imposition and the resulting separation of families. In response, the British GOI empowered the Commissioner of Labour and the Government of Madras to grant individual exemptions and the commissioner decided that, in general, wives and minor children or dependent non-working parents should be able to join male workers in Ceylon. It was expected that, on the same principle, dependents in Ceylon wishing to join their male relatives in India would be enabled to do so.[63] Moreover, those arriving in the five months before the imposition of the ban could also be granted exemptions.

However, no provisions were made for repatriations since officials and planters feared a mass exodus and, thus, a shortage of labour, and as a result, many migrants, often debt-ridden, were forced to stay in Ceylon. Again, given the separation of families, the Commissioner of Labour as well as estate superintendents in "deserving cases" could grant exemptions provided that the visit to India was brief and the return to Ceylon was certain.[64] The Protector of

61 *Confidential Report of the Agent of GOI in Ceylon of Events During the Period January-July, 1934*, NAI.

62 *Annual Report of Planter Association of Ceylon for 1939*, Overseas Section, 1940, NAI.

63 From August 1939 to February 1940, the applications for exemptions numbered 4,166, of which the Commissioner of Labour, exercising his discretionary powers, granted 1,289. *ARAGOIC for 1939*, 1940, NAI.

64 *ARAGOIC for 1939*, 1940, NAI.

Ceylon

India Bans Migration Of Workers

An almost complete ban has been placed by the Government of India on the emigration of unskilled Indian labourers to Ceylon (says Reuter). This ban has been imposed owing to the position created by the Ceylon Government's decision to terminate immediately the employment of a large number of Indians engaged on unskilled work in Ceylon.

By an Indian Correspondent

"CEYLON for the Sinhalese and the Sinhalese alone!" is the slogan heard in that island today.

Yet the Sinhalese actually form only 58 per cent. of the population.

The others include 858,000 Indians, mostly workers on the British-owned rubber and tea plantations, the Tamils of Jaffna in the north, the Moors and Malays scattered all over the island, and the Burghers of Colombo.

DISFRANCHISED

There has been persistent propaganda against Indian workers.

"The Indian," it is said, "has caused unemployment among the Sinhalese. He is the cause of the misery of the Sinhalese masses, and he must be got rid of as soon as possible."

It is after months of propaganda on these lines that Ministers have decided to repatriate nearly 8.000 Indian workers.

The Indian labourer on the plantations is to be disfranchised and left to the mercy of the planter.

He has already been excluded from the franchise for local bodies by the Village Communities Ordinance of last year.

FIGURE 18.5 *News Chronicle*, 1 August 1939
SOURCE: PJ DEPT., IOR: L/PJ/8/203, BL, UK

Emigrants at both Mandapam and Tuticorin ensured that no unskilled persons crossed over to Ceylon under the guise of skilled workers. In the complex bureaucracy, the agency issued credentials to bona fide Indian merchants, businessmen, and skilled workers to cross if they furnished proof that they did not fall under the ban or had special permission from the Commissioner of Labour, Madras, or other authorities. The Government of India, in September 1942, facilitated customary visits with the clause of return to Ceylon.

9 Conclusion

The economic depression of the 1930s brought the interaction between planter capital interests, labour migration, and demands for self-rule both in India and in Ceylon to the forefront – as in Malaya and Burma. Popular antagonism against Indians, privileged by the British colonizer administration, targeted migrants. However, in Ceylon as in other British colonies, migrant workers had been and were agents of development as they filled jobs the respective resident populations did not wish to accept. Despite this role in the global cash crop market and the important contribution to the circuit of global capitalism, emigrant Indian labour remained a highly exploited segment of global labour forces. From recruitment in India to deployment in a colony, the labourers faced exploitative conditions that were regulated, both formally and informally, by the networks of intermediaries, the plantocracy as well as the colonial bureaucracy. Despite official attempts to remove irregularities both in mobility and employment, malpractices continued to exist, mainly because of colonial officials' complicity with planters. Procuring more labourers and extracting maximum productivity increased tax revenues. In this context, the kangany system, once considered a facilitating institution, came to be widely criticized. However, it was the interface between anti-Indian and anti-immigration sentiments and rising ethnonationalism in Ceylon as well as Indian nationalists' pressure to secure equal rights and better working conditions for Indian migrant workers that shifted the colonial discourse from the regulation of the system to the restriction of labour mobility. Hence, in a way, the Ceylonese nationalists' demand for the restriction of immigration and the Indian nationalists' demand for the restriction of emigration coalesced and the ban on unskilled labour migrations, as well as the formal demise of the kangany systems, were the result of the larger anti-colonial movements in this region. The final ban had persisting aftereffects such as the separation of families, restrictions on the cross-territorial labour movement, citizenship concerns, and dilemmas of longing and belonging which resulted in a renewed set of conflicts in the postcolonial period. While the kangany and maistry systems formally ended in the 1940s in both Ceylon and Malaya, much of the system of advances, middlemen recruiters, indebtedness and bondage continued in India in renewed forms.[65]

65 Jan Breman, Isabelle Guerin, and Aseem Prakash, eds., *India's Unfree Workforce of Bondage Old and New* (Oxford: Oxford University Press, 2009).

PART 5

Workingmen's and -women's Agency in Globally Interconnected Spaces

CHAPTER 19

Introduction

Dirk Hoerder and Lukas Neissl

Human beings develop capabilities for agency in the processes of socialization in childhood, in their families, and in their local-regional cultures in the frames set by the larger society-economy-polity. Migrants, thus, approach their society (or societies) of destination with pre-migration mental settings, unconsciously internalized or consciously acquired, and activate and adapt them in post-arrival local cultures and economies. In the course of their migration from one embeddedness to another, they develop bi- or, perhaps, multi-cultural identifications and personalities. This multifaceted process in parlance is artificially separated by the standard usages of (fixed) ethnic and place references: Vietnamese in France, Chinese in Indonesia, Italians in Little Italy in New York, for example.

Self-decided migrants prepare for their future, select a destination, and depart because they intend to leave unacceptable aspects of their culture or place of origin. Although refugees or forced workers cannot prepare in the same way, they still have to come to terms with the conditions at their destination. All arrive in a neighbourhood (or barrack compound) and a worksite whether mine, plantation, domestic job or other. They do not arrive in a state, whole society, or so-called national economy. A "South African mine" is a mine more than a South African state. Hence, unless the local-to-local trajectories are made explicit, analyses of migrants' acculturation or of state-side integration policies remain abstract.

The chapters in this section, encompass experiences in the Philippines and Japan, Hawai'i and the US (West Coast variant) as well as Canada (Quebec variant), Austria, Yugoslavia and Turkey (urban and rural variant), Denmark (urban variant), and Ukraine (rural variant). While analyses require precision and detail, the communication of their results requires simplification. Communication necessarily reduces complexity to permit the addressee to understand the core of the issues at hand. To use the Ukraine-to-Quebec case, scholars not specialized in either society will neither have sufficient knowledge of the villages of departure and, perhaps, Tsarist Russian domination of the region nor will they be able to place the Thetford asbestos mines in context. Scholars and authors thus constantly walk a fine line between presenting precise details and simultaneously conveying these in a comprehensible format.

 | DOI:10.1163/9789004686991_020

This issue has been overlooked for as long as scholarship was nationally-bounded and nation-inspired – the now criticized methodological nationalism and territorialism. Comparative and global approaches transcend such narrow limitations but need to introduce their audience to the complexities of human agency in multiple cultures.

Yukari Takai (Chapter 20) analyses how rural families in southwestern Japan had to gauge Pacific-island and transpacific options to find wage labour on Hawaiian plantations or at worksites on the northwest coast of Canada and the US. The Meiji central government imposed the push framework – through debilitating taxes on agriculture to finance the modernization of the nascent imperial state – that hinged on militarization and industrialization. In many other states, too, taxation of peasant families or undervaluation of their products on regional, state-wide, and global markets pushed rural people out of the polity to which, by birth and residence, they belonged. The Japanese state, at the beginning of the movement toward widespread emigration, assisted the departure of its subjects. At the time, many other governments, such as those of Poland and Italy discussed in Chapter 7, also turned to ex-porting populations. The assistance was meant to channel the "surplus" of southern Japanese agriculturalists to Hawaiian plantations and their exploitative labour regime. However, the migrant workers, collecting information, quickly understood that wages were better in Vancouver and Seattle and decided to migrate onward. Their comparative assessment of working conditions was similar to that of Southern Chinese migrants who preferred British-imperial labour markets to French-imperial ones (Chapter 8). Such decisions required functioning information flows from trusted persons rather than official advertisements or interest-driven recruiting schemes. Many migrants who signed the customary contracts for plantation labour in Hawai'i had no intention to submit to the working conditions offered by US-capital-owned plantations. To move on, they required the help of middlemen – facilitators, mediators – and, for a fee, well-informed Japanese hotel owners in Hawai'i helped and cooperated with US law firms and Japanese interpreters. All those involved, namely the hotel owners, lawyers, and interpreters, profited from the trans-shipment business within limits and, in contrast to the South Indian-Ceylon kanganies (Chapter 18), did not cheat: Through the backward linkage of information flows, cheated migrants would have warned subsequent migrants about dishonest hotel keepers and, thus, would have deprived them of any future business. While the three state governments (Japanese, Canadian, and the US) involved attempted to regulate migration, the – from the point of view of state authorities lowly – immigrant hotel owners undercut governments' power in the interest of both the migrants at their destination and their remittance-dependent families in the southwestern Japanese prefectures. As the saying goes: Learn well all the rules, so as to know, how to break them in a proper manner. In a further comparison, not included in this volume, the stance of the hotel owners in the Pacific ports resembles that of hotel owners in the port of Bremen, Northern Germany, who accommodated East European migrants before their embarkation for the transatlantic voyage. To keep their business, they treated migrants fairly (and provided them with writing paper to inform their co-villagers of this). Additionally, Bremen state's authorities – dependent on taxes from the emigration business – turned a blind eye to the emigration of young men of draft age prohibited by other Hohenzollern-German or Romanov-Russian imperial governments. Hence, migrant agency in state-set frames was (and is) considerably more complex than administrators imagine.

The relationship between state authority and migrant agency is also the topic of Geoffrey Ewen's study of a strike in wartime 1915, begun by Ukrainian immigrant workers, in the French-speaking and, at the time, rigorously Catholic Canadian province of Quebec (Chapter 21). When the owners of the asbestos mines in Thetford reduced wages in a concerted action, the Ukrainian workers, intending to resist, had to communicate with their co-workers in Quebec French, an archaic French dialect dating back to the original French-imperial seventeenth-century state-sponsored migration. Not of the Roman Catholic faith, they had to deal with Catholicism at a time when the Quebec Church held complete control over the province's education system and thus dominated the childhood socialization of native Quebec workers. The Ukrainian immigrants from Tsarist Russia did carry with them experiences as supporters of socialist and, perhaps, anti-clerical parties, and, if arriving after 1905, experiences of worker strikes and peasant revolts in the course of the first Russian revolution. Those arriving from the Habsburg Empire had witnessed socialist and social democratic organizing. All such experiences had to be translated into Quebec-North American practices and class convictions – or the lack of the latter. The striking workers at first received support from liberal-minded administrators, indicating that "the state" was not as monolithic as the conservative majority believed. Small- and medium-town administrators and businessmen in North America often did support strikes: They knew what a living wage was and storekeepers supplying immigrant families would go down if capitalist wage cuts reduced incomes – and thus spending money for livelihoods.

Similarly, city authorities knew that below-subsistence wages would increase the demand for poor relief. Both shopkeepers and city administrators were aware that in several of the Thetford mines, workers had to buy provisions in company stores, just as South Indian workers had to do in plantation stores in Ceylon (as discussed in Chapter 18). To break the strike, the Catholic Church and the capital owners need the help of the secular Federal Government which – since asbestos was a raw material used for arms production – invoked war-time legislation to end the collective agency of the workers. In addition, the Federal Government sent interned Ukrainian working-class immigrants as forced labourers to replace the strikers. Since they were interned because of their origin in the – now war-time enemy – Habsburg Empire, the men were class-conscious and immediately joined the strike. While the migrants wanted to blend in to develop life prospects that they could not achieve under Tsarist Russian rule, the Catholic Quebec ruling elite used all its power to crush working-class agency.

Veronika Helfert (Chapter 22) engages with a different aspect of working-class agency: The conflicting interests of different class segments. While Chapter 11 illustrates the spectrum from (working-class) exclusionism to solidarity through reference to debates in the Second International, this chapter explores migrant women workers in the Austrian textile industry within the context of the considerably institutionalized (and hierarchical) Austrian labour movement and Austrian state policies after the Second World War. Labour relations in post-war Austria were characterized by strong corporatist cooperation mechanisms between capital and labour and when the Austrian state and industry and other capitalist European countries succeeded in establishing a *Gastarbeitsregime* in the 1960s, this specific labour migration regime was shaped by the male-centred institutional framework of Austrian social partnership. Thus, the migrating women workers, mostly from Yugoslavia and Turkey, faced a double marginalization within the Austrian labour movement, both as women and as (newly arriving) migrants. Their specific concerns were barely considered in official trade union policies and the institutional racism, expressed in the repressive (labour) legislation against non-Austrian workers, additionally hindered their integration into the Austrian labour movement. Thus, their agency – their "spaces of activism" – was shaped by a high degree of precarity.

Today, most of the worksites of these (former) migrant women no longer exist. Beginning in the 1970s, the global textile industry underwent significant changes leading to major shifts in the composition of the industry on a global scale. Within a relatively short period of time, Asia – after the British-Empire-imposed hiatus of nearly two centuries – again became the centre of global textile production. Beginning with the global economic crisis in the 1970s – which ended the cycle of capital accumulation driven by post-war reconstruction in capitalist Europe – capital(ist) owners developed new strategies to keep up their profits. While the economic growth period after the Second World

War was characterized by strategies to mobilize (the) labour (of workingmen and -women) to worksites in the capitalist centres, capital was now migrated to the peripheries and semi-peripheries of the global economy. In different phases, capital(ist) owners relocated the labour-intensive steps of textile production from Europe to global peripheries, mainly to Asia and, initially, also to Northern Africa, and after 1989, to Eastern Europe. In Asia, first the Republic of Korea, Singapore, Hồng Kong (then still part of the British colonizer empire) and Taiwan, later the Philippines, Indonesia, Thailand, and Malaysia, and subsequently Bangladesh, Pakistan, Sri Lanka, and Vietnam became centres of global textile production, under the command of multinational companies with headquarters as well as research and marketing facilities in the Global North. Following these distinctive political and economic developments of many of Asia's states, it was China which – after the capital(ist)-oriented reforms in the late 1970s – became the largest producing and exporting state of textiles on the globe by far.

In various parts of the world and in different time settings, issues of exploitation, migration, insertion into worksites and union structures were similar. Studying women migrants connecting the Philippines and Denmark, Nina Trige Andersen (Chapter 23) briefly frames out-migration from the Philippines since the US war against Spain (usually labelled "Spanish-American war") and the annexation and occupation of "the Philippines" – meaning the Tagalog-speaking people of many cultures. After an early and, at first, sporadic migration to the US, oceanic and European destinations also grew in importance: Men were hired in the global shipping industry, and since the 1960s women were employed in the worldwide domestic, care, and service labour markets. In Denmark, with a rapid expansion of business travel and tourism since the 1960s, the hotel sector, in the capital Copenhagen in particular, expanded and needed workers capable of communicating in English with international clients. While most Danish workers were unable to fulfil this requirement, for Filipinas, given the US rule and subsequent influence over their country, English was a language of communication. At the same time, the old-style Danish labour organization remained distant from the new in-migrating workers. As a result, the women – "chamber*maids*" – in the hotel cleaning operations, on the one hand, could only rely on their own initiatives and, on the other, had to come to understand labour rights and union organization. A double process of change subsequently commenced: The women developed their organizational capabilities, and a new generation of Danish labour activists reshaped the labour movement. From a global perspective, the cleaning staff in Los Angeles (Chapter 14) as in many states-societies-economies faced similar exploitation by mobile capital that was fugitive from social obligations and began struggles specific to their space, experience, and frames.

The workers in the Copenhagen and Los Angeles labour market sectors, like others in other sectors, sent part of their wages back home to sustain their families. This system has been called "economies of absence" in which important contributors to economic survival are absent from the social-economic spaces where their remittances are put to use. In this context, we might better speak of a "double location" of economic activity and impact. While this discussion has referred to individual migrants and migrant families, the sum of migrants' and migrant families' remittances sustains whole state economies, whether the Philippines, Bangladesh, Pakistan or others, as in the past in the case of Poland and Italy (Chapter 7). The migrant workingmen and -women discussed in these chapters are, to use the recently introduced label, essential workers for all of the world economy and the many individual state economies involved.

CHAPTER 20

Between Migrants and States

Japanese Entrepreneurs and Professionals in Two Port Cities in the Pacific World, 1880s to 1920s

Yukari Takai

Abstract

At the turn of the twentieth century, tens, if not hundreds of thousands of Japanese migrants left Japan and landed in Hawai'i only to depart for North America either immediately or after varying periods of time. Many chose to move on in search of higher wages and better working conditions. The extent of their transmigration depleted the labour supply in Hawai'i's sugar cane fields and alarmed plantation owners, diplomats, immigration authorities and policymakers, whether Japanese, Canadian or American. This chapter examines the role of previously underexamined parties of migration, such as Japanese immigrant hotel owners and boardinghouse keepers along with their partners in business, Japanese translators and their white American associates. Situated between migrants and state regulators – the two more familiar parties of migration – these brokers of migration, I suggest, facilitated, regulated and profited from Japanese workers' mobility in an increasingly racialized and exclusionary Pacific world.

Keywords

Hawai'i – Japanese hotels in Honolulu – Japanese in Seattle – Japanese in Vancouver – Japanese migrants – translocal – transpacific migration – transpacific world

At the turn of the twentieth century, tens, if not hundreds of thousands of Japanese migrants left their island nation and landed in Hawai'i, only to depart for Seattle, San Francisco, Vancouver, or Victoria either immediately or after varying periods of time. Many *issei*, as the first-generation Japanese-born workers were called, chose to move on in search of higher wages and better working conditions. The extent of the transmigration of Japanese, or *tenkō imin* as they were familiarly referred to, depleted the much-needed labour supply in Hawai'i's sugar cane fields and alarmed plantation owners, diplomats,

 | DOI:10.1163/9789004686991_021

immigration authorities and Japanese, American,[1] and Canadian policymakers. This chapter examines the role of Japanese immigrant hotel owners and boardinghouse keepers along with their partners in business, Japanese translators, and their American associates, in Honolulu and Vancouver. They shaped the transpacific circuits of issei workers at the very time when governments in Tokyo, Washington, DC, and Ottawa enacted increasingly tight immigration and emigration laws and regulations for those crossing the Pacific. I argue that the proprietors of immigrant hotels and their associates were central in collaborating with, acquiescing in, or undercutting the power of the state authorities and of Hawai'i's economic and political powerhouse, the sugar plantation owners.

As facilitators, profit-makers or even exploiters, immigrant hotelkeepers, translators and attorneys in Honolulu and Vancouver enmeshed their business activities, their translocal networks, and their professional knowledge with or against workers' agency for the passages across the Pacific. Situated between migrants and state regulators – the two more familiar parties of migration – these entrepreneurs and professionals were an important yet understudied aspect of the migration process. Through an in-depth analysis of these brokers of mobility as well as by drawing on transpacific and translocal perspectives, I aim to further our understanding of the power of capital and nation-states. Rather than delving into the agency of migrant workers alone, I seek to illuminate the world in which small capital owners, translators and paralegals of Japanese background together with American attorneys both served and profited from new Japanese arrivals. In so doing, I suggest that as facilitators, regulators, and profiteers of mobility they navigated a shifting world and easily crossed the boundary between facilitation and exploitation.

A translocal perspective helps us understand the dynamic connections between people and places below and above the level of the national. Since the spatial turn in historical writing, the transnational as an analytical concept has framed voluminous works on the movements of people, goods, money, and ideas, both in the past and the present. While acknowledging the force of transnational history, I take its critics seriously who highlight the fact that transnational history and its variants are less suited to establishing links below the elite level.[2] An overwhelming majority of people who migrated overseas

1 In this chapter "American," according to contemporary usage, refers to "US" or "US citizen."

2 Ulrike Freitag and Achim von Oppen, *Translocality: The Study of Globalising Processes from a Southern Perspective* (Leiden: Brill, 2010). For a critique of transnationalism from the perspective of transcultural societal studies, see Dirk Hoerder, *"To Know Our Many Selves": From the Study of Canada to Canadian Studies* (Edmonton: Athabasca University Press, 2010).

from Japan were peasants, workers, traders, and various non-professional women and men.

The islands of Hawai'i were the leading destination for Japanese migrant workers since 1885 when the Japanese government, in agreement with its Hawaiian counterpart, shipped the first contingent of government-contract labourers or *kan'yaku imin*. They were destined to work on sugar cane plantations for three years, thereby replenishing a source of labour power that Kānaka Maoli (native Hawaiians) and Chinese workers had provided earlier, and that Filipinos and other workers would do later. A steady flow of labour migration from Japan continued until the end of *kan'yaku imin* in 1894. The number of arrivals increased during the periods of the private contract system and free, i.e., non-contracted migration (from 1894 to 1900 and 1901 to 1907, respectively). In 1907 and 1908, the so-called Gentlemen's Agreement between the US and Japan stopped labour migration from Japan. By this time, the Japanese constituted the largest ethnic group in Hawai'i, and over 200,000 Japanese arrived there in the period spanning 1885 to 1924 when the US Congress barred Japanese immigration to the US.[3]

An overwhelming majority of the Japanese arrivals in Hawai'i during the government-sponsored migration period were landless farmers, mostly men, whose lives were devastated by the heavy taxation, severe deflation, and transformation of the local economy under the Meiji government.[4] Most came from the southwestern prefectures – especially in the early years of the government-sponsored migration – and from very clearly defined villages, although the tendency toward migration gradually spread throughout the archipelago. This points to the importance of local connections, the strength of chain migration and the extent of the so-called migration fever. From the perspective of the Meiji imperial government, the popularity of *kan'yaku imin* points to a measure of success in their efforts to turn Hawai'i into a new site to ease the problems of an alleged surplus population and the impoverishment of rural peasant families after the launch of the colonization of Hokkaido.[5] The private emigration system counted a relatively greater proportion of members of a more affluent

3 Franklin Odo and Kazuko Shinoto, *Zusetsu Hawai nihonjinshi 1885–1924* (Honolulu: Bishop Museum Press, 1985), 13.

4 Martin Dusinberre, *Hard Times in the Hometown: A History of Community Survival in Modern Japan* (Honolulu: University of Hawai'i Press, 2012), 88–89.

5 Between 1885 and 1894, over 29,000 Japanese people arrived in Hawai'i. Alan Takeo Moriyama, *Imingaisha: Japanese Emigration Companies and Hawaii, 1894–1908* (Honolulu: University of Hawai'i Press, 1985), xviii; Okabe Makio, *Umi wo watatta nihonjin*, 2nd ed. (Tokyo: Yamakawa shuppan), 29–30.

class, including once prosperous landowning households, who were willing to pay for the journey and could do so without government subsidies.[6]

In the years leading to 1907, Japanese migrants transformed Hawai'i once again, whereby it ceased to be the primary destination for a growing number of Japanese labourers and instead became a temporary stopover for a longer trans-pacific voyage to Seattle, San Francisco, Vancouver, and Victoria. From 1902 to 1907, at the height of the transmigration movement, 40,000 Japanese left the Hawaiian islands for the continent.[7] During a mere ten-month period from January to October 1907, out of the 8,125 Japanese who arrived in Vancouver and Victoria in British Columbia, only one out of five had travelled directly from Japan, while as many as one out of three had travelled from Hawai'i, only a minute number (nine individuals) first went to Mexico before crossing the borders into Canada. Furthermore, of all Japanese who landed at the Canadian ports in question, only a little over one-half (55 percent or 4,429 individuals) remained in Canada while 45 percent or 3,619 individuals immediately went to the US.[8] The arrival of tens of thousands of Japanese transmigrants inflamed both anti-Japanese and anti-Asian feelings among the white residents on the Pacific coast on both sides of the Canada-US border and subsequently a series of race riots erupted in San Francisco, Bellingham and Vancouver in the spring and the autumn of 1907.[9]

Japanese labourers in Hawai'i were aware of the wages on the continent and were able to gauge them against the meagre pay they earned on the sugar cane fields. Informed by friends and families and facilitated but also exploited by Japanese hotels, labour recruiters and white American barristers, Japanese workers, after various lengths of stay in Hawai'i, left in droves for the continent. They both knew about and wanted higher wages and better working conditions, or so they were promised, in railroad maintenance, orchards and mining on the Pacific coast and inland. The annexation of Hawai'i by the US in 1898 was a disaster for the native kingdom of Kānaka Maoli and a mixed blessing

6 Kimura Kenji, *Kindai nihon no imin to kokka, chi'ikishakai* (Tokyo: Ochanomizu shuppan, 2021), 76.

7 Yukari Takai, "Bridging the Pacific: Diplomacy and the Control of Japanese Transmigration via Hawai'i, 1890–1910," in *Entangling Migration History: Borderlands and Transnationalism in the United States and Canada,* ed. Benjamin Bryce and Alexander Freund (Gainesville: University Press of Florida, 2015), 141–161.

8 Canada, Royal Commission, *Report of W. L. Mackenzie King, C. M. G. Commissioner Appointed to Enquire into the Methods by Which Oriental Labourers Have Been Induced to Come to Canada* (Ottawa, 1907), 24. Hereafter referred to as the *Report.*

9 Among the several studies on the subject, see for example Erika Lee, "Hemispheric Orientalism and the 1907 Pacific Coast Race Riots," *Amerasia Journal* 33, no. 2 (2007): 19–47.

for Asians in Hawai'i. Under the new regime, the former plantation workers became free workers since the US Alien Contract Labour Law of 1885 barred the use of contract labourers. As a result, after the annexation, the Japanese in Hawai'i were legally at liberty to move to the mainland because such a move was a matter of relocation within US borders without having to undergo a second series of immigration procedures, including a medical examination, quarantine and a customs check in the continental US, once they had been admitted to Hawai'i.[10]

In comparison to men, only a small number of Japanese women travelled from Hawai'i to the continent. However, women accounted for a higher percentage among Hawai'i-bound migrants in comparison to their counterparts migrating to the continent. This reflected, to some extent, the Japanese government's policy and the Hawaiian sugar planters' preference for family migration for the sugar cane field workers. Unfortunately, the available sources that I relied on – including the Japanese language newspapers, immigrant publications, photographs and ephemera, as well as diplomatic records housed at the Diplomatic Archives of the Ministry of Foreign Affairs in Japan (DAMFA) – do not provide a gender breakdown for the transmigration from Hawai'i to the continental destinations. Due to the dearth of available sources on women in the hotel business in Hawai'i as elsewhere, the discussion in the following sections is therefore limited to issei men despite the importance of women's role in this business and the gender dimensions of transnational migration.

1 Brokerage at the Front Line: Japanese Hotel and Boardinghouse Keepers

The first series of full-fledged Japanese immigrant hotels in Honolulu opened for business in the 1890s.[11] New hotels subsequently sprang up, doubling in number from 11 in 1899 to 22 in 1908 and they thrived until 1924 when the US federal government banned the admission of any Japanese or even any Asians to the country. Around 1893, some 16 Japanese hotel owners in Honolulu formed

10 Takai, "Bridging the Pacific," 144–146.

11 Gaimushō tsūshōkyoku, *Tsūshōisan*, no. 37 (March 1896), no. 29 (May 1908), no. 55 (October 1909). Cited in Iida Kōjirō, *Honolulu no nikkeijin no rekishichiri* (Kyoto: Nakanishiya Shuppan, 2013), 128, 137. Yamashiro Matsutarō, "Nihonjin ryokan no hensen wo kataru," *Jitsugyō no Hawai*, 1 August 1913, 83; see also the issues of 1 September 1917, 148, and 1 February 1935, 48, 49; Sōga Keihō, *Gojyūnenkan no Hawai kaiko* (Honolulu: Gojyūnenkan no Hawai kaiko kankōkai, 1953), 14–142.

the first Japanese business association, the Japanese Hotel Association (ホノルル日本人旅館組合), with the two-fold aim to standardize the services – the accommodations and accompanying businesses – among its member hotels and to serve newly arriving compatriots.[12] Allegedly to promote the interests of its members, this cartel of small enterprises set a standard rate for room and board and, for example, for commissions on steamship ticket sales for the transpacific liners.

Significantly, Japanese hotel owners in Honolulu and Vancouver, as well as in many other places in and around the Pacific, played roles far beyond simply providing a place to stay. They acted as surrogate notaries, travel agents, job placement agents and at times, temporary clinics for issei labourers. An advertisement for the Japanese Hotel Association of Honolulu in one of the city's Japanese-language daily newspapers provides a glimpse into their services.[13] For a fee, some members assisted their fellow countrymen and -women with acquiring the official papers for registering at the Japanese consulate, for sending for wives and children, or requests for the deferral of conscription to the town hall or village office in Japan. Some also helped immigrants with the withdrawal of deposits from a Japanese emigration bank, a deposit some emigration companies required. Others sold cut-rate steamship tickets to Japan or the continent. They commonly took care of the safekeeping of personal documents, including the passports and family registries of issei workers. This practice facilitated their assisting working-class compatriots both with formalities with the local consulate and their home village offices. In this way, they cemented their role as an indispensable conduit bridging the Japanese authorities (representing the state, local consulates, towns, or villages) and individual immigrant men and women abroad.

12 Kimura Yoshigorō and Inoue Tanebumi, *Saishin seikaku Hawai tokō an'nai,* (Tokyo: Hakubunkan, 1904), 54; Yamashiro Matsutarō, "Nihonjin ryokan no hensen wo kataru," *Jitsugyō no Hawai,* 1 February 1935; Nihon jijisha, ed., *Kan'yaku nihon imin hawai tokō gojjyu-shūnen kinenshi* (Honolulu: Nihon jijisha, 1935), 116, cited in Iida, *Honolulu,* 128, 149, 159; "Honolulu nihonjin ryokan kumiai no rekishi to jigyō," in *Nippu jiji Hawai nenkan,* ed. Nippu jijisha (Honolulu: Nippu jijisha, 1941), 44–45. The association renamed itself to the Honolulu Japanese Hotel Association after the First World War.

13 Iida, *Honolulu,* 129; *Jitsugyō no hawai,* 1 August 1913, page number unavailable, 1 September 1913, p. 148; Kimura and Inoue, *Saishin seikaku,* 54–55. For advertisements of Komatsuya Ryokan and Yamashiro Ryokan, see for example Nippu jiji sha, ed., *Hawai dōhō hatten kaikōshi* (Honolulu: Nippu jiji sha, 1921), 20, 289; Saitō Miki, "Hawai zaijyū honpō rōdōsha wo beikoku ni yushutsusuru mono zōka no ken, oyobi kore ni taishi ryōjikan narabini waga imingaisha ga sono seishisaku wo hodokoshitaru no ken," 2 December 1903, Gaikōbunsho, 3.8.2.168 Hawai imin beikoku tenkō kinshi ikken.

One hotel near the port of Vancouver opened its lobby for the treatment of trachoma-infected new arrivals from Japan to substitute for an ophthalmologist's clinic distant from the port. Trachoma eye infection was a leading cause for US immigration authorities to bar entry.[14] On one occasion, the Japanese Boardinghouse Keepers Union in Vancouver, well aware that the newcomers would have little difficulty in finding immediate employment, advanced a total of $ 3,000 in cash for the landing money requirement that Canadian immigration regulations imposed at a rate of CA$ 25 per person on would-be workers.[15] This led to other sources of revenue, such as commissions for services and possibly for subsequent business dealings. The extent to which the hotel owners assisted with the needs of immigrant compatriots, the formalities of the governments, and the business interests of various parties were such that one Japanese journalist in Honolulu claimed – albeit with some exaggeration – that the Japanese consulate, emigration companies, and steamship companies all kowtowed to the Japanese Hotel Association.[16]

While the research emphasizes the national or racial aspects, what was crucial (although often overlooked) is the local or more precisely, the translocal aspects. Many among the immigrant hotel owners were former government-contract immigrants who had left Japan to work on the sugar cane plantations for three years. A fair number originated, as mentioned earlier, from southwestern Japan, landed in Hawai'i between 1885 and 1894, and subsequently rose above their later arriving compatriots.[17] The early migrants-turned-owners capitalized on close ties with their villages, prefectures, or regions of origin in

14 Nakayama Jinshirō, *Kanada no hōko,* ge (Tokyo: Japan Taimususha, 1922), in *Nikkei imin shiryoshū,* ed. Sakata Yauo, 1, Hokubei hen 2, vol. 11 (Tokyo: Nihon tosho sentā, 1994), 1714–1715.

15 Mackenzie King, *Report,* 57; Tairiku nippōsha, ed., *Kanada dōhō hattenshi* (Vancouver: Tairiku nippōhsa, 1909), 67, 68; Patricia Roy, *A White Man's Province: British Columbia Politicians and Chinese and Japanese Immigrants 1858–1914* (Vancouver: University of British Columbia Press, 1989), 188; Ninette Kelley and Michael J. Trebilcock, *The Making of the Mosaic: A History of Canadian Immigration Policy* (Toronto: University of Toronto Press, 1998), 147. The first hotel association, Kanada yadoya kumiai or Canada Inn Association, was founded in the 36th year of Meiji (1903). A group of members dissatisfied with the leadership branched off to establish its own association, Kanada ryokan kumiai or Canada Hotel Union, in May during the 39th year of Meiji (1906). The two associations merged in 1907 as the Japanese Boardinghouse Union of Vancouver. Nakayama Jinshirō, *Kanada no hōko*: 1709–1716.

16 *Jitsugyō no hawai,* 1 September 1917, 148.

17 For a discussion of boardinghouse proprietors and their associations in San Francisco, Los Angeles and Honolulu, see Yūji Ichioka, *The Issei: The World of the First Generation Japanese Immigrants, 1885–1924* (New York: Free Press, 1988), 65.

Japan to recruit clients. While such "capitalization" practices were by no means unique to Japanese immigrants,[18] the translocal connections among Japanese hotel proprietors and their clients remained particularly strong as is reflected in the fact that among the inns and hotels in Honolulu in the early twentieth century, there was likely at least one that carried the name of the newcomers' home prefecture.[19]

An example of this is found in the life of Kawasaki Kiyozō, the owner of one of the oldest and most well-established hotels in Honolulu. In 1885, the first year of government-sponsored emigration, he had left his native village of Kuka on the island of Suō Ōshima in the inland sea of Setonaikai or Setouchi in southwestern Japan.[20] Dubbed the "Hawai'i of the Setocuchi inland sea," the island of 130 square kilometres was home to a substantial number of Hawai'i-bound emigrants at the time and one out of three among the first contingent of 944 *kan'yaku imin* was a Suō Ōshimarite. Having worked on a plantation on the Island of Kaua'i for three years, Kawasaki moved to Honolulu and worked at the Japanese consulate before opening a small hotel in 1891. In the following year, he became a co- and then full owner of another hotel, which he named Kawasaki Ryokan. One of many who stayed at the hotel was a co-islander Katamoto Ichisuke, arriving eleven years later, who probably learned about Kawasaki through local connections from his home island.[21]

Drawing on a shared local origin, familiar dialect, and networks of kin and co-villagers, some hotels used newspaper advertisements or brochures to highlight their connections among co-regionals. The Higoya Ryokan or Higo

---

18 For example, Italians also valued networks of family, kin, and co-villagers across the Atlantic and similarly profited from the extended webs of human relations. Robert Harney, "Men without Women," in *The Italian Immigrant Women in North America*, ed. Betty Boyd Caroli, Robert F. Harney, and Lydio F. Tomasi (Toronto: Multicultural History Society of Ontario, 1977), 79–102. For a critical assessment of earlier discussions, see Nancy M. Forestell, "Bachelors, Boarding-Houses, and Blind Pigs: Gender Construction in a Multi-Ethnic Mining Camp, 1909–1920," in *A Nation of Immigrants: Women, Workers, and Communities in Canadian History, 1840s-1960s*, ed. Franca Iacovetta with Paula Draper and Robert Ventresca (Toronto: University of Toronto Press, 1998), 251–290, especially 259–263.

19 This strategy, common among many Japanese hotelkeepers from the leading home prefectures in southwestern Japan (Yamaguchi, Hiroshima, Kumamoto, for example), was also used by others from numerically less important prefectures such as Fukuoka. From Matsubara to Hayashi, confidential no. 22, 6 November 1906, *Nihon gaiko bunsho* (1906), 303–306. Iida, *Honolulu*, 127–134.

20 Okuizumi Eizaburō, ed., *Shoki zaihokubei nihonjin no kiroku*, vol. 26 (Tokyo: Bunseishoten, 2015), 15–17; Iida, *Honolulu*, 133–134.

21 Murakami Wakako, "Hawai gaeri no tōmintachi: Imin no shima Suō Ōshima," *Jinbunken kiyō* 83 (2016), 181–198, especially 189–190.

Hotel – with Higo being the ancient designation for the Kumamoto prefecture on Kyūshū island, which was a leading prefecture of origin for southern Japanese migrants – printed its business address and phone number in Honolulu, in addition to the names and the addresses in the presumably native hamlets in Higo of the hotel owner Takagi Gentarō and a full-time staff member.[22] Using this information, Takagi sought to entice his fellow country-, or rather, local men and fellow provincials.

The clients of the Japanese immigrant hotels, inns, and boardinghouses were by no means limited to their owners' hometown or prefecture of origin, however. As part of their advertising efforts, several hotels printed multicoloured leaflets for prospective migrants. For example, a brochure of the Ebisuya Hotel included a photo of its newly completed two-story building along with detailed instructions to the new arrivals about what to say (or not to say) and what to carry (or not to carry) at various points of arrival, whether the US immigration station and customs office, passport check, office of the sugar planters' association, or the registration at the Japanese consulate in Honolulu.[23]

2 Agents of Mobility

Japanese hotels, inns, and boardinghouses capitalized on the transmigration of Japanese labourers as a vital source of income. They were constantly fully occupied with labourers either directly from Japan or from the outer Hawaiian islands waiting for departure to a continental destination. In a rare first-hand account, hotel owner Yamashiro Matsutarō related his dealings with Japanese transmigrants from Hawai'i. Originating from Hiroshima prefecture, southwestern Japan, he had arrived in Hawai'i in 1890 with the fourteenth shipment of government-contract migrants. Having worked on two sugar cane plantations on the island of Maui, Yamashiro moved to Honolulu and purchased a hotel from a compatriot. In 1900, a considerable portion of the city's Chinese, Japanese and Kānaka quarters – including Yamahiro's hotel – burnt down when Hawai'i's Board of Health set a fire in an attempt to quell an outbreak

22 From Matsubara Kazuo to Hayashi Tadashi, Nihon imin hawai chakugo no kōdō jyōkyō narabi sonotaisaku ni kanshi rinshin no ken, confidential no. 22, 6 November 1906, *Nihon gaiko bunsho* (1906), 303–306.

23 Ebisuya ryokan, Hawai tokō an'nai, circa 1904, Hawai ni okeru honpō imin kankei zakken hōkoku no bu, 3.8.2.41, (1904), vol. 3, Diplomatic Archives of the Ministry of Foreign Affairs of Japan (DFMFA). The same file (1904) also includes photos of several other Japanese immigrant hotels in Honolulu.

FIGURE 20.1 Advertisement for the Ebisuya Hotel in Honolulu
SOURCE: THE DIPLOMATIC ARCHIVES OF THE JAPANESE MINISTRY OF FOREIGN AFFAIRS, NIHON GAIKŌ BUNSHO, VOL. 3, 3-8-2-41. COURTESY OF THE DIPLOMATIC ARCHIVES OF THE MINISTRY OF FOREIGN AFFAIRS OF JAPAN IN TOKYO

of the bubonic plague. Yamashiro subsequently relocated closer to downtown and built the Yamashiro Ryokan or Yamashiro Hotel[24] after which he began to transport issei workers to the continental US.[25] Most of these men arrived with passports stating their destination as being "Hawai'i only" and spent ten days in quarantine before moving on.

Yamashiro was not alone in capitalizing on his capacity to arrange for the transmigration of issei labourers, as Japanese immigrant hotels promised a "huge discount" for continent-bound steamship travellers and other services. This was facilitated by the fact that Japanese hotels in Honolulu and, for

24 Iida, *Honolulu*, 133.
25 *Hawai dōhō hatten kaikōshi*, 227, 228; Iida, *Honolulu*, 134.

example, San Francisco obtained special rates from steamship companies for the bulk sale of tickets.[26]

The business interests of the hotel and boardinghouse owners clashed with the regulations of the Japanese, American, and Canadian states, as well as with the local power of the Hawaiian Sugar Planters' Association. Among those at the front line in challenging the power and authority of the regulators was Haga Kusaka, who owned Kanjō Ryokan *a.k.a.* Shikokuya (Shikoku being one of the four main islands of Japan and Haga's home island) in Honolulu. In 1906, Haga was harshly reprimanded for prompting a branch manager of the Japanese emigration company Tairiku Shokumin Gōshi Kaisha (Continental Emigration Co & Lit.) on his home island to distribute handbills among Honolulu-bound Japanese. Haga's act was in defiance of the Foreign Ministry's ban on such practices.[27]

Haga's bid to utilize his connections, whether translocal and transpacific, personal and professional, for the potentially highly lucrative venture of transmigration also led him to engage in another scheme. In collaboration with the Seattle-based Japanese labour contract and supply company, the Oriental Trading Company, he chartered the steamship *Olympia* for three shipments of issei labourers out of Honolulu.[28] The outcome of this venture was mixed, as after successfully transporting 600 labourers to Seattle, Haga was unable to recruit the projected numbers for the two remaining voyages.[29] However, in both his own and in the issei workers' interests, through this action he

26 The Boardinghouse Keepers Association in San Francisco induced the Pacific Mail Steamship Company to provide them with a reduced rate. *Yamato Shinbun*, 13 February 1906. Ichioka, *Issei*, 65; Saitō Miki to Komura, 28 May 1902, enclosure, Alex. Centre to H. Hackfield and Co., n.d., Japanese American Research Project, University of California Los Angeles, DFMFA, reel 12.

27 Handbill of Kanjō ryokan, Hawai imin beikoku tenkō kinshi ikken, 3.8.2.168.1, vol. 1 (1902), *Nihon gaikō bunsho* (1906), 318, 319; from Saitō to Hayashi, confidential no. 22, 6 November 1906, *Nihon gaikō bunsho* (1906), 303.

28 Iriye Toraji, *Hōjin Kaigai Hattenshi* (Tokyo: Hara Shobo, 1981; original, Tokyo: Ida Shoten, 1942), 449, 450. From Matsubara to Ministry of Foreign Affairs Saionji Kinmochi, "Zaihawai nihonjin wo beihondo ni sasoi dashi no tame rinjisen raifu no ken," 13 March 1906, public no. 60, *Nihon gaikō bunsho* (1906), 314. Ichioka, *Issei*, 66.

29 From Matsubara to Ministry of Foreign Affairs Saionji Kinmochi, "Zaihawai nihonjin," 13 March 1906, *Nihon gaikō bunsho* (1906), 314. See also *The Issei*, 66; Kornel S. Chang, *Pacific Connections: The Making of the U.S.-Canada Borderlands* (Berkeley: University of California Press, 2012), 75–76.

deliberately and successfully challenged the Japanese foreign office and the powerful Hawaiian Sugar Planters' Association.[30]

The hotel owners' initiatives were not always aligned with those of local Japanese communities. A case in point was negotiations between Japanese Boardinghouse Union of Vancouver and the fishermen's society in Steveston, a thriving fishing village 20 kilometres to the south. In July 1907, Nakayama Jinshirō, the director of the Japanese Boardinghouse Union, attempted to persuade the executives of the Japanese Fishermen's Benevolent Society to house stranded recent Japanese arrivals from Honolulu whose numbers by far exceeded the capacity of Vancouver's Japanese hotels. Many of Steveston's fisher families hailed from the fishing village of Mio in Wakayama prefecture, southwestern Japan. The Vancouver hotel and boardinghouse proprietors, for their part, counted a fair portion of descendants of Ōmi *shōnin* traders from a wealthy and powerful merchant class of a long-standing in Shiga prefecture, also in southwestern Japan, dating from the thirteenth century.[31] Director Nakayama decided to curry favour with the fishermen's association by bridging their local and professional differences with a rhetoric of patriotism, nationalism, and imperial solidarity. At first, one of the representatives from the fishermen's association – who was to serve as its head later – noted drily that they heard phrases such as "*yamato minzoku* (Japanese race)," "brethren," and "imperial subjects" of the Japanese Empire far too many times. Still, they finally if grudgingly agreed to collaborate with the boardinghouse owners. The latter reaped an immediate profit by collecting a fee of CA$ 1 per day from each immigrant who went to Steveston, news that the fishermen's association learned only later.[32]

The initial reactions to this development among the executives of the fishermen's association point to a strain of class antagonism and geographical friction; it also suggests a limit in the extent to which the recently minted notion of imperial Japanese subjects gained traction among ordinary migrants in the early twentieth century. To be certain, commoners in Japan were increasingly exposed to the new, top-down discourse of national belonging as imperial subjects during and immediately after the years of imperial Japan's first two major

30 From Matsubara to Ministry of Foreign Affairs Saionji Kinmochi, "Zaihawai nihonjin," 13 March 1906, *Nihon gaikō bunsho* (1906), 314. See also Ichioka, *Issei*, 66; Chang, *Pacific Connections*, 75–76.

31 Kobayashi Teiji, *Sutebusuton gyosha jizen dantai sanjū gonenshi* (Tokyo: Sutebusuton Gyosha Jizen Dantai, 1935), 163–166; reprint in Sasaki Toshiji, ed., *Kanada iminshi shiryō* (Tokyo: Fuji Shuppan, 1995), vol. 4.

32 Kobayashi, *Sutebusuton gyosha jizen dantai*, 163–166.

international wars, namely the Sino-Japanese War (1894–1895) and the Russo-Japanese War (1904–1905). However, the sense of being imperial subjects had a long way to go before it seeped in deeply and, if ever, evenly among the population, including among men and women overseas such as fishers in Steveston. While the director of Vancouver's Japanese Boardinghouse Union attempted to capitalize on the imperial discourse, the men of the fishermen's union probably helped because of a sense of compassion and obligation towards their stranded co-nationals. Hence, the fishermen's executives had little choice but to accept, if reluctantly, such a call to duty.

Nakayama, for his part, was seemingly aware of the private business-state conflict between the issei and the Canadian government when he flatly denied that his Union played any role in the Hawai'i-to-Vancouver transmigration. He may have wanted to avoid any association between the Boardinghouse Union and the increasingly contentious issue of the "importation of Oriental labourers" amid the Royal Commission investigation of Canada's Deputy Minister of Labour, Mackenzie King (later Canada's longest-serving Prime Minister) and the subsequent publication of his report. To avoid any blame being allocated to his activities, Nakayama thus decided to implicate his colleagues in Honolulu in the extensive transmigration that was taking place. In 1921, however, Nakayama published a more than 2,000-page encyclopaedia in the Japanese language about Japanese in Canada, in which he boasted that the Japanese Boardinghouse Union of Vancouver together with the Vancouver-based labour contracting firm Nikka Yotashi Kaisha were accountable for the successful settlement of Japanese from Hawai'i.[33] His double discourse served two audiences separately, Japanese compatriots and Anglo-Canadian authorities, and such an approach was imperative for a community leader at a time of worsening anti-Japanese antagonism within white societies and their governments.

3 Brokering Knowledge: Japanese Interpreters and American Attorneys

Whereas translocal connections and personal networks to home villages, towns, or regions in Japan were crucial to both immigrant entrepreneurs and newly arriving migrants, both needed Japanese interpreters and American attorneys to provide professional knowledge and connections – whether linguistic, legal, or financial – and to orchestrate the actual flows of money,

33 Nakayama, *Kanada no hōko*, 1719.

services, and people across the Pacific Ocean. In so doing, these professionals brokered, mediated, or manipulated the desires of immigrants in search of higher wages, of hotel proprietors in the quest for greater profit, and of the nation-states that were intent on curbing the mobility of those they deemed undesirable.

The legal systems in early twentieth-century Hawai'i and North America were essentially white[34] and institutional racism denied the Japanese the right to practice law or to serve on juries, just like it excluded the First Nations peoples and Chinese immigrants.[35] It was in this context that Japanese interpreters and paralegals such as Maruyama Kin'ichirō and Makino Frederick Kinzaburō worked as translators and paralegals in Honolulu in partnership with white American solicitors such as Charles F. Chillingworth and A. V. Geer.[36] Together, the Japanese-American syndicates calibrated the logistics for transportation, transferred money from one locality to another and, when necessary, even travelled with Japanese labourers on board a steamship to accomplish their business goals.[37]

In 1907, Chillingworth and Maruyama chartered a steamship, the *Kumeric*, for the transmigration of Japanese labourers out of Hawai'i.[38] Collaborating with Japanese hotel and boardinghouse owners in Honolulu, they sold steamship tickets at a price of US$ 36 per passenger. While this was higher than the regular charge for steerage passage (US$ 30) the price also covered additional

---

34 The government of British Columbia excluded the Japanese population in the province from the voters' list in 1895 and thus disqualified them from serving as jurors or entering the legal profession. Kelly and Trebilcock, *The Making of the Mosaic*, 146–147. Most US states barred non-US citizens from practicing law. Lisa Mar, *Brokering Belonging: Chinese in Canada's Exclusion Era, 1885–1945* (New York: Oxford University Press, 2010), 50, note 4. See also A. M. Hendrickson, *Rules for Admission to the Bar in the Several States and Territories of the United States in Force January 1, 1922*, 11th ed. (St. Paul, MN: West, 1922), 3–221. Under the Nationality Acts of 1790 and 1870, the US federal law restricted the right of naturalization to aliens who were either "free white" or of "African nativity and descent." However, the vagueness of the "free white" concept left open the possibility for Japanese immigrants to become naturalized citizens. On 13 November 1922, the landmark US Supreme Court case of Ozawa v. United States denied eligibility for citizenship to the Japanese-born immigrants (issei) in the US. Nisei Veterans Legacy, accessed 29 February 2020, https://www.nvlchawaii.org/issei-not-eligible-us-citizenship.

35 Mar, *Brokering Belonging*, 52.

36 *Nippu Jiji*, 9 December 1911, 17 December 1934.

37 *Nippu Jiji*, 24, 26, 27, 28 April 1916.

38 Mackenzie King, *Report*, 56, 57.

fees including the departure tax of US$ 5 at the port of Honolulu,[39] whereby the hotel owners kept US$ 1 per passenger as a commission. Maruyama and Chillingworth collected, held, or even lent money to prospective Japanese passengers for the purchase of steamship tickets and to fulfil the requirement of a minimum sum of CA$ 25 ("show money") required by the government officials for entry in Vancouver or Victoria. Chillingworth scrupulously recorded the varying amounts he advanced to each out-bound Japanese passenger without sufficient funds and issued receipts while Maruyama accompanied the labourers on board the *Kumeric* to collect the money after passing admission. Both used their social and cultural assets in the service of their clients, namely the hotel keepers and labourers, during a time when all three governments (Japanese, American, and Canadian) sought to limit the mobility of foreigners or nationals deemed undesirable based on race, class, or gender.

Naturally, both Maruyama and Chillingworth provided the services outlined with their own financial interest in mind, and they subsequently also established connections with the Honolulu-based Theodore Davies & Company (Davies & Co.), one of the "Big Five" oligarchies among the sugar cane processing companies. Davies & Co. would send money to an agent in Vancouver who would distribute the legally required amounts of funds that were to be shown to the Canadian immigration authorities to the Japanese passengers. After admission, the money was to be returned and sent back to Honolulu, possibly for another round of the transhipment of passengers.

However, the plan failed miserably for two reasons. Firstly, Canadian and Japanese authorities became aware that the entire scheme was dubious. Dr Munro, a Canadian medical inspector and immigration agent in Vancouver, discovered that the money did not belong to the passengers and that it literally was "show money."[40] As a result, in an extraordinary step, the Consul General of Japan in Vancouver, Morikawa, boarded the ship and instructed the Japanese passengers to submit the money along with their passport to a consulate official once they had shown it to the Canadian immigration officials.[41] However, the sight of Japanese immigrants each dropping CA$ 25 into a sack held by a staff member of the Japanese consulate resulted in an outcry from local Members of Parliament and city councillors. Dr Munro ordered the money to be returned to the transmigrant labourers, who in their turn kept it

39 Mackenzie King, *Report*, 57, 59. The cost of passage for a steamer from Honolulu to Seattle was US$ 39. A letter from Hamamura Kyōichi, the owner of Ebisuya Hotel, Honolulu to Ōta Rikizō, 30 August 1906, Gaikō bunsho, record number unknown.

40 Mackenzie King, *Report*, 56, 58.

41 Mackenzie King, *Report*, 59; Roy, *White Man's Province*, 187–188.

to use as starting capital. In an additional transoceanic twist, the hotel owners in Honolulu, having sold tickets for the passage from Honolulu to continental North America, had to deal with the seething discontent of many Japanese labourers who remained in Honolulu and who wanted reimbursement for the cancelled transpacific voyage for which they had paid. As many as 250 were refused to board on the *Kumeric* in Honolulu because the ship had smallpox-infected Portuguese labourers from Madeira on board on its way to Honolulu, labourers whom the Planters' Association had been importing and who were rejected of landing. Ironically, the Japanese were to board the very ship that the sugar planters chartered to make up for the labour shortage because of the departure of Japanese sugar plantation workers in the first place. Chillingworth and the Japanese entrepreneurs needed to reimburse – via the Japanese hotel owners – the discontented Japanese ashore in Honolulu but were unable to do so because the two professional brokers had already transferred the money from the ticket sale to Vancouver, distributed part of it among the Japanese for show money, and were thus unable to collect it.[42]

However, for the Japanese labourers who made their way to Vancouver, the venture was anything but a failure as landing at the Canadian port fulfilled their initial desire to leave the sugar cane plantations behind and opened up new choices to settle in Vancouver or its vicinity or to move on to yet another destination. Moreover, each new arrival had CA$ 25 in their possession, not a small sum for a former sugar plantation labourer. An unintended result of this was that several new arrivals from Honolulu might have breathed an air of freedom as they spurned offers from members of the Japanese Boardinghouse Union of Vancouver to stay at one of their hotels or boardinghouses.[43]

Once established in a wage-providing job, remittances tightened migrants' ties to their hometowns or villages in a concrete manner. Despite numerous differences in their level of power, standing, and capacity to manage their affairs in the English language in their immediate habitat, Japanese labourers, entrepreneurs, and professionals abroad, including those in Hawai'i, sent remittances home, even though not everyone was able to contribute.[44] Overall, the total amount of remittances and cash sent home grew over the years. During

42 Roy, *White Man's Province*, 188; *The San Francisco Call*, 23 October 1907; *Nippu Jiji*, 8 December 1934, accessed 10 April 2019; Mackenzie King, *Report*, 55.

43 Mackenzie King, *Report*, 59.

44 For example, among the expatriates in Brazil from Tōwa cho village on Suō Ōshima Island in the 1920s through the 1930s, few reported having sent remittances to their home village. Miyamoto Tsuneichi and Okamoto Sadamu, *Tōwa chō shi* (Yamaguchi ken Ōshima gun Tōwa chō, 2004), 669.

the first five years of the government-sponsored migration system (1885–1889), the Honolulu Consul General reported a total of US$ 830,000 transferred to home prefectures. Over the following six years (1889–1894), the amount more than doubled to US$ 1,810,000.[45] In 1891 alone, the Hawaiian *dekasegi* (or temporary migrant) workers from Hiroshima prefecture contributed a total of US$ 747,000 (or an equivalent of 440,455 yen), either as remittances or cash brought home.[46] In 1905, immediately after the end of the Russo-Japanese war, the value of the contributions from abroad to Hiroshima reached nearly double the annual revenue of the prefecture. Two years later, the amount of the contributions rose to two and a half times that of the prefectural revenue.[47]

Regardless of the differences in the amounts of the contributions, the ability to contribute money to their families or communities of origin must have filled migrant workers, entrepreneurs, and settler colonists with a sense of pride, relief, or satisfaction because for many this had been the primary reason for going abroad. For the struggling families who stayed behind, these remittances could mean the difference between survival and death as the money sent by their relatives working abroad repaid debts, built houses, bought parcels of land or simply clothed members of the family during the government-sponsored migration period. Later, during the so-called private and free migration periods (1894–1900 and 1901–1907, respectively), remaining families invested a growing proportion of the remittances received in savings, while the need to pay off debt continued to be an important reason for going abroad. When injury, sickness, or death struck a family member abroad, or when a person indulged in alcohol or gambling, this could devastate the family back home. In 1897, an overwhelming majority (a total of 24 out of 30 households in 1892) of the families of Hawaiian returnees in the hamlet of Hésaka-mura in Hiroshima prefecture reported that they had barely lived from hand to mouth before the migration of a family member to Hawai'i, but that after their family member's return, they no longer struggled.[48] For the families with a higher level of assets, the remittances either sustained their standard of living or raised it even further. One such family in the same village related the story of a family member

45 Kodama Masaaki, *Nihon iminshi kenkyū josetsu* (Hiroshima: Keoisuisha, 1992), Tables 2–28, 385–386. Based on Nijū nananen chū hawai koku honpō ijūmin no keikyō, *Tūshōisan*, no. 17 (Report of Consul General of Japan in Honolulu, 1 April 1895).

46 *Hiroshima ijūshi, shiryōhen*, 70–72. See also Kodama, Tables 1–71 and 1–72, in *Nihon iminshi*, 225–227.

47 Kodama, *Nihon iminshi*, 555, 556; Hiroshimaken, *Hiroshimaken ijyūshi. Tsūshi hen* (Hiroshima: Daiichi hōki shuppan gaisha, 1993), 166.

48 Hatsukaichi shi, Hiroshima ken, Meiji 24-nen, bunsho hassō hikae. Miyauchimura (1891). Cited in Kodama, *Nihon iminshi*, 226–228.

who went to Hawai'i and contributed a total of 650 yen, remittances and cash combined. As a result, the household assets more than doubled (from 358 yen to 780 yen) over the time period in question.[49]

Remittances also benefited the communities of origin as the money invested built elementary schools, repaired village shrines and temples, and purchased rare luxuries such as pianos and gramophones that were otherwise never seen in the villages or towns of origin.[50] The town offices, local temples, and newsletters for the villagers and expatriates published or displayed handwritten lists of the donors, with their names, the amount of the donation in US or Canadian dollars and their locations abroad, whereby the latter ranged from Hawai'i to Korea to Taiwan, among many other places. The local temple on the island of Okikamuro in Yamaguchi prefecture, for example, listed donors for the rebuilding of its Ontaishido Hall, which counted 40 of its top contributors as living in Hawai'i.[51] Remittances and donations not only strengthened the translocal ties of the migrants but also raised the level of their social recognition and that of their families among the people back home to whom they were connected.

Finally, remittances helped replenish the foreign reserve of the home country. Since the late nineteenth century, politicians, policymakers, and intellectuals in Japan were constantly concerned with two issues, namely the alleged surplus population and the shortage in foreign currency reserves. Outmigration and remittances, they considered, helped alleviate both problems. It was against this background that the Japanese government first engaged in government-sponsored migration and, after the mid-1890s, in the oversight of private migration. However, the heightening tension resulting from white racism against Asians, which transmigration exacerbated, pressured Tokyo to modify and subsequently abandon these policies in the first decade of the new century.

---

49 Kodama, *Nihon iminshi*, 226–228.

50 Hiroshima ken, *Hiroshimaken ijūshi. Shiryōhen* (Hiroshima: Daiichi hōki shuppan gaisha, 1991), 74–75.

51 Miyamoto Tsuneichi, *Watashi no nihon chizu* (Tokyo: Miraisha, 2008), vol. 9 Setonaikai III Suō Ōshima: 186–187; Miyamoto and Okamoto, *Tōwa chōshi*, 679; Yasui Manami, "Hawai to kokyō no shima wo musubu: Yamaguchi ken Okikamuro jima no zasshi 'Kamuro' yori," *Ritsumeikan Studies in Language and Culture* 31, no. 1 (2019): 83–94.

4 Conclusion

A close examination of the transpacific mobility of issei labourers and the activities of a range of brokers who helped steer it, reveals a complex interplay of forces that shaped and were shaped by local, regional, and global networks and by the professional knowledge of the parties involved. It also points to the power and limitations of the nation-states that sought to regulate the mobility of those deemed undesirable into and out of their sovereign territories. Japanese immigrant hotels and boardinghouses in Honolulu and Vancouver thrived at a key juncture of this dynamism between the initiatives of migrant workers and the intensification of the nation-states' exclusionary and discriminatory regulations from the late 1880s onward. The US and Canadian ban on transmigration in 1907 and 1908 profoundly reduced the operations of the hotel businesses. Until then, the small business owners of immigrant hotels and boardinghouses profited – and fulfilled demand – by inciting issei labourers to leave Hawai'i's sugar plantations for a continental destination. Together with Japanese interpreters and paralegals and Anglo-American barristers, the owners of immigrant hotels and boardinghouses placed their legal, linguistic, and cultural knowledge at the disposal of the enterprise of transmigration. For the small – and larger – capitalists, the service to transmigrants was lucrative, albeit risky. However, for governments, attempts to curtail migrants' decision-making were also not without risks, and the agency of transpacific migrants – like that of transoceanic ones in general – undercut capital and government strategies, if in limited ways.

CHAPTER 21

Deterring Free and Deploying Interned Migrant Ukrainian Workers

The Catholic Church, the Canadian State, and the Quebec Asbestos Strikes of 1915 and 1916

Geoffrey Ewen

Abstract

The Thetford Mines asbestos strikes of 1915 and 1916 and the formation of a Western Federation of Miners (WFM) local prompted the formation of a Catholic union in opposition to the secular North American "international unions" and led to intense inter-union rivalry. The chapter examines the neglected role of Ukrainian migrants, who often were militant socialists and free thinkers. Despite comprising only a small minority among the miners, they were able to forge solidarity across ethnic, linguistic, national, political, and religious lines. Acknowledging the central role of East European workers facilitates an enhanced understanding of the strategy used by the Catholic Church and its union to encourage employers to fire and replace active free Ukrainian union supporters with French Canadian Catholics. In addition, the Canadian Federal government undermined the WFM by blocking a legal strike and by furnishing German and Austrian civilian internees, mostly recent Ukrainian immigrants, as unfree labour to one large mining company.

Keywords

Catholic social action – Catholic unions – international unions – Quebec labour – Thetford asbestos strike – Ukrainian immigrants – Western Federation of Miners

On the morning of 18 October 1915, both immigrant and Canadian-born Ukrainians working at the Jacob Asbestos Mine in Thetford Mines, Quebec, went on strike and immediately won an increase of ten cents a day. Even more impressive, their example and leadership led to the first general strike among asbestos miners and the first major wartime uprising in the munitions industry. In this case, a small percentage of migrant workers were able to establish

 | DOI:10.1163/9789004686991_022

solidarity in a multinational workforce dominated by Canadian-born employees. This surprised employers, government officials, and churchmen who expected national, religious, and ethnic differences among workers to prevent unified action. Although Ukrainians – whether Orthodox, Protestant, Eastern Catholic or Roman Catholic – made up more than 10 percent of the total labour force, they played a role that far exceeded their numbers in this instance. However, despite their impact, they have received little attention in historical research. While there were also smaller numbers of other immigrants working in the asbestos mines in Thetford Mines, Quebec, notably Polish and Italian, as well as some anglophone Canadians, most of the miners were Catholic French Canadians largely recruited from nearby farms.

At the time, the Province of Quebec was rigorously Roman Catholic and over 80 percent of the population was francophone Catholic, which rose to 86 percent Roman Catholic when anglophones were included. Many of Quebec's institutions, including educational establishments, hospitals, and social services were organized along confessional lines. To take one example, public schools were either Catholic or Protestant and the clergy had a significant presence and influence on Catholic school boards. As a result, Quebec was the one place in Canada and the United States that established a separate Catholic labour movement.

Most of the research on the asbestos strikes of 1915 and 1916 to date has focused on the Catholic Church's efforts to build a confessional trade union movement. This was the first bout of inter-union rivalry in the Quebec Archdiocese between the secular US-based "international" and the emerging Catholic labour movement – "international" unions were based in the US but had locals in Canada. While the clergy had established a small number of Catholic unions elsewhere in Quebec since 1907, it was during the war years that Catholic and national unions became a serious rival to the international unions primarily represented by the American Federation of Labor (AFL). Perhaps the principal reason for the lack of research on immigrant workers is the focus of scholars on Quebec's Quiet Revolution of the 1960s, during which society secularized and the state took over many of the functions of the Church and became involved in the economy and social policy while challenging the role of Canada's Federal government. At the time of the emergence of labour and working-class history in the 1970s, both intellectuals and historians were preoccupied with the national question, namely whether Quebec, as the only province with a francophone majority, should seek its independence from anglophone Canada or not. The national and Catholic labour movement of the early twentieth century, unique to Quebec, would lead to the formation of the Confédération des travailleurs catholiques du Canada (CTCC) in 1921, which was renamed the nationalist Confédération des syndicats nationaux (CSN) in 1960.[1]

Even migration historians have tended to ignore Ukrainian workers in Quebec, while devoting substantial attention to Ukrainian migrants to Western Canada and to cities such as Winnipeg, Manitoba, or Toronto, Ontario.[2] For Quebec, research has largely focused on the early twentieth-century Jewish and Italian migrants. Yiddish-speaking migrants and refugees had a strong presence in the garment industries and a reputation, among those involved in the labour movement, for radicalism and militancy.[3] In contrast, Italians, the next largest group, according to Bruno Ramirez had little interest in organized labour or collective action.[4] Research on both groups also reflects the fact that they mainly settled in Montreal, Quebec, Canada's largest industrial and commercial city, as scholars have largely neglected smaller industrial centres such as Thetford Mines in the Eastern Townships, an area southwest of Quebec City. Too often, Quebec historiography outside of the metropolis of Montreal has neglected the activities of migrant workers, socialists, and free thinkers.

The major primary sources for this chapter are newspaper articles, especially from *Le Canadien*, the only daily newspaper in Thetford Mines and ardent supporter of Catholic unionism and *L'Action catholique* published in Quebec City and owned by the Archdiocese of Quebec. While both provide some first-hand accounts from a Catholic viewpoint, no English or French language labour or

1 For examples of studies that focus on the national question, see Jacques Rouillard, *Les syndicats nationaux au Québec, 1900–1930* (Quebec: Presses de l'Université Laval, 1974) and Jacques Rouillard, *L'Expérience syndicale au Québec: Ses rapports avec l'état, la nation et l'opinion publique* (Montreal: vlb éditeur, 2008).

2 For recent works on Ukrainian Canadians, see Rhonda Hinther, *Perogies and Politics: Canada's Ukrainian Left, 1891–1991* (Toronto: University of Toronto Press, 2018); Kassandra Luciuk, "Reinserting Radicalism: Canada's First National Internment Operations, the Ukrainian Left, and the Politics of Redress," in *Civilian Internment in Canada: Histories and Legacies*, ed. Rhonda Hinther and Jim Mochoruk (Winnipeg: University of Manitoba Press, 2020); Kassandra Luciuk, "'More Dangerous Than Many a Pamphlet or Propaganda Book': The Ukrainian Canadian Left, Theatre, and Propaganda in the 1920s," *Labour/Le Travail* 83 (2019): 77–103; Rhonda Hinther and Jim Mochoruk, eds., *Reimagining Ukrainian Canadians: History, Politics, and Identity* (Toronto: University of Toronto Press, 2011); Vadim Kukushkin, *From Peasants to Labourers: Ukrainian and Belarusian Immigration from the Russian Empire to Canada* (Montreal: McGill-Queen's University Press, 2007).

3 For an example on wartime garment strikes, see Gerald Tulchinsky, "Corner of Pain and Anguish," in *Canada's Jews: A People's Journey* (Toronto: University of Toronto Press, 2008), 126–164.

4 Bruno Ramirez, "Workers Without a Cause: Italian Immigrant Labour in Montreal, 1880–1930," in *Arrangiarsi: The Italian Immigration Experience in Canada*, ed. Roberto Perin and Franc Sturino (Montreal: Guernica, 1989), 119–134.

socialist newspaper existed in Quebec before the appearance of the bilingual *Le monde ouvrier/The Labour World* of the AFL-affiliated Montreal Trades and Labour Council in the early spring of 1916. This weekly offered a labour perspective, albeit one in which the voices of Ukrainian socialists were absent. These sources, however, were subject to wartime censorship by a central government that feared that any publicity given to walkouts in munitions industries might spread to other locales. It is thus likely that the correspondence of the Royal Commission[5] that resolved the August 1916 strike was read into the House of Commons *Debates* to get around these restrictions. Finally, the records of the Federal Department of Labour, in particular its strike and lockout files, also proved invaluable, as did the convention proceedings of the Trades and Labour Congress of Canada, a central labour body affiliated with the AFL.

1 The Role of Ukrainians in the Asbestos Mines

This chapter examines the predominant role of Ukrainian workers in Thetford. The Ukrainians provided experienced activists, organizers, and speakers who were able, initially at least, to galvanize the whole workforce into staging a general strike. In Ukraine, many had already been members or followers of socialist and anti-clerical parties, such as the Ukrainian Social Democratic Union of the Russian Social Democratic Party and had experienced worker strikes and peasant revolts during the Russian revolution of 1905. Migrants from the Habsburg Empire had also experienced the emergence of socialist and social democratic parties, such as the Ruthenian-Ukrainian Radical Party, and unions. Significantly, many more Ukrainian migrants were radicalized in Canada by the poor living and working conditions in the new country.[6] While Catholic union promoters attacked international unions and their organizers as socialists, they were, in fact, loyal followers of AFL policies that left-wing activists considered altogether too moderate, if not reactionary, within the North American labour movement. In the case of the Thetford asbestos mines, the actions and militancy of very determined socialists, mostly Ukrainian, as

5 A Royal Commission is an official and public government inquiry to investigate and make non-binding recommendations to the government on matters of national concern. It is established by the Crown at the advice of the Prime Minister, and this reminds us that Canada was and is a monarchy, then part of the British Empire, and inherited many of its institutions.

6 Hinther, *Perogies and Politics*, 16–24, 52–53; Ian McKay, *Reasoning Otherwise: Leftists and the People's Enlightenment in Canada, 1890–1920* (Toronto: Between the Lines, 2008), 410.

well as of free thinkers drew the attention of Catholic clergy and, subsequently the state in its Canadian federal incarnation.

Asbestos was an essential wartime material used in naval and submarine construction, for making gloves for handling rapid-fire cannons and constructing filters for gas masks. It had long been known as a "miraculous" mineral that could be woven into a fireproof cloth. Thetford Mines, one of the most important asbestos mining regions in the world, was surrounded by satellite mining communities spanning an approximate forty-mile radius.[7] It was a one-industry town with five large mines and some smaller ones, mostly open-pit. The workforce grew from roughly 3,000[8] in 1914 to between 5,000 and 6,000 by 1919 and comprised French Canadians, anglophone Canadians, Eastern European immigrants, mostly Ukrainian – often described as Russian because they came from the Russian Empire – and Polish, as well as some Italians. However, the latter two groups were rarely mentioned in the sources.[9] Work was organized along gender lines and men worked in the mines, while both men and women were employed in the town's two refining mills. All the workers in the King and Johnson Mines had to buy provisions in the two company stores. Mining also involved a good deal of railway construction that employed Ukrainian workers whom the Canadian Pacific Railway often hired directly from Eastern Europe.[10]

At the beginning of the First World War, Canada had been in a depression. Since 1913, unemployment was high, business prospects uncertain, and a short-lived embargo banned asbestos exports to the US. As a result, capital stood against labour and many employers reduced wages; the Thetford miners

7 Royal Commission on Industrial Relations, Evidence given by D. H. Pennington, Quebec City, 11 June 1919, 4017–4018 (henceforth cited as "Mathers Commission" after its chair Manitoba Chief Justice Thomas Graham Mathers). Robert Armstrong, "L'industrie de l'Amiante au Québec 1878–1929," *Revue d'histoire de l'Amérique française* 33, no. 2 (1979): 187–195.

8 Jean Gérin-Lajoie, "Histoire financière de l'industrie de l'amiante," in *La grève de l'amiante*, ed. Pierre Elliot Trudeau (Montreal: Cité libre, 1956), 105.

9 While the Eastern European and Italian workers accounted for approximately 10 percent of the workforce in 1919, their number was considerably larger during the early war years. Mathers Commission, Evidence by D. H. Pennington, Quebec City, 11 June 1919, 4017–4018. In one mine, immigrants accounted for a third of the workers before the war. Kraig Schwartz, "Empowerment and Class Struggle: Factors Influencing Class Formation in the Asbestos Industry of Quebec: A Case Study of Thetford Mines," (PhD diss., University of Maine, 1997), 175. On immigrants in the nearby Asbestos mining community of Black Lake, see Clément Fortier, *Black Lake – Lac d'amiante 1882–1982*, vol. 2 (Black Lake: C. Fortier, 1986), 191–210.

10 In 1920, Ukrainians were the single largest national group in railway construction in Canada. Orest T. Martynowych, "The Ukrainian Socialist Movement in Canada 1900–1918," *Journal of Ukrainian Graduate Studies* 1, no. 1 (1976): 28.

suffered a 14 percent wage cut. The large companies colluded to set the scale, and the smaller firms followed the pattern, as did the municipal government with its own employees.[11] The companies kept wages low even as military demand increased production, encouraged fragmentation along ethnic lines to discourage the solidarity necessary for unionization, and in a hierarchical division of labour, they placed immigrants in the worst jobs. At least one of the larger companies, Jacob Asbestos, paid different wage scales to Eastern European and French-Canadian workers.[12] Soon most families were in debt and widespread and general hostility towards the employers and mine managers mounted. By late 1915, however, the economy was recovering as munitions production ramped up and men either found work or enrolled in the army. Employers' profits increased, and the labour market tightened.

While a close examination of the 1915 strikes illuminates the importance of Ukrainian socialist leadership, this was not the first indication of left-wing activity in the region. In 1915, two miners, Nicolas Tkachuk and Ivan Chaprun formed a branch of the Ukrainian Social Democratic Party (USDP) in Thetford. Established in Canada in 1914 as a socialist political party that encouraged members to join revolutionary unions such as the Industrial Workers of the World (IWW), which had a strong presence in Western Canada, the Western Federation of Miners (WFM), or the militant United Mine Workers of America (UMWA). It offered relief to unemployed and injured workers, and cultural and educational activities to its members.[13] The USDP was a revolutionary Marxist organization undergoing increasing Bolshevization after 1914.[14] The Canadian state, under the guise of nationalism and wartime exigencies, rounded up and interned many jobless left-wing young Ukrainian men from the

11 Mathers Commission, Evidence by D. H. Pennington, Quebec City, 11 June 1919, 4017–4018.

12 Fernand Dumont, "Histoire du syndicalisme dans l'industrie de l'amiante," in Trudeau, ed., *La grève de l'amiante*, 125–126.

13 Luciuk, "Reinserting Radicalism," 54–55. For some recent works on the IWW in Canada, see Duff Sutherland, "'Sentiment Very Good for the IWW': The Kootenay Logger Strikes of 1923 and 1924," *BC Studies* 206 (2020): 89–119; David Schulze, "The Industrial Workers of the World and the Unemployed in Edmonton and Calgary in the Depression of 1913–1915," *Labour/Le Travail* 25 (1990): 47–75; Lytton N. McDonnell, "Wet and Wobbly Harmonies: Music and Saloon-life in the Industrial Workers of the World, 1905–1920," *Labor History* 60, no. 6 (2019): 779–791; Evelyne Stitt Pickett, "Hoboes Across the Border: A Comparison of Itinerant Cross-Border Laborers Between Montana and Western Canada," *Montana: The Magazine of Western History* 49, no. 1 (1999): 18–31; Mikhail Bjorge, "'They Shall Not Die!' Anarchists, Syndicalists, Communists, and the Sacco and Vanzetti Solidarity Campaign in Canada," *Labour/Le Travail* 75 (2015): 43–73. "Language locals" refers to organization along linguistic lines.

14 Martynowych, "The Ukrainian Socialist Movement," 27–28.

Austro-Hungarian Empire at the beginning of the war. Although many of them hoped that the war would bring about the liberation of Ukraine from Tsarist or Habsburg rule, they formally were "enemy aliens." These rigorous national security measures radicalized many, as did the biased and blatantly pro-employer policies of the Canadian Federal as well as provincial governments.

The catalyst for the general strike was the industrial action at the Jacobs Asbestos Mine on the morning of 18 October 1915. While the Ukrainian workers immediately received an increase in their daily wage from $ 1.55 to $ 1.65,[15] the company management left the wages of other workers – mostly French Canadians – at the original rate of $ 1.55 per day.[16] The latter, expecting higher wages than immigrants, were enraged and demanded a return to pre-war wages of $ 1.75 a day and they walked out when the company management refused. What followed set the basis for solidarity across ethnic, national, political, linguistic, and religious lines which was remarkable, especially given the ethnic hierarchization of workers that prevailed across Canada at the time. In Thetford, the Ukrainian workers joined forces with the Canadian ones and raised the same demand. The Ukrainian Socialist spokespeople, with leadership qualities suggesting previous strike experience, went from mine to mine to bring their fellow pit men out and within an hour all mining operations stopped. Once the demands were drawn up, Tkachuk and Chaprun led the strikers to the two refining mills to shut them down. Next, discussions followed about closing the company stores,[17] and about extending the strike to the whole district and halting the train shipments. This first general strike in Thetford's history quickly involved more than 2,000 workers.[18] The representatives of capital were surprised by the strike's spontaneity and the rapidity with which it spread. Indeed, secrecy, timing and spontaneity were key elements for the workers to prevent employers from preparing for the walk-out. Tkachuk and Chaprun organized several large demonstrations.

Despite not having a union, on the Monday morning of 18 October 1915, the strikers left the pits idle and approached the local state: A crowd descended on the City Hall to meet with Thetford Mayor Carreau and City Councillor J. Lacasse Rousseau, an electrical contractor sympathetic to organized labour, later twice elected as a labour mayor of Thetford. The strikers formed a

15 All currency references in this chapter are in Canadian dollars (CA$).

16 *Le Canadien*, 21 October 1915.

17 *Le Soleil*, 19 October 1915; Peter Melnycky, "Badly Treated in Every Way: The Internment of Ukrainians in Quebec During the First World War," in *The Ukrainian Experience in Quebec*, ed. Alexandra Biega and Myroslav Diakowsky (Quebec: Basilian Press, 1994).

18 *Le Soleil*, 19 October 1915.

committee of 18 miners from all the mines, including Tkachuk and Chaprun representing the Ukrainians, presided over by Mayor Carreau with Councillor Rousseau as Secretary. During a large demonstration that evening, all four addressed the crowd.[19]

The strikers drew up a list of demands that included a wage increase, an end to the compulsory use of company stores, and reinstatement of all strikers. On behalf of the miners, J. L. Rousseau approached each company's managers: Like most miners, he was French Canadian and was not employed as a miner and would therefore not face discrimination in the form of losing his job. Within the space of a week, all the companies agreed to the wage increase but only gave a qualified promise to take back all striking workers. Considering this a victory, the strikers thanked Councillor Rousseau and, notably, the Canadians then thanked the Ukrainians for their support. At the same meeting, the lawyer Girouard announced that the strikers had general support in the community and, in a one-industry town, both small businesses and professionals could side with the miners. This success inspired other groups of workers and Thetford municipal workers, including members of the police and firefighters who had suffered from wage cuts at the start of the war, who threatened a strike and got a 14 percent increase.

The strikers, however, did not get all that they wished and the momentum for spontaneous pressure tactics created by the Ukrainian leaders appears to have stalled soon after the committee was formed. Its members rapidly drew up the demands with the pit workers uppermost in mind and before mill strikers, including women cobblers, could add their specific demands. Since the committee negotiators did not want to add new demands to the initial ones, Councillor Rousseau merely hoped that mill workers would also get the proposed wage increase.[20] The Ukrainian strike leaders recognized that the list of demands left much to be desired[21] as the mill workers' interests, both those of men and women, appeared as an afterthought. The direct action that some strikers proposed, such as expanding the work stoppage to the whole mining region or stopping trains, was abandoned for limited negotiations. In the following weeks, no solidarity with women, or mill workers in general, appears to have emerged, and while solidarity cut across ethnic divisions it may have worked only one way when it came to gender lines, as women mill workers went out on strike in solidarity with male miners but ultimately their demands were not backed up by the pit men. Both Ukrainian socialists and Canadian-born

19 *Le Canadien*, 21 October 1915.

20 *Le Canadien*, 21 October 1915.

21 *Le Canadien*, 27 October 1915.

miners demonstrated a hegemonic masculinity that placed men's interests ahead of women's demands.[22] Even though the cobblers were most likely unmarried and childless, their earnings were still viewed by almost all men as supplementary to male breadwinner wages. Unfortunately, the sources used in this work do not provide any indication of the views of women workers and there is no further mention of them. The current status of research also shows that the labour of women in the Thetford mills and their interconnectedness or the everyday situation of the miners' families has still not received attention. At the beginning of the strike, the socialist Ukrainians played a major role and provided an example of militancy that was subsequently emulated by French-Canadian and English-Canadian miners. It was the Ukrainians who laid the basis for solidarity within a multinational workforce, one that was religiously, linguistically, and politically diverse. This strike and the ones that followed it in Thetford in 1916 were part of the transcontinental and transatlantic uprising that witnessed revolutions and workers' revolts in North America and Europe during the years from 1915 to 1919.

On Sunday 24 October 1915, once the strike was settled, Tkachuk and Chaprun called a meeting to decide to establish a union. After first debating whether to form a union at all, those assembled went on to argue whether it should be a Catholic or an international, and, in the latter case, a socialist union. The Ukrainian strike leaders wanted a local of the Western Federation of Miners that had a history and reputation for militancy, radicalism, and serving as a revolutionary platform. At the time, it was affiliated with the AFL with jurisdiction over miners outside of coal production. The threat of a militant industrial international union galvanized one local notable into action. Publisher Alfred Frenette had recently moved to Thetford from Trois-Rivières, an industrial town on the St. Lawrence River halfway between Quebec City and Montreal. He actively campaigned for a Catholic labour organization, having been one of the founders and an executive member of the Corporation ouvrière catholique (COC) in Trois-Rivières as well as president of its typographers' union.[23] The COC, which never called out a strike in its entire existence, was founded to offer a Catholic alternative to the secular AFL. In Thetford, Frenette, who openly identified with the clergy and mining companies, had recently purchased the town's newspaper, *Le Canadien*. He feared the loss of printing contracts with the mine owners since, if an international union was established, this would force the companies to use a print shop with AFL union

22 For a discussion of masculinity among Ukrainian socialists, see Hinther, *Perogies and Politics*, 6–9.

23 *Le Canadien*, 27 October, 11, 25 November 1915.

labour.[24] At the meeting, Frenette propounded the advantages of a Catholic organization. Tkachuk and Chaprun explained the need for a union to defend workers' rights and avoid troubles with owners[25] and indicated that working-class interests were the same across religious and ethnic lines.[26] Jointly with Councillor Rousseau, they argued that miners had to be in the same organization to be effective. Their argument won the day, the assembled workers almost unanimously supported founding an international union,[27] and they pitched in to collect funds to permit Tkachuk to travel to Montreal to secure international union organizers. The next day, both parish priests in Thetford appealed to the Archdiocese for help: "The winds of revolution are blowing through our small town." one warned while the other argued that "[t]he Austrians who are the cause of the strike should be imprisoned. The employers will notice only too late that they never should have hired these immigrants in preference to our good Catholic workers."[28] Given the presence of Ukrainian socialists and the arrival of AFL organizers Arthur Martel, Narcisse Arcand and G. R. Brunet, veterans of the international unions in Quebec, the Church sent in heavy reinforcements from Quebec City.[29]

2 Enter the Quebec Catholic Church

The following week, Mgr. Paul-Eugène Roy, the auxiliary Archbishop of the Archdiocese of Quebec, and Father Maxime Fortin, the recently appointed director of the Archdiocese's l'Action sociale catholique, an organization established in 1907 to consolidate and promote Catholic causes ranging from temperance to Catholic unionism, arrived in Thetford. The Archdiocese had also founded a daily, widely circulating newspaper in 1907, entitled *L'Action sociale* – known as *L'Action catholique* from 1915 onward. Fortin would prove to

24 *Le Canadien*, 18, 25 November 1915; Archives de la Confédération des syndicats nationaux (henceforth CSNA), Flyer "Pourquoi le Journal 'Le Canadien' est contre les Mineurs Unis d'Amérique," signed by W. A. Aubert, 8 November 1915.

25 *Le Canadien*, 27 October 1915.

26 *Le Canadien*, 28 October 1915.

27 *Le Canadien*, 27 October 1915.

28 Centre d'archives de la région de Thetford Mines, Fonds de correspondance de l'Abbé Joseph-Eugène-Théophile Proulx, aumônier de l'Union catholique des ouvriers de Thetford Mines, 1915–1916, J. G. Goudreau to Mgr. P.-E. Roy, 25 October 1915; Théo. Houle to Mgr. C. O. Gagnon, 25 October 1915 (author's translations).

29 Dumont, "Histoire du syndicalisme dans l'industrie de l'amiante," 127; *Le Canadien*, 4 November, 2 December 1915.

be one of the most influential Catholic union promoters in the early years of the movement and he would become the first chaplain of the CTCC in 1921. The Church opposed international unions as secular, socialist, anti-clerical, anti-Catholic, and a threat to private property and hence Mgr. Roy warned against anything but a purely Canadian organization. At one meeting, some of the approximately 1,500 international union supporters, undoubtedly including many Ukrainians, heckled Archbishop Roy with whistling and shouts, openly expressed rage, used vulgar language, and exhibited riotous conduct – at least according to Catholic newspapers. They implied that the hecklers were not from Thetford. While the interruption may have been personal, it may also indicate a challenge to the role of the Church, which for several decades had done nothing to alleviate the plight of the workers and now intended to divide working-class forces. Even the relatively conservative AFL had called for workers to join the same unions regardless of religious differences.[30]

While the radicalism of the workers paralleled that of those in other parts of the Atlantic world and (as other chapters in this volume indicate) in Asia, Africa, and South America, the Quebec Church was a latecomer to working-class issues. Twenty-five years earlier, in 1891, the papal encyclical *Rerum novarum* had demanded, from a transatlantic perspective, that attention be paid to the social problems of industrialization.[31] However, the Quebec hierarchy – in close association with state and capital – had refused to take action. Forced to react by the strike, the Quebec Church energetically embraced only selected aspects of the encyclical, namely the protection of private property, condemnation of socialism, and avoidance of class conflict and it only slowly began to pay attention to the amelioration of workers' living and working conditions. From 1907, the clergy had organized a few Catholic unions, but none went on strike before 1919. Their aim was to destroy the international unions, and the argument used to convince workers was that strikes, the most visible sign of class conflict, would involve wage loss and thus counter the workers' material interests. A turning point in the power relations between the Church and unions came in 1917 when the clergy convinced Quebec City's national unions, long rivals of the much larger AFL and its affiliates, to become Catholic institutions. The combination of the Church's resources and a workers' movement with some history of militancy led the confessional unions to seek collective agreements and, after a delay of several years, to become more militant in the defence of their members' wages and workplace conditions.

30 *Le Canadien*, 4, 11 November 1915; *L'Action catholique*, 4 November 1915.

31 Rerum novarum or Rights and Duties of Capital and Labor, is an encyclical issued by Pope Leo XIII on 15 May 1891.

The Church hierarchy labelled French-Canadian AFL activists such as Arcand and Martel, actively practising Catholics, as irreligious and socialist. They, like others, advocated reforms such as the municipalization of public services or free and compulsory education but did not demand the replacement of the Church-dominated educational regime, a demand far too radical even for many of the international unions' members. These AFL activists considered themselves labourists and tried to avoid associating with those who were manifestly socialist.[32]

Simultaneously, religious authorities and Catholic union promoters exerted pressure on Catholic workers to resist international union drives. In December 1916, at the first anniversary of the establishment of the Catholic union in Thetford, Father Fortin insisted that Catholic union members abstain from any theory or act that ran counter to the teachings and orders of the Church.[33] Such statements prompted Montreal's *Le monde ouvier/The Labor World* in its turn to insist that the international unions were not adversaries to good religious observance.[34] Indeed, most French-Canadian workers were practising Catholics and even Alfred Charpentier, who later played a leading role in the Catholic labour movement as president of the CTCC, stated that he would not have tolerated any criticism of his religious convictions when he had been a member of an international union.[35] When Father Fortin declared before the Royal Commission on Industrial Relations in Quebec City in 1919 that AFL organizers were preaching revolutionary, anti-religious, and anti-clerical doctrines, the international unions' Quebec and Lévis Trades and Labor Council was indignant and demanded to know exactly whom he had in mind.[36] One enraged worker even wrote to Chicoutimi's Bishop Lapointe in September 1917 defending both his faith and his membership in an international union.[37]

While Ernest Bélanger, the president of the Conseil général des unions ouvrières de Québec, a National Union Labour Council close to clerical union promoters, on a visit to Thetford in 1916 claimed that international union

32 On labourism, see Craig Heron, "Labourism and the Canadian Working Class," *Labour/Le Travail* 13 (1984): 45–76.

33 *Le monde ouvrier/The Labor World*, 23 December 1916.

34 *Le monde ouvrier/The Labor World*, 26 May 1917.

35 Alfred Charpentier, *Cinquante ans d'action ouvrière: Les mémoires d'Alfred Charpentier* (Quebec: Presses de l'Université Laval, 1971), 15.

36 CSNA, Box 1650, File Correspondance de l'abbé Maxime Fortin, aumônier de la CTCC 1917–1921, Gaud. DesBiens to Maxime Fortin, 12 June 1919; for Fortin's statement see Mathers Commission, Evidence by Maxime Fortin, Quebec City, 11 June 1919, 4061.

37 Robert Parisé, *Le fondateur du syndicalisme catholique au Québec, Mgr Eugène Lapointe: Sa pensée et son action syndicales* (Montreal: Presses de l'Université du Québec, 1978), 42.

leaders were non-believers who attacked the clergy,[38] most French-Canadian union organizers remained practising Catholics and only a few were free thinkers.[39] It is among the immigrants that one would find socialists, perhaps anarchists among the Italian miners, and larger numbers who were free thinkers and who could be militantly anti-clerical. Certainly, socialism and free thinking were on the rise in the Canadian Ukrainian community.

The Ukrainian community in Canada was one in which intense religious controversies and violent divisions between the Orthodox, Protestant, Eastern Catholic rite, and Roman Catholic churches were played out – disputes that were also expressed in print. Significantly, serious tensions emerged between Ukrainian Catholic immigrants and French-Canadian Catholic bishops. While the immigrant socialists might have largely been free thinkers, atheists, agnostics, or have unusual spiritual ideas, many of the religious also vociferously protested the role of the Quebec Roman Catholic Church in industrial affairs. The Socialist newspaper *Robochyi narod* (Working People), initially published in Montreal and later in Winnipeg, complained about the clergy's indifference to the plight of unemployed workers. Certainly, socialists and Ukrainian Protestants accused the clergy of colluding with capitalists and serving the interests of their employers.[40]

During the meetings in the aftermath of the Thetford strike, Mgr. Roy and Father Fortin, for their part, were also willing to use invectives and shoving. The day after their meeting was disrupted, they stormed into an international union meeting and Roy forced his way past workers blocking his path. In a raucous affair, they confronted the organizers and eventually ordered workers who did not wish to join a Catholic union to leave the hall. He may have hoped that those remaining would favour a Catholic union as only some 200 workers, perhaps one-eighth of those attending, left. However, as later occurrences testified, this was not a good poll of Catholic union support.[41]

38 Schwartz, "Empowerment and Class Struggle," 216 fn. 3.

39 Free thinkers were relatively rare in francophone Quebec, especially outside of Montreal. For an example of a free-thinking journalist in Montreal, see Andrée Lévesque, *Éva Circé-Côté: Libre-penseuse 1871–1949* (Montreal: Les éditions du remue-ménage, 2010).

40 Orest T. Martynowych, *Ukrainians in Canada: The Formative Period, 1891–1924* (Edmonton: Canadian Institute of Ukrainian Studies Press, 1991); on religious turmoil, see Chapters 7, 8 and 14, and on accusations of supporting employers, see 388–389.

41 La Renaissance catholique au Canada, Études spéciales, L'Action sociale et catholique de Mgr. Paul-Eugène Roy, III. Le syndicalisme ouvrier, accessed 10 February 2022, http://crc-canada.net/études-spéciales/action-catholique-quebec/mgr-roy.html.

In the following weeks, both the *Union catholique des ouvriers mineurs* (UCOM) and a local of the WFM were formally established.[42] Some of the Catholic union's leaders were miners who had not participated in the recent strike.[43] Father Théodore Proulx, a priest, was appointed as chaplain to the union. This development marked the start of open warfare between the rival movements, and the beginning of large-scale inter-union rivalry, during which Chaplain Proulx did his utmost to destroy the WFM local. He privately urged mine owners to openly support the UCOM and fire influential members of the international union, albeit only a few at a time so as not to arouse opposition from fellow workers. Father Houle of Saint-Maurice parish in Thetford approvingly noted that the Ukrainians at the Jacob Asbestos mine, including the most active union leaders, were being fired and replaced. Indeed, Nicolas Tkachuk and Ivan Chaprun may have been among those fired as they disappeared from the record. When the WFM demanded a daily wage increase of 75 cents, Proulx had the Catholic union petition for a 25 cents per day raise to forestall the internationalists and undermine the higher demand. The companies obliged and later adopted the smaller increase. In February 1916, when Ukrainian workers demanded the reinstatement of fired union leaders, the chaplain provided UCOM members as strikebreakers to the Jacob Asbestos company at the request of the mine manager. All these steps were taken with the full knowledge of the Church hierarchy and were sanctioned by the l'Action sociale catholique of the Archdiocese.[44]

Catholic union promoters were aware that the international union had the support of workers who were neither Catholic nor Canadian[45] and they claimed that the "foreign" element was the active strike organizers. The clergy feared the militant Ukrainians and assumed that they would spread socialism, class consciousness, and militancy. Already in November 1915, Mgr. Roy had declared that an international union would mean an increase in foreign or migrant workers and that the "Canadiens" – meaning Catholic French Canadians – would be forced to side with them or leave their homes and city.[46] As a result, replacing Ukrainian workers and forcing them to leave Thetford

42 Sr. M.-Amadeus Welton, *Mgr Paul-Eugène Roy Archevêque de Québec* (Quebec: Éditions de l'action Catholique 1941), 159; Rouillard, *Syndicats Nationaux*, 196; *Le Canadien*, 4 November 1915.

43 Schwartz, "Empowerment and Class Struggle," 198.

44 Dumont, "Histoire du syndicalisme dans l'industrie de l'amiante," 128–129; *Le Canadien*, 4 November 1915, notes that the two Ukrainian leaders have troubles and that all that is left for them is to pack up and leave. They then disappear from the records.

45 *L'Action catholique*, 26 October 1915.

46 *L'Action catholique*, 4 November 1915.

became a central part of the Church's campaign to destroy international unionism.

To summarize: Throughout 1916, the WFM, attractive to an ethnically diverse workforce with 900 members enjoyed the support of most organized miners in Thetford compared to 200 to 300 for the Catholic union, with the latter representing a mere minority of the French Canadians.[47] Hence, the international union had more support even among French Canadians and shared workplace experience provided solidarity across ethnic and linguistic lines within the WFM. The new WFM local prepared a list of demands that included union recognition, a closed shop, a system by which workers' union dues were automatically checked off by the companies and remitted to the local, an eight-hour day, and an increase in the daily wage from $ 1.75 to $ 2.50.[48] It also prepared for another strike, all in the face of the active campaign by the UCOM to undermine its efforts.[49]

3 Enter the State in the Form of the Secular Federal Government

At this point, the Federal Canadian state intervened by passing new labour legislation. With growing unrest in munitions factories, the government attempted to prevent, discourage, or at least regulate strikes. On 23 March 1916, it extended the Industrial Disputes Investigation Act (IDIA) of 1907 to all war-related industries. The IDIA was the main piece of Federal legislation governing labour disputes and imposed compulsory conciliation before a legal strike or lock-out in public utilities, such as gas, water and electric services, and in industries considered essential to Canada's economic development such as railways, coal, and metal mining. The act required a tripartite conciliation board, with one member chosen by employers and another by workers, who were then to agree on a third to act as an impartial chair. These conciliation boards investigated disputes and could issue a public report with non-binding recommendations.

47 The degree of support for the WFM is disputed. Narcisse Arcand claimed that there were 900 members after checking the books of the local whereas Kraig Schwartz concluded that this was inflated since no more than 350 paid dues in 1916. Schwartz, "Empowerment and Class Struggle," 220, fn. 10. In this context, it is important to note that the payment of dues is not a reliable gage of support as it was notoriously difficult to collect dues before the automatic check-off, even amongst workers who would solidly back their local or a strike.

48 *Montreal Star*, 26 August 1916; Dumont, "Histoire du syndicalisme dans l'industrie de l'amiante," 128.

49 *Le monde ouvrier/The Labor World*, 5 August 1916.

While the boards attempted to resolve disputes, organized labour was ambivalent. Some argued that the process could prove useful in certain circumstances if amended to remove biases favouring employers; others opposed the act and advocated for its abolition because it often worked to the employer's advantage. Although work stoppages were illegal while the conciliation board conducted its investigation, there were no sanctions against employers who dismissed union activists or supporters, or who changed the terms of employment. Boards also tended to accept employer refusals to deal with unions, did not recommend direct negotiations, union recognition or automatic dues check-off, and frequently encouraged settlements with committees of the firm's employees, thereby bypassing labour organizations altogether while they usually restricted their efforts to merely finding a compromise on wages and hours. The effectiveness of strikes often depended on timing and an element of surprise, and the IDIA cancelled both of these advantages.[50]

The WFM local in Thetford was willing to comply with the IDIA. In June 1916, the Department of Labour sent a fair-wages officer to try to mediate, the first step when a dispute seemed imminent. The despatched officer, Narcisse Arcand, had long been an effective organizer for the United Brotherhood of Carpenters and Joiners (UBCJ). Rebuffed by the companies, Arcand explained to the WFM how to apply for conciliation under the IDIA. The Department of Labour also warned that non-compliance would result in the rigid enforcement of the Criminal Code penalties provided by the act. Two weeks later, the Department of Labour suddenly removed Arcand following a complaint from the mine companies' lawyer. Arcand believed this was motivated by a desire to prevent conciliation and, aghast at the degree of employer influence over the government, he resigned and returned to his former position as UBCJ organizer.[51]

Next, the Federal Minister of Labour, Thomas Crothers, personally intervened. Meeting with mine owners and union representatives, Crothers asked the miners to drop most of their demands, arguing that an IDIA board could not deal with either recognition or dues check-off and that there was no advantage in seeking a new increase of 50 cents when the company had recently granted one of 25 cents. When the local made a formal request for an IDIA

50 On the IDIA, see Jeremy Webber, "Compelling Compromise: Canada Chooses Conciliation over Arbitration, 1900–1907," *Labour/Le Travail* 28 (1991): 15–57; Judy Fudge and Eric Tucker, *Labour Before the Law: The Regulation of Workers' Collective Action in Canada, 1900–1948* (Toronto: University of Toronto Press, 2001).

51 *Le monde ouvrier/The Labor World*, 30 September 1916; Trades and Labour Congress of Canada (henceforth TLCC), *Proceedings*, 1916, 107.

board, Crothers suggested that a committee of employees from each mine meet separately with the mine managers, which was the process favoured by the companies. The minister assured the local that WFM secretary and municipal councillor J. L. Rousseau, their principal spokesperson, could accompany each committee.[52] While the union considered this approach to be more appropriate for unorganized workers, it nevertheless complied. However, despite Crothers' promise, some companies refused to admit Rousseau to the fruitless discussions.[53] When the WFM made a second request under the IDIA, it asked for a single conciliation board to deal with the six employers as a group. In fact, in other industries, a single conciliation board had dealt with unions whose members worked in 500 different shops. The Department of Labour refused this proposal on the grounds that the companies could not agree on a single representative, although, as the WFM pointed out, the six companies under three controlling capital interests[54] had formed a united front by hiring a single lawyer to act on their behalf. The union concluded that Crothers was willing to reinterpret the IDIA to suit capital and that his opinion neither conformed to the spirit nor the letter of the law. Rousseau warned the Labour Department that the union leadership had proven its patriotism by preventing a strike for as long as they had and might be unable to postpone a strike any further.[55]

Never far in the background, the Catholic union did its utmost to undermine both the WFM and the IDIA: In July 1916, the UCOM formed committees of workers from each company to negotiate with their respective employers. WFM members thwarted this attempt by attending the UCOM meeting in large numbers. The 1,200 miners present at the gathering nominated three representatives to speak to all the companies on their behalf, including WFM secretary J. L. Rousseau and an Eastern European immigrant.[56] UCOM's Father Théodore Proulx urged UCOM members to resist international union appeals and to remain at work in the event of a walkout. The Catholic union declared

52 F. A. Acland, Deputy-Minister of Labour, and Clerk of the Commission of Conciliation and Enquiry to J. L. Rousseau, 24 July 1916, in Canada, House of Commons, *Debates*, 4 May 1917, 1115.

53 J. L. Rousseau to the Clerk of the Commission of Conciliation and Inquiry, 28 July 1916, in Canada, House of Commons, *Debates*, 4 May 1917, 1115–1117.

54 Canada, Chambre des communes, *Débats*, 4 May 1917, 1153–1154; TLCC, *Proceedings*, 1916, 107; Canada, House of Commons, *Debates*, 4 May 1917, 1119.

55 J. L. Rousseau to the Clerk of the Commission of Conciliation and Enquiry, 28 July 1916, in Canada, Chambre des communes, *Débats*, 4 May 1917, 1148. It is not clear whether Crothers had ever informed the union that it had to apply for a separate board to deal with each company. Canada, House of Commons, *Debates*, 4 May 1917, 1119.

56 *Le Canadien*, 3 August 1916.

that its members were satisfied with the conditions and were grateful for what the employers had already done for the workers. Furthermore, the UCOM resolved that, in case of a strike, they would support the employers.[57]

At this point, the Federal government went even further in aiding one mining company. It furnished the Asbestos Corporation with a new pool of labour, comprising 250 Austrian and German civilian internees, mostly if not all Ukrainian speakers, who were escorted to Thetford by the militia to work under the supervision of 50 armed private detectives – i.e., one guard for every five workers.[58] These "Austrian" and "German" internees were, in fact, subjects of the Habsburg and Hohenzollern emperors and many were opposed to these empires. While Minister of Labour Crothers claimed that they were sent because of a shortage of labour, the union saw this as a deliberate attempt at intimidation and the initial reception of the new recruits was hostile. Montreal's *Le monde ouvrier/The Labor World* called for their removal, warning that "enemy aliens" as miners that were charged with handling dynamite and other explosives during wartime might present a security threat.[59] The indignation of the local community, which had sent 200 volunteers to fight with the Canadian Expeditionary Force in Europe, prompted Narcisse Arcand, back in Thetford to help the union, to declare at a protest meeting that "the men might just as well get their guns and fight against alien enemies at home as go to Europe to do their fighting."[60]

However, the position of the civilian internees soon changed and historian Kassandra Luciuk showed that internment was used in a very selective manner. Approximately 4,000 Ukrainians out of a total immigrant population of 170,000 were interned, generally comprising young, single, vulnerable, and often unnaturalized individuals. Many, impoverished and unemployed, were disappointed with their Canadian experience, working in mining, lumber, manufacturing, and railway construction under harsh and dangerous conditions, earning poor wages, and being subject to employment insecurity, they had frequently been rounded up while engaged in protesting unemployment

57 Dumont, "Histoire du syndicalisme dans l'industrie de l'amiante," 112, 129–131; TLCC, *Proceedings*, 1916, 176.

58 *Le monde ouvrier/The Labor World*, 15 July 1916, 30 September 1916; Canada, House of Commons, *Debates*, 4 May 1917, 1119. On internment during the First World War in Canada, see Bohdan S. Kordan, *Enemy Aliens: Prisoners of War: Internment in Canada during the Great War* (Montreal/Kingston: McGill-Queen's University Press, 2002); Frances Swyripa and John Hern Thompson, eds., *Loyalties in Conflict: Ukrainians in Canada During the Great War* (Edmonton: Canadian Institute of Ukrainian Studies, 1983).

59 *Le monde ouvrier/The Labor World*, 15 July 1916.

60 TLCC, *Proceedings*, 1916, 111.

and the lack of relief. Essentially, internment targeted proletarian and radical Eastern Europeans and denied them their civil rights and liberties, thereby radicalizing large numbers of Ukrainian speakers that were not yet politicized. Ukrainian Social Democratic Party members were among the interned in many of the camps, including the Spirit Lake Camp in Quebec where internees cut wood and cleared the land. The USDP organized reading groups and the camps provided fertile ground for the building of a class-conscious socialist movement as it was poor – in fact often brutal – treatment by guards that led to camp strikes.[61] At Spirit Lake, authorities left strikers without heat or rations and, once released on parole to an employer, they could be threatened with re-internment or prison if they did not work.[62] Thus, unsurprisingly, they turned to industrial unions with a reputation for militancy. The use of internment may be viewed as the start of state persecution of ethnic radicals in Canada,[63] which marks the advent of Canada's long history of organized repression of communism and the working-class left.

In Thetford, sympathy soon developed between union members and the internees, many of whom had union cards and did not want to scab. They expressed their dissatisfaction with the dangerous mining conditions that resulted in at least one death among them, and they wanted to return to the internment camp. The companies, already deducting the cost of travel from the internment camp from their pay, threatened to withhold food if they joined the union.[64] Ethnic ties played a role as most of the internees and many of the strikers were Ukrainian speakers. In this case, workplace contact and the shared experience of obnoxious company tactics and dangerous working conditions produced solidarity not just amongst those who spoke Ukrainian but among workers from numerous national backgrounds. The deployment of the interned civilians thus increased the number of socialists in Thetford.

On 3 August 1916, still without a conciliation board, some 900 members of the WFM stopped production at six mines, despite facing the mine owners, the government, and the Catholic union. Without going through the IDIA process, the strike was illegal. The companies refused to negotiate with the WFM, and the Catholic UCOM asked the owners to reopen the mines and supplied strikebreakers. After several weeks, the WFM had to surrender and it offered to

61 Luciuk, "Reinserting Radicalism," 49–69.

62 Bohdan S. Kordan, *No Free Man: Canada, the Great War, and the Enemy Alien Experience* (Montreal/Kingston: McGill-Queen's University Press, 2016), 185, 211; for the Spirit Lake Camp strike, see Melnycky, "Badly Treated in Every Way."

63 Hinther and Mochoruk, *Civilian Internment in Canada*, 2, 8.

64 Schwartz, "Empowerment and Class Struggle," 225; TLCC, *Proceedings*, 1916, 107–109.

return to work if there was no discrimination against the strikers. Determined to be rid of the strike leaders, the company waited for a complete capitulation, effectively imposing a lock-out, and then drew up a blacklist.[65] In the end, the state in the form of the Federal government in Ottawa facilitated the outcome desired by the capitalist companies. C. A. E. Blanchet, a one-person Royal Commission, was dispatched by the Department of Labour to end the strike.[66] As with an IDIA board, a Royal Commission could compel people to testify but in practice, Blanchet acted as a mediator. As the strike was collapsing, he arranged for the companies to sign a single "agreement" that was in their words "made with the employees individually." It was signed by twelve miners, two from each mine, none representing a union. One lawyer, J. A. Lane, signed for all companies.[67] Minister of Labour Crothers described the settlement as "perfectly satisfactory."[68] However, WFM secretary J. L. Rousseau felt that the minister had deceived the miners. The Federal government had postponed the strike, twice refused to appoint conciliation boards under the IDIA, supplied interned aliens as labour to one of the companies, forced the miners into an illegal walkout, and helped work out a settlement on the employers' terms that ignored the union.[69]

4 Conclusion

This defeat had long-term consequences, as worker organization and militancy took decades to fully recover. The 1916 strike left a legacy of bitterness and division in Thetford. While the WFM and the Catholic union both survived for some years, the level of labour organization in Thetford declined after 1916 and then virtually disappeared in the 1920s, like many other union locals.[70] Asbestos miners would have to wait until 1949 before there would be another large and significant general strike.

The Ukrainian workers in Thetford – like all of their co-workers regardless of their religious affiliation and ethnic culture – not only faced the opposition

65 Dumont, "Histoire du syndicalisme dans l'industrie de l'amiante," 112, 129–131; TLCC, *Proceedings*, 1916, 176.

66 *Le monde ouvrier/The Labor World*, 23 September 1916.

67 Library and Archives Canada (henceforth LAC), Strike and Lockout files, RG 27, vol. 304, Strike 5, contains a copy of the agreement.

68 For Crothers' justification and labour's reaction, see TLCC, *Proceedings*, 1916, 107–109.

69 *Le monde ouvrier/The Labor World*, 23 September 1916.

70 Dumont, "Histoire du syndicalisme dans l'industrie de l'amiante," 128–136.

of the employers, notoriously intransigent in the mining industry, but also of a government that favoured capital and of a Church that undermined working-class self-organization. While in the following decade little union activity could take place, the repression may have contributed to a legacy of class consciousness and direct action. To give one example, in the early 1920s, 400 unorganized miners fed up with one obnoxious mine manager forced him onto a train out of town and, when he tried to return with 40 armed guards, the strikers offered large-scale resistance, even raiding the local hardware stores for guns. It was only through the intervention of local notables who persuaded the manager and his guards to leave for good that violence was prevented.[71]

This period of conflict has usually been studied because it marked the first major inter-union conflict between an embryonic Catholic labour movement and the long-established international unions. In this context, it is important to note that it was not only the AFL that prompted the Church's offensive but rather it was the presence of determined socialists, mostly Ukrainian, that upset the Catholic clergy. The Thetford asbestos mines and the workers in them were part of a worldwide war, of socialist and labour developments in Europe and North America, and of the Catholic Church's attempt to destroy and replace international and secular unions in Quebec. The Church's reactionary actions during these incidents even appear at odds with some of the elements of support expressed for workers' organizations and improved living and working conditions in *Rerum novarum*. Despite the appeals made in this document, the only elements of the encyclical that the Quebec Church vigorously retained were the condemnation of socialism and class conflict. These events demonstrated workers' agency as did other activities around the globe.

71 LAC, Strike and Lockout files, RG 27, vol. 330, strike 22.

CHAPTER 22

A "Special Category of Women" in Austria and Internationally

Migrant Women Workers, Trade Union Activists, and the Textile Industry, 1960s to 1980s

Veronika Helfert

Abstract

At the beginning of the 1960s, Austria joined Western and Northern European states in recruiting temporary migrant workers. While the European "guestworker" and migrant labour regimes have been subject to multiple studies in the last 40 years, migrant women have rarely been at the centre of these investigations, although their specific issues have comprised a facet of the international labour movement since the 1970s. Female migrant workers faced a double marginalization in the labour movement, both as migrants and as women. By analysing printed source material, archival documents, and interviews with women trade unionists, this chapter examines this specific double marginalization; how gender, class, and ethnicity shaped the labour activism of domestic and migrant working women; and how the international, national, and local levels interacted in the context of the deindustrialization of the Austrian textile industry.*

Keywords

Austria – deindustrialization – gender – labour migration – textile industry – trade unions

In 1981, in the International Labour Organization (ILO) news bulletin *Women at Work*, Yugoslav politician Vida Tomšič[1] pointed out that over 30 percent of

* This chapter is part of a project that has received funding from the European Research Council (ERC) under the European Union's Horizon 2020 research and innovation programme (Grant agreement No. 833691 – ZARAH). I would like to thank Susan Zimmermann and the rest of the ZARAH Team (https://zarah-ceu.org/team-members/) for their comments.

1 Mateja Jeraj, "Vida Tomšič," in *A Biographical Dictionary of Women's Movements and Feminisms: Central, Eastern and South Eastern Europe, 19th and 20th Centuries*, ed. Francisca

the Yugoslav workers employed abroad were women. She went on to show how women workers differed from their male counterparts by region of origin, type of education, and age structure, and outlined various measures that would be taken in Yugoslavia to support these women – and their families – before leaving and after returning: "Special attention is devoted to the specific problems of women in connection with maternity."[2] The memories of Slobodanka Kudlaček-Ritopečki, a Serbo-Croatian interpreter at the Chamber of Labour for Vienna in the 1970s correspond with these assertions. On the one hand, pregnancy was a period that made migrant women workers particularly vulnerable to exploitation,[3] and on the other hand, policies related to the raising of children were a particularly harsh instrument of the Austrian labour migration regime. "But as an individual woman, there wasn't much you could do," she noted on this pivotal issue.[4] Kudlaček-Ritopečki arrived in 1972, at the peak of workers' recruitment abroad for work in Austrian industries such as construction or the textile and garment sector with a large proportion of women being hired.[5] While agreements to promote the rights of migrant workers as well as (working) women were already being advanced at the international level in the 1960s,[6] an increased awareness of the differences between women became prominent in the late 1970s and early 1980s[7] – which also was, probably not coincidentally, the United Nations (UN) Decade for Women.[8] As historian Eileen Boris argued recently, it was in this period that a "construction of a category within a category, 'women in developing countries,' as the

de Haan, Krasimira Daskalova, and Anna Loutfi (Budapest: Central European University Press, 2006), 575–579.

2 Vida Tomšič, "Women as Migrant Workers from Yugoslavia," *Women at Work: An ILO News Bulletin,* no. 1 (1981): 12.

3 Institut für Historische Sozialforschung (IHSF), Archive, Chamber of Labour, Vienna, "Ausschüsse für Frauenarbeit und Familienpolitik, 1963–1994," Minutes of a meeting between trade unionists and functionaries of the Chambers of Labour concerning the consultation on the amendment of the Maternity Protection Act, 9 November 1971, 11–13.

4 Slobodanka Kudlaček-Ritopečki, interview by Veronika Helfert, 18 November 2021, transcript with the author, audio, 22:16. All translations from German into English are by the author.

5 Eleonore Kofman et al., *Gender and International Migration in Europe: Employment, Welfare and Politics* (London/New York: Routledge, 2000), 3–8.

6 Dorothy Sue Cobble, *For the Many: American Feminists and the Global Fight for Democratic Equality* (Princeton, NJ/Oxford: Princeton University Press, 2021), 339–379.

7 Eleonore Kofman, "Female 'Birds of Passage' a Decade Later: Gender and Immigration in the European Union," *International Migration Review* 33, no. 2 (1999): 269–270.

8 Eileen Boris, Dorothea Hoehtker, and Susan Zimmermann, "Introduction" to *Women's ILO: Transnational Networks, Global Labour Standards and Gender Equity, 1919 to Present* (Leiden: Brill, 2018), 10–11.

other of the woman worker" became hegemonic in ILO policy papers.[9] The assessments of activists in and from Yugoslavia,[10] both in Austria as well as at the international level indicated that issues affecting women workers, in general, proved even more precarious for migrant women and were purposefully instrumentalized by migration regimes such as that in Austria. Female immigrant workers faced a double marginalization as migrants and as women, not only in the labour market but also in relation to trade unions and the state. The concept of double marginalization is based on the insight that categories of social inequalities are "interlocking" and "interactive";[11] an understanding that has produced rich theoretical and empirical scholarship since the 1980s under the term *intersectionality*.[12]

While the European "guestworker" and migrant labour regimes have been subject to multiple studies in the last 40 years, migrant women have rarely been at the centre of investigation, although their specific issues have been present in the international labour movement since the 1970s. This chapter explores the relationship between women migrant workers from mainly Yugoslavia and, to a lesser degree, Turkey and Austrian trade unionists from the 1960s to the 1980s, a period first shaped by rising labour demand and subsequently by rationalization and deindustrialization. Moreover, by analysing printed source materials such as company newspapers, minutes from the Trade Union Women's Congress, and yearly reports of trade union branches, as well as archival documents and by conducting interviews with women trade unionists, the interconnections of the local, national, and international levels will be examined. This chapter's first section depicts labour migration and the effect of deindustrialization on the workforce and trade unionism in the Austrian textile and garment industry. It highlights the working conditions in a sector that

9 Eileen Boris, *Making the Woman Worker: Precarious Labor and the Fight for Global Standards, 1919–2019* (New York: Oxford University Press, 2019), 91.

10 The perspective of the sending country will not be discussed. See, however, Brigitte Le Normand, *Citizens without Borders: Yugoslavia and Its Migrant Workers in Western Europe* (Toronto: University of Toronto Press, 2021).

11 Evelyn Nakano Glenn, "From Servitude to Service Work: Historical Continuities in the Racial Division of Paid Reproductive Labor," *Signs* 18, no. 1 (1992): 1.

12 While authors in the US such as bell hooks or Angela Davis already voiced their critique of feminist and Marxist writers as excluding the histories and experiences of Black and marginalized women, the term "intersectionality" was introduced by Kimberlé Crenshaw in 1989 in "Demarginalizing the Intersection of Race and Sex: A Black Feminist Critique of Antidiscrimination Doctrine, Feminist Theory, and Antiracist Politics," *University of Chicago Legal Forum,* no. 5 (1989): 139–167. On the development of the term see: Sara Salem, "Intersectionality and its Discontents: Intersectionality as Traveling Theory," *European Journal of Women's Studies* 25, no. 4 (2018): 403–418.

was overwhelmingly dependent on women and migrant workers. The second section places the Austrian labour migration regime ("*Gastarbeitsregime*")[13] in a historical and international context. In this context, the Austrian model of regulating temporary contract work,[14] with its strong involvement of trade unions and workers' representatives, proves to be particularly protectionist. The ILO's debates on the special protection of female labour migrants since the mid-1970s hardly appear in the policies. This is no coincidence, as the following section argues, given that labour migration has been misconstrued as male with the result of marginalizing migrant women in policies, trade union movements, and, ultimately, in historiographic discourse. Our analysis of the activities of Austrian women trade unionists in works councils and as top-level functionaries in the Austrian Textile, Garment, and Leather Workers Union (Gewerkschaft Textil, Bekleidung, Leder; TBL) as well as the women's local and national departments of the Austrian Trade Union Federation (Österreichischer Gewerkschaftsbund, ÖGB) reveals that especially those from regions with a significant textile industry, particularly in Vorarlberg, spoke out very early against the admission of foreign workers. They identified the "guestworker problem" as one of the central problems of working women. This section traces organized labour's vacillation between institutional exclusion and the selective inclusion of migrant (male) workers as "guestworker spokespersons." The double marginalization in the labour movement in conjunction with the structural racism of the Austrian labour migration regime reduced activism to precarious spaces as will be explored in the last section.

1 Labour Migration, Deindustrialization and Rationalization in the Textile Industry

The Austrian textile industry centred in Vorarlberg, Lower Austria, and Tyrol had a long history of internal and international labour migration since the nineteenth century.[15] After the Second World War, the economic situation

13 Kenneth Horvath, *Die Logik der Entrechtung: Sicherheits- und Nutzendiskurse im österreichischen Migrationsregime* (Göttingen: V&R Unipress, 2014), 129–159.

14 Mahua Sarkar, "Introduction" to *Work Out of Place* (Berlin/Boston: De Gruyter Oldenbourg, 2018), 3.

15 Sylvia Hahn, "Migration und Ökonomie: Über den Zusammenhang von Industrialisierung, Deindustrialisierung und Zuwanderung," in *"Vom selben Schlag": Migration und Integration im niederösterreichischen Industrieviertel*, ed. Thomas Schmidinger (Wiener Neustadt: Verein Alltag Verlag, 2008), 15–31.

and labour market conditions were tense. Since the Austrian state considered young, unskilled women as a surplus population that was not needed for the economy, these women subsequently looked for work in Switzerland, Germany, or Great Britain.[16] Due to higher wages and better job opportunities, many of those who lived in the Austrian-Swiss and Austrian-German border regions crossed the border (*Grenzgänger*).[17] Both locally and in global perspective, the textile industry's workforce was shaped by migration. To maximize profits, companies in the Global North, initially in the 1950s and 1960s, sought to bring in temporary migrant labour, then changed to outsource part of the production to countries such as Yugoslavia or Hungary and, in a further step, relocated production to the Global South.[18]

The working conditions in the labour-intensive textile industry became increasingly strenuous in the face of relentless economic pressure. The textile industry was characterized by numerous high occupational strains: heavy physical work, often one-sided exposure, noise, dust, the stress involved in doing piecework and night as well as shift work – and it was also one of the worst-paying industries.[19] Piecework wages were common in many companies, as were complicated systems that calculated wages based on performance, length of employment, absenteeism, etc. According to a study from the 1980s, far more women than men worked on piecework wages, as indicated by a distribution of 66 percent in contrast to 21 percent.[20]

The piecework system rested on competition among workers that often created boundaries based on gender, age, or origin. Austrian workers, for example, referred to temporary migrant workers as "piecework pushers" (*Akkordtreiber*) because they knew they would only be doing the work for a short time and

---

16 IIHS Amsterdam, ILO 93, Report on requirements on foreign manpower and on resources available for emigration in European countries, 7. With thanks to Olga Gnydiuk. Ute Sonnleitner, Anita Ziegenhofer, and Karin M. Schmidlechner, "Aufbruch als Chance: Steirische Arbeitsmigration in die Schweiz 1945–1955," *Jahrbuch für Geschichte des ländlichen Raumes*, no. 11 (2014): 56.

17 Felix Butschek, "Österreichische Arbeitskräfte im Ausland," *Monatsberichte des österreichischen Instituts für Wirtschaftsforschung* 37, no. 10 (1964): 389–394.

18 Beth English, "Global Women's Work: Historical Perspectives on the Textile and Garment Industries," *Journal of International Affairs* 67, no. 1 (2013): 67–82; Chiara Bonfiglioli, *Women and Industry in the Balkans: The Rise and Fall of the Yugoslav Textile Sector* (London: I. B. Tauris, 2020), 87–95.

19 Dieter Bichlbauer, Ingrid Frassine, and Angelika Laburda, *Arbeitsbedingungen und Gesundheit der Arbeiterinnen und Arbeiter in der Textilindustrie* (Vienna: Federal Ministry of Labour and Social Affairs, 1988), 8–12.

20 Bichlbauer, Frassine, and Laburda, *Arbeitsbedingungen*, 164.

therefore wanted to get the most money out of it.[21] The resentment of Austrian workers in this regard did not necessarily correspond to reality – not least because many labour migrants only returned to their countries of origin after long periods or ultimately remained in Austria. (Austrian) workers in the industry protested against evaluation systems that were not comprehensible, targets that could not be met due to technical problems and poor organization, errors in accounting, and individual discrimination. Abuses regularly occurred, and it was not always easy for works councils to determine whether the wages paid correctly corresponded to the performed work.[22] Due to the high level of physical exertion that the work entailed, older female workers experienced a drop in performance and thus lower wages that were only rarely compensated through "loyalty bonuses." This contrasts with the experiences of older male colleagues as men could more easily have careers within the company or be transferred to less strenuous jobs once their performance decreased. Furthermore, they generally tended to work in departments with hourly rather than piecework wages.[23] Many textile companies worked with two-shift or three-shift schedules and working hours were sometimes scheduled to accommodate the care duties of women workers.[24] In regions where childcare facilities were inadequate, as in Vorarlberg, the shift system offered many families the opportunity to share childcare between spouses.[25] Therefore, textile trade unionists protested when some employers, referring to global competition, urged the introduction of a four-shift schedule and Sunday work as this would further complicate the precarious balancing act of factory work, housework and (sparse) free time.

The international fluctuations in the textile sector, especially the 1940s and 1950s up-and downswings, also affected the Austrian producers. In the 1960s,

---

21 Maria Madlener, Greter Starzer, and Josef Weidenholzer, *Die Situation der Fabrikarbeiterin in Oberösterreich: Erfahrungsberichte vom Studientag am 15. März 1980 an der Universität Linz* (Vienna/Graz: Leykam, 1980), 27–28.

22 Bichlbauer, Frassine, and Laburda, *Arbeitsbedingungen*, 131–139; see also Andrea Nogler-Stark, interview by Veronika Helfert, 10 February 2022, transcript with the author, audio. The long-standing women's chairwoman of the TBL, Nogler-Stark, was a member and then chairwoman of the works council at the Vorarlberg textile company Huber Tricot from 1986 to 2019. In company newspapers such as the *Dreihammer: Zeitschrift für die Mitarbeiter der F. M. Hämmerle Textilwerke AG Dornbirn – Feldkirch – Wien*, comprehensive explanations of the composition of wages were published in Serbo-Croatian and Turkish in the 1980s.

23 Bichlbauer, Frassine, and Laburda, *Arbeitsbedingungen*, 118–119.

24 Vorarlberger Wirtschaftsarchiv, Feldkirch, A/9615, Arbeitszeitenvergleichssammlung des Textilunternehmers Franz M. Rhomberg.

25 Nogler-Stark, interview; Bichlbauer, Frassine, and Laburda, *Arbeitsbedingungen*, 119.

with steadier growth and a simultaneous shortage of workers, the industry became unable to meet domestic demand and failed to be competitive in the world market. Companies reacted by increasing rationalization and investment in modern high-output machinery on the one hand, and by recruiting workers from abroad on the other hand.[26] Upon achieving full (male) employment, the booming economies of Western Europe sought to meet labour needs by recruiting foreign workers,[27] only to use them as a manoeuvring mass in times of economic crises and rising unemployment rates among domestic workers, or by increasing the participation of women in the labour market. Within Europe, labour migrants moved from the South to the North.[28]

With the advent of labour migration under the "guestworker" scheme, migrant working men and women filled the lower-paid, unskilled jobs in the industry (usually "women's jobs"), while non-migrant women workers moved on to other sectors.[29] When the global economic crisis of the 1970s hit the Austrian textile industry particularly hard, this had a major impact on women's jobs which subsequently affected migrant women differently from Austrian women. Studies have shown how deindustrialization enforced social inequalities and had different effects depending on gender, class, race and/or ethnicity.[30] Many of the big textile companies went bankrupt or closed their production sites in Austria (e.g., Vöslauer Kammgarn filed for bankruptcy in 1978).[31] Despite various attempts to counter these developments, including the consolidation of individual companies (*Textillösung Ost* and *Textillösung West*), the pressure of global economic trends could only be relieved in the short term. Only a few, such as F. M. Hämmerle, survived to the mid-2000s, or are still operating by having moved most of their production sites abroad.

26 Franz Rauter, *Das Fremdarbeiterproblem in Innsbrucker Textil- und Bekleidungsbetrieben* (Innsbruck: Wagner, 1972), 12.

27 Herman Obdeijn, "Les migrations vers l'Europe: Un mouvement d'émancipation du Tiers Monde," in *Les migrations du travail en Europe*, ed. Klaus Morgenroth (Bern: Lang, 2003), 36.

28 James F. Hollifield, *Immigrants, Markets, and States: The Political Economy of Postwar Europe* (London: Harvard University Press, 1992), 15.

29 Erika Thurner, *Der "goldene Westen"? Arbeitszuwanderung nach Vorarlberg seit 1945* (Bregenz: Vorarlberger Autoren Gesellschaft, 1997), 24.

30 Tim Strangleman, James Rhodes, and Sherry Linkon, "Introduction to Crumbling Cultures: Deindustrialization, Class, and Memory," *International Labor and Working-Class History* 84 (2013): 7–22.

31 Doris Schwaiger, "Krisenstrategien industrieller Unternehmungen und ihre wirtschaftsgeographischen Auswirkungen: Versuche zur Sanierung einer Textilindustrie im Rahmen der Textillösung Ost" (Diploma thesis, University of Vienna, 1984), 1–23.

During these relocations and restructuring processes, migrant workers (both male and female) and women workers were fired first.

Work in the textile and garment industry was also affected by technologization and rationalization.[32] In her report to the ÖGB women's congress in 1983, Maria Metzker, head of the ÖGB women's department, warned that indeed the "technologization of women's workplaces" particularly in the textile industry will not only lead to a shift in women's employment but also to a decrease of women's participation in the workforce; a problem with "unforeseen abysses."[33] Since the 1970s, a continuous loss of workplaces in the textile and garment industry amounted to a yearly decrease of 3 percent in garment making until 1983.[34] Between 1977 and 1983, 25 percent of all jobs in the textile industry and 23 percent in the garment industry were lost. Between 1983 and 1987, the unemployment rate of women rose by 43 percent, whereas that of men only increased by 14 percent.[35] In 1976, for the first time, more women were employed as white-collar workers than as blue-collar workers at a national level.[36] In parallel, textile unionists lost their prominent influence in the trade union movement and with the deindustrialization processes, union membership continuously declined.

2 The Austrian Labour Migration Regime in a European Context

The movement of labour to industrial centres, which had shaped European societies since the seventeenth century,[37] was disrupted by the First World War. In the new nation-states, labour migration subsequently became an urgent issue for industries, governments, and national as well as international labour movements.[38] After the collapse of the Habsburg monarchy in 1918, the

32 "New Technologies and Women's Jobs," *Women at Work*, no. 2 (1980): 5–6.

33 Maria Metzker, Report on the Activities of the Women's Department, in *Stenographisches Protokoll: 9. Frauenkongreß des Österreichischen Gewerkschaftsbundes vom 18. bis 20. Mai 1983*, ed. ÖGB Frauenabteilung (Vienna: ÖGB-Verlag, 1983), 32.

34 Debate contribution by Anneliese Pulkrab (Gewerkschaft TBL), in *9. Frauenkongreß des Österreichischen Gewerkschaftsbundes*, 137.

35 Hilde Seiler, Report on the Activities of the Women's Department, in *Stenographisches Protokoll: 10. ÖGB-Frauenkongreß vom 2. bis 4. Juni 1987*, ed. ÖGB Frauenabteilung (Vienna: ÖGB-Verlag, 1987), 34.

36 "Die Frau am Arbeitsmarkt," in *Frauenarbeit in den Gewerkschaften: Bericht über das Jahr 1976* (Vienna: ÖGB-Verlag), 3–11.

37 Sylvia Hahn, *Migration – Arbeit – Geschlecht: Arbeitsmigration in Mitteleuropa vom 17. bis zum Beginn des 20. Jahrhunderts* (Göttingen: V&R Unipress, 2008), 157–244.

38 Ahmet Akgündüz, "Guest Worker Migration in Post-War Europe (1946–1974): An Analytical Appraisal," in *An Introduction to International Migration Studies: European*

traditional short-distance internal migrations of seasonal labour on which many sectors – agriculture in particular – relied, now involved crossing state borders and became international migrations. However, protectionist laws, especially the Domestic Worker Protection Act (*Inlandarbeiterschutzgesetz*) of 1925, closed off the Austrian labour market to non-Austrian citizens.[39] Austria's labour migration regime was characterized by the involvement of various interest groups. Since the First World War and, similarly, after 1945 mainly social democratic politicians and trade unionists insisted on state regulation of employment permits for foreign citizens to prevent exploitation of workers and disadvantages for domestic workers. In this context, anti-Slavic resentments also comprised part of the argument.[40] Such attitudes already characterized the standpoints of the Austrian delegates during the debates on labour migration at the congresses of the Second International (see Chapter 11 in this volume).[41]

After the end of the Second World War, especially since the 1950s, international labour mobility to Western Europe increased considerably.[42] Most states resumed labour regimes and migrants embarked on their routes. While West and North European states aimed for controlled recruitment of workers in South European countries, non-state-regulated migration paths via tourist visas and individual job searches were commonplace throughout Europe.[43] As described by Simon Goeke in his study on West Germany,[44] the official recruitment paths for migrant workers were only one of the multiple entryways to segments of the labour markets.[45]

Perspectives, ed. Marco Martinello and Jan Rath (Amsterdam: Amsterdam University Press, 2012), 182–186.

39 Jessica Richter, "Das österreichische Inlandarbeiterschutzgesetz von 1925 und die LandarbeiterInnen: Zur Organisation des 'nationalisierten' Arbeitsmarkts," in *Rural History Yearbook / Jahrbuch für Geschichte des ländlichen Raums*, no. 15 (2018): 281–296.

40 Horvath, *Die Logik der Entrechtung*, 173.

41 Lucas Poy, "La Segunda Internacional y la cuestión de las migraciones a comienzos del siglo XX," *Revista Izquierdas*, no. 50 (2021): 1–23.

42 Klaus J. Bade, "L'Europe, continent d'immigration: Migrations et intégration à la fin du XXe siècle," in Morgenroth, *Les migrations du travail*, 4–5.

43 Christoph Rass, "Temporary Labour Migration and State-Run Recruitment of Foreign Workers in Europe, 1919–1975: A New Migration Regime?," *International Review of Social History* 57, no. 20 (2012): 191–224.

44 Simon Goeke, "*Wir sind alle Fremdarbeiter!" Gewerkschaften, migrantische Kämpfe und soziale Bewegungen in Westdeutschland 1960–1980* (Paderborn: Ferdinand Schöningh, 2020).

45 *Gastarbeiter in österreichischen Betrieben*, ed. Verein für ökonomische und soziologische Studien (Vienna: 1972), 6.

Although it was more of an emigration country in the 1950s, Austria joined states such as Germany and Switzerland in establishing a "guestworker programme" targeting recruitment for specific economic sectors within the framework of the *Raab-Olah-Agreement* of 1961/1962[46] whereby labour recruitment agreements were concluded with Spain, Yugoslavia, and Turkey.[47] These programmes served to maintain control over the sectors and periods of employment, thereby "immigrants who could be made to leave"[48] as Cindy Hahamovitch put it. While in countries with a colonial past, such as France or Great Britain, this heritage and associated legislation framed the specifics of the immigration regimes,[49] in Austria the legacies of the Habsburg Empire and the national socialist past framed both labour migration and labour activism.[50] The newly recruited migrant workers arrived in a post-Nazi (*postnazistisch*) and post-genocidal society that had until recently benefited from the exploitation of forced labour.[51] In short, national socialist legacies and legal continuities shaped the Austrian labour migration regime.[52] The "guestworker programme" of the Second Austrian Republic, founded in 1945, continued interwar policies but also took "international standards of labour migration" into account.[53] These programmes consisted of an annual quota (*Kontingente*) of labourers to be recruited for specific industries, negotiated and established by trade unions and employer representatives. They mandated compulsory health examinations before recruitment, the provision of housing by employers, a rotation

46 This agreement formalized the social partnership in Austria comprising cooperative relationships between employers' and employees' associations such as the ÖGB, the Chamber of Labour or the employers' Economic Chamber (*Wirtschaftskammer*) with the aim of preventing conflicts through consensus building.

47 Anne Unterwurzacher, "'The Other Colleagues': Labor Migration at the Glanzstoff-Fabrik in St. Pölten from 1962 to 1975," in *Migration in Austria*, ed. Günter Bischof and Dirk Rupnow (New Orleans: University of New Orleans Press, 2017), 139–159.

48 Cindy Hahamovitch, "Creating Perfect Immigrants: Guestworkers of the World in Historical Perspective," *Labor History* 44, no. 1 (2003): 72.

49 Hollifield, *Immigrants,* 38.

50 Continuities are visible even on the architectural level as the – often desolate – tenements for migrant textile workers in the nineteenth century were re-used 100 years later for "guestworkers." Sylvia Hahn, "Migration und Ökonomie."

51 Dirk Rupnow, "Deprovincializing Contemporary Austrian History: Plädoyer für eine transnationale Geschichte Österreichs als Migrationsgesellschaft," *zeitgeschichte* 40, no. 1 (2013): 12.

52 Vida Bakondy and Renée Winter, "Schweigen und Profitieren: Überlegungen zur Fortwirkung von Strukturen nationalsozialistischer Zwangsarbeit nach 1945," in Schmidinger, *"Vom selben Schlag,"* 57–64.

53 Rass, "Temporary Labour Migration," 200.

principle – i.e., the issuance of work permits limited to one year – and the prohibition of employing recruited workers during strikes.[54]

When, as a consequence of the economic crisis of 1973, European states discontinued labour recruitment on the international labour market,[55] the Austrian Act Governing the Employment of Foreign Nationals (*Ausländerbeschäftigungsgesetz*) of 1975 aimed at regulating and reducing the migrant workforce. Labour migrants contested the laws but received almost no support from the trade unions.[56] Roughly at the same time, in 1977, several members of the Council of Europe agreed on a convention on migrant workers (European Treaty Series No. 93) aiming to ensure that workers, who were nationals of member states "are treated no less favourably than workers who are nationals of the receiving state in all aspects of living and working conditions."[57] The convention highlighted problem areas such as violations of the rights of migrant workers during their recruitment and in their working and living conditions (housing, family reunions, education or unemployment) and social rights.[58] The Convention Concerning Migrations in Abusive Conditions and the Promotion of Equal Opportunity and Treatment of Migrant Workers (No. 143) of the ILO of 1975 and the ILO Migrant Workers Recommendation (No. 151) aimed even more strongly towards equal treatment of domestic and foreign workers. However, Austria neither signed the ILO's nor the Council of Europe's Convention (during the period under review)[59] and Austrian workers' representatives expressed reservations, particularly regarding the right

54 Sylvia Hahn, "Geschichte der Arbeitsmigration in Österreich," in *50 Jahre jugoslawische Gastarbeit in Österreich*, ed. Ali Özbaş, Joachim Hainzl, and Handan Özbaş (Graz: Clio, 2016), 32. For a historical overview, see Hahn, *Migration – Arbeit – Geschlecht*, 139–155.

55 Among others, see Mirjana Morokvasic, "Birds of Passage are also Women," *International Migration Review* 18, no. 4 (1984): 888.

56 August Gächter, "Die Einwanderung aus der Türkei und was aus ihr wird," in *50 Jahre türkische Gast (?) Arbeit in Österreich: Wissenschaftliche Analysen – Lebensgeschichten / Avusturya'da 50 yıllık misafir (?) işçi: bilimsel analizler – hayat hikayeleri*, ed. Ali Özbaş, Joachim Hainzl, and Handan Özbaş (Graz: Leykam, 2014), 50.

57 European Convention on the Legal Status of Migrant Workers / Convention Européenne Relative au Statut Juridique du Travailleur Migrant, European Treaty Series no. 93, December 1977.

58 Emmanuel Comte, *The History of the European Migration Regime: Germany's Strategic Hegemony* (London/New York: Routledge, 2018).

59 Stefan Rosenmayer, "Die öffentlich-rechtliche Stellung von Gastarbeitern, insbesondere das Aufenthaltsrecht," in *Ausländische Arbeitskräfte in Österreich*, ed. Hannes Wimmer (Frankfurt/Main: Campus Verlag, 1986), 95–97.

of migrant workers to run for office in interest groups as outlined in the ILO Convention No. 143 and Recommendation 151.[60]

These international policy instruments of the late 1970s addressed the unequal treatment of workers due to citizenship but made little reference to the circumstances of women. Within the ILO, for example, no conventions and recommendations on the issues of migrant women workers were produced until 1990, apart from policies against trafficking women and girls and for the rights of the family members of migrant workers.[61]

Only instruments concerning women included them as the "special category of women" and the European Commission called migrant women "disadvantaged women," together with "single-parent families, single women, immigrant women, women returning to the labour market after a career break, physically and mentally handicapped women, self-employed women."[62] As late as 1980, the Committee of Ministers of the Council of Europe adopted the "Recommendation concerning migrant women calling for effective equality of opportunity and treatment with national women and advocating special measures in their favour."[63] Five years earlier, the ILO's "Plan of Action with a view to promoting equality of opportunity and treatment for women workers" (1975) adopted measures to promote the equal participation of women in the (national) workforce. Policymakers and labour representatives should "ensure adequate and appropriate attention to all special categories of women who may encounter particular difficulties, such as migrant women who are frequently the victims of discrimination and exploitation and who also run social risks"[64] – a clause that had been proposed by the workers' members in the Committee on Equality for Women Workers, among them the head of the ÖGB women's department, Maria Metzker.[65]

60 IHSF Archive, Chamber of Labour, Vienna, AC SV/AUS 2.1.5.24/K/R1: "Ausschüsse für Sozialpolitik, 1963–1994," Summary minutes of the meeting of the Social Policy Committee, 10 May 1976, 4.

61 Sonya Michel, "Mothers Working Abroad: Migrant Women Caregivers and the ILO, 1980s-2010s," in Boris, Hoehtker, and Zimmermann, *Women's ILO*, 321–323.

62 "Commission of the European Communities: Medium-Term Community Programme, 1986–90," *Women at Work*, no. 1 (1986): 65.

63 "Council of Europe: Recommendation Concerning Migrant Women," *Women at Work*, no. 1 (1980): 50.

64 "Resolution on Equality of Opportunity and Treatment for Women Workers," *Women at Work*, no. 2 (1977): 22.

65 "Eighth Item on the Agenda: Equality of Opportunity and Treatment for Women Workers, Report of the Committee on Equality for Women Workers," *International Labour Conference 60th Session, Geneva, 1975, Records of the Proceedings*, 776–777.

3 The Misconstruction of Labour Migration as a Male Phenomenon

For a long period, Yugoslavian citizens accounted for the largest group of migrant workers in Austria, with a share of 76.4 percent (66,400 persons) in 1970.[66] Although most labour migrants in the 1960s and 1970s were men, the proportion of women was higher than assumed in public narratives and frequently repeated in scholarship. In the 1970s, according to Sylvia Hahn, 35 percent of Yugoslav migrants were female, which increased to up to 40 percent in the 1980s.[67] Even if women entered Austria as relatives or wives, they still sought employment and thus need to be considered within the context of labour migration.[68] Significantly, employment rates among migrant women were higher than among Austrian women: In 1971, for example, the employment rate was 80 percent for Yugoslav women as compared to 48 percent for Austrian women. Migrants were primarily employed as unskilled workers, leading to shifts in the gender ratios in certain sectors and the emergence of an ethnically divided labour market.[69] An example from the historic Vöslauer Kammgarn AG – a worsted yarn factory near Vienna – illustrates this development. While the proportion of women among Austrian nationals employed fell from 74 to 69 percent between 1965 and 1974, the proportion of migrant women in the company's workforce remained stable at approximately 50 percent with, however, a peak of around 60 percent during the recession period from 1966 to 1968.[70] The number of Austrian citizens among the company's workforce decreased from 2,344 (91.4 percent) to 910 (68.7 percent) from 1965 to 1975. In 1973 – the year in which the highest number of migrant workers were recruited – migrant workers accounted for 50.6 percent of all workers.[71]

66 Caroline Hornstein Tomić and Katica Ivanda Jurčević, "Gäste auf Zeit – Grenzgänger – transkulturelle Vermittler: Identitätsbildung in der Migration," in *Gast:arbeit: Gehen – Bleiben – Zurückkehren: Positionen zur Arbeitsmigration im Raum Ex-Jugoslawien*, ed. Jörn Nuber and Angelika Welebil (Vienna: Edition Art Science, 2012), 177.

67 Hahn, "Geschichte der Arbeitsmigration," 33; Tomšič, "Women as Migrant Workers from Yugoslavia," 12.

68 Christiane Harzig, "Immigration Policies: A Gendered Historical Comparison," in *Crossing Borders and Shifting Boundaries I: Gender on the Move*, ed. Mirjana Morokvasic, Umut Erel, and Kyoko Shinozaki (Wiesbaden: Springer, 2003), 48–54.

69 Stefanie Mayer, "Migration & Labor Markets: Political Discourse in Austria," in *Debating Migration: Political Discourse on Labor Immigration in Historical Perspective*, ed. Stefanie Mayer and Mikael Span (Innsbruck: Studien-Verlag, 2009), 37–40.

70 Akgündüz, "Guest Worker Migration," 186.

71 Percentages calculated from the numbers provided in Ulla Fischer-Westhauser, "Actien-Gesellschaft der Vöslauer Kammgarn-Fabrik: Ein Beispiel alter österreichischer Industriegeschichte" (PhD diss., University of Vienna, 1994), Appendix 45–47. Note that the numbers refer to blue-collar workers and not to all employees at the Kammgarn AG.

The Vöslauer Kammgarn is representative of the textile industry as a whole: At the beginning of the 1970s between 40 and 60 percent of the workers in the sector were migrants.[72]

However, despite these indications, it is not possible to present exact numbers of foreign women employed in the textile and garment industry, since the statistics rarely noted gender ratios.[73] The Austrian census of 1981, for the first time, registered the gender of labour migrants.[74] While the annual reports of the women's departments of the trade unions monitored and documented women's employment rates, they did not provide the numbers of non-Austrian female nationals with the exception of the years 1965 and 1966 when approximately 20 percent of the 34,098 and 49,102 recruited workers were women.[75] Subsequently, the data concerning the women employed included non-Austrian citizens without further specification and the total number of "guestworkers" was provided without any gender specification. Only the reports of the ÖGB women's committee in Vorarlberg continuously show the proportion of women among labour migrants, which amounted to one-third throughout the 1970s. However, the published data does show that economic sectors with a high percentage of female labour were among those which recruited large numbers of labour migrants – in particular, the textile and garment industry in Vorarlberg and elsewhere in Austria.[76]

The absence of data shows to what degree the cliché of guestworker migration as being a largely male phenomenon has hampered research.[77] Only a few studies from the late 1960s onwards focused on the lives of women "guestworkers,"[78] and few journalists such as Henriette Werner or Ilse Beheim wrote on

---

72 Friedrich Fürstenberg, "Die Integration von Gastarbeitern in unsere Gesellschaft," in *Die Problematik der Gastarbeiter: Enquete der Kammer für Arbeiter und Angestellte für Oberösterreich und des Österreichischen Gewerkschaftsbundes* (Linz: Kammer für Arbeiter und Angestellte für Oberösterreich, 1973), 15.

73 Among others, see Erich Lehner, "Die Gastarbeiter im Rahmen des österreichischen Arbeitsmarktes," in *Die Problematik der Gastarbeiter.*

74 August Gächter, "50 Jahre jugoslawische Gastarbeit in Österreich" in Özbaş, Hainzl, and Özbaş, *50 Jahre jugoslawische Gastarbeit in Österreich*, 50.

75 *Frauenarbeit in den Gewerkschaften (1965)*, 3; and *Frauenarbeit in den Gewerkschaften (1966)*, 3.

76 Ilse Beheim, "Die Gastarbeiterin in Österreich," *Arbeit und Wirtschaft* 23, no. 12 (December 1969): 53.

77 Elisabeth Koch et al., "Migrationsforschung und Geschlecht: Über den Wandel von Darstellungen von Migrantinnen," in Nuber and Welebil, *Gast:arbeit*, 313; María do Mar Castro Varela and Dimitria Clayton, eds., *Migration, Gender, Arbeitsmarkt: Neue Beiträge zu Frauen und Globalisierung* (Königstein/Taunus: Helmer Verlag, 2003); Morokvasic, "Birds of Passage," 899–900.

78 Koch et al., "Migrationsforschung und Geschlecht."

the issue in leading trade union publications, such as “Arbeit und Wirtschaft.”[79] However, the publications usually focused less on the specific multiple burdens faced by migrant women workers than on racist stereotypes that attributed the issues arising from unequal job opportunities to a supposedly more patriarchal culture of origin.[80] Migration and gender scholar Eleonore Kofman has aptly called this tendency the “orientalizing of immigrant women.”[81] This also concerns texts that criticized prejudices of the majority society and that portrayed the difficult working and living conditions in Austria.

To conclude: Reinforced by the pictorial representation and the linguistic reduction to the generic masculine (characteristic of the German language) in most publications on migrant workers, women workers only appeared sporadically in the scholarly and public sphere, historiography included, and, if mentioned, female migration was primarily associated with care workers and domestic servants.

4 The Double Marginalization of Migrant Women Workers in Trade Unionism

Once Austria became a receiving country of labour migration in the 1960s – after post-war emigration from Austria had abated – trade union attitudes were ambivalent. On the one hand, trade unions across West and North European countries voiced concerns that migrant workers would reduce the influence of trade unions and endanger the gains made in labour rights by acting as competitors in the labour market.[82] On the other hand – to counteract such a development – the unions established a variety of information and service offers and recruited migrant workers as members.[83] As “organizations aiming to regulate and mitigate competitive relations among workers in the labor market,”[84] the ÖGB and its branch unions sought to prevent unequal

79 Beheim, “Die Gastarbeiterin,” 53–55; Henriette Werner, “Gastarbeiter,” *Arbeit und Wirtschaft* 19, no. 9 (September 1965): 19.

80 For a similar insight, see Morokvasic, “Birds of Passage,” 889.

81 Kofman, “Female ‘Birds of Passage’,” 285.

82 Johan Svanberg, “International Trade-Unionism and Migration: European Integration and the Post-War ‘Free’ Movement of Labour,” *Labor History* 62, no. 5–6 (2021): 671–687.

83 Jan Kreisky, “Migration und Gewerkschaft: Skizze einer widerspruchvollen und wechselhaften Geschichte,” in *Wissenschaft über Gewerkschaft: Analysen und Perspektiven*, ed. Brigitte Pellar (Vienna: ÖGB-Verlag), 171–172; Hannes Wimmer, “Zur Ausländerbeschäftigungspolitik in Österreich,” in Wimmer, *Ausländische Arbeitskräfte*, 18–26.

84 Julia Soul, “Local Unions in a Transnational Movement: The Role of Mexican Unions in the Making of International Networks,” *Labor and Society* 22, (2019): 26.

treatment of domestic and foreign workers and thus avoid negative impacts on labour standards and wage development. However, they also frequently adopted a protectionist position against the recruitment of migrant workers. As early as 1955 – before the recruitment agreements – the ÖGB women's conference in Vorarlberg protested against an "intended taking in of women workers from abroad (*Fremdarbeiterinnen*) for the Vorarlberg textile industry"[85] and presented a motion to that intent at the national women's congress in the same year. The motion was only adopted after discussion and with some opposing votes and abstentions.[86] In 1961, the Vorarlberg women trade unionists demanded a law to regulate the employment of foreign citizens and also wanted co-determination regarding the number of foreign women recruited.[87] The issue remained present at their and other Austrian states' (*Länder*) conferences until the late 1960s, especially among trade union women in Tyrol.[88] A leading Vorarlberg unionist, Lotte Eß, became the first female vice-president of the Chamber of Labour for Vorarlberg in 1967 and like Grete Rehor, another prominent textile unionist and Austrian Minister of Social Affairs from 1966 to 1970, she pursued exclusionary policies. The union women wanted to reduce the number of foreign workers, which they labelled the "guestworker problem" (*Gastarbeiterproblem*), and to improve the vocational training of girls and young women, as well as their employment opportunities and the medical infrastructure in rural areas.[89] Rehor, a member of the conservative Austrian People's Party (Österreichische Volkspartei, ÖVP), successfully advocated for more difficult access to the payment (and stricter control) of family allowances for migrant workers,[90] a sensitive field to ensure strict migration policies.

The "guestworker problem" (*Gastarbeiterproblem*) found institutional expression in the trade union system through the establishment of special committees at the state level, in the Chambers of Labour or in individual trade unions. The Vorarlberg textile trade union established such committees in the late 1960s and the regional Chamber of Labour in the late 1970s.[91] Unfortunately, no minutes of the committee meetings have been preserved or are accessible

85 *Frauenarbeit in den Gewerkschaften* (*1955*), 24.

86 *Stenographisches Protokoll: 2. Frauenkongreß des Österreichischen Gewerkschaftsbundes: 14. und 15. Oktober 1955*, ed. ÖGB Frauenabteilung (Vienna: ÖGB-Verlag, 1955), 184–185.

87 *Frauenarbeit in den Gewerkschaften* (*1961*), 54.

88 *Frauenarbeit in den Gewerkschaften* (*1962*), 46–47; *Frauenarbeit in den Gewerkschaften* (*1969*), 50.

89 Report from Vorarlberg, compiled by Lotte Eß, *Frauenarbeit in den Gewerkschaften* (*1982*), 76–78.

90 Karl von Vogelsang Archive, Vienna, File no. 2586.

91 *Frauenarbeit in den Gewerkschaften* (*1980*), 74.

and the printed reports of the TBL, for example, mainly contain information on the quotas of migrant workers in various sectors and do not reveal whether other topics were discussed. Migrants had, at best, a minor role in these committees, constituting a maximum of 46 percent, and finally, from 1980 to 1989, a mere 20 percent in the labour migration committee (*Gastarbeiterausschuss*) of the ÖGB in Vorarlberg. Among the migrant members, there were never more than two women, and sometimes none.[92]

This peripheral presence reflected the ÖGB position until the 1990s: "Austrian works councils are quite capable of imparting their knowledge to the foreigners, they could do this much better than if the foreigners themselves elected works councils."[93] Trade union functionaries understood their role as being to advise and represent all colleagues equally, albeit without the representation of workers of non-Austrian citizenship, who received the right to vote in works council elections in 1976 but could not stand for office.[94]

In some companies, however, "guestworker spokespersons" (*Gastarbeitersprecher*) could be appointed. Their task was to help with matters related to the workplace and, in addition, with issues specific to migrant workers, such as passport extensions. The ÖGB in Vorarlberg offered special courses for Yugoslav and Turkish spokespersons in the late 1970s and early 1980s, to "avoid difficulties between works councils and foreign workers, which are rooted partly in the language."[95] The training sessions covered general Austrian labour law, specific legislation such as the Act Governing the Employment of Foreign Nationals, issues around leave from work and vacations, wage tax issues, various social security topics, and German language courses. While publications suggest that only men served as spokespersons, the reports show that (a few) women were enrolled in these courses in some years.[96]

The Austrian state, in its turn, considerably restricted the possibilities of political articulation for non-citizens and, in addition to the limitation on voting rights, participation in demonstrations was curtailed. Foreign citizens were not allowed to act as organizers, overseers, or leaders of a public assembly.[97]

92 Information compiled from the reports of the ÖGB in Vorarlberg published between 1980 and 1989.

93 *Problematik der Gastarbeiter*, 65–66.

94 Kurt Prokop, "Die Gastarbeiter aus der Sicht der Arbeitnehmer," in *Problematik der Gastarbeiter*, 53–62; Kreisky, "Migration und Gewerkschaft," 174–175.

95 *Bericht 1977*, ed. ÖGB Vorarlberg (Vienna: ÖGB-Verlag, 1977), 20.

96 ÖGB Vorarlberg, *Bericht 1977*, 20–21, 24.

97 Hüsseyin Uz, "Organisation gegen Isolation: Migrantische Selbstorganisation zwischen Interessensvertretung und Parallelgesellschaft," in Schmidinger, *"Vom selben Schlag,"* 221–222.

These mechanisms of exclusion, together with the fact that until the mid-2000s only Austrian citizens were allowed to be elected as works council members, reinforced the division between the trade union movement and workers without Austrian citizenship.[98] For Austrians, membership in a works council was often a first step towards a trade union career.

Many trade unionists considered migrant workers difficult to organize, notwithstanding all evidence to the contrary. Very few – such as former anti-fascist resistance fighter and socialist journalist Henriette Werner[99] – took into consideration that precarious employment conditions (caused by fixed-term employment contracts with great dependence on the employer) made labour activism harder for migrant workers. Attempts to agitate in the languages of migrant workers, beyond the publication of certain trade union information, are not recorded. Resentment among many works councils against the "enemies of organized workers,"[100] as migrant workers were sometimes called, was evident.[101]

Thus, all evidence supports the hypothesis of the double marginalization of migrant women in the structures of trade unions and Chambers of Labour. In the few areas in which migrant workers were able to assume formal functions, women were either barely present or not represented at all while in the organizational structures created for and by union women, the issues of labour migrants were only discussed in "a discourse of problems."[102] Interpreter Slobodanka Kudlaček-Ritopečki did not recall any contacts with trade union women's representatives during her years of work, and the minutes of the committee of women's work in the Chamber of Labour in Vienna as well as of the ÖGB women's congresses show almost no contributions regarding the topic.[103]

98 The right of foreign citizens to stand as candidates in elections to the Chamber of Labour and works councils was pushed through by migrant activists who took legal action all the way to the European Court of Justice and the UN Human Rights Committee. Franz Fischill, "Antidiskriminierung: MigrantInnen in der Gewerkschaft," accessed 28 February 2022, https://www.oegb.at/themen/gleichstellung/antidiskriminierung/migrantinnen-in-der-gewerkschaft.

99 "Kotlan-Werner, Henriette," accessed 28 February 2022, http://biografia.sabiado.at/kotlan-werner-henriette/.

100 Werner, "Gastarbeiter," 20.

101 Also see the remarks in Madlener, Starzer, and Weidenholzer, *Die Situation der Fabrikarbeiterin,* 21; Hans Peter Martin, *Nachtschicht: Eine Vorarlberger Betriebsreportage*, 2nd ed. (Vienna: Sensen-Verlag, 1979), 25–26.

102 Svanberg, "International Trade-Unionism and Migration," 684.

103 Kudlaček-Ritopečki, interview. Similarly, the native textile unionists I interviewed could not recall having been in contact or especially engaged with women labour migrants, also see Nogler-Stark, interview; Sophie Bauer, interview by Veronika Helfert, 6 October 2021,

5 Precarious Spaces of Activism

The problems caused by the extremely restrictive Austrian legislation regarding works council elections and the positions taken by the trade union movement did concern the textile industry. In some companies, such as the large Austrian textile manufacturer F. M. Hämmerle, female white-collar workers were voted into the blue-collar works councils, since "the many foreign workers in our production units do not have the right to stand for election, it is very difficult to find suitable candidates for the works council."[104] Women trade unionists also pointed to the fact that it was difficult to hold works council elections in companies with an 80 percent non-Austrian workforce such as F. M. Hämmerle.[105]

Organizing required resources: time, networks, language, and other skills. And since the nineteenth century, women trade unionists had pointed out that involvement was challenging for many women regardless of their background because of the allocation of family responsibilities. "You'll rarely find a works council who can be present full-time and who is married and has a family to take care of," noted an anonymous woman trade unionist in 1980: "That's just not happening."[106] This was even more difficult for migrant women on short employment contracts or, if on longer contracts, who had only been working in the company for a short time.[107] A close reading of the company newspaper of F. M. Hämmerle reveals that it was only in 1989 that two women were elected as works council members. Most likely they were Yugoslav migrant workers and could only stand for election after having acquired Austrian citizenship.[108]

The activities that were undertaken in several locations throughout Austria by the ÖGB, its trade unions, and the Chambers of Labour to organize "the foreign colleagues as members,"[109] included providing information in

---

transcript with the author, audio; IHSF Archive, Chamber of Labour, Vienna, "Ausschüsse für Frauenarbeit," 3 Boxes.

104 "Vier Frauen im Betriebsrat stellen ihren Mann," *Dreihammer* 35, no. 1 (January/February 1982).

105 *Frauenarbeit in den Gewerkschaften* (1973), 53; "Wir sprechen mit Erich Mauracher," *Der Aufstieg: Organ der Gewerkschaft der Textil-, Bekleidungs-, und Lederarbeiter*, no. 7/8 (July/August 1974): 10.

106 Madlener, Starzer, and Weidenholzer, *Die Situation der Fabrikarbeiterin*, 52.

107 See the discussions in *Frauenarbeit in den Gewerkschaften* (1963), 59; and *Frauenarbeit in den Gewerkschaften* (1965), 60.

108 *Dreihammer* 41, no. 4 (October/November/December 1988): 11; *Dreihammer* 42, no. 1 (January/February/March 1989): 5.

109 Prokop, "Die Gastarbeiter," 61.

Serbo-Croatian, Turkish – and less frequently in Italian – and hiring interpreters with weekly office hours.[110] This service continued in the 1970s as "a large proportion of the appearing guest workers are women."[111] However, there were limits to what the interpreters could do, since they were not allowed to undertake independent consultations. Nevertheless, some of them, like Slobodanka Kudlaček-Ritopečki, acquired extensive knowledge over time that supported migrant women in their claims.[112]

Other initiatives of the late 1980s followed models introduced in Germany and Australia, and in Vienna and Vorarlberg, foreigners' counselling centres (*Ausländerberatungsstellen*) were founded, or co-founded, by migrant actors themselves. The respective association in Vorarlberg did include representatives from the trade unions and the regional Chamber of Labour but worked independently. It offered extensive counselling and support in Turkish and Serbo-Croatian. The association, which existed from 1986 to 2000, fundamentally changed its character when, in the mid-1990s, it was assigned to the regional office of the Public Employment Service in Vorarlberg.[113] More far-reaching, albeit short-term, attempts to compensate for the lack of suffrage rights for foreign citizens at the municipal level were realized in the 1990s in the form of foreigners' advisory committees (*Migrantenbeiräte/Ausländerbeiräte*). Such councils were also introduced in other countries with varying degrees of autonomy and decision-making power.[114]

However, to deal with issues of daily life and political participation, many migrant women organized autonomously, and associations of various kinds – sports, cultural or even political – were an essential component of their activism whereby clubs such as *Jedinstvo Beč* played an important role in establishing and maintaining socio-political networks.[115] Some of these activities were funded by the ÖGB.[116] In their leisure time, migrant women workers were often involved in activities to foster the culture of their countries of origin. The circulation of knowledge and everyday support formed part of this activism – often

110 For example, *Frauenarbeit in den Gewerkschaften* (1972), 52.

111 *Frauenarbeit in den Gewerkschaften* (1972), 62.

112 Kudlaček-Ritopečki, interview.

113 Vorarlberger Landesarchiv, Bregenz, Ausländerberatungsstelle, 3 Boxes.

114 Vorarlberger Landesarchiv, Bregenz, Ausländerberatungsstelle, Box 3, Initiative für AusländerInnenbeiräte in Vorarlberg, "AusländerInnen-/ImmigrantInnen-/Minderheitenbeiräte, Infopaket."

115 Lutger Pries, *Internationale Migration* (Bielefeld: Transcript Verlag, 2015), 34.

116 *Frauenarbeit in den Gewerkschaften* (1976), 57. An event in cooperation with Radio-TV Zagreb in Vorarlberg in 1977 was, for example, attended by 2,600 people. ÖGB Vorarlberg, *Bericht 1977*, 24.

complementing or even taking over parts of the responsibilities of state institutions, such as school education or finding help in dealing with authorities. Due to the limited time resources, the investment in such activities competed with the level of involvement in labour activism. In this context, Ljubomir Bratić also argues that these associations had a difficult position at the intersection of different fields of interest. Mainly founded as grassroots organizations in the late 1960s by Yugoslav workers themselves, they experienced a boom in the 1970s and were supported by the institutions and governments of both countries involved.[117] In contrast, the associations established by and for Turkish migrant women mainly started to emerge in the 1980s.[118] While the Austrian labour migration regime, with its institutional racism and sexism, left women migrant workers little room for manoeuvre, they did show agency as translators, advisors, or in self-organized activities – all of which were performed on a voluntary and unpaid basis alongside their wage and care work.

6 A "Special Category of Women": Conclusion

Since the 1970s, the ILO has repeatedly pointed to the fact that indeed "special categories" of women exist, "who, because of their special characteristics, are experiencing not only common problems but also specific difficulties due to their socio-economic condition, age, minority status or a combination of these factors."[119] The UN Decade of Women brought the issue of migrant women into the focus of social scientists and labour activists at the international level, addressing – in addition to their class exploitation – the double discrimination they faced as women and as migrants.[120] Earlier migrant women had been understood as a problem category together with older female workers or young

117 Ljubomir Bratić, "Der Name Jugo," in Özbaş, Hainzl, and Özbaş, *50 Jahre jugoslawische Gastarbeit*, 68–71; Verena Lorber, "'Jeden Samstag und Sonntag haben wir im Klub verbracht': Die Beschäftigungssituation und das Alltagsleben von jugoslawischen Arbeitsmigrantinnen in der Steiermark von 1960 bis 1919," in Özbaş, Hainzl, and Özbaş, *50 Jahre jugoslawische Gastarbeit*, 130–140; Ljubomir Bratić, "Soziopolitische Netzwerke der MigrantInnen aus der ehemaligen Sozialistischen Föderativen Republik Jugoslawien (SFRJ) in Österreich," in *Österreichischer Migrations- und Integrationsbericht: Demographische Entwicklungen – sozioökonomische Strukturen – rechtliche Rahmenbedingungen*, ed. Heinz Fassmann and Irene Stacher (Klagenfurt/Celovec: Verlag Drava, 2003), 385–409.

118 Hüseyin A. Şimşek, *50 Jahre Migration aus der Türkei nach Österreich* (Vienna: Lit-Verlag, 2017), 402–417.

119 "Special Categories," *Women at Work*, no. 2 (1985): 17.

120 Morokvasic, "Birds of Passage," 891.

people; as a "special category," a deviation from the norm of the male (non-migratory) worker, but also from the woman worker – who in herself is already a "special category" of worker.

The "special category of women," or the "other of the women worker," to use the words of Eileen Boris, appeared not only in public discourse in Austria but also in the writings of socialist journalists and publications of sociologists. Although women trade unionists – especially in the top echelons – certainly followed the international discussions and social science studies, this, according to the accessible publications and minutes, had no impact on daily policymaking and trade union work. On the contrary, the trade unions' active opposition to labour migration and their ambivalent policies and organizational strategies shaped attitudes toward domestic and migrant workers alike. The exclusionary access of female TBL trade unionists, especially in Vorarlberg, was intensified by the pressure on jobs during the restructuring processes since the 1970s. Resolutions adopted at the international level found little or no echo in the women's departments of the Austrian Chambers of Labour and trade unions. The vulnerable position of migrant women workers was rarely addressed publicly, with one exception being the intervention of trade unionist Gabriele Traxler in the 1988 parliamentary debate on the Act Governing the Employment of Foreign Nationals in which she highlighted the multiple burdens of care work and wage work and the often-precarious working conditions.[121] The concept of "the special category of women" has not been a major subject of debate among Austrian trade unionists. However, if women were already subject to ongoing exclusion in the trade unions, even in those sectors in which they constituted the majority of workers, this affected migrant women all the more. Under the double marginalization in the Austrian institutionalized labour movement, their concerns were not given attention in the specific women's committees of trade union organizations nor in the bodies that dealt with the concerns of migrant workers. Under the government's restrictive labour migration regime, they also faced difficulties in articulating their interests within social partnership institutions. The spaces of their activism – be it on an institutional level or in self-organized spaces – remained highly precarious. However, some still circumvented all restrictions and dealt with concrete matters of their own everyday life, as illustrated by examples of activism in migrant workers' clubs or foreigners' counselling centres.

121 Stenographic minutes, Austrian Parliament, XVIIth legislative period, 59th session, 21 April 1988, 6802–6803.

CHAPTER 23

Filipina Chambermaids in Denmark

Organizing Within and Outside the Copenhagen Hotel and Restaurant Workers' Union, 1960s to 1990s

Nina Trige Andersen

Abstract

From the 1960s, Copenhagen hotels started recruiting workers from the Philippines, and by 1970, Filipinos in Denmark were sufficiently numerous to form the first Filipina/o Association of Denmark (FAD). For the "Filipino Pioneers," as the arrivals from 1960 to 1973 referred to themselves, there were numerous reasons for migrating, especially due to the volatile economic and political conditions in the Philippines at the time. During those years, the Philippine Department of Labor increased its engagement in state-managed labour export. In Denmark, although most Filipinas/os joined trade unions on arrival, their integration as active trade union militants was delayed by the weakness of the Hotel and Restaurant Workers' Union (HRF/RBF) and a generally hesitant attitude on the part of the Danish trade union movement towards migrants. This chapter investigates the strategies of the trade union and Filipina hotel workers to organize a sector that is notoriously precarious, with the recruitment of migrants as one of several management strategies to keep labour costs low.

Keywords

Denmark – labour export – labour migration – labour organizing – Philippines – service work – trade union history

1 Introduction

This chapter investigates an understudied aspect of labour migration from the Philippines, namely that of women recruited for the service sector in Northern Europe in the second half of the twentieth century. More specifically, the chapter focuses on the recruitment of Filipinas to Copenhagen hotels from the 1960s to the 1990s, and the relations between these migrant

 | DOI:10.1163/9789004686991_024

women workers and the Danish Hotel and Restaurant Workers Union (HRF/RBF, Hotel-og Restaurationspersonalets Forbund/Restaurations-og Bryggeriarbejderforbundet – later merged into 3F, Fagligt Fælles Forbund [United Federation of Danish Workers]). Much has been written on labour migration from the Philippines, both in colonial times – under US rule since the defeat of Spain as a colonizer power in 1898 – and after the declaration of the independent republic in 1946.[1] Research on twentieth-century migration has centred on the US and, later, the oil-producing economies of the Persian Gulf as well as East Asia. However, even before the Philippine Labor Code of 1974 systematized and scaled up state-managed labour export, and countries such as the oil-producing Arab states started recruiting hundreds of thousands of workers from the Philippines, Europe emerged as a destination of large-scale migration in the 1960s.

To understand the dynamics and drivers of how the Philippine state and society became suppliers of labour power to the world, the early stages of European recruitment and the experiences of workers in Europe provide an instructive case. In the 1960s to the mid-1970s, Filipinos and Filipinas were to some extent hired for industrial manufacturing jobs, but primarily for the service sector.[2] One of the countries that recruited Filipino workers from the 1960s onwards – and was assisted in this endeavour by the Philippine state – was Denmark. In fact, although overlooked in most industry-focused research on the so-called guestworker era, the European service (and healthcare) sectors recruited migrant labour on a massive scale during the 1960s and 1970s, predominantly women and many of them from Southeast Asia.[3] They performed

1 See, for example, Catherine Ceniza Choy, *Empire of Care: Nursing and Migration in Filipino American History* (Durham, NC: Duke University Press/Quezon City: Ateneo de Manila University Press, 2003); Robyn Magalit Rodriguez, *Migrants for Export: How the Philippine State Brokers Labor to the World* (Minneapolis: University of Minnesota Press, 2010); Filomeno V. Aguilar, Jr., *Migration Revolution: Philippine Nationhood and Class Relations in a Globalized Village* (Manila: Ateneo de Manila University Press, 2014); Filomeno V. Aguilar, Jr., ed., *Filipinos in Global Migrations: At Home in the World?* (Quezon City: Philippine Social Science Council, 2002). Furthermore, the Scalabrini Migration Center, Quezon City, is one of the important research hubs concerning this topic. See, for example, Graziano Battistella and Anthony Paganoni, eds., *Philippine Labor Migration: Impact and Policy* (Quezon City: Scalabrini Migration Center, 1992).

2 Thousands of Filipinos were also recruited to work on ships owned by European and other companies in the same period. While some Filipina hotel workers in Copenhagen married Filipino sailors, the working conditions of the latter are beyond the scope of this research project.

3 Nina Trige Andersen, *Labor Pioneers: Economy, Labor, and Migration in Filipino-Danish Relations 1950–2015* (Quezon City: Ateneo de Manila University Press, 2019), 1–29.

vital functions in the local economies of their destination countries and, in the case of Denmark, they also came to play a central role in the development of trade unions' attitudes to migrant labour as well as in specific labour struggles by tackling a changing labour market in the emerging neoliberal restructuring of the economy.

This chapter draws on a larger research project on the economy, labour, and migration in Filipino-Danish relations from the mid-twentieth century until the present.[4] It focuses on the labour organizing aspects of Filipinas working as hotel chambermaids in Copenhagen from the 1960s to the 1990s and on the trade union of the hotel and restaurant sector, HRF, which became part of RBF, and since the early 2000s has been a sector group in 3F, which is one of the largest unions in Denmark today. The story of migrant worker conditions and labour struggles will be contextualized by a brief account of why and how labour migration from the Philippines to Denmark commenced and developed, including the motivations of Filipinas/os for migrating to Denmark.

2 The Filipino Pioneers in Denmark – in Global Perspective

Philippine migration to Denmark is part of the rapidly increasing migration within the sectors of care, domestic and service work as well as of so-called "marriage migration." The first generations of Filipino workers arrived in the 1960s and early 1970s before the formal ban on new work permits for third-country nationals was adopted by the Danish parliament in November 1973. Under the impact of the economic crisis in the mid-1970s, most other European countries adopted similar restrictions. Those arriving in Denmark between 1960 and 1973 usually refer to themselves as the "Filipino Pioneers" and the "Vanguards of the Seventies." Among them were small clusters with a shared history, for example, 49 women were recruited at the same time in 1973 for one-year contracts at the newly constructed Hotel Scandinavia in Copenhagen, and were subsequently known as "the 49ers."

The focus on this comparatively small number of migrants will permit a detailed, oral history-based study of insertion as well as exclusion, including an analysis of the slow entry into the union movement, a process in which both migrants and younger open-minded activists had to overcome the total disinterest of the old union leadership. From a global perspective, the migration of

4 The research project commenced in 2010 and the outputs include two books and several journal articles as well as newspaper articles, see www.filippinernesdanmarkshistorie.dk.

multiple small numbers, as well as large-volume movements, add up to millions – of which each person has to find a way to become part of their society of arrival. In 2020, according to official data more than 12 million Filipinos and Filipinas – out of a total Philippine population of approximately 110 million – lived overseas. Just over half were men, while 48 percent of the migrants were women. Due to the long US rule of the Philippine archipelago, more than 4 million had settled and formed families in the US,[5] 1.1 million in Canada, more than 3.3 million in the Arab Gulf states, where family formation was almost impossible, and less than 0.7 million have selected Malaysia, Singapore, Hong Kong, and Macau as destinations.[6] On the oceans, men from the Philippines account for almost one-quarter of the shipping crews, whether on container carriers or cruise ships.[7] In Europe, Great Britain and France are the main destinations with perhaps 200,000 in-migrants each, followed by Italy and Spain with 150,000–165,000 each. Quantitatively, this makes the migration to Denmark marginal. However, in the mid-1970s, Europe was the destination of one in every four registered temporary Philippine migrant workers,[8] and Denmark was on the list of countries served by the state agencies managing labour migration from the beginning. For every migrant, the place and space of arrival is his or her centre of life and for the Danish receiving society, the number of Philippine migrants was (and still is) significant. Most migrants continue to relate to their families and regional-local cultures of origin and the latter are numerous in the Philippine urban and island societies with high levels of internal migrations. Migrant women and men may also relate to siblings, cousins as well as other kin and friends at other destinations. As a result, the networks and relationships of Philippine migrants in Denmark may be global,

5 While early labour recruitment from the Philippines to the US territories was to the agriculture, fishing, and military industries, recruitment of nurses also played a central role, especially in the mid-twentieth century. Choy, *Empire of Care*.

6 For the diversity of Philippine migration during the twentieth century, see Aguilar, *Filipinos in Global Migrations*.

7 On the colonial roots of seafarer migration, see Filomeno V. Aguilar, Jr., “Manilamen and Seafaring: Engaging the Maritime World Beyond the Spanish Realm,” *Journal of Global History* 7, no. 3 (2012): 364–388, and on the contemporary impact of seafarer migration, see Roderick R. Galam, *Women Who Stay: Seafaring and Subjectification in an Ilocos Town* (Quezon City: Ateneo de Manila University Press, 2018).

8 Aniceto Orbeta, Jr., and Michael Abrigo, *Philippine International Labor Migration in the Past 30 Years: Trends and Prospects*, Discussion Paper 2009–33 (Makati City: Philippine Institute for Development Studies, 2009); Alcestis Abrera-Mangahas, *Response to New Market Opportunities: The Case of the Overseas Employment Sector*, Working Paper 89–11 (Makati City: Philippine Institute for Development Studies, 1989). Of those registered as temporary migrant workers, many did not return even if they had originally intended to.

even if their life projects have to be local. This points to one difference in comparison to the majority society: For non-migrating residents the local and, perhaps, the national is paramount.

Each trajectory of the "Filipino Pioneers" – a reference that came to include all Denmark-bound migrants of the sixties and seventies – began in the respective home community: Some were encouraged by family members or inspired by family histories of migrating abroad and they took it as an opportunity for adventure and saving money. Others were pressured by acute economic hardship. Another group used migration as a way out of a politically volatile situation, particularly since the early 1970s when protests against the Marcos regime grew more intense and president Ferdinand Marcos put the "country," meaning each and every inhabitant, under martial law in September 1972. Many of the Filipinas/os who migrated to Denmark came from the provinces where job opportunities were scarce and, had they stayed in the country, many would have had to migrate to the capital to find work – or to the US military bases and the special economic zones in the Philippines. In that light, going to another country, even as far as Denmark, could present itself as the safer, saner, and – not least – more promising option.[9]

In Denmark, hotels, especially in the capital Copenhagen, faced a sudden shortage of workers in the 1960s and 1970s. One reason for this was a rapid expansion of the sector as the economic boom and the globalization of the economy implied more travelling, both for business and leisure. New and unprecedentedly large hotels were constructed in Copenhagen, thereby creating an instant demand for workers to service them. At the same time, the economic boom made it possible for Danish-born workers to "advance" to jobs with better conditions and wages than the hotel sector typically offered and hence recruiting migrant labour was a way for the hotel owners to avoid or at least postpone improving wages and working conditions. Furthermore, since the expanding hospitality sector aimed to cater to an international audience, hotel managements were interested in workers who could communicate with international guests and at this time, few Danes spoke English at the desired level. Recruiting staff from the Philippines came with a linguistic advantage, since most Filipinas/os, especially from urban areas, speak fluent English as a second language.

The case of "the 49ers" provides an instructive example of cooperation between globally positioned management, a labour-exporting state, and

9 These generalizations are based on oral history collected among dozens of people from the pioneer generation. See Andersen, *Filipino Pioneers*, part I and II, for an in-depth account of the motivations and routes.

potential migrants. The recruitment of workers for the Hotel Scandinavia involved global corporation networks, local "drummers" (private recruiters who did not work for agencies), the Philippine Department of Labor as a facilitating institution, Danish employers' labour needs and recruitment efforts, as well as individual and collective initiatives. The hotel in Copenhagen had been built as a joint venture between Scandinavian Airlines and the American-owned hotel chain Western International, for which it was to be the entry point to the Northern European market. The job interviews held in Manila in 1973 were conducted by the human resource manager of the Singaporean Shangri La Hotel, who was a former colleague of the American CEO, Mr. Ellis, hired by the chain to run the Danish hotel. A number of the 49 women had been recommended for the job interview by relatives already working in hotels and restaurants in Denmark; some had been flagged by local agents in their villages; and others were referred by the Philippine Department of Labor. An official from the department, the acting manager of the Manila Employment Office, Ester Garcia, accompanied the group on their journey to Denmark to ensure that what had been offered in the job interviews in Manila would also materialize upon arrival in Copenhagen.

By the early 1970s, several hundred workers from the Philippines had arrived to work in Copenhagen and, in 1970, had founded their first organization, the Filipino Association of Denmark. A campaign letter by a team that ran for office in 1972 mentioned "the almost 300 Pinoys scattered in this tiny and oldest kingdom of the world, Denmark."[10] By "Pinoy" or, feminine "Pinay," the migrants refer to themselves as Fili*pino/a* with the "y" added. Although Danish government statistics do not provide accurate counts of the numbers of Filipinas/os arriving during the 1960s and 1970s, figures from 1980 onward are available in the national statistics online service StatBank. While earlier data from the Central Register in Denmark lists 473 resident Filipinas/os in 1975 and 666 in 1979, this does not reflect gross arrivals and departures.[11] In addition, some of the workers who arrived between 1960 and 1975 never officially resided in Denmark but arrived on tourist visas and worked with or without permits for limited periods of time, and then moved on to destinations in, for instance, Canada, Norway, and the US. The practice of entry via tourist

10 Filipino Association of Denmark, archival material: Campaign letter indicating Elmo Carino running for president and his team presenting their platform, November 1972 (kindly donated to Filippinernes Danmarkshistorie by Luz Hammer).

11 E-mail from the Senior Head Clerk, Population and Education, Statistics Denmark, Dorthe Larsen, to author, 31 May 2016.

visa continued throughout the 1970s, although migration restrictions made it increasingly difficult.

Many of the pioneers had arrived with the intention to remigrate when they had accumulated some savings and when the situation in their country of origin had improved. However, not only did the situation not improve but political repression grew more intense and so did the economic crisis. Thus, the Filipino Pioneers became the backbone of a community in Denmark that would quietly grow during the following decades.

3 Institutionalizing Labour Export

While European states were recruiting migrant labour for a booming economy in the 1960s and 1970s, the Marcos regime's Minister of Labor, Blas F. Ople, reorganized the Labor Department under the influence of "export orientation" advice from international institutions such as the International Labour Organization (ILO), the World Bank, and the International Monetary Fund (IMF). In Ople's interpretation, "export" involved commodified segments of the state's population[12] and, drawing on experiences and practices from colonial times and the more recent years of close ties to the US economy, the Labor Department retooled its management of sending labour abroad. With the Labor Code of 1974, the state-managed labour export was systematized and scaled up by the creation of the Overseas Employment Development Board (OEDB, today POEA – Philippine Overseas Employment Administration). (For other European cases of labour export economies, see Chapter 7 in this volume.)

Denmark was one of the countries served by the Philippine Department of Labor, both before and after 1974[13] and OEDB placements of workers – also in those countries of Europe that formally adopted bans on migration from third countries in the mid-1970s – grew from year to year. In 1979, the OEDB facilitated the placement of workers in France, Denmark, Switzerland, West Germany, and England as the top recruiters. When, from 1980 onward, the OEDB-facilitated migration faded, this merely reflected the fact that private

12 Nina Trige Andersen, "Laboring Pioneers and Pioneers of Labor Export," *IIAS Newsletter* 84 (2019), https://www.iias.asia/the-newsletter/article/laboring-pioneers-and-pioneers-labor-export.

13 Department of Labor and Employment, *Annual Report* (Manila: Department of Labor and Employment, 1973), 18; Overseas Employment Development Board, *Annual Report* (Mandaluyong: OEDB, 1978).

agencies were formally allowed to re-enter the overseas labour recruitment market and quickly outcompeted the state agency. In addition, increasing numbers of potential migrants did not need intermediaries but could make use of their own networks of friends and relatives already residing abroad.

4 Migrants Marginalized in the Danish Trade Union Movement

While most migrants in Denmark during the so-called guestworker era – including Filipinas/os – joined trade unions shortly after taking up work, few experienced direct contact with their unions in the first years. Some of the Filipino Pioneers remember having discussed work and wage conditions with Danish colleagues, and some received help from a local shop steward to gain the same rights as Danish workers. A few involved themselves in local labour struggles. However, it would be several decades before the Danish trade unions systematically attempted to involve foreign-born workers as potential members in their activities and began to communicate in languages familiar to them. For instance, for Filipinas, English was their language of choice, although most learned Danish in time.

Many migrant workers joined the unions in the 1960s and 1970s, not because of any organizing efforts but rather because they were obliged to join, or at least thought this to be the case. While it was mandatory to join the unemployment insurance administered by the unions, this obligation did not extend to actual union membership although this distinction was not easy for foreigners to understand. Furthermore, some workplaces had so-called exclusive agreements (later banned by European Union regulations), which meant that employers were not allowed to hire non-unionized workers. Thus, the unions technically did not have to actively recruit foreign workers, and, in practice, this became an excuse to not make the effort.

The 49ers, for example, unionized for these reasons but experienced no connections to the Hotel and Restaurant Workers' Union (HRF) other than paying membership fees. The 49er Josie Høgh, working at Hotel Scandinavia, recalls a gap between migrants and the union because, among what she calls the "ordinary workers," there were no Danes. Waiters and those in other more prestigious jobs did not interact with the chambermaids. For their part, the 49ers did not contact the union, partly because "everything was new: the language, the environment" and partly because they were on a one-year contract. Looking back, Josie Høgh feels the migrants were let down by the labour union. The Filipina chambermaids would, for example, have needed help to sort out overtime pay and the right to paid holidays – in both respects the management often cheated.[14]

Viewed from a stateside perspective, the Philippine government did not encourage migrants to engage in collective efforts to improve their working conditions in their countries of destination but instead underlined their "responsibility" to subject themselves to the authority of their employers and thereby showcase that Filipino manpower was both loyal and productive. One of the 49ers, for example, in the pre-OEDB arrangements, had participated in an "Overseas Service Workers' Training Course" organized by the National Manpower and Youth Council, Office of Manpower Services, and Bureau of Women and Minors.[15] Before departing, she received a letter from the Department of Labor lamenting that she had to go abroad but expressing its understanding of the necessity and encouraging her to give a good example by performing her "duties and responsibilities" well and showing that "Filipinos are a hard-working, industrious, honest, loyal, self-reliant and self-respecting people." She was never to forget that whatever she did abroad would "reflect upon our country." With this message, she departed for the one-year contract – together with her 48 compatriots – but ended up serving Hotel Scandinavia for her entire working life.[16]

Like Josie Høgh, many of the pioneers expected their work abroad to be temporary and most had plans of either migrating on to other (preferably English-speaking) countries or of re-migrating to the Philippines. However, many reasons induced them to decide to stay: Some wanted to save more, some found opportunities in Denmark to be more promising than, for instance, in the US, and others realized that the conditions they had left in the Philippines had not improved, while a few had fallen in love in Denmark or had been joined by family members.

However, only 21 days after the arrival of the 49ers, the Danish government adopted the so-called immigration stop and when their employer, Hotel Scandinavia, applied with the Danish authorities to prolong their work permits, this was denied. Instead, the women had to seek employment in private

14 Interviews with Josephine "Josie" Høgh from Santo Niño, Paranaque, conducted at her home in Frederiksberg, Copenhagen, and during reunions of the 49ers in the years between 2010 and 2015, followed up by informal conversations and e-mail correspondence. The main interviews were conducted on 4 November 2010, 21 June 2011, and 15 January 2012.

15 Documents from the Soliman private archive (kindly lent to the author by Mona Soliman, daughter of a 49er).

16 Documents from the Soliman private archive.

households as domestic workers, which remained one of the few legal options to stay (apart from marrying a Danish citizen or someone with permanent residence). Some of the women, however, continued to work shifts in the hotel, unaware that this was technically illegal. The HRF union noticed this at a time when the union movement as a whole, sceptical of foreign workers from the start, assumed a more hostile attitude towards the "guestworkers" who had not left when the economic crisis in the mid-1970s began to translate into rising unemployment. In early 1973, the chairperson of HRF Copenhagen, Elsa Hansen, had still written: "Wretched be the day when we, as one can observe in for instance the United States, would become some kind of racists because we have to associate with the guestworkers in the workplaces. The right to work, to exist, is a human right, regardless of race, colour, and nationality."[17] However, at the beginning of 1975 when the labour union had been informed that some of the Philippine chambermaids were working in private homes while still doing shifts at the hotels, the same Elsa Hansen wrote:

> I can't believe that foreigners 'illegally' and through the backdoor find their way to those jobs that Danish workers could take on. This is exactly what brings about aversion to foreigners [...] One suspects that certain individuals within the sector are behind these manoeuvres of 'storing' the named chambermaids in the private households only to retrieve them later on [...] but we have the names of these people, and we will follow them closely, and if they show their faces again in the hotels, we will retaliate. There you have it.[18]

5 The HRF Transforms Through Filipina Organizing

Many other pioneers had similar experiences: They paid membership fees but heard nothing, other than receiving membership magazines and occasionally an information letter, all of it in Danish, that few of them could read in the first years.

However, in 1978 the national conflict in the hotel and restaurant sector became a turning point for the attitude of the HRF towards migrant colleagues. Some of the pioneers remember having been active in the conflict, and a scrapbook in the archive of what today is 3F documents shows that Filipinas/

17 *HRF-bladet* 3, no. 9 (1973): 20–21, translation by the author.
18 *3 Kuverter* (January 1975): 21, translation by the author.

os were manning picket lines.[19] The conflict could have shaken the employers: picket lines all over Copenhagen – also manned by Filipinas/os – at Hotel d'Angleterre, Sheraton, Restaurant Felix, and in front of Copenhagen Central Station. As a result of the mass action, hotel owners quickly had trouble sustaining operations. The 49er Pinay Valenzuela remembers that most of the picketers in front of Hotel Sheraton were "internationals," as she phrases it.[20] Today she recalls the joy of being in a country where "even ordinary workers" could express themselves and fight for their rights without repercussions. Her brother in the Philippines was imprisoned without trial during those years for having organized a strike at Subic Naval Base.

However, while ordinary HRF members were picketing, the union leaders signed a deal with their employers. On the night of 4 May 1978, after two weeks of conflict that practically shut down all hotels, restaurants, and ferries in Denmark, the two top leaders of the union together with a high-placed union secretary from the coalition of labour unions in Denmark (LO, Landsorganisationen i Danmark today FH, Fagbevægelsens Hovedorganisation) settled with the employers' association (AHR, Arbejdsgiverforeningen af Hoteller og Restauranter [Employers' Association of Hotels and Restaurants]) without the knowledge of the union members – not even of their negotiating committee.[21] While the chambermaids did get a raise, more importantly, thousands of hotel and restaurant workers gained their first labour struggle experiences. The dissatisfaction with HRF leadership had been brewing for some time and after the highly unpopular deal, the dissatisfied members took over the organization. The new guard – despite being all-white Danes themselves – had the mobilization of migrant members at the very top of its agenda. Approximately one in eight HRF union members on the national scale and almost half of all members in Copenhagen were migrants and, without them, the union would never develop clout. However, it would take a decade before the HRF was able to put its words into action.

Through their own efforts and those of their Danish colleagues with a new agenda, Filipina hotel workers became involved in the labour movement from the 1980s and, peaking in the 1990s, in intense labour struggles. In the process, they became core unionists. In fact, the HRF, which had limited impact on

19 The scrapbook containing photos, leaflets, newspaper clippings, strike songs, etc. was found in the basement of the 3F headquarters.

20 Collective interview with Josie Høgh, Christina Madsen, Leticia Valencia, and Rufina Valenzuela during a visit of Hotel Scandinavia, 18 December 2011. The only 49er who still worked at the hotel showed us around.

21 Documents from the scrapbook.

improving the working conditions of Danes or migrants during the first half of the twentieth century, by the 1980s and 1990s came to pioneer new strategies for both. Through the experiences of Filipina chambermaids, it organized migrant workers in the face of a changing economy marked by subcontracting and ever-changing company ownership. The labour conflicts that dominated the Copenhagen hotels during these decades revolved around a wave of outsourcing, in particular of the cleaning functions which entailed an atomization of the chambermaid profession.

When one of the opposition leaders, Bent Moos from Aarhus, was elected president of the HRF on a national level in 1982, this caused anxiety in the social democratic-dominated labour union movement, because Moos was known as a "communist."[22] In the new agenda, migrant mobilization had top priority. The Aarhus branch, in a critique of the old HRF presidency, pointed out that:

> 1. The annual report does not at all touch upon one of the most pressing issues for labour struggle [mest påtrængende faglige problemer]: The intrusion of cleaning companies in our sector.
> 2. The annual report says nothing of the mounting problems faced by our foreign members during the crisis.
> 3. The annual report does in no way reflect the fact that 87 percent of the members are women.[23]

Two years after the opposition took over national leadership, the HRF was the only union other than Specialarbejderforbundet i Danmark (SiD) for unskilled workers in the private sector including factories, to establish so-called immigrant committees in each local branch because, in Bent Moos' words, "immigrants constituted such a central part of our membership base, and no one had bothered to mobilize them before."[24]

---

22 Bent Moos was co-founder of a Leninist faction in an organization called *Venstresocialisterne* (Left Socialists) which he left in 1973 with the *Kommunistisk Forbund* (Communist Union), a splinter which reunited with *Venstresocialisterne* in 1980.

23 From the HRF archive in Århus Amt, quoted in Søren Federspiel, *Vi, der går køkkenvejen: Hotel-og Restaurationspersonalets Forbund 1933–1990* [We Who Enter Through the Kitchen Door: The Hotel and Restaurant Workers' Union 1933–1990] (Copenhagen: Knuths Forlag, 1998), 165.

24 Based on an interview conducted at the 3F headquarters in Copenhagen on 10 August 2015, as well as prior and subsequent conversations and e-mail correspondence. Moos was president of the HRF and vice-president of Samvirket from 1982 to 1988, president of Samvirket from 1988 to1990, and president of the RBF from 1990 to 1994. He has since worked in various positions in the labour union. In his last position with the Private Service, Hotel and Restaurant branch in the merged 3F labour union coalition, he paid

6 Pirate Companies and Chambermaids

The inclusion of migrant workers into the union occurred in the context of a transformation of the entire Danish labour market from the mid-1980s onwards, which intensified during the 1990s. The rapidly expanding subcontracting involved so-called triangle situations: Employer A outsources to subcontractor B, who takes over the workers and the collective agreement between the workers and A. Then A terminates the contract with B and contracts with C, who has no relation either to the workers or the collective agreement. In this way A can get rid of both workers and collective agreements.[25]

"Pirate" companies – semi-legal companies who "boarded" on bigger companies – aggressively undermined the Danish model of "flexicurity" based on a high level of workers' and employers' organization, including collective agreements and mutual recognition between employer associations and labour unions. The model, which was prevalent since the beginning of the twentieth century, expressed "big class compromises involving in particular the working class, the farmers and, at times, also the capitalist bourgeoisie."[26]

The triangle procedure undermined the class compromise and the HRF uncovered clandestine operations under the auspices of seemingly respectable companies. Surreptitiously as early as the 1970s and openly during the 1990s "pirate cleaners" – and, in its more violent and organized form, the "cleaning mafia" – had begun to encroach on the cleaning contracts at hotels and restaurants (see Chapter 14 in this volume for similar developments in California). While organizing workers in this fluctuating sector in regular companies had been difficult for the HRF, organizing people who worked for dubious subcontractors in an increasingly complex underworld was close to impossible. At its national congress in 1985, the HRF called the outsourcing schemes its "evil spirit" and accused the employers of a deliberate union-busting strategy.[27]

At this point, with the HRF still beset by internal struggles, the (new) national leaders knew that the migrant workers had to be involved. "We had all the right intentions, but no flesh and blood," according to Bent Moos. "There were no

special attention to seamen, including Filipinos. He retired in June 2015 and organized the 3F archive until his death in the spring of 2022.

25 For an account of a labour struggle around a triangle manoeuvre in which Filipinas were in the frontline, see Chapter 13 in Andersen, *Labor Pioneers*.

26 Niels Finn Christiansen and Pirjo Markkola, "Introduction," in *The Nordic Model of Welfare: A Historical Reappraisal*, ed. Niels Finn Christiansen et al. (Copenhagen: Museum Tusculanum Press, 2006), 18.

27 *3 Kuverter*, no. 3 (1986): 4–5.

immigrants among the elected officials in HRF, and almost no immigrant shop stewards. We had to change all that. A major plug in the system remained in the Copenhagen branch leadership – the only part of the old guard who had survived the takeover of HRF by our opposition. Copenhagen was crucial; this was where most immigrant members were."[28] In 1990, the opposition finally won and the new Copenhagen chairperson, Eva Høgskov, also from the Aarhus section, recalls:

> The old ones knew their time was up and they withdrew voluntarily, giving the new leadership their blessing, so outwardly it all looked nice and neat. But it was the result of years of struggle, and the old branch leadership knew they were cornered. [In the union office, the new leaders were in for a surprise.] We couldn't believe it – boxes and piles everywhere with member cases. We just started at one end and kept going. It was cases worth millions of unpaid wages and benefits, most of them belonging to Filipina chambermaids.[29]

For decades, the previous leaders had ignored the Filipina chambermaids in particular, and the organizing efforts in general, and worked with a bureaucratic perspective that as long as there were collective agreements on paper, they did not have to check whether the rights of the workers were respected in practice. Among those who for years had tried to get local trade union representatives to help file cases against their employer was Ruth Theil, a Filipina chambermaid at Hotel Sheraton from Davao, Mindanao. She had arrived in Denmark in late 1985 and, since early 1986, worked as a chambermaid at the Sheraton, Marriott, and Dan hotels. She was elected shop steward and subsequently became a member of the RHF-Copenhagen board. She remembers her surprise at being called to the branch office in 1990: "And there was Eva with all the paperwork I had collected." By this time, migrant workers had realized that union membership was not mandatory, and since they received few benefits from paying their fees, many had opted to leave. "Eva told me: 'You've got to organize them, Ruth.' And I said: 'How? They barely dare talk to me.' But we waited until the right moment came."[30]

28 Interview Moos 2015.

29 Interview conducted at her home, 11 March 2015, as well as prior phone conversation. Eva Høgskov was a member of the Hotel and Restaurant Workers' Union HRF/Samvirket since the 1970s and chair of the HRF Copenhagen branch 1991–1998.

30 Interviews conducted together with Violeta Jensen, 16 March 2016 and 4 April 2016 in central Copenhagen.

If the new labour union leadership was taken aback by the piles of unresolved cases, so were the employers when subpoenas started piling up on their desks. In 1992, at least 35 cases were won against hotels, restaurants, and cleaning companies; the single biggest victory was against the cleaning company Steward Service for unpaid wages, lack of job contracts, and unpaid overtime and holiday supplements amounting to a total of 400,000 Danish Kroner, equalling more than 30 months of wages.[31] Hotel d'Angleterre, Sheraton, and Imperial – all main employers of Filipinas – were sentenced to paying fines to the union for unpaid wages and overtime.[32] The union won so many cases that they could not keep up with distributing the money rolling in. "We worked hard to get in touch with all the chambermaids. Not all of them were members, but it was still their money," Eva Høgskov said and added:

> We offered three months of free membership, no fees, and if people were not happy with the union, they could just leave with their compensation from the cases. We owed them that much, the union having collected membership fees from so many workers for so many years without doing anything. Most of the new members stayed, though, I think we ended up with 95 percent coverage of the Filipina chambermaids in Copenhagen. Our membership numbers skyrocketed.[33]

The membership in HRF Copenhagen increased from 1,900 in 1991 to 3,600 in 1996[34] and much of this success was due to the organizing efforts of Filipinas. By 1996, 43 percent of all chambermaids in Copenhagen were covered by collective agreements with the RBF, up from less than 15 percent in 1994. Another 33 percent of the chambermaids were covered by a competing union, the Women Workers' Union in Denmark (KAD – Kvindeligt Arbejderforbund i Danmark).[35]

In the early 1990s, the (by then) well-organized Filipina chambermaids were facing new and dangerous adversaries and the labour struggles intensified at a moment when the hotel sector was going through yet another crisis, more

31 RBF *Afdelingsnyt*, no. 1 (1992): 5, 9.

32 RBF *Afdelingsnyt*, no. 3 (1992): 4, and no. 2 (1992): 4.

33 Interview Høgskov 2015.

34 RBF *Afdelingsnyt* (February 1996): 3.

35 The rest of the workers were either covered by so-called yellow unions – unions historically created by the employers that do not take action such as strikes – or employed at workplaces under picketing campaigns, or employed at hotels with fewer than 20 workers, which were too small to be included in the survey (Rengøringsselskaberne i tal februar 1997, Thorkild Holmboe-Hay archive).

complex than that of the 1970s, since every other hotel was either not making profits or running a deficit, and one in three was close to bankruptcy. One of the major causes of the crisis was overcapacity as a result of speculation in constructing new hotels.[36] This crisis led the management of hotels to look for cost-cutting opportunities through every legal – and illegal – measure.

The HRF under Eva Høgskov understood that inter-union cooperation was mandatory and she thus summoned the other unions operating in the hotel and restaurant industry. "[W]e have launched a battle against the part of the cleaning sector that bases itself on fraud and scamming. Several initiatives have been tried out and more are coming, so we'll have a busy time ahead of us," she wrote to her union colleagues in KAD, SiD, Lager og Handel (Warehouse and Trade), and Sanitørernes Fagforening (Union of Cleaners) in February 1992.[37] With the joint meeting to coordinate activities, a decade-long struggle to "clean up" the cleaning sector began with Filipina chambermaids at the centre.

7 "Filipinas Have Always Been the Easiest to Organize"

In March 1993, Olivia Medgyesi – a Filipina who had worked as a chambermaid at Hotel Phoenix and Hotel Østerport and was recruited by HRF/RBF as an organizer and central activist in the anti-pirate campaign – together with Ruth Theil and a handful of other chambermaid colleagues started the Philippine Network in RBF, centred on HRF Copenhagen.[38] Within a month, they had more than 100 active members, many of them elected shop stewards at the hotels.[39] The network became one of the most remarkable examples of self-organized migrant workers in Danish labour history.

According to Olivia Medgyesi, her Filipina colleagues were often hesitant to push cases, just as Ruth Theil had experienced at Hotel Sheraton. They joined the union but "they were so afraid to lose their income that they'd rather stay quiet. [...] But I was determined to use my new influence on the labour union board to strengthen their voice." Lone Søgaard, who was hired as an organizer

36 *Hotel, Restaurant & Fritid*, no. 10 (1992): 8–9; HOREFA Beretning (1991–1993): 3.

37 Brev vedrørende: Rengøringsfirmaerne i København, København 23.2.92 (Thorkild Holmboe-Hay archive), translation by the author.

38 The HRF had merged into the RBF.

39 Course of events based on interview with Olivia Medgyesi (Copenhagen, 2013) and Ruth Theil, and on articles in the RBF-bladet: January 1992 (1), June-July 1992 (5), and May 1993 (4), as well as the written account of the first ordinary congress of the RBF 1990–1994, 46.

in the Copenhagen branch in 1993, recalls how Filipinas became the most active members during those years:

> On my first day of work, on 1 July 1993, someone at the union office whispered to me: 'I think you should drop by Hotel Sheraton. There are things happening this morning.' When I arrived, the Filipina chambermaids were already forming picket lines. They were angry about the way they were being treated by the matron who did not respect their work and used offensive language. During that decade there were struggles in several major hotels in town. Filipinas have always been the easiest to organize, and we doubled our membership during the first years under the new leadership who realized the importance of involving the non-Danish speaking workers. Soon, we had Filipina shop stewards from the hotels elected for the main board as well. Those years were a grand time for the union.[40]

"Olivia Medgyesi was the first to argue that we had to organize people according to nationality and to educate shop stewards in their own languages," recounted Thorkild Holmboe-Hay, a former shop steward at Hotel d'Angleterre and later, as a trade union employee, responsible for the anti-pirate campaign.[41] Olivia Medgyesi also organized social and cultural events among the migrant members and shared Filipino recipes, such as kare-kare stew, in the union magazine.[42] The first general assembly of the network, which was held on 29 March 1993, elected Olivia Medgyesi as president and Ruth Theil as vice president. Other officials included the Filipino Pioneers Manuel Villanueva and Jorge Abainza. Thus, the network crosscut old divides between pioneers and the next generation: Both Ruth and Olivia had arrived in Denmark in the late 1980s and had obtained legal residence through marriage.

At the congress of the national union in 1998, HRF Copenhagen had finally, 30 years after migrants started to enter the union, achieved a representation that matched realities, as approximately half of the congress participants from

40 Interview at the 3F headquarters, 15 December 2015. Lone Søgaard worked in various positions for the Hotel and Restaurant Workers' Union (HRF/RBF/PSHR – Privat-, Service-, Hotel-og Restaurationsgruppen – 3F) since 1993, particularly with Filipina chambermaids.

41 Primary interview conducted at his home, 26 February 2014, as well as prior phone interviews and subsequent e-mail correspondence and follow-up interviews at his office. Thorkild Holmboe-Hay, former vice-chair of the HRF Copenhagen branch, was in charge of the campaign against the pirate cleaning companies. He has since been employed by PSHR 3F.

42 RBF *Afdelingsnyt*, no. 4 (1992): 8.

the branch had a non-Danish background.[43] This was the joint achievement of the Filipina chambermaids and the new leadership. Soon the membership magazine was also printed in languages other than Danish and at large meetings and general assemblies, translations were offered and, according to the members' needs, English was supplemented with Arabic and Turkish.

Olivia Medgyesi faced problems even with the new leadership. She wanted the HRF/RBF and KAD to work together for the benefit of migrant members, especially regarding jobs that (Filipina) migrants most frequently occupied, namely that of hotel cleaners and chambermaids. The HRF/RBF and KAD, however, were either not able to or not interested in establishing cooperative practices. Instead, they often seemed to place obstacles in each other's paths and fought so-called border conflicts (*grænsekonflikter*) over which union had the right to organize the chambermaids. The HRF/RBF felt that all work at the hotel was under their jurisdiction, whereas the KAD maintained that once chambermaid work was outsourced to private cleaning companies, it belonged to the KAD.

The Philippine Network in the RBF, which assisted Filipinas/os who were afraid of joining the union, only existed for a few years. It is unclear why it was dissolved as the explanations from former members of the network and Danish trade unionists vary and several elements as outlined here seem to have played a role.[44] The network not only consisted of different generations but also of what one could call different traditions within the Philippine population in Denmark. Political disagreements and religious differences played a role and, according to some informants, one of the factions was more secular than the other. There were also some disagreements on tactics and the degree of patience necessary when working with the cumbersome structures of the Danish labour unions and labour laws. The network may also have been destabilized by the fact that one of the founders, Victoria DeVera, fell critically ill and had to withdraw.

Connie Mendoza, who had come to Denmark in 1990 and who had been mobilized for trade union work during the conflict at her first workplace, had been treasurer of the network and recalls that the relationship between the

43 Ringbind med papirer fra HR-Gruppens 3. ordinære gruppekongres, October 1998, Aalborg (Thorkild Holmboe-Hay archive).

44 The information and assessments were derived from interviews the author conducted with several people involved in the network, with Danish trade unionists who had close contacts to the network, and from written contemporary accounts from, for example, members' magazines.

Philippine members and the RBF was not without friction. "There was always a limitation to the welcome feeling," as she put it, elaborating:

> On the good side, being at union meetings was always very lively, very educational; we learned about rights, about activism, how we could improve the organization, the recruitment. On the bad side were some of the officials [...] if you asked a question after a meeting, sometimes you would get the answer: 'What – didn't you listen!? That was explained already!' Sometimes you would hear some racist remark, *eller de snakker dansk; siger til os vi skal snakke dansk* ['or they start to speak Danish; they tell us to speak Danish'[45]]. But they should just be grateful for us foreigners in the union. We were more members and more money for the union.[46]

Other trade unionists, however, were welcoming: "It was different with Thorkild and Eva – with them you just knew that they would help anyone regardless of nationality."

For all activists in the network, the classic problem of a double or triple workload was also at play: Many members had more than one job and also had a family to take care of – some both in Denmark and in the Philippines. Working more than one job was the consequence of the traditional precarity in the sector that became more acute during the 1980s and 1990s economic restructuring. The chambermaid profession, which was particularly under attack, often involved part-time or on-call work instead of full-time work, which meant that a full-time income had to be assembled by working for several employers. While most people needed a full-time income to make ends meet, this was even more urgent for those who did not only sustain themselves and their families in Denmark but regularly sent money to relatives abroad, as many Filipinas continued to do even after decades of living abroad. As a result, it was difficult to find time for trade union work. In effect, most of the leading members of the network were either single or divorced, or their children were already adults. The number of potential leading activists was thus small and most of the daily work rested on just a handful of people.

In sum, while it is difficult to ascertain the exact impact of the Philippine Network on the ability of the RBF to mobilize amongst Philippine workers and members, during the years in which the network was active it did engage

45 Mendoza in the interview switches to Danish when recalling what she experienced as racist behaviour, thus demonstrating that she does in fact speak Danish.

46 Interview at her home on 9 October 2015. Although she previously was active in the HRF/RBF, by the time of interview, she had retired.

people who otherwise probably would not have taken an active part in unionizing activities. The network organized parties and fundraisings, and the trade union thus also came to represent the kind of social glue and safety net that the Philippine associations had represented since the early 1970s. In a way, the network along with the Philippine associations outside of the union played a role in making Denmark, Copenhagen, and the workspaces a new home or social anchor point for workers of Filipino origin.

Similarly, the fact that the RBF encouraged and supported the existence of such a network served as a message to migrant members that they were – in all respects – welcome in the trade union; they did not have to try to adapt or look alike in certain ways but could use their particularities as resources instead. The Philippine Network also solidified the practice that the HRF/RBF began to pioneer: It was both possible and fruitful to communicate in languages spoken and understood by the members, instead of insisting on a concept of "equal treatment" that, in effect, meant that the practices – including language usage – of people born and raised in Denmark were the standard for all. While the RBF allocated substantial resources to engaging its migrant members, the equal treatment/no special treatment position was maintained by both KAD and SiD. For many years, this constituted a major obstacle to the mobilization of migrants and was even reflected in the occupational health (or lack thereof) of migrants.[47] Only a decade later, both organizations, by then fused into 3F, began to publish materials in multiple languages and to hire and educate migrants to organize their compatriots. One of the important resources of the RBF's Philippine Network was, as Eva Høgskov had noticed early, in Connie Mendoza's words: "Sheraton, d'Angleterre, Scandinavia – they were all connected by workers. We Filipinos always knew someone at the other hotels."[48]

8 Conclusion

Compared to the many other destinations of migrants from the Philippines, the story of the Filipina trade union organizing in Denmark is a story with its

47 Jesper Nielsen and Karen Winding, "Har indvandrere et arbejdsmiljø? Rapport om en undersøgelse af arbejdsmiljø og arbejdsskader blandt indvandrere fra 3. lande på det danske arbejdsmarked" [Do Immigrants Have Occupational Health? Report on a Study of Occupational Health and Industrial Injuries Among Immigrants from Third Countries on the Danish Labour Market] (Copenhagen: Center for Alternativ Samfundsanalyse, 1994), 46–47.

48 Interview Mendoza 2015.

own specificities. Significantly, it is also a story of migrant organizing as such whereby the initiatives are similar but the contexts vary according to the state and social space of arrival. In addition, it shows workers mobilizing on their own initiative rather than waiting for the protection of their rights by an institutional bargaining system.

At the same time, the recollection of the story of these achievements is symptomatic for many labour organizations and, despite the remarkable organizing efforts of Filipina chambermaids, they were largely omitted from the official history of the HRF until recently. In *Vi, der går køkkenvejen* (We Who Enter Through the Kitchen Door), labour historian Søren Federspiel hardly mentioned migrant workers and, if mentioned, they were depicted as a "challenge" to the union. He summarized: "If the immigrant members caused problems, it was nothing, though, compared to the illegal immigrants who became employed in the hotel and restaurant industry […] By the first half of the 1970s, cases of Filipina chambermaids began to emerge."[49]

Federspiel completed his research at the very moment when Filipinas had become a central militant force in the HRF, and Olivia Medgyesi and Ruth Theil had been elected to the board of the Copenhagen branch. When, in the 2010s, the author of this chapter approached the successor of the HRF/RBF, the PSHR group in 3F, the union had almost forgotten this part of their very recent history, even though several of its employees had been active in the 1980s and 1990s. The new PSHR leadership considered the archives of the struggles lost, except for some materials in the private homes of trade unionists. It was the retired former national president of the HRF, Bent Moos, who on the author's request "unearthed" the files in the basement of the 3F headquarters. While the PSHR was thrilled to have the stories recounted, it is remarkable how easily the organizing experiences of migrant workers can be erased from history – and thus from the active memory of the trade unions.

As for developments in the Philippines, the state-managed labour export, systematized and expanded by the Department of Labor under the Marcos regime from the late 1960s, had initially been presented as a "temporary" measure to alleviate unemployment and secure the inflow of foreign currency. However, it was never terminated. Today, the workers who leave the country through official channels and thus the mediation of the POEA, leave with messages similar to the one written by Ester Garcia from the Manila Employment Office to a 49er in 1973: They are to represent their country well through serving foreign employers with loyalty and hard work. However, as the role of Filipina

49 Federspiel, *Vi, der går køkkenvejen*, 141–142.

chambermaids in Copenhagen shows, migrants can combine hard work with the other virtues of, in Garcia's words, "self-reliance" and "self-respect." Migrants thus may and do demand respect in the destination countries – from employers, trade unions, and society as a whole.

Selective Bibliography

Abrera-Mangahas, Alcestis. *Response to New Market Opportunities: The Case of the Overseas Employment Sector*. Working Paper 89–11. Makati City: Philippine Institute for Development Studies, 1989.

Abu-Lughod, Janet L. *Before European Hegemony: The World System A.D. 1250–1350*. New York: Oxford University Press, 1989.

Afonso, Alexandre, and Camilla Devitt. "Comparative Political Economy and International Migration." *Socio-Economic Review* 14, no. 3 (2016): 591–613.

Afonso, Alexandre. "Migrant Workers or Working Women? Comparing Labour Supply Policies in Post-War Europe." *Journal of Comparative Policy Analysis: Research and Practice* 21, no. 3 (2019): 251–269.

Aguilar, Filomeno V., Jr. "Manilamen and Seafaring: Engaging the Maritime World Beyond the Spanish Realm." *Journal of Global History* 7, no. 3 (2012): 364–388.

Aguilar, Filomeno V., Jr., ed. *Filipinos in Global Migrations: At Home in the World?*. Quezon City: Philippine Social Science Council, 2002.

Ahmad, Attiya. "Beyond Labour: Foreign Residents in the Persian Gulf States." In *Migrant Labour in the Persian Gulf*, edited by Mehran Kamrava and Zahra Babar, 21–40. London: Hurst, 2012.

Aleinikoff, T. Alexander, and Douglas Klusmeyer, eds. *Citizenship Today: Global Perspectives and Practices*. Washington, DC: Carnegie Endowment for International Peace, 2001.

Altan, Selda. "Politics of Life and Labor: French Colonialism in China and Chinese Coolie Labor During the Construction of the Yunnan-Indochina Railway, 1898–1910." *International Labor and Working-Class History* 101 (2022): 1–23.

Andersen, Nina Trige. *Labor Pioneers: Economy, Labor, and Migration in Filipino-Danish Relations 1950–2015*. Quezon City: Ateneo de Manila University Press, 2019.

Arrighi, Giovanni. "Labour Supplies in Historical Perspective: A Study of the Proletarianization of the African Peasantry in Rhodesia." *Journal of Development Studies* 6, no. 3 (1970): 197–234.

Atabaki, Touraj. "Indian Migrant Workers in the Iranian Oil Industry 1908–1951." In *Working for Oil: Comparative Social Histories of Labor in the Global Oil Industry*, edited by Touraj Atabaki, Elisabetta Bini, and Kaveh Ehsani, 189–226. London: Palgrave Macmillan, 2018.

Austen, Ralph. *African Economic History: Internal Development and External Dependency*. London: James Currey, 1987.

Austin, Gareth, Ewout Frankema, and Morten Jerven. "Patterns of Manufacturing Growth in Sub-Saharan Africa: From Colonization to Present." In *The Spread of*

Modern Industry to the Periphery Since 1871, edited by Kevin Hjortshøj O'Rourke and Jeffrey Gale Williamson, 345–374. Oxford: Oxford University Press, 2017.

Bade, Klaus. *Migration in European History*, trans. Allison Brown. Malden, MA/ Oxford: Blackwell, 2003.

Balibar, Étienne, and Immanuel Wallerstein. *Race, Nation, Class: Ambiguous Identities*. London: Verso, 1991.

Balibar, Étienne, Monique Chemillier-Gendrerau, Jacqueline Costa-Lascoux, and Emmanuel Terray. *Sans-papiers: L'archaïsme fatal*. Paris: La Découverte, 1999.

Bauböck, Rainer, Bernhard Perchinig, and Wiebke Sievers. *Citizenship Policies in the New Europe*. Amsterdam: Amsterdam University Press, 2009.

Belich, James. *The World the Plague Made: The Black Death and the Rise of Europe*. Princeton, NJ: Princeton University Press, 2022.

Berger, Elena. *Labour, Race and Colonial Rule: The Copperbelt from 1924 to Independence*. Oxford: Clarendon Press, 1974.

Biega, Alexandra, and Myroslav Diakowsky, eds. *The Ukrainian Experience in Quebec*. Quebec: Basilian Press, 1994.

Bischof, Günter, and Dirk Rupnow, eds. *Migration in Austria*. New Orleans: University of New Orleans Press, 2017.

Blum, Jerome. *Lord and Peasant in Russia: From the Ninth to the Nineteenth Century*. Princeton, NJ: Princeton University Press, 1961.

Bolland, O. Nigel. *The Politics of Labour in the British Caribbean: The Social Origin of Authoritarianism and Democracy in the Labour Movement*. Kingston: Ian Randle, 2001.

Boris, Eileen, Dorothea Hoehtker, and Susan Zimmermann, eds. *Women's ILO: Transnational Networks, Global Labour Standards and Gender Equity, 1919 to Present*. Leiden: Brill, 2018.

Boris, Eileen. *Caring for America: Home Health Workers in the Shadow of the Welfare State*. Oxford: Oxford University Press, 2012.

Boris, Eileen. *Making the Woman Worker: Precarious Labor and the Fight for Global Standards, 1919–2019*. New York: Oxford University Press, 2019.

Bosma, Ulbe, Gjis Kessler, and Leo Lucassen, eds. *Migration and Membership Regimes in Global and Historical Perspective: An Introduction*. Leiden: Brill, 2013.

Bosma, Ulbe. "Beyond the Atlantic: Connecting Migration and World History in the Age of Imperialism, 1840–1940." *International Review of Social History* 52, no. 1 (2007): 116–123.

Bosma, Ulbe. *The Making of a Periphery: How Island Southeast Asia Became a Mass Exporter of Labor*. New York: Columbia University Press, 2019.

Bradley, Joseph. *Muzhik to Muscovite: Urbanization in Late Imperial Russia*. Berkeley: University of California Press, 1985.

Breman, Jan, and Marcel van der Linden. "Informalizing the Economy: The Return of the Social Question at the Global Level." *Development and Change* 45, no. 5 (2014): 920–940.

Breman, Jan, Isabelle Guerin, and Aseem Prakash, eds. *India's Unfree Workforce of Bondage Old and New*. Oxford: Oxford University Press, 2009.

Brown, Carolyn. "Mining." In *General Labour History of Africa: Workers, Employers and Governments, 20th-21st Centuries*, edited by Stefano Bellucci and Andreas Eckert, 151–176. Woodbridge, UK: James Currey, 2019.

Campbell, Gwyn, and Alessandro Stanziani, eds. *The Palgrave Handbook of Bondage and Human Rights in Africa and Asia*. New York: Palgrave Macmillan, 2020.

Campbell, Persia Crawford. *Chinese Coolie Emigration to Countries Within the British Empire*. London: P. S. King & Son, Ltd., 1923.

Carens, Joseph H. *Culture, Citizenship, and Community: A Contextual Exploration of Justice as Evenhandedness*. Oxford: Oxford University Press, 2000.

Caroli, Betty Boyd, Robert F. Harney, and Lydio F. Tomasi, eds. *The Italian Immigrant Women in North America*. Toronto: Multicultural History Society of Ontario, 1977.

Carter, Marina. *Voices from Indenture: Experiences of Indian Migrants in the British Empire*. London: Leicester University Press, 1996.

Castles, Stephen, and Ozkul Deriya. "Circular Migration: Triple Win, or a New Label for Temporary Migration?" In *Global and Asian Perspectives on International Migration*, edited by Graziano Battistella, 27–49. Basel: Springer, 2014.

Chalcraft, John. "Migration and Popular Protest in the Arabian Peninsula and the Gulf in the 1950s and 1960s." *International Labor and Working-Class History* 79 (2011): 28–47.

Chan, Shelly. *Diaspora's Homeland: Modern China in the Age of Global Migration*. Durham, NC: Duke University Press, 2018.

Chang, Kornel S. *Pacific Connections: The Making of the U.S.-Canada Borderlands*. Berkeley: University of California Press, 2012.

Chen, Ta. *Chinese Migration, With Special Reference to Labor Conditions*. Honolulu: University of Hawai'i Press, 2015.

Chowdhury, Mehdi, and S. Irudaya Rajan, eds. *South Asian Migration in the Gulf*. London: Palgrave Macmillan, 2018.

Choy, Catherine Ceniza. *Empire of Care: Nursing and Migration in Filipino American History*. Durham, NC: Duke University Press/Quezon City: Ateneo de Manila University Press, 2003.

Christiansen, Niels Finn, Klaus Petersen, Niels Edling, and Peer Haave, eds. *The Nordic Model of Welfare: A Historical Reappraisal*. Copenhagen: Museum Tusculanum Press, 2006.

Cleveland, Todd Charles. "Rock Solid: African Laborers on the Diamond Mines of the Companhia de Diamantes de Angola (Diamang), 1917–1975." PhD diss., University of Minnesota, 2008.

Cobble, Dorothy Sue. *For the Many: American Feminists and the Global Fight for Democratic Equality*. Princeton, NJ/Oxford: Princeton University Press, 2021.

Colucci, Michele. *Lavoro in movimento*. Rome: Donzelli editore, 2008.

Cometti, Elizabeth. "Trends in Italian Emigration." *Western Political Quarterly* 11, no. 4 (1958): 820–834.

Cooper, Frederick. *Decolonization and African Society: The Labor Question in French and British Africa*. Cambridge: Cambridge University Press, 1996.

Costa, Daniel, and Philip Martin. *Temporary Labor Migration Programs: Governance, Migrant Worker Rights, and Recommendations for the UN Global Compact for Migration*. Washington, DC: Economic Policy Institute, 2018.

Cross, Gary S. *Immigrant Workers in Industrial France: The Making of a New Laboring Class*. Philadelphia: Temple University Press, 1983.

Crush, Jonathan, Alan Jeeves, and David Yudelman. *South Africa's Labor Empire: A History of Black Migrancy to the Gold Mines*. Cape Town: David Philip Publishers, 1991.

Curthoys, Ann, and Andrew Markus, eds. *Who Are Our Enemies? Racism and the Australian Working Class*. Sydney: Hale & Iremonger, 1978.

Denning, Michael. "Wageless Life." *New Left Review* 66 (2010): 79–97.

Duignan, Peter, and L. H. Gann, eds. *Colonialism in Africa 1870–1960*. Vol. 4: *The Economics of Colonialism*. Cambridge: Cambridge University Press, 1975.

Dusinberre, Martin. *Hard Times in the Hometown: A History of Community Survival in Modern Japan*. Honolulu: University of Hawai'i Press, 2012.

Düvell, Franck. "Clandestine Migration in Europe." *Social Science Information* 47, no. 4 (2008): 479–497. https://doi.org/10.1177/0539018408096442.

Düvell, Franck. "Paths into Irregularity: The Legal and Political Construction of Irregular Migration." *European Journal of Migration and Law* 13 (2011): 275–295. https://doi.org/10.1163/157181611X587856.

Düvell, Franck. "Transit Migration: A Blurred and Politicised Concept." *Population, Space and Place* 18, no. 4 (2012): 415–427. https://doi.org/10.1002/psp.631.

Elkan, Walter. "Migrant Labor in Africa: An Economist's Approach." *American Economic Review* 49, no. 3 (1959): 188–197.

Elsner, Lothar, and Joachim Lehmann. *Ausländische Arbeiter unter dem deutschen Imperialismus 1900 bis 1985*. Berlin: Dietz, 1988.

Emmer, Pieter C., and Magnus Mörner, eds. *European Expansion and Migration: Essays on the Intercontinental Migration from Africa, Asia and Europe*. New York: Berg, 1992.

Engel, Barbara. *Between the Fields and the City: Women, Work, and the Family in Russia, 1861–1914*. Cambridge: Cambridge University Press, 1994.

Enloe, Cynthia. *Bananas, Beaches and Bases: Making Feminist Sense of International Politics*. Berkeley: University of California Press, 1990.

Errichiello, Gennaro. "Foreign Workforce in the Arab-Gulf States (1930–1950): Migration Patterns and Nationality Clause." *International Migration Review* 46, no. 2 (2012): 389–413.

Feinstein, Charles. *An Economic History of South Africa: Conquest, Discrimination, and Development*. Cambridge: Cambridge University Press, 2005.

Ferguson, James. *Expectations of Modernity: Myths and Meanings of Urban Life on the Zambian Copperbelt*. Berkeley: University of California Press, 1999.

Forberg, Martin. "Ausländerbeschäftigung, Arbeitslosigkeit und gewerkschaftliche Sozialpolitik: Das Beispiel der Freien Gewerkschaften zwischen 1890 und 1918." *Archiv für Sozialgeschichte* 27 (1987): 51–81.

Frank, Andre Gunder, and Barry K. Gills, eds. *The World System: Five Hundred Years or Five Thousand?*. London: Routledge, 1993.

Frank, Andre Gunder. *Capitalism and Underdevelopment in Latin America*. New York: Monthly Review Press, 1967.

Frank, Andre Gunder. *ReOrient: Global Economy in the Asian Age*. Berkeley: University of California Press, 1998.

Freund, Bill. *The African City: A History*. Cambridge: Cambridge University Press, 2007.

Fröbel, Folker, Jürgen Heinrichs, and Otto Kreye. *The New International Division of Labour: Structural Unemployment in Industrialised Countries and Industrialisation in Developing Countries*. Cambridge: Cambridge University Press, 1980.

Fudge, Judy, and Eric Tucker. *Labour Before the Law: The Regulation of Workers' Collective Action in Canada, 1900–1948*. Toronto: University of Toronto Press, 2001.

Gabaccia, Donna R. "The 'Yellow Peril' and the 'Chinese of Europe': Global Perspectives on Race and Labor, 1815–1930." In *Migration, Migration History, History: Old Paradigms and New Perspectives*, edited by Jan Lucassen and Leo Lucassen, 177–196. Bern: Lang, 2005.

Gabaccia, Donna R., and Dirk Hoerder, eds. *Connecting Seas and Connected Ocean Rims: Indian, Atlantic, and Pacific Oceans and China Seas Migrations from the 1830s to the 1930s*. Leiden: Brill, 2011.

Gabaccia, Donna R., and Franca Iacovetta, eds. *Women, Gender, and Transnational Lives: Italian Workers of the World*. Toronto: University of Toronto Press, 2002.

Gabaccia, Donna R., and Fraser M. Ottanelli, eds. *Italian Workers of the World: Labor, Migration and the Making of Multi-Ethnic States*. Urbana: University of Illinois Press, 2001.

Galam, Roderick R. *Women Who Stay: Seafaring and Subjectification in an Ilocos Town*. Quezon City: Ateneo de Manila University Press, 2018.

García, María Cristina. *Seeking Refuge: Central American Migration to Mexico, the United States, and Canada*. Berkeley: University of California Press, 2006.

Gardner, Andrew. "Engulfed: Indian Guest Workers, Bahraini Citizens, and the Structural Violence of the Kafala System." In *The Deportation Regime: Sovereignty, Space and the Freedom of Movement*, edited by Nicholas De Genova and Nathalie Peutz, 196–223. Durham, NC/London: Duke University Press, 2010.

Glickman, Rose. *Russian Factory Women: Workplace and Society, 1880–1914*. Berkeley: University of California Press, 1984.

Goeke, Simon. *"Wir sind alle Fremdarbeiter!" Gewerkschaften, migrantische Kämpfe und soziale Bewegungen in Westdeutschland 1960–1980*. Paderborn: Ferdinand Schöningh, 2020.

Grandin, Greg. *Empire's Workshop: Latin America, the United States, and the Rise of the New Imperialism*. New York: Owl Books, 2007.

Green, Nancy L., and Francois Weil, eds. *Citizenship and Those Who Leave: The Politics of Emigration and Expatriation*. Urbana: University of Illinois Press, 2007.

Haas, Hein de, Stephen Castles, and Mark J. Miller. *The Age of Migration: International Population Movements in the Modern World*. London: Red Globe Press, 2020.

Haas, Michiel de, and Ewout Frankema, eds. *Migration in Africa: Shifting Patterns of Mobility from the 19th to the 21st Century*. London: Routledge, 2022.

Hahamovitch, Cindy. "Creating Perfect Immigrants: Guestworkers of the World in Historical Perspective." *Labor History* 44, no. 1 (2003): 69–94.

Hahamovitch, Cindy. *No Man's Land: Jamaican Guestworkers in America and the Global History of Deportable Labor*. Princeton, NJ: Princeton University Press, 2011.

Hahn, Sylvia. *Migration – Arbeit – Geschlecht: Arbeitsmigration in Mitteleuropa vom 17. bis zum Beginn des 20. Jahrhunderts*. Göttingen: V&R Unipress, 2008.

Hansen, Erik. "Marxists and Imperialism: The Indonesian Policy of the Dutch Social Democratic Workers Party, 1894–1914." *Indonesia* 16 (1973): 81–104.

Harris, Nigel. *The New Untouchables: Immigration and the New World Worker*. New York: I. B. Tauris, 1995.

Hatton, T. J., and Jeffrey G. Williamson. *The Age of Mass Migration: Causes and Economic Impact*. New York: Oxford University Press, 1998.

Haupt, Georges, and Madeleine Rebérioux, eds. *La deuxième Internationale et l'Orient*. Paris: Cujas, 1967.

Haupt, Georges, Michael Löwy, and Claudie Weill. *Les Marxistes et la question nationale, 1848–1914*. Paris: Maspero, 1974.

Herbert, Ulrich. *A History of Foreign Labor in Germany, 1880–1980: Seasonal Workers, Forced Laborers, Guest Workers*. Translated by William Templer. Ann Arbor: University of Michigan Press, 1990.

Hinther, Rhonda, and Jim Mochoruk, eds. *Civilian Internment in Canada: Histories and Legacies*. Winnipeg: University of Manitoba Press, 2020.

Hinther, Rhonda, and Jim Mochoruk, eds. *Reimagining Ukrainian Canadians: History, Politics, and Identity*. Toronto: University of Toronto Press, 2011.

Hinther, Rhonda. *Perogies and Politics: Canada's Ukrainian Left, 1891–1991*. Toronto: University of Toronto Press, 2018.

Hirschman, Alfred. "Exit, Voice, and the State." *World Politics* 31, no. 1 (1978): 90–107.

Hochschild, Adam. *King Leopold's Ghost: A Story of Greed, Terror and Heroism in Colonial Africa*. Boston/New York: Houghton Mifflin Harcourt, 1998.

Hoerder, Dirk, and Amarjit Kaur, eds. *Proletarian and Gendered Mass Migrations: A Global Perspective on Continuities and Discontinuities from the 19th to the 21st Century*. Leiden: Brill, 2013.

Hoerder, Dirk, with Inge Blank and Horst Rössler, eds. *Roots of the Transplanted*. 2 vols. New York: Columbia University Press, 1994.

Hoerder, Dirk. "From Migrants to Ethnics: Acculturation in a Societal Framework." In *European Migrants: Global and Local Perspectives*, edited by Dirk Hoerder and Leslie Page Moch, 211–262. Boston: Northeastern University Press, 1996.

Hoerder, Dirk. *Cultures in Contact: World Migrations in the Second Millennium*. Durham, NC: Duke University Press, 2002.

Hollifield, James F. *Immigrants, Markets, and States: The Political Economy of Postwar Europe*. London: Harvard University Press, 1992.

Hyslop, Jonathan. "The Imperial Working Class Makes Itself 'White': White Laborism in Britain, Australia, and South Africa Before the First World War." *Journal of Historical Sociology*, 12, no. 4 (1999): 398–421.

Iacovetta, Franca, with Paula Draper and Robert Ventresca, eds. *A Nation of Immigrants: Women, Workers, and Communities in Canadian History, 1840s-1960s*. Toronto: University of Toronto Press, 1998.

Ichioka, Yūji. *The Issei: The World of the First Generation Japanese Immigrants, 1885–1924*. New York: Free Press, 1988.

International Labour Organization. *Global Estimates on International Migrant Workers*. Geneva: International Labour Office, 2021.

Irick, Robert L. *Ch'ing Policy Toward the Coolie Trade, 1847–1878*. Taipei: Chinese Materials Center, 1982.

Isajiw, Wsevolod W. *Understanding Diversity: Ethnicity and Race in the Canadian Context*. Toronto: Thompson, 1999.

Jaiswal, Ritesh Kumar. "Ephemeral Mobility: Critical Appraisal of the Facets of Indian Migration and the Maistry Mediations in Burma (c.1880–1940)." *Almanack* (2018): 80–118.

Janowska, Alina. *Emigracja zarobkowa z Polski 1918–1939*. Warsaw: Państwowe Wydawnictwa Naukowe, 1981.

Johnson, Chalmers. *Blowback: The Costs and Consequences of American Empire*. 2nd ed. New York: Henry Holt, 2004.

Jureidini, Ray, and Said Fares Hassan, eds. *Migration and Islamic Ethics: Issues of Residence, Naturalisation and Citizenship*. Leiden: Brill, 2019.

Kaczmarczyk, Pawel, Enrique Aldaz-Carroll, and Paulina Hołda. "Migration and Socio-Economic Transition: Lessons from the Polish Post-EU Accession Experience." *East European Politics and Societies* 34, no. 4 (2020): 910–936.

Kasaba, Reşat. *A Moveable Empire: Ottoman Nomads, Migrants, and Refugees.* Seattle: University of Washington Press, 2009.

Katzenellenbogen, Simon. "The Miners' Frontier: Transport and General Economic Development." In *Colonialism in Africa 1870–1960*. Vol. 4: *The Economics of Colonialism,* edited by Peter Duignan and L. H. Gann, 360–426. Cambridge: Cambridge University Press, 1975.

Kelley, Ninette, and Michael J. Trebilcock. *The Making of the Mosaic: A History of Canadian Immigration Policy*. Toronto: University of Toronto Press, 1998.

Kessler, Gijs, Christine Moll-Murata, and Karin M. Hofmeester, eds. "Conquerors, Employers and Arbiters: States and Shifts in Labour Relations, 1500–2000." *International Review of Social History* 61, no. S24 (2016).

Khalaf, Abdulhadi, Omar AlShehabi, and Adam Hanieh, eds. *Transit States: Labour, Migration and Citizenship in the Gulf.* London: Pluto Press, 2014.

Kicinger, Anna. *Polityka emigracyjna II Rzeczpospolitej.* CEFMR Working Paper 4. Warsaw: University of Warsaw, 2005.

King, Russell, Gabriella Lazaridis, and Charalambos Tsardanidis, eds. *Eldorado or Fortress? Migration in Southern Europe*. London: Palgrave MacMillan, 2000.

Klein, Naomi. *The Shock Doctrine: The Rise of Disaster Capitalism*. London: Penguin, 2008.

Kleßmann, Christoph. *Polnische Bergarbeiter im Ruhrgebiet 1870–1945: Soziale Integration und nationale Subkultur einer Minderheit in der deutschen Industriegesellschaft.* Göttingen: Vandenhoeck & Ruprecht, 1978.

Kofman, Eleonore, Annie Phizacklea, Parvati Raghuram, and Rosemary Sales. *Gender and International Migration in Europe: Employment, Welfare and Politics.* London/New York: Routledge, 2000.

Kofman, Eleonore. "Female 'Birds of Passage' a Decade Later: Gender and Immigration in the European Union." *International Migration Review* 33, no. 2 (1999): 269–299.

Kordan, Bohdan S. *No Free Man: Canada, the Great War, and the Enemy Alien Experience.* Montreal/Kingston: McGill-Queen's University Press, 2016.

Kulczycki, John J. *The Foreign Worker and the German Labor Movement: Xenophobia and Solidarity in the Coal Fields of the Ruhr, 1891–1914*. Oxford: Berg, 1994.

Lake, Marilyn, and Henry Reynolds. *Drawing the Global Colour Line: White Men's Countries and the International Challenge of Racial Equality*. Cambridge: Cambridge University Press, 2008.

Lee, Erika. "Hemispheric Orientalism and the 1907 Pacific Coast Race Riots." *Amerasia Journal* 33, no. 2 (2007): 19–47.

Lee, Suzy K. "The Three Worlds of Emigration Policy: Towards a Theory of Sending State Regimes." *Journal of Ethnic and Migration Studies* 43, no. 9 (2017): 1453–1471.

Li, Guotong. *Migrating Fujianese: Ethnic, Family, and Gender Identities in an Early Modern Maritime World*. Leiden: Brill, 2016.

Linden, Marcel van der, and Karl Heinz Roth, eds. *Beyond Marx: Theorising the Global Labour Relations of the Twenty-First Century*. Leiden: Brill, 2013.

Linden, Marcel van der. "Enjeux pour une histoire mondiale du travail." *Le Mouvement Social* 241, no. 4 (2012): 3–29.

Linden, Marcel van der. "Labour History: The Old, the New and the Global." *African Studies* 66, no. 2–3 (2007): 169–180.

Lipietz, Alain. *Mirages and Miracles: The Crisis in Global Fordism*. Translated by David Macey. London: Verso, 1987.

Lucassen, Jan, and Leo Lucassen, eds. *Globalising Migration History: The Eurasian Experience (16th-21st Centuries)*. Leiden: Brill, 2014.

Lucassen, Jan, Leo Lucassen, and Patrick Manning, eds. *Migration History in World History: Multidisciplinary Approaches*. Leiden: Brill, 2010.

Mabogunje, Akin L. "Systems Approach to a Theory of Rural-Urban Migration." *Geographical Analysis* 2, no. 1 (1970): 1–18.

Machado, Pedro, Steve Mullins, and Joseph Christensen, eds. *Pearls, People, and Power: Pearling and Indian Ocean Worlds*. Athens: Ohio University Press, 2020.

Mahmood, Mamdani. *Citizen and Subject: Contemporary Africa and the Legacy of Late Colonialism*. Princeton, NJ: Princeton University Press, 1996.

Mar, Lisa. *Brokering Belonging: Chinese in Canada's Exclusion Era, 1885–1945*. New York: Oxford University Press. 2010.

Martynowych, Orest T. *Ukrainians in Canada: The Formative Period, 1891–1924*. Edmonton: Canadian Institute of Ukrainian Studies Press, 1991.

Mau, Steffen. *Sortiermaschinen: Die Neuerfindung der Grenze im 21. Jahrhundert*. Munich: Beck, 2021.

McCartin, Joseph A. *Collision Course: Ronald Reagan, the Air Traffic Controllers, and the Strike That Changed America*. Oxford: Oxford University Press, 2013.

McKeown, Adam. "Global Migration, 1846–1940." *Journal of World History* 15, no. 2 (2004): 155–189.

McKeown, Adam. "The Social Life of Chinese Labor." In *Chinese Circulations: Capital, Commodities, and Networks in Southeast Asia*, edited by Eric Tagliacozzo and Wen-chin Chang, 62–83. Durham, NC: Duke University Press, 2011.

Milkman, Ruth, ed. *Organizing Immigrants: The Challenge for Unions in Contemporary California*. Ithaca, NY: ILR Press, 2000.

Miller, Sally. *Race, Ethnicity, and Gender in Early Twentieth-Century American Socialism*. New York: Garland, 1996.

Moch, Leslie Page. *Moving Europeans: Migration in Western Europe since 1650.* Bloomington: Indiana University Press, 2003.

Morawska, Ewa. "Labor Migrations of Poles in the Atlantic World Economy, 1880–1914." *Comparative Studies in Society and History* 31, no. 2 (1989): 237–272.

Morokvasic, Mirjana. "Birds of Passage are also Women." *International Migration Review* 18, no. 4 (1984): 886–907.

Murphy, Richard Charles. *Guestworkers in the German Reich: A Polish Community in Wilhelmine Germany*. Boulder, CO: East European Monographs, 1983.

Nederveen Meerkerk, Elise van. *Women, Work and Colonialism in the Netherlands and Java: Comparisons, Contrasts, and Connections, 1830–1940*. Cham, CH: Palgrave Macmillan, 2019.

Ngai, Mae M. *Impossible Subjects: Illegal Aliens and the Making of Modern America.* Princeton, NJ: Princeton University Press, 2014.

Ngai, Mae. *The Chinese Question: The Gold Rushes and Global Politics*. New York: W. W. Norton, 2021.

Nichtweiß, Johannes. *Die ausländischen Saisonarbeiter in der Landwirtschaft der östlichen und mittleren Gebiete des Deutschen Reiches: Ein Beitrag zur Geschichte der preußisch-deutschen Politik von 1890 bis 1914*. Berlin: Rütten & Loening, 1959.

Northrup, David. "Indentured Indians in the French Antilles." *Outre-Mers: Revue d'histoire* 87, no. 326 (2000): 245–271.

Northrup, David. *Indentured Labor in the Age of Imperialism, 1834–1922.* Cambridge: Cambridge University Press, 1995.

Okolski, Michael. "Przepływ siły roboczej w świetle niemiecko-polskiej umowy dwustronnej opracownikach sezonowych." In *Polscy pracownicy na rynku Unii Europejskiej,* edited by Pawel Kaczmarczyk and Wojciech Łukowski, 23–37. Warsaw: Scholar, 2004.

Ong, Aihwa. *Neoliberalism as Exception: Mutations in Citizenship and Sovereignty.* Durham, NC: Duke University Press, 2006.

Orbeta, Aniceto, Jr., and Michael Abrigo. *Philippine International Labor Migration in the Past 30 Years: Trends and Prospects*. Discussion Paper 2009–33. Makati City: Philippine Institute for Development Studies, 2009.

Peebles, Patrick. *The Plantation Tamils of Ceylon*. London/New York: Leicester University Press, 2001.

Phimister, Ian. *An Economic and Social History of Zimbabwe, 1890–1948: Capital Accumulation and Class Struggle*. New York: Longman, 1988.

Pietraszek, Edward. "Zwischen Geldverdienen und Aufstieg: Polnische Arbeitsmigranten in Deutschland von 1870 bis 1939." In *Vom Wandergesellen zum "Green Card" Spezialisten: Interkulturelle Aspekte der Arbeitsmigration im östlichen Mitteleuropa,* edited by Klaus Roth, 107–133. Münster: Waxmann, 2003.

Piketty, Thomas, with Facundo Alvaredo, Lucas Chancel, Emmanuel Saez, and Gabriel Zucman. *Rapport sur les inégalités mondiales 2018*. Paris: Le Seuil, 2018.

Piketty, Thomas. *Le Capital au XXIe siècle*. Paris: Le Seuil, 2013.

Pilkington, Hilary. *Migration, Displacement and Identity in Post-Soviet Russia*. London: Routledge, 1998.

Piven, Frances Fox, and Richard Cloward. *Regulating the Poor: The Functions of Public Welfare*. 2nd ed. New York: Vintage Books, 1993.

Plascencia, Luis F. B. "State-Sanctioned Coercion and Agricultural Contract Labor: Jamaican and Mexican Workers in Canada and the United States, 1909–2014." In *On Coerced Labor: Work and Compulsion after Chattel Slavery*, edited by Marcel van der Linden and Magaly Rodríguez García, 225–265. Leiden: Brill, 2016.

Portes, Alejandro, Manuel Castells, and Lauren A. Benton, eds. *The Informal Economy: Studies in Advanced and Less Developed Countries*. Baltimore: Johns Hopkins University Press, 1989.

Randolph, John, and Eugene M. Avrutin, eds. *Russia in Motion: Cultures of Human Mobility since 1850*. Urbana: University of Illinois Press, 2011.

Reyneri, Emilio. *Migrants' Involvement in Irregular Employment in the Mediterranean Countries of the European Union*. Geneva: ILO, 2002.

Robinson, Geroid T. *Rural Russia under the Old Regime: A History of the Landlord-Peasant World and a Prologue to the Peasant Revolution of 1917*. Berkeley: University of California Press, 1967.

Rodriguez, Robyn Magalit. *Migrants for Export: How the Philippine State Brokers Labor to the World.* Minneapolis: Minnesota University Press, 2010.

Roller, Kathrin. *Frauenmigration und Ausländerpolitik im Deutschen Kaiserreich: Polnische Arbeitsmigrantinnen in Preußen*. 2nd ed. Berlin: Bertz, 1994.

Romero, Federico. "Migration as an Issue in European Interdependence and Integration: The Case of Italy." In *The Frontier of National Sovereignty: History and Theory 1945–1992*, edited by Alan S. Milward, Frances M. B. Lynch, Federico Romero, Ruggero Ranieri and Vibeke Sørensen, 33–58. London/New York: Routledge, 1992.

Rossum, Matthias van. "Coolie Transformations – Uncovering the Changing Meaning and Labour Relations of Coolie Labour in the Dutch Empire (18th and 19th Century)." In *Bonded Labour: Global and Comparative Perspectives (18th-21st Century)*, edited by Sabine Damir-Geilsdorf, Ulrike Lindner, Gesine Müller, Oliver Tappe, and Michael Zeuske, 83–102. Bielefeld: Transcript Verlag, 2016.

Rouillard, Jacques. *Les syndicats nationaux au Québec, 1900–1930*. Quebec: Presses de l'Université Laval, 1974.

Roy, Patricia. *A White Man's Province: British Columbia Politicians and Chinese and Japanese Immigrants 1858–1914*. Vancouver: University of British Columbia Press, 1989.

Ruíz, Vicki L. *From Out of the Shadows: Mexican Women in Twentieth-Century America*. 10th anniversary ed. Oxford: Oxford University Press, 2008.

Rye, Johan Fredrik, and Karen O'Reilley, eds. *International Labour Migration to Europe's Rural Regions*. London: Routledge, 2021.

Rye, Johan Fredrik, and Sam Scott. "International Labour Migration and Food Production in Rural Europe: A Review of the Evidence." *Sociologia Ruralis* 58, no. 4 (2018): 928–952. https://doi.org/10.1111/soru.12208.

Sánchez-Alonso, Blanca. "The Age of Mass Migration in Latin America." *Economic History Review* 72, no. 1 (2019): 3–31.

Sarkar, Mahua, ed. *Work Out of Place*. Berlin/Boston: De Gruyter Oldenbourg, 2018.

Sarkar, Mahua. "Constrained Labour as Instituted Process: Transnational Contract Work and Circular Migration in Late Capitalism." *European Journal of Sociology* 58, no. 1 (2017): 171–204.

Sarkar, Mahua. "The Flipside of the Integration Question: Guestworker Regimes and Temporary Circular/Managed Migration in History." *Refugee Watch: A South Asian Journal on Forced Migration* 49 (2017): 1–25.

Sassen, Saskia. "Women's Burden: Counter-Geographies of Globalization and the Feminization of Survival." *Journal of International Affairs* 53, no. 2 (2000): 503–524.

Schmitter Heisler, Barbara. "Sending Countries and the Politics of Emigration and Destination." *International Migration Review* 19, no. 3 (1985): 469–484.

Schwartz, Kraig. "Empowerment and Class Struggle: Factors Influencing Class Formation in the Asbestos Industry of Quebec: A Case Study of Thetford Mines." PhD diss., University of Maine, 1997.

Seccombe, Ian J., and Richard I. Lawless. "The Gulf Labour Market and the Early Oil Industry: Traditional Structures and New Form of Organization." In *The Gulf in the Early 20th Century: Foreign Institutions and Local Responses*, edited by Richard I. Lawless, 91–124. Durham, NC: University of Durham, Occasional Papers Series 31, 1986.

Shaw, Randy. *Beyond the Fields: Cesar Chavez, the UFW, and the Struggle for Justice in the 21st Century*. Berkeley: University of California Press, 2008.

Siegelbaum, Lewis H. "Those Elusive Scouts: Pioneering Peasants and the Russian State, 1870s-1950s." *Kritika: Explorations in Russian and Eurasian History* 14, no. 1 (2013): 43–48.

Siegelbaum, Lewis H., and Leslie Page Moch. *Broad Is My Native Land: Repertoires and Regimes of Migration in Russia's Twentieth Century*. Ithaca, NY: Cornell University Press, 2014.

Singha, Radhika. "The Great War and a 'Proper' Passport for the Colony: Border-Crossing in British India, c.1882–1922." *Indian Economic and Social History Review* 50, no. 3 (2013): 289–315.

Srivastava, Ravi. "Labour Migration in India: Recent Trends, Patterns and Policy Issues." *Indian Journal of Labour Economics* 54, no. 3 (2011): 411–440.

Stanziani, Alessandro. *Labor on the Fringes of the Empire*. Basingstoke, UK: Palgrave Macmillan, 2018.

Strangleman, Tim, James Rhodes, and Sherry Linkon. "Introduction to Crumbling Cultures: Deindustrialization, Class, and Memory." *International Labor and Working-Class History* 84 (2013): 7–22.

Strikwerda, Carl. "Tides of Migration, Currents of History: The State, Economy, and the Transatlantic Movement of Labor in the Nineteenth and Twentieth Centuries." *International Review of Social History* 44, no. 3 (1999): 367–394.

Surak, Kristin. "Guestworkers: A Taxonomy." *New Left Review* 84 (2013): 84–102.

Szczepański Maciej. "Analiza polityki państwa wobec migracji powrotnych: Przypadek Polski." In *Polityka państwa wobec migracji powrotnych własnych obywateli: Teoria i praktyka*, edited by Magdalena Lesińska, 16–38. CMR Working Papers 44/102. Warsaw: University of Warsaw, 2010.

Takai, Yukari. "Bridging the Pacific: Diplomacy and the Control of Japanese Transmigration via Hawai'i, 1890–1910." In *Entangling Migration History: Borderlands and Transnationalism in the United States and Canada*, edited by Benjamin Bryce and Alexander Freund, 141–161. Gainesville: University Press of Florida, 2015.

Tetzlaf, Stefan. "The Turn of the Gulf Tide: Empire, Nationalism, and South Asian Labor Migration to Iraq, c. 1900–1935." *International Labor and Working-Class History* 79 (2011): 7–27.

Tinker, Hugh. *A New System of Slavery: The Export of Indian Labour Overseas, 1830–1920*. London: Oxford University Press, 1974.

Tintori, Guido, and Michele Colucci. "From Manpower Export to Brain Drain? Emigration and Italy, between Past and Present." In *Routledge Handbook of Contemporary Italy: History, Politics, and Society,* edited by Andrea Mammone, Ercole Giap Parini, and Giuseppe Veltri. New York: Routledge, 2015.

Tintori, Guido. "Italy: The Continuing History of Emigrant Relations." In *Emigration Nations: Policies and Ideologies of Emigrant Engagement,* edited by Michael Collyer, 126–152. Basingstoke, UK: Palgrave Macmillan, 2013.

Torpey, John. *The Invention of the Passport: Surveillance, Citizenship and the State*. New York: Cambridge University Press, 2000.

Urbansky, Sören. *Beyond the Steppe Frontier: A History of the Sino-Russian Border.* Princeton, NJ: Princeton University Press, 2020.

Valdez, Inés. "Socialism and Empire: Labor Mobility, Racial Capitalism, and the Political Theory of Migration." *Political Theory* 49, no. 6 (2021): 902–933.

Ventresca, Roberto. "Italian Migration Policies at the Beginning of the European Integration Process: Fruitless Attempts?." In *Peoples and Borders: Seventy Years of Migration in Europe, from Europe, to Europe [1945–2015]*, edited by Elena Calandri, Simone Paoli and Antonio Varsori, 57–76. Baden-Baden: Nomos, 2017.

Vito, Christian G. de, and Anne Gerritsen. "Micro-Spatial Histories of Labour: Towards a New Global History." In *Micro-Spatial Histories of Global Labour*, edited by Christian G. de Vito and Anne Gerritsen, 1–28. Basingstoke, UK: Palgrave Macmillan, 2018.

Vito, Christian G. de. "History Without Scale: The Micro-Spatial Perspective." *Past and Present* 242, Supplement 14 (2019): 348–372.

Waijenburg, Marlous van. "Financing the African Colonial State: The Revenue Imperative and Forced Labor." *Journal of Economic History* 78, no. 1 (2018): 40–80.

Wallerstein, Immanuel M. *The Modern World-System*. 3 vols. New York/San Diego: Academic Press, 1974–1989.

Ward, Kathryn, ed. *Women Workers and Global Restructuring*. Ithaca, NY: Cornell University Press, 1990.

Webber, Jeremy. "Compelling Compromise: Canada Chooses Conciliation over Arbitration, 1900–1907." *Labour/Le Travail* 28 (1991): 15–57.

Weill, Claudie. *L'Internationale et l'autre: Les relations inter-ethniques dans la II° Internationale*. Paris: Arcantere, 1987.

Westad, Odd Arne. *The Global Cold War: Third World Interventions and the Making of Our Times*. Cambridge: Cambridge University Press, 2005.

Whitol de Wenden, Catherine. "Citizenship and Migration in a Globalized World." *Rechtstheorie* 51 (2020): 7–13.

Williams, Michael. *Returning Home with Glory: Chinese Villagers around the Pacific, 1849 to 1949*. Hong Kong: Hong Kong University Press, 2018.

Wimmer, Andreas, and Nina Glick Schiller. "Methodological Nationalism and Beyond: Nation-Building, Migration and the Social Sciences." *Global Networks* 2, no. 4 (2002): 301–334.

Wimmer, Andreas, and Nina Glick Schiller. "Methodological Nationalism, the Social Sciences, and the Study of Migration: An Essay in Historical Epistemology." *International Migration Review* 37, no. 3 (2003): 576–610.

Yen, Ching-Hwang. *Coolies and Mandarins: China's Protection of Overseas Chinese During the Late Ch'ing Period*. Singapore: Singapore University Press, 1985.

Yun, Lisa. *The Coolie Speaks: Chinese Indentured Laborers and African Slaves in Cuba*. Philadelphia: Temple University Press, 2008.

Zachariah, Kunniparampil Curien, and Sebastian Irudaya Rajan. *Kerala's Gulf Connection, 1998–2011: Economic and Social Impact of Migration*. Hyderabad: Orient Blackswan, 2012.

Zahra, Tara. *The Great Departure: Mass Migration from Eastern Europe and the Making of the Free World*. New York/London: W. W. Norton, 2017.

Index of Human Geography

Note: All references to a culture are listed under one entry (e.g. "Poland," "Poles," and "Polish" are listed under "Poland"). The geographical location of cities and regions in brackets (with very few exceptions) refers to present-day internationally accepted state borders.

www.ingramcontent.com/pod-product-compliance
Lightning Source LLC
LaVergne TN
LVHW010623300926
849162LV00001B/42
* 9 7 8 9 0 0 4 6 8 6 9 8 4 *